AF819979

Recommended by **Teachers**
Trusted by **Toppers**

All in One

BIOLOGY
Class 12

EVERYTHING YOU NEED TO SCORE

- Simplified NCERT Theory
- In-text & Chapter Exercises
- All Types of Exam Pattern Questions
- CBQs; MCQs, A-R, Case Based
- Board Questions Upto 2025
- Sample Question Papers

CBSE Exams 2026

Recommended by **Teachers**
Trusted by **Toppers**

All in one®

BIOLOGY
Class 12

EVERYTHING YOU NEED TO SCORE

- Simplified NCERT Theory
- In-text & Chapter Exercises
- All Types of Exam Pattern Questions
- CBQs; MCQs, A-R, Case Based
- Board Questions Upto 2025
- Sample Question Papers

CBSE Exams 2026

Authors
Himanshi Gambhir,
Anushri Sharma

arihant
SUCCESS AND NOTHING LESS

ARIHANT PRAKASHAN
(School Division Series)

ADMINISTRATIVE & PRODUCTION OFFICES

Regd. Office

'Ramchhaya' 4577/15, Agarwal Road, Darya Ganj, New Delhi -110002
Tele: 011- 47630600, 43518550; Fax: 011- 23280316

Head Office

Kalindi, TP Nagar, Meerut (UP) - 250002, Tel: 0121-7156203, 7156204

SALES & SUPPORT OFFICES

Agra, Ahmedabad, Bengaluru, Bareilly, Chennai, Delhi, Guwahati, Hyderabad, Jaipur, Jhansi, Kolkata, Lucknow, Nagpur & Pune.

PO No : TXT-XX-XXXXXXX-X-XX

Published By Arihant Publications (India) Ltd.

For further information about the books published by Arihant, log on to www.arihantbooks.com or e-mail at info@arihantbooks.com

Follow us on

PRICE ₹450.00

PRODUCTION TEAM

Publishing Managers
Mahendra Singh Rawat & Keshav Mohan

Cover Designer
Salman Shaikh

Inner Designer
Ankit Tyagi

Project Head
Shiva Choudhary

Page Layouting
Naresh Kumar

Proof Reader
Nidhi

Index *cum* Study Planner

			Studied	Revised	Exam ready
1.	**Sexual Reproduction in Flowering Plants**	**1-35**			
	Flower	1-2	☐	☐	☐
	Pre-Fertilisation: Structures and Events	2-7	☐	☐	☐
	Pollination	7-11	☐	☐	☐
	Double Fertilisation	12	☐	☐	☐
	Post-Fertilisation : Structures and Events	12-15	☐	☐	☐
	Some Special Mechanisms of Reproduction	15-16	☐	☐	☐
	Mind Map	17	☐	☐	☐
	Exam Pattern Questions	18-33	☐	☐	☐
	Self Assessment Test	34-35	☐	☐	☐
2.	**Human Reproduction**	**36-66**			
	Human Reproductive System	36-41	☐	☐	☐
	Gametogenesis	41-43	☐	☐	☐
	Menstrual Cycle	43-45	☐	☐	☐
	Fertilisation	45	☐	☐	☐
	Embryonic Development	46-47	☐	☐	☐
	Mind Map	48	☐	☐	☐
	Exam Pattern Questions	49-64	☐	☐	☐
	Self Assessment Test	65-66	☐	☐	☐
3.	**Reproductive Health**	**67-88**			
	Reproductive Health: Problems and Strategies	67-73	☐	☐	☐
	Sexually Transmitted Diseases (STDs)	73	☐	☐	☐
	Infertility	73-74	☐	☐	☐
	Mind Map	75	☐	☐	☐
	Exam Pattern Questions	76-86	☐	☐	☐
	Self Assessment Test	87-88	☐	☐	☐
4.	**Principles of Inheritance and Variation**	**89-129**			
	Mendelian Inheritance	89-93	☐	☐	☐
	Mendel's Laws of Inheritance	93-94	☐	☐	☐
	Deviations from Mendelian	94-96	☐	☐	☐
	Chromosomal Theory of Inheritance	96-97	☐	☐	☐
	Linkage and Recombination	97-98	☐	☐	☐
	Sex-Determination	98-101	☐	☐	☐
	Mutation	101	☐	☐	☐
	Pedigree Analysis	101-102	☐	☐	☐
	Genetic Disorders	102-105	☐	☐	☐
	Mind Map	106	☐	☐	☐
	Exam Pattern Questions	107-127	☐	☐	☐
	Self Assessment Test	128-129	☐	☐	☐
5.	**Molecular Basis of Inheritance**	**130-177**			
	The DNA and RNA World	130-133	☐	☐	☐
	Packaging of DNA Helix	133-134	☐	☐	☐
	The Search for Genetic Material	134-137	☐	☐	☐
	Central Dogma	137-138			

		Studied	Revised	Exam ready
Replication of DNA	138-139			
Transcription	140-142			
Genetic Code	142-144			
Translation	144-145			
Regulation of Gene Expression	145-147			
Human Genome Project (HGP)	147-149			
DNA Fingerprinting	149-150			
Mind Map	151			
Exam Pattern Questions	152-175			
Self Assessment Test	176-177			
6. Evolution	**178-205**			
Origin of Life	178-180			
Evidences of Evolution	180-184			
Theories of Evolution	184-187			
Account of Evolution	187-189			
Origin and Evolution of Human	189-190			
Mind Map	191			
Exam Pattern Questions	192-203			
Self Assessment Test	204-205			
7. Human Health and Diseases	**206-240**			
Health	206-207			
Disease	207-211			
Immunity	211-215			
Acquired Immuno Deficiency Syndrome (AIDS)	215-216			
Cancer	216-217			
Adolescence : Drug and Alcohol Abuse	217-220			
Mind Map	221			
Exam Pattern Questions	222-238			
Self Assessment Test	239-240			
8. Microbes in Human Welfare	**241-265**			
Introduction	241			
Microbes in Household Products	241-242			
Microbes in Industrial Products	242-244			
Microbes in Sewage Treatment	244-245			
Microbes in Production of Biogas	245-246			
Microbes as Biocontrol Agents	246-247			
Microbes as Biofertilisers	247-248			
Mind Map	249			
Exam Pattern Questions	250-263			
Self Assessment Test	264-265			
9. Biotechnology: Principles and Processes	**266-296**			
Principles of Biotechnology	266-267			
Tools of Recombinant DNA Technology	268-272			
Processes of Recombinant DNA Technology	272-275			
Mind Map	276			
Exam Pattern Questions	277-294			
Self Assessment Test	295-296			

		Studied	Revised	Exam ready
10. Biotechnology and Its Applications	**297-324**			
Biotechnological Applications in Agriculture	297-300	☐	☐	☐
Biotechnological Applications in Medicine	300-303	☐	☐	☐
Transgenic Animals	303-304	☐	☐	☐
Ethical Issues	304-305	☐	☐	☐
Mind Map	306	☐	☐	☐
Exam Pattern Questions	307-322	☐	☐	☐
Self Assessment Test	323-324	☐	☐	☐
11. Organisms and Populations	**325-348**			
Populations	325-329	☐	☐	☐
Population Interactions	329-332	☐	☐	☐
Mind Map	333	☐	☐	☐
Exam Pattern Questions	334-346	☐	☐	☐
Self Assessment Test	347-348	☐	☐	☐
12. Ecosystem	**349-370**			
Introduction	349-350	☐	☐	☐
Ecosystem : Structure and Function	350-351	☐	☐	☐
Productivity	351-352	☐	☐	☐
Decomposition	352-353	☐	☐	☐
Energy Flow	353-356	☐	☐	☐
Ecological Pyramids	356-357	☐	☐	☐
Mind Map	358	☐	☐	☐
Exam Pattern Questions	359-368	☐	☐	☐
Self Assessment Test	369-370	☐	☐	☐
13. Biodiversity and Its Conservation	**371-395**			
Levels of Biodiversity	371-372	☐	☐	☐
Magnitude of Biodiversity	372-373	☐	☐	☐
Patterns of Biodiversity	373-374	☐	☐	☐
Loss of Biodiversity	374-376	☐	☐	☐
Biodiversity Conservation	376-378	☐	☐	☐
Mind Map	379	☐	☐	☐
Exam Pattern Questions	380-393	☐	☐	☐
Self Assessment Test	394-395	☐	☐	☐
CBSE Examination Paper 2025	**396-403**			
Sample Question Papers (1-3)	**404-418**			

One Book- Endless Features
to Help you Succeed

01

CHAPTER

Sexual Reproduction in Flowering Plants

All living organisms produce their progenies via asexual and sexual reproduction. The process of sexual reproduction is mostly seen in higher organisms such as flowering plants. This process involves the fusion of male and female haploid (n) gametes to form a diploid ($2n$) zygote.
In this chapter, we will discuss all the aspects of sexual reproduction in the flowering plants.

- 1.1 Flower
- 1.2 Pre-Fertilisation: Structures and Events
- 1.3 Pollination
- 1.4 Double Fertilisation
- 1.5 Post-Fertilisation : Structures and Events
- 1.6 Some Special Mechanisms of Reproduction

- Objective Type Questions (43 Qs ; MCQs, A-R
- Case Based Questions (2)
- Subjective Type Questions (29 VSAs, 47 SAs, 20 LAs)

1.1 Flower

- It is a main reproductive organ in angiospermic plant.
- Flower is a modified shoot in which internodes are highly condensed and leaves are modified into floral parts.
- A typical flower consists of four distinct parts or whorls, i.e. **calyx, corolla, androecium** and **gynoecium**.
- All these parts are attached to a base called **receptacle** or **thalamus**.

Chapter Intro

A quick information about the coverage of the chapter to explain students about what they are going to study.

1.1 Flower

- It is a main reproductive organ in angiospermic plant.
- Flower is a modified shoot in which internodes are highly condensed and leaves are modified into floral parts.
- A typical flower consists of four distinct parts or whorls, i.e. **calyx, corolla, androecium** and **gynoecium**.
- All these parts are attached to a base called **receptacle** or **thalamus**.
- Out of these, calyx and corolla are sterile and considered as **non-essential** or **accessory whorls**, whereas androecium and gynoecium are fertile and considered as **essential** or **reproductive whorls**.

Simplified Theory

It contains the necessary study material well supported by Definitions, Facts, Figures, Flowcharts, etc.

TEACHER'S TIP
Tapetal cell become binucleate due to **endomitosis**, where they duplicate their chromosome without dividing, resulting in two nuclei per cell.

Teacher's Tip

Important Points related to given concept to bring students focus on important points.

Quick Test 1

1. How many microsporangia can be observed in a cross-section of the bilobed structure of a male reproductive organ of a flower?
2. An anther with malfunctioning tapetum often fails to produce viable male gametophytes. Give any one reason.
3. Arrange the following terms in a correct developmental sequence.
   Pollen grain, sporogenous tissue, microspore tetrad, pollen mother cell, male gametes. *NCERT*
4. Give an example of a plant which came into India as a contaminant and is a cause of pollen allergy.
5. **State True or False.**
   The male gametophyte of angiosperms can be stored for several years in liquid nitrogen.

Quick Tests

To make students understand the chapter in a smooth part-by-part manner, Quick Tests have been given in each chapter. These Exercises help students to assess the understanding of related concepts at regular interval.

One Book- Endless Features
to Help you Succeed

Illustrative Figures

To make the concepts completely visible, illustrative diagrams have been given at various place.

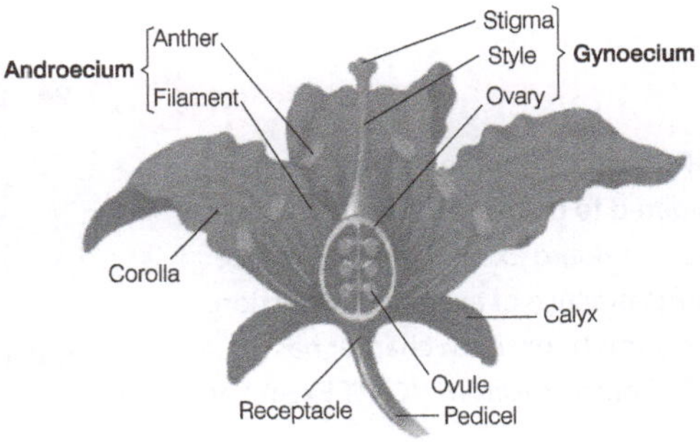

Fig. 1.1 Structure of a flower

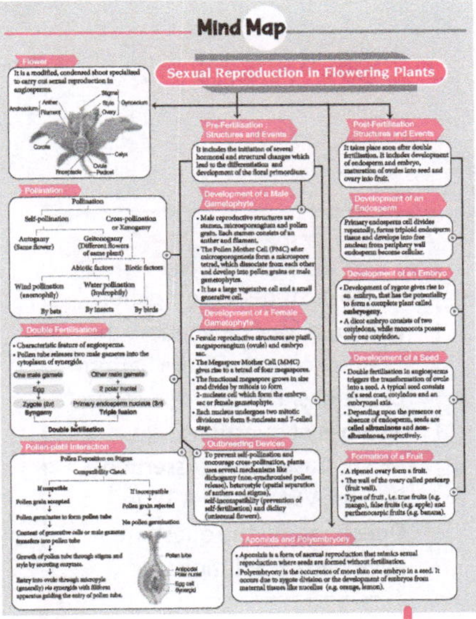

Mind Map

A quick revision visual tool for the complete chapter.

NCERT Questions

To make students completely understand NCERT books, solutions of selected NCERT questions have been given in each chapter.

12. Differentiate between microsporogenesis and megasporogenesis. Which type of cell division occurs during these events? Name the structure formed at the end of these two events. **NCERT**

Ans.

Microsporogenesis	Megasporogenesis
In this process, haploid microspores are formed from diploid microspore mother cell.	In this process haploid megaspore is formed from diploid megaspore mother cell.

The cell division that occurs during these events is meiosis.

Pollen grain and female gametophyte or embryo sac. (1 × 3)

13. With a neat labelled diagram explain the 7-celled, 8-nucleate nature of the female gametophyte. **NCERT**

Ans. Refer to a e no. 7 dia ram 19.

17. Many of the flowering plants producing hermaphrodite flowers have developed many devices to discourage self-pollination and to encourage cross-pollination. Given below is a picture of one such outbreeding device in a flowering plant. Study the picture and answer the questions that follow: **CBSE 2025**

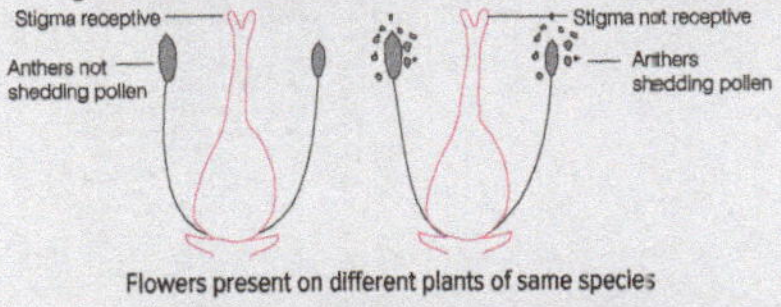

Flowers present on different plants of same species

Ans. (i) The given type of pollination is cross-pollination, where flowers on different plants of the same species exchange pollen. This is advantageous as it promotes genetic variation, leading to better adaptability, disease resistance, and healthier offspring compared to self-pollination.

Board Exams' Questions

Solving Board Exams' Questions while studying the chapters, always prove to be confidence booster. For this purpose, each chapter has selected Questions from last 10 years Board Exams upto 2025.

One Book- Endless Features

to Help you Succeed

NCERT Exemplar Problems

NCERT Exemplar Problems are considered to be the best problem books for School/Board Examinations. To make students practice of exemplary questions given in this book, each chapter has selected problems from NCERT Exemplar.

24. In a fertilised embryo sac, the haploid, diploid and triploid structure are **NCERT Exemplar**

(a) synergid, zygote and primary endosperm nucleus
(b) synergid, antipodal and polar nuclei
(c) antipodal, synergid and primary endosperm nucleus
(d) synergid, polar nuclei and zygote

Ans. (*a*)

Sample Question Papers

To make students practice of examination in real sense, there are 3 Sample Question Papers at the end. All these Sample Questions Papers are exactly prepared on the latest syllabus & pattern of examination.

SAMPLE QUESTION PAPER 1

A Highly Simulated Sample Question Paper for CBSE Class XII Examination

BIOLOGY

Time : 3 Hours **Max. Marks : 70**

General Instructions

1. All questions are compulsory.
2. The question paper has five sections and 33 questions.
3. Section-A has 16 questions of 1 mark each; Section-B has 5 questions of 2 marks each; Section-C has 7 questions of 3 marks each; Section-D has 2 case-based questions of 4 marks each; and Section-E has 3 questions of 5 marks each.
4. There is no overall choice. However, internal choices have been provided in some questions. A student has to attempt only one of the alternatives in such questions.
5. Wherever necessary, neat and properly labelled diagrams should be drawn.

Section-A

1. A female was incapable of producing ovum, but can provide suitable environment for fertilisation. Out of the options given below, select the correct method suggested by the doctors for successful results?
(a) IUD (b) GIFT
(c) IUI (d) ICSI

2. Given below are four reproductive stages and their sites of occurrence.

	Stages		Sites of Occurrence
A.	Fertilisation	1.	Ampulla of oviduct
B.	Cleavage	2.	Isthmus of oviduct
C.	Blastocyst	3.	Cervix
D.	Parturition	4.	Uterine wall

How many pairs are correctly matched?
(a) 1 (b) 2 (c) 3 (d) 4

3. Which one of the following correctly describes the homologous structure?
(a) Organs with anatomical similarities, but performing different functions
(b) Organs with anatomical dissimilarities, but performing same function
(c) Organs that have not function now, but had an important function in ancestor
(d) Organs appearing only in embryonic stage and disappearing later in the adult

4. The gene disorder phenylketonuria is an example for
(a) multiple factor (b) multiple allelism
(c) pleiotropy (d) polygenic inheritance

5. Smoking is not socially acceptable as it has greater risk to human health. Identify the type of cancer caused by smoking and the main component for this case.

	Cancer	Component
(a)	Lung	Carbon dioxide
(b)	Throat	Carbon monoxide
(c)	Lung	Tar
(d)	Throat	Nicotine

6. In order to activate the immune system and destroy tumour, which of the following substances are given to cancer patients?
(a) Histamine
(b) Interleukin
(c) α-interferon
(d) Morphine

Exam Pattern Questions

To make students completely prepared for examination, this Exercise contains Exam Pattern Questions. This exercise covers all types of questions, like; MCQs, Case Based, Assertion-Reason, VSA, SA & LA Type Questions. All the questions have Hints & Solutions. .

EXAM PATTERN QUESTIONS

Objective Type Questions

Multiple Choice Questions

1. Identify *A* to *G* in following figure and answer accordingly.

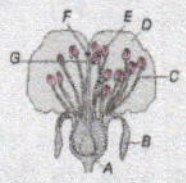

(a) *A*–Ovary, *B*–Filament, *C*–Sepal, *D*–Petal, *E*–Style, *F*–Stigma, *G*–Anther
(b) *A*–Sepal, *B*–Ovary, *C*–Petal, *D*–Filament, *E*–Anther, *F*–Stigma, *G*–Style
(c) *A*–Ovary, *B*–Sepal, *C*–Filament, *D*–Petal, *E*–Anther, *F*–Stigma, *G*–Style
(d) *A*–Petal, *B*–Anther, *C*–Stigma, *D*–Style, *E*–Filament, *F*–Sepal, *G*–Ovary

Ans. (*c*)

2. A typical angiosperm anther is dithecous which means that it is
(a) one lobed and the lobe has two theca
(b) two lobed and each lobe has one theca
(c) two lobed and each lobe has two theca
(d) four lobed and each lobe has two theca

Ans. (*c*)

4. What is the characteristics of tapetum?
(a) It is uninucleated
(b) It is multinucleated
(c) It is binucleated
(d) It provide nourishment to the megaspore.

Ans. (*b*)

5. Which of the following is correct with respect to microsporogenesis?
(a) The cells of sporogenous tissue divide and form pollen mother cells.
(b) Pollen mother cells are formed form a tetrad
(c) Inside the microsporangium several thousand male gamete are present
(d) Both (a) and (c)

Ans. (*d*)

6. How many pollen mother cells should undergo meiotic division to produce 48 pollen grains?
(a) 8 (b) 12 (c) 16 (d) 24

Ans. (*b*) Each pollen mother cell produces 4 haploid pollen grains during meiosis. Thus, 12 pollen mother cells are required to produce 48 pollen grains.

7. 60% of the angiosperms shed their pollens at the
(a) 2-celled stage (b) 3-celled stage
(c) 4-celled stage (d) 1-celled stage

Ans. (*a*)

Latest Course Structure

Paper: One	Time: 3 Hrs	Max. Marks : 70

Units		Marks
VI	Reproduction	16
VII	Genetics and Evolution	20
VIII	Biology and Human Welfare	12
IX	Biotechnology and its Applications	12
X	Ecology and Environment	10
	TOTAL	**70**

UNIT VI Reproduction

Chapter 1 : Sexual Reproduction in Flowering Plants

Flower structure; development of male and female gametophytes; pollination - types, agencies and examples; out breeding devices; pollen-pistil interaction; double fertilisation; post-fertilisation events - development of endosperm and embryo, development of seed and formation of fruit; special modes- apomixis, parthenocarpy, polyembryony; Significance of seed dispersal and fruit formation.

Chapter 2 : Human Reproduction

Male and female reproductive systems; microscopic anatomy of testis and ovary; gametogenesis -spermatogenesis and oogenesis; menstrual cycle; fertilisation, embryo development upto blastocyst formation, implantation; pregnancy and placenta formation (elementary idea); parturition (elementary idea); lactation (elementary idea).

Chapter 3 : Reproductive Health

Need for reproductive health and prevention of Sexually Transmitted Diseases (STDs); birth control - need and methods, contraception and Medical Termination of Pregnancy (MTP); amniocentesis; infertility and assisted reproductive technologies - IVF, ZIFT, GIFT (elementary idea for general awareness).

UNIT VII Genetics and Evolution

Chapter 4 : Principles of Inheritance and Variation

Heredity and variation: Mendelian inheritance; deviations from Mendelism – incomplete dominance, co-dominance, multiple alleles and inheritance of blood groups, pleiotropy; elementary idea of polygenic inheritance; chromosome theory of inheritance; chromosomes and genes; Sex determination - in humans, birds and honeybee; linkage and crossing over; sex linked inheritance - haemophilia, colour blindness; Mendelian disorders in humans - thalassemia; chromosomal disorders in humans; Down's syndrome, Turner's and Klinefelter's syndromes.

Chapter 5 : Molecular Basis of Inheritance

Search for genetic material and DNA as genetic material; Structure of DNA and RNA; DNA packaging; DNA replication; Central Dogma; transcription, genetic code, translation; gene expression and regulation - *lac* operon; Genome, Human and rice genome projects; DNA fingerprinting.

Chapter 6 : Evolution

Origin of life; biological evolution and evidences for biological evolution (paleontology, comparative anatomy, embryology and molecular evidences); Darwin's contribution, modern synthetic theory of evolution; mechanism of evolution - variation (mutation and recombination) and natural selection with examples, types of natural selection; Gene flow and genetic drift; Hardy - Weinberg's principle; adaptive radiation; human evolution.

UNIT VIII Biology and Human Welfare

Chapter 7 : Human Health and Diseases

Pathogens; parasites causing human diseases (malaria, dengue, chikungunya, filariasis, ascariasis, typhoid, pneumonia, common cold, amoebiasis, ring worm) and their control; Basic concepts of immunology - vaccines; cancer, HIV and AIDS; Adolescence - drug and alcohol abuse.

Chapter 8 : Microbes in Human Welfare

Microbes in food processing, industrial production, sewage treatment, energy generation and microbes as bio-control agents and bio-fertilisers. Antibiotics; production and judicious use.

UNIT IX Biotechnology and Its Applications

Chapter 9 : Biotechnology - Principles and Processes

Genetic Engineering (Recombinant DNA Technology).

Chapter 10 : Biotechnology and its Application

Application of biotechnology in health and agriculture: Human insulin and vaccine production, stem cell technology, gene therapy; genetically modified organisms - *Bt* crops; transgenic animals; biosafety issues, biopiracy and patents.

UNIT X Ecology and Environment

Chapter 11 : Organisms and Populations

Population interactions - mutualism, competition, predation, parasitism; population attributes - growth, birth rate and death rate, age distribution.

Chapter 12 : Ecosystem

Ecosystems: Patterns, components; productivity and decomposition; energy flow; pyramids of number, biomass, energy

Chapter 13 : Biodiversity and its Conservation

Biodiversity-Concept, patterns, importance; loss of biodiversity; biodiversity conservation; hotspots, endangered organisms, extinction, Red Data Book, Sacred groves, biosphere reserves, national parks, wildlife sanctuaries and Ramsar sites.

Practicals

Practicals should be conducted alongside the concepts taught in theory classes

List of Experiments

Evaluation Scheme		Marks
One Major Experiment 5		5
One Minor Experiment 2 & 3		4
Slide Preparation 1& 4		5
Spotting		7
Practical Record + Viva Voce	(Credit to the student's work over the academic session may be given)	4
Investigatory Project and its Project Record + Viva Voce		5
Total		30

A. List of Experiments

1. Prepare a temporary mount to observe pollen germination.
2. Study the plant population density by quadrat method.
3. Study the plant population frequency by quadrat method.
4. Prepare a temporary mount of onion root tip to study mitosis.
5. Isolate DNA from available plant material such as spinach, green pea seeds, papaya, etc.

B. Study and observer the following (Spotting):

1. Flowers adapted to pollination by different agencies (wind, insects, birds).
2. Pollen germination on stigma through a permanent slide or scanning electron micrograph.
3. Identification of stages of gamete development, i.e., T.S. of testis and T.S. of ovary through permanent slides (from grasshopper/mice).
4. Meiosis in onion bud cell or grasshopper testis through permanent slides.
5. T.S. of blastula through permanent slides (Mammalian).
6. Mendelian inheritance using seeds of different colour/sizes of any plant.
7. Prepared pedigree charts of any one of the genetic traits such as rolling of tongue, blood groups, ear lobes, widow's peak and colour blindness.
8. Controlled pollination - emasculation, tagging and bagging.
9. Common disease causing organisms like *Ascaris, Entamoeba, Plasmodium,* any fungus causing ringworm through permanent slides, models or virtual images or specimens. Comment on symptoms of diseases that they cause.
10. Models specimen showing symbolic association in root modules of leguminous plants, and parasitic mode of nutation shown by *Cuscuta* on host, lichens.
11. Flash cards/models showing examples of homologous and analogous organs.

01 CHAPTER

Sexual Reproduction in Flowering Plants

All living organisms produce their progenies *via* asexual and sexual reproduction. The process of sexual reproduction is mostly seen in higher organisms such as flowering plants. This process involves the fusion of male and female haploid (n) gametes to form a diploid ($2n$) zygote.

In this chapter, we will discuss all the aspects of sexual reproduction in the flowering plants.

YOUR STUDY GOALS

- 1.1 Flower
- 1.2 Pre-Fertilisation: Structures and Events
- 1.3 Pollination
- 1.4 Double Fertilisation
- 1.5 Post-Fertilisation : Structures and Events
- 1.6 Some Special Mechanisms of Reproduction

YOUR PRACTICE GOAL

- Objective Type Questions (43 Qs ; MCQs, A-R
- Case Based Questions (2)
- Subjective Type Questions (29 VSAs, 47 SAs, 20 LAs)

1.1 Flower

- It is a main reproductive organ in angiospermic plant.
- Flower is a modified shoot in which internodes are highly condensed and leaves are modified into floral parts.
- A typical flower consists of four distinct parts or whorls, i.e. **calyx, corolla, androecium** and **gynoecium**.
- All these parts are attached to a base called **receptacle** or **thalamus**.
- Out of these, calyx and corolla are sterile and considered as **non-essential** or **accessory whorls**, whereas androecium and gynoecium are fertile and considered as **essential** or **reproductive whorls**.

- The different parts of a flower are discussed below in brief.

Calyx

- It is the outermost whorl of the flower.
- Calyx is made up of several functional units called **sepal**.
- These are generally green, leaf-like structures, which protect the flower in the bud stage.

Corolla

- It is the second whorl of flower that arises inner to the calyx.
- Individual units of corolla are called **petals**.
- These are brightly coloured and fragrant, making the flower attractive and helping in pollination.

Androecium

- It is the male reproductive organ consisting of whorl of stamens.
- Each stamen consists of an **anther** and **filament**.
- It helps in the production of microspores, i.e. pollen grains, containing male gametes within the anther lobes.

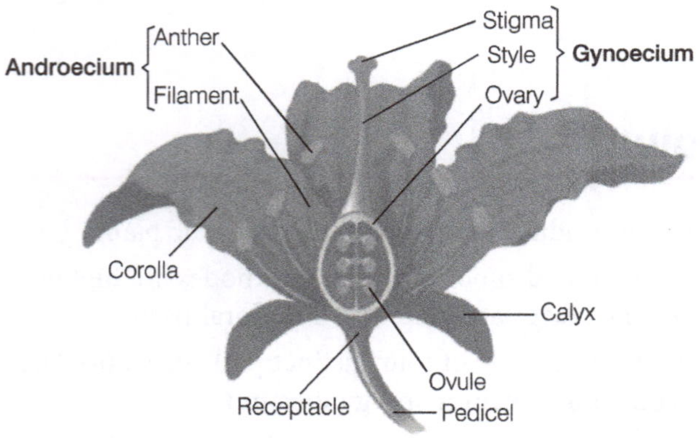

Fig. 1.1 Structure of a flower

Gynoecium

- It is the female reproductive organ.
- The gynoecium is made up of one or more **carpels**.
- A carpel consists of three parts, i.e. **stigma** (receptive part), **style** (a long tube beneath stigma) and **ovary** (basal part of style that bears ovules).
- It helps in the production of female gametes.

1.2 Pre-Fertilisation: Structures and Events

- The events which occur before the fertilisation are called **pre-fertilisation events**.
- During this process several hormonal and structural changes occur, which lead to the differentiation and development of floral organ or flower.
- In the flower, the **androecium** (male reproductive part) and **gynoecium** (female reproductive part) differentiate and develop to form male and female gametophytes, respectively.
- Different structures and events involved in pre-fertilisation are discussed below.

Stamen, Microsporangium and Pollen Grain

These are described below in brief

Stamen

- It is the **male reproductive unit** of an angiosperm.
- A stamen consists of two parts
  - **Filament** It is a long and slender stalk. The proximal end of the filament is attached to the thalamus or the petal of the flower.
  - **Anther** It is the terminal structure which is generally bilobed.
- The number and length of the stamens vary in flowers of different species.

Structure of an Anther

- A typical angiospermic anther is a **bilobed** structure with each lobe having two **theca** (dithecous).
- These two theca are separated by a longitudinal groove running lengthwise.
- In a cross section, the anther appears as four-sided (tetragonal) structure consisting of four **microsporangia** located at the corners, two in each lobe.
- Later, the microsporangia develop and become **pollen sacs**.

- They extend longitudinally all through the length of an anther and are packed with the pollen grains.

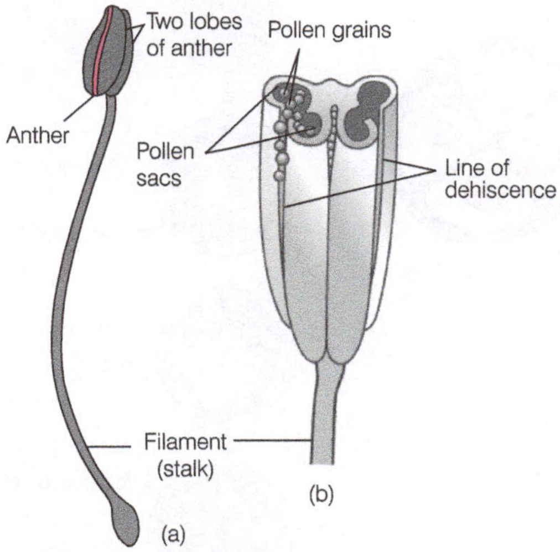

Fig. 1.2 (a) A typical stamen, (b) Three-dimensional cut section of an anther

Structure of a Microsporangium

- A typical microsporangium appears circular in transverse section and is surrounded by four wall layers, i.e. the **epidermis, endothecium, middle layers** and the **tapetum**.

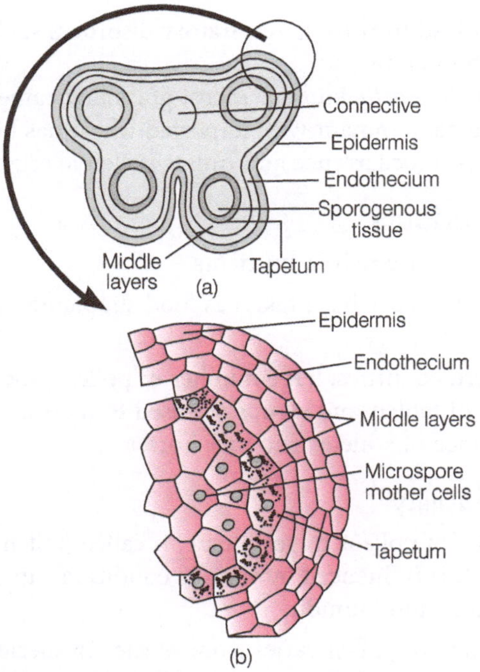

Fig. 1.3 (a) Transverse section of a young anther, (b) Enlarged view of a microsporangium

- The **outer three wall layers** are protective in function and help in dehiscence of anther to release pollen grains.
- The **innermost layer** (tapetum) nourishes the developing microspores or pollen grains.
- The cells of tapetum possess dense cytoplasm and generally have more than one nucleus.

> **TEACHER'S TIP**
> Tapetal cell become binucleate due to **endomitosis**, where they duplicate their chromosome without dividing, resulting in two nuclei per cell.

- When the anther is young, a group of compactly arranged homogenous cells called the **sporogenous tissue** occupies the centre of each microsporangium.

Microsporogenesis

- The process of formation of microspore from a pollen mother cell *via* meiosis is called microsporogenesis.
- Each diploid cell of the sporogenous tissue grows and is capable of transforming into **microspore** or **Pollen Mother Cells** (PMC).
- The PMC divides by meiosis to produce four haploid microspores, which are arranged in a cluster of four cells called **microspore tetrad.**
- As the anthers mature and dehydrate, the microspores dissociate from each other and develop into pollen grains.
- Inside each microsporangium, several thousands of **microspores** or **pollen grains** are formed.

Sporogenous tissue $(2n) \rightarrow$ PMC $(2n) \rightarrow$ Microspore tetrad $(n) \rightarrow$ Pollen grains (n)

- The dehiscence of anther leads to the release of pollen grains.

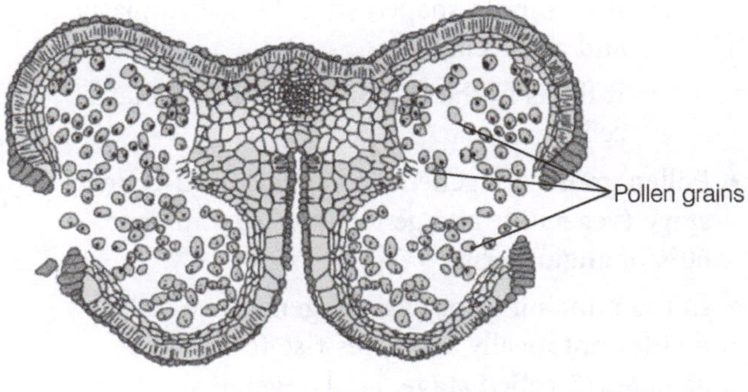

Fig. 1.4 A mature dehisced anther

Pollen Grains

- These are also known as male gametophyte.
- Pollen grains are haploid and minute spores that contain male gamete, essential for the reproduction.
- They vary in their size, shape, colour, design, etc., from species to species.

Structure of Pollen Grain

- Pollen grains are generally spherical measuring about 25-50 micrometer in diameter.
- The wall of pollen grains is comprises of two layers, i.e.
  - **Outer Hard Layer** (Exine) It is made up of **sporopollenin**, the most resistant organic material that can withstand high temperatures, strong acid and alkali.
    - No known enzyme can degrade sporopollenin that is why pollens are well-preserved as fossils.
    - Pollen grains have prominent aperture called **germ pore**, where sporopollenin is absent.
  - **Inner Layer** (Intine) It is a thin and continuous layer, chiefly composed of **cellulose** and **pectin**.
    The cytoplasm of pollen grain is surrounded by a plasma membrane.
- Pollen grains undergo mitotic division to give rise to two unequal cells.
  - **Vegetative Cell** This cell is bigger in size. It has abundant reserve food material and a large nucleus, which is irregular in shape.
  - **Generative Cell** This cell is small in size.
    - It is spindle-shaped with dense cytoplasm and a nucleus.
    - It floats in the cytoplasm of the vegetative cell.
- Pollen grains are generally shed at this **2-celled stage** (vegetative and generative cells) in over 60% of angiosperms.
- In the remaining species, the generative cell divides mitotically and gives rise to two male gametes (**3-celled stage**, i.e. 1 vegetative cell and 2 male gametes) before pollen grains are shed.
- The vegetative cell grows further to form pollen tube.

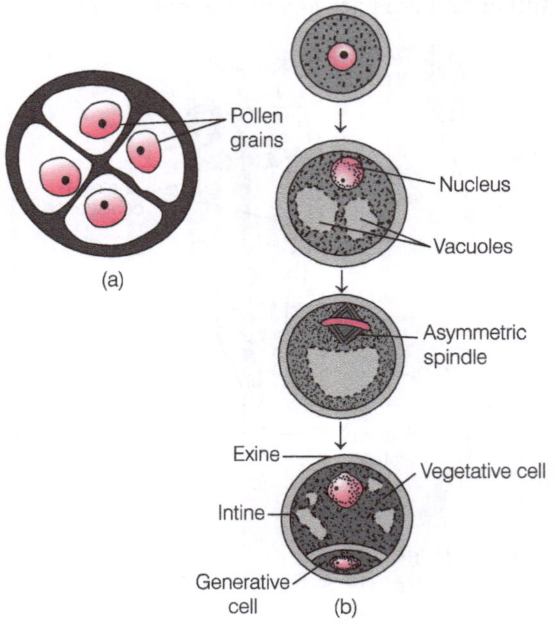

Fig. 1.5 (a) Enlarged view of a pollen grain tetrad, (b) Stages of a microspore maturing into a pollen grain

Pollen Allergy

- Pollen grains of several plant species may cause severe allergies and bronchial affliction.
- This may lead to chronic respiratory disorders such as asthma, bronchitis, etc.
  For example, *Parthenium* or carrot grass that came to India as a contaminant with imported wheat has became ubiquitous in occurrence and causes pollen allergy.

Pollen Products

- Pollen grains are rich in nutrients.
- Pollen tablets have been taken as food supplements in recent years.
- In Western countries, large number of pollen products in the form of tablets and syrups are used to increase the performance of athletes and race horses.

Pollen Viability

- The ability of pollens to germinate, is called pollen viability. It is influenced by various conditions, including temperature and humidity.
- The viability of pollen varies from species to species, e.g. 30 minutes in case of wheat, rice and several months in some members of Solanaceae, Rosaceae, Leguminosae, etc.

- It is possible to store pollen grains for years in liquid nitrogen (–196°C) in pollen banks for later use in plant breeding programmes.

Quick Test 1

1. How many microsporangia can be observed in a cross-section of the bilobed structure of a male reproductive organ of a flower?
2. An anther with malfunctioning tapetum often fails to produce viable male gametophytes. Give any one reason.
3. Arrange the following terms in a correct developmental sequence.
   Pollen grain, sporogenous tissue, microspore tetrad, pollen mother cell, male gametes. *NCERT*
4. Give an example of a plant which came into India as a contaminant and is a cause of pollen allergy.
5. **State True or False.**
   The male gametophyte of angiosperms can be stored for several years in liquid nitrogen.

Pistil, Megasporangium and Embryo Sac

These are described below in brief

Pistil

- The **gynoecium** represents the female reproductive part of the flower.
- Gynoecium may consist of one pistil or carpel (called **monocarpellary**), two carpels (called **bicarpellary**), three carpels (called **tricarpellary**) or many carpels (called **multicarpellary**).
- Pistil may be **syncarpous**, i.e. more than one pistils fused together, e.g. in *Papaver* or may be **apocarpous,** i.e. carpels remain free, e.g. in *Michelia* (Fig. 1.6).
- A typical pistil consists of following parts
  - **Stigma** It receives the pollen grains. It has sticky surface on which pollen grains get stuck during pollination.
  - **Style** It is an elongated slender part beneath the stigma. It connects the stigma with ovary. Pollen tube grows through the style and reaches to the ovary.
  - **Ovary** It is basal swollen part which contains ovules and eggs. Inside the ovary, **ovarian cavity** (locule) is present. The **placenta** is located inside the ovarian cavity.

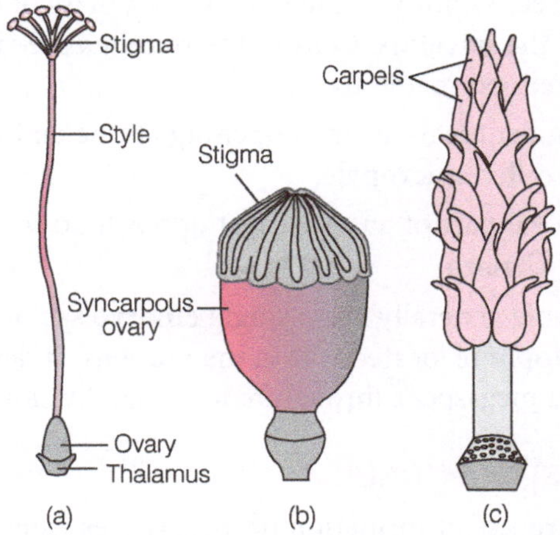

Fig. 1.6 (a) A dissected flower of *Hibiscus* showing pistil (other floral parts have been removed); (b) Multicarpellary, syncarpous pistil of *Papaver;* (c) Multicarpellary, apocarpous gynoecium of *Michelia*

- Ovule commonly known as **megasporangia** arise from the placenta.
- The number of ovule in an ovary may be one, e.g. wheat, paddy, mango, etc., or many, e.g. papaya, watermelon, orchids, etc.

Structure of Megasporangium (Ovule)

- The ovule is a small structure attached to the placenta by means of a stalk called **funicle**. It develops into a seed after fertilisation.
- The body of ovule fuses with funicle in the region called **hilum**. It represents the junction between an ovule and funicle.

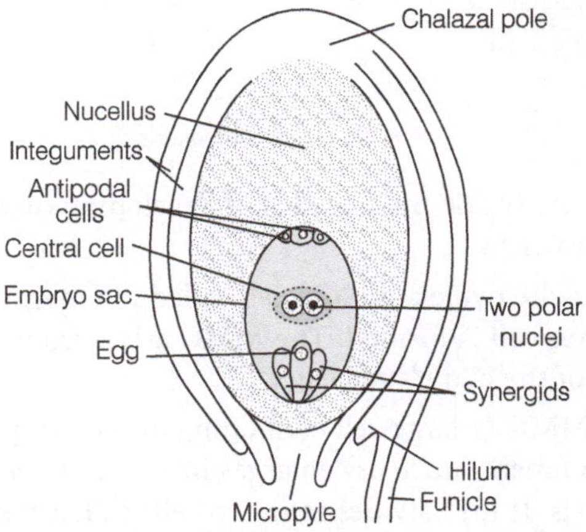

Fig. 1.7 Diagrammatic view of a typical anatropous ovule

- Each ovule has one or two protective envelops called **integuments.**
- Enclosed within the integuments is a mass of cells called the **nucellus.** Cells of the nucellus are rich in reserve food materials.
- Integument leave a small opening at one end of the ovule called **micropyle.**
- The basal part of an ovule just opposite to micropyle is called **chalaza.**
- An ovule generally has a single **embryo sac** or **female gametophyte** located within the nucellus. It develops from a megaspore through reductional division.

Megasporogenesis

- The process of formation of megaspores from **Megaspore Mother Cell** or **MMC** (diploid) is called megasporogenesis.

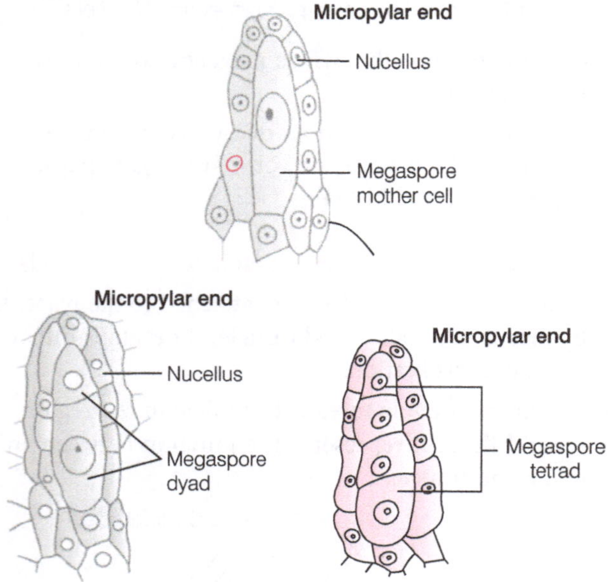

Fig. 1.8 Megasporogenesis

- It occurs inside the nucellus of developing ovule of angiosperms.
- Inside the ovule a diploid cell called the **megaspore mother cell** is formed. The MMC arises from the initial cells of the ovule's nucellus.
- The MMC (a large cell containing dense cytoplasm and a prominent nucleus) enlarges in size and divides by meiosis. It first divides into two cells called **megaspore dyad.**
- These two cells divide again and form, a linear row of four haploid cells called **megaspore tetrad.**

Female Gametophyte (Embryo Sac)

- In majority of flowering plants, out of the four megaspores, only one remains functional and develop into **female gametophyte,** while the other three gradually degenerate.
- This process of embryo sac formation from a single megaspore is termed as **monosporic development.**
- Formation of female gametophyte, i.e. embryo sac is termed as **megagametogenesis.**

Development of Female Gametophyte

Following are the different stages in the development of female gametophyte.

- The functional haploid megaspore is the first cell of female gametophyte of angiosperms.
- It enlarges in size to form the female gametophyte, also called **embryo sac.**
- Its nucleus undergoes mitotic division to form 2-nuclei that move to opposite poles forming **2-nucleate** embryo sac.
- This **2-nucleate** embryo sac undergoes two more sequential mitotic divisions, giving rise to the **4-nucleate** stage and later **8-nucleate** stage of embryo sac.
- All these mitotic divisions are strictly **free-nuclear,** i.e. nuclear division are not followed immediately by cell wall formation.
- After the 8-nucleated stage, cell walls are laid down leading to the organisation of typical female gametophyte.
- Six of the eight nuclei get surrounded by cell walls and get organised into cells. The remaining two nuclei are known as **polar nuclei.**
- Three cells are grouped together towards the micropylar end, constitute the **egg apparatus.** It consists of two **synergids** and one **egg cell.**
- The synergids have special cellular thickenings at the micropylar tip called **filiform apparatus,** which play an important role in guiding the pollen tube into synergids.
- Remaining three cells are grouped the chalazal end and are called the **antipodals.**

- The large central cell, situated below the egg apparatus, contains 2 polar nuclei.
- Thus, a typical angiospermic **embryo sac** or **female gametophyte** at maturity consists of **eight nuclei** and **seven cells**.

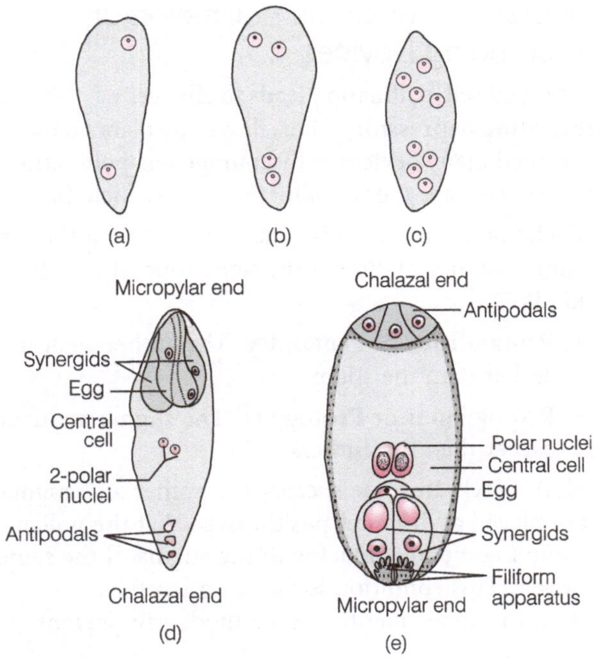

Fig. 1.9 (a) 2-nucleate stage of embryo sac, (b) 4-nucleate stage of embryo sac, (c) 8-nucleate stage of embryo sac, (d) Cell formation in embryo sac, (e) A diagrammatic representation of mature embryo sac

MMC ($2n$) $\xrightarrow{\text{Meiosis}}$ 4 megaspores (n) $\longrightarrow$ 1 functional megaspore (n) $\xrightarrow{\text{Mitosis (3x)}}$ 7-celled, 8 nucleated sac

Quick Test 2

1. Mention one similarity between the carpel of *Papaver* and *Michelia*.
2. Name the part of flower that act as the landing platform for pollen grains.
3. What will be the ploidy of nucellus and functional megaspore of a tetraploid plant?
4. Name the cells present at the chalazal end of the embryo sac.
5. **State True or False.**
   The functional megaspore undergoes free nuclear meiotic division to form an 8-nucleate and 7-celled structure.

1.3 Pollination

- The male and female gametes (non-motile) formed in their respective gametophytes are brought together for fertilisation *via* pollination.
- The transfer of pollen grains from the anther of a flower to the receptive stigma of the same or other flower is called pollination.
- Flowering plants have evolved an amazing array of adaptations to achieve pollination.
- Depending upon the source of pollen grains, pollination is of following three types

Autogamy (Self-Pollination)

- It is the kind of pollination that is achieved within the same flower.
- In this, the pollens from the anthers of a flower are transferred to the stigma of the same flower.
- It is possible only when anther and stigma are in close contact and there is synchrony in pollen release and stigma receptivity.
- Some plants like *Viola* (common pansy), *Oxalis* and *Commelina* produce two types of flower.
- These are as follows
  - **Chasmogamous Flowers** These are open flowers with exposed sex organs. On these flowers pollens from another flower can land on the stigma as well, e.g. *Catharanthus* and *Mirabilis*.

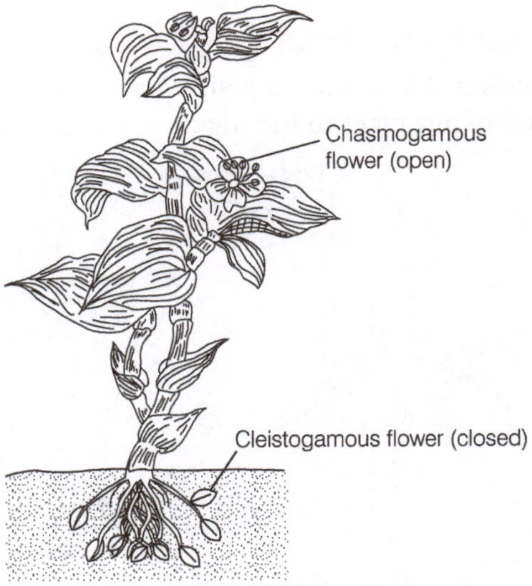

Fig. 1.10 Chasmogamous and cleistogamous flowers in *Commelina benghalensis*

- **Cleistogamous Flowers** These are closed flowers with their anthers and stigma lying close to each other. These flowers produce an assured seed set even in the absence of pollinators. Almost all the cleistogamous flowers are invariably autogamous as there is no chance of cross-pollination, e.g. *Commelina*.

Geitonogamy

- It is a kind of self-pollination where the pollen grains from the anther of a flower are transferred to the stigma of another flower of the same plant.
- It is functionally a type of cross-pollination (involving a pollinating agent), but genetically it is similar to autogamy (since pollen grains come from the same plant).

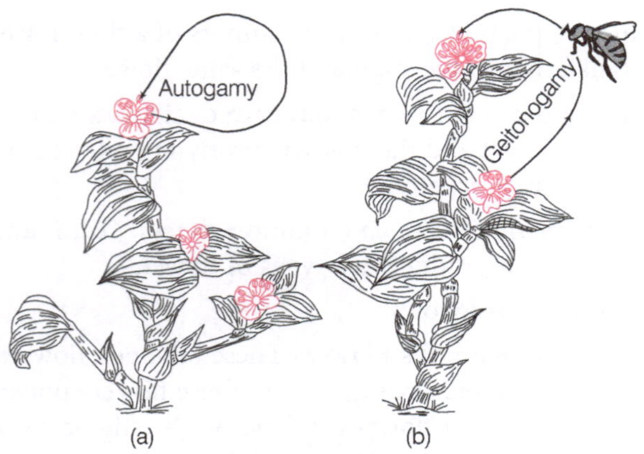

Fig. 1.11 Self-pollination : (a) Autogamy, (b) Geitonogamy

Xenogamy (Cross-pollination)

- It involves the transfer of pollen grains from the anther of one plant to the stigma of another plant.

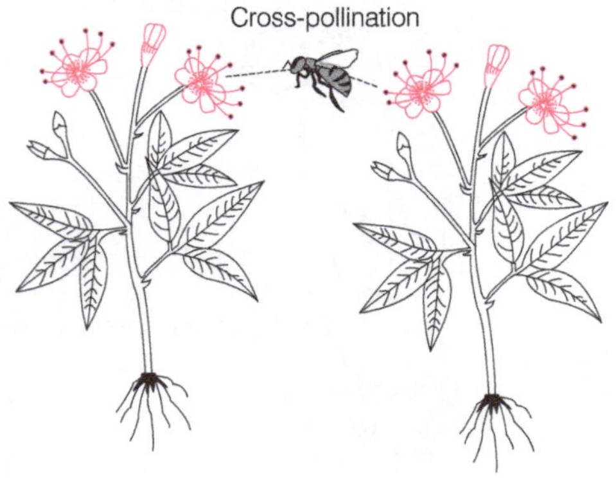

Fig. 1.12 Cross-pollination

- This is the only type of pollination which brings genetically different types of pollen grains to the stigma.
- Cross-pollination occurs with the help of biotic and abiotic agents.

Adaptations for Cross-pollination or Outbreeding Devices

Continued self-pollination leads to chances of **inbreeding depression**. Thus, flowering plants have developed many devices to discourage self-pollination and to encourage cross-pollination. These include

- **Dichogamy** In some bisexual flowers, the anther and stigma do not mature at the same time. It is of two kinds
  - **Protandrous** or **Protandry** The anthers mature earlier than the stigma.
  - **Protogynous** or **Protogyny** The stigma matures earlier than the anthers.
- **Heterostyly** In some species, the anther and stigma are placed at different positions, so that the pollen cannot come in contact with the stigma of the same flower. This condition is called heterostyly.
  Both the above mentioned methods will prevent autogamy.

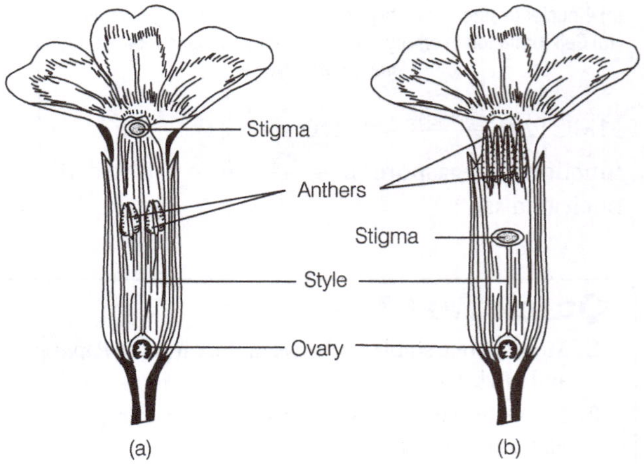

Fig. 1.13 Flowers exhibiting heterostyly : (a) Long-styled flower, (b) Short-styled flower

- **Self-incompatibility** It is a genetic mechanism of preventing the pollen from fertilising ovules of the same flower or another flower of the same plant by inhibiting pollen germination or pollen tube growth in the pistil.

- **Dicliny or Unisexuality** It refers to the production of only unisexual flowers. If both male and female flowers are present on the same plant (monoecious), it prevents autogamy, but not geitonogamy, e.g. castor, maize, etc.
- **Dioecy** In this, both autogamy and geitonogamy are prevented. In several species like papaya, male and female flowers are present on different plants, i.e. each plant is either male or female. This condition is called dioecy.

Agents of Cross-pollination

- Pollen cannot be transferred from the anther to the stigma on its own. So, majority of plants relies on other agents to transfer the pollens.
- These agents of pollination in angiosperms have been grouped into two main categories

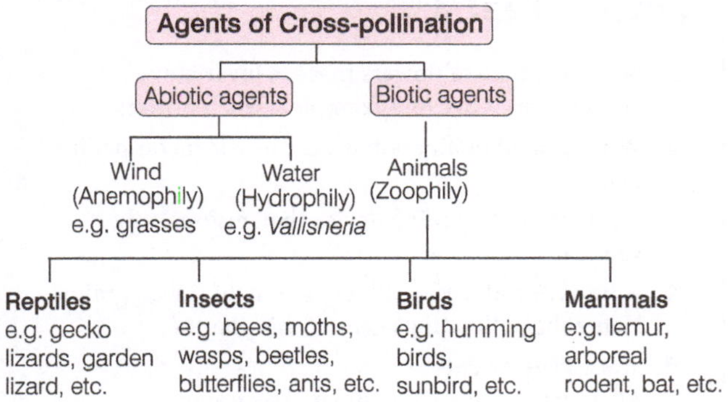

- Majority of plants use biotic agents for pollination.
- Only some partions of plants use abiotic agents as pollen grains coming in contact with the stigma is a chance factor in both wind and water pollination.
- To increase the chances of pollen grains meeting with stigma and reduce associated loss of pollen grains, the plants have adopted various ways.

Adaptations for Wind Pollination

Wind pollination or **anemophily** is the most common abiotic pollination. The adaptations of wind pollinated flowers are as follows

- Flowers are small, colourless, inconspicuous and nectarless.
- Wind pollinated flowers often have a single ovule in each ovary and numerous flowers packed into an inflorescence (cluster of flowers) such as the tassels of corn cob (i.e. stigma and style).
- The stamens are well-exposed for the easy dispersal of pollen grains.
- Pollen grains are small, light, dry, dusty, non-sticky and sometimes even winged.
- The stigmas are large, hairy and feathery or branched to catch the air-borne pollen grains.
- Common examples of wind pollinated flowers are grasses, maize, etc.

Fig. 1.14 A wind pollinated plant showing compact inflorescence and well-exposed stamens

Adaptations for Water Pollination

Pollination by water or **hydrophily** is quite rare in flowering plants and is limited to about 30 genera, mostly monocotyledons. The adaptations of water pollinated flowers are as follows

- It is very common in lower plant groups such as algae, bryophytes and pteridophytes.
- Flowers are small, colourless, inconspicuous, odourless and nectarless.
- In most of the water pollinated species, pollen grains are protected from getting wet by mucilaginous covering.
- In *Vallisneria*, female flowers reach the surface of water by the long stalk and male flowers or pollen

grains are released on to the surface of water. They are then carried passively by water currents.

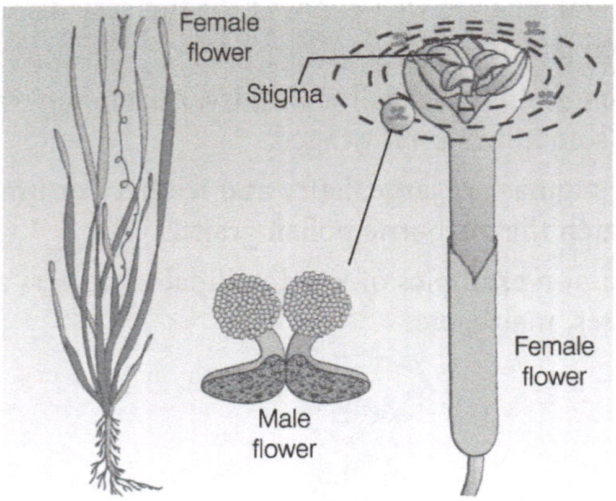

Fig. 1.15 Hydrophily in *Vallisneria*

- In plants like sea grasses, female flowers remain submerged in water and the pollen grains are released inside the water. In such species, pollen grains are long, ribbon-like and are carried passively inside the water to reach stigma and achieve pollination.
- Common examples of water pollinated plants are *Vallisneria* and *Hydrilla* which grow in freshwater and several marine sea grasses such as *Zostera*.
- Whereas not all aquatic plants use water for pollination. In a majority of aquatic plants, the flowers emerge above the surface level of water and are pollinated by insects or wind as in land plants, e.g. water hyacinth and water lily.

Adaptations for Insect Pollination

Pollination by insects is also termed as **entomophily**. Among the animals insects, particularly bees are the dominant biotic pollinating agent. The adaptations of insect pollinated flowers are as follows

- Insect pollinated flowers are large, colourful, fragrant and rich in nectar.
- A number of flowers are clustered into an inflorescence to make them conspicuous, when the flowers are small.
- Flowers have nectar glands and are highly fragrant to attract, insects.
- The surface of pollen grains is sticky due to exine layer, which gets attached to the insects body.
- The flowers pollinated by flies and beetles secrete foul odour to attract these insects.
- To sustain animal visits, flowers have to provide rewards. Nectar and pollen grains are floral rewards for the insect pollinators.
  For example, in some species, floral rewards are to provide safe place for laying eggs, e.g. *Amorphophallus* (the tallest flower about 6 feet in height).
- In the plant *Yucca*, both the species, i.e. moth and the plant cannot complete their life cycles without each other. The moth deposits its eggs in the locule of the ovary and the flower, in turn, gets pollinated by the moth. The larvae of the moth come out of the eggs as the seeds start developing.
- Many insects may consume pollen or the nectar without bringing about pollination. These floral visitors are referred to as **pollen/nectar robbers**.

Quick Test 3

1. Name the type of flowers that are invariably autogamous. Give one example of such flowers.
2. What type of pollination occurs in self-incompatible plants?
3. Name the outbreeding device that ensures only xenogamy.
4. A flower produces small, dry and light pollen grains. Name the pollinating agent of this plant.
5. **State True or False.**
   All aquatic plants are pollinated by water.

Pollen-Pistil Interaction

- The events from the deposition of pollen on the stigma till the entry of pollen-tube into the ovule are collectively called **pollen-pistil interaction**.
- It is a dynamic process involving pollen recognition followed by either the inhibition or promotion of pollen germination.
- This phenomena is an essential step in fertilisation of angiosperms and determines the compatibility and incompatibility of pollen and pistil.
- It includes following steps

1. Recognition of Compatible Pollen

- The pistil has the ability to recognise and accept the right pollen (compatible pollen of the same species as the stigma) and to reject wrong pollen (incompatible pollen grains that may or may not be of the same species).

- Compatibility is the result of continuous dialogue mediated by chemical components of the pollen interacting with those of the pistil.
- The pistil rejects the incompatible pollen by preventing pollen germination on the stigma or pollen tube growth in the style.
- After recognition of the correct pollen, pistil promotes post-pollination events that lead to fertilisation.
- The knowledge gained in this area would help the plant breeder in manipulating pollen-pistil interaction, even in incompatible pollinations to get desired hybrids.

2. Growth of a Pollen Tube

- The pollen grains reach the receptive stigma through pollination. Pollen grains after landing on the stigma absorb water and swell.
- These pollen grains germinate on the stigma to produce a pollen tube through one of the germ pores. The contents of the pollen grain then move into this tube.
- The pollen tube grows through the tissues of stigma and style by secreting certain hydrolytic enzymes and reaches the ovary.

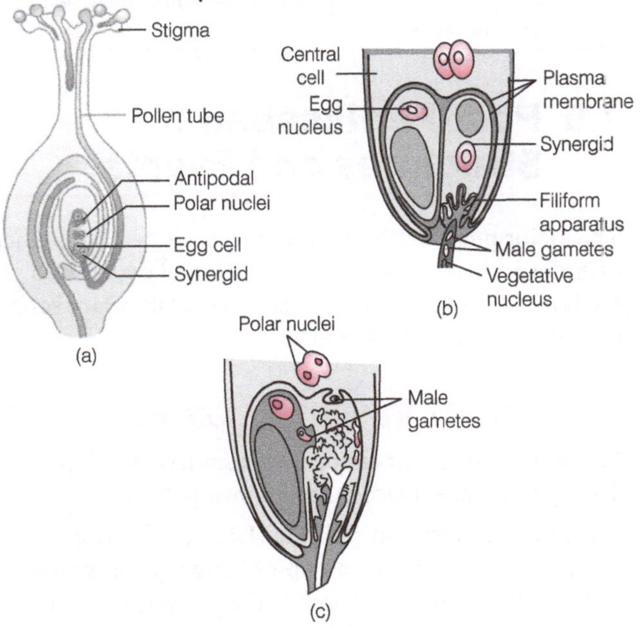

Fig 1.16 (a) LS of a pistil showing growth of pollen tube, (b) Enlarged view of an egg apparatus showing entry of pollen tube into a synergid, (c) Discharge of male gametes into a synergid and the movements of the gametes, one into the egg and the other into the central cell

- In some plants pollen grains shed at 2-celled condition (vegetative cell and generative cell). In such plants, the generative cell divides and forms the two male gametes during the growth of pollen tube in the stigma.
- Plants in which pollens are shed at 3-celled condition, pollen tube carries two male gametes from the beginning.

3. Entry of Pollen Tube into the Ovule

- After reaching the ovary, the pollen tube usually enters the ovule through the micropylar end.
- It then enters one of the synergids through the filiform apparatus present at micropylar end.
- The filiform apparatus directs the growth of pollen tube by secreting some chemical substances.

> **TEACHER'S TIP**
> In most plants, the pollen tube enters the ovule through the **micropyle**. However, in some species, it can enter the ovule through regions other then the micropyle, such as the **chalazal end**. This type of pollen tube entry is referred to as **chalazogamy.**

Artificial Hybridisation

- It is the crossing of different species and often genera to combine desirable characters to produce commercially superior varieties.
- This approach have been used by the plant breeders for crop improvement programmes.
- It is achieved by the following methods
    - **Emasculation** The anther is removed from the bud before it dehisces using a pair of forceps. It is mainly done when the female parent bears bisexual flowers.
    - **Bagging** The emasculated flower is covered by a bag of suitable size generally made up of butter paper, so as to prevent contamination of the stigma by unwanted pollen grains.
      When the stigma of bagged flower becomes receptive, the mature and desired pollen grains are dusted onto the stigma, the flower is rebagged and the fruits are allowed to develop.
- If the female parent is unisexual, emasculation is not necessary.
- In this case, the female bud is directly bagged and when the stigma turns receptive, suitable pollen grains are dusted onto it, so as to allow germination and the flowers are rebagged. This method ensures that the fertilisation occurs with desired pollen.

1.4 Double Fertilisation

- In angiosperms, there is a fusion of two male gametes with two different cells of the same female gametophyte in order to produce two different structures.
- This process is known as double fertilisation which is unique to the angiospermic plants.
- The pollen tube that enters the ovule, releases the two male gametes into the cytoplasm of the synergid. The penetrated synergid then starts degenerating.
- One of the two male gametes fuse with the egg cell and forms a diploid ($2n$) zygote. This process is called **syngamy**. The diploid zygote develops into an embryo.
- The second male gamete fuses with the two polar nuclei or secondary nucleus in the central cell to form the triploid **Primary Endosperm Nucleus** (PEN).
- This process is called **triple fusion** as three haploid nuclei are involved in the fusion.
- The process of double fertilisation can be understand by the help of the diagram given below

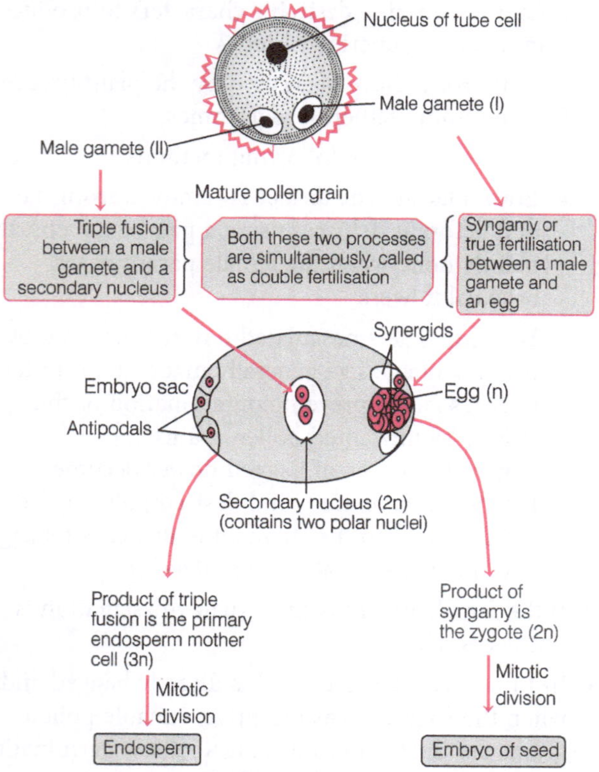

Fig 1.17 Steps of double fertilisation

- After triple fusion, the central cell becomes the **Primary Endosperm Cell** (PEC). The PEC gives rise to the endosperm.
- As both the fusions, syngamy and triple fusion, occur in an embryo sac, the phenomenon is termed as **double fertilisation**.

Syngamy	Ist male gamete + Female gamete $\rightarrow$ Zygote ($2n$) $\rightarrow$ Embryo
Triple fusion	IInd male gamete + 2 polar nuclei $\rightarrow$ PEN ($3n$) $\rightarrow$ Endosperm ($3n$)

Quick Test 4

1. Which part of the flower has the ability to determine the compatible nature of pollen?
2. Will fertilisation take place if the stigma is removed from the pistil?
3. How many pollen tubes carry the two male gametes to the embryo sac?
4. **State True or False.**
   Emasculation can be done in both unisexual and bisexual flowers.
5. What will be the number of chromosomes in each cell of angiospermic leaves if its endosperm contain 36 chromosomes?

1.5 Post-Fertilisation : Structures and Events

The major **post-fertilisation events** include development of endosperm and embryo, maturation of ovules into seeds and ovary into fruit. These events take place soon after the double fertilisation.

Development of Endosperm

Endosperm development proceeds embryo development. This process takes place in the following steps

- Primary endosperm cell [Fig. 1.18 (a)] divides repeatedly and forms a **triploid endosperm tissue.** The cells of this tissue are filled with reserve food materials and are used for the nutrition of the developing embryo.
- Generally, primary endosperm tissue undergoes successive free nuclear divisions to give rise to free nuclei. At this stage, it is called **free-nuclear endosperm**.

- After this cell wall formation takes place and the endosperm becomes **cellular**.
- The number of free nuclei formed before cellularisation varies greatly.
- The coconut water from tender coconut is nothing, but free-nuclear endosperm (made up of thousands of nuclei). The surrounding white kernel is the cellular endosperm.

Development of an Embryo

- The zygote gives rise to an organised mass of cells called the **embryo**, at the micropylar end of embryo sac.
- This embryo has the potential to form a complete plant.
- Most zygotes divide only after certain amount of endosperm is formed to assure that proper nutrition is provided to the developing embryo.
- In majority of angiosperms, the zygote (fertilised egg) divides by an asymmetric mitotic division and generates two cells with two different fates.
  - The smaller daughter cell with dense cytoplasm is situated towards the chalazal pole. It is called **apical cell** or **embryonal cell**.

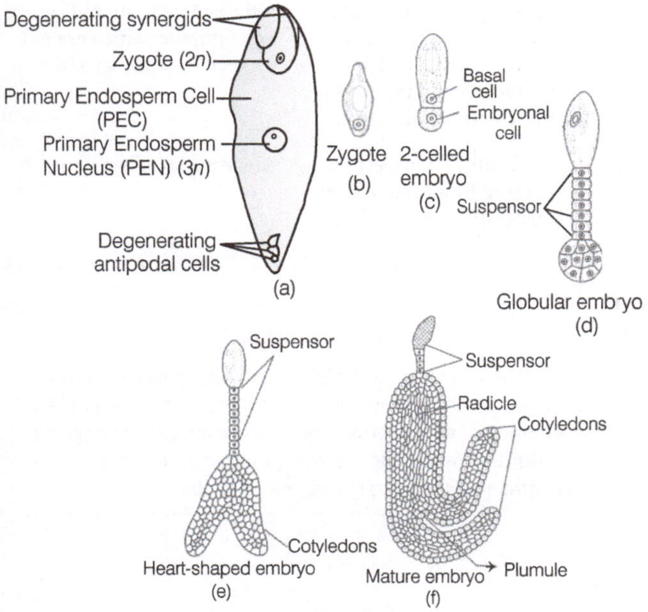

Fig. 1.18 (a) Fertilised embryo sac showing zygote and primary endosperm nucleus, (b-f) Stages of embryo development in a dicot plant

  - Another comparatively larger daughter cell situated towards the micropylar end, is called **basal cell**. This cell divides transversely and gives rise to **suspensor cells**.

  The zygote gives rise to the **proembryo** and subsequently to the **globular**, **heart-shaped** and **mature embryo**.

  Though, the seeds differs greatly, the early stages of embryo development (embryogeny) are similar in both monocots and dicots.

Structure of Dicot and Monocot Embryos

- A typical **dicotyledonous embryo** consists of an **embryonal axis** and two **cotyledons**.

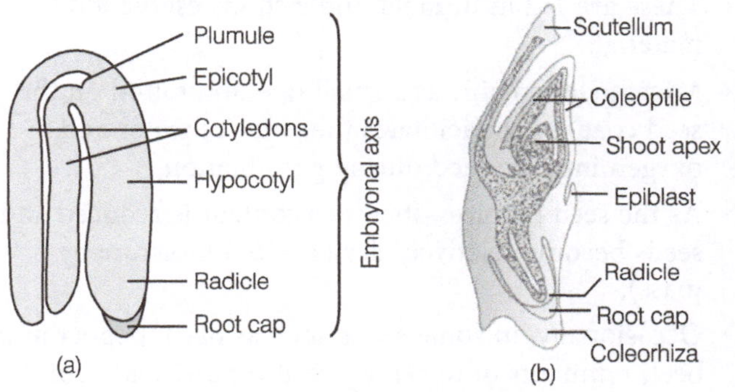

Fig. 1.19 (a) A typical dicot embryo, (b) LS of an embryo of grass (monocot embryo)

- The portion of the embryonal axis above the level of cotyledons is the **epicotyl**, which terminates in the **plumule** or stem tip.
- The cylindrical portion below the level of cotyledons is **hypocotyl** that terminates in the **radicle** or **root tip**.
- The root tip is covered with a **root cap**.
- **Embryo of monocots** possesses only one cotyledon at one end (lateral) of the embryonal axis and this cotyledon is called **scutellum** (in grass family).
- At the lower end, the embryonal axis has radical and root cap enclosed in an undifferentiated sheath called **coleorhiza**.
- The portion of the embryonal axis above the level of attachment of scutellum is the **epicotyl**.
- The epicotyl has a shoot apex and a few leaf primordia enclosed in a hollow foliar structure called **coleoptile.**

Seed

- In angiosperms, seed is the final product of sexual reproduction.
- It is often described as fertilised ovule. These seeds are formed inside the fruits.

Structure of a Seed

- A typical seed consists of a **seed coat, cotyledon** and **an embryonal axis**. The seed coat is often double layered, formed by the integuments.
- The outer integument forms the outer seed coat or **testa**, which is hard and inner integument forms the inner **seed coat** or **tegmen**. Both are protective in function.
- The cotyledons (embryonic leaves) are simple structures that are generally thick and swollen with food materials (as in legumes).
- These are 1-2 in number and rich in reserve food material.
- **Micropyle** remains as a small opening found on the seed coat which facilitates the entry of water and oxygen into the seed during germination.
- As the seed matures, its water content is reduced and seeds become relatively dry (10-15% moisture by mass).
- Occasionally, in some seeds such as black pepper and beet, remnants of nucellus are also persistent. This residual, persistent nucellus is the **perisperm**.

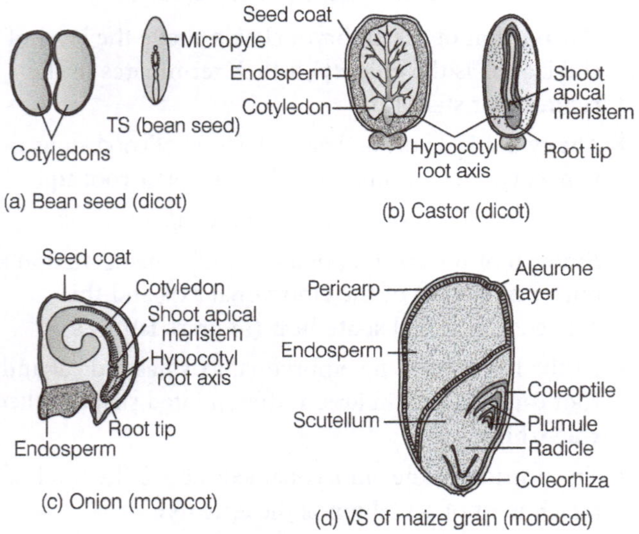

Fig. 1.20 Internal structure of some seeds

Types of Seeds

- Depending upon the presence or absence of endosperm, seeds can be divided into following types
  - **Endospermic or Albuminous Seed** Endosperm is present in this seed, as it is not completely used up during embryo development, e.g. wheat, maize, coconut, barley, castor, etc.
  - **Non-albuminous or Ex-albuminous Seed** Endosperm is absent in this seed as it is completely consumed during embryo development, e.g. pea, bean, groundnut, etc.
- Depending upon the number of cotyledons seeds can be monocots and dicots.
- The major differences between monocot and dicot seeds are as follows

Monocot Seeds	Dicot Seeds
The embryo possesses only one cotyledon.	The embryo possesses two cotyledons.
The reserve food material is usually stored inside the endosperm.	The reserve food material is stored either in cotyledons or inside the endosperm.
The embryonal axis is differentiated into radicle and plumule. Radicle is protected by a sheath, coleorhiza and plumule is protected by coleoptile.	The embryonal axis is differentiated into radicle and plumule, which are not protected by any sheath.
Seed laden endosperm is covered by aleurone layer, made up of protein rich cells.	Aleurone layer is absent.

Seed Dormancy

Sometimes the general metabolic activity of the embryo slows down and it may enter into a state of inactivity called **dormancy** or **seed dormancy**. When favourable conditions are available (adequate moisture, oxygen and suitable temperature), the seed germinates into plants.

Advantages of Seeds

Following are the advantages of seeds

- They are the basis of our agriculture.
- The stored food in seeds supports the its growth till they become nutritionally independent.
- Seeds can be stored for longer time as food source and also to raise the crop in the next season.
- Seeds of a large number of species can live for several years, e.g. *Lupinus arcticus* of Arctic Tundra (oldest viable seed remained dormant for 10,000 years), date palm (*Pheonix dactylifera*) of King Herod's Palace near the Dead sea (viable seed of 2000 year old).
- Seeds are the products of sexual reproduction, so they generate genetic combination leading to variations.
- Seeds have better adaptation to facilitate dispersal strategies to form new plant colonies.

Seed Dispersal

It is the movement or transport of seeds away from the parent plant. This allows seeds to spread in a large geographical area.

Significance of Seed Dispersal

- Seed dispersal is important because if the seeds are not dispersed, many germinating seedlings will grow very close to the parent plant.
- Seedlings growing close to parent plant results in competition between seedlings as well as with parent plant. The competition is for light, space, water and nutrients.
- Competition for the above factors affects the growth of plant.

Formation of a Fruit

- A **fruit** is formed after fertilisation as a result of cell division and differentiation in the ovary, i.e. a ripened ovary forms a fruit.
- It may be **fleshy**, e.g. guava, orange and mango or may be dry, e.g. groundnut, mustard, etc.
- The wall of the ovary develops into the fruit wall called **pericarp**. It has three layers, i.e. **epicarp**, **mesocarp** and **endocarp**.

Significance of Fruit Formation

- Fruits protect the seed from mechanical injury.
- Fleshy fruits provide food to animals who also act as dispersal agents of their seeds.
- Fruits are also consumed by humans.

Types of Fruits

On the basis of formation, fruits are of following types

- **True Fruits** The fruit derived from ovary of a flower and not associated with any non-carpellary part is termed as true fruit, e.g. mango and tomato.
- **False Fruits** The fruit derived from ovary along with other accessory floral parts like thalamus is called false fruit, e.g. apple, cashewnut, strawberry, etc.

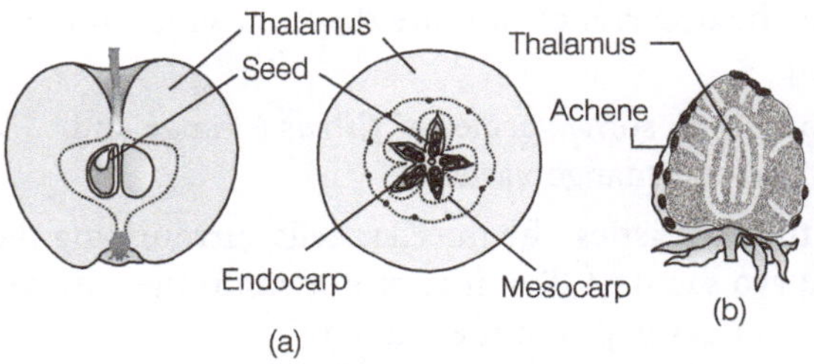

Fig. 1.21 False fruits: (a) Apple and (b) Strawberry

- **Parthenocarpic Fruits** Some fruits develop without undergoing fertilisation, these are called parthenocarpic fruits, e.g. banana.
  This process of formation of fruits without fertilisation in plants is known as **parthenocarpy**. It can be induced through the application of growth hormones and such fruits are seedless.

1.6 Some Special Mechanisms of Reproduction

Although, seeds in general are the products of fertilisation, but a few flowering plants have evolved special mechanisms to produce seeds or to develop many embryos from a single fertilised egg.

These methods are discussed below

1. Apomixis

- It is a form of asexual reproduction that mimics sexual reproduction and produces seeds without fertilisation.

- It does not involve the formation of zygote through the gametic fusion. It occurs in some species of Asteraceae and grasses.
- Apomictic seeds are viable seeds produced without pollination or sexual reproduction.
- In some species, the diploid egg cell is formed without reductional division and develops into embryo without fertilisation.
- Apomixis is extensively used in hybrid seed industry.
- Production of hybrid seeds is costly, if hybrids are made into apomicts, there is no segregation of characters in the hybrid progeny. Then the farmers do not need to buy hybrid seeds year after year and can use apomictic seeds to raise new crops every year.

2. Polyembryony

- It is the occurrence of more than one embryo in a seed.
- It occurs in some species of *Citrus* (orange and lemon) and mango varieties.
- In these varieties, the nucellar cells surrounding the embryo sac start dividing, protude into the embryo sac and develop into the embryos.

3. Parthenocarpy

- The production and development of seedless fruit is called parthenocarpy. It is of two types, vegetative and stimulative.
- In **vegetative parthenocarpy**, the seedless fruits can develop even without the stimulus of pollination, e.g. pear.
- In **stimulative parthenocarpy**, the stimulus of pollination is required without actual process of fertilisation, e.g. grapes.

Quick Test 5

1. Give the name of the common functions that cotyledons and nucellus perform. *NCERT Exemplar*
2. Name the part of embryo sac that develops into seed coat.
3. Seeds are fertilised mature ovule which possess stored food. In what category will a castor seed be placed?
4. Which part of the flower give rise to the fleshy part of the apple?
5. **State True or False.**
   Pollination and fertilisation is not necessary in apomixis.

Mind Map

Sexual Reproduction in Flowering Plants

Flower

It is a modified, condensed shoot specialised to carry out sexual reproduction in angiosperms.

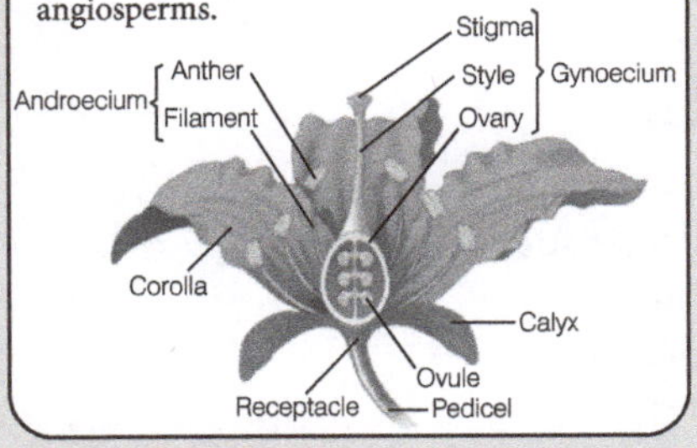

Pollination

Pollination

- Self-pollination
  - Autogamy (Same flower)
  - Geitonogamy (Different flowers of same plant)
- Cross-pollination or Xenogamy
  - Abiotic factors
    - Wind pollination (anemophily)
    - Water pollination (hydrophily)
  - Biotic factors
    - By bats
    - By insects
    - By birds

Double Fertilisation

- Characteristic feature of angiosperms.
- Pollen tube releases two male gametes into the cytoplasm of synergids.

One male gamete + Egg → Zygote ($2n$) — **Syngamy**

Other male gamete + 2 polar nuclei → Primary endosperm nucleus ($3n$) — **Triple fusion**

Double fertilisation

Pollen-pistil Interaction

Pollen Deposition on Stigma
↓
Compatibility Check

If compatible
↓
Pollen grain **accepted**
↓
Pollen germinates to form **pollen tube**
↓
Content of generative cells or male gametes **transfers** into pollen tube
↓
Growth of pollen tube through stigma and style by secreting enzymes.
↓
Entry into ovule through micropyle (generally) *via* synergids with filiform apparatus guiding the entry of pollen tube.

If incompatible
↓
Pollen grain **rejected**
↓
No pollen germination

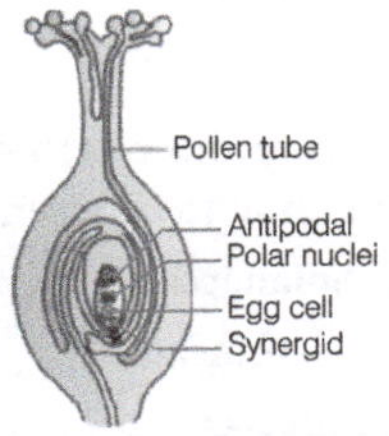

Pre-Fertilisation : Structures and Events

It includes the initiation of several hormonal and structural changes which lead to the differentiation and development of the floral primordium.

Development of a Male Gametophyte

- Male reproductive structures are stamen, microsporangium and pollen grain. Each stamen consists of an anther and filament.
- The Pollen Mother Cell (PMC) after microsporogenesis form a microspore tetrad, which dissociate from each other and develop into pollen grains or male gametophytes.
- It has a large vegetative cell and a small generative cell.

Development of a Female Gametophyte

- Female reproductive structures are pistil, megasporangium (ovule) and embryo sac.
- The Megaspore Mother Cell (MMC) gives rise to a tetrad of four megaspores.
- The functional megaspore grows in size and divides by mitosis to form 2-nucleate cell which form the embryo sac or female gametophyte.
- Each nucleus undergoes two mitotic divisions to form 8-nucleate and 7-celled stage.

Outbreeding Devices

To prevent self-pollination and encourage cross-pollination, plants uses several mechanisms like dichogamy (non-synchronised pollen release), heterostyle (spatial separation of anthers and stigma), self-incompatiblity (prevention of self-fertilisation) and dicliny (unisexual flowers).

Post-Fertilisation Structures and Events

It takes place soon after double fertilisation. It includes development of endosperm and embryo, maturation of ovules into seed and ovary into fruit.

Development of an Endosperm

Primary endosperm cell divides repeatedly, forms triploid endosperm tissue and develops into free nuclear; from periphery wall endosperm become cellular.

Development of an Embryo

- Development of zygote gives rise to an embryo, that has the potentiality to form a complete plant called **embryogeny.**
- A dicot embryo consists of two cotyledons, while monocots possess only one cotyledon.

Development of a Seed

- Double fertilisation in angiosperms triggers the transformation of ovule into a seed. A typical seed consists of a seed coat, cotyledon and an embryonal axis.
- Depending upon the presence or absence of endosperm, seeds are called **albuminous** and **non-albuminous,** respectively.

Formation of a Fruit

- A ripened ovary form a fruit.
- The wall of the ovary called **pericarp** (fruit wall).
- Types of fruit , i.e. true fruits (e.g. mango), false fruits (e.g. apple) and parthenocarpic fruits (e.g. banana).

Apomixis and Polyembryony

- Apomixis is a form of asexual reproduction that mimics sexual reproduction where seeds are formed without fertilisation.
- Polyembryony is the occurrence of more than one embryo in a seed. It occurs due to zygote division or the development of embryos from maternal tissues like nucellus (e.g. orange, lemon).

EXAM PATTERN QUESTIONS

Objective Type Questions

Multiple Choice Questions

1. Identify *A* to *G* in following figure and answer accordingly.

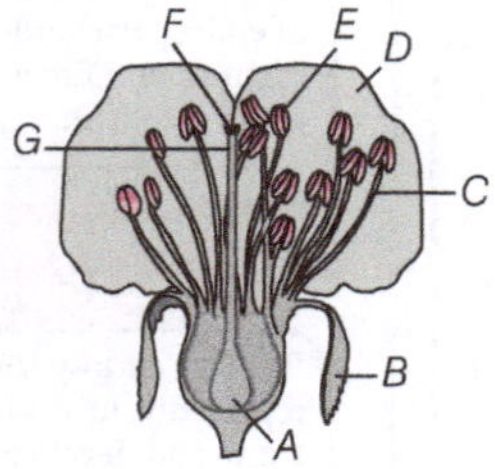

(a) *A*–Ovary, *B*–Filament, *C*–Sepal, *D*–Petal, *E*–Style, *F*–Stigma, *G*–Anther
(b) *A*–Sepal, *B*–Ovary, *C*–Petal, *D*–Filament, *E*–Anther, *F*–Stigma, *G*–Style
(c) *A*–Ovary, *B*–Sepal, *C*–Filament, *D*–Petal, *E*–Anther, *F*–Stigma, *G*–Style
(d) *A*–Petal, *B*–Anther, *C*–Stigma, *D*–Style, *E*–Filament, *F*–Sepal, *G*–Ovary

Ans. (*c*)

2. A typical angiosperm anther is dithecous which means that it is

(a) one lobed and the lobe has two theca
(b) two lobed and each lobe has one theca
(c) two lobed and each lobe has two theca
(d) four lobed and each lobe has two theca

Ans. (*c*)

3. In the transverse section of a young anther shown below, identify the correct sequence of wall layers. **CBSE 2021 Term-I**

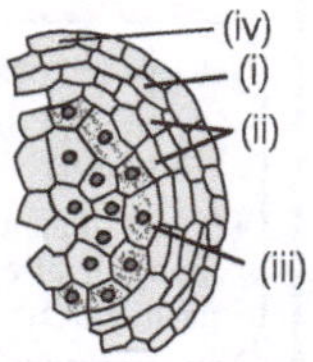

	(i)	(ii)	(iii)	(iv)
(a)	Middle layers	Endothecium	Epidermis	Tapetum
(b)	Tapetum	Middle layers	Endothecium	Epidermis
(c)	Epidermis	Endothecium	Middle layers	Tapetum
(d)	Endothecium	Middle layers	Tapetum	Epidermis

Ans. (*d*)

4. What is the characteristics of tapetum?

(a) It is uninucleated
(b) It is multinucleated
(c) It is binucleated
(d) It provide nourishment to the megaspore.

Ans. (*b*)

5. Which of the following is correct with respect to microsporogenesis?

(a) The cells of sporogenous tissue divide and form pollen mother cells.
(b) Pollen mother cells are formed form a tetrad
(c) Inside the microsporangium several thousand male gamete are present
(d) Both (a) and (c)

Ans. (*d*)

6. How many pollen mother cells should undergo meiotic division to produce 48 pollen grains?

(a) 8 (b) 12 (c) 16 (d) 24

Ans. (*b*) Each pollen mother cell produces 4 haploid pollen grains during meiosis. Thus, 12 pollen mother cells are required to produce 48 pollen grains.

7. 60% of the angiosperms shed their pollens at the

(a) 2-celled stage (b) 3-celled stage
(c) 4-celled stage (d) 1-celled stage

Ans. (*a*)

8. Which of the following statement is incorrect?

(a) Pollen grains of many species like *Parthenium* may become a cause of severe allergies
(b) Period for which the pollens remain viable is fixed for all types of angiosperms
(c) Pollens, in case of paddy, lose their viability within 30 minutes of their release
(d) Stored pollens can be used as pollen banks and can be further made use in production of improved crop varieties

Ans. (*a*)

9. Pollen grains retain viability for months in plants belonging to different families given below.

I. Solanaceae II. Leguminosae
III. Gramineae IV. Rosaceae
V. Liliaceae

The correct option is **CBSE 2021 Term-I**

(a) I, II and V (b) I, II and IV
(c) II, IV and V (d) I, III and V

Ans. (*b*)

10. Match the following columns.

	Column I (Ovary)		Column II (Pistil)
A.	Monocarpellary	1.	Free pistil
B.	Multicarpellary	2.	Fused pistil
C.	Syncarpous	3.	Many pistil
D.	Apocarpous	4.	Single pistil

Codes

	A	B	C	D
(a)	1	2	3	4
(b)	4	3	2	1
(c)	3	4	2	1
(d)	4	3	1	2

Ans. (*b*)

11. Which condition of gynoecium (pistil) is shown in the figures (i) and (ii)? **CBSE 2021 Term-I**

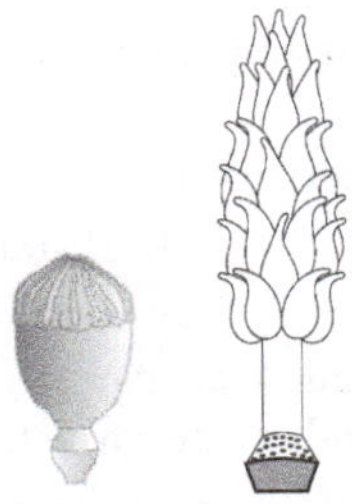

(i) (ii)

(a) (i) Multicarpellary apocarpous,
(ii) Multicarpellary syncarpous
(b) (i) Multicarpellary syncarpous,
(ii) Multicarpellary apocarpous
(c) (i) Bicarpellary apocarpous,
(ii) Bicarpellary syncarpous
(d) (i) Bicarpellary syncarpous,
(ii) Bicarpellary apocarpous

Ans. (*b*)

12. Enclosed within the integuments of a typical anatropous ovule is a diploid mass of cellular tissue known as **CBSE 2021 Term-I**

(a) megaspore mother cell
(b) nucellus
(c) synergids
(d) embryo sac

Ans. (*b*)

13. In the figure of anatropous ovule given below, choose the correct option for the characteristic distribution of cells within the typical embryo sac.

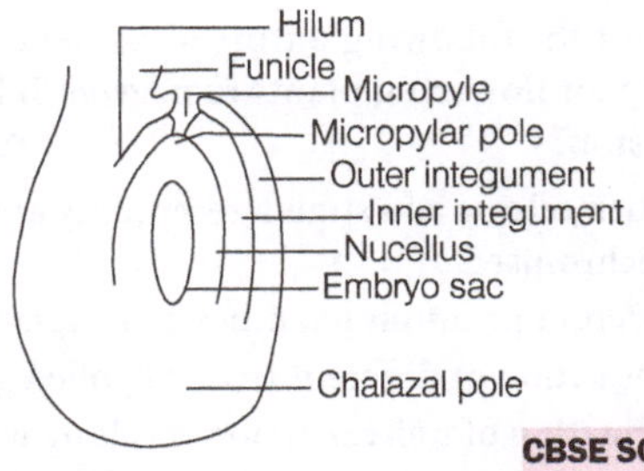

CBSE SQP 2021 Term-I

	Number of cells at chalazal end	Number of cells at micropylar end	Number of nuclei left in central cell
(a)	3	2	3
(b)	3	3	2
(c)	2	3	3
(d)	2	2	4

Ans. (*b*)

14. A botanist studying *Viola* (common pansy) noticed that one of the two flower types withered and developed no further due to some unfavourable condition, but the other flower type on the same plant survived and it resulted in an assured seed set. Which of the following will be correct? **CBSE SQP 2021 Term-I**

(a) The flower type which survived is cleistogamous and it always exhibits autogamy
(b) The flower type which survived is chasmogamous and it always exhibits geitonogamy
(c) The flower type which survived is cleistogamous and it exhibits both autogamy and geitonogamy
(d) The flower type which survived is chasmogamous and it never exhibits autogamy

Ans. (*a*)

15. In which of the following plant both male and female flowers are born on the same plant and the mode of pollination can be geitonogamy or xenogamy?

(a) Papaya (b) Date palm (c) Maize (d) Spinach

Ans. (*c*)

16. Consider three plants with the following modes of pollination. **Competency Based Que.**

Plant P: Autogamy, Plant Q: Xenogamy

Plant R: Geitonogamy

Which of the above case/s is/are most likely to not show genetic variation in the offspring?

(a) Only P (b) Only Q (c) P and R (d) Q and R

Ans. (*c*) Plant P and R are most likely to not show genetic variation because they perform autogamy and geitonogamy, respectively in which genetic contribution comes from the same plant which shows low genetic variation.

17. **Which of the following outbreeding devices are used by majority of flowering plants to prevent inbreeding depression?** CBSE 2021 Term-I

I. **Pollen release and stigma receptivity are not synchronised.**
II. **Different positions of anther and stigma.**
III. **Production of different types of pollen grains.**
IV. **Formation of unisexual flowers along with bisexual flowers.**
V. **Preventing self-pollen from fertilising the ovules by inhibiting pollen germination.**

(a) I, II and V (b) II, III and V
(c) I, III and V (d) III, IV and V

Ans. (*a*)

18. **Long ribbon-like pollen grains are seen in some.** CBSE 2024 C

(a) Aquatic plants (b) Wind-pollinated grasses
(c) Gymnosperms (d) Bird-pollinated flowers

Ans. (*a*)

19. **In the dioecious aquatic plant shown, identify the characteristics of the male flowers that reach the female flowers for pollination.** CBSE SQP 2021 Term-I

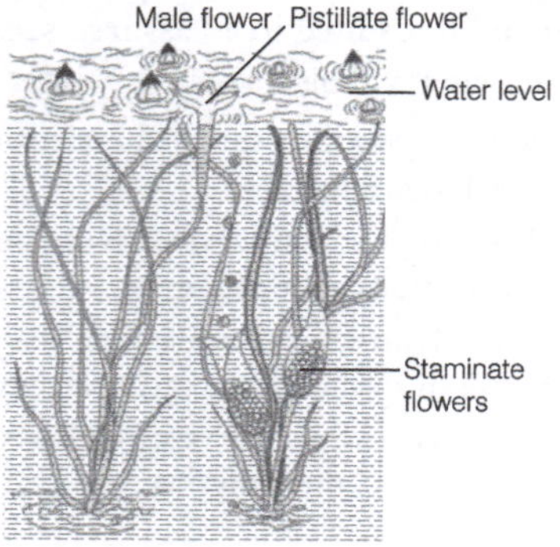

	Size of the flower	Colour of the flower	Characteristic features of pollen grain
(a)	Small	Brightly coloured	Light weight and non-sticky
(b)	Large	Colourless	Large and sticky
(c)	Small	White	Small, covered with mucilage
(d)	Large	Colourless	Non-sticky

Ans. (*c*)

20. **Select the statements that are true for pollination mechanism in flowering plants from the given options.** CBSE 2025

I. **In *Vallisneria*, the female flowers are pollinated by pollen grains inside the water.**
II. **In *Zostera*, pollen grains are released on the surface of water.**
III. **In most of the water-pollinated species, pollen grains are covered by a mucilaginous coating.**
IV. **Pollination by water is quite rare and limited to about 30 genera.**

Choose the correct answer.

(a) I and II (b) II and III
(c) III and IV (d) I and IV

Ans. (*c*) Statements III and IV are correct, but statements I and III are incorrect and can be corrected as

- In *Vallisneria*, the female flowers are pollinated by pollen grains on the water surface.
- In *Zostera*, pollen grains are released inside the water and carried by water currents.

21. **Select the following statements that are true for insect pollinated flowers from the given options.** CBSE 2025

I. **Majority of these flowers are large, colourful and rich in nectar.**
II. **Nectars and seeds are usual floral rewards to attract insects for pollination.**
III. **Pollen grains of these flowers are generally mucilaginous so as to stick to the body of the insects.**
IV **A foul odour is emitted by some flowers to attract flies and beetles.**

Choose the correct answer.

(a) I and II (b) II and III
(c) III and IV (d) I and IV

Ans. (*d*) Statements I and IV are correct, but statements II and III are incorrect and can be corrected as

- Nectar, not seeds, serves as the primary floral reward to attract insects for pollination.
- Pollen grains of insect pollinated flowers can be sticky, but they are not necessarily mucilaginous.

22. **To overcome incompatible pollinations so as to get desired hybrids, a plant breeder must have the knowledge of ....** CBSE 2021 Term-I

(a) pollen-nucellar interaction
(b) pollen-egg cell interaction
(c) pollen-pistil interaction
(d) pollen-embryo sac interaction

Ans. (*c*)

23. **While planning for an artificial hybridisation programme involving dioecious plants, which of the following steps would not be relevant?** NCERT Exemplar

(a) Bagging of female flower
(b) Dusting of pollen on stigma
(c) Emasculation
(d) Collection of pollen

Ans. (*c*) If the female parent produces unisexual flower, so there is no need for emasculation.

24. In a fertilised embryo sac, the haploid, diploid and triploid structure are NCERT Exemplar

(a) synergid, zygote and primary endosperm nucleus
(b) synergid, antipodal and polar nuclei
(c) antipodal, synergid and primary endosperm nucleus
(d) synergid, polar nuclei and zygote

Ans. (*a*)

25. In flowering plants, the endosperm develops from which of the following?

(a) Zygote (b) Synergids
(c) Polar nuclei (d) Egg cell

Ans. (*c*)

26. Identify the correct labellings in the figure of a fertilised embryo sac of an angiosperm given below. CBSE SQP 2024

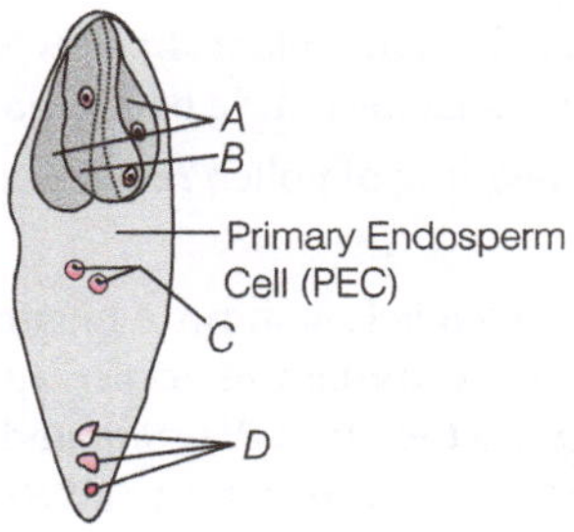

(a) *A* - Zygote, *B* - Degenerating synergids, *C* - Degenerating antipodals, *D*- PEN
(b) *A* - Degenerating synergids, *B* - Zygote, *C* - PEN, *D*- Degenerating antipodals
(c) *A* - Degenerating antipodals, *B* - PEN, *C* - Degenerating synergids, *D*- Zygote
(d) *A* - Degenerating synergids, *B*-Zygote, *C*-Degenerating antipodais, *D*-PEN

Ans. (*b*)

27. Choose the correct labellings for the parts *X*, *Y* and *Z* in the given figure of the stages in embryo development in a dicot. CBSE 2021 Term-I

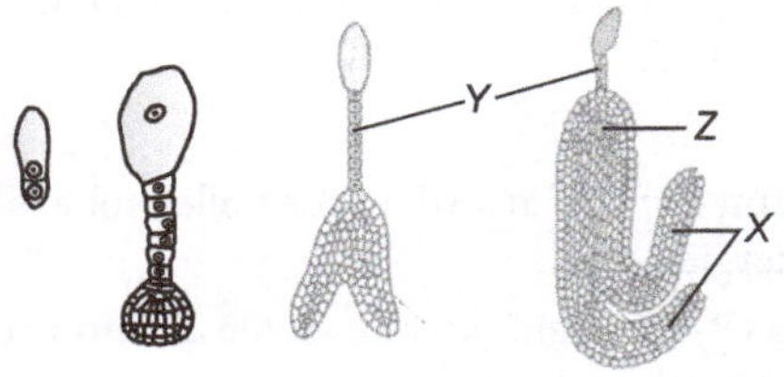

(a) *X* is suspensor, *Y* is radicle and *Z* is cotyledon
(b) *X* is radicle, *Y* is cotyledon and *Z* is suspensor
(c) *X* is cotyledon, *Y* is suspensor and *Z* is radicle
(d) *X* is zygote, *Y* is radicle and *Z* is cotyledon

Ans. (*c*)

28. Select the option that shows the correctly identified *U*, *X*, *Y* and *Z* in a developing dicot embryo. CBSE 2023

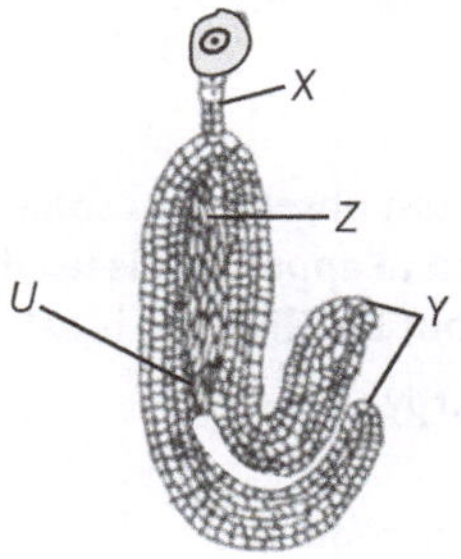

(a) *X*–Plumule (2*n*), *Y*–Suspensor (*n*), *Z*–Cotyledon (2*n*), *U*–Radicle (2*n*)
(b) *X*–Plumule (2*n*), *Y*–Suspensor (2*n*), *Z*–Radicle (2*n*), *U*–Cotyledon (2*n*)
(c) *X*–Suspensor (2*n*), *Y*–Cotyledon (2*n*), *Z*–Radicle (2*n*), *U*–Plumule (2*n*)
(d) *X*–Cotyledon (2*n*), *Y*–Radicle (*n*), *Z*–Plumule (*n*), *U*–Suspensor (*n*)

Ans. (*c*)

29. Which of the following statements are true related to seed *X* and *Y*? CBSE SQP 2021 Term-I

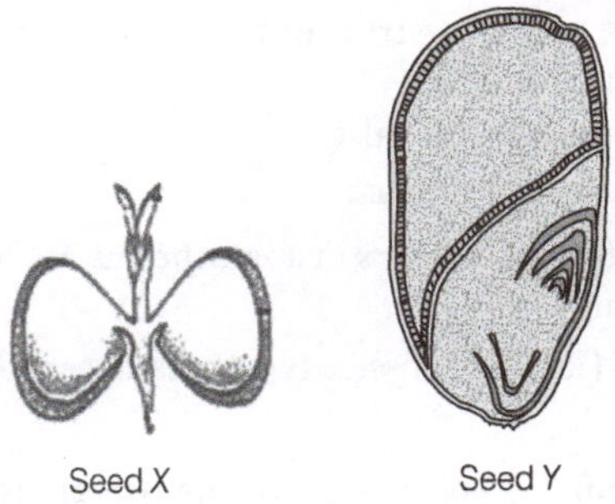

I. Seed *X* is dicot and endospermic or albuminous.
II. Seed *X* is dicot and non-endospermic or non-albuminous.
III. Seed *Y* is monocot and endospermic or albuminous.
IV. Seed *Y* is monocot and non-endospermic or non-albuminous.

Choose the correct option with respect to the nature of the seed.

(a) I and III (b) II and III
(c) I and IV (d) II and IV

Ans. (*b*)

30. In angiosperms, the integuments of the ovule develop into which structure after fertilisation?

(a) Seed coat (b) Endosperm
(c) Cotyledon (d) Fruit

Ans. (*a*)

31. The part of the fruit that develops from the ovary wall is known as the

(a) exocarp (b) endocarp

(c) mesocarp (d) pericarp

Ans. (*d*)

32. The phenomenon observed in some plants where in parts of the sexual apparatus is used for forming embryos without fertilisation is called NCERT Exemplar

(a) parthenocarpy

(b) apomixis

(c) vegetative reproduction

(d) sexual reproduction

Ans. (*b*) Apomixis is the phenomenon of formation of seeds without fertilisation. These embryos are genetically identical to the parental plant.

Assertion-Reason Questions

Direction (Q. Nos. 1-11) *In each of the following questions, a statement of Assertion (A) is given followed by corresponding statement of Reason (R). Of the statements, mark the correct answer as*

(a) Both A and R are true and R is correct explanation of A

(b) Both A and R are true, but R is not the correct explanation of A

(c) A is true, but R is false

(d) A is false, but R is true

1. Assertion (A) Anthers in angiosperms are bilobed and dithecous.

Reason (R) They possess two theca in each lobe.

Ans. (*a*)

2. Assertion (A) Pollen grain of angiosperm is considered as the male gametophyte.

Reason (R) Pollen grain contains stigma, style and ovary.

Ans. (*c*) A is true, but R is false and R can be corrected as Pollen grain contains one vegetative cell and one generative cell.

3. Assertion (A) Some plants shed pollen at the 3-celled condition.

Reason (R) These plants carry 3 male gametes since the beginning of reproductive process.

Ans. (*c*) A is true, but R is false. R can be corrected as

Some plant shed pollen at three cell stage in which 1 is vegetative cell and 2 male gametes are present.

4. Assertion (A) *Parthenium* is known to cause pollen allergy.

Reason (R) It is not a native plant species.

Ans. (*b*)

5. Assertion (A) Megaspore mother cell undergoes meiosis to produce four megaspores.

Reason (R) Megaspore mother cell and megaspore both are haploid.

Ans. (*c*) A is true, but R is false and R can be corrected as Megaspore mother cell is diploid. It undergoes meiosis to produce megaspores which are haploid.

6. Assertion (A) Embryo sac development is monosporic in *Polygonum*.

Reason (R) In this development, only one functional megaspore is present at chalazal end.

Ans. (*a*)

7. Assertion (A) Cleistogamous flowers produce assured seed set even in the absence of pollinators.

Reason (R) Cleistogamous flowers do not open at all.

Ans. (*a*)

8. Assertion (A) Flowering plants have evolved an amazing array of adaptations to achieve pollination.

Reason (R) Shedding of pollen requires external agents.

Ans. (*c*)

9. The diagram given below shows a phenomenon known as epihydrophily (Pollination occurring over the water surface). Refer to the given diagram and comment upon the appropriateness of Assertion and Reason.

Assertion (A) Hydrophily is an uncommon mode of pollination exhibited by aquatic plants.

Reason (R) Pollens are distributed through water bodies to other plants.

Ans. (*b*)

10. Assertion (A) The growth of the pollen tube is arrested in the synergid.

Reason (R) Synergids secretes some chemotropically active substance.

Ans. (*b*)

11. Assertion (A) Non-albuminous seeds have no residual endosperm.

Reason (R) The endosperm is completely consumed during embryo development.

Ans. (*a*)

Subjective Questions

Very Short Answer Type Questions

1. Plants have two phases in their life cycle: sporophytic phase and gametophytic phase. The sporophytic phase is diploid and vegetative, while the gametophytic phase is haploid and reproductive. From this information, identify the male gametophyte in angiosperms. Competency Based Que.

Ans. Pollen grain is the male gametophyte in angiosperms.

2. Write down the ploidy of the cell of microspore tetrad.

Ans. Cells of microspore tetrad are formed by meiosis. Therefore, they are haploid (n) in nature.

3. Give an example of a plant which came into India as a contaminant and is a cause of pollen allergy.

Ans. *Parthenium* or Carrot grass is a major contaminant which came to India and caused pollen allergy.

4. What do you mean by pollen viability? Diksha

Ans. The period for which the pollen grains can retain the ability to germinate is called pollen viability.

5. Suggest one method to preserve pollen grains. Why do we store pollen grains? Diksha

Ans. Cryopreservation can be used to preserve pollen grains. It can be used as pollen banks in crop breeding programmes. (½+½)

6. Name the parts of an angiosperm flower in which development of male and female gametophyte take place. NCERT

Ans. The development of male and female gametophyte takes place in anther and ovary, respectively.

7. Why do we call embryo sac monosporic?

***Or* What is meant by monosporic development of female gametophyte?** NCERT

Ans. An embryo sac is called monosporic because it develops from one of the four megaspores formed from the division of megaspore mother cell.

8. Name all the haploid cells present in an unfertilised mature embryo sac of a flowering plant.

Ans. All the cells of the embryo sac are haploid, except the central cell which is first binucleate and then becomes diploid due to the fusion of polar nuclei. The haploid cells are the egg cells, synergids and antipodal cells.

9. What is the function of filiform apparatus found in mature embryo sac of an angiosperm?

Ans. Filiform apparatus are special cellular thickenings present in synergids at the micropylar end and helps in guiding the entry of pollen tubes into the synergids.

10. How many pollen grains and ovules are likely to be formed in the anther and the ovary of an angiosperm bearing 25 microspore mother cells and 25 megaspore mother cells, respectively? CBSE SQP 2019

Ans. 100 pollen grains and 25 ovules are likely to be formed in the anther and the ovary of an angiosperm bearing 25 microspore mother cells and 25 megaspore mother cells, respectively.

11. In angiosperms, the male gametophyte has a simple structure while the female gametophyte has a much more complex structure with multiple supporting cells in it. How does such a structural difference help each gametophyte perform their functions better? Competency Based Que.

Ans. The pollen grain needs to be transferred to the stigma. Hence, smaller size makes it easier for the movement. While, the ovule develops into the seed and supports the growing embryo. The supporting cells provide nourishment to the growing embryo. (½+½)

12. Geitonogamy is considered as xenogamy as well as autogamy. Give reason.

Ans. Geitonogamy is considered as xenogamy because a pollinating agent is required for pollination. It is considered as autogamy because pollen grains come from the same plant.

13. Name an out breeding device which prevents both autogamy and geitonogamy. Diksha

Ans. Dioecious condition.

14. What is self-incompatibility? NCERT Exemplar

Ans. It is a genetic mechanism which prevents self-pollen from fertilising the ovules by inhibiting pollen germination or pollen tube growth in the pistil.

15. How does pollination take place in water hyacinth and water lily? CBSE SQP 2023

Ans. In water hyacinth and water lily, pollination occurs by insects or wind, because the flowers of these plants emerge above the level of water surface.

16. Give an example for a symbiotic relationship existing between a plant and a pollinating agent. How it is mutually benefitted? Diksha

Ans. *Yucca* plant and moth. Moth deposits its eggs in the locule of the ovary at the same time the flower gets pollinated by the moth.

17. Pistil can identify a right type of pollen grain from a wrong type. Is it possible?

Ans. The pistil can identify the correct type of pollen grain by pollen–pistil interaction. When compatible pollen lands on the stigma it binds to the stigma and sends biochemical signals that promote pollen tube growth.

18. Which is the triploid tissue in a fertilised ovule? How is the triploid condition achieved? NCERT Exemplar

Ans. Endosperm is the triploid tissue. It results from triple fusion involving union of one male gamete and two haploid polar nuclei. (½ + ½)

19. Mention the reason of difference in ploidy of zygote and PEN in angiosperms.

Ans. Zygote is formed when male and female gametes (both haploid) fuse. Thus, it is diploid ($2n$) in nature.

PEN is formed by the fusion of secondary diploid nucleus ($2n$) with one of the male gamete (n). Thus, it is triploid. (½ + ½)

20. Why does endosperm development precede embryo development? CBSE SQP 2021

Ans. Endosperm development precede the embryo development because it provides nutrition to the developing embryo.

21. Endosperm is a mass of nutritive cell. What impact would lack of endosperm create on the growing embryo?

Ans. Endosperm stores carbohydrates, fats, proteins, etc. In the absence of endosperm, growth of embryo would be poor. This would further result in the formation of non-viable seeds.

22. Identify *A* in the figure, showing a stage of embryo development in a dicot plant and mention its function.

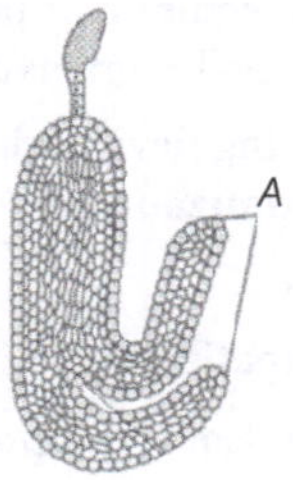

Ans. *A* is cotyledon. It is the storehouse of food in seeds. (½ + ½)

23. How many meiotic divisions are required to produce 76 seeds in a guava fruit? CBSE SQP 2021

Ans. 95 meiotic divisions are required to produce 76 seeds in a guava fruit. (1)

24. Name the homologous structures of embryo of a typical dicot and embryo of grass.

Ans. The cotyledons of a typical dicot embryo and scutellum of a grass embryo are homologous structures.

25. Given below is a section of maize grain. Identify *A* and state its function.

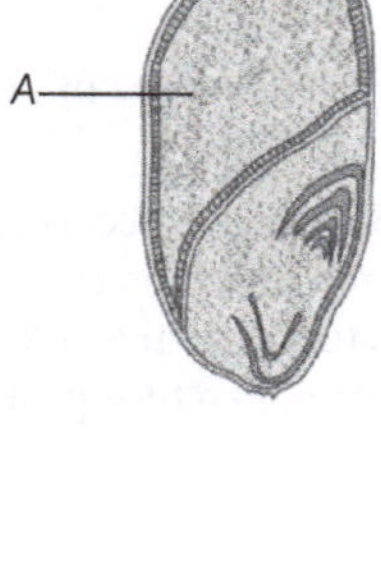

Ans. *A* is endosperm. It provides nutrition to the developing embryo. (½ + ½)

26. Name two plants where remnants of nucellus can be found in seeds.

Ans. In black pepper and beet, remnants of nucellus are found in seeds.

27. Give the name of any two seeds which do not retain their nutritive tissue as they attain maturity.

Ans. Pea and groundnut. (½ + ½)

28. What is non-albuminous seed?

Ans. Non-albuminous seeds have no residual endosperm as it is completely consumed during embryo development (e.g. pea, groundnut).

29. Mention one similarity and one difference between the processes of apomixis and polyembryony. Competency Based Que.

Ans. **Similarity** Both apomixis and polyembryony results in the production of genetically identical individuals.

Difference Apomixis refers to a mode of reproduction in which seeds are produced without the process of fertilisation, whereas in polyembryony multiple embryos develop from single fertilised egg. (½ + ½)

Short Answer Type Questions

1. Why are angiosperm anthers called dithecous? Describe the structure of microsporangium.

Ans. The anthers of angiospermic flowers are bilobed and each lobe is divided into two parts or theca. Thus, the anther of angiosperms are dithecous. For structure of microsporangium, refer to text on page no. 3. (1 × 2)

2. In the TS of a mature anther given below, identify '*a*' and '*b*' and mention their functions. CBSE 2019

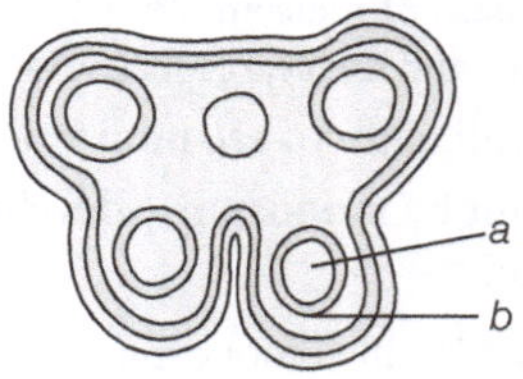

Ans. In the given figure *a* is sporogenous tissue and *b* is tapetum.

(i) **Sporogenous tissue** has cells which are potential Pollen Mother Cell (PMC) or microspore mother cell and give rise to microspore tetrad.

(ii) **Tapetum** nourishes the developing microspores or pollen grains. (1 + 1)

3. Explain the role of tapetum in the formation of pollen grain wall. NCERT

Ans. Tapetum is the innermost layer of the microsporangium. It produces the exine layer of the pollen grains, which is composed of the sporopollenin, the most resistant organic material. During microsporogenesis, the cells of tapetum produce various enzymes, hormones, amino acids and other nutritious materials required for the development of pollen grains.

4. What is microsporogenesis? Where does it occur in angiosperms?

Ans. Refer to text on page no. 3.

5. What is the importance of microspore mother cell undergoing meiosis?

Ans. Refer to text on page no. 3.

6. (i) Name the organic material that the exine of pollen grain is made up of. How is this material advantageous to pollen grain?

(ii) Exine does not form a continuous layer around the pollen grain. Give reason.

(iii) How are 'pollen banks' useful?

Ans. (i) The exine of pollen grain is made up of sporopollenin. It is the most resistant biological material so far known. It protects pollen grains from any environmental damages.

(ii) Exine on pollen grain is not a continuous layer. It is thin at places and pollen tube germinates by growth of intine through these thin parts of exine called germ pores.

(iii) Pollen banks can be used for storing pollen grains for years and for crop breeding programmes. (1 × 3)

7. A pollen grain in angiosperm at the time of dehiscence from an anther could be 2-celled or 3-celled. Explain, how are the cells placed within the pollen grain when shed at a 2-celled stage. Competency Based Que.

Ans. At the time of dehiscence, a pollen grain in angiosperms can be 2-celled. In this stage, the pollen grain consists of two cells: a vegetative (tube) cell, which is larger and will later form the pollen tube and a generative cell, which is smaller and located inside the vegetative cell. The generative cell will divide to form two sperm cells during fertillisation. When the pollen is shed from the anther the generative cell remains inside the vegetative cell and the division to form sperm cells occurs after pollination. (1 + 1)

8. Write a short note on pollen product and pollen allergy.

Ans. Refer to text on page no. 4.

9. Pollen banks are playing a very important role in promoting plant breeding programme over the world. How are pollens preserved in the pollen banks? CBSE 2019

Ans. Pollen grains are stored for years in liquid nitrogen (−196°C) in pollen banks for later use in plant breeding programmes. Plant breeding is a technique of manipulation of plant species in order to create desired plant types that are better suited for cultivation, give better yield and are disease resistant.

The objectives of such pollen banks include incorporation of certain traits or characters into crop plants in order to enhance the food production. (1 + 1)

10. With a neat and labelled diagram, describe the parts of a typical angiosperm ovule. NCERT

Ans. Refer to page no. 5 diagram 1.7.

11. In a flowering plant, a microspore mother cell produces four male gametophytes while a megaspore mother cell forms only one female gametophyte. Explain.

Ans. In flowering plants, microspore mother cells undergo meiosis and form microspore tetrad. After attaining maturity, these microspores separate from each other and each microspore develops into a male gametophyte. On the other hand, megaspore mother cell divides by meiotic division to produce four megaspores. From these, three degenerate while the one undergoes further development and mitotic divisions to produce female gametophyte.

12. Differentiate between microsporogenesis and megasporogenesis. Which type of cell division occurs during these events? Name the structure formed at the end of these two events. NCERT

Ans.

Microsporogenesis	Megasporogenesis
In this process, haploid microspores are formed from diploid microspore mother cell.	In this process haploid megaspore is formed from diploid megaspore mother cell.

The cell division that occurs during these events is meiosis.

Pollen grain and female gametophyte or embryo sac. (1 × 3)

13. With a neat labelled diagram explain the 7-celled, 8-nucleate nature of the female gametophyte. NCERT

Ans. Refer to page no. 7 diagram 1.9.

14. Write the location and functions of synergid.

Ans. Synergid cells are two specialised cells that lie adjacent to the egg cell in the female gametophyte of angiosperms.
Functions of synergids are as follows

(i) They nourishes the ovum and give direction to the pollen tube.

(ii) The filiform apparatus located inside synergids secretes chemical substance that helps in attracting the pollen tube towards the embryo sac. (1+1)

15. List the different types of pollination depending upon the source of pollen grain.

Ans. Depending on the source of pollen grain, pollination can be classified into following types

(i) **Autogamy** It is the transfer of pollen grain from anther to the stigma of the same flower.

(ii) **Geitonogamy** It is the transfer of pollen grains from anther of one flower to the stigma of another flower on the same plant.

Geitonogamy is functionally cross-pollination involving pollinating agent, but genetically it is equivalent to autogamy since, the pollen grains come from the same plant.

(iii) **Xenogamy** It is the transfer of pollen grains from anther to the stigma of different plant. It brings genetically different types of pollen grains to the stigma. (1×3)

16. What are chasmogamous flowers? Can cross-pollination occur in cleistogamous flowers? Give reasons for your answer. NCERT

Ans. Chasmogamous flowers are open flowers with exposed anthers and stigma.

Cross-pollination cannot occur in cleistogamous flowers because they remain in bud stage throughout their life and form seeds *via* self-pollination. (1 + 1)

17. Many of the flowering plants producing hermaphrodite flowers have developed many devices to discourage self-pollination and to encourage cross-pollination. Given below is a picture of one such outbreeding device in a flowering plant. Study the picture and answer the questions that follows CBSE 2025

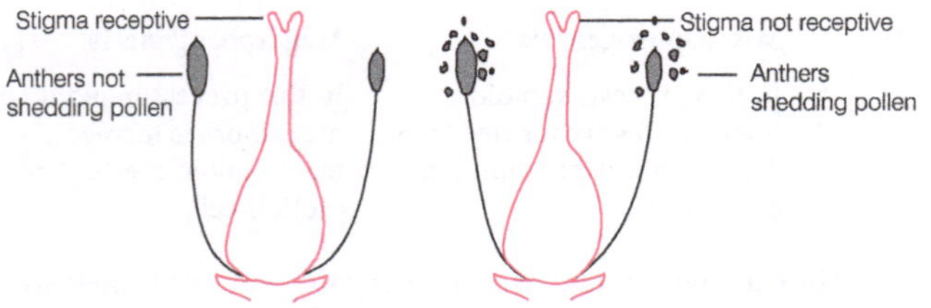

(i) Explain how the given type of pollination is advantageous to the plant.

(ii) Can this flowering plant show geitonogamy? Justify your answer.

Ans. (i) The given type of pollination is cross-pollination, where flowers on different plants of the same species exchange pollen. This is advantageous as it promotes genetic variation, leading to better adaptability, disease resistance and healthier offspring compared to self-pollination.

(ii) No, this flowering plants cannot show geitonogamy because geitonogamy involves pollination between different flowers on the same plant. Here, flowers are present on different plants of the same species, which ensures xenogamy (true cross-pollination) instead of geitonogamy.

18. Mention two strategies evolved to prevent self-pollination in flower. NCERT

Ans. Two strategies to prevent self-pollination in flower are as follows

(i) Production of unisexual flowers.

(ii) Maturation of anthers and stigma at different time in a bisexual flower. (1 + 1)

19. What is self-incompatibility? Why does self-pollination not lead to seed formation in self-incompatible species?

Ans. Refer to text on page no. 8. NCERT

Due to inhibition of self-fertilisation, self pollination does not lead to seed formation.

20. Explain the process of pollination in *Vallisneria*.

Ans. In *Vallisneria*, the female flower reaches the surface of water by a long stalk and the pollen grains are released on the surface of water. The pollen grains are then carried passively by water currents and reach the stigma eventually.

21. (i) Flowers are known to reward their insect pollinators. Explain.

(ii) Who are called pollen robbers?

Ans. (i) Refer to text on page no. 10 (Adaptations for insect pollination).

(ii) Refer to text on page no. 10 (Adaptations for insect pollination).

22. How many cellular nuclei does the pollen tube of angiosperm have? What is the ploidy of each of the nuclei? What is the function of tube cell nucleus?

Ans. The pollen tube of mature male gametophyte of angiosperms has three cellular nuclei-two sperms nuclei and one tube cell nucleus. All those nuclei are part of the male gametophyte of the plant and each of them is haploid (n). (2)

Tube cell nucleus is the vegetative nucleus, that guides the growth of the pollen tube when it enters into the pistil. (1)

23. One of the major approaches of crop improvement programme is artificial hybridisation. Explain the steps involved in making sure that only the desired pollen grain pollinate the stigma of a bisexual flower by a plant breeder. CBSE 2023

Ans. When the desired pollen grains are used for pollination and fertilisation, to get desired progeny, it is called artificial hybridisation.

Steps of artificial hybridisation

(i) **Emasculation** In this step, the anthers (male part) are removed from a bisexual flower to avoid unwanted fertilisation from the anthers of the same flower. Unisexual flowers do not require this step.

(ii) **Bagging** In this step, the flowers are covered with a bag to avoid landing of unwanted pollen grains on the stigma. The bagging is done till the flower attains receptivity.

(iii) **Pollination** Pollens with desired traits are dusted onto the flower after the flower is ready to receive the pollens. (1×3)

24. What is meant by emasculation? When and why does a plant breeder employ this technique? NCERT

Ans. Emasculation is the process of removal of stamens from a bisexual flower before they shed pollen in order to prevent self-pollination and permit cross-pollination of stigma with desired pollen. During breeding, the breeder wants to make sure that the desired pollen grains are used for pollination and the stigma is protected from contamination (from an unwanted pollen.) (2)

A plant breeder employs this technique to select and incorporate specific traits in the progeny. (1)

25. What is bagging technique? How is it useful in a plant breeding programme? NCERT

Ans. Refer to text on page no. 11.

26. Mention the advantages of emasculation and bagging in artificial hybridisation in plants bearing unisexual and bisexual flowers. CBSE 2020

Ans. Emasculation is the removal of anthers from bud before its dehiscence. In unisexual plants, it is not required while in bisexual plants, it helps in preserving pollens and preventing unwanted pollination. Bagging is advantageous in both type of plants. This protects them from any contamination by pollen grains.

27. Emasculation and bagging are the two important steps carried during artificial hybridisation to obtain superior varieties of desired plants. Explain giving reasons, in which types of flowers and at what stages are the two processes carried out. CBSE 2019

Ans. Refer to text on page no. 11 (Artificial hybridisation).

28. (i) **Can a plant flowering in Mumbai be pollinated by pollen grains of the same species growing in New Delhi? Provide explanation to your answer.** Competency Based Que.

(ii) **Draw the diagram of a pistil where pollination has successfully occurred. Label the parts involved in reaching the male gametes to its desired destination.**

Ans. (i) Yes, a plant flowering in Mumbai can be pollinated by pollen grains of the same species growing in New Delhi. It is mainly possible due to artificial hybridisation. In this the pollens are collected from the source plant in Mumbai and dusted on the emasculated flower growing in New Delhi. (1)

(ii) The parts involved in transferring the male gametes to their desired destination are stigma, style, micropyle, filiform apparatus and synergids. For LS of post-pollinated pistil refer to fig. 1.16 on page no. 11. (2)

29. What does the interaction between pollen grains and its compatible stigma result in after pollination? List two steps in sequence that follow after the process.

Ans. The interaction between a pollen grain and the stigma after pollination results in the germination of pollen grain.

When the pollen grains fall on the compatible stigma, the pollen tube grows and enters one of the synergids and releases two male gametes.

(i) One of the male gametes moves towards the egg cell and fuses with it to complete syngamy to form the zygote.

(ii) The other male gamete fuses with the two polar nuclei and forms triploid Primary Endosperm Nucleus (PEN). This is termed as triple fusion.

Since, two kinds of fusion–syngamy and triple fusion take place, the process is known as double fertilisation and is characteristic of flowering plants. (1 × 3)

30. What is triple fusion? Where and how does it take place? Name the nuclei involved in triple fusion. NCERT

Ans. Triple fusion is the process in which one male gamete fuses with two polar nuclei and forms primary endosperm nucleus. It takes place inside the embryo sac of angiospermic plant. Three nuclei are involved in triple fusion, i.e. two polar nuclei and one male gamete. (1 + 2)

31. (i) **Describe the endosperm development in coconut.**

(ii) **Why is tender coconut considered a healthy source of nutrition?**

(iii) **How are pea seeds different from castor seeds with respect to endosperm?**

Ans. (i) In coconut, endosperm formation is of nuclear type. The primary endosperm nucleus undergoes repeated nuclear division without cell wall formation. (1)

(ii) Tender coconut is an endosperm. It is rich in nutrients like fats, proteins, carbohydrates, minerals, vitamins, etc. Hence, it is considered as a healthy source of nutrition. (1)

(iii) Refer to text on page no. 14 (Types of seeds). (1)

32. Why do you think that the zygote is dormant for sometime in a fertilised ovule? NCERT

Ans. There is an adaptation in angiospermic plants to provide assured nutrition to the developing embryo. Most zygotes divide only after certain amount of endosperm is formed. Therefore, zygote remains dormant for sometime in a fertilised ovule.

33. In the majority of angiosperms, the zygote divides by an asymmetric mitotic division and generates two cells. Discuss the fates of these cells.

Ans. Refer to text on page no. 13 (Development of an embryo).

34. Starting with the zygote, draw the diagrams of the different stages of embryo development in a dicot. NCERT Exemplar

Ans. Refer to fig 1.18 on page no. 13.

35. Give one word for the following statements.

(i) **Embryonal axis above the level of cotyledons.**

(ii) **Embryonal axis below the level of cotyledons.**

(iii) **The simple structure that are swollen with reserve food material.**

Ans. (i) Epicotyl (ii) Hypocotyl (iii) Cotyledons (1×3)

36. Scutellum is the single cotyledon found in the monocot embryo only. Explain using diagram.

Ans. Refer to text on page no. 13 (Structure of monocot embryo). For diagram refer to diagram 1.20 (d) on page no. 14.

37. (i) Draw a diagram of pistil showing pollen tube growth in angiosperm and label
(a) stigma, (b) male gametes,
(c) pollen tube and (d) ovule.
(ii) Write the function of micropyle.

Ans. (i) Refer to fig. 1.16 (a) on page no. 11. (1½)

(ii) The micropyle helps in absorbing the water at the time of germination of seed. It is through the micropylar end that the pollen tube enters the ovule. (1½)

38. Micropyle is the single opening found on the seed coat. Do you agree? Also, state its function.

Ans. Yes, micropyle is the single opening found on the seed coat. Refer to text on page no. 14 (Structure of a seed).

39. In the diagram given below, identify the parts of the flowers and mention the post-fertilisation changes shown in the parts. **Competency Based Que.**

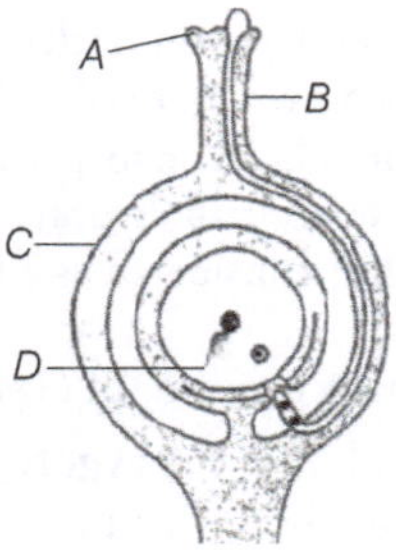

Ans.

Parts	Post-fertilisation change
A – Stigma	Both degenerate
B – Style	
C – Ovary	Fruit
D – Ovule	Seed

40. Differentiate between endosperm and perisperm, give one example of each.

Ans. Differences between endosperm and perisperm are as follows

Endosperm	Perisperm
It develops from primary endosperm nuclei.	It represents the persistent remains of the nucellus in the seed.
Endosperm develops first, followed by an embryo development.	It is a part that belongs to the seed.
It is usually in fluid form or it is dry.	It is usually dry.
It is triploid , e.g. coconut.	It is diploid, e.g. black pepper.

41. Double fertilisation is reported in plants of both castor and groundnut. However, the mature seeds of groundnut are non-albuminous and castor are albuminous. Explain the post-fertilisation events that are responsible for it.

Ans. Double fertilisation is reported in both castor and groundnut, but their mature seeds are different in terms of endosperm. PEN undergoes repetitive division to form a free nuclei after that cell wall forms, which giving rise to cellular endosperm.

Endosperm may be completely utilised by the developing embryo before the maturation of seeds as in groundnut. Such seeds are called non-albuminous or non-endospermic seeds. In some seeds, a portion of endosperm remains in the seed and is used up during seed germination. Such seeds are called albuminous or endospermic seeds, e.g. castor. (1 × 3)

42. Explain any three advantages that seeds offer to angiosperms.

Ans. Refer to text on page no. 15.

43. Why is apple called a false fruit? Which part(s) of the flower forms the fruit? **NCERT**

Ans. Apple is called false fruit because it is derived from the ovary along with other accessory floral parts. In apple, thalamus and ovary of the flower forms the fruit. (1 + 1)

44. If one can induce parthenocarpy through the application of growth substances, which fruits would you select to induce parthenocarpy and why? **NCERT, Competency Based Que.**

Ans. Only fleshy fruits like orange, watermelon, lemon, etc. should be selected as parthenocarpic fruits. Here, seeds of fruits are irritant during consumption, so seeds are removed. Thus, to make the fruits even more valuable. (2)

45. What is apomixis and what is its importance? **NCERT**

Ans. Apomixis is a type of asexual reproduction that mimics sexual reproduction. Here, the embryos can develop directly from the nucellus, integuments or synergid of a diploid embryo sac.

The plants produced by apomixis are genetically similar to the parent plant. They maintain and exhibit all the good characteristics of the parent plant without any risk of segregation of hybrid characters.

The information gained from genetics of apomixis can be commercially used in the transfer of apomictic genes into hybrid varieties. (1+2)

46. How are parthenocarpic fruits produced by some plants and apomictic seeds by some other? Explain.

Ans. The fruits which develop without undergoing fertilisation, are called parthenocarpic fruits, e.g. banana. Parthenocarpy can be induced through the application of growth hormones and such fruits are seedless.

Apomixis It is a form of asexual reproduction that mimics sexual reproduction, but produces seeds without fertilisation. It occurs in some species of Asteraceae and grasses. Apomictic seeds are viable and produced without pollination or sexual reproduction.

47. The image below shows two germinated seeds *X* and *Y* which belong to the same species. Seed *X* is produced by apomixis whereas seed *Y* is a product of sexual reproduction. CBSE SQP 2024

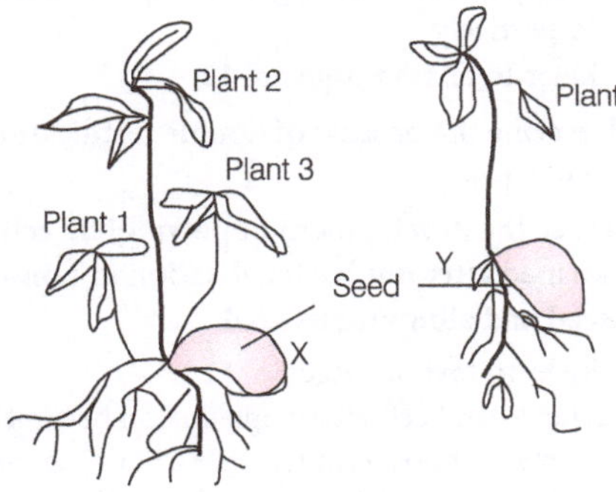

(i) **Write the number of embryo (s), embryo sac (s) and ovule(s) in the ovary of seed *X*.**

(ii) **How multiples embryos are formed in *Citrus* fruits?**

(iii) **What advantage will plants developed from seed *Y* have over seed *X*?**

Ans. (i) Seed *X*- 3 embryos; 1 embryo sac; 1 ovule.

(ii) The nucellar cells grow mitotically and develop into the embryos by asexual reproduction.

(iii) The plants growing from seed *X* will have to share the resources/endosperm so there is a possibility of some plant being undernourished while in seed *Y* only one plant will use the entire endosperm for its growth. The plants of seed *X* are clones, so they will not show variation whereas plants from seed *Y* will have genetic variation and so can show greater adaptability. (1 × 3)

Long Answer Type Questions

1. (i) **Explain the development of male gametophyte in an angiosperm.**

(ii) **Draw a labelled diagram of a three-celled male gametophyte.** CBSE 2024

Ans. (i) Refer to text on page no. 3.

(ii)

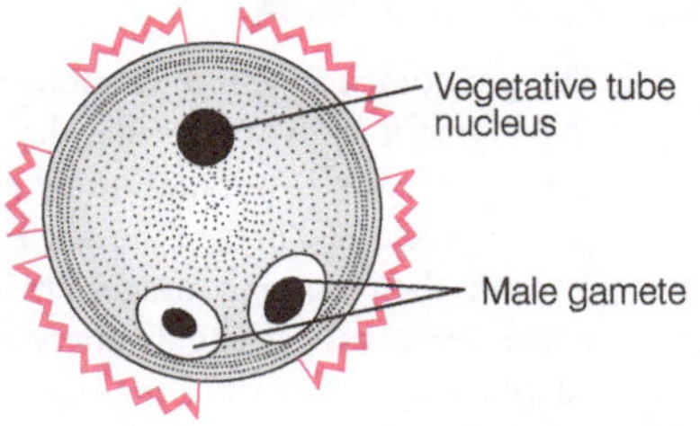

2. Trace the development of a 2-celled pollen grain of an angiosperm within an anther. Draw a labelled diagram to substantiate your answer. CBSE 2020

Ans. Refer to text on page no. 3-4 and refer to figure 1.5(b). (5)

3. (i) **Describe the process of megasporogenesis, in an angiosperm.**

(ii) **Draw a diagram of a mature embryo sac of angiosperm, label its any six parts.** CBSE 2020

Or **With a neat labelled diagram describe the part of a typical angiosperm ovule.** NCERT

Ans. (i) Refer to text on page no. 6-7.

(ii) Refer to figure no. 1.9 (e) on page no. 7. (2+3)

4. (i) **Explain the monosporic development of embryo sac in the ovule of an angiosperm.**

(ii) **Draw a diagram of the mature embryo sac of an angiospermic ovule and label any four parts in it.**

Ans. (i) Refer to text on page no. 6. CBSE 2023

(ii) Refer to figure 1.9 (e) on page no. 7. (3+2)

5. Describe the structure of the embryo sac of a mature angiosperm. Explain the role of synergids in it. Diksha

Ans. Refer to text on page no. 6-7.

6. (i) **State one difference and one similarity between geitonogamy and xenogamy.**

(ii) **Explain any three devices developed in flowering plants to discourage self-pollination and encourage cross-pollination.**

Ans. (i) Refer to text on page no. 8.

(ii) Refer to text on page no. 8.

7. (i) **Explain the significance of each of the following features present in plants given below.**

(a) **In rose-bay plant the stamens ripen before the stigma.**

(b) **In certain species of primrose, the flowers have short stamen and long style.**

(c) **The bisexual flower of mustard exhibits rejection of self-pollen grain.**

(ii) Explain how autogamy is prevented in castor and papaya plant, respectively. **CBSE SQP 2024**

Ans. (i) (a) The phenomenon where stamens mature before the stigma is known as protandry. This timing helps prevent self-pollination by ensuring that the pollen is released before the stigma is receptive. As a result, the plant encourages cross-pollination, which increases genetic diversity and enhances adaptability.

(b) In species of primrose, the presence of short stamens and long styles promotes heterostyly. This arrangement physically separates the pollen and stigma, reducing the likelihood of self-pollination. By facilitating cross-pollination with pollen from different plants, this feature helps to enhance genetic variation, which can lead to improved resilience and adaptability in the population.

(c) The rejection of self-pollen grains in bisexual mustard flowers is a form of self- incompatibility. This mechanism ensures that the plant does not fertilise itself, promoting cross-pollination instead. The genetic diversity resulting from cross-pollination is advantageous for the overall health and survival of the species, as it increases variability in traits that can help plants adapt to environmental changes. (1×3)

(ii) In castor plants, autogamy is prevented through dicliny; that is, castor plants have separate male and female flowers. This separation ensures that autogamy is prevented. Papaya exhibits a unique approach to prevent autogamy. In papaya male and female flower grow on different plants. This condition is called dioecy. (2)

8. **(i) Plan an experiment and prepare a flowchart of the steps that you would follow to ensure that the seeds are formed only from the desired sets of pollen grains. Name the type of experiment that you carried out.**

(ii) Write the importance of such experiments.

Ans. (i) Artificial hybridisation is carried out to ensure that seeds are formed from the desired set of pollen grains. This is done by emasculation and bagging.

The flowchart below shows the steps to be followed

Anther is removed in bud condition from a bisexual flower (Emasculation)

↓

Female flower is obtained

↓

Emasculated flower is enclosed in a bag made up of butter paper or plastic (Bagging)

↓

Mature and viable pollen grains are collected from desired male plants

↓

Bag is opened and pollen grains are dusted on the stigma

↓

Bag is replaced immediately

↓

Artificial pollination takes place (3)

(ii) Importance of such experiments are as follows

(a) Creation of new genetic recombination with better qualities.

(b) Incorporation of a large number of desirable characters into a single variety. (2)

9. **(i) Name the nuclei that fuse to form PEN.**

(ii) What is the ploidy of PEN and zygote?

(iii) Explain the development of endosperm from PEN.

Ans. (i) Two polar nuclei and one male gamete. (1)

(ii) Ploidy of PEN and zygote is triploid and diploid respectively. (2)

(iii) Refer to text on page no. 12. (2)

10. **(i) Describe the process of double fertilisation in angiosperms.**

(ii) Trace the development of polyploidal cell that is formed after double fertilisation in non-albuminous seed and albuminous seed. **CBSE 2020**

Ans. (i) Refer to text on page no. 12. (2½)

(ii) The central cell after triple fusion becomes the Primary endosperm Cell (PEC) and develops into the endosperm which is triploid nutritive tissue. In albuminous seed the endosperm persists even at maturity as developing embryo does not consume it completely as in castor and coconut.

In non-albuminous seed the endosperm is completely consumed by the developing embryo. So, endosperm is not present at maturity as in pea, groundnut, etc. (2½)

11. **(i) Draw a labelled diagram of a ferillised embryo sac of an angiosperm (label any four parts).**

(ii) Explain double fertillisation in angiospermic plant. **CBSE 2024 C**

Ans. (i) For fig refer to figure. 1.9(e) on page no. 7.

(ii) Refer to text on page no. 12.

12. **Explain the post-pollination events leading to seed production in angiosperms.**

Ans. The major events in post-fertilisation include development of endosperm and embryo, maturation of ovules into seeds and ovary into fruit. They take place soon after the double fertilisation. These are as follows

Development of an Endosperm The development of endosperm precedes embryo development. The primary endosperm cell divides repeatedly to form a **triploid endosperm tissue.**

In most of the cases, the PEN undergoes successive nuclear divisions without cytokinesis, to give rise to **free**

nuclear endosperm. Subsequently, cell wall formation starts from the periphery and the endosperm becomes completely cellular, e.g. coconut.

Development of an Embryo The embryo develops at the micropylar end of the embryo sac where the zygote is situated. Most zygotes divide only after certain amount of endosperm is formed. The nutrition for the development of embryo is provided by the endosperm. The zygote gives rise to proembryo and subsequently to the globular, heart-shaped and mature embryo.

Development of a Seed Double fertilisation in angiosperms triggers the transformation of ovule into a seed. Seeds are formed inside the fruits.

Formation of a Fruit A fruit is formed as a result of cell division and differentiation in the ovary, which is transformed into fruit as a result of stimuli received from pollination as well as from developing seed. (5)

13. (i) With labelled diagrams, depict stages in embryo development in a dicotyledonous plant.

(ii) Endosperm development precedes embryo development. Why? CBSE SQP 2023

Ans. (i) Refer to fig. 1.18 on page no. 13. (2½)

(ii) Endosperm is formed during the double fertilisation wherein one of the two male gametes fuses with two polar nuclei. The development of endosperm precedes that of the embryo in angiosperm seeds, because the endosperm cells provide nutrition to the developing embryo. In mature albuminous seeds, endosperm exists as storage tissue. It stores starch and fat. (2½)

14. Describe the difference between the structures of a dicot embryo and monocot embryo. Also draw LS of monocot and dicot seeds.

Ans. Refer to text on page no. 13 and fig. 1.19.

15. Read the statement and answer the questions that follows

A flower of brinjal has 520 ovules in its ovary. However, it produces a fruit with only 480 viable seeds.

(i) What could have prevented the rest of the 40 ovules from maturing into viable seeds? Explain giving a reason. Competency Based Que.

(ii) Describe the development of a dicot embryo in a viable seed.

(iii) Why certain angiospermic seeds are albuminous, while others are ex-albuminous? Explain.

Ans. (i) Ovules can develop into viable seeds having the ability to germinate under suitable environmental conditions. However, ovules often do not develop in viable seeds because of the following reasons

(a) Excessive dry weather or high temperature.

(b) Damage embryo.

(c) Starvation due to exhaustion of food in ovule. (2)

(ii) Refer to text on page no. 13. (1)

(iii) In flowering plants, during the development of seeds, along with embryo, a nutritive tissue called endosperm is also formed. During embryo development, endosperm degenerates to release its content that helps in the growth of embryo. In some plants, the endosperm is completely used up in embryo development. In such seed endosperm is absent, e.g. pea, gram, beans, etc. These seeds are called ex-albuminous seeds.

On the other hand, in some plants, the endosperm tissue persists in the viable seeds. These are called as albuminous seeds, e.g. castor. (2)

16. Read the following statement and answer the questions that follows.

'A guava fruit has 200 viable seeds'.

(i) What are viable seeds?

(ii) Write the total number of

(a) Pollen grains

(b) Gametes producing 200 viable guava seeds. Competency Based Que.

(iii) Prepare a flowchart to depict the post-pollination events leading to viable seed production in a flowering plant.

Ans. (i) Viable seeds are seeds having the ability to germinate when favourable conditions are present. (1)

(ii) (a) Numbers of pollen grains = 200

(b) Gametes producing 200 viable guava seeds = 400 (2)

(iii) The process of post-pollination events is as follows

Pollen grain germinates on stigma

↓

Pollen tube carrying the male gametes, reaches the ovule

↓

It discharges the male gametes into the embryo sac

↓

Fusion of male gametes with egg cell occurs (syngamy) to form zygote

↓

PEN form by the fusion of male gamete with two polar nuclei (triple fusion)

↓

Ovules develops into seed (2)

17. A flower of tomato plant following the process of sexual reproduction produces 240 viable seeds.

Answer the following questions giving reasons

(i) What is the minimum number of pollen grains that must have been involved in the pollination of its pistil?

(ii) What would have been the minimum number of ovules present in the ovary?

(iii) How many megaspore mother cells were involved?

(iv) **What is the minimum number of microspore mother cells involved in the above case?**

(v) **How many male gametes were involved in this case?**

Ans. (i) The minimum number of pollen grains that must have been involved are 240, as 240 viable seeds are formed.

(ii) The minimum number of ovules would also have been 240, as 240 viable seeds are formed. After fertilisation, the ovule turns into seed.

(iii) 240 megaspore mother cells were involved. They undergo meiotic division to form 4 haploid megaspores. Out of them only 1 becomes functional megaspore and rest 3 degenerate.

(iv) The minimum number of microspore mother cells in the above case would be 60. This is because each microspore mother cell gives rise to 4 microspores.
Thus, to obtain 240 microspores, 60 microspore mother cells are required.

(v) The number of male gametes involved would be 480. It is because each pollen grain has two male gametes. One male gamete fuses with egg cell, while second male gamete fuses with two polar nuclei. (1 × 5)

18. **Differentiate between**

(i) **Hypocotyl and epicotyl**

(ii) **Coleoptile and coleorhiza**

(iii) **Integument and testa**

(iv) **Perisperm and pericarp** NCERT

Ans. (i) Differences between hypocotyl and epicotyl are as follows

Hypocotyl	Epicotyl
The portion of the embryonal axis below the level of cotyledons is called the hypocotyl.	The portion of the embryonal axis above the level of cotyledons is called the epicotyl.
It terminates at its lower end in the radicle or root tip covered with a root cap.	It terminates with the plumule.

(1)

(ii) Differences between coleoptile and coleorhiza are as follows

Coleoptile	Coleorhiza
It is a conical protective sheath over the epicotyl bearing the shoot apex and leaf primordia.	It is a protective sheath over the radicle and root cap.
It comes out of the soil.	It remains inside the soil.
It protects the plumule during its emergence from the soil.	It protects the radicle during its passage into the soil.

(1½)

(iii) Differences between in integument and testa are as follows

Integument	Testa
It is the protective covering of the ovule.	It is the protective covering of the seed.
It is a thin covering.	It is a thick covering.
The cells are living.	The cells are dead.
It is a pre-fertilisation structure.	It is a post-fertilisation structure.

(1)

(iv) Differences between perisperm and pericarp are as follows

Perisperm	Pericarp
It represents residual persistent nucellus.	It represents the fruit wall derived from the ovary wall.
It is part of the seed.	It is part of the fruit.
It is generally dry.	It can be dry or fleshy.
It is often non-functional for the seed.	It acts like a protective covering, helps in dispersal and providing nutrition.
It is present only in few seeds.	It is found in all fruits.

(1½)

19. (i) **Explain the structure of a typical monocotyledonous embryo of a flowering plant.**

(ii) **How are multiple embryos formed in a citrus fruit? What is the mechanism known as?** CBSE 2025

Ans. (i) A typical monocotyledonous embryo consists of several distinct parts. It has a single cotyledon, known as the scutellum, which is specialised for absorbing nutrients from the endosperm during seed germination.
The plumule, which develops into the shoot, is protected by a sheath called the coleoptile, while the radicle, which develops into the root, is covered by the coleorhiza. The embryo also has an epicotyl, which is the region above the scutellum that leads to shoot development, and a hypocotyl, the region between the scutellum and radicle. These structures help in the proper development of the seedling after germination. (2½)

(ii) In some citrus varieties, certain nucellar cells surrounding the embryo sac start dividing and protrude into the embryo sac, developing into embryos.
As a result, each ovule contains multiple embryos. The occurrence of more than one embryo in a seed is known as polyembryony. (2½)

20. (i) **Explain any two ways by which apomictic seed can develop.**
(ii) **List one advantage and one disadvantage of a apomictic crop.**
(iii) **Why do farmers find production of hybrid seeds costly?** **CBSE 2019**

Ans. (i) Apomictic seed can develop in two ways as follows
(a) In some species, nucellus and integuments extend into the embryo sac and develops an embryo.
(b) In some species, the diploid egg cell is formed without reduction division and develops into embryo without fertilisation. (2)

(ii) **Advantage of Apomictic Crop** Apomixis ensures genetic uniformity, retains hybrid vigour and reduces dependence on polination.
Disadvantage of Apomictic Crop During the production of apomictic crop, there is no genetic diversity in the progeny. (2)

(iii) Production of hybrid seed is a costly process. Since, hybrid seeds do not maintain hybrid characters. These seeds are to be produced year after year. This is the reason why farmer find production of hybrid seeds costly. (1)

Source Based/Case Based/Passage Based Questions

1. **Refer to the two graphs given below. Graph *A* represents rate of pollination with respect to insect pollinated flowers and graph *B* represents the same in wind pollinated flowers.**

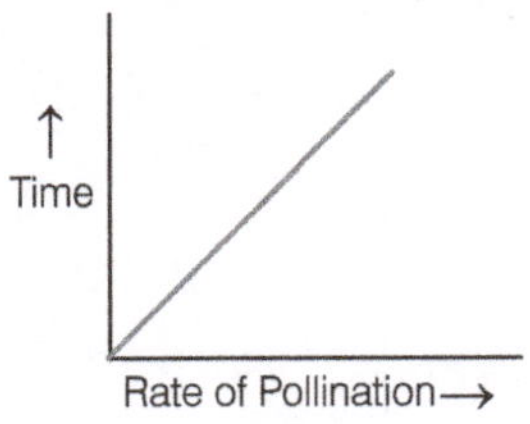

(A)

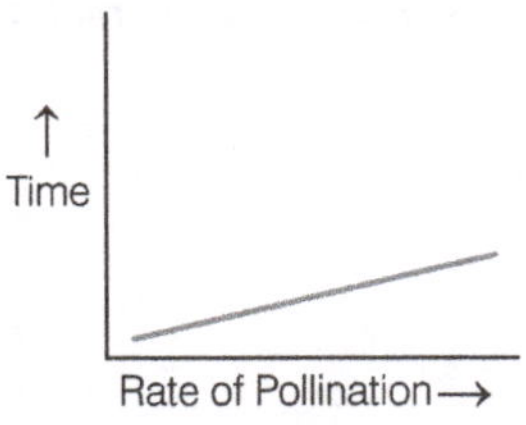

(B)

Study the above two graphs and answer the questions that follows.
(i) **What do you infer from the two graphs ?**
(ii) **Give reason as for why the other mode is not an efficient mode of pollination.**
(iii) **State two features of wind pollinated flowers.**

Or

(iii) **Name any two factors that affect pollination.**

Ans. (i) We infer that rate of pollination is successful or more in case of insect pollinated flowers (graph *A*). (1)
(ii) The other mode is not efficient because in anemophily (graph *B*), several pollen grains are lost mid-way without fulfilling the purpose of pollination. (1)
(iii) Two features of wind pollinated flowers are
(a) Light and non-sticky pollen grains.
(b) Feathery stigma to trap pollen grains. (2)

Or

(iii) Temperature, floral morphology and number of pollinators, etc., affect pollination. (2)

2. **A study examined the seed dormancy period of *Helianthus annuus* (sunflower) in two environments a temperate region (region *A*) and a tropical region (region *B*).**
Data collected in the study is given below.
Competency Based Que.

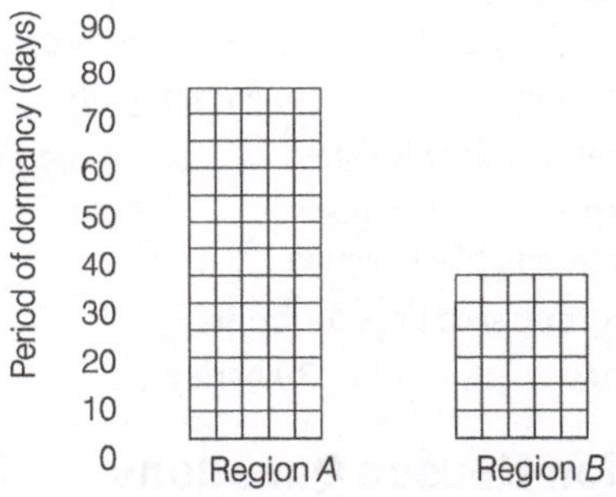

(i) **Which region has high rate of seed dormancy? Why?**
(ii) **Why do the integuments of an ovule harden and the water contents gets highly reduced as the seed matures?**
(iii) **What are albuminous seeds? Explain it with the help of examples.**

Ans. (i) The dormancy rate is higher in the temperate region. Temperate regions experience distinct seasons, including cold winters. Seeds enter dormancy to survive unfavourable conditions until temperature rise and moisture becomes available in spring. (2)
(ii) Integuments of an ovule harden and the water contents gets highly reduced to keep the seed dry and maintained the dormant stage. (1)
(iii) Albuminous seeds retain a part of endosperm as it is not completely used during embryo development, e.g. wheat, barly, maize, castor. (1)

SELF ASSESSMENT TEST

Multiple Choice Questions

1. The outermost and innermost wall layers of microsporangium in an anther are
(a) endothecium and tapetum respectively
(b) epidermis and endodermis, respectively
(c) epidermis and middle layer, respectively
(d) epidermis and tapetum, respectively

2. During microsporogenesis, meiosis occurs in
(a) endothecium
(b) microspore mother cells
(c) microspore tetrads
(d) pollen grains

3. What is the function of filiform apparatus in an angiospermic embryo sac?
(a) Brings about opening of the pollen tube
(b) Guides the pollen tube into a synergid
(c) Prevents entry of more than one pollen tube into a synergid
(d) None of the above

4. The female gametophyte of a typical dicot at the time of fertilisation is
(a) 8–celled (b) 7–celled (c) 6–celled (d) 5–celled

5. Spiny or sticky pollen grains and large, attractively coloured flowers are associated with
(a) hydrophily (b) entomophily (c) ornithophily (d) anemophily

6. Persistent nucellus is called as .... and is found in ....
(a) perisperm, black pepper
(b) perisperm, groundnut
(c) endosperm, black pepper
(d) endosperm, groundnut

7. Endospermic seeds are found in
(a) castor (b) barley (c) wheat (d) All of these

Assertion-Reason Questions

Direction (Q. Nos. 8-11) *In each of the following questions, a statement of Assertion (A) is given followed by corresponding statement of Reason (R). Of the statements, mark the correct answer as*

(a) If both A and R are true and R is the correct explanation of A.
(b) If both A and R are true, but R is not the correct explanation of A.
(c) If A is true, but R is false.
(d) If A is false, but R is true.

8. **Assertion** (A) Cells of tapetum have more than one nucleus.
Reason (R) They undergo meiosis without cytokinesis.

9. **Assertion** (A) Self-pollination can lead to reduced genetic diversity in plant populations.
Reason (R) Self-pollination limits the mixing of genetic material, making offspring more similar to the parent plant.

10. **Assertion** (A) Emasculation is a technique used to promote hybridisation in flowering plants.
Reason (R) Emasculation prevents self-pollination by bagging the anthers from flowers.

11. **Assertion** (A) Seed dispersal mechanisms are vital for the survival of plant species.
Reason (R) Effective seed dispersal reduces competition among seedlings and allows plants to colonise new areas.

Very Short Answer Type Questions

12. Name the part of flower that the tassels of corn cob represents.
13. Give the scientific name for the outbreeding device that promotes development of unisexual flowers in different plants.
14. You are given castor and bean seeds which one of the two would you choose to observe the endosperm?
15. Name the type of pollination occurs in *Zostera*.

Short Answer Type Questions

16. Describe the structure of pollen grain and write any one advantage and disadvantage of pollen grains.
17. Explain the following terms.
    (i) Monocarpellary (ii) Multicarpellary (iii) Syncarpous
18. What are chasmogamous and cleistogamous flowers?

Long Answer Type Questions

19. Explain the adaptation of wind pollination in brief.
20. Draw a neat, labelled diagram of an ovule and describe the parts of a typical angiosperm ovule.
21. Explain the structure of monocot and dicot embryo.

Case Based Question

22. Sudha cracked open a coconut and found the following content as shown in the image below

(i) Identify the parts of the seed labelled as P and Q.
(ii) What is most likely to have happened to the coconut water?
(iii) What is the ploidy of the coconut water that we drink from the tender coconut? Justify.

Answers

1. (d)	2. (b)	3. (b)	4. (b)	5. (b)	6. (a)	7. (d)
8. (c)	9. (a)	10. (c)	11. (a)			

02 CHAPTER

Humans are sexually reproducing **viviparous** (i.e. give birth to young ones) organisms. They are also **unisexual**, i.e. male and female sexes are separate and each sex has their own reproductive organs (gonads), reproductive ducts and accessory structures.

Human Reproduction

YOUR STUDY GOALS

2.1 Human Reproductive System
2.2 Gametogenesis
2.3 Menstrual Cycle
2.4 Fertilisation
2.5 Embryonic Development

YOUR PRACTICE GOAL

- Objective Type Questions (37 Qs ; MCQs, A-R) Case Based Questions (8)
- Subjective Type Questions
- (25 VSAs, 42 SAs, 15 LAs)

Reproduction is the biological process by which organisms produce offspring to ensure the survival of their species.

The reproductive events in humans include gametogenesis, insemination, fertilisation, implantation, gestation and parturition. Although these events occur after puberty, but there are remarkable differences between the reproductive events in male and female.

In this chapter, we will study about the different reproductive systems in male and female and also the various events of human reproduction.

2.1 Human Reproductive System

- Human beings show prominent sexual dimorphism where males and females differ from each other by a number of primary and secondary sexual characteristics.
- **Primary sex characters** are those which are present in both males and females since birth, like external genitalia.
- **Secondary sex characters** are those characters, which appear after puberty and include a number of traits like presence of thick facial hairs, low pitched voice, etc., in males and well-developed mammary glands, high pitched voice, etc., in females.

- The organs that participate in all activities related to reproduction are called **reproductive organs**. On the basis of their functions, they are classified as primary sex organs and secondary sex organs.
  (i) **Primary Sex Organs** These are also called gonads. The process of gamete formation and secretion of hormones occur in these organs, e.g. testis (in males) and ovary (in females).
  (ii) **Secondary Sex Organs** These do not produce gametes or sex hormones, but play an important role in reproduction. Thus, also known as **accessory sex organs**.

Male Reproductive System

It is located in the **pelvis region** of the body. It consists of a pair of testes, accessory ducts, glands and the external genitalia. These structures are discussed below in details.

Primary Sex Organ

Testes are the primary sex organs in men. These occur in pair.

Testes

- These are the **male gonads**, i.e. the site where the male gametes or sperms are produced.
- In adults, each testis is oval in shape, with a length of about 4-5 cm and width of 2-3 cm.
- These are situated outside the abdominal or pelvic cavity within a darkly pigmented sac of skin called **scrotal sac** or **scrotum**.

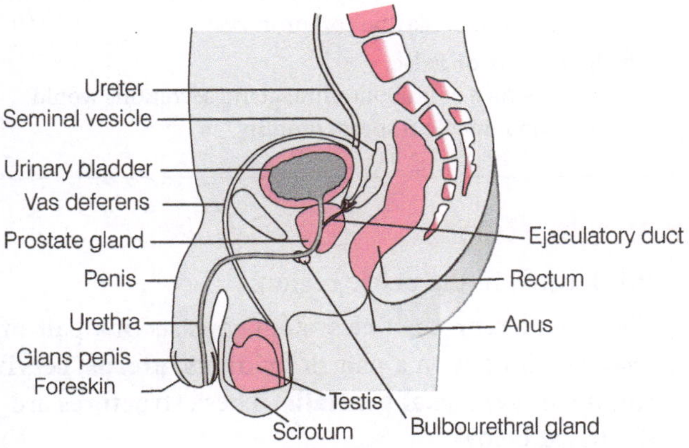

Fig. 2.1 Sectional view of male pelvis showing reproductive system

- Scrotum acts as thermoregulator and keeps the testicular temperature 2-2.5° C lower than the normal internal body temperature. This temperature is necessary for sperm production, i.e. spermatogenesis.
- The testis is surrounded by three dense protective coverings.
- Each testis is divided into 250 compartments called **testicular lobules**. Each lobule contains 1-3 highly coiled **seminiferous tubules**.

Seminiferous Tubule

- It is the structural and functional unit of testis in which sperms are produced.
- Each seminiferous tubule is lined on its inside by two types of highly specialised cells, which are given below
  - **Male Germ Cells** (Spermatogonia) These cells undergoes meiotic division, leading to the formation of sperms.
  - **Sertoli Cells** (Nurse cells) These cells provide nutrition to the developing germ cells.

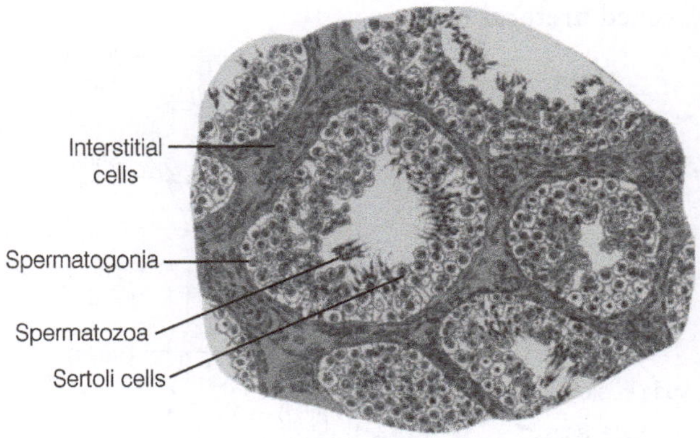

Fig. 2.2 Diagrammatic sectional view of seminiferous tubule

- The regions outside the seminiferous tubules called **interstitial spaces**, contain small blood vessels and masses of cells called **interstitial cells** or **Leydig cells.**
- These cells synthesise and secrete the testicular hormones called **androgens**.
- Leydig cells are endocrine in function and thus regulate and maintain male sex characters.
- Other immunologically competent cells are also present in this region.

Secondary Sex Organs

They consist of the following structures

Accessory Duct System

It consist of series of ducts that store and transport the sperms from the testis to the outside through urethra.

The male accessory ducts include, **rete testis, vasa efferentia, epididymis, vas deferens** and **urethra.**

- **Rete Testis** The seminiferous tubules are present in testis and open into vasa efferentia through rete testis.
- **Vasa Efferentia** It exits the testis and open into the epididymis.
- **Epididymis** It is a long, coiled tube that is located along the posterior surface of each testis and leads to the vas deferens.
- **Vas Deferens** It ascends to the abdomen, loops over the urinary bladder, receives a duct from the seminal vesicles and opens into the urethra as the ejaculatory duct.
- **Urethra** It originates from the urinary bladder and extends through the penis to its external opening called **urethral meatus.**

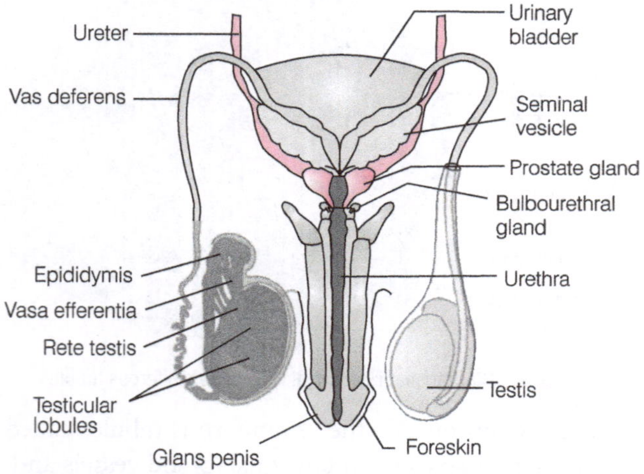

Fig. 2.3 Diagrammatic view of male reproductive system (part of testis is open to show inner details)

Accessory Glands

The accessory glands or the secondary glands are described below

- **Prostate Gland** This gland is situated around the first part of urethra and secretes a milky, slightly alkaline fluid that contains lipids, enzymes, citric acid, etc.
- **Seminal Vesicles** These are paired tubular glands, present below the urinary bladder. These secrete mucus and a watery alkaline fluid that contains fructose (an energy source for the sperms).
- **Bulbourethral or Cowper's Gland** These glands are situated beneath the prostate gland and near the base of penis. Cowper's gland secrete mucus and an alkaline fluid, which helps in the lubrication of the penis.
- Secretion of these glands constitute seminal plasma which is rich in fructose , calcium and certain enzymes.

External Genitalia (Penis)

- The penis is the external genitalia of males, made up of specialised tissue that enables erection and facilitates insemination.
- It's enlarged tip, called the **glans penis,** is covered by a loose fold of skin known as the **foreskin.**

Quick Test 1

1. Name the cells which are responsible for providing support and nourishment to the developing sperm in the testis.
2. **State True or False.**
   Regular hot baths can positively affect male fertility by increasing testicular temperature.
3. A couple is experiencing difficulties in conceiving and the male partner has been found to have low testosterone levels. Which specific cells in the testes are responsible for the given condition?
4. If a male semen lacks prostatic secretions, which accessory duct may be compromised?
5. **State True or False.**
   The absence of bulbourethral gland secretions would have no impact on sperm motility.

Female Reproductive System

- It is located in the pelvic region.
- The female reproductive system consists of a pair of **ovaries**, along with a pair of **oviducts**, **uterus**, **cervix**, **vagina** and **external genitalia**. These structures are discussed below

Primary Sex Organs

Ovaries are the primary sex organs of female. Their description is given below

Ovaries

- They produce female gametes (ovum) and several steroid hormones (ovarian hormones).
- The ovaries are located one on each side, in the lower part, of the abdomen.

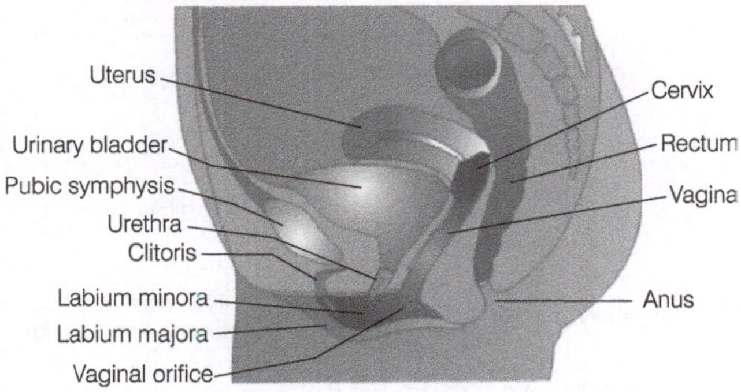

Fig. 2.4 Diagrammatic sectional view of female pelvis showing reproductive system

- Each ovary is about 2-4 cm in length and is connected to the uterus and pelvic wall by ligaments.
- It is covered by a thin epithelium enclosing **ovarian stroma**, which contains connective tissues, blood vessels and mature follicles.
- The stroma is divided into two parts, i.e. a peripheral **cortex** and an inner **medulla**.

Secondary Sex Organs

These consist of the following structures

Accessory Ducts

The following parts constitute the accessory ducts in females

(i) **Oviducts** (Fallopian Tubes)

- These are two small tubes of about 10-12 cm in length and lies on either sides of uterus.
- These tubes carry the egg from the periphery of ovary to the uterus and also provide the appropriate environment for fertilisation.
- The Fallopian tubes or oviducts is differentiated into infundibulum, ampulla and isthmus.
- **Infundibulum** is broad and funnel-shaped part that is closest to the ovary. Its edges bear motile, finger-like projections called **fimbriae.** They help in the collection of ovum after ovulation.
- **Ampulla** is the long, wide, thin-walled part of the Fallopian tube that lie next to the infundibulum.
- **Isthmus** has short-narrow lumen. It follows ampulla and joins the uterus.

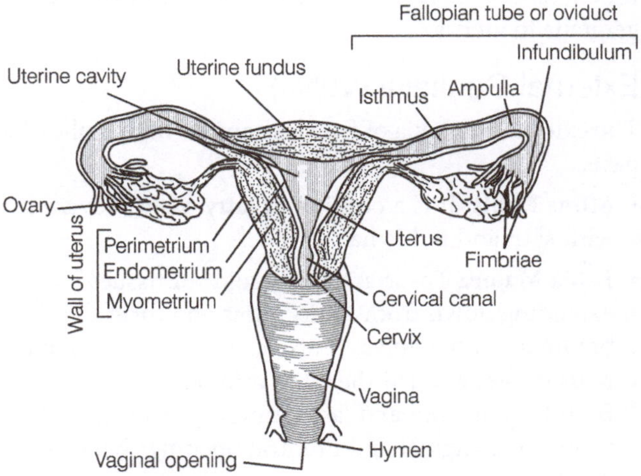

Fig. 2.5 Diagrammatic sectional view of female reproductive system

(ii) **Uterus** (Womb)

- It is single, muscular inverted pear-shaped structure.
- It is supported by ligaments attached to the pelvic wall.
- It lies between the urinary bladder and rectum and has a thick, highly vascular wall, composed of three layers of tissues.
  - **Outer Perimetrium** A thin membranous covering of uterus wall.
  - **Middle Myometrium** A thick layer of smooth muscle fibres, which contracts strongly during delivery of the baby.
  - **Inner Endometrium** A thick glandular layer that lines the uterine cavity and have many blood vessels. It undergoes cyclic changes during the menstrual cycle.
- Uterus receives the ovum from the Fallopian tube. An egg after being fertilised gets implanted in the uterus. It forms placenta for the development of foetus and also expels the young one at the time of birth.
- **Cervix** is the narrow entrance of the uterus into the vagina. The cavity of cervix is called **cervical canal,** which along with vagina forms the **birth canal.**

(iii) Vagina

It is about 10 cm long and acts as a receptacle for the penis during copulation as well as allows a passage for menstrual flow and foetus during parturition. It functions as a passage way that connects the external genitalia to uterus.

External Genitalia (Vulva)

The external genitalia of females consists of the following parts

- **Mons Pubis** It is a cushion of fatty tissue, covered with skin and pubic hairs.
- **Labia Majora** These are fleshy folds of tissues extending down from mons pubis and form the boundary of the vulva. It also covers two additional folds of tissue called the **labia minora**.
  Both labia majora and labia minora surround and protect the vaginal and urethral openings beneath them.
- **Clitoris** It is the small finger-like structure. It lies at the upper junction of the two labia minora above the urethral opening.
- **Hymen** It is a thin mucous membrane, which partially covers the vaginal opening.
- It is often torn during the first coitus (intercourse) and may be present in some women even after coitus.
- It can also get stretched or broken by sports activities such as horseback riding, cycling, etc., or even by a sudden fall or jolt, therefore the presence or absence of hymen is not an accurate indicator of a woman's virginity or sexual experience.

Mammary Glands

- Functional mammary glands are the characteristic feature of all female mammals.
- These are paired structures (breasts) that contain glandular tissue and variable amount of fat.
- The glandular tissue of each breast is divided into 15-20 **mammary lobes**, which contain clusters of cells known as **alveoli.**
- The cells within the alveoli produce milk, which is stored in the cavities, or lumens, of the alveoli.
- The alveoli open into **mammary tubules**.
- The tubules of each lobe join to form a **mammary duct**.
- Several mammary ducts join to form a wider **mammary ampulla** which is connected to **lactiferous duct** through which milk is sucked out.

Alveoli → Mammary tubules → Mammary duct → Mammary ampulla → Lactiferous duct

Fig. 2.6 Pathway of milk through the mammary gland

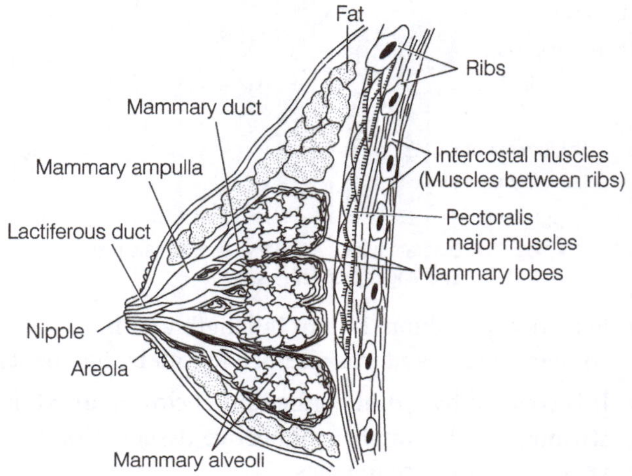

Fig. 2.7 Diagrammatic sectional view of mammary glands

TEACHER'S TIP

Mammary glands are referred to as secondary sexual characteristics. As they develop during puberty and are linked to sexual differentiation and reproduction, though they do not directly participate in the reproductive process. .

Quick Test 2

1. **State True or Talse.**
   The fimbriae are responsible for moving the egg through the Fallopian tube after it has been captured from the ovary.
2. During labour, dysfunction of which uterine layer can lead to prolonged labour?.
3. If a woman experiences a shorter menstrual period (3 days instead of 5), which layer of the uterine lining might be affected?
4. '*X*' is a thin membranous structure which partially covers the vaginal opening, identify '*X*'.
5. Name the structure which is formed by the union of several mammary ducts.

2.2 Gametogenesis

The process of formation of haploid gametes from the undifferentiated diploid germ cells in the gonads, for sexual reproduction, is called **gametogenesis.**

In human beings gametogenesis is of two types, i.e. **spermatogenesis** (in males) and **oogenesis** (in females).

Spermatogenesis

- It is the process of formation of spermatozoa (sperms) in seminiferous tubules of testes.
- These tubules are lined by a **germinal epithelium.**
- The process of spermatogenesis begins at puberty (Fig 2.8). It includes the following stages

1. Multiplication Phase

- The undifferentiated germ cells are called **spermatogonia** (sing : spermatogonium) or **sperm mother cells.**
- Spermatogonia are present on the inside wall of seminiferous tubules.
- They increase in number by repeated mitotic divisions.
- The newly formed spermatogonium possesses the same number of chromosomes as parent cell. Each spermatogonium is diploid and contains 46 chromosomes.

2. Growth Phase

Some of the spermatogonia differentiate to form **primary spermatocytes.**

3. Maturation Phase or Formation of Spermatids

- Each of these primary spermatocytes undergoes first meiotic division and produces two equal haploid cells called **secondary spermatocytes** (23 chromosomes each).
- Each of secondary spermatocytes further undergoes second meiotic division to produce four equal haploid **spermatids.**

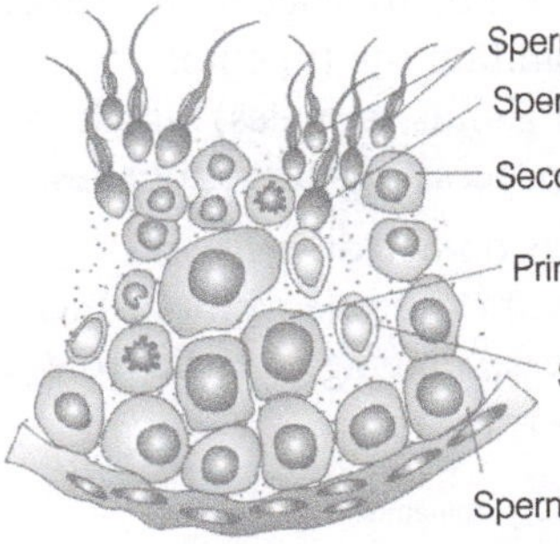

Fig. 2.8 Diagrammatic sectional view of a seminiferous tubule (enlarged)

4. Differentiation Phase

- The spermatids transform into **spermatozoa** (sperms) by the process called **spermiogenesis.**
- After spermiogenesis, sperm heads get embedded in the Sertoli cells and are finally released from the seminiferous tubules by the process of **spermiation.**

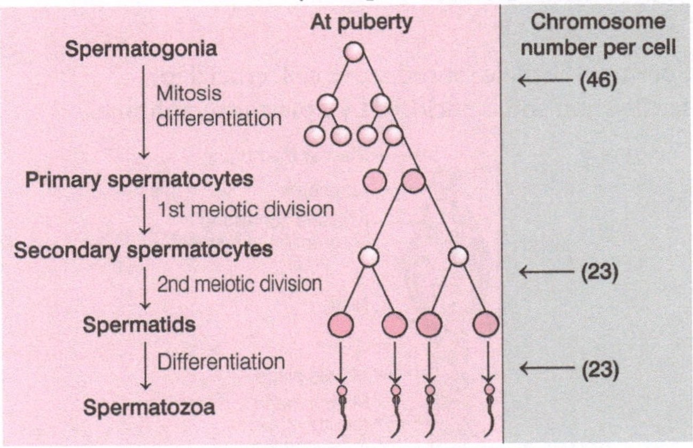

Fig. 2.9 Schematic representation of spermatogenesis in human male

Hormones Control for Spermatogenesis

- Spermatogenesis initiates due to a significant increase in the secretion of **Gonadotropin Releasing Hormone** (GnRH) by hypothalamus at the age of puberty.
- The increased level of GnRH acts on anterior pituitary, which further stimulates the secretion of two gonadotropins, i.e. **Luteinising Hormone** (LH) and **Follicle Stimulating Hormone** (FSH).

- LH acts on the Leydig cells, stimulating the synthesis and secretion of androgens (testicular hormone, which maintain the function of accessory ducts and glands in males) which in turn, stimulate the process of spermatogenesis.
- In addition, FSH acts on Sertoli cells and stimulates the secretion of some factors which help in spermiogenesis, playing a crucial role in the formation of sperm.

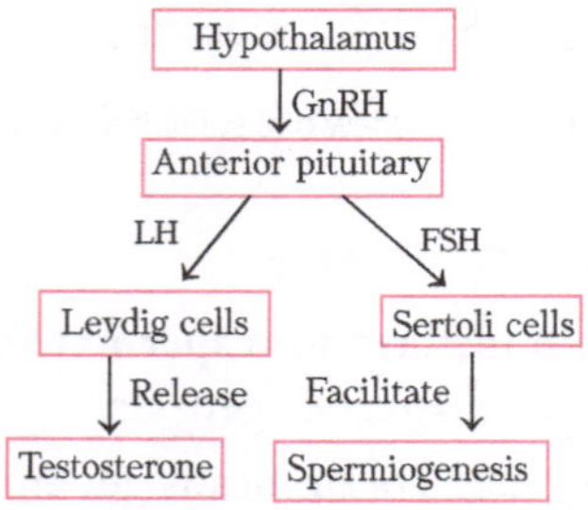

Fig. 2.10 Hormonal control of spermatogenesis

Structure of a Sperm (Spermatozoa)

Sperm is the male reproductive cell, crucial for fertilisation and is enclosed by a plasma membrane.

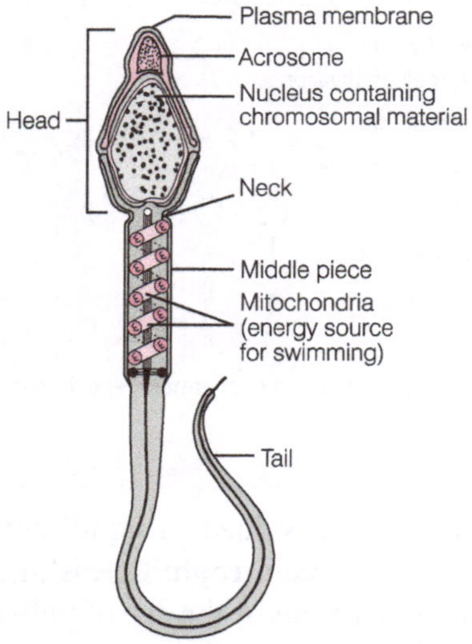

Fig. 2.11 Structure of a human sperm

- It is a microscopic structure consisting of a head, neck, middle piece and a tail.
  - **Head** It is oval in shape and composed of a elongated haploid nucleus and a small anterior cap-like structure, called **acrosome**.
    The acrosome contains **hydrolytic enzymes,** which is used to penetrate the egg (ovum) during fertilisation.
  - **Neck** It is located between the head and middle piece.
  - **Middle Piece** It possesses several mitochondria to produce energy for the movement of the tail.
  - **Tail** It facilitates the sperm motility which is crucial for fertilisation.
- The human male ejaculates about 200-300 million sperms during a coitus.
- For normal fertility, about 60% of them must have normal shape and size and atleast 40% of them must show vigorous motility.
- Secretions of epididymis, vas deferens, seminal vesicles and prostate are essential for motility and maturation of sperm. The seminal plasma along with sperm constitutes the **semen**.

Oogenesis

- It is the process of formation of a mature female gamete and takes place in ovaries.
- The production of eggs in females begins before birth, i.e. during the embryonic development stage.
- Although, the development is completed only after fertilisation.
- The process undergoes following phases

1. Multiplication Phase

- Cells in germinal epithelium undergo mitotic division producing undifferentiated germ cells called **oogonia** or **egg mother cells** within each fetal ovary; no more oogonia are added after birth.
- These cells start dividing and enter prophase-I of meiotic division.
- They get temporarily arrested at this stage and are known as **primary oocytes.**

2. Growth Phase

- During this phase, primary oocyte is surrounded by a single layer of granulosa cells and is called the **primary follicle**.
- About millions of these follicles exist in females before birth. A large number of these follicles degenerate during the phase from birth to puberty. Therefore, at puberty only 60,000-80,000 primary follicles are left in each ovary.

- The **primary follicles** get surrounded by more layers of granulosa cells and a new theca to form **secondary follicles.**
- The secondary follicle transforms into tertiary follicle, which are characterised by a fluid cavity called **antrum.**
- The theca layer is organised into an inner **theca interna** and an outer **theca externa.**

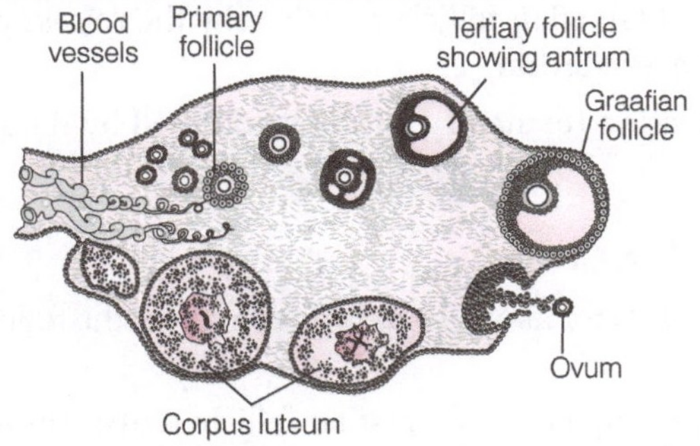

Fig. 2.12 Diagrammatic sectional view of ovary showing different stages

3. Maturation Phase

- Two meiotic divisions *viz*, meiosis-I and meiosis-II occur during this phase.
- **Meiosis-I** The primary oocyte within this tertiary follicle grows in size.
  - The fully grown primary oocyte completes its first meiotic division producing two unequal daughter cells.
  - Among them the larger haploid cell is called **secondary oocyte** (ovum) and the tiny one is called **first polar body.**
  - The secondary oocyte retains bulk of the nutrient rich cytoplasm of primary oocyte.

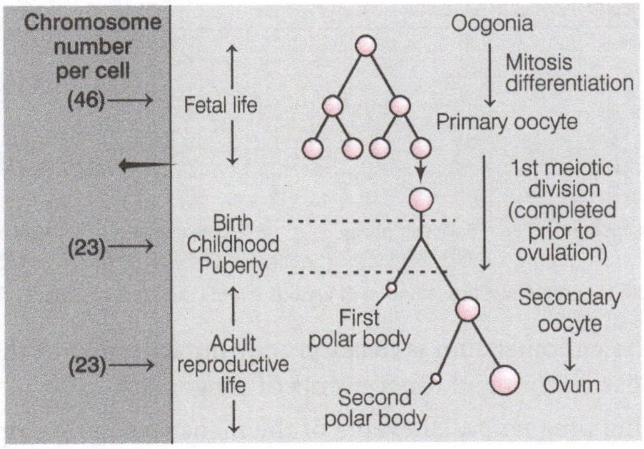

Fig. 2.13 Schematic representation of oogenesis in human female

- **Meiosis-II** The secondary oocyte starts its second meiotic division but remains suspended in it, till the sperm enters inside it.
- The tertiary follicle further changes into a mature follicle or **Graafian follicle.** The secondary oocyte forms a new membrane called **zona pellucida** surrounding it.
- At this stage, the Graafian follicle, ruptures to release the secondary oocyte from the ovary. The process of release of the secondary oocyte from the ovary is called **ovulation.**

Hormonal Control of Oogenesis

- The growth, maintenance and functions of the female reproductive organs are under the hormonal control.
- GnRH is secreted by the hypothalamus. It stimulates the anterior lobe of pituitary gland to secrete LH and FSH.
- FSH stimulates the growth of the ovarian follicle. It also increases the development of egg/oocyte within the follicle.
- LH induces ovulation and stimulates the corpus luteum to secrete progesterone.

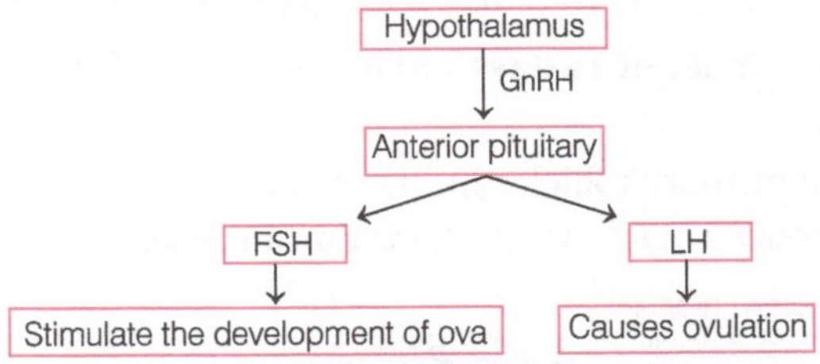

Fig. 2.14 Hormonal control of oogenesis

- Together these hormones coordinate the complex hormonal interactions that leads to the cyclical changes in the ovaries and the endometrium during menstrual cycle.

2.3 Menstrual Cycle

- It is the reproductive cycle in female primates, e.g. monkeys, apes and human beings.
- The first menstruation, known as **menarche,** begins at puberty. While its stoppage around 50 years of age is called **menopause.**
- The cyclic menstruation is an indication of normal reproductive phase and extends between menarche and menopause.

- In human females, menstruation is repeated at an average interval of about 28/29 days.
- The cycle of events starting from one menstruation till the next one is called **menstrual cycle.**
- One ovum is released during the middle of each menstrual cycle. The menstrual cycle consists of following four phases

1. Menstrual (Bleeding) Phase

- The cycle starts with menstrual phase. It lasts for about **3-5 days.**
- During this phase the endometrial lining of the uterus breaks down due to the deficiency of progesterone and is sloughed off. Blood vessels rupture, causing bleeding through vagina. The process is called **menstruation** or **menstrual flow**. It occurs only when ovum is not fertilised.
- Lack of menstruation may be indicative of pregnancy. However, it may also be caused due to some other underlying causes like stress, poor health, etc.

2. Follicular (Proliferative) Phase

It lasts for **about 14 days** and involves the following events

- The primary follicles in the ovary grow to become a fully mature **Graafian follicle**.

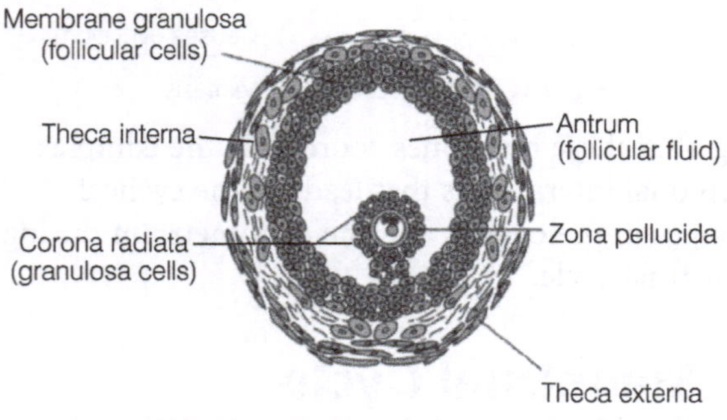

Fig. 2.15 Structure of a Graafian follicle

- Simultaneously, the endometrium of uterus regenerates through proliferation.
- The changes in the ovary and the uterus are induced by changes in the levels of pituitary and ovarian hormones, i.e. FSH and oestrogen, respectively.
- The secretion of gonadotropins (LH and FSH) increases gradually during the follicular phase.
- This stimulates follicular development as well as secretion of oestrogen by the growing follicles.

3. Ovulatory Phase

- Both LH and FSH attain a peak level in the middle of cycle (about 14th day).
- Rapid secretion of LH leading to its maximum level during the mid-cycle is called **LH surge**. It induces rupture of Graafian follicle and thereby the release of ovum, i.e. **ovulation**.
- The ovulation (ovulatory phase) is followed by the **luteal phase**.

4. Luteal (Secretory) Phase

This phase lasts for about **10 days** and involves the following events

- The remaining parts of Graafian follicle transform into the **corpus luteum**.
- The corpus luteum secretes large amounts of progesterone essential to maintain endometrium.

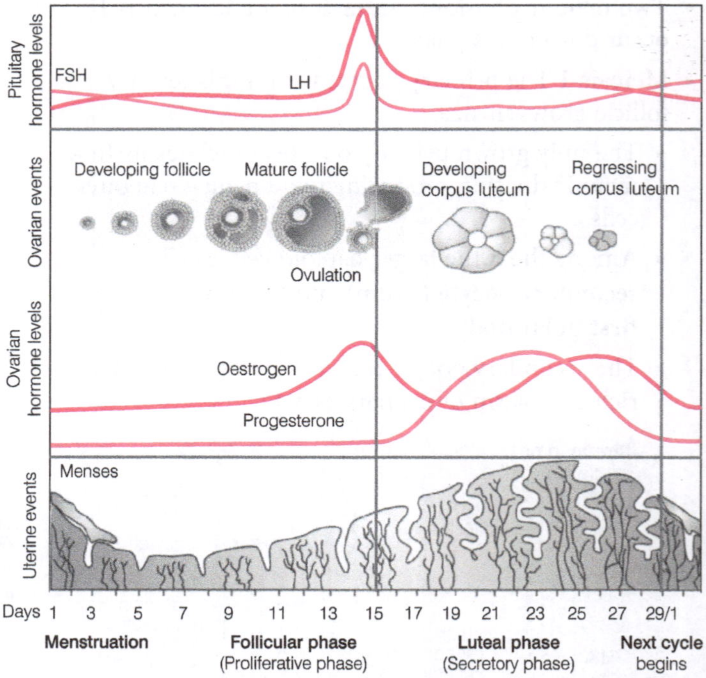

Fig. 2.16 Diagrammatic presentation of various events during menstrual cycle

- As the endometrium is necessary for implantation of the fertilised ovum and other events of pregnancy.
- During pregnancy, all events of the menstrual cycle stop and there is no menstruation.

- In the absence of fertilisation, the corpus luteum degenerates.
- The disintegration of endometrium leading to the menstruation, marking a new cycle.

Menstrual Hygiene

Maintenance of hygiene and sanitation during menstruation is very important. To promote health and prevent infections, it is crucial to adhere to the following practices

- Take bath and clean yourself regularly.
- Use sanitary napkins or clean homemade pads.
- Change sanitary napkins or homemade pads after every 4–5 hrs as per the requirement.
- Dispose the used sanitary napkins properly by wrapping it with a used paper.
- Do not throw the used napkins in the drainpipe of toilets or in the open area.
- After handling the napkin, wash hands with soap.

Quick Test 3

1. In spermatogenesis, if there is a deficiency of Follicle-Stimulating Hormone (FSH), which stage of sperm development is most likely affected, potentially leading to infertility?
2. A man with a mutation that prevents the mitotic division of spermatogonia would likely experience what effect on his sperm production?
3. If a woman has 10 primary oocytes in her ovaries, how many ova can potentially be produced during her reproductive life?
4. **State True or False.**
   If a woman has short menstrual cycle (e.g., 21 days), this suggests that the secretory phase of her cycle is prolonged.
5. If a woman has a short luteal phase (less than 10 days), secretion of which hormone will get affected?

2.4 Fertilisation

- The process of fusion of a sperm with an ovum is called **fertilisation**.
- The discharge of semen, by the penis, into the female's vagina close to the cervix during coitus (copulation) is called **insemination**.
- After insemination, the motile sperms move through the cervix, enter the uterus and finally reach the junction of the isthmus and ampulla (ampullary-isthmis junction) of the Fallopian tube.
- The ovum released from the ovary also reaches the ampullary-isthmic junction, where fertilisation takes place.
- Fertilisation can only occur if the ovum and sperms are transported simultaneously to this junction. This explains why all copulations do not lead to fertilisation and pregnancy.
- The events leading to fertilisation are as follows
  - A sperm, during fertilisation, comes in contact with the **zona pellucida** of the ovum. This induces changes in the membrane, which blocks the entry of the other sperms. Thus, ensuring that only one sperm can fertilise an ovum.

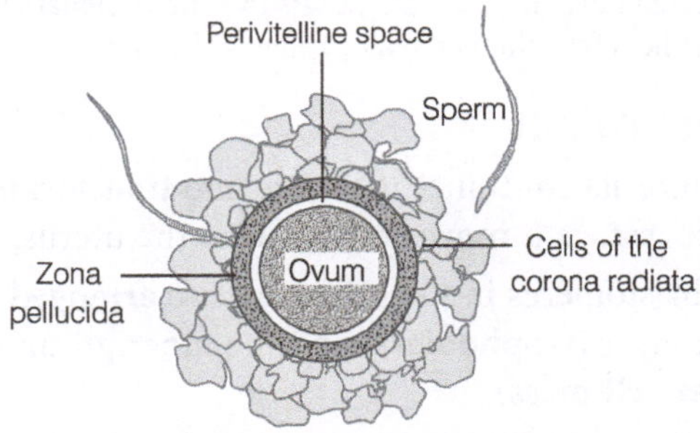

Fig. 2.17 Ovum surrounded by few sperms

  - The secretions of the acrosome help the sperm to enter into the cytoplasm of the ovum through zona pellucida and the plasma membrane.
  - This induces the completion of meiotic division of the secondary oocyte. The second meiotic division is also unequal and results in the formation of a **secondary polar body** and a **haploid ovum** (ootid).
  - Eventually, the haploid nucleus of the sperm and that of ovum fuse together to form a **diploid zygote**.

Sex-Determination

Sex of the baby is decided at embryonic stage only. After fusion of the male and female gametes, the zygote would carry either XX or XY. It depends on whether the sperm carrying X or Y-chromosome fertilised the ovum. The zygote carrying XX would develop into a female baby and XY would form a male baby.

2.5 Embryonic Development

The development of embryo from fertilised ovum involves the following events

1. Cleavage

- The mitotic division starts as the zygote (fertilised ovum) gradually moves through the isthmus of the oviduct towards the uterus.
- This event results in the formation of 2, 4, 8, 16 daughter cells called **blastomeres.**
- This process is called **cleavage.** The embryo with 8-16 blastomeres is called a **morula.**

TEACHER'S TIP

During cleavage, the size of the zygote does not increase. Instead, the zygote undergoes rapid mitotic divisions to form smaller cells called **blastomeres** without a corresponding increase in overall size. This results in a multicellular embryo, while the total volume remains roughly the same.

2. Blastulation

- The morula continues to divide and transforms into **blastocyst,** as it moves further into the uterus.
- The blastomeres in the blastocyst are arranged into an outer layer (**trophoblast**) and the inner group of cells (**inner cell mass**).
- This inner group of cells is attached to trophoblast.

3. Implantation

- The trophoblast layer then gets attached to the endometrium and the inner cell mass differentiates into the **embryo.**
- After attachment, the uterine cells divide rapidly and covers the blastocyst.
- As a result, the blastocyst becomes embedded in the endometrium of the uterus. This is called **implantation** and it leads to pregnancy (i.e. the time from conception to birth).
- Immediately after implantation, the inner cell mass (embryo) differentiates into an outer layer called **ectoderm** and an inner layer **endoderm.** A **mesoderm** soon develops between the ectoderm and endoderm.
- The process of transforming the blastocyst into a 3-layered structure called **gastrula** is called **gastrulation.**
- These three layers give rise to all tissues and organs in an adult.
- Inner cell mass contains certain cells called **stem cells,** which have the potency to give rise to all the tissues and organs.

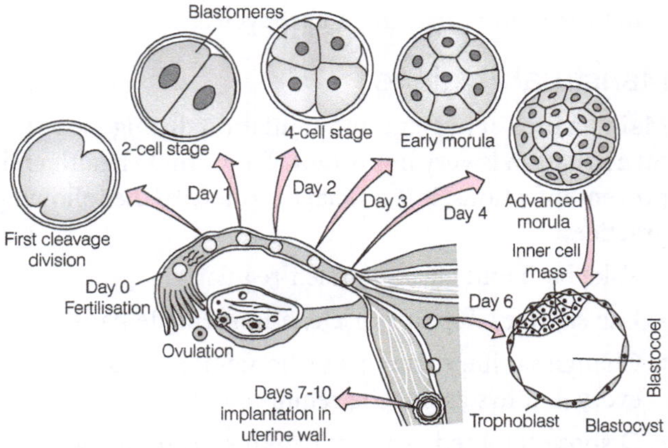

Fig. 2.18 Fetal development during the first and second weeks

Changes During Pregnancy

- After implantation, finger-like projections called **chorionic villi,** appear on the trophoblast.
- These are surrounded by the uterine tissue and maternal blood.
- The chorionic villi and the uterine tissue become inter-digitated with each other and jointly form a structural and functional unit between foetus and maternal body called **placenta.**

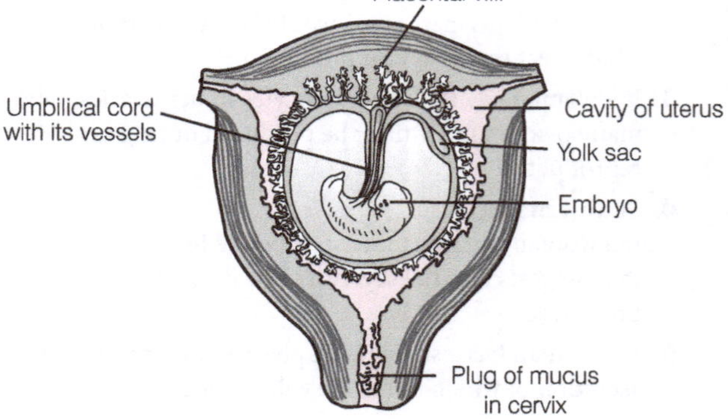

Fig. 2.19 The human foetus within the uterus

- The placenta performs the following functions
  - It facilitates the supply of oxygen and nutrients to the embryo.
  - It aids in the removal of carbon dioxide and waste materials produced by the foetus.
  - It is connected to the embryo through the **umbilical cord,** which helps in the transport of substances to and from the embryo.

- Placenta also acts as an endocrine tissue and produces several hormones like **human Chorionic Gonadotropin** (hCG), **human Placental Lactogen** (hPL), **oestrogen**, **progestogens**, etc.
- It is important to note that hCG, hPL and relaxin are produced in women only during pregnancy.
- In the later phase of pregnancy, a hormone called **relaxin** is also secreted by the ovary.
- In addition, the levels of other hormones like estrogens, progestogens, cortisol, prolactin, thyroxine, etc., are increased several times in the maternal blood during pregnancy.
- This increased production is necessary to support fetal growth, metabolic changes in the mother and maintenance of pregnancy.

Changes in Embryo

- In humans, pregnancy lasts for 9 months and after one month of pregnancy, embryo **heart** is formed.
- The first sign of growing foetus may be noticed by listening to the heart sound carefully through stethoscope.
- By the end of **second month**, the foetus develops **limbs** and **digits**. By the end of 12 weeks (first trimester), major **organ systems** and **external genitalia** are well-developed.
- The first movement of the foetus and **appearance of hair** can be observed during the **fifth month**.
- By the end of **24 weeks** (second trimester), the body is covered with fine hairs, eyelids get separated and eyelashes are formed.
- By the end of nine months of pregnancy, the foetus becomes fully developed and is ready for delivery.

Parturition

- The time period during which the embryo remains in the uterus, i.e. after the last day of menstruation to the day of parturition is called **gestation**.
- This period in humans is about of 9 months.
- The vigorous contraction of the uterus at the end of pregnancy causes expulsion/delivery of the foetus.
- This process of delivery of the foetus (childbirth) is called **parturition.** It is induced by a complex neuroendocrine mechanism.
- The signals of parturition originate from the fully developed foetus and the placenta, which induce mild uterine contractions called **foetal-ejection reflex.**
- This triggers the release of **oxytocin** from the maternal pituitary.
- It promotes contractions of uterine muscles, which inturn stimulate further secretion of oxytocin.
- The stimulatory reflex between the uterine contraction and oxytocin secretion continues resulting in stronger and stronger contractions.
  This leads to the expulsion of the baby out of the uterus through the birth canal.
- Soon after the birth of baby, placenta is also expelled out of the uterus.

Lactation

- The mammary glands in females undergo differentiation during pregnancy.
- The production and release of milk by the mammary glands of female after birth of a young one is called **lactation.**
- The first milk, which comes out from the mother's mammary glands during initial few days of lactation is called **colostrum.**
- It is rich in proteins and energy along with the several antibodies that provide passive immunity to the newborn.
- Breastfeeding during the initial period of infant growth is highly recommended by the doctors for bringing up a healthy baby.

Quick Test 4

1. **State True or False.**
   Once the egg reaches the ampulla, fertilisation is guaranteed to occur.
2. Mention the number of chromosomes of zygote if two sperms fertilise a single ovum.
3. At which location in the female reproductive tract would a blastula with 36 blastomeres most likely be found?
4. The foetus is observed to have fully developed eyelashes and eyebrows. At what stage of development is this most likely to occur?
5. **State True or False.**
   Colostrum is the first milk produced after childbirth and contains more fat than mature breast milk.

Mind Map

Human Reproduction

Reproductive System

Male Reproductive System

- Primary sex organs, i.e. testes.
- Secondary sex organs
  - Accessory ducts, i.e. rete testis, vasa efferentia, vas deferens and epididymis.
  - Accessory glands, i.e. seminal vesicle, prostate and Cowper's gland.
- External genitalia, i.e. vulva.

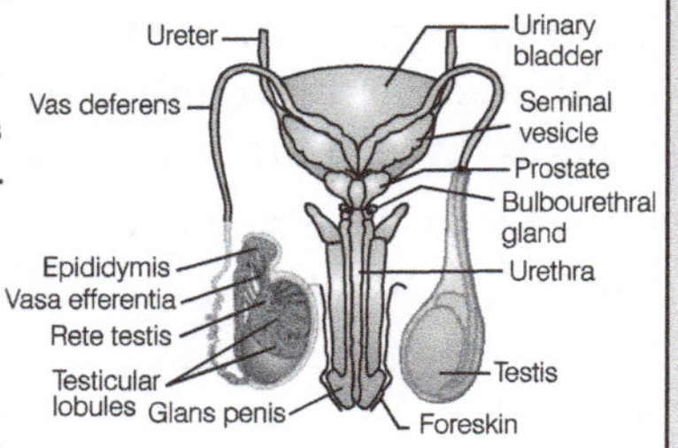

Female Reproductive System

- Primary sex organs, i.e. ovaries.
- Secondary sex organs
  - Accessory ducts, i.e. pair of oviducts (Fallopian tubes), uterus and cervix.
  - Accessory glands, i.e. mammary glands.
- External genitalia, i.e. vulva.

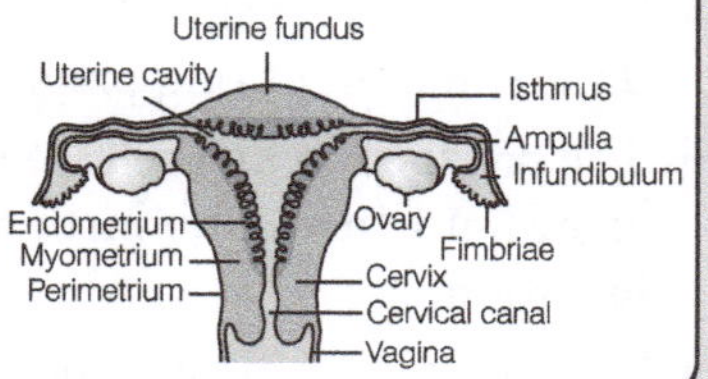

Menstrual Cycle

- It is the reproductive cycle in female primates, e.g. monkeys, apes, human beings.
- It begins at puberty, i.e. menarche and stops around 50 years of age, i.e. menopause.
- It consists of the four phases: menstrual phase, follicular phase, ovulatory phase and luteal phase.

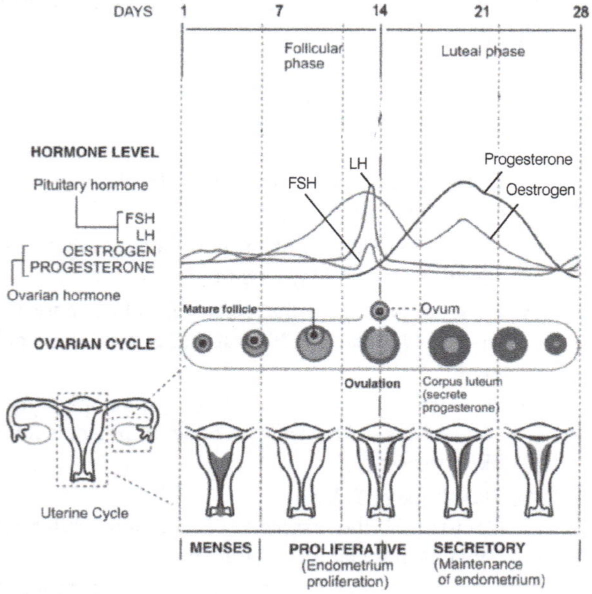

Gametogenesis

Formation of haploid gametes from the undifferentiated diploid germ cells in the gonads.

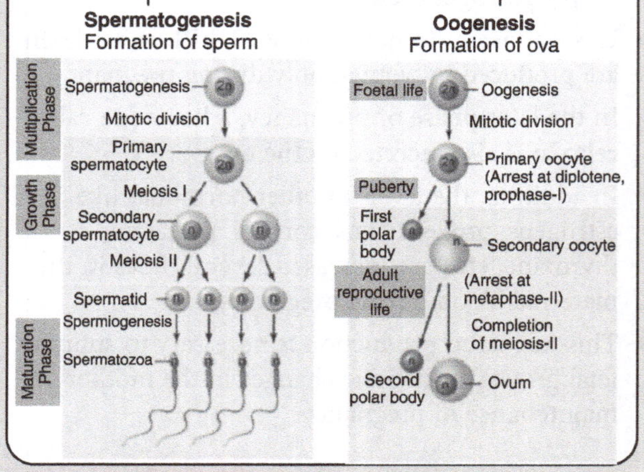

Fertilisation

It is the process of fusion of sperm and egg (ovum) to produce zygote.

Implantation

Zygote undergoes repeated mitotic divisions to form a blastocyst, which is implanted in the uterus resulting into pregnancy.

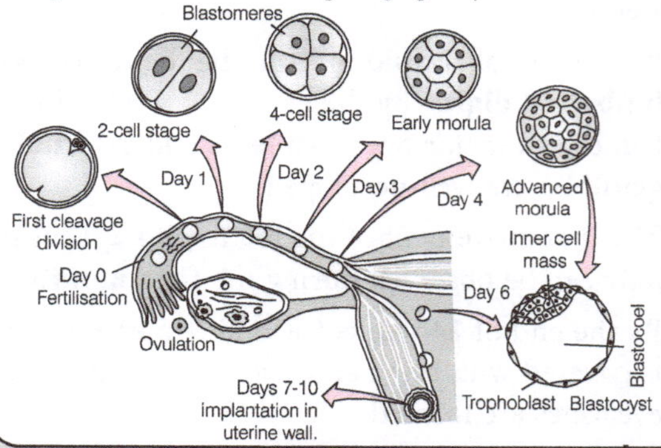

Embryonic Development

- The embryo after implantation differentiates into ectoderm (outer layer), mesoderm (middle layer) and endoderm (inner layer).
- These layers give rise to specific tissues, organs and organ system.
- One month : Heart formed.
- Second month end : Developed limbs and digits.
- First trimester : Major organ system formed.
- Fifth month : First movement and hair on head.
- Second trimester end : Fine hair, separate eye lid and eye lashes formed.
- Nine months : Foetus fully developed.

Parturition

Process of delivery of foetus (child birth), induced by complex neuro-endocrine complex.

Lactation

The production and release of milk by the mammary glands of female after birth of young one.

EXAM PATTERN QUESTIONS

Objective Type Questions

Multiple Choice Questions

1. What is the principal role of scrotum?

(a) To regulate the temperature of the testis
(b) To regulate the overall body temperature
(c) To regulate the secretion of growth hormone
(d) To regulate the production of male hormones

Ans. (*a*)

2. Given below is a diagrammatic view of the human male reproductive system. CBSE 2021 Term-I

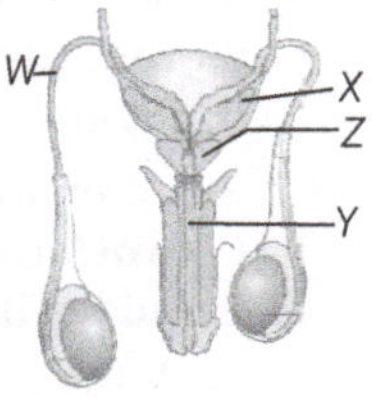

Identify the correct labelling for *W*, *X*, *Y* and *Z* and choose the correct option from the table below.

	W	*X*	*Y*	*Z*
(a)	Epididymis	Prostate gland	Glans penis	Bulbourethral gland
(b)	Bulbourethral gland	Glans penis	Prostate gland	Epididymis
(c)	Vas deferens	Seminal vesicle	Urethra	Prostate gland
(d)	Rete testis	Bulbourethral gland	Epididymis	Glans penis

Ans. (*c*)

3. If for some reason, the vasa efferentia gets blocked, the gametes will not transported from

(a) testes to epididymis
(b) epididymis to vas deferens
(c) ovary to uterus
(d) testes to seminiferous tubule

Ans. (*a*) If the vasa efferentia gets blocked, the gametes (sperm) cannot move from the testes to the epididymis because the vasa efferentia are the conduits that transport sperm from the seminiferous tubules, where sperm are produced, to the epididymis, where they are mature and stored.

4. Seminal plasma, the fluid part of semen is formed by Diksha

(a) seminal vesicle and bulbourethral gland
(b) bulbourethral gland and prostate
(c) prostate and seminal vesicle
(d) seminal vesicles, prostate and bulbourethral gland

Ans. (*d*)

5. The following diagram refers to the female reproductive system of humans. Identify *A* to *F*. Competency Based Que.

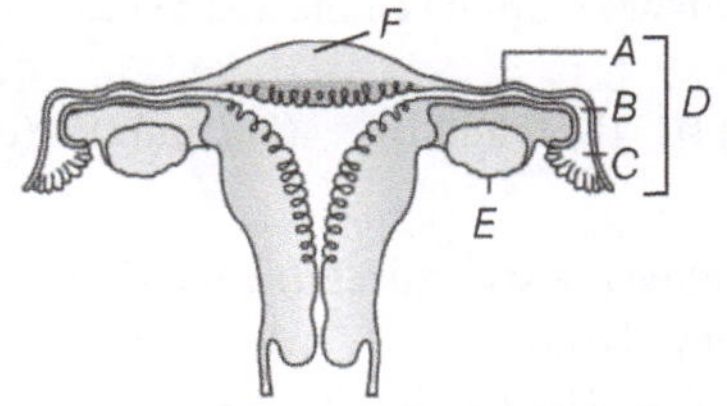

(a) *A*–Ampulla, *B*–Isthmus, *C*–Infundibulum, *D*–Fallopian tube, *E*–Ovary, *F*–Uterine fundus
(b) *A*–Isthmus, *B*–Infundibulum, *C*–Ampulla, *D*–Fallopian tube, *E*–Ovary, *F*–Uterine fundus
(c) *A*–Isthmus, *B*–Ampulla, *C*–Infundibulum, *D*–Fallopian tube, *E*–Ovary, *F*–Uterine fundus
(d) *A*–Ampulla, *B*–Infundibulum, *C*–Isthmus, *D*–Fallopian tube, *E*–Ovary, *F*–Uterine fundus

Ans. (c)

6. Given below are few statements with reference to the uterus in the female reproductive system: CBSE 2025

I. The myometrium exhibits strong contractions during the delivery of the baby.
II. The uterus opens into the cervix through a narrow opening called vagina.
III. The cavity of the cervix and the vagina forms the birth canal.
IV. The outermost layer of uterus is a thin membranous perimetrium.
V. The uterus is supported by tendons attached to the pelvic wall.

Choose the option with all true statements from the given options

(a) I, II and IV (b) II, III and V
(c) II, IV and V (d) I, III and IV

Ans. (*d*) Statements I, III and IV are correct, while statements II and V are incorrect and can be corrected a

The uterus opens into the cervix through a narrow opening called the cervical canal.

The uterus is supported by ligaments attached to the pelvic wall.

7. Fleshy folds of tissue which extends down the mons pubis and surrounds the vaginal opening are called

(a) labia minora (b) labia majora
(c) hymen (d) clitoris

Ans. (*b*)

8. Choose the correct option for the features of functional mammary gland of all female mammals from the statements below.

I. Glandular tissue with variable amount of fat.
II. Mammary lobes, 30-40 in number called alveoli.
III. Mammary ducts joining to form mammary tubules.
IV. Mammary ampulla connected to lactiferous duct.

CBSE 2021 Term-I

(a) I and III (b) II and III (c) I and IV (d) II and IV

Ans. (*c*)

9. Given below are structural details of a human mammary gland.

I. The glandular tissue in the breast has 15-20 clusters of cells called alveoli.
II. The milk is stored in the lumen of alveoli.
III. The alveoli join to form the mammary ducts.
IV Mammary ampulla is connected to lactiferous ducts.

Choose the option that gives the correct detail of human mammary gland. **CBSE 2023**

(a) I and II (b) II and III (c) II and IV (d) I and III

Ans. (*c*)

10. During spermatogenesis, the maturation phase includes

(a) transformation of gonocytes into spermatogonia through mitosis
(b) the growth of spermatogonia into primary spermatocyte
(c) conversion of primary spermatocytes into spermatids *via* meiosis
(d) formation of oogonia from the spermatocytes *via* meiosis

Ans. (*c*)

11. During spermatogenesis, which cells are the first to contain haploid number of chromosomes?

(a) Spermatogonium (b) Primary spermatocyte
(c) Secondary spermatocyte (d) Spermatid

Ans. (*c*) Secondary spermatocytes are the first cells, during spermatogenesis, in which the chromosome number. becomes half. Thus, they contain haploid number of chromosomes.

12. The nature of meiotic division during oogenesis in a human female is **CBSE 2021 Term-I**

(a) equal cell division (b) suspended cell division
(c) continuous cell division (d) rapid cell division

Ans. (*b*) Meiotic division during oogenesis in human females is suspended to preserve oocytes for a long time, starting from foetal development until ovulation.

Primary oocytes are arrested in prophase-I and remain dormant until puberty. This ensures that eggs are available for fertilisation at the right time and helps to maintain egg quality, preventing premature ageing or chromosomal errors.

13. The correct sequence of hormone secretion from beginning of menstruation is **CBSE SQP 2021 Term-I**

(a) FSH, progesterone, oestrogen
(b) Oestrogen, FSH, progesterone
(c) FSH, oestrogen, progesterone
(d) Oestrogen, progesterone, FSH

Ans. (*c*)

14. Some important events in the human female reproductive cycle are given below. Arrange the events in a proper sequence.

A-Secretion of FSH, B-Growth of corpus luteum, C-Growth of the follicle and oogenesis, D-Ovulation, E-Sudden increase in the levels of LH

(a) A, C, E, D, B
(b) A, D, C, E, B
(c) B, A, C, D, E
(d) C, A, D, B, E

Ans. (*a*)

15. Given below are few statements with reference to the major events in the menstrual cycle of a human female **CBSE 2025**

(i) During the follicular phase, the primary follicles grow to become a Graafian follicle.
(ii) Gonadotropins FSH and progesterone stimulate follicular development during the follicular phase.
(iii) LH surge induces rupture of Graafian follicle thereby releasing the corpus luteum.
(iv) Progesterone released by corpus luteum is essential for maintenance of endometrium.
(v) Both LH and progesterone attain a peak level in the middle of the cycle.

Choose the option with all true statements from the given options

(a) I, II and IV (b) II, III and V
(c) II, IV and V (d) I, III and IV

Ans. (*d*) Statements I, III and IV are correct, while statements II and V are incorrect and can be corrected as

FSH and LH stimulate follicular development during the follicular phase.

LH peaks in the middle of the cycle, whereas progesterone peaks in the luteal phase.

16. **Match the following columns and choose the correct answer from the codes given below.**

	Column I		Column II
A.	Proliferative phase	1.	Breakdown of endometrial lining
B.	Secretory phase	2.	Follicular phase
C.	Menstruation	3.	Luteal phase

Codes

	A	B	C
(a)	2	3	1
(b)	1	3	2
(c)	3	2	1
(d)	3	1	2

Ans. (*a*)

17. **Which of the following is correct regarding the role of acrosomal reaction?**

(a) Contact of sperms with eggs
(b) Digestion of zona pellucida
(c) Disintegration of acrosome
(d) Contact of acrosome and nucleus of egg

Ans. (*b*) Acrosomal reaction is the digestion of the zona pellucida. It involves the progressive fusion of the acrosomal membrane with the plasma membrane of the sperm. It creates pores through which the acrosomal enzymes can be released by exocytosis. These enzymes allow the sperm to digest and create a path through the zona pellucida to the oocyte.

18. **Given is the stage of growing embryo and different regions of the Fallopian tube marked as *A, B, C* and *D*.**

Competency Based Que.

Where do you think the given stage of embryo will be seen in the Fallopian tube?

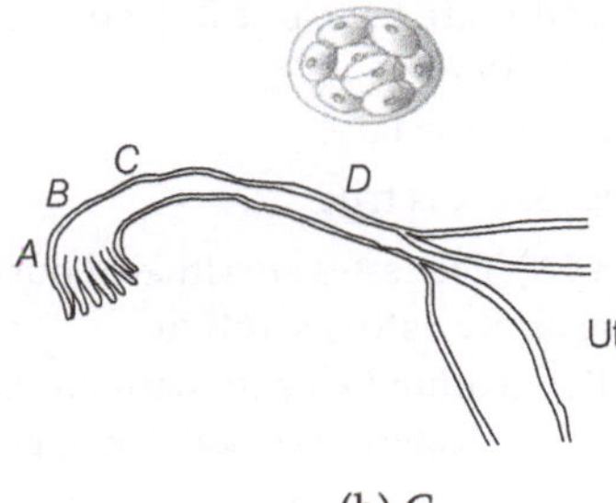

(a) *A* (b) *C*
(c) *B* (d) *D*

Ans. (*d*)

19. **Figure *A* shows the front view of the human female reproductive system and figure *B* shows the development of a fertilised human egg cell.**

Competency Based Que.

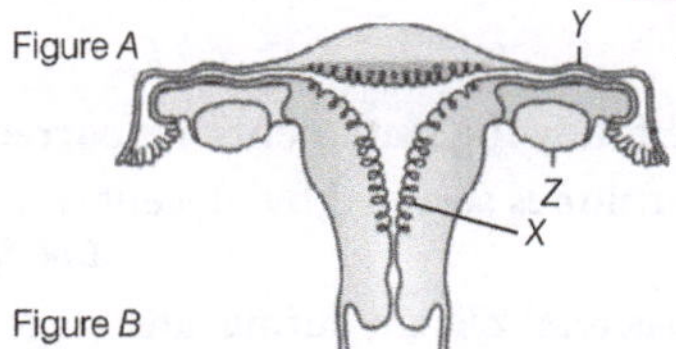

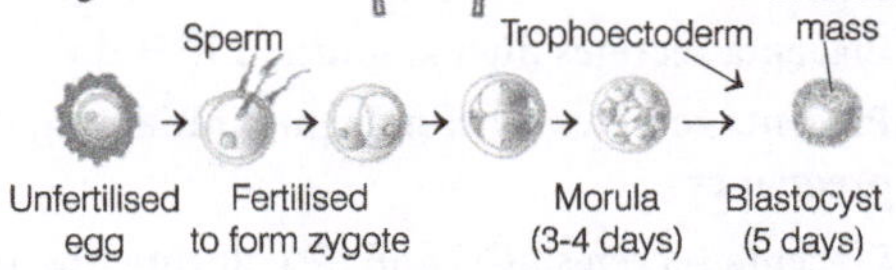

Identify the correct stage of development of human embryo (Figure *B*) that takes place at the site *X, Y* and *Z*, respectively in the human female reproductive system (Figure *A*).
Choose the correct option from the table below.

	X	*Y*	*Z*
(a)	Morula	Fertilised egg	Blastocyst
(b)	Unfertilised egg	Fertilised egg	Morula
(c)	Blastocyst	Fertilised egg	Unfertilised egg
(d)	Fertilised egg	Morula	Blastocyst

Ans. (*c*)

20. **Identify the human development stage shown below as well as the related right place of its occurrence in a normal pregnant woman and select the right option for the two together.**

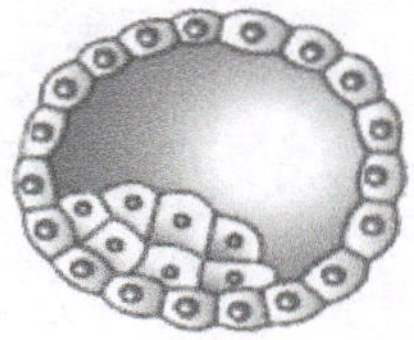

Competency Based Que.

	Developmental stage	Site of occurrence
(a)	Blastocyst	Uterine wall
(b)	8- celled morula	Starting point of Fallopian tube
(c)	Late morula	Middle part of Fallopian tube
(d)	Blastula	End part of Fallopian tube

Ans. (a)

21. **Chorionic villi and uterine tissue become inter- digitated with each other and jointly form**

(a) trophoblast (b) inner cell mass
(c) placenta (d) implantation

Ans. (*c*)

22. **Which of the following statements are correct with respect to hormones secreted by placenta?** **CBSE SQP 2021 Term-I**

I. **Placenta secretes relaxin during later stage of pregnancy.**
II. **Placenta secretes high amount of FSH during pregnancy.**
III. **Placenta secretes relaxin during initial stage of pregnancy.**
IV. **Placenta secretes hCG and hPL during pregnancy.**

(a) I and IV (b) I, II and IV
(c) III and IV (d) II, III and IV

Ans. (*a*)

23. **Which one of the following hormone is secreted by the human placenta that helps in the maintenance of pregnancy ?** **CBSE 2024**

(a) Relaxin
(b) Human chorionic gonadotropin
(c) Oxytocin
(d) Human placental lactogen

Ans. (*b*)

24. **Concentration of which of the following substances will decrease in the maternal blood as it flows from embryo to placenta through the umbilical cord?** **Competency Based Que.**

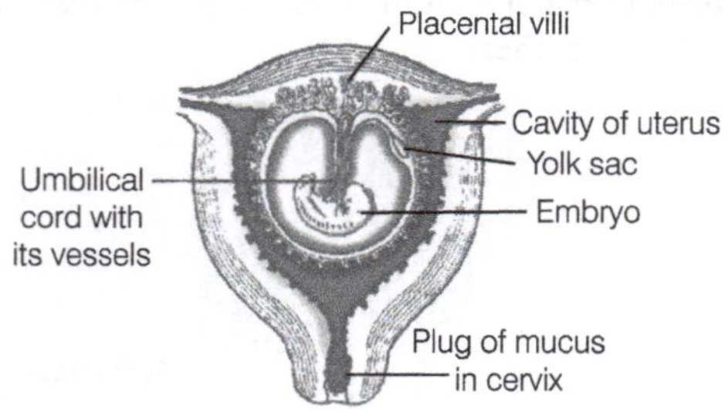

I. **Oxygen** II. **Amino acids**
III. **Carbon dioxide** IV. **Urea**

(a) I and II (b) II and IV
(c) III and IV (d) I and IV

Ans. (*a*) As maternal blood flows through the umbilical cord to the placenta, oxygen and amino acids diffuse from the maternal blood to the foetal blood, decreasing their concentration in maternal blood. While, carbon dioxide and urea diffuses from foetal blood to maternal blood, increasing their concentration in maternal blood.

25. **During human embryonic development, the heart in the embryo is formed after** **CBSE 2021 Term-I**

(a) 15 days of pregnancy
(b) 30 days of pregnancy
(c) 45 days of pregnancy
(d) 60 days of pregnancy

Ans. (*b*)

26. **Signals for parturition in human female originate from**

(a) fully developed foetus only **CBSE SQP 2024**
(b) Both placenta as well as fully developed foetus
(c) placenta only
(d) oxytocin released from maternal pituitary

Ans. (*b*)

27. **Colostrum is important for newly born because**

(a) it contains essential antigen
(b) it contains essential antibodies
(c) it contains milk protein and antigen molecule
(d) it has more nutrients than ordinary milk

Ans. (*b*) Colostrum is the milk produced during the initial few days of lactation. It contains several essential antibodies, which are absolutely essential to develop resistance against pathogenicity in newborn. So, it is recommended by doctors to feed breast milk to newborn during the initial period of infant growth.

Assertion-Reason Questions

Direction (Q. Nos. 1-10) *In each of the following questions, a statement of Assertion (A) is given followed by corresponding statement of Reason (R). Of the statements, mark the correct answer as*

(a) Both A and R are true and R is correct explanation of A
(b) Both A and R are true, but R is not the correct explanation of A
(c) A is true, but R is false
(d) A is false, but R is true

1. **Assertion** (A) The testes are situated outside the abdominal cavity within scrotum.
Reason (R) Scrotum helps to maintain low temperature of testes, necessary for spermatogenesis.

Ans. (*a*)

2. **Assertion** (A) The Sertoli cells are present in seminiferous tubules.
Reason (R) Sertoli cells provide nutrition to the germ cells and spermatozoa.

Ans. (*b*)

3. Assertion (A) Interstitial spaces outside the seminiferous tubule have blood vessels and Sertoli cells.

Reason (R) Sertoli cells provide nutrition to the germ cells. **CBSE 2021 Term-I**

Ans. (*d*) A is false, but R is true. A can be corrected as

The interstitial spaces outside the seminiferous tubules contain blood vessels and Leydig cells. Sertoli cells are found inside the seminiferous tubules and support spermatogenesis.

4. Assertion (A) The bulbourethral gland is a male accessory gland.

Reason (R) Its secretion helps in the lubrication of the penis, thereby facilitating reproduction.

Ans. (*a*)

5. Assertion (A) Production of FSH and LH increases in the ovulation phase.

Reason (R) Due to decrease in the level of LH, ovulation (releasing of ova) takes place.

Ans. (*c*) A is true, but R is false. R can be corrected as

Due to increase in the level of LH ovulation takes place, triggering the release of the mature egg from the ovary.

6. In the given figure showing schematic representation of a menstrual cycle in human female. Refer to the three phases *A*, *B* and *C* of menstrual cycle and comment upon the appropriateness of Assertion and Reason.

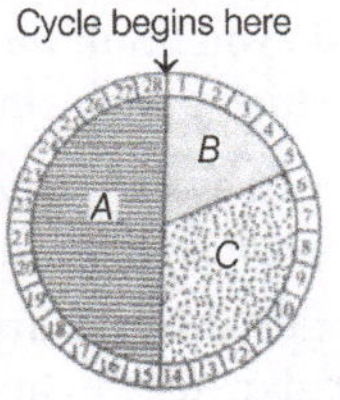

Competency Based Que.

Assertion (A) Ovulation takes place during the end of phase *C*.

Reason (R) The level of FSH is low during this period.

Ans. (*c*)

7. The diagram given below shows the events of cleavage. Refer to the diagram and comment upon the appropriateness of Assertion and Reason.

Competency Based Que.

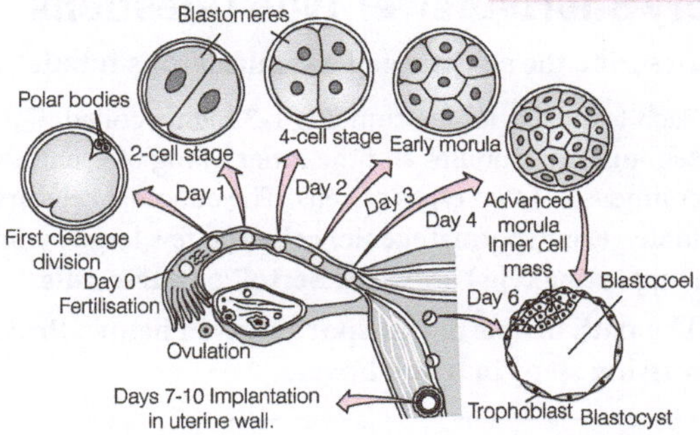

Assertion (A) During cleavage, the cells divide rapidly and continue to rise in number, but the mass of protoplasm remains same.

Reason (R) With each consecutive sub-division there is approximately half the cytoplasm in each daughter cell.

Ans. (*b*)

8. Assertion (A) Placenta is an endocrine gland.

Reason (R) Placenta secretes many hormones essential for pregnancy.

Ans. (*a*)

9. Assertion (A) Parturition is induced by a complex neuroendocrine mechanism.

Reason (R) At the end of gestation period, the maternal pituitary releases prolactin which causes uterine contractions. **CBSE SQP 2021 Term-I**

Ans. (*c*)

10. Assertion (A) Colostrum provides nutrition and helps the new born baby to develop resistance for healthy growth.

Reason (R) Colostrum contains proteins, lactose and antibodies such as IgA.

Ans. (*a*)

Subjective Questions

Very Short Answer Type Questions

1. Describe the structure of a seminiferous tubule. NCERT

Ans. Each testicular lobule contains 1-3 highly coiled seminiferous tubules and the inner lining of each tubule is composed of two types of cells. The cuboidal cells are called **male germ** (spermatogenic) **cells** and few large pyramidal (supporting cells) are called **Sertoli** or **nurse cells.**

2. The path of sperm transport is given below. Provide the missing steps in blank boxes.

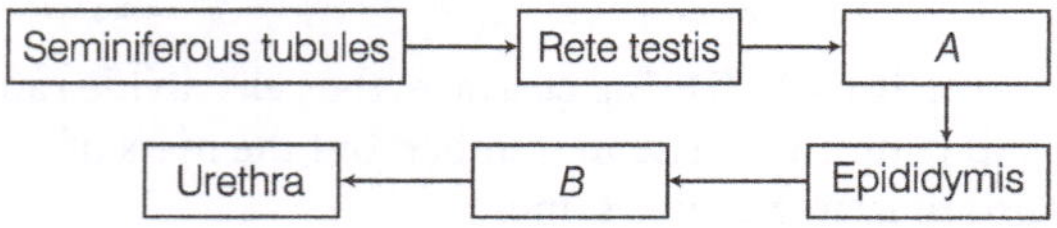

NCERT Exemplar

Ans. *A* – Vasa efferentia, *B* – Vas deferens (½ × 2)

3. What are the major components of the seminal plasma? NCERT

Ans. Seminal fluid is a secretion of accessory sex glands of male, that is, seminal vesicles, prostate gland and Cowper's glands. It is rich in fructose, calcium and certain enzymes.

4. List the different parts of human oviduct through which the ovum travels till it meets the sperm for fertilisation.

Ans. The different parts of human oviduct through which the ovum travels till it gets fertilised are

Fimbriae → Infundibulum → Ampulla → Isthmus (1)

5. What is the role of cervix in the human female reproductive system? NCERT Exemplar

Ans. Cervix helps in regulating the passage of sperms into the female uterus. It also forms the birth canal along with vagina to facilitate parturition.

6. Are male and female gametes haploid or diploid?

Ans. Male and female gametes are haploid.

7. The Leydig's cell as found in the human body are the secretory source of which hormone?

Ans. Androgens

8. Name the hormones involved in regulation of spermatogenesis. NCERT

Ans. GnRH (Gonadotropin Releasing Hormone), LH (Luteinizing Hormone) and FSH (Follicle Stimulating Hormone) are involved in regulation of spermatogenesis.

9. Name the process of release of spermatozoa from Sertoli cells into cavity of seminiferous tubule.

Ans. Spermiation (1)

10. Spermatids possess haploid number of chromosome. Explain.

Ans. Spermatids are produced by meiosis during spermatogenesis. Thus, they possess haploid number of chromosomes.

11. On the basis of the functions mentioned below, identify each one correctly.

(i) It helps in the movement of spermatozoan in a fluid medium.

(ii) It contains hydrolytic enzymes and is used to contact and penetrate the egg during fertilisation.

Ans. (i) Sperm tail (ii) Acrosome (½ × 2)

12. Sperms have a tail whereas egg does not. Why?

Ans. Sperms have to swim in female reproductive tract to reach the ovum, by moving their tail in the fluid, while eggs do not require it.

13. How many ova will be produced by one fully grown primary oocyte?

Ans. Only one ova is produced by one fully grown primary oocyte. (1)

14. How many primary follicles are left in each ovary at puberty?

Ans. 60,000-80,000. (1)

15. How many eggs do you think were released by the ovary of a female dog which gave birth to 6 puppies? NCERT

Ans. Six eggs were released by the ovary of a female dog, if it gave birth to six puppies. (1)

16. List the changes that the primary oocyte undergoes in the tertiary follicular stage in human embryo.

Ans. In human females, the primary oocyte grows in size, completes meiosis-I and divide to forms a larger cell, the secondary oocyte and a smaller cell, the first polar body.

17. Given below is a flowchart showing ovarian change during menstrual cycle. Fill in the spaces with the hormonal factor(s) responsible for the events shown.

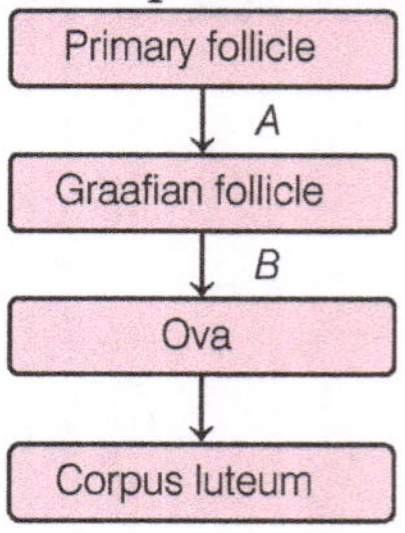

Ans. *A* – FSH and oestrogen

B – LH

18. State the name of the hormone, which is secreted by corpus luteum.

Ans. Progesterone

19. The diagram shows the female reproductive system. Where do fertilisation and implantation occur?

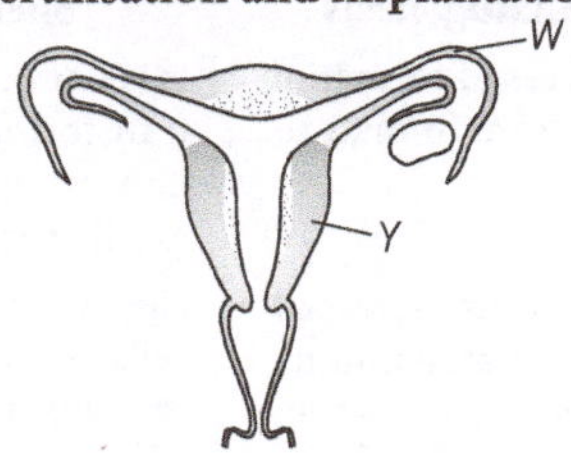

Ans. Fertilisation takes place in Fallopian tube (*W*) and implantation takes place in uterus (*Y*). (½ × 2)

20. What do you call the layer of cells forming the outer wall of the blastocyst?

Ans. Trophoblast

21. State the function of trophoblast in human embryo.

Ans. Trophoblast forms chorionic villi, which become part of the placenta.

22. A woman passes out hCG in the urine during the pregnancy. Why?

Ans. Placenta forms during pregnancy releases hCG, which comes out in urine of pregnant woman. The presence of human Chorionic Gonadotropin (hCG) is the basis of pregnancy test.

23. What stimulates pituitary to release the hormone responsible for parturition?

Ans. The signal from the fully developed foetus and placenta induces mild uterine contractions called fetal-ejection reflex. This triggers release of oxytocin from the maternal pituitary. (1)

24. Given below are the stages in human reproduction. Write them in correct sequential order. Insemination, Gametogenesis, Fertilisation, Parturition, Gestation, Implantation. NCERT Exemplar

Ans. Gametogenesis → Insemination → Fertilisation → Implantation → Gestation → Parturition.

25. Name the mammary gland secretion which provides resistance to diseases in a newborn.

Ans. Colostrum.

Short Answer Type Questions

1. Why are the human testes located outside the abdominal cavity? Name the pouch in which they are present.

Ans. Human testes are located outside the abdominal cavity to maintain a temperature that is optimal for sperm production. The ideal temperature for spermatogenesis is slightly lower than the normal body temperature. Thus, these are located outside the abdominal cavity in sac-like structure called scrotum.

2. Draw a labelled diagram of male reproductive system. NCERT

Or **Draw a labelled diagram to show inter-relationship of four accessory ducts in a human male reproductive system.**

Ans. Refer to fig. 2.3 on page no. 38.

3. Draw a sectional view of a seminiferous tubule of human. Label Sertoli cell, spermatogonia and Leydig cell on it and write their functions.

Ans. Refer to fig. 2.2 on page no. 37.

4. Write the location and function of the following in human testes.

(i) Sertoli cells **(ii) Leydig cells**

Ans. (i) **Sertoli cells** are found in seminiferous tubule and nourish the male gametes.

(ii) **Leydig cells** are found in interstitial region between seminiferous tubules and secrete androgens. (1×2)

5. What are the major functions of male accessory ducts and glands? NCERT

Or **Name the male accessory glands in humans and write their functions.**

Ans. The male accessory ducts are rete testis, vasa efferentia, epididymis and vas deferens. These ducts store and transport the sperms from the testes to the outside through the urethra. The male accessory glands are paired seminal vesicles, a prostate gland and paired bulbourethral glands. The secretion of these glands forms seminal plasma, which is rich in fructose, calcium and certain enzymes. The secretion of bulbourethral glands lubricates the glans penis.

6. How the spermatozoa reaches the epididymis?

Ans. Spermatozoa or sperm formed in the seminiferous tubules reaches the vasa efferentia through rete testis. Several vasa efferentia open into the epididymis and carry sperm outside the body. (2)

7. Write two major functions each of testis and ovaries. NCERT

Ans. Testis and ovaries are the primary sex organs in the males and females, respectively. Each testis bears large number of seminiferous tubules, which are the spermatogenic tissue of the testis. Similarly, ovaries bear the Graafian follicle or the ovarian follicles, which ultimately give rise to ovum. The testes secrete testosterone and the ovaries secrete estrogen and progesterone. (1½ + 1½)

8. Describe the functions of the following

(i) Epididymis **(ii) Vas deferens**

(iii) Seminiferous tubules **(iv) Vagina**

(v) Uterus

Ans. For (i-iii) refer to text on page no. 38-39, for (iv-v) refer to text on page no. 39-40. (3)

9. Compare the secondary sex organs of males and females in detail.

Ans. Refer to text on page no. 38-40. (3)

10. Mark the odd one in each series.

(i) **Scrotum, rete testis, Fallopian tube, vas deferens**
(ii) **Ovary, uterus, vagina, ejaculatory duct**
(iii) **Prostate, testis, seminal vesicles, Cowper's gland**
(iv) **Fallopian tubes, vagina, uterus, ovaries**

Ans. (i) Fallopian tube (ii) Ejaculatory duct
(iii) Testis (iv) Ovaries (1/2×4)

11. Draw a labelled diagram of female reproductive system. NCERT

Ans. Refer to fig 2.5 on page no. 39.

12. Given below is the diagram showing a part of the reproductive system of a human female.

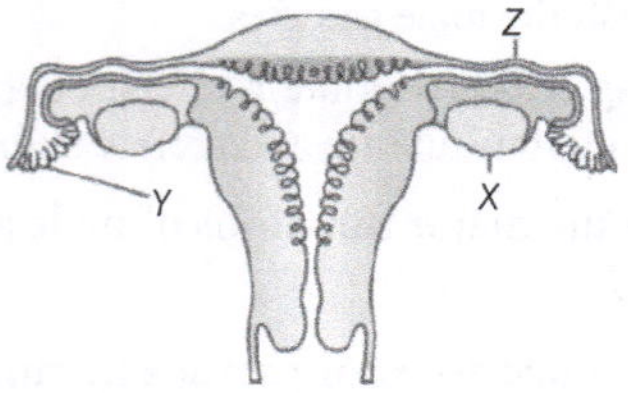

(i) **Identify 'Y' and write its function.**
(ii) **Identify 'Z' and write the events that may occur here.**
(iii) **Mention the stage at which the process of oogenesis temporarily gets arrested and name the cells thus formed in the 'X' of a baby girl at the time of her birth.**

Ans. (i) *Y* represents ovary. The ovary produces and releases eggs (oocytes) during ovulation and secretes hormones such as estrogen and progesterone.
(ii) *Z* represents fallopian tube. Fertilization of the egg by the sperm typically occurs in the fallopian tube. If fertilization occurs, the zygote begins its journey to the uterus for implantation.
(iii) Oogenesis temporarily gets arrested at the prophase I stage of meiosis-I. Cells formed in '*X*' (ovary) is primary oocyte. (1× 3)

13. Name and explain the role of the inner and middle walls of the human uterus.

Or **State the cellular nature and functions of myometrium and endometrium.** CBSE 2024 C

Ans. Refer to text on page no. 39 (Uterus). (2)

14. What is the number of chromosomes in the following cells of a human male?

(i) Spermatogonial cells (ii) Spermatids
(iii) Primary spermatocytes
(iv) Sertoli cells

Ans. (i) 46 (ii) 23 (iii) 46 (iv) 46 (½ × 4)

15. Differentiate between spermatogenesis and spermiogenesis.

Ans. Differences between spermatogenesis and spermiogenesis are as follows

Spermatogenesis	Spermiogenesis
It is a process of formation of sperms from immature germ cells.	It is a process of transformation of a non-motile spermatid in to a motile spermatozoa.
Number of cells increased as each spermatogonium produces four spermatids.	No change in number of cells as only one spermatid develops into a spermatozoa.

(1 + 1)

16. Define spermiogenesis and spermiation. NCERT

Ans. **Spermiogenesis** The transformation of spermatids into mature sperm, involving changes like formation of tail and acrosome.

Spermiation The release of mature sperm from Sertoli cells into the seminiferous tubules for further transport. (1 + 1)

17. Draw a diagram of a mature human sperm. Label any three parts and write their functions.

Or **Draw a well-labelled diagram of sperm.** NCERT

Ans. Refer to fig. 2.11 on page no. 42.

18. (i) **When and where does spermatogenesis occur in a human male?**
(ii) **Draw the diagram of a mature human male gamete. Label the following parts–Acrosome, nucleus, middle piece and tail.**
(iii) **Mention the functions of acrosome and middle piece.**

Ans. (i) Spermatogenesis occurs at the age of puberty in testes of human male.
(ii) Refer to fig. 2.11 on page no. 42.
(iii) Refer to text on page no. 42. (1×3)

19. Identify A, B, C and *D* with reference to gametogenesis in humans in the flowchart given below.

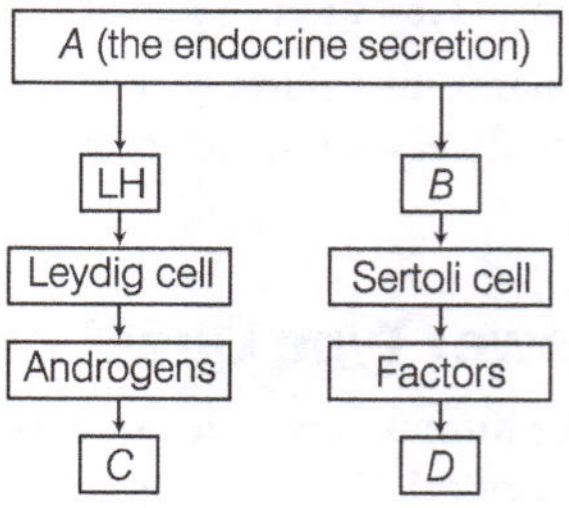

Ans. *A*—GnRH *B*—FSH
C—Spermatogenesis *D*—Spermiogenesis (½×4)

20. **(i) Differentiate between vasa efferentia and vasa deferentia.**

(ii) Distinguish between spermatocytes and oocytes.

Ans. (i) Differences between vasa efferentia and vasa deferens are as follows

Vasa efferentia	Vasa deferens
They arise from the rete testes.	They arise from the epididymis.
Fine and convoluted ductules vary from 15-20 in number.	Thick and coiled ductules, only 2 in number.
Carry spermatozoa from rete testes to epididymis.	Carry spermatozoa from epididymis to ejaculatory ducts.

(2)

(ii) Spermatocyte is a male gametocyte from which a sperm develops, while oocyte is a female gamete which leads to the development of an egg. (1)

21. **Draw a labelled diagram of a section through ovary.** NCERT

Ans. Refer to fig. 2.12 on page no. 43.

22. **What is the difference between a primary oocyte and a secondary oocyte?** NCERT Exemplar

Ans. Primary oocyte is a diploid cell formed in foetal ovary when the gamete mother cell, oogonia is arrested at prophase-I of meiosis. Secondary oocyte is the haploid cell formed from primary oocyte that completes its first meiotic division, during puberty. The secondary oocyte produces the female gamete ova (n). (1 × 2)

23. **Meiotic arrest is a phenomenon noticed during oogenesis in human females where oocytes are arrested in the primary oocyte stage.** Competency Based Que.

(i) What is the chromosomal count of these primary oocytes?

(ii) How are these primary oocytes converted to ovum?

Ans. (i) The chromosomal count of these primary oocytes is 46. (1)

(ii) The primary oocytes are transformed into ova through the following processes

- At puberty, Follicle-Stimulating Hormone (FSH) stimulates the growth of primary oocytes, leading to the formation of primary follicles.
- Each primary follicle develops into secondary and then tertiary follicles. This process involves the proliferation of granulosa cells and the formation of an antrum.
- In the tertiary follicle, the primary oocyte resumes meiosis and undergoes the first meiotic division, resulting in a secondary oocyte and a polar body.
- The secondary oocyte is released during ovulation. If fertilisation occurs, it completes the second meiotic division, forming an ovum and another polar body. (2)

24. **Write the effect of the high concentration of LH on a mature Graafian follicle.**

Ans. High level of LH ruptures the Graafian follicles and thereby releases the ovum. Refer to text on page no. 43. (2)

25. **Draw a labelled diagram of a Graafian follicle.** NCERT

Ans. Refer to fig. 2.15 on page no. 44.

26. **How many eggs are released by a human ovary in a month? How many eggs do you think would have been released if the mother gave birth to identical twins? Would your answer change if the twins born were faternal?** NCERT

Ans. Only one egg is released by a human ovary in a month. Only one egg is released if the mother gave birth to identical twins. Yes, two or more eggs are released in case of faternal twins. (1 × 3)

27. **What is menstrual cycle? Which hormones regulate menstrual cycle?** NCERT

Ans. For menstrual cycle, refer to text on page no. 43-44.

The hormones involved in the process are

(i) **FSH, LH** stimulate growth of follicle and maturation of ovum.

(ii) **Oestrogen** stimulate endometrial repair and growth.

(iii) **Oestrogen and progesterone** together prepare endometrium and other parts of the body for pregnancy. (1 × 3)

28. **Explain the role of pituitary and ovarian hormones in the menstrual cycle of humans females.** CBSE 2020

Ans. The menstrual cycle is controlled by rhythmic synthesis and release of ovarian hormones under feedback control of the hormones of anterior pituitary. These are discussed below

(i) **Pituitary Hormones** The gonadotroph cells of anterior pituitary secrete FSH and LH in females. Their role in menstrual cycle are as follows

(a) **Follicle Stimulating Hormone** (FSH) It is secreted during the follicular phase of the cycle and is responsible for follicular development.

(b) **Luteinizing Hormone** (LH) It triggers ovulation and stimulate the formation of corpus luteum and secretion of estradiol and progesterone from ovary. (1½)

(ii) **Ovarian Hormones** Ovary secretes the following hormones under the effect of FSH and LH.

(a) **Oestrogen** It influences proliferation of the uterine endometrium to prepare for implantation of the fertilised oocyte.

(b) **Progesterone** It is secreted from corpus luteum under the influence of LH, maintains endometrium for implantation. Its rising level inhibits LH. (1½)

29. The graph given below shows the number of primordial follicles per ovary in women at different ages. Study the graph and answer the questions that follow. CBSE 2023, Competency Based Que.

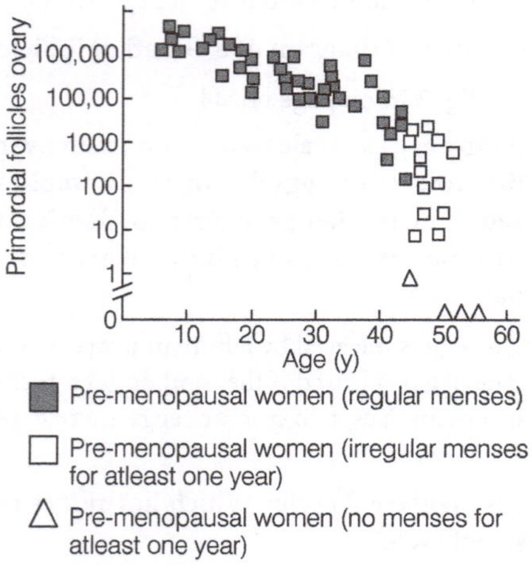

(i) What is the average age of the women at the onset of menopause?

(ii) At what age are maximum primordial follicles present in the ovary, according to the given graph?

Ans. (i) It is clear from the graph that the primordial follicles per ovary starts decreasing rapidly after the age of 35-40 years and reaches almost zero by the age of 50 years. Therefore, the average age of women at the onset of menopause can be estimated to be around 50 years. (1)

(ii) According to the given graph, the maximum number of primordial follicles per ovary is present at birth. After birth, this number decreases gradually and by the age of 20 years, the number of follicles reduces to approximately 1,00,000. After the age of 20 years, the number of follicles decreases at a faster rate and by the age of 40 years, the number of follicles reduces to approximately 10,000. Therefore, the maximum number of primordial follicles per ovary is present at birth. (1)

30. The events of the menstrual cycle are represented as follows.

(i) Menstrual phase (ii) Follicular phase
(iii) Ovulatory phase (iv) Luteal phase

Recall these events and state the levels of hormones (FSH, LH and progesterone) simply by mentioning high or low.

(a) On 5th day (b) On 14th day (c) On 21st-23rd day

Ans.

	Hormones	5th day	13-14th day	21st-23rd day
(a)	FSH	Low	High	Low
(b)	LH	Low	High	Low
(c)	Progesterone	Low	Low	High

(1 × 3)

31. Corpus luteum in pregnancy has a long life. However, if fertilisation does not take place, it remains active only for 10-12 days. Why? NCERT Exemplar

Ans. During pregnancy, there is no menstruation. The corpus luteum secretes large amount of progesterone. This is required to maintain the endometrium during early pregnancy.

In the absence of fertilisation, the corpus luteum cannot be maintained more than 10-12 days leading to its degeneration.

32. (i) The human male ejaculates about 200 to 300 million sperm during a coitus, however the ovum is fertilised by only one sperm. How does the ovum block the entry of additional sperms?

(ii) All copulations will not lead to fertilisation. Why? CBSE SQP 2024

Ans. (i) During fertilisation, a sperm comes in contact with the zona pellucida membrane of the ovum and induces changes in the membrane that blocks the entry of other sperms. (1)

(ii) All copulations does not lead to fertilisation, as for fertilisation to occur, both ovum and sperms should be transported simultaneously to the ampullary-isthmic region of the Fallopian tubule. (1)

33. Where does fertilisation occur in humans? Explain the events that occur during this process.

Ans. Fertilisation in human beings takes place in the ampullary-isthmic junction of the Fallopian tube.

The events/steps of fertilisation are as follows

Discharge of semen into female vagina.

↓

Movement of sperms to reach ampullary-isthmic junction of fallopian tube.

↓

Release and transport of ovum at the same junction.

↓

Fusion of sperm and ovum. (1 + 2)

34. In our society, the women are often blamed for giving birth to daughters. Can you explain why this is not correct? NCERT

Ans. In our society, the women are blamed for giving birth to daughters. This is wrong because sex of the baby is determined by the male sperm that can have either X or Y-chromosome.

Since, women have only one type of chromosome (X) in all the ova.

If the sperm having X-chromosome fertilises the ovum (X), the resulting zygote (XX) will become a female.

If the sperm having Y-chromosome fertilises the ovum (X), the resulting zygote (XY) will become a male. (1½ + 1½)

35. A series of events occur untill the implantation of the blastocyst in the uterus. State them sequentially.

Ans. Refer to text on page no. 46.

36. Name the embryonic stage that gets implanted in the uterine wall of the human female. Also draw its diagram.

Ans. The blastocyst gets embedded in the endometrium of the uterus. This process is called implantation and it leads to pregnancy. Refer to fig 2.18 on page no. 46. (1½ + 1½)

37. (i) A blood test reported negative for hCG. What does negative hCG imply? Name the tissue which produces hCG.

(ii) If a blood test reported positive for hCG in a person, then which other hormones would also be secreted by the tissue secreting hCG? **CBSE SQP 2024**

Ans. (i) Negative hCG implies no pregnancy. It is produced from the placenta. (1)

(ii) If a blood test reported positive for hCG in a person, then other hormones that would also be secreted by the placenta will be human Placental Lactogen (hPL), oestrogen and progestogen. (1)

38. When and how does placenta develop in human female?

Ans. Refer to text on page no. 46.

39. When and where do chorionic villi appear in humans? State their function.

Ans. Chorionic villi appear just after implantation. They appear as finger-like projections on the trophoblast and become interdigitated with the surrounding uterine tissues and form the placenta.

40. What are the major changes that take place in the foetus during second trimester of the pregnancy?

Ans. Refer to text on page no. 47.

41. What is parturition? Which hormones are involved in induction of parturition? **NCERT**

Or

Describe the process of parturition in humans.

Ans. Refer to text on page no. 47.

42. Explain the neuroendocrine mechanism involved in the process of parturition in a human female leading to the expulsion of the baby out of the uterus through the birth canal. **CBSE 2025**

Ans. Refer to text on page no. 47.

Long Answer Type Questions

1. (i) What is spermatogenesis? Briefly describe the process of spermatogenesis. **NCERT**

Or

(i) Where and how in the testes process of spermatogenesis occur in humans?

(ii) Draw diagram of human sperm and label four parts. **CBSE 2020**

Ans. (i) Refer to text on page no. 41.

(ii) Refer to fig. 2.11 on page no. 42.

2. (i) Draw a labelled diagram of a cross-section of human seminiferous tubule. (label any four parts)

(ii) Explain the hormonal regulation of spermatogenesis. **CBSE 2024 C**

Ans. (i) Refer to fig. 2.2 on page no. 37.

(ii) Refer to text on page no. 41 and 42.

3. (i) Name and explain the structural organisation of the male sex accessory ducts in the human male reproductive system.

(ii) Describe the role of gonadotropin FSH in the regulation of spermatogenesis. **CBSE 2025**

Ans. (i) Refer to text on page no. 38.

(ii) Refer to text on page no. 42.

4. What is oogenesis? Give a brief account of oogenesis.

Ans. Refer to text on page no. 42 and 43. **NCERT**

5. (i) Draw a diagrammatic sectional view of ovary of human female and label the following.

(1) Blood vessels (2) Primary follicle

(3) Tertiary follicle (4) Ovum

(ii) At which stage of life are primary follicles formed in a human female?

(iii) Explain the events (both hormonal and structural) that occur at the time of ovulation till the onset of the next menstrual cycle. **CBSE 2024**

Ans. (i) Refer to fig 2.12 on page 43.

(ii) The primary follicles formed in a human female at embryonic stage. (1)

(iii) Both LH and FSH attain a peak level in mid of menstrual cycle. The rapid secretion of LH, leading to its maximum level is called LH surge, which induces rupture of Graafian follicle and cause ovulation. Ovulatory phase is followed by luteal phase during which remaining parts of Graafian follicle transform as corpus luteum. It produces large amount of progesterone needed for maintaining endometrium. In the absence of fertilisation corpus luteum degenerates which causes disintegration of the endometrium leading to menstruation. (2)

6. Explain the development of a secondary oocyte (ovum) in a human female from the embryonic stage upto its ovulation. Name the hormones involved in this process.

Or **When does oogenesis start in humans? Name the three hormones and their sources, linked with oogenesis. How do they influence the process of oogenesis? Explain.**

Ans. The process of formation of a mature female gamete is called **oogenesis.** This process starts during embryonic stages where millions of gamete mother cells, oogonia are formed in foetal ovary.

Oogonia starts division and enters **prophase-I** and gets temporarily arrested at this stage to form **primary oocytes**. Each primary oocyte gets surrounded by a layer of granulosa cells forming **primary follicle.**
From birth to puberty, large number of follicles degenerate (follicular atresia) and at puberty 60,000-80,000 follicles are left in each ovary.

Primary follicles form **secondary follicles,** surrounded by more layers of granulosa cells.
Secondary follicle transforms into tertiary follicle with a fluid-filled cavity called antrum, having theca externa and theca interna. The primary oocyte completes Ist meiotic division (grows in size) forming two unequal haploid cells, large haploid secondary oocyte and a tiny first polar body.

Tertiary follicle transforms into mature Graafian follicle, which ruptures to release ovum/secondary oocyte (ovulation).

The hormones involved are FSH (Follicle Stimulating Hormone) and LH (Luteinizing Hormone) secreted by anterior pituitary in response to production of GnRH (Gonadotropin Releasing Hormone).
FSH stimulates follicular growth and maturation of oocyte. Granulosa cells of follicles produce oestrogen. In the presence of both LH and oestrogen, ovulation occurs. (3+2)

7. Name the functions of the following.

(i) Corpus luteum **(ii) Endometrium**
(iii) Acrosome **(iv) Sperm tail**
(v) Fimbriae NCERT

Ans. (i) **Corpus Luteum** It secretes progesterone required for the maintenance of endometrium.

(ii) **Endometrium** It is the innermost layer of uterus. It provides nutrition for the development of foetus. Implantation of blastocyst occurs in endometrium.

(iii) **Acrosome** It contains hydrolytic enzymes required to dissolve the membranes of the ovum for fertilisation.

(iv) **Sperm tail** It helps in the movement of sperm in the female genital tract for fertilisation.

(v) **Fimbriae** It is present at the opening of oviduct and helps in collection of egg after ovulation. (1×5)

8. How is 'oogenesis' marked different from spermatogenesis with respect to the growth till puberty in the humans?

Ans. Differences between spermatogenesis and oogenesis are as follows

Spermatogenesis	Oogenesis
It begins and gets completed in the testis only.	It begins in the ovary and is completed in the Fallopian tube of female reproductive tract.
Spermatogonia change to primary spermatocytes.	Oogonia change to primary oocytes.
A primary spermatocyte divides to form two secondary spermatocytes.	A primary oocyte divides to form the secondary oocyte and one polar body.
The secondary spermatocyte divides to form two spermatids.	A secondary oocyte divides to form one ootid and one polar body.
A spermatogonium forms four spermatozoa.	An oogonium forms one ovum.

(5)

9. Meiotic division during oogenesis is different from that in spermatogenesis. Explain how and why. NCERT Exemplar

Ans. Meiotic division during oogenesis is different from that of spermatogenesis in the following ways

Meiotic division in spermatogenesis	Meiotic division in oogenesis
Million of sperms generated at a time.	Only one mature ovum is generated at a time, every month.
After two complete meiotic divisions, four equal sized cells are produced.	After completion of two meiotic division one big cell with almost all the cytoplasm and two very small-sized cells are produced.
They mature into flagellated and motile cell.	Mature ovum is non-flagellated and non-motile.

Refer to fig. 2.9 on page no. 41 and 2.13 on page 43. (2½)

(i) Unequal cell division makes the ovum much larger than the other two polar bodies. As, ovum has more cytoplasm and more organelles, it has a better chance of survival than the sperm.

(ii) The male makes millions of tiny sperms, while the female makes only one egg per month that also arrested in second meiotic division, until just before fertilisation. This is a way of conserving energy.

(iii) Sperm is smaller and motile as it has to move out of male system to female reproductive system. Larger egg has abundant reserve food, so that embryo starts developing right after fertilisation. (2½)

10. Study the graph given below related with menstrual cycle in females. **Competency Based Que.**

(i) Identify ovarian hormones *X* and *Y* mentioned in the graph and specify their source.

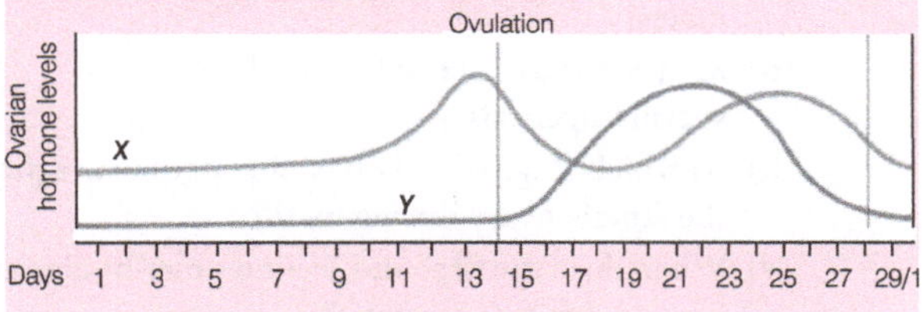

(ii) Correlate and describe the uterine events that take place according to the ovarian hormones label *X* and *Y* mentioned in the graph on

(a) 6–15 days **(b) 16–25 days**

(c) 26–28 days (when ovum is not fertilised)

Ans. (i) In the given graph,

X is oestrogen that is secreted by the growing follicles in the ovary during the follicular phase of menstrual cycle. *Y* is progesterone that is secreted by the corpus luteum during luteal phase of menstrual cycle. (2)

(ii) Uterine events that take place according to the ovarian hormones labelled as *X* and *Y* during different days of menstrual cycle are as follows

(a) **6–15 days** Endometrium of the uterus regenerates by proliferation under the influence of oestrogen. (1)

(b) **16–25 days** Under the influence of progesterone, the endometrium of the uterus is maintained for implantation of fertilised ovum and other events of pregnancy. (1)

(c) **26–28 days** If the ovum is not fertilised, corpus luteum degenerates which causes disintegration of endometrium thus, leading to menstruation and marking a new cycle. (1)

11. Explain the role of pituitary gonadotropins during the follicular and ovulatory phases of the menstrual cycle. Describe the shifts in steroidal secretions. **Diksha**

Ans. The menstrual cycle is controlled through the pituitary gland by the hypothalamus. Changes in the ovary and uterus during the menstrual cycle is due to the fluctuation in the levels of ovarian and pituitary hormones. Towards the end of the menstrual phase, the pituitary FSH eventually increases which causes the development of the follicles inside the ovaries. During the maturation of follicles, more oestrogen is secreted , triggering a positive feedbock loop, leading to surge in GnRH, which then cause surge in FSH and LH secretion from the anterior pituitary. Both the FSH and LH attain a peak level during the mid of the cycle. This speedy secretion of LH leads to LH surge which induces rupture of Graafian follicle and hence the ovulation. The LH hormone causes the conversion of the empty follicle into the corpus luteum. The corpus luteum produces steroidal hormones-progesterone and oestrogen. (5)

12. Where does fertilisation occur in the oviduct of a human female ? Explain the embryonic development from fertilised ovum up to its implantation. **CBSE 2020**

Ans. Refer to text on page no. 45-46.

13. (i) Explain the formation of placenta after the implantation in a human female.

(ii) Draw a diagram showing human foetus within the uterus and label any four parts in it. **CBSE 2023**

Ans. (i) The development of the placenta is called placentation. In humans, placental formation starts in the third week of pregnancy. At this stage, the embryo has two different cell types, i.e. trophoblast cells and inner cell mass. The inner cell mass forms the foetus and the trophoblast forms the placenta. From trophoblast, some processes develop that connect with the uterine wall. The umbilical cord developed from the placenta also connected to the foetus and helps in the transport of substances to and from the embryo. (2½)

(ii) Refer to fig. 2.19 on page no. 46. (2½)

14. What are the major features of embryonic development at various months of pregnancy?

Ans. Refer to text on page no. 47.

15. (i) Arrange the following hormones in the sequence of their secretion in a pregnant woman.
hCG, LH, FSH, Relaxin

(ii) Mention their source and the function they perform.

Ans. (i) The sequence of secretion of the given hormones in a pregnant woman is

$$\text{FSH} \rightarrow \text{LH} \rightarrow \text{hCG} \rightarrow \text{Relaxin} \quad (2)$$

(ii)

Hormones	Sources	Functions
FSH	Anterior pituitary lobe	Stimulates the growth of ovarian follicles in ovary.
LH	Anterior pituitary lobe	It triggers ovulation.
hCG	Placenta	It stimulates the corpus luteum to secrete progesterone.
Relaxin	Ovary	It facilitates parturition by softening the connective tissue of pubic symphysis. (3)

Source Based/Case Based/Passage Based Questions

1. Study the given figure.

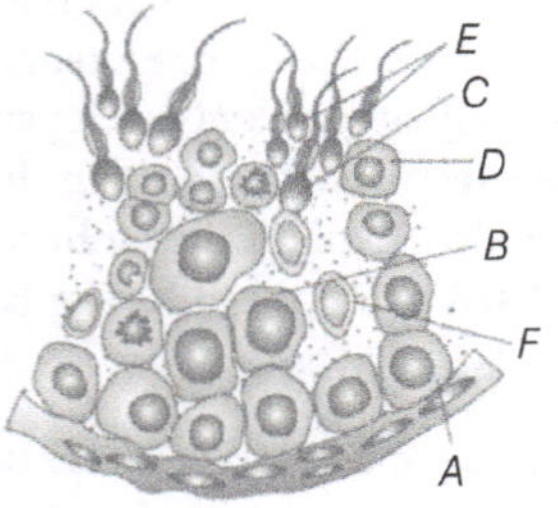

(i) Pick out and name the cells that undergo spermiogenesis.

(ii) Name 'A' and 'B' cells. What is the difference between them with reference to the number of chromosomes?

(iii) Pick out and name the motile cells.

(iv) What is 'F' cell? Mention its function.

Ans. (i) *C*–Spermatids, undergo spermiogenesis

(ii) *A*–Spermatogonium,

B–Primary spermatocyte

Both spermatogonium and primary spermatocyte contain 46 chromosomes.

(iii) *E*–Spermatozoa, are motile cells.

(iv) *F*–Sertoli cell, it provides nutrition to the germ cells. (1×4)

2. The hormones that play an active role in spermatogenesis are Gonadotropin Releasing Hormone (GnRH), Luteinizing Hormone (LH) and Follicle Stimulating Hormone (FSH). Observe the given flowchart and answer the questions accordingly.

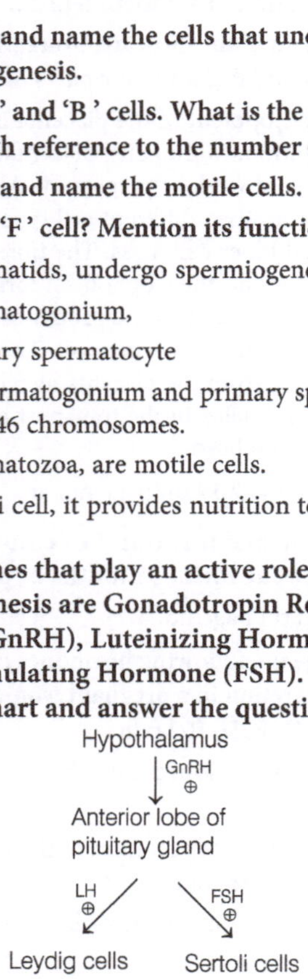

(i) Does increased secretion from hypothalamus have any effect on Sertoli cells?

(ii) What is the effect of LH on Leydig cells?

(iii) How does FSH help in the process of spermiogenesis?

Ans. (i) Yes, increased secretion of GnRH from hypothalamus does have a effect on Sertoli cells. (1)

(ii) LH acts on the Leydig cells and stimulates the synthesis and secretion of androgens, which in turn stimulate the process of spermatogenesis. (2)

(iii) FSH acts on Sertoli cells and stimulates the secretion of some factors which help in spermiogenesis. (1)

3. While teaching the concepts of gametogenesis, teacher told students that oogenesis and spermatogenesis differ significantly.

Teacher also told them that unlike spermatogenesis, oogenesis begin during the foetal life of female. However, in both the process, LH and FSH play a major role.

(i) When and where does spermatogenesis begin in males?

(ii) Mention the effect of LH and FSH on spermatogenesis.

(iii) At which stage of cell division, oogonia are present in the female ovary during birth?

(iv) When does the first and second polar bodies are formed during oogenesis?

Ans. (i) In males, spermatogenesis begins during puberty in the seminiferous tubules of testes.

(ii) LH acts on Leydig cells and stimulates the synthesis and secretion of androgens. FSH acts on Sertoli cells and stimulates the secretion of factors, which promote spermiogenesis.

(iii) At birth, ovary contains primary oocytes arrested at prophase-I of meiotic division.

(iv) First polar body is formed during first meiotic division, when secondary oocyte is formed. Second polar body is extruded when ovum is formed from secondary oocyte. (1×4)

4. The graph given below depicts the average number of eggs of female possess throughout their life. Observe the graph and answer the following questions.

Competency Based Que.

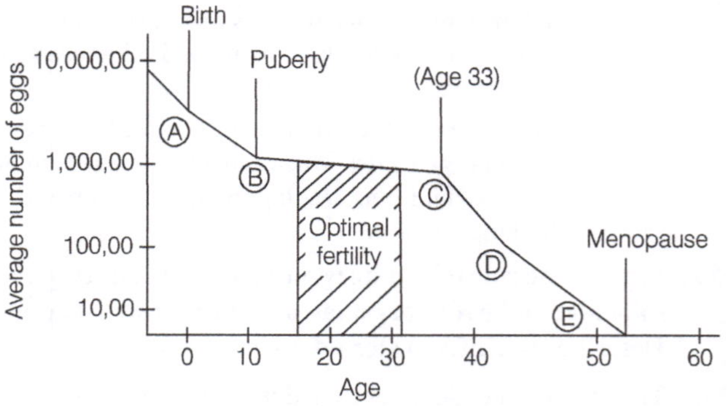

(i) How many eggs are female born with?

(ii) The time interval between the age 18 to 32 is considered as the phase of optional fertility. Give reason.

(iii) Referring to the above graph, state the phase in which fertility declines.

(iv) What are the effects experienced by a female after post-menopause ?

Ans. (i) During foetal development, a female have about 6 million eggs. At birth, these are about 5-6 lakh (approximately 1 million) eggs left.

(ii) Females become fertile in their teens following puberty. The beginning of reproductive years marked by the onset of ovulation and menstruation. During their reproductive years, women have regular monthly menstrual periods. This enhances the chances of fertility. Thus, the age 18 to 32 is considered as the phase of optimal fertility.

(iii) Generally, reproductive potential decreases as women get older. It can be expected to end 5 to 10 years before menopause, i.e. *C* to *D* in the above graph.

(iv) The time of a women's life following menopause is called post-menopause. As a result of several factors, including lower level of oestrogen, the post-menopausal womens are at higher risk of osteoporosis and heart diseases. (1 × 4)

5. Refer to the figure given below and answer the questions that follows

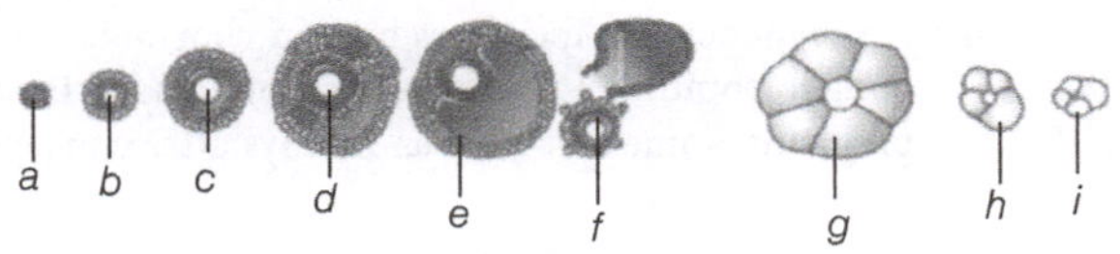

(i) **Which hormone is responsible for the process occurring in stage labelled as *f*?**

(ii) **Why is there a decrease in size of *g* in further stages?**

(iii) **What will be the conclusion, if the label marked as *h* and *i* retain their size same as *g*?**

Ans. (i) The process shown in stage labelled as *f* is ovulation. It is the release of mature egg from the ovary in the female body. The Luteinizing Hormone (LH) regulates the menstrual cycle and causes release of egg from the ovary. (1)

(ii) Corpus luteum, a temporary endocrine structure degenerates in the absence of fertilisation. If pregnancy does not occur, the corpus luteum degenerates in 12-14 days. (1)

(iii) The stages labelled as *g*, *h* and *i* are the corpus luteum. If the size of *g* is maintained for a duration, it suggests that fertilisation has occur. As corpus luteum is responsible for the production of progesterone in early pregnancy. (2)

6. Given below is the diagram of a human ovum surrounded by a few sperms. Study the diagram and answer the following questions.

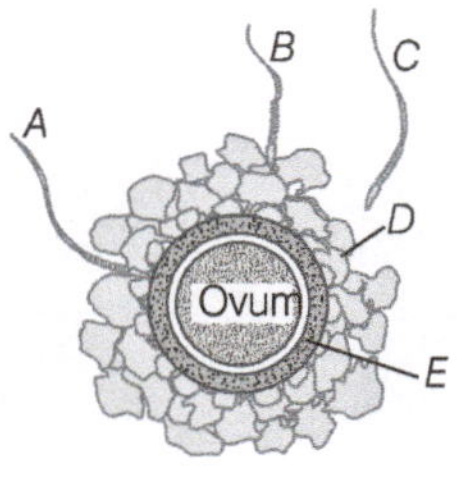

(i) **Which one of the sperms would reach the ovum earlier?**

(ii) **Identify '*D*' and '*E*'. Mention the role of '*E*'.**

Or (ii) **Mention what helps the entry of sperm into the ovum and write the changes occurring in the ovum during the process.**

(iii) **Name the specific region in the female reproductive system where the event represented in the diagram takes place.**

Ans. (i) The sperm '*A*' would reach the ovum earlier. (1)

(ii) *D*–Corona radiata, *E*–Zona pellucida.
During fertilisation, a sperm comes in contact with zona pellucida layer of the ovum and induces changes in the membrane that block the entry of additional sperms. (2)

Or (ii) The secretions of the acrosome help the sperm enter into the cytoplasm of the ovum through the zona pellucida and the plasma membrane. This induces the completion of the meiotic division of the secondary oocyte. (2)

(iii) These events takes place in the Fallopian tube of uterus. (1)

7. The graph given below shows how the lining of the uterus, in a female who has achieved puberty, varies with time. Examine the graph and answer the following questions. **Competency Based Que.**

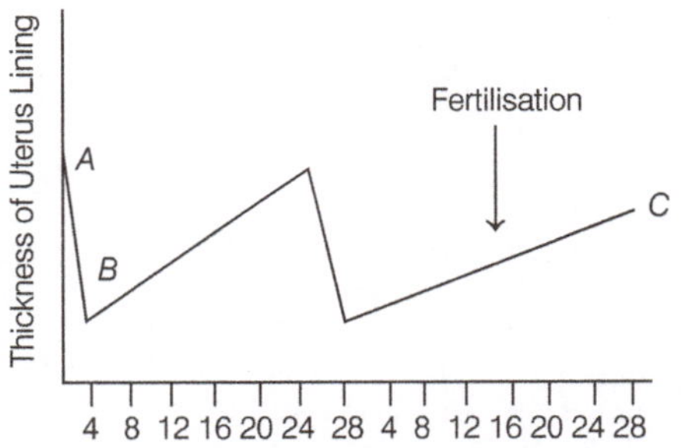

(i) **What is happening between *A* and *B*?**

(ii) **When the ovulation will take place? Surge of which pituitary hormone is required for ovulation?**

(iii) **Fertilisation occurs on the 16th day of the second menstrual cycle. How do you expect the graph to behave after points *C*? Will the pattern of the first and second months be followed?**

(iv) **Write the role of yolk sac.**

Ans. (i) It represents menstrual flow. During this phase, the uterus lining is shed along with the blood and moves out of the body in the form of bleeding. (1)

(ii) 14th day or in the mid of the cycle. LH surge (Luteinizing hormone increases) of pituitary hormone is required for ovulation. (1)

(iii) As fertilisation occurs on the 16th day, the graph after point C will be straight lined. Because once fertilisation occurs, the uterus lining is retained and no bleeding menstrual flow occurs during that period. (1)

(iv) It provides nutrition and facilitate gas exchange between mother and developing embryo before the placenta forms. (1)

8. The graph given below is showing the levels of hCG, oestrogen and progesterone during pregnancy. Observe the graph carefully and answer the questions that follows. **Competency Based Que.**

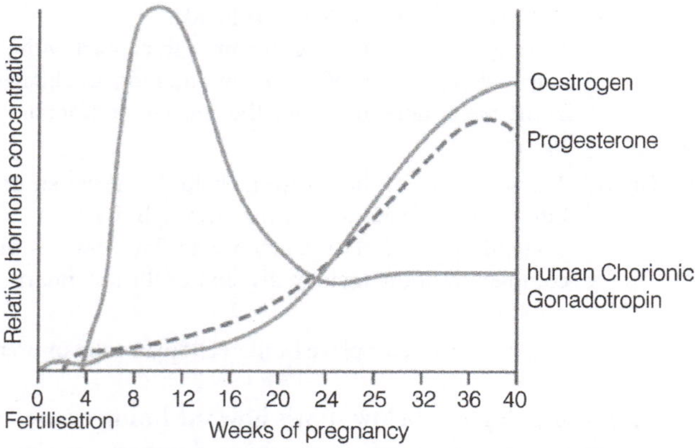

(i) What are the sources of these three hormones during the first 7-8 weeks of pregnancy?

(ii) A part from the above three hormones shown in the above graph. What are the other hormones present in the female body ? Also write their functions.

(iii) Which of the above given hormones checked for the confirmation of pregnancy ?

Ans. (i) Corpus luteum is the source of oestrogen and progesterone during the first few weeks of pregnancy. Whereas placenta is the main source of human Chorionic Gonadotropin (hCG) hormone in the later stages of pregnancy. (1)

(ii) A part from oestrogen, progesterone and hCG, the other hormones are as follows

(a) **Prolactin** It is the main hormone needed to produce breast milk. It prepares mammary glands for milk production.

(b) **Relaxin** It relaxes the joints of the pelvis and soften the cervix during birth.

(c) **Oxytocin** The levels of this hormone rise at the start of labour. It stimulates the contraction of uterine muscle, necessary for parturition. (2)

(iii) A pregnancy test measures human chorionic gonadotropin. It appears in the blood and urine of pregnant women as early as 10 days after conception. (1)

SELF ASSESSMENT TEST

Multiple Choice Questions

1. Which of the following option accurately depicts the path of sperm in the male reproductive system?
(a) Testes → Epididymis → Vas deferens → Seminal vesicles → Prostate gland → Urethra
(b) Epididymis → Testes → Seminal vesicles → Prostate gland → Vas deferens → Urethra
(c) Vas deferens → Epididymis → Testes → Prostate gland → Urethra → Seminal vesicles
(d) Testes → Seminal vesicles → Vas deferens → Epididymis → Prostate gland → Urethra

2. Select the incorrect pair from the following.
(a) Infundibulum – Funnel-shaped structure
(b) Fimbriae– Finger-like projection
(c) Ampulla – Narrow part of the oviduct
(d) Uterus – Pear-shaped structure

3. Several mammary ducts join to form a wider mammary ampulla which is connected to
(a) mammary lobes
(b) alveoli
(c) lactiferous duct
(d) nipple

4. During spermatogenesis, which cells are the first to contain a haploid number of chromosomes?
(a) Spermatogonium
(b) Secondary spermatocyte
(c) Primary spermatocyte
(d) Spermatids

5. Identify the incorrect statement.
(a) The process of oogenesis gets started during the embryonic development.
(b) The number of primary follicles increases from the birth till the puberty.
(c) Tertiary follicle is characterised by the fluid filled cavity called antrum.
(d) The meiotic division in oogenesis is unequal.

6. Which of the following correctly represents the function of the part labelled as *A*?

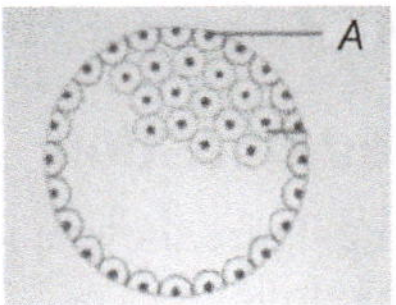

(a) Gets differentiated as embryo
(b) Responsible for the production of hCG
(c) Helps in attachment to the endometrium
(d) Facilitate the supply of oxygen and nutrients to the embryo

7. Signals from fully developed foetus and placenta ultimately lead to parturition, which is facilitated by the release of
(a) oestrogen from placenta
(b) oxytocin from maternal pituitary
(c) oxytocin from foetal pituitary
(d) maternal progesterone

Assertion-Reason Questions

Direction (Q. Nos. 8-11) *In each of the following questions, a statement of Assertion (A) is given followed by corresponding statement of Reason (R). Of the statements, mark the correct answer.*
(a) Both A and R are true and R is the correct explanation of A.
(b) Both A and R are true, but R is not the correct explanation of A.
(c) A is true, but R is false.
(d) A is false, but R is true.

8. **Assertion** (A) The male reproductive system is regulated by hormones.
Reason (R) Hormones such as Luteinizing Hormone (LH) and Follicle-Stimulating Hormone (FSH) from the pituitary gland control testosterone production and spermatogenesis in the testes.

9. **Assertion** (A) The vagina serves multiple functions in the female reproductive system.
Reason (R) Vagina produces hormones that regulate the menstrual cycle and facilitate ovulation.

10. **Assertion** (A) Once fertilisation occurs, the zygote immediately implants in the uterus.
Reason (R) After fertilisation blastocyst travels to the uterus for implantation.

11. **Assertion** (A) The first trimester is a critical period in pregnancy.
Reason (R) During first trimester most major organs and systems of the foetus begin to develop.

Very ShortAnswer Type Questions

12. Name two types of cells of germinal epithelium present in the mammalian testes.
13. How many sperms will be produced from 20 primary spermatocytes?
14. In ovary which structure gets transformed into the corpus luteum and name the hormone secreted by the corpus luteum.
15. Name the hormone responsible for the uterine contractions during parturition.

Short Answer Type Questions

16. Mention the function of acrosome and tail in human sperm.
17. How does zona pellucida of ovum helps in preventing polyspermy?
18. Define lactation. Why colostrum is good for the health of new born babies?

Long Answer Type Questions

19. What is spermatogenesis? Give a brief account of spermatogenesis.
20. Draw a sectional view of human ovary showing three different stages of developing follicles, corpus luteum and ovulation.
21. Mention the fate inner cell mass after implantation in the uterus. Draw a well-labelled diagram showing the transport of the zygote from 2- celled stage to the 16-celled stage in the female reproductive system.

Case Based Question

22. The following figure shows a foetus within the uterus. On the basis of the given figure, answer the questions that follows.

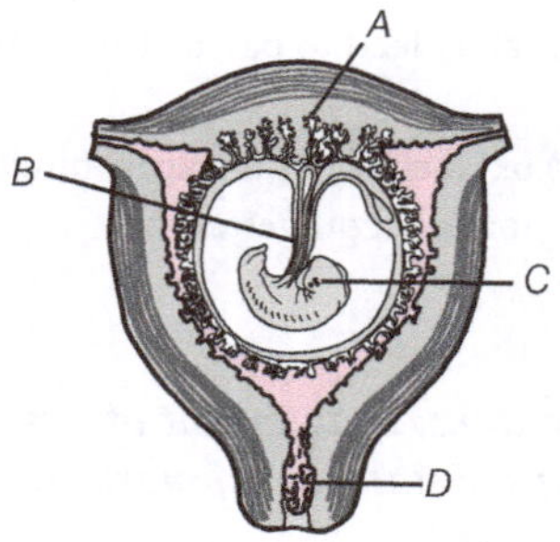

(i) In the above figure, label the parts *A*, *B*, *C* and *D*.
(ii) In the above figure, choose and name the correct part (*A*, *B*, *C* or *D*) that act as temporary endocrine gland and substantiate your answer.
(iii) Mention the role of the *B* in the development of the embryo.

Answers

1. (a)	2. (c)	3. (c)	4. (b)	5. (b)	6. (c)	7. (b)	8. (a)
9. (c)	10. (d)	11. (a)					

03
CHAPTER

Reproductive Health

The term 'reproductive health' refers to the state of healthy reproductive organs with normal functions.
According to the **World Health Organisation** (WHO), reproductive health can be defined as the total well-being in all aspects of reproduction. These include physical, emotional, behavioural and social well-being

YOUR STUDY GOALS

3.1 Reproductive Health: Problems and Strategies
3.2 Sexually Transmitted Diseases (STDs)
3.3 Infertility

YOUR PRACTICE GOAL

- Objective Type Questions (49 Qs ; MCQs, A-R) Case Based Questions (3)
- Subjective Type Questions
- (14 VSAs, 49 SAs, 6 LAs)

- A society with people having physically and functionally normal reproductive organs and emotionally and behaviourally normal interactions among them in all sex-related aspects is called a reproductively healthy society.
- In this chapter, we will discuss various aspects on which healthcare programmes should focus, methods of contraception, STDs and infertility problems and methods to tackle them in order to achieve reproductive health of each and every individual of society.

3.1 Reproductive Health : Problems and Strategies

- India was amongst the first few countries to initiate action plans and programmes at the national level to attain total reproductive health as a social goal.
- These programmes called **family planning** were initiated in 1951 and were periodically assessed over past decades.
- Improved programmes covering reproduction related areas are currently in operation under the name **Reproductive** and **Child Healthcare** (RCH) **programmes**.

Reproductive and Child Healthcare (RCH) Programmes

Major tasks of RCH programmes include

- Creating awareness among people about various aspects of reproduction.
- Providing facilities and support to build-up a reproductively healthy society.

In order to create awareness among people regarding a reproductive healthy society the government has initiated some measures. These are as follows

- The government and non-government agencies use audio-visual and print media for creating awareness among people about reproduction related aspects.
- Slogans like '**hum do hamare do**' and the adoption of one child norm are also promoted.
- Introduction of sex education in schools to provide right information to young minds, so as to discourage them from believing in myths and misconceptions about sex-related issues.
- Proper information about reproductive organs, adolescence and related changes, safe and hygienic sexual practices and **Sexually Transmitted Diseases** (STDs) like, AIDS would help people, specifically adolescents, to lead a reproductively healthy life.
- Educating people, especially fertile couples and those in marriageable age groups about birth control options, care of pregnant mothers, post-natal care of mother and child, importance of breastfeeding, equal opportunities for male and female child.
- Awareness of problems due to uncontrolled population growth, social evils like sex abuse and sex-related crimes, etc. should be created to enable people to think and take up necessary steps to build a reproductive healthy society.
- Statutory ban on **amniocentesis**, massive child immunisations, etc., are some programmes which need to be adopted.
- Research in development of better reproductive strategies are encouraged by the government and other agencies. For example, development of new user friendly methods of contraception.
  Successful implementation of various action plans to attain reproductive health requires strong infrastructure, medical facilities, professional expertise and material support.

Amniocentesis

- It is a medical procedure used in pre-natal diagnosis of chromosomal abnormalities, resulting in genetic disorders like haemophilia, Down's syndrome, sickle-cell anaemia, etc.
- In this procedure, small amount of amniotic fluid surrounding the developing foetus is taken and examined for genetic abnormalities.
- This technique is being misused for sex-determination and if the developing foetus turns out to be a girl, people undertake actions that lead to female foeticide. Thus, this procedure has certain legal restrictions in gender based countries.

Population Explosion

- **Population** represents the total number of individuals of a species living in an area.
- In last century, all-around development in various fields significantly improved people's quality of life.
- At the same time, increased health facilities along with better living conditions had an explosive impact on the growth of population.
- This rapid increase in population over a relatively short period is called **population explosion**.
- The world population, which was around 2 billion (2000 million) in 1900 rocketed to about 6 billion by 2000 and 7.2 billion in 2011.
- A similar trend was observed in India as well. Our population, which was approximately 350 millions at the time of our independence, has outcrossed the population of China recently.

Reasons for Population Explosion

- Expected reasons for the population explosion may be
  - Rapid decline in **death rate**, i.e. **Maternal Mortality Rate** (MMR) and **Infant Mortality Rate** (IMR).
  - Increase in number of people of reproducible age.
- Thus, natality (birth rate) and mortality (death rate) are the two basic processes, which plays a key role in regulating population size.

Consequences of Overpopulation

- According to 2011 census report, the population growth rate was less than 2 per cent, i.e. 20/1000/year.
- The population growth at such an alarming rate can lead to absolute scarcity of even the basic requirements.
- Some of the direct consequences of over population are given below as
  - **Shortage of Food Supply** This occurs when the population keeps on increasing, but the production of food does not increase in a similar proportion.
  - **Unemployment** As number of people increase, demand for jobs will also increase. But when sufficient number of jobs are not available this would cause unemployment.
  - **Education** With increasing population, more people need to be educated. This creates difficulties for the government to provide proper education to all.
  - **Poverty** Family tends to become poor, if there are more people in it and the income is less.
  - **Insufficient Shelters** An increasing population always results in shortage of space to dwell in as the area does not grow/expand with the increasing population.
  - **Lack of Clothing** A rise in population leads to increasing poverty in a country or an area. This directly affects the capability of an individual to deal with his daily expenses including clothing.

Control of Population Growth

Steps undertaken by government to control population growth are as follows

- Statutory raising of marriageable age of girls to 18 years and 21 years in case of boys.
- Giving incentives to the couples with small families.
- Motivating smaller families through media outlets like advertisements, posters and bill boards, etc., by encouraging the use of various contraceptive methods.

Quick Test 1

1. Name the program that focuses on creating reproductive and child health awareness among people.
2. Which technique is used to diagnose genetic diseases like sickle-cell anaemia in a baby before birth?
3. State one reason that led to India overtaking China as the world's most populous country.
4. State one direct consequence of an alarming increase in population growth.
5. **State True or False.**
   Raising the marriageable age can reduce overpopulation by delaying child birth.

Birth Control (Contraception)

- The regulation of conception by using preventive methods or devices that limit the number of offsprings is called **birth control** or **contraception.**
- An ideal contraceptive should be
  - User-friendly
  - Easily available
  - Effective
  - Reversible with no or least side effects.
  - Non-interfering with the sexual drive, desire and/or the sexual act of the user.

Methods of Birth Control

The presently available, wide range of contraceptive methods could be broadly grouped under the following categories

1. Natural/Traditional Methods

These methods are based on the principle of avoiding chances of sperms and ovum meeting.
Some of them are as follows

(i) **Periodic Abstinence** It is a method in which couples avoid coitus (intercourse) from 10th to 17th day of the menstrual cycle. This is because ovulation occur mostly during this time.

- Since, chances of fertilisation are high during this time interval, it is called the **fertile period.**

- Thus, by abstaining from coitus during this period, conception could be prevented.

(ii) **Coitus Interruptus or Withdrawal** In this method, the male partner withdraws his penis from the vagina just before ejaculation, to avoid insemination.

(iii) **Lactational Amenorrhoea** (Absence of menstruation) It refers to the absence of menstruation during the period of intense lactation after parturition.

- Since, ovulation does not occur in this period, the chances of conception are almost nil.
- This method is reliable for a maximum period of six months after parturition.
- Side effects are almost nil, since no medicines are used, but chances of failure of this method are high.

2. Barrier Methods

- In such methods, sperms and ovum are prevented from physically meeting with the help of barriers in order to prevent fertilisation.
- These methods are available for both males and females. These are as follows

(i) **Condoms** These barriers are made up of thin rubber or latex sheath and are used to cover the penis in males or vagina and cervix in females.

- These are used during coitus, so that ejaculated semen would not enter into the female reproductive tract.
- **Nirodh** is a popular brand of condom used by males. Female condoms are known as **femidoms**.
- Use of condoms has increased in recent years due to its additional benefit of providing protection to the user against STDs and AIDS.
- Moreover, they are easily disposable and can be self-inserted, providing privacy to the user.

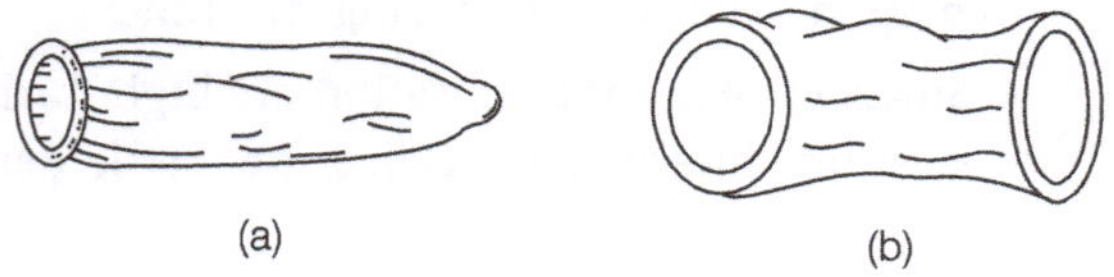

Fig 3.1 Barrier method: (a) Condom for male (b) Femidom for female

(ii) **Cervical Caps, Diaphragms and Vaults** These are also made of rubber and are inserted into the female reproductive tract to cover the cervix during intercourse.

They prevent conception by blocking entry of sperms through cervix. These are reusable.

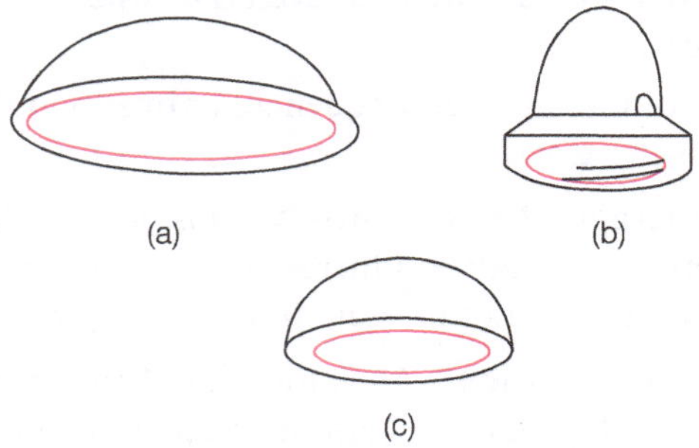

Fig 3.2 Barrier method : (a) Diaphragms, (b) Cervical cap, (c) Vault

(iii) **Spermicidal Creams, Jellies and Foams** (chemical methods) These are usually used along with the above stated barrier methods to increase their contraceptive efficiency.

These are applied at the surface of the vagina before intercourse to prevent sperm entry.

3. Intra Uterine Devices (IUDs)

- These devices contain either copper or progesterone and are inserted by doctors or expert nurses in the uterus through vagina.
- IUDs are ideal contraceptives for females who want to maintain space among children and/or delay pregnancy.
- It is one of the most widely accepted methods of contraception in India.
- IUDs increase phagocytosis of sperms within the uterus.
- These are categorised as long term contraceptive methods and can be further divided into

(i) **Copper Releasing IUDs** Cu-T, Cu-7 and Multiload 375 are some of the Cu-releasing IUDs. Cu ions released, suppress sperm motility and their capacity to fertilise.

(ii) **Hormone Releasing IUDs** Progestasert, LNG-20 are some of the well known hormone releasing IUDs.

They make uterus unsuitabe for implantation and cervix hostile to sperms.

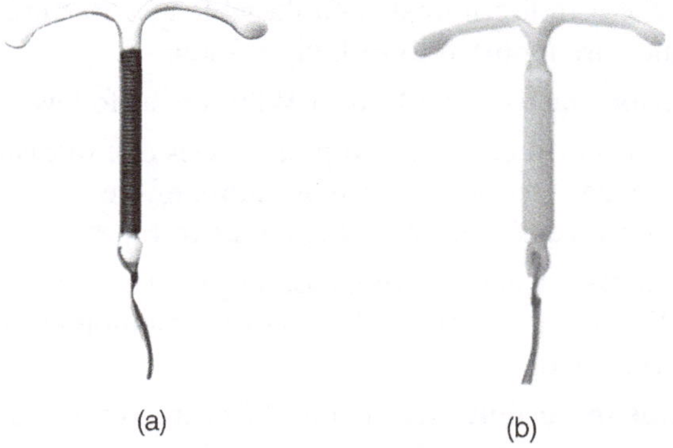

Fig 3.3 Intra Uterine Devices (IUDs) : (a) Copper IUD, (b) Hormonal IUD

(iii) **Non-medicated IUDs**, e.g. Lippes loop.

4. Oral Contraceptives

- These are the preparations of hormones either progestogens or progestogen-oestrogen combinations in the form of **pills** (tablets).
- This contraceptive method is used by the females.
- They alter or inhibit ovulation and implantation and also modify the quality of cervical mucus to prevent or retard the entry of sperms.
- Oral pills are generally taken daily for a period of 21 days starting within the first five days of menstrual cycle.
- After a gap of 7 days (during which menstruation occurs), it has to be repeated in the same pattern till female desires to prevent conception.
- These are well-accepted as they are very effective with lesser side effects. These pills are very popular among urban women. Most common example is '**Saheli**'.
- **Saheli** is a new oral contraceptive for females that contains a non-steroidal preparation.
- It is once a week pill with few side effects and high contraceptive value. It was developed by **CDRI** (Central Drug Research Institute), **Lucknow**.

5. Injectables and Implants

- Progestogens (may/may not be combined with oestrogen) can also be used by females as injections or implants under the skin.
- Their mode of actions is similar to that of pills, but their effective periods are much longer.

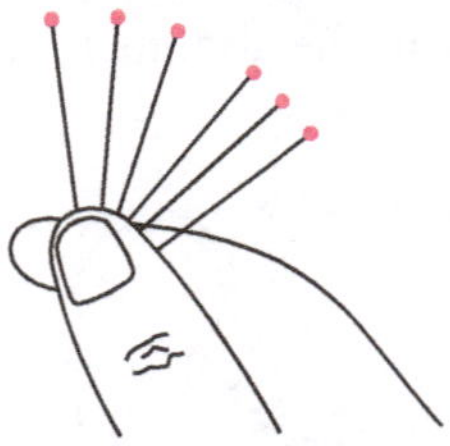

Fig 3.4 Implants

> **TEACHER'S TIP**
> **Injectables** and **implants** are both hormonal methods of contraception, but differ in their administration and duration of effectiveness. Injectables are administered via a needle, typically every 1 to 3 months, and provide temporary contraception for a few months at a time. In contrast, implants are small rods or devices inserted under the skin, releasing hormones gradually over a period of 3 to 5 years.

6. Emergency Contraceptives (Morning After Pills)

- These are medications that primarily prevents or delays ovulation.
- These are combination of progestogen-oestrogen.
- These pills, if taken within 72 hours of coitus are highly effective as emergency contraceptives, helping to prevent pregnancy in case of rape or casual unprotected intercourse.

7. Surgical (Sterilisation) Methods

- These are the terminal methods used by male/female partner to prevent any more pregnancies.
- These are the permanent methods, which block the transport of gametes and thereby prevent conception.
- Surgical methods are available in the form of **vasectomy** in men and **tubectomy** in women.

(i) **Vasectomy** (in males) A small part of the vas deferens is removed or tied up through a small incision on the scrotum in males.

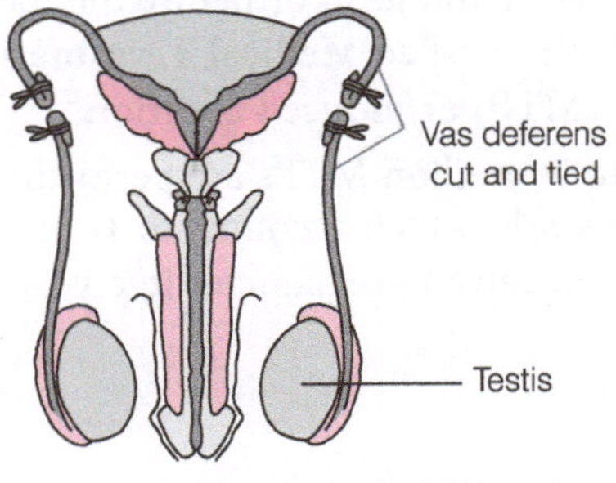

Fig. 3.5 Sterilisation method: Vasectomy

(ii) **Tubectomy** (in females) A small part of the Fallopian tube is removed or tied up through a small incision in the abdomen or through vagina in female.

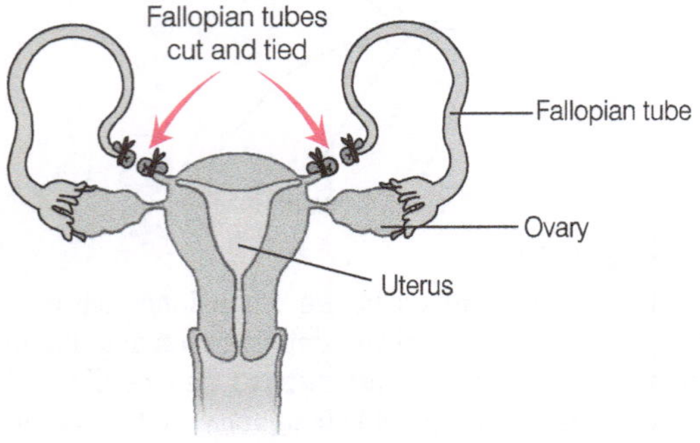

Fig. 3.6 Sterilisation method: Tubectomy

- Both these techniques are known to be highly effective, but are poorly reversible.

Responsible use of Contraceptives

- One should keep in mind that contraceptives are not regular requirements for maintaining reproductive health.
- They are practiced against natural reproductive events like conception or pregnancy.
- There may be personal reasons to adopt these methods like to prevent pregnancy or to delay or space pregnancy.
- However, their possible ill effects like nausea, abdominal pain, breakthrough bleeding, irregular menstrual bleeding or even breast cancer, should not be totally ignored.
- Still on the counterpart, these methods have significant role in checking growth of population.

Medical Termination of Pregnancy (MTP)

- Intentional or voluntary termination of pregnancy (abortion) before full term or before the foetus becomes viable is called **Medical Termination of Pregnancy** (MTP) or induced abortion.
- Nearly 45 to 50 million MTPs are performed in a year all over the world which accounts to 1/5th of the total number of conceived pregnancies in a year.
- Government of India legalised MTP in 1971 with some strict conditions to avoid its misuse, especially to check indiscriminate and illegal female foeticides, which are reported to be high in India.
- **Various factors** that lead to MTPs are as follows
  - To get rid of unwanted pregnancies due to casual unprotected intercourse or failure of the contraceptive used during coitus or rapes.
  - In cases where continuation of pregnancy is harmful either to the foetus or to the mother or even both.
- **Some important facts** about MTPs are as follows
  - MTPs are considered relatively safe upto 12 weeks of pregnancy (first trimester). It becomes more riskier after the first trimester as the foetus becomes intimately associated with maternal tissue.
  - It is being misused (*via* amniocentesis) to abort even the normal female foetuses.
  - Majority of MTPs are performed illegally by unqualified quacks which may be fatal.
- Illegal abortions can be dangerous for young mother as well as the foetus. So, effective counselling is needed before adopting MTPs as it will help in reducing such cases.

MTP Amendment Act, 2017

- The Medical Termination of Pregnancy (Amendment) Act of 2017 was enacted by Indian government.
- According to this act, a pregnancy can be terminated on a certain considered ground within the first 12 weeks of pregnancy on the opinion of one registered medical practitioner, while two opinions are required if pregnancy is between first 12 weeks to 24 weeks.
- The grounds for such termination of pregnancies are
  - Continuation of pregnancy is a health risk to mother.
  - Foetus is at substantial risk of physical or mental abnormalities leading to his/her being seriously handicapped.

Quick Test 2

1. Can periodic abstinence be considered an ideal contraceptive method?
2. Mention the part of the female reproductive system where the cervical caps and diaphragms are inserted.
3. **State True or False.**
   The contraceptive pill developed by CDRI has irreversible effects on the female body.
4. Which part of the male reproductive system is surgically altered during a vasectomy?
5. Is it safe for a 7-month pregnant woman to terminate her pregnancy *via* MTP?

3.2 Sexually Transmitted Diseases (STDs)

- These are the diseases that are mainly passed from one person to another during sexual intercourse.
- They are also known as **Sexually Transmitted Infections** (STIs) or **Venereal Diseases** (VDs) or **Reproductive Tract Infections** (RTIs).
- Genital herpes, syphilis, gonorrhoea, chlamydiasis, genital warts, trichomoniasis, hepatitis-B and infection of HIV leading to AIDS are some common STDs.
- These diseases are major threat to a healthy society and are reported to be high among individuals in the age group of 15-24 years.
- Except for hepatitis-B, genital herpes and HIV infections, all other diseases are completely curable, if detected early and treated properly.

Transmission of STDs

- STDs are transmitted through various means, primarily involving sexual contact.
- STIs like hepatitis-B and HIV can also be transmitted by
  - Sharing of contaminated injection or needles, surgical instruments, etc., with infected persons.
  - Transfusion of blood.
  - From infected mother to foetus.

Symptoms of STDs

- The early symptoms of STDs are minor and include itching, fluid discharge, slight pain, swellings, etc., in the genital region.
- Infected females may often be asymptomatic and hence may remain undetected for long.
- Absence or less significant symptoms may lead to complications later, which include **Pelvic Inflammatory Diseases** (PIDs), abortions, still births, ectopic pregnancies, infertility or even cancer of the reproductive tract.
- The patients also remain undetected due to the following reasons
  - The absence or less significant symptoms in early stages of infection.
  - Social stigma attached to the STDs.

Preventive Measures for STDs

- Prevention or early detection and cure of STDs is given prime consideration under the RCH programmes.
- One should not panic because prevention from STDs is possible and one could be free of these infections by following these simple principles, which are given below
  - Avoid sex with unknown/multiple partners.
  - Avoid unprotected sexual intercourse, always use condoms.
  - Use sterilised needles and syringes.
  - In case of doubt, consult a doctor as early as possible for early detection and get completely treated if diagnosed with disease.

3.3 Infertility

- The biological inability of a person to conceive inspite of regular unprotected coitus is referred to as **infertility**. It is also one of the major aspects of reproductive health.
- A large number of couples all over the world including India are infertile.
- The reasons for infertility could be related to many individual aspects such as physical, congenital, diseases, drugs, immunological or even psychological.
- In India, for the couple being child less, only the female is blamed, but the problem may also lie in the male partner.
- Specialised infertility clinics could help these couples in diagnosis and provision of proper treatment, thus enabling them to have children.
- This can be done with the help of the following techniques

Assisted Reproductive Technologies (ARTs)

- The infertile couples could be assisted to have children in special healthcare units (infertility clinics, etc.) through certain special techniques called **Assisted Reproductive Technologies** (ARTs).
- This is done after diagnosis of reproductive disorders.
- ART is also used for couples, who are suffering from certain diseases like AIDS to reduce the risk of infection to child, when the pregnancy is desired.
- Some of the prominent techniques under ART are as follows

1. *In Vitro* Fertilisation (IVF) or Test Tube Baby Programme

- It is a technique of initiating the fertilisation process outside the female body.
- In IVF method, ova from the wife or a female donor and the sperms from the husband or the male donor are collected and are induced to form a zygote under simulated conditions *in vitro* (outside the female body).
- It is also termed as **test tube baby programme** as the initial process is carried out in laboratory.
- The zygote or early embryo with upto 8 blastomeres is then transferred inside the body of female for further development.

2. ZIFT and IUT

- When the 8-celled blastomere stage of embryo, obtained by *in vitro* fertilisation is transferred into the Fallopian tube, the process is termed as **Zygote Intra Fallopian Transfer** (ZIFT).
- On the other hand, when the embryo with more than 8-celled blastomere stage is placed directly into the lining of the uterus to complete its further development, it is termed as **Intra Uterine Transfer** (IUT).

3. *In Vivo* Fertilisation

- This involves formation of embryo within the female body once the gametes have fused successfully.
- Embryos thus formed could also be used for such transfer to assist those females who cannot conceive.
- A developing embryo is implanted in the uterus of another female.
- A woman who substitutes or takes place of the real mother to nurse the embryo is called **surrogate mother**.

4. Gamete Intra-Fallopian Transfer (GIFT)

In this technique, the ovum collected from donor is transferred to the Fallopian tube of another female, who cannot produce ova, but can provide a suitable environment for fertilisation and further development.

5. Intra-Cytoplasmic Sperm Injection (ICSI)

- In this, a single sperm is carefully injected into an egg in laboratory using a micro needle.
- It is beneficial in case of male infertility, where sperm count is low or in case of absence of sperms.

6. Artificial Insemination (AI) Technique

- In AI, the semen is collected either from the husband or a healthy donor and then artificially introduced into the vagina or into the uterus, i.e. **IUI** (**Intra Uterine Insemination**) of the female.
- It is commonly used in cases where male partners are unable to inseminate the female due to very low sperm counts in the ejaculate.
- All these techniques require extremely high precision, specialised persons and expensive instruments. Therefore, there are only few such centres in the country and hence their benefits are obtained only by limited persons.

> **Quick Test 3**
>
> **1. State True or False.**
> Gonorrhoea and chlamydiasis can be transferred by sharing contaminated injections.
>
> **2.** State one symptom that may be caused if an STD remains undetected for a long time.
>
> **3.** If a woman is unable to conceive because of the administration of contraceptive pills, is she considered infertile?
>
> **4.** Suggest an appropriate ART for a couple in which the female is unable to produce ova, but can provide a suitable medium for fertilisation and implantation.
>
> **5.** Name the technique in which sperm is injected into
> (i) the vagina of the female (ii) the egg of the female

Mind Map

Reproductive Health

Reproductive and Child Healthcare Programme

It is a part of family planning programme initiated in India (1951) to attain total reproductive health as social goal.

Population Explosion

It is a rapid increase in population over a relatively short period. Reasons for the population explosion may be
(a) Decline in mortality, MMR and IMR.
(b) Inclination in number of people in reproducible age.

Population Growth

- Natality and immigration contribute to increase in the population size.
- Whereas, mortality and emigration contribute to decrease in the population.

Measures to Control Population Growth

- Raising of marriageable age of girls to 18 years and 21 years in case of boys.
- By giving incentives to the couples with small families.
- Motivate small families by using various contraceptive methods.

Sexually Transmitted Infections (STIs)

- Also called **Venereal Disease** (VD) or **Reproductive Tract Infection** (RTI)
- STIs is caused by
  - **Bacteria** - Gonorrhea, syphilis, chlamydiasis
  - **Viruses** - Genital herpes, genital warts, HIV-AIDS, hepatitis-B
  - **Protozoa** - Trichomoniasis
- Except for hepatitis-B, genital herpes and HIV infection, other diseases are completely curable, if treated early and properly.

Preventive Measures for STDs

- Avoiding sex with unknown/multiple partners.
- Always use condoms during coitus.
- Use sterilised needles and syringes.
- Awareness about STDs.
- Consult a doctor as early as possible for detection and get completely treated if diagnosed with disease.

Birth Control

Regulation of conception by preventive methods or devices that limit the number of offspring.

Methods of Birth Control

Natural Method
- **Periodic Abstinence**
  - Avoiding coitus during fertile period (from 10-17 days of menstrual cycle).
- **Coitus Interruptus**
  - Withdrawal of penis from vagina just before ejaculation.
- **Lactational Amenorrhea**
  - Absence of menstruation during period of intense lactation following parturition.

Barrier Method
- **Condoms**
  - For both males and females.
- **Diaphragms, Cervical Caps and Vaults.**
  - Inserted into female reproductive tract.
- **Spermicidal creams, jellies and foams.**

Intra-Uterine Devices
- Inserted into the uterus through vagina.
- **Non-medicated IUDs** (Increase phagocytosis of sperms within uterus, e.g. Lippes loop)
- **Copper releasing IUDs** (Copper suppresses sperm motility, e.g. CuT, Multiload 375).
- **Hormone releasing IUDs** (Make uterus unsuitable for conception, e.g. Progestasert, LNG -20).

Chemical Method
- To prevent ovulation
- **Oral Contraceptives**
  - Progestogen or Progestogen+ Oestrogen combination pill (e.g. Mala-D).
  - Non-steroidal pill (e.g. Saheli).
- **Emergency pills**
  - within 72 hrs of coitus.
- **Injections**
  - Progestogen/Progestogen-oestrogen (every 3 months).
- **Implants**
  - Progestogen
  - Progestogen-oestrogen patches (under skin).

Surgical/Sterilisation Method
- Highly effective, but poor reversibility.
- **Tubectomy**
  - A small part of Fallopian tube is removed or tied.
- **Vasectomy**
  - A small part of vas deferens is removed or tied.

Infertility

- It is the biological inability of a person to conceive inspite of regular unprotected coitus.
- It is mainly of two types, i.e. primary and secondary infertility.

Medical Termination of Pregnancy (MTP)

- Voluntary or intentional abortion performed to terminate pregnancy before completion of full term.
- Legalised by Indian government in 1971.
- **Safer during the first trimester of pregnancy**
- Illegal use of MTP - After misuse of amniocentesis for female foeticide.

Assisted Reproductive Technology

It is the methods used to achieve pregnancy by artificial means to help infertile couples in having children.

Techniques of ARTs

In Vitro Fertilisation (IVF)
- Fertilisation outside the body in simulated conditions followed by embryo transfer.
- **Test Tube Baby Program**
  - Collection of ova (♀) and sperm (♂)

IVF
↓
Embryo Transfer

- Upto 8 blastomeres → ZIFT (Zygote Intra Fallopian Transfer)
- More than 8 blastomeres → IUT (Intra Uterine Transfer)

Gamete - Intra Fallopian Transfer (GIFT)

Transfer of an ovum collected from a donor to Fallopian tube of another female who cannot produce ova, but can provide suitable conditions for fertilisation and further development of foetus.

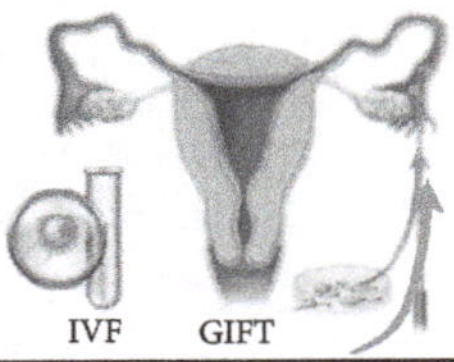

IVF GIFT

Intra Cytoplasmic Sperm Injection (ICSI)

Sperm is directly injected into the ovum to form an embryo in the laboratory followed by embryo transfer.

ICSI

Artificial Insemination
- Used in case of low sperm count and inability of male to inseminate the females.
- Semen → artificially introduced into vagina or uterus (IUI).

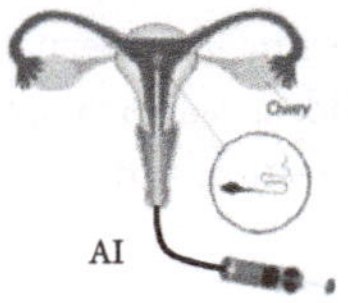

AI

EXAM PATTERN QUESTIONS

Objective Type Questions

Multiple Choice Questions

1. Which of the following statement is incorrect regarding reproductive health?

(a) A society with people having physically normal reproductive organs is one of the important aspect of being reproductively healthy.

(b) According to health association reproductive health is the well being of physical and behavioural aspect

(c) Functionally normal reproductive organs and normal emotional and behavioural interaction is also associated with reproductive health.

(d) Family planning programme was initiated in 1951 to attain total reproductive health as a social goal.

Ans. (*b*)

2. Amniocentesis is a medical procedure where some of the amniotic fluid of the developing foetus is drawn to analyse the foetal cells and dissolved substances. It was banned in India around 1994 under the Pre-conception and Prenatal Diagnostic Techniques Act in order to stop female foeticides. Which of the following highlight the importance of amniocentesis despite the ban? CBSE CFPQ

(a) Identification of a decline in sex ratio

(b) Prevention of sexually transmitted diseases

(c) Determination of biological sex of the unborn baby

(d) Detection of genetic disorders

Ans. (*d*)

3. Amniocentesis is a technique that is used to CBSE 2024 C

(a) determine any disease of the heart

(b) determine any genetic disorder of the foetus

(c) determine any disorder of the brain

(d) detect any abnormality in the bone formation

Ans. (*b*)

4. Which of the following is an indicator of a reproductively unhealthy society? Competency Based Que.

(a) Increase in infant mortality rate

(b) Decline in maternal mortality rate

(c) Widespread awareness of contraceptive methods

(d) Detection and cure of sexually transmitted diseases

Ans. (*a*)

5. Increased IMR and decreased MMR in a population will NCERT Exemplar, Competency Based Que.

(a) cause rapid increase in growth rate

(b) result in decline in growth rate

(c) not cause significant change in growth rate

(d) result in an explosive population

Ans. (*c*) **IMR** (Infant Mortality Rate) and **MMR** (Maternal Mortality Rate) both are responsible for affecting the growth rate inversely. It means decline in IMR as well as MMR will result in high population growth and *vice-versa.*

Therefore, in the above situation, if IMR has been increased and MMR has been decreased in a population, it will not cause any significant change in growth rate.

6. All of the following are the consequences of over population except

(a) it increases the poverty of a country

(b) it leads to the shortage of food supply

(c) it results in unemployment

(d) it contributes to economic growth

Ans. (*d*)

7. Intensely lactating mothers do not generally conceive due to the NCERT Exemplar, Competency Based Que.

(a) suppression of gonadotropins

(b) hypersecretion of gonadotropins

(c) suppression of gametic transport

(d) suppression of fertilisation

Ans. (*a*) Breastfeeding reduces fertility by affecting the production of certain reproductive hormones. It is known to suppress the production of **Gonadotropin Releasing Hormone** (GnRH) and **Follicle Stimulating Hormone** (FSH) which triggers ovulation. It also leads to increased level of prolactin, a hormone that inhibits ovulation.

8. Diaphragms are contraceptive devices used by the females. Choose the correct option from the statements given below.

I. They are introduced into the uterus.

II. They are placed to cover the cervical region.

III. They act as physical barriers for sperm entry.

IV. They act as spermicidal agents.

(a) I and II (b) I and III (c) II and III (d) III and IV

Ans. (*c*)

9. **Choose the correct option from *A*, *B* and *C*.**

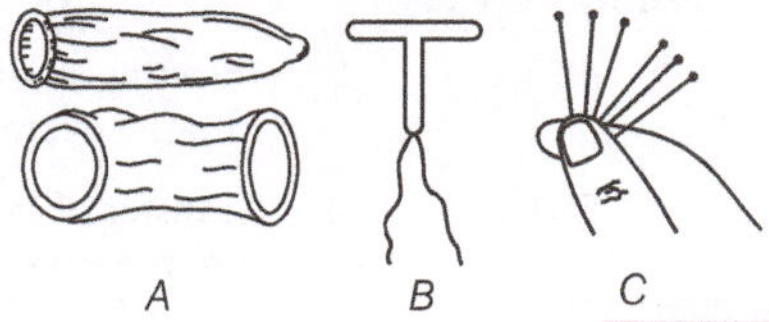

Competency Based Que.

(a) *A*–Condoms, *B*–Copper-T, *C*–Implants
(b) *A*–Tubectomy, *B*–Implants, *C*–Copper-T
(c) *A*–Vasectomy, *B*–Condoms, *C*–Copper-T
(d) *A*–Copper-T, *B*–Condoms, *C*–Implants

Ans. (*a*)

10. **The mode of action of the copper ions in an IUD is to**

CBSE SQP 2021 Term-I

(a) increase the movement of sperms
(b) decrease the movement of the sperms
(c) make the uterus unsuitable for implantation
(d) make the cervix hostile to the sperms

Ans. (*b*)

11. **An IUD recommended to promote the cervix hostility to the sperms is** CBSE 2021 Term-I

(a) Cu-T (b) Multiload-375 (c) LNG-20 (d) Cu-7

Ans. (*c*)

12. **Which of the following is hormone releasing IUD?**

(a) LNG-20 (b) Multiload-375
(c) Lippes loop (d) Cu-7

Ans. (*a*)

13. **Identify the correct statements with respect to Saheli?**

I. It is twice a week pill with very few side effects.
II. It was developed by CDRI, Lucknow.
III. It is an oral pill containing non-steroidal preparations.
IV. This pills are for women, but have low contraceptive value.

Choose the correct option.

(a) I and II (b) II and III (c) II and III (d) III and IV

Ans. (*c*)

14. **Sterilisation techniques are generally full proof methods of contraception with least side effects. Yet, this is the last option for the couples because**

I. it is almost irreversible.
II. of the misconception that it will reduce sexual urge/drive.
III. it is a surgical procedure.
IV. of lack of sufficient facilities in many parts of the country.

Choose the correct option.

(a) I and III (b) II and III
(c) II and IV (d) I, II, III and IV

Ans. (*a*)

15. **Given below are the four methods and their modes of action in achieving contraception. Select their correct matching from the four options that follows.**

Column I (Birth control measures)		Column II (Modes of action)	
A.	Pill	1.	Prevents sperms reaching cervix
B.	Condom	2.	Prevents implantation
C.	Vasectomy	3.	Prevents ovulation
D.	Copper-T	4.	Semen contains no sperms

Codes

	A	B	C	D		A	B	C	D
(a)	3	4	1	2	(b)	2	3	1	4
(c)	3	1	4	2	(d)	4	1	2	3

Ans. (*c*)

16. **Following statements are given regarding MTP. Choose the correct option given below.**

I. MTPs are generally advised during first trimester.
II. MTPs are used as a contraceptive method.
III. MTPs are always surgical.
IV. MTPs require the assistance of qualified medical personnel.

(a) II and III (b) II and III (c) I and IV (d) I and II

Ans. (*c*)

17. **Given below are four aspects of reproductive health in Column I and their related information in Column II.** CBSE 2023

Column I (Terms used in reproductive health)		Column II (Significant information)	
A.	MTP	1.	Analysing foetal cells from amniotic fluid of the foetus
B.	Amniocentesis	2.	Legalised in 1971
C.	Saheli	3.	Programme initiated in 1951
D.	Family planning	4.	Non-steroidal oral contraceptive

Codes

	A	B	C	D		A	B	C	D
(a)	4	2	3	1	(b)	2	1	4	3
(c)	1	3	2	4	(d)	2	1	3	4

Ans. (*b*)

18. **Identify the disease which is not a sexually transmitted disease.** CBSE 2021 Term-I

(a) Gonorrhoea (b) Syphilis
(c) Amoebiasis (d) Chlamydiasis

Ans. (*c*)

19. **A couple can be infertile because of**

A. physical defect

B. congenital defect

C. psychological defect

D. genetic haemolysis

V. Down's syndrome

(a) A, C, D, E (b) B, C and E

(c) C, D and E (d) A, B and C

Ans. (*d*)

20. **Assisted reproductive technology does not include**

(a) zygote extra Fallopian transfer

(b) *in vitro* fertilisation and embryo transfer

(c) artificial insemination

(d) gamete intra Fallopian transfer

Ans. (*a*)

21. **Choose the correct statement regarding the ZIFT procedure.**

(a) Ova collected from a female donor are transferred to the Fallopian tube to facilitate zygote formation

(b) Zygote is collected from a female donor and transferred to the Fallopian tube

(c) Zygote is collected from a female donor and transferred to the uterus

(d) Ova collected from a female donor and transferred to the uterus

Ans. (*b*)

22. **Embryo with more than 16 blastomeres formed due to *in vitro* fertilisation is transferred into**

(a) uterus (b) Fallopian tube

(c) fimbriae (d) cervix

Ans. (*a*)

23. **A female undergoing IVF treatment has blocked Fallopian tubes. The technique by which the embryo with more than 8 blastomeres will be transferred into the female for further development is** **CBSE SQP 2021 Term-I**

(a) ZIFT (b) GIFT (c) IUT (d) AI

Ans. (*c*)

24. **Given below are Column I with a list of certain Assisted Reproductive Technologies (ARTs) and in Column II the procedures followed during ART.** **CBSE 2023**

	Column I (Names of ART)		Column II (Procedures)
A.	GIFT	1.	Transfer of ovum from a donor into the Fallopian tube of another female.
B.	ICSI	2.	Transfer of semen from the donor into the vagina of the female.
C.	ZIFT	3.	Injecting sperms directly into the ovum.
D.	IUI	4.	Transfer of early embryos into the Fallopian tube.

Choose the option where ART correctly matches with the procedure.

	A	B	C	D		A	B	C	D
(a)	1	2	3	4	(b)	4	1	2	3
(c)	4	3	1	2	(d)	1	3	4	2

Ans. (*d*)

Assertion-Reason Questions

Direction (Q. Nos. 1-15) *In each of the following questions, a statement of Assertion (A) is given and followed by corresponding statement of Reason (R). Of the statements, mark the correct answer as*

(a) If both A and R are true and R is the correct explanation of A.

(b) If both A and R are true, but R is not the correct explanation of A.

(c) If A is true, but R is false.

(d) If A is false, but R is true.

1. **Assertion** (A) Reproductive and Child Healthcare (RCH) programme is for reproduction related areas.

Reason (R) It deals with creating awareness among various reproduction related aspects.

Ans. (*a*)

2. **Assertion** (A) Amniocentesis is often misused.

Reason (R) It is meant for determining the genetic disorders in the foetus, but it is being used to determine the sex of the foetus, leading to increase in the female foeticide.

Ans. (*a*)

3. **Assertion** (A) Family planning is done by using contraceptive methods.

Reason (R) Natural contraceptive methods include condoms, diaphragms, etc., while barrier methods include periodic abstinence, lactational amenorrhea, etc.

Ans. (*c*)

4. **Assertion** (A) Periodic abstinence is a method in which couples avoid coitus from day 10 to 17 of menstrual cycle.

Reason (R) Periodic abstinence has limited effectiveness because menstrual cycles are not always regulaer. **CBSE 2024 C**

Ans. (*a*)

5. Assertion (A) Periodic abstinence is a natural method of birth control where couples avoid intercourse from day 10 to 17 of the menstrual cycle.

Reason (R) Ovulation occurs around the middle of the menstrual cycle. **Competency Based Que.**

Ans. (*a*)

6. Assertion (A) Lactational amenorrhea is the natural method of contraception.

Reason (R) It increases the phagocytosis of sperm. **CBSE SQP 2021 Term-I**

Ans. (*c*)

7. Assertion (A) Contraceptives are methods to prevent unwanted pregnancies.

Reason (R) Unwanted pregnancies can only be prevented by using oral contraceptives.

Ans. (*c*)

8. Assertion (A) Cu-T, Cu-7 and LNG-20 are the most widely used copper-releasing IUDs.

Reason (R) Cu-ions in IUDs effectively suppress sperm motility and the fertilising capacity of sperms. **CBSE 2025**

Ans. (*d*) A is false, and R is true. A can be corrected as Cu-T and Cu-7 are copper-releasing IUDs, while LNG-20 is a hormone-releasing IUD.

9. Assertion (A) Saheli, an oral contraceptive for females, contains a steroidal preparation.

Reason (R) It is 'once a week' pill with very few side effects. **CBSE SQP 2021 Term-I**

Ans. (*d*) A is false, but R is true. A can be corrected as Saheli, an oral contraceptive for females, contains non-steroidal preparation.

10. Assertion (A) Mode of action of pills and implants/injectables is similar.

Reason (R) The effective period of pills is much longer as compared to implants/injectables. **CBSE 2025**

Ans. (*d*)A is true and R is false and R can be corrected as, The effective period of implants/injectables is much longer compared to pills.

11. Assertion (A) Sterilisation is a surgical method of contraception.

Reason (R) It blocks gamete transport and thereby prevents conceptin.

Ans. (*a*)

12. Assertion (A) Vasectomy is a sterilisation procedure advised for females as a terminal method.

Reason (R) In vasectomy, a small part of the vas deferens is removed or tied by blocking gamete transport therefore preventing conception. **CBSE 2021 Term-I**

Ans. (*d*)

13. Assertion (A) Determining the sex of an unborn child followed by MTP is an illegal practice.

Reason (R) Amniocentesis is a practice to test the presence of genetic disorders also. **CBSE 2023**

Ans. (*b*)

14. Assertion (A) Very often persons suffering from Sexually Transmitted Diseases (STDs) do not go for timely detection and proper treatment.

Reason (R) Absence or less significant symptoms in the early stages of STDs and the social stigma attached to the disease. **CBSE 2021 Term-I**

Ans. (*a*)

15. Refer to the given diagrams of *in vitro* fertilisation technique used to help couples with fertility. Comment upon the appropriateness of the Assertion and the Reason. **Competency Based Que.**

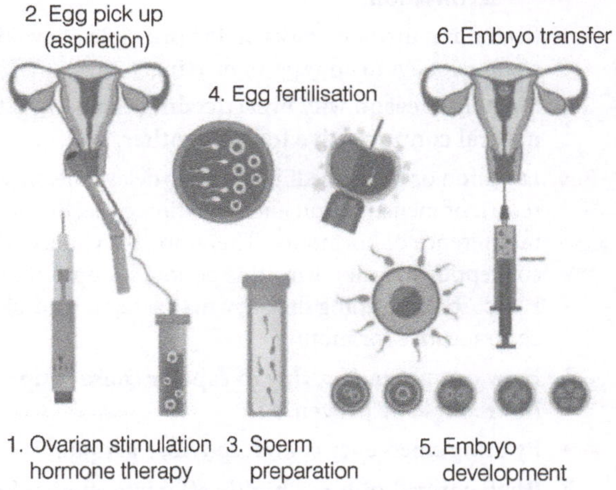

Assertion (A) IVF is one of the widely known types of ART.

Reason (R) It guarantees the chance of conceiving and thereby pregnancy.

Ans. (*c*) A is true, but R is false. R can be corrected as IVF is definitely known to increase chances of fertility in couples which fail to be parents, however the technique does not guarantee the pregnancy as the technique does not work for everybody.

Subjective Questions

Very Short Answer Type Questions

1. Reproductive health refers only to healthy reproductive functions. Comment. NCERT Exemplar

Ans. No, reproductive health refers to the total well-being in all aspects of reproduction, i.e. physical, emotional, psychological and social.

2. In which year, a national level approach to build up a reproductively healthy society was taken up in our country?

Ans. 1951

3. Overpopulation has become a serious problem in the developing countries. Tell us why?

Ans. Overpopulation can exhaust natural resources and create severe complication for survival, socio-economic problems, pollution, etc.

4. Which of the following is true for the natural method of birth control?

(i) They employ barriers to prevent fertilisation.

(ii) They avoid chance meeting of gametes to prevent fertilisation.

Ans. (ii) Natural method works on the principle of avoiding the chances of ovum and sperm meeting.

5. State one reason why breastfeeding the baby acts as a natural contraceptive for the mother.

Ans. Lactation or breastfeeding the baby delays the onset or return of menstruation and ovulation cycle, due to interference of hormones. Therefore, the chances of conception are nil during this period, i.e. upto six months. Hence, breastfeeding the baby may act as a natural contraceptive for mother.

6. How can pregnancy due to rape or causal unprotected intercourse be prevented?

Ans. By using emergency contraceptives, e.g. i-pill.

7. Birth control pills are highly effective when taken regularly. Name the contraceptive recently developed at CDRI, Lucknow.

Ans. Saheli is an once a week oral contraceptive developed at CDRI, Lucknow.

8. Why is tubectomy considered a contraceptive method?

Ans. In tubectomy, a small part of the Fallopian tube is cut and tied up. This prevents egg to reach Fallopian tube, thus help in contraception.

9. Give two reasons why a person infected with a venereal disease does not go for timely detection and treatment of it.

Ans. Two reasons are as follows

(i) Absence of significant symptoms at earlier stage.

(ii) Social stigma attached to the STDs. (½ × 2)

10. Name the complication that arises due to late detection of STDs.

Ans. Late detection of STDs leads to pelvic inflammatory diseases, abortions, still birth, ectopic pregnancies, infertility or even cancer of reproductive tract.

11. State the statement given below as true/false with explanation.
Infertility is defined as the inability to produce a viable offspring and is always due to abnormalities/defects in the female partner. NCERT

Ans. False, infertility is defined as biological inability of a person to conceive inspite of regular unprotected coitus and often female is blamed for the couple being childless, but more often the problem lies in male partner.

12. Give some reasons for infertility among young couples.

Ans. Drugs, congenital disease and smoking, etc.

13. Name the assisted reproductive technology depicted in the image given below. Competency Based Que.

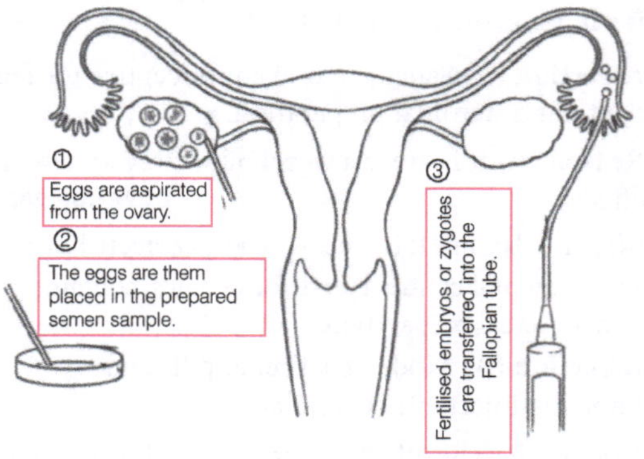

Ans. ZIFT (Zygote Intra Fallopian Transfer) is depicted in the image given in question.

14. What is the method of directly injecting a sperm into ovum called as?

Ans. Intra-cytoplasmic sperm injection

Short Answer Type Questions

1. Briefly describe the aims and measures of reproductive and child healthcare programmes in India.

Or **Comment on the Reproductive and Child Healthcare Programme of the government to improve the reproductive health of the people.** NCERT Exemplar

Ans. Refer to text on page no. 67 and 68.

2. What are the 4 major objectives of RCH? **Diksha**

Ans. Refer to text on page no. 68.

3. Suggest some important steps that you would recommend to be taken to improve the reproductive health standards in India.

Ans. Some important steps to improve the reproductive health standards in India are as follows

- Creation of awareness in reproductive and child healthcare.
- Proper medical and emotional support to infertile couples.
- Introduction of sex education in school.
- Educating people about birth control method, safe and hygienic sexual practices, etc. (½ × 4)

4. Discuss the reproduction related aspects for which counselling should be provided at the school level.

Ans. Refer to text on page no. 68.

5. Is sex education necessary in schools? Why? **NCERT**

Ans. Yes, sex education is necessary in schools because

(i) The children should know about sex-related issues and problems like adolescence changes, menstrual cycle, menstrual problems, unwanted pregnancy, unsafe abortion, reproductive tract infections and STDs.

(ii) They should be aware of changes happening in their body and should be taught about healthy habits including personal cleanliness and hygiene.

(iii) Counselling and awareness regarding reproductive organs, safe and hygienic sexual practices will play an important role in making people reproductively healthy. (1 × 3)

6. What do you think in the significance of reproductive health in a society? **NCERT**

Ans. Significance of reproductive health in a society are as follows

(i) Control over the transmission of STDs.

(ii) Less deaths due to reproduction related diseases like AIDS, cancer of reproductive tract.

(iii) Control in population explosion.

(iv) Reproductive health of men and women will affects the health of the next generation in a positive way. (½ × 4)

7. Suggest the aspects of reproductive health which need to be given special attention in the present scenario. **NCERT**

Ans. Special attention needs to be given to the following aspects

(i) Educating people (starting from age group above 12 years) about reproductive system, processes and practices and importance of safe and responsible sex. (1)

(ii) Providing education about harmful sexual practices, unwanted pregnancy, unsafe abortion, reproductive tract infections and cancers, gender based responsibilities and gender equality in making decisions about sex, etc. (1)

(iii) Establishing proper systems of education, counselling, prevention, detection and management of health problems, care and rehabilitation and ensuring easy accessibility of appropriate services. (1)

8. Do you think that reproductive health in our country has improved in the past 50 years? If yes, mention some such areas of improvement. **NCERT**

Ans. Yes, the reproductive health has improved in India, in terms of

(i) reduced maternal and infant mortality rates.

(ii) early detection and cure of STDs.

(iii) assistance to infertile couples.

(iv) availability of a variety of methods for family planning.

(v) availability of maternal and child healthcare programmes.

(vi) introduction of sex education in schools. (½ × 6)

9. Consider the given image and answer the questions that follows. **Competency Based Que.**

(i) Identify and describe the procedure as shown.

(ii) How this procedure is being misused?

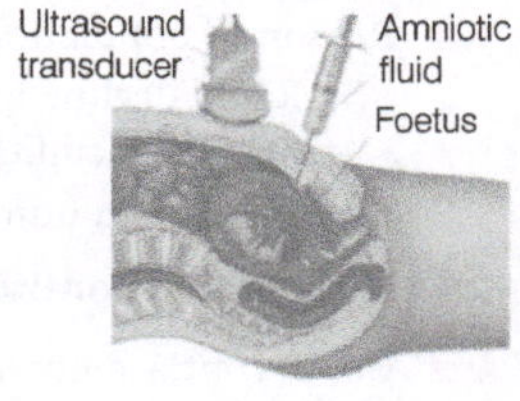

Ans. (i) Amniocentesis is depicted in the given image. In this technique small amount of amniotic fluid surrounding the developing foetus is taken and is then examined for genetic abnormalities.

(ii) This technique is misused for sex-determination followed by abortion of female foetus (female foeticide) (1)

10. Explain what is meant by the term amniocentesis. How is this technique misused in India.? **CBSE 2025**

Ans. Amniocentesis is a foetal sex-determination test based on the chromosomal pattern in cells extracted from the amniotic fluid, surrounding the developing embryo. It is misused for determining the sex of the foetus and aborting the child if it is a female. (1 + 2)

11. If implementation of better techniques and new strategies are required to provide more efficient care and assistance to people, then why is there a statutory ban on amniocentesis? Write the use of this technique and give reason to justify the ban.

Or **Amniocentesis for sex-determination is banned in our country. Is this ban necessary? Comment.** **NCERT**

Or **Do you justify the statutory ban on amniocentesis in our country? Gives reasons.** **NCERT Exemplar**

Ans. Refer to text on page no. 68.

12. (i) List the four major causes of increasing population in our country that you would like to speak on to your fellow students.

(ii) **Write any two steps that you would stress upon to control the population explosion.** **CBSE 2020**

Ans. (i) Four major causes of increasing population in our country are
(a) Ignorance and complete lack of awareness about the adverse effects of increasing population especially in rural regions.
(b) Increase in the population of young reproductive age group.
(c) Social stigmas about girl child and desire to have boy child.
(d) Rapid decline in death rate and increase in birth rate. (½ × 4)

(ii) Two steps that can control population explosion
(a) Planning small families.
(b) Use of contraceptives like condoms to avoid unwanted pregnancies. (1)

13. What are the suggested reasons for the population explosion? **NCERT**

Ans. Reason of population explosion are
(i) Rapid decline in the overall death rate because of better medical facilities.
(ii) Increase in number of people in reproducible age. (1×2)

14. Is the use of contraceptives justified? Give reasons. **NCERT**

Ans. Use of contraceptives is justified due to the following reasons
(i) In the absence of contraceptives, the population growth rate will rise at an explosive rate and there will be scarcity of even the basic necessities.

As Earth's resources are limited. We have already started facing the problems of overcrowding, food price inflation, power and water shortage, etc. Further increase in population will only aggrevate the situation.

(ii) Contraceptives provide an option for planning the family by spacing the pregnancies and avoiding unwanted pregnancies.
(iii) Contraceptives also guard against STDs to some extent. (1×3)

15. Mention two advantages of lactational amenorrhea as a contraceptive method. **NCERT Exemplar**

Ans. The two advantages of lactational amenorrhea as a contraceptive method are mentioned as below
(i) If the mother is breastfeeding completely, she would not ovulate, so chances of conception would be low.
(ii) She would not need to use any pill or devices for birth control. So, there will be no side effects. (1×2)

16. (i) List any four characteristics of an ideal contraceptive.
(ii) Name two intra uterine contraceptive devices that affect the motility of sperms.

Ans. (i) Refer to text on page no. 69. (½ × 4)
(ii) Refer to text on page no. 70. (1)

17. (i) Name any two copper releasing IUDs.
(ii) Explain how do they act as effective contraceptives in human females.

Ans. (i) Cu-T, Cu-7 and Multiload-375. (1)
(ii) IUDs function by either of the following mechanisms
(a) Suppress sperm motility or fertilising capacity of sperms.
(b) Increase phagocytosis of sperms within the uterus. (1 + 1)

18. Answer the following
(i) What are IUDs?
(ii) List out its types with examples.
(iii) How do they prevent conception?

Ans. Refer to text on page no. 70. (1×3)

19. (i) Explain the mode of action of Cu^{++} releasing IUDs as a good contraceptive. How is hormone releasing IUD different from it ?
(ii) Why is 'Saheli' a preferred contraceptive by women (any two reasons)? **CBSE 2020**

Ans. (i) Cu^{++} ions-releasing IUDs are more efficient methods of contraception because
(a) Cu^{++} ions suppress sperm motility and fertilising capacity of sperms.
(b) It increases phagocytosis of sperms within the uterus.
(c) It is one of the safest, long-term, most effective, convenient and least expensive and reversible contraceptives available.

The hormone releasing IUDs on the other hand make the uterus unsuitable for implantation and the cervix hostile to sperms. (2)

(ii) Saheli is a preferred contraceptive method by women because
(a) It is taken once in a week.
(b) It has very few side effects and high contraceptive value. (1)

20. How do 'implants' act as an effective method of contraception in human females ? Mention their one advantage over contraceptive pills. **CBSE 2024 C**

Ans. Contraceptives in the form of progestogen or a combination of progestogen and oestrogen can also be used as injections or implants under the skin. These implants are very effective because they stop ovulation and block sperm from reaching the egg. They either prevent fertilisation or stop the embryo from attaching to the uterus. The implants also help the egg move quickly through the Fallopian tube and uterus before fertilisation can happen.

Advantage: One advantage of implants is that they are effective for up to 72 hours after intercourse.

21. State the composition and principle of oral pills as a contraceptive measure taking the example of Saheli. CBSE SQP

Ans. Saheli is a non-steroidal preparation that carries out effective contraceptive functions. These pills inhibit ovulation and implantation and alter the quality of cervical mucus to prevent or retard the entry of sperms.

22. Name two hormones that are constituents of contraceptive pills. Why do they have high and effective contraceptive value? Name a commonly prescribed non-steroidal oral pill. CBSE 2016

Ans. Two hormones that are constituents of contraceptive pills are progestogen or progesterone-oestrogen combination. (1)

These hormones have high and effective contraception value, since they inhibit ovulation or implantation or alter the quality of cervical mucus to retard the entry of sperm and prevent conception. A commonly prescribed non-steroidal oral pill is Saheli. (2)

23. Explain the mode of action of contraceptive pills taken by human females. Mention the schedule to be followed for effective outcome. CBSE 2024

Ans. Pills contain progestogens or progestogen–oestrogen combination. They inhibit ovulation, and implantation as well as, alter the quality of cervical mucus to prevent or retard the entry of sperms.

Pills have to be taken daily for a period of 21 days starting within first five days of menstrual cycle. After a gap of 7 days it has to be repeated in the same pattern till the female desires to prevent conception.

24. Correct the following statements.
 (i) Surgical methods of contraception prevent gamete formation.
 (ii) Oral pills are very popular contraceptives among the rural women. NCERT

Ans. Correct statements are given below
 (i) The surgical methods of contraception prevent gamete transfer from the organs of production to the site of fertilisation.
 (ii) Oral pills are very popular contraceptives among the urban women. (1+1)

25. Name and explain a surgical contraceptive method that can be adopted by the male partner of a couple. CBSE 2023

Ans. The surgical contraceptive method adopted by the male partner is vasectomy.

In vasectomy a surgical expert cut the vas deferens and ties the ends to stop the transport of sperms from the epididymis to the ejaculatory duct. Thus, it ensures the absence of sperm in the male ejaculation to prevent unwanted pregnancies. This procedure is performed on both the vas deferens. It is an irreversible procedure. (1+2)

26. Fed up of a large family, a couple wanted to adopt a terminal method of contraception. Describe the process conducted by the doctor in either of the cases- male /female partner. Also mention one advantage and one disadvantage of this method.

Ans. For terminal method of contraception in males and females, refer to text on page no. 71-72.

27. Given below are two statements. State whether each of them is true or false and justify, using examples.
 (i) All contraceptives have the added advantage of protection against sexually transmitted diseases.
 (ii) Natural birth control methods have negligible side effect. Competency Based Que.

Ans. (i) False, contraceptives like IUDs and pills do not protect against STDs.
 (ii) True, natural birth control methods have negligible side effect as no medicines or devices are used in natural birth control options Periodic abstinence, lactational amenorrhea and coitus interruptus are some examples of natural birth control method. (1×2)

28. Removal of gonads cannot be considered as a contraceptive option. Why? Competency Based Que., NCERT

Ans. Removal of gonads cannot be considered as a contraceptive option because it not only stops the production of gametes, but also stops the secretion of many other hormones required for normal body function.

Also, this is an irreversible method. It means once removed, gonads cannot be replaced and the person will remain infertile for whole life.

29. Observe the relation between first two words given below and give suitable word for blank. Competency Based Que.
 (i) Male : Vasectomy : : Female : …… .
 (ii) Condom : Nirodh : : Oral pill : …… .

Ans. (i) Tubectomy
 (ii) Saheli (1×2)

30. Identify *A*, *B*, *C* and *D* in the following table with reference to birth control. Competency Based Que.

Methods	Examples
A	Diaphragm
Female sterilisation	*B*
C	Saheli
D	Cu-T

Ans. *A*–Barrier, *B*–Tubectomy, *C*–Oral pill, *D*–Cu releasing IUD (½ × 4)

31. Strict conditions are to be followed in Medical Termination of Pregnancy (MTP) procedures, mention two reasons. NCERT Exemplar

Ans. Refer to text on page no. 72.

32. For performing medical termination of pregnancy strict conditions are to be followed by both the medical practitioner and the patient. Discuss why has this become necessary in India?

Ans. Refer to text on page no. 72.

33. State true/false with explanation.

(i) Natural abortions could happen spontaneously too.

(ii) Complete lactation could help as a natural method of contraception.

(iii) Creating awareness about sex-related aspects is an effective method to improve reproductive health of the people. NCERT

Ans. (i) True, natural abortion (miscarriage) also happens. This may be due to poor health of mother or poor development of foetus. Sometimes, the uterus of mother is not well developed to continue pregnancy.

(ii) True, complete lactation has been reported to be effective, but only upto a maximum period of six months following parturition.

(iii) True, awareness of sex-related issues will lead to reduction of unhealthy reproductive practices. (1 × 3)

34. All Reproductive Tract Infections (RTIs) are STDs, but all STDs are not RTIs. Justify with example.

Ans. Among the common STDs, hepatitis-B and AIDS are not infections of the reproductive organs though their mode of transmission could be through sexual contact also.

All other diseases like gonorrhoea, syphilis, genital herpes, hepatitis-B are transmitted through sexual contact and are also infections of the reproductive tract, so these are STDs as well as RTIs, whereas AIDS and hepatitis are STDs, but not RTIs. NCERT Exemplar

35. Given below are some diseases caused by different pathogens (bacteria, virus, protozoans, etc.) Syphilis, Hepatitis-B, Diphtheria, Hepatitis-A Gonorrhoea, Anthrax, Trichomoniasis.

(i) How many of these are sexually transmitted?

(ii) Give symptoms of any one of the diseases.

Ans. (i) Four among the given diseases are sexually transmitted diseases. These are syphilis, hepatitis-B, gonorrrhoea and trichomoniasis.

(ii) The symptoms of STDs include itching, fluid discharge, slight pain, swelling, etc., in the genital region. (1+1)

36. Name any two VDs which might occur in a human female. State any two complications in a female if it is left untreated. CBSE 2025

Ans. Two venereal diseases (STDs) that may occur in females are syphilis and gonorrhea. If left untreated, these can lead to Pelvic Inflammatory Disease (PID), causing infertility, chronic pelvic pain, and ectopic pregnancy. Additionally, they can result in pregnancy complications, including miscarriage, premature birth, and congenital infections in newborns. (1+1)

37. STDs can be considered as self-invited diseases. Comment. NCERT Exemplar

Ans. Sexually Transmitted Diseases (STDs) can be considered self-invited diseases because these diseases develop due to our own unsafe habits.

But one could be free of these infections by following the simple principles given below

(i) Avoid sex with unknown partners/multiple partners.

(ii) Always use condoms during coitus.

(iii) In case of doubt one should go to a qualified doctor for early detection and get complete treatment if diagnosed with disease.

If all the above said precautions are not strictly adopted by people, they are inviting STDs to infect them. (1×3)

38. An individual has tested positive for AIDS infection.

(i) Discuss the ways in which the individual could have caught this infection.

(ii) State two ways of prevention from AIDS.

Ans. (i) The ways in which the individual could have caught AIDS are as follows

- Transfusion of HIV positive blood.
- Sexual intercourse with infected partner.
- Sharing needles or surgical instruments. (2)

(ii) AIDS can be prevented by

- Avoiding intercourse with unknown/multiple partners.
- Using condoms during intercourse. (1)

39. STDs can be prevented by self-consciousness. Comment.

Ans. Refer to text on page no. 73.

40. What are the measures one has to take to prevent from contracting STDs? NCERT

Ans. Refer to text on page no. 73. (3)

41. Write the basic steps followed in the Assisted Reproductive Technologies (ARTs) programme to help childless couples. Why is it also known as test tube baby programme? CBSE 2024

Ans. Basic steps followed in Assisted Reproductive Technology are as follows

- Ova from wife or female donor and sperm from husband or male donor are collected and induced to form a zygote under simulated conditions in the laboratory (*in vitro*).
- Zygote or embryo are transferred into the female body for development. `
- It is also known as test tube baby programme because the initial process is carried out in the laboratory / *in vitro*.

(1 × 3)

42. After a brief medical examination a healthy couple came to know that both of them are unable to produce functional gametes and should look for an 'ART' (Assisted Reproductive Technique). Name the 'ART' and the procedure involved that you can suggest them to bear a child.

Ans. The ART that can be suggested to the couple in the given situation is IVF (*In Vitro* Fertilisation).

Refer to text on page no. 74.

43. (i) **Explain steps involved in *in vitro* fertilisation popularly known as test tube baby programme.**

(ii) **State the importance of this programme.**

Ans. Refer to text on page no. 74.

44. Mention the primary aim of the 'Assisted Reproductive Technology' (ART) programme. **NCERT Exemplar**

Ans. Refer to text on page no. 74.

45. An infertile couple has agreed for a test tube baby programme. Describe the procedures adopted for such technologies.

Ans. Refer to text on page no. 74.

46. Why ZIFT is a boon to childless couples? Explain the procedure.

Ans. Zygote Intra Fallopian Transfer (ZIFT) is a boon to the couple where the female cannot conceive naturally.

In this method, fertilisation is carried out *in vitro* (in the laboratory conditions) and the zygote or early embryo, formed (with upto 8-celled blastomeres) is then transferred into the Fallopian tube. (1+1)

47. Correct the following statements. **NCERT**

(i) **All STDs are completely curable.**

(ii) **In ET techniques, embryos are always transferred into the uterus.** **Competency Based Que.**

Ans. Correct statements are as follows

(i) Only a few STDs are completely curable that too, if diagnosed early and treated appropriately. (1)

(ii) In ET techniques 8-celled embryos are transferred into the Fallopian tubes and more than 8-celled embryos are generally transferred into the uterus. (1)

48. 'Intra-Cytoplasmic Sperm Injection (ICSI)' and 'Gamete Intra-Fallopian Transfer (GIFT)' are two assisted reproductive technologies. How is one different from the other?

Ans. In GIFT, the ovum from a healthy female donor is transferred to the Fallopian tube of a female, who cannot produce ova, but can provide suitable environment for fertilisation and embryo development (*in vivo* fertilisation).

While in ICSI, sperms from a donor are injected directly into the ovum, *in vitro* under simulated conditions. The embryo is later transferred to uterus or Fallopian tube for further development. (1+1)

49. In which method semen is artificially introduced into vagina? In which cases is this method adopted?

Ans. Refer to text on page no. 74.

Long Answer Type Questions

1. Discuss in your own words why the government is popularising the slogan-'Hum Do Humare Do' in both rural and urban areas of the country.

Ans. Refer to text on page no. 68-69 (Population explosion).

2. (i) **Explain one application of each one of the following**

(a) **Amniocentesis** (b) **Lactational amenorrhea**

(ii) **Prepare a poster for the school programme depicting the objectives of "Reproductive and Child Healthcare Programme".** **CBSE 2019**

Ans. (i) (a) Refer to text on page no. 68. (Amniocentesis).

(b) Refer to text on page no. 70. (Lactational amenorrhea). (2)

(ii) Student can take the help of their teacher or draw on their own. (3)

3. (i) **Name a terminal method to prevent pregnancy in humans.**

(ii) **Describe the procedure of the terminal method carried in human male and female.**

Ans. (i) A terminal method to prevent pregnancy in human is vasectomy (males) or tubectomy (females). (1)

(ii) Refer to text on page 71-72. (2+2)

4. List any four major categories into which contraception methods could be broadly classified. Explain briefly each category giving one example of each.

Ans. Refer to text on page no. 69 to 71.

5. Answer the following questions on Medical Termination of Pregnancy (MTP).

(i) **Though MTP can check population growth, it is not meant for this purpose. Give reason.**

(ii) **Why MTP is not legalised in many countries of the world?**

(iii) **Why MTP is legalised in India?**

(iv) **Is MTP considered safe at all stages of pregnancy? Comment.**

Ans. Refer to text on page no. 72.

6. Suggest some methods to assist infertile couples to have children. **NCERT**

Ans. Infertile couples can have children by using Assisted Reproductive Technologies (ARTs). Refer to text on page no. 74.

Source Based/Case Based/Passage Based Questions

1. The histogram given below shows the population of a country 'X' during different years. **Competency Based Que.**

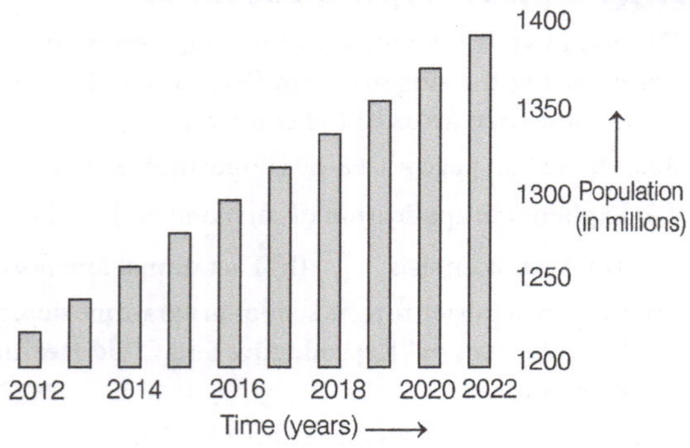

(i) What does the above graph show ?

(ii) Why do you think there is a constant increase in the size of population from 2012-2022 ?

(iii) Can you think of ways in which this growing population be controlled ? Mention any two.

Or **(iii) Is the government taking necessary steps to prevent population explosion ? Mention two such steps.**

Ans. (i) The given graph shows increase in population of the country with respect to time. (1)

(ii) Population has constantly increased due to better medical facilities leading to decreased mortality rates. Also, number of births has increased. Both of these reasons have contributed in the population growth. (1)

(iii) Growing population can be controlled by the following ways

- Practicing and encouraging birth control methods like using condoms, femidoms.
- Promoting sex education in school and raising minimum age of marriage for both boys and girls. (2)

Or (iii) Yes, the government is taking necessary steps in order to prevent population explosion. Some of these are

- Providing incentives to couples with small families.
- Statutory raising of marriageable age of girls to 18 years and that of boys to 21 years. (2)

2. A newly married couple was afraid of using contraceptive and IUDs. So, they opted for natural methods of contraception. During a random counselling session, the couple found that natural contraception is not reliable, instead they can use barrier contraceptives.

(i) Name two natural methods of contraception that could be used by this couple.

(ii) What does the contraceptive pill Saheli contain?

(iii) Mention the benefits of using barrier contraceptives.

Or (iii) Give example of any two barrier contraceptives that can be used by females (other than condoms). How they can prevent conception?

Ans. (i) Coitus interruptus and periodic abstinence are the two natural methods of contraception. (1)

(ii) Saheli is once a week contraceptive pill, which contain a non-steroidal preparation. (1)

(iii) Barrier contraceptives, i.e. condoms prevent the ovum and sperm from physical meeting to prevent fertilisation. It also protects the user from contracting sexually transmitted diseases. (2)

Or (iii) Diaphragms, cervical caps and vaults. They can prevent conception by blocking entry of sperms through cervix. (2)

3. The data given below shows the rates of sexually transmitted infections from the year 2014 to 2018.

Refer to the given data and answer the following questions.

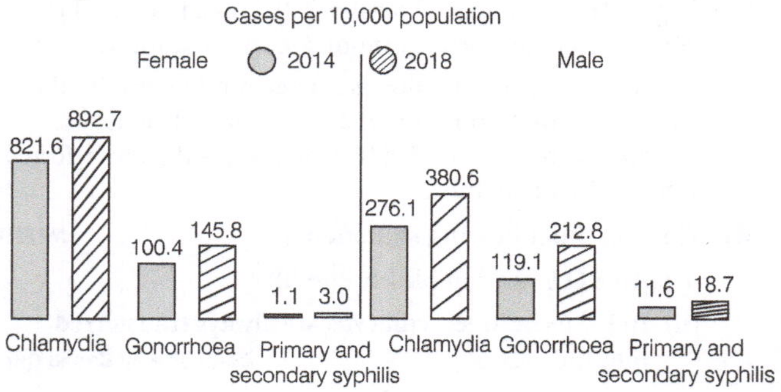

(i) Why do you think rates of STIs have increased in the duration of four years (2014-18) ?

(ii) What can be the major causes of sexually transmitted diseases/infections ?

(iii) What kind of symptoms does one experience to suspect an STI ?

Or **(iii) How can you prevent STDs ? Mention any two ways.**

Ans. (i) Rates of sexually transmitted diseases/infections have increased as people are getting less precautious. They are not using any kind of precautions like condoms in order to prevent spread of STDs. (1)

(ii) Sexually transmitted diseases/infections are mainly caused by various bacteria, viruses and some yeasts. (1)

(iii) Symptoms that one experiences to suspect sexually transmitted infection include

(a) Burning/itching in vaginal areas.

(b) Unusual discharge from the penis.

(c) Pain in pelvic/ abdominal region.

(d) Fluid discharge from the genital area. (2)

Or (iii) STDs/STIs can be prevented by the following two ways

(a) Avoiding sex with unknown/multiple partners.

(b) Using condoms during intercourse. (2)

SELF ASSESSMENT TEST

Multiple Choice Questions

1. Which of the following statements correctly represents the ideal contraceptive ?
   I. It should be easily available. II. It should be user friendly.
   III. It should be irreversible and effective. IV. It should have side effects.
   (a) I and II (b) III and IV (c) III and IV (d) I and IV
2. Which of the following is commonly called withdrawal method?
   (a) Lactational amenorrhea (b) Coitus interruptus
   (c) Periodic abstinence (d) Rhythmic method
3. Choose the right one among the statements given below. **NCERT Exemplar**
   (a) IUDs are generally inserted by the user itself (b) IUDs increase phagocytosis reaction in the uterus
   (c) IUDs suppress gametogenesis (d) IUDs once inserted need not to be replaced
4. Select the incorrect pair.
   (a) Copper releasing IUD- Multiload 375 (b) Hormone releasing IUD-Cu-7
   (c) Non-medicated IUD- Lippes loop (d) Oral pills – Saheli
5. The mode of action of oral pill is to
   (a) decrease the movement of the sperms (b) increase the movement of sperm
   (c) decrease the fertilising capacity of the sperm (d) alter the quality of cervical mucus
6. Consider the diagram given below and identify which type of contraception would be used in the part marked as *A*?

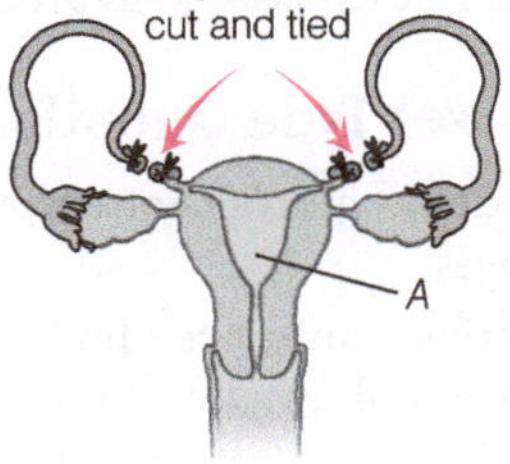

   (a) Diaphragms and vaults
   (b) LNG-20 and Cu-T
   (c) Implants and injectable
   (d) Spermicidal creams and jellies
7. Which of the following statement correctly describes artificial insemination?
   (a) It involves placing sperm directly into the female's reproductive tract to achieve pregnancy without natural mating.
   (b) It requires the extraction of eggs from the female, which are then fertilised in a laboratory.
   (c) It is a method of genetic engineering used to produce genetically modified offspring.
   (d) It refers to the introduction of sperm from a donor into the female reproductive system through natural mating.

Assertion-Reason Questions

Direction (Q. Nos. 8-11) *In each of the following questions, a statement of Assertion (A) is given followed by corresponding statement of Reason (R). Of the statements, mark the correct answer as*

(a) If both A and R are true and R is the correct explanation of A.
(b) If both A and R are true, but R is not the correct explanation of A.
(c) If A is true, but R is false.
(d) If A is false, but R is true.

8. **Assertion** (A) The rapid population growth in many countries has led to a strain on natural resources and environmental degradation.

   Reason (R) Population explosion is often caused by high birth rates, improved healthcare and lack of family planning, leading to an unsustainable increase in population.

9. **Assertion** (A) Barrier methods of contraception prevent fertilisation by physically blocking the passage of sperm into the female reproductive tract.

   Reason (R) Barrier methods, such as condoms and diaphragms, work by preventing the release of eggs from the ovaries during ovulation.

10. **Assertion** (A) Sterilisation is a permanent method of contraception.

    Reason (R) Sterilisation involves the use of hormonal injections that prevent the release of eggs or sperm during ovulation.

11. **Assertion** (A) Zygote Intra-Fallopian Transfer (ZIFT) is an advanced method of Assisted Reproductive Technology (ART) used to treat infertility.

    Reason (R) In ZIFT, fertilisation of the egg occurs outside the body and the resulting zygote is then placed into the Fallopian tube.

Very Short Answer Type Questions

12. What is the primary cause of population explosion?
13. How do oral contraceptive pills prevent pregnancy?
14. Write any two common symptoms of Sexually Transmitted Diseases (STDs).
15. At what stage embryo can be introduced in the fallopian tube in ZIFT?

Short Answer Type Questions

16. Distinguish between

    (i) Copper releasing IUDs and hormone releasing IUDs   (ii) Vasectomy and tubectomy
17. How can Sexually Transmitted Diseases (STDs) be prevented?
18. What is the role of Assisted Reproductive Technology (ART) in treating infertility?

Long Answer Type Questions

19. Explain various types of contraceptive methods along with their mechanisms of action, advantages and disadvantages.
20. Explain sterilisation as a method of contraception. Describe the different types of sterilisation procedures in both males and females with their respective labelled diagrams.
21. What is Assisted Reproductive Technology (ART)? Describe the various types of ART procedures including their advantages and disadvantages.

Case Based Question

22. Shown below are some details pertaining to an oral contraceptive pill. Carefully study them and answer the questions that follows.

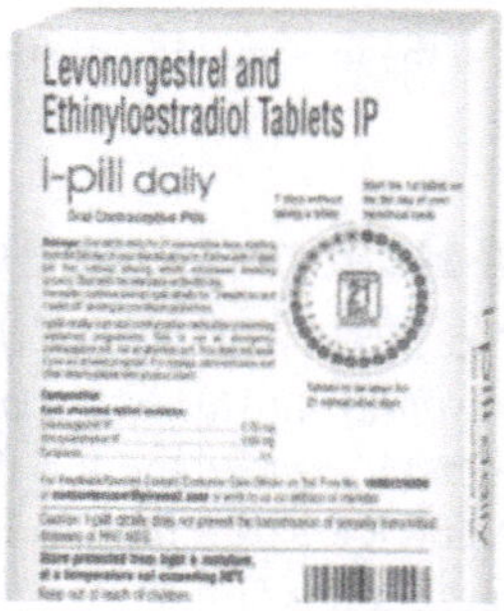

    (i) Name any two reproductive processes blocked by the oral pill shown in the diagram.

    (ii) A patient *X* took the pills as instructed for one month. Why is there a gap of 7 days after 21st day indicated on the pack?

    (iii) Patient *X* suspects that her partner is suffering from hepatitis-B. In such a situation

    (a) Would you recommend her to use oral pills shown above as the only contraceptive? Support your answer with a reason.

    (b) What is an alternative contraceptive that can be suggested to patient *X* and her partner?

Answers

1. (a)	2. (b)	3. (b)	4. (b)	5. (d)	6. (b)	7. (a)	8. (b)
9. (c)	10. (c)	11. (a)					

04

CHAPTER

Mendelian inheritance is the basis of classical genetics. It explains how traits are passed from parents to offspring.
In this chapter, we will study about the basics of genetics involving Mendelism, sex-determination, genetic disorders, etc.

YOUR STUDY GOALS

4.1 Mendelian Inheritance
4.2 Mendel's Law of Inheritance
4.3 Deviations from Mendelism
4.4 Chromosomal Theory of Inheritance
4.5 Linkage and Recombination
4.6 Sex-Determination
4.7 Mutation
4.8 Pedigree Analysis
4.9 Genetic Disorders

YOUR PRACTICE GOAL

- Objective Type Questions (42 Qs ; MCQs, A-R) Case Based Questions (4)
- Subjective Type Questions
- (41 VSAs, 68 SAs, 24 LAs)

Principles of Inheritance and Variation

- Living beings produce offspring of their own kinds through the process of reproduction.
- These offsprings resemble their parents in most of the characteristics.
- The phenomenon of transmission of characters from parents to offsprings is called **heredity**.
- The process by which the characters pass from one generation to another is called **inheritance**. It froms the basis of heredity.
- In addition to similarities, offsprings also display certain differences either among themselves or between them and their parents. This degree of differences whether among offsprings or between offspring and parents is called **variation**.
- The branch of science which deals with the study of heredity and variation is known as **genetics**.

4.1 Mendelian Inheritance

To understand the mechanism of transmission of characters from one generation to another, one must understand the terminology used in genetics as given below

- **Gene** (unit factor) It is considered as the determinant of a characteristic pertaining to a particular organism. Mendel used the word factors for the units that control various traits.

- **Character** It is the feature or characteristic of an individual like height, colour, shape, etc.
- **Trait** It is an inherited character, i.e. the feature, which is normally inherited and has its detectable variant too.
- **Gene Locus** It is the particular position of a gene on a chromosome.
- **Alleles** It is an alternate forms or varieties of genes in a particular gene pair that occupies the same locus (position) on homologous pair of chromosome.
- **Homozygous** When a gene pair in an organism contains two identical alleles, which control similar trait of a character, then the organism is considered as homozygous for that particular trait.
- **Heterozygous** When a gene pair contains two different alleles, which control different traits of a character in an organism, then the organism is considered as heterozygous for that particular trait.
- **Dominant Allele** An allele which expresses itself phenotypically whether present in homozygous or in heterozygous conditions.
- **Recessive Allele** An allele which expresses itself phenotypically when present only in homozygous condition, but it remains suppressed in heterozygous conditions.
- **Genotype** It is the complete genetic constitution of an individual.
- **Phenotype** It is the physical appearance of an individual.
- **Hybrid** The literal meaning of this word is mixture. In genetics, it can be define as an offspring, which is obtained from a cross between two genetically different parents.
- **F_1-generation** First filial (*filial*–offspring) generation.
- **F_2-generation** Second filial generation.
- **Back Cross and Test Cross** Back cross is a cross between F_1-progeny and one of its parents.
  A special back cross to the recessive parent is known as **test cross**. This method was devised by Mendel to determine whether the dominant phenotype is homozygous or heterozygous.
- **Punnett Square** It is a grid devised by a British geneticist **RC Punnett**. It is used to determine the various genotypes and phenotypes resulting from the combination of all possible gametes.

Mendel and his Experiments

- **Gregor Johann Mendel** was the pioneer of classical geneticists.
- He was the first to conduct the experiments on the pattern of inheritance and variations in living things.
- His observations became the foundation of modern genetics and study of heredity.
- Therefore, he is also known as '**Father of Genetics**'.
- He conducted hybridisation experiments on **garden pea** (*Pisum sativum*) for **seven years** (1856-1863) and proposed the laws of inheritance in living organisms.

Rediscovery of Mendel's Work

- Though, Mendel published his work on inheritance of characters in 1865. It remained unrecognised for several reasons till 1900. Some of them are as follows
  - Communication was difficult, so his work could not be widely publicised.
  - His concept of genes as stable non-blending units contradicted the continuous variation observed in nature and was not accepted by contemporaries.
  - His approach of using mathematics to explain biological phenomenon was totally new and unacceptable.
  - He could not provide any physical proof for the existence of factors.
- In 1900, **Hugo de Vries, Correns** and **von Tschermak** rediscovered Mendel's results independently.
- Later they converted two of the Mendel's generalisation as the law of segregation and law of independent assortment.

Quick Test 1

1. Name the allele that is always suppressed in a heterozygous condition.
2. **State True or False.**
   A person with a dominant allele for a trait will always pass that allele on to their offspring.
3. Identify the method used to determine whether an individual with a dominant phenotype is homozygous or heterozygous.
4. **State True or False.**
   Alleles of a gene occupy different loci on the same chromosome.
5. For how many years does Mendel conducted his hybridisation experiment?

Mendel's Experiments

- Mendel conducted artificial/cross-pollination experiments by performing **emasculation** (removal of anthers) on several true-breeding pea lines.
- In order to test the purity of plants, he self-crossed the offsprings (or progeny) for several generations.
- His experiment had a large sampling size, which gave greater credibility to the data he collected.
- He also maintained the statistical record of all the experiments for analysis.

Mendel's Experimental Material

Mendel selected garden pea plant as his experimental material due to the following reasons

- Pea plants are readily available on large scale and has bisexual cleistogamous (closed) flowers.
- Pea plants are predominantly self-pollinated, but they can also be cross-pollinated to produce fertile hybrids.
- These are annual plants with short life cycle. So, several generations can be studied within a short period.
- Pea plants could be easily raised, maintained and they produce large number of seeds.
- Pea plants have distinct and easily detectable contrasting characteristics.
- Mendel selected **14 true-breeding pea plant varieties** as pairs. These were similar except for one character with contrasting traits.

The contrasting traits are listed in the table given below

Characters	Contrasting Traits	
	Dominant Trait	Recessive Trait
Shape of the seeds	Round	Wrinkled
Colour of the seeds	Yellow	Green
Shape of the pods	Inflated	Constricted
Colour of the pods	Green	Yellow
Colour of the flowers	Violet	White
Position of the flower	Axial	Terminal
Height of the stem	Tall	Dwarf

Mendel's Experimental Procedure

Mendel performed experiments in following three stages

- **Selection of Pure Breeds** Mendel observed and selected one trait or character at a time, e.g. he crossed tall and dwarf pea plants to study the inheritance of one gene.
- **Hybridisation** He hybridised plants with constracting forms of a single trait (**monohybrid cross**). The seeds produced by these crosses were grown to develop into plants of **Filial 1 progeny** or **F_1-generation** (F_1-plants). In later experiments, Mendel also crossed pea plants with two contrasting characters (**dihybrid cross**).
- **Self-pollination** He then self-pollinated the F_1-plants to produce plants of **Filial 2** progeny or F_2-generation (F_2-plants).

Mendel's Observation

- In F_1-generation, Mendel found that all pea plants were tall, like one of its parent and none was dwarf.
- In F_2-generation, he found that some of the offspring were 'dwarf'. Hence, the characters which were not seen in F_1-generation were expressed in F_2-generation.

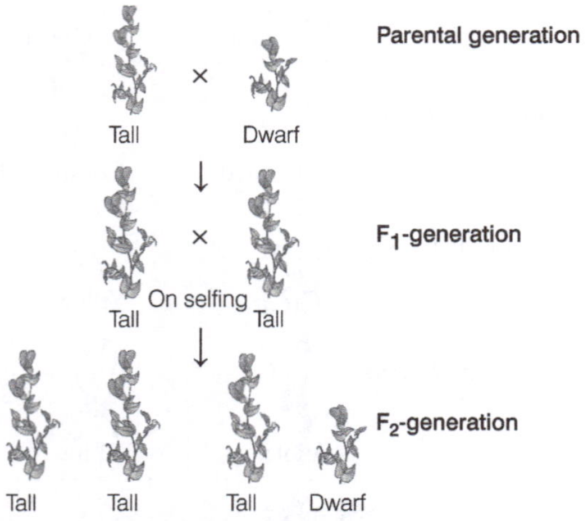

Fig. 4.1 Diagrammatic representation of monohybrid cross

- The proportion of plants that were dwarf was 1/4th of the F_2-plants, while 3/4th of the F_2-plants were tall.
- These contrasting traits (tall/dwarf) did not show any blending (mixing) either in F_1 or in F_2-generation as none were of intermediate height.
- Similar results were obtained with the other traits studied by Mendel. Only one of the parental traits was expressed in F_1-generation, while in F_2-generation, both the traits were expressed in the ratio of 3:1.
- Mendel also found identical results in dihybrid cross as in monohybrid cross.

> Mendel self-pollinated the F_2 plants and found that dwarf F_2 plants continued to generate dwarf plants in F_3 and F_4 generations.

Mendel's Inferences

Following inferences were made by Mendel based on his observations

- He proposed that some 'factors' passed down unchanged from parent to offspring through the gametes over successive generations. Now-a-days, these factors are known as **genes**, are hence the units of inheritance.
- When tall (TT) and dwarf (tt) plants produce gametes by the process of meiosis, the alleles of the parental pair segregate and only one of the allele gets transmitted to a gamete. Thus, there is only 50% chance of a gamete containing either allele, as segregation is a random process.
- During fertilisation, two alleles, 'T' from one parent and 't' from other parent are united to produce a zygote, that has one 'T' and one 't' allele or the hybrids have Tt.
- Since, these hybrids contain alleles which express **contrasting traits**, such plants are heterozygous.

Mathematical Interpretation

In mathematical terms, the result can be written as follows

- 1/4th of the random fertilisation lead to TT. 1/2 lead to formation of Tt and 1/4th to tt genotype.
- The 1/4 : 1/2 : 1/4 ratio of TT : Tt : tt is mathematically condensable in the form of the binomial expression $(ax + by)^2$, that has the gametes bearing genes T or t in equal frequency of 1/2.

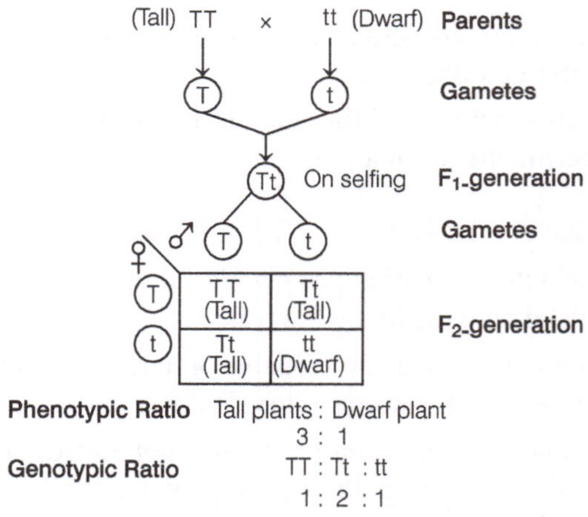

Fig. 4.2 A monohybrid cross of true breeding pea plant

- The expression is expanded as $(1/2T + 1/2t)^2$

$$= (1/2T + 1/2t) \times (1/2T + 1/2t)$$
$$= \frac{1}{4}TT + 1/2\,Tt + 1/4\,tt$$

- Though the genotypic ratios can be calculated using mathematical probability, but it is not possible to know genotypic composition by looking at the phenotype of a dominant trait.
- Therefore, to solve this problem Mendel devised test cross.

Test Cross

- In a standard test cross, an organism (such as pea plants) with a dominant phenotype (whose genotype is unknown) is crossed with a recessive parent, instead of being self-crossed.
- By analysing the offspring of this cross, the genotype of the test organism can be determined.
  There can be two possible genotypes of an unknown dominant phenotype as illustrated below
  - If the unknown is homozygous violet (WW) then crossing with white recessive (ww) gives all violet offsprings (i.e. all Ww).
  - If the unknown is heterozygous violet (Ww) then crossing with white recessive (ww) results in violet (Ww) and white (ww) progeny in 1 : 1 ratio.

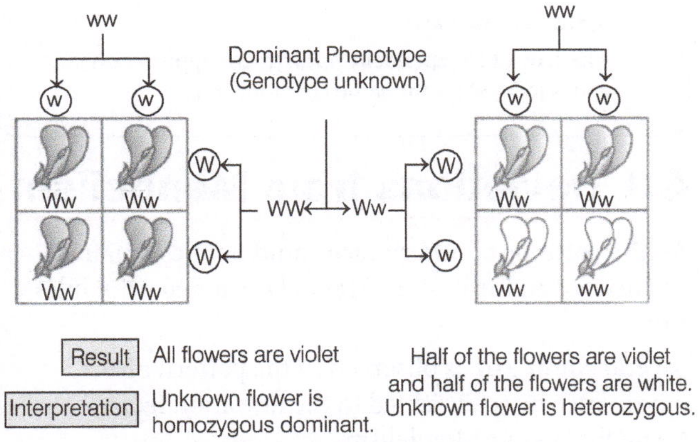

Fig 4.3 Diagrammatic representation of a test cross

> **Quick Test 2**
>
> 1. What technique did Mendel use to remove the anthers from flowers to control pollination?
> 2. **State True or False.**
>   True breeding plants can only be used to study dominant traits, as they cannot produce recessive traits.
> 3. What term describes the process of crossing two genetically distinct individual to produce offspring with a combination of traits?
> 4. **State True or False.**
>   Mendel concluded that offspring inherit one allele, for each trait, from each parent.
> 5. In a test cross, if the dominant phenotype individual is homozygous, what will the offspring's genotypic ratio be?

4.2 Mendel's Laws of Inheritance

Based on the study of one and two gene inheritance, Mendel proposed following laws

Inheritance of One Gene

- It involves the study of inheritance of a single pair of alleles or factors for one character at a time (monohybrid cross).
- Based on his observations on monohybrid crosses, Mendel proposed two general rules in order to consolidate his understanding of inheritance in monohybrid crosses.
- Today, these rules are called the principles or laws of inheritance which are discussed below.

Law of Dominance (First Law)

- This law states that characters are controlled by discrete units called factors, which usually occur in pairs.
- When two contrasting characters are crossed, only the one character appear in F_1 generation (hybrid). The one which is able to express its phenotypic effect is called **dominant character.**
- In contrast, the other factor which remain suppressed is called **recessive character.**
- For example, in the monohybrid cross, when dwarf plant is crossed with tall plant, the F_1-generation have all tall plants. This shows that allele for tallness is dominant.

Law of Segregation (Second Law)

- This law states that, at the time of gamete formation, two factors of a character segregate independently.
- Hence, the gamete receive only one factor or allele for a character.
- The alleles do not show any blending and both the characters are recovered as such in the F_2-generation, though one of these is not seen in the F_1-generation.
- This law is also called **law of purity of gametes.**

Inheritance of Two Genes

- It involves the study of inheritance of two pairs of alleles for two different characters at a time (dihybrid cross).

- Mendel found that inheritance of one pair of allele (one trait) does not interfere in the inheritance of other pair of allele (second trait).
- This can be understand by the following example
  - When a plant having round and yellow seeds is crossed with the plant having wrinkled and green seeds, only round and yellow hybrid is produced in F_1-generation.
  - However, in F_2-generation, four types of plants appear because each pair of dominant and recessive factors are inherited independently.
  - Based upon this, Mendel proposed a second set of generalisations or postulates which is called **law of independent assortment.**

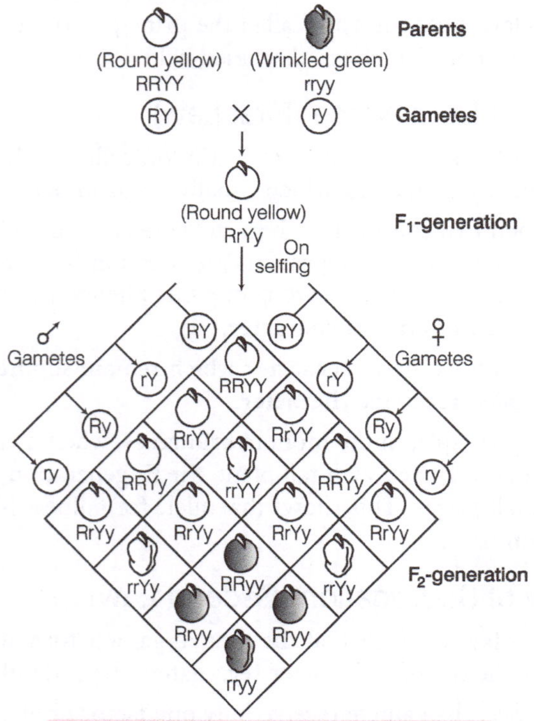

Phenotypic Ratio Round yellow : Round green : Wrinkled yellow : Wrinkled green = 9 : 3 : 3 : 1

Fig. 4.4 Result of dihybrid cross where the two parents differed in two pairs of contrasting traits, i.e. seed colour and seed shape

Law of Independent Assortment (Third Law)

- This law states that at the time of gamete formation, two factors of different characters assort independently.
- Later, they get randomly rearranged in the offspring to produce both parental and new combinations of characters.

Quick Test 3

1. Which principle states that the tall plant trait will be expressed over the dwarf trait in a heterozygous individual?
2. **State True or False.**
   According to the Law of Segregation, an organism with a heterozygous genotype will pass on both alleles for a trait to its offspring.
3. Do genes located on different chromosomes assort independently in the F_2-generation, leading to four possible plant types?
4. Name the process which is commonly used to predict genetic outcomes based on independent assortment?
5. **State True or False.**
   The Law of Independent Assortment applies only to genes located on the same chromosome.

4.3 Deviations from Mendelism

All the patterns of inheritance could not be explained exclusively on the basis of Mendel's original principles alone.

Several complexities observed in the pattern of inheritance by scientist led to the deviation from Mendel's laws or Mendelism.

Incomplete Dominance

- It is a phenomenon in which phenotype of the F_1-hybrid does not resemble any of the parent.
- Instead, it is an intermediate between the expression of two alleles in their homozygous state.
- Here, although the phenotypic ratio deviates from Mendel's monohybrid ratio, but the parental characters reappear in F_2-generation.
- For example, in **snapdragon** (dog flower, *Antirrhinum majus*), there are two types of flower colour in pure state. These are red coloured flowers and white coloured flowers.
- Upon crossing the pure breeding red flowered and white flowered plants, hybrids of F_1-generation possess pink flowers.

- For further selfing F_1-plants, F_2-generation possess 1 red (RR): 2 pink (Rr) : 1 white (rr) flowered plants.
- Here, pink flower colour appear due to the incomplete dominance of red flower trait over white flower trait.

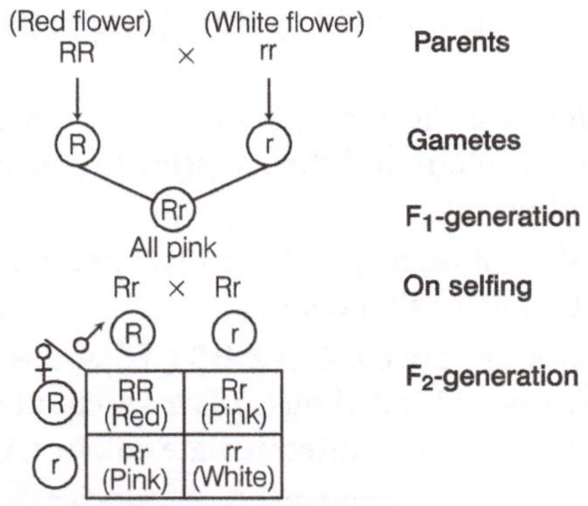

Phenotypic Ratio : Red : Pink : White
1 : 2 : 1
Genotypic Ratio : RR : Rr : rr
1 : 2 : 1

Fig. 4.5 Monohybrid cross in snapdragon, where one allele is incompletely dominant over the other allele

Explanation of Incomplete Dominance

- A diploid organism contains two copies of genes in the form of alleles (homozygous and heterozygous), which carries the information to express a particular trait.
- The pair of alleles may be dissimilar due to some changes in one of them, which modifies the information that particular allele contain.
- For instance, the normal allele produces the regular enzyme required to transform a substrate (S) whereas, the modified allele could lead to the production of a normal or less efficient enzyme, a non-functional enzyme, or no enzyme at all.
- If the modified allele produces a functional but less efficient enzyme, it will not change the organism's phenotype.
- But if it produces a non-functional enzyme or no enzyme, the organism's traits may be affected.
- The phenotype/trait will only be dependent on the functioning of the unmodified allele.
- The unmodified allele is the dominant allele and modified allele is generally the recessive allele.
- Thus, incomplete dominance result due to the production of non-functional enzyme or no enzyme by the recessive allele.

Codominance

- It is the phenomenon in which two alleles express themselves independently when present together in an organism.
- In other words, it is the phenomenon in which offspring (F_1-generation) shows resemblance to both the parents, e.g. ABO blood grouping system in humans.
- ABO blood groups (in humans) are controlled by the gene I. Which exhibit three alleles- I^A, I^B and i. I^A and I^B are codominant alleles and both are dominant over i.
- The plasma membrane of the red blood cells has sugar polymers that protrude from its surface and the kind of sugar is controlled by the gene I.
- The alleles I^A and I^B produce a slightly different form of the sugar, while allele i does not produce any sugar.
- When I^B and i are present, only I^B expresses (because i does not have any sugar), same in the case with I^A and i.
- But when I^A and I^B are present together, they both express their own types of sugars, this is due to codominance. Therefore, the red blood cells have both A and B types of sugars.
- Since, there are three different types of alleles, there can be six different combinations of these three alleles.
- Hence, a total of six different genotypes of the human ABO blood types are present as given below in the table.

Genetic Basis of Blood Groups in Human Population

Allele from Parent 1	Allele from Parent 2	Genotype of Offsprings	Blood Types of Offsprings
I^A	I^A	I^AI^A	A
I^A	i	$I^A i$	A
I^A	I^B	I^AI^B	AB
I^B	I^A	$I^A I^B$	AB
I^B	I^B	I^BI^B	B
I^B	i	I^Bi	B
i	i	ii	O

Multiple Alleles

- When more than two alternative forms (allele) of a gene occupy the same locus on a chromosome within a population, these are known as **multiple alleles**.
- The ABO blood grouping is a good example of multiple alleles.
- In this case, more than two, i.e. three alleles (I^A, I^B, i) governing the same character.
- Multiple alleles can be found only when population studies are carried out.

Pleiotropy

- It is the phenomenon in which a single gene product may produce multiple or more than one phenotypic effect.
- Pleiotropic gene manifests its effect on the metabolic pathways, which inturn contributes to development of different phenotypes.
- **For example**
  - **Phenylketonuria** is a disorder, which is caused due to the mutation in the gene that codes the enzyme phenylalanine hydroxylase (single gene mutation). The affected individuals show reduced hair and skin pigmentation as well as mental retardation.
  - In garden pea various characters like, starch synthesis, size of starch grains and the shape of seeds are controlled by one gene. The genotypes and phenotypes for the traits are as follows
    BB – Round seeds, large starch grains.
    Bb – Round seeds, intermediate size starch grains.
    bb – Wrinkled seeds, small starch grains.
- Therefore, it can be said that dominance is not an autonomous feature of the gene, or its product. Infact it depends on the gene product and production of a particular phenotype from this product.

Polygenic Inheritance

- It refers to the inheritance of traits that are controlled by three or more genes (polygenic traits).
- The genes which control and regulate the polygenic traits are called **polygenes.**
- In polygenic inheritance, one polygene controls a partial expression of trait.
- Together, several polygenes produce a cumulative effect and thus governs quantitative characters.
- Since, the phenotype shows participation of each allele and is also influenced by the environment, it is called **quantitative inheritance** as the character/phenotype can be quantified.
- For example, human skin colour is determined by the presence of a pigment melanin and the quantity of melanin is determined by three pairs of polygenes (A, B and C).
- The dominant forms A, B and C are responsible for dark skin colour and the recessive forms for the light skin colour.
- The effect of each allele is additive and reflects in varied range of skin colours.
- If a black or very dark (AA BB CC) and white or very light (aa bb cc) individuals marry each other, the offspring will show intermediate colour (Aa Ba Ca).

Quick Test 4

1. Name the phenomenon taking place when a heterozygous organism displays a phenotype that is a blend of the two parent traits?
2. **State True or False.**
   In codominance, the offspring will show a blend of both parental traits.
3. If there are four alleles of a gene, how many possible genotypes can be formed?
4. If an allele results in a less efficient enzyme, how would the phenotype likely be affected?
5. **State True or False.**
   Polygenic traits typically show a limited number of distinct phenotypes.

4.4 Chromosomal Theory of Inheritance

- It was proposed independently by **Walter Sutton** and **Theodore Boveri** in 1902.
- They stated that behaviour of chromosome (coloured bodies as they were visualised by staining) was parallel to behaviour of genes and used chromosome movement to explain Mendel's law.
- Sutton united the knowledge of chromosomal segregation with Mendelian principles and called it as **chromosomal theory of inheritance**.
- According to this theory,
  - All hereditary characters must be associated with sperms and egg cells as they act as a bridge between generations.

- The hereditary factors must be carried by the nuclear material.
- Like the Mendelian alleles, chromosomes are also found in pairs.
- The two alleles of a gene pair are located on homologous sites on the homologous chromosomes.
- Homologous chromosomes form synapsis during meiosis and get separated to pass into different cells.
- The sperms and eggs have haploid sets of chromosomes, which fuse to re-establish the diploid state of zygote. This is the basis for segregation and independent assortment.
- The genes are carried onto the chromosomes.

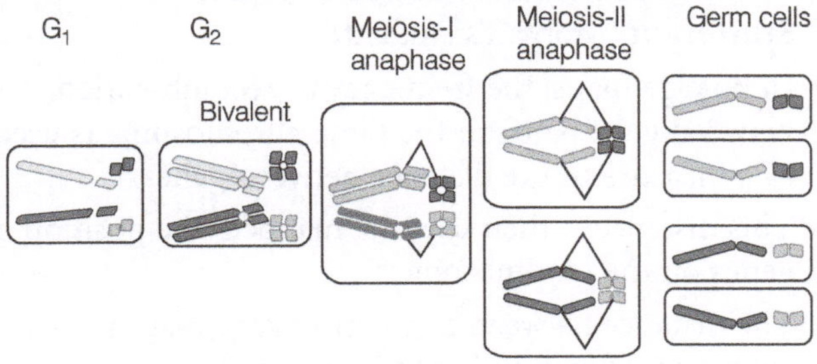

Fig. 4.6 Meiosis and germ cell formation in a cell with four chromosomes

Comparison between the Behaviour of Chromosomes and Genes

Chromosomes	Genes
These occur in pairs.	These also occur in pairs.
Segregate at the time of gamete formation such that only one of each pair is transmitted to a gamete.	Segregate during gamete formation and only one of each pair is transmitted to a gamete.
One pair segregates independently of other pair.	One pair segregates independently of another pair situated on different chromosome. However, segregation of linked genes shows dependency on each other.

Experimental Verification of Chromosomal Theory of Inheritance

- It was done by **Thomas Hunt Morgan** and his colleagues.
- His discoveries confirmed that genes are located on the chromosomes.
- Before Morgan's work, the idea that gene were carried on chromosomes was a hypothesis.
- Through his experiments with *Drosophila melanogaster*, Morgan was able to demonstrate that inheritance patterns could be explained by the behaviour of chromosomes during meiosis.
- Moreover, he observed that the two genes under consideration, did not segregate independently as in the case of characters studied by Mendel.
- It further led to the discovery of the basis for the variation that are produced during sexual reproduction.
- Morgan selected fruit fly, *Drosophila melanogaster* for his experiments because
    - They could be grown on simple artificial medium in the laboratory.
    - Their life cycle is only about two weeks.
    - A single mating could produce a large number of flies.
    - It has four pairs of chromosomes, which differ in size.
    - There was a clear differentiation of the sexes, i.e. male (smaller) and female (bigger).
    - It has many types of hereditary variation which can be easily seen through low power microscope.

4.5 Linkage and Recombination

- Morgan conducted dihybrid crosses in *Drosophila* to study sex-linked gene, similar to Mendel's dihybrid crosses in peas, i.e. the genes present on the X-chromosome.
- They hybridised yellow-bodied and white-eyed females with brown-bodied and red-eyed males (wild type) and intercrossed their F_1-progeny (Cross A).
- It was observed that the two genes did not segregate independently of each other and the F_2-ratio deviated significantly from 9 : 3 : 3 : 1 ratio.
- Morgan and his group analysed that in *Drosophila*, when the two genes in a dihybrid cross were situated on the same chromosome, the proportion of parental gene combinations were much higher than the non-parental type.

- Morgan attributed this due to the physical association of the two genes on a chromosomes and termed this association linkage.
- The term '**recombination**' was coined to describe the generation of non-parental gene combinations. (Fig 4.7)
- Thus, linkage is a phenomenon of genetic inheritance in which genes of a particular chromosome show their tendency to inherit together.
- Morgan and his group also found that even when genes were grouped on the same chromosome, some genes were tightly linked, i.e. linkage is stronger between two genes, and the frequency of recombination is low (Fig 4.7, Cross A).
- Whereas, the frequency of recombinations is higher, if genes are loosely linked, i.e. linkage is weak between two genes (Fig 4.7, Cross B).
- For example, he found that the genes white and yellow were very tightly linked and showed only 1.3 per cent recombination, while white and miniature wing showed 37.2 percent recombination.
- Recombination of linked genes occurs due to crossing over (exchange of corresponding parts between the chromatids of homologous chromosomes).

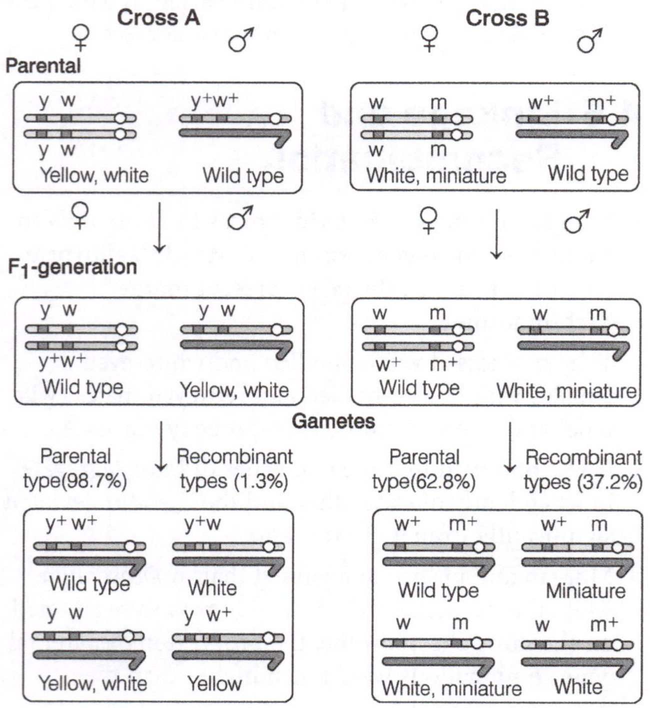

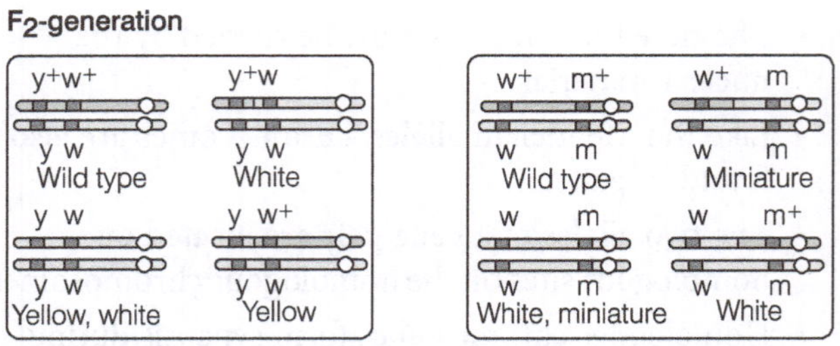

Fig. 4.7 Linkage : Results of two dihybrid crosses conducted by Morgan. Cross 'A' shows crossing between genes y and w ; Cross 'B' shows crossing between genes w and m. Here, dominant wild type alleles are represented with (+) sign in superscript

Chromosome Maps or Linkage Maps

- These maps were constructed by **Alfred Sturtevant** (Morgan's student).
- In linkage maps, the frequency of recombination between gene pairs on the same chromosome is used as a measure of the distance between genes.
- This distance is then used to 'mapped' the position of genes on the chromosome.
- The distance between genes in linkage map is expressed as map unit or Morgan unit.
- Genetic maps are now used as a basis in the sequencing of whole genomes, e.g. human genome sequencing project.

Quick Test 5

1. **State True or False.**
   According to the chromosomal theory of inheritance, traits are inherited independently of the chromosomes.
2. **State True or False.**
   Drosophila males have larger bodies than females.
3. What term describes the exchange of genetic material between linked chromosomes?
4. In a test cross between a heterozygous individual and a homozygous recessive, what would be the expected result if the genes are linked?
5. What does a 1% recombination frequency between two genes on a chromosomal map represent?

4.6 Sex-Determination

The establishment of sex through differential development in an individual at the time of zygote formation is called **sex-determination**.

Mechanisms of Sex-Determination

- **Henking** in 1891, traced a specific nuclear structure through spermatogenesis in few insects.
- He also observed that 50% of sperms received this specific structure after spermatogenesis, whereas the other 50% of sperms did not receive it.
- He named this structure as **X-body**, but could not explain its signficance.
- Scientists further explained that X-body was a chromosome and called it as **X-chromosome**.
- Due to the involvement of X-chromosome in the determination of sex, it was named as sex chromosome.
- The other chromosomes, which determine the somatic characters were named as **autosomes** (AA).
- Thus, on the basis of the type of sex chromosome present in the gamete, the parents can be of two types
  - **Homogametic,** i.e. producing similar gametes.
  - **Heterogametic,** i.e. producing different gametes.
- Various sex-determination mechanisms are observed in organisms are discussed below

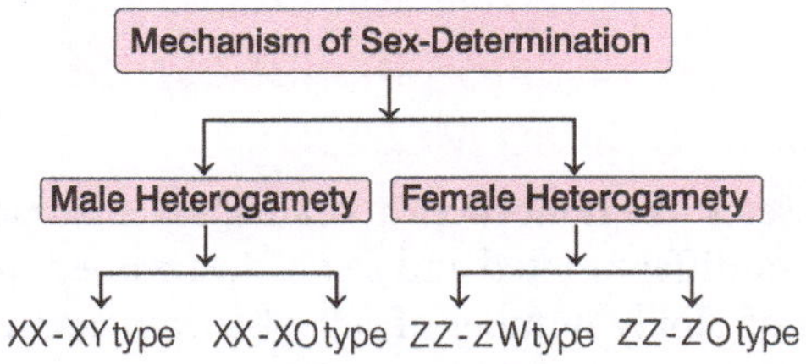

Fig. 4.8 Mechanism of sex-determination

Male Heterogamety

- The mechanism in which male produces two different types of gametes in following way
  - Either with or without X-chromosome.
  - Some gametes with X-chromosome and some with Y-chromosome.
- Let us study the following two cases in detail.

1. XX-XY Type

- This type of sex-determination is found in certain insects like *Drosophila melanogaster* and mammals, including human.
- In these organisms both males and females bear same number of chromosomes.
- However, the males have autosomes (AA) along with a pair of XY-chromosome and females have autosomes along with XX-chromosomes.
- Hence, the males produce two types of gametes containing X or Y sex chromosome.
- In contrast, the females produce only one type of gametes with an X-chromosome (homogametic).

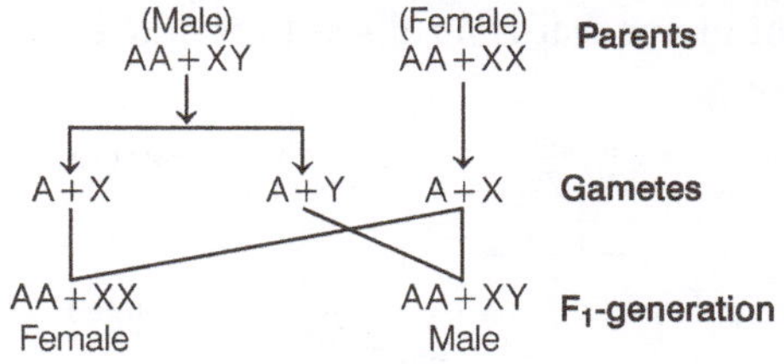

Fig. 4.9 Determination of sex in *Drosophila*

Thus, in this type of sex-determination, the presence of Y-chromosomes which is smaller than X-chromosome determines the maleness.

2. XX-XO Type

- This type of sex-determination is found in a large number of insects, e.g. grasshopper, etc.
- In these organisms, males have only one X-chromosome and produce two types of sperms, i.e. 50% with X-chromosome and 50% without X-chromosome.
- On the contrary, females have a pair of X-chromosomes and produce homogametic eggs.

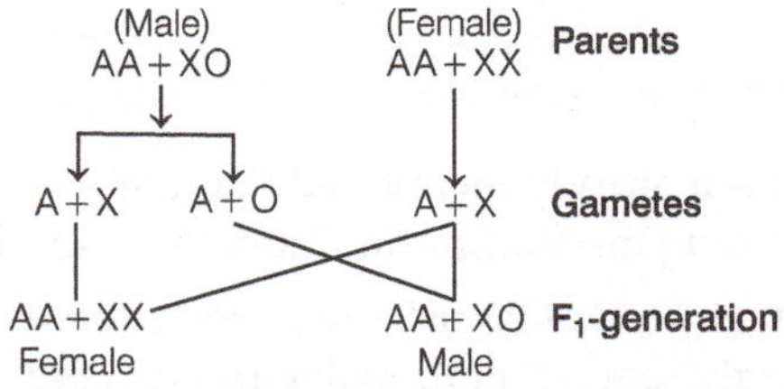

Fig. 4.10 Determination of sex in grasshopper

- Eggs fertilised by sperms having an X-chromosome become females and those fertilised by sperms which do not possess X-chromosome become males.

Female Heterogamety

- In this case, the total number of chromosomes are same in both males and females.
- But two different types of gametes, due to different sex chromosomes, are produced by females.

1. ZZ-ZW Type

- This method of sex-determination is seen in birds, fowls and fishes.
- Females have one Z and one W-chromosome along with autosomes whereas males have a pair of Z-chromosomes (i.e. homogametic).
- Thus, the sex of an organism is determined by the type of ovum that is fertilised to produce an offspring.

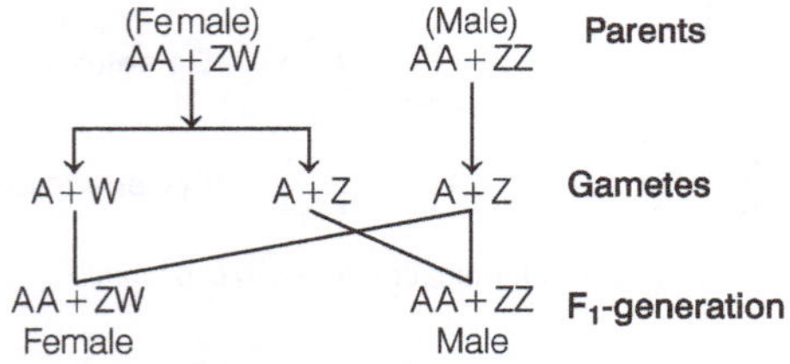

Fig. 4.11 Determination of sex in birds

2. ZZ-ZO Type

- In this method of sex-determination, the female is heterogametic (ZO) and male is homogametic (ZZ).
- It occurs in certain butterflies and moths.

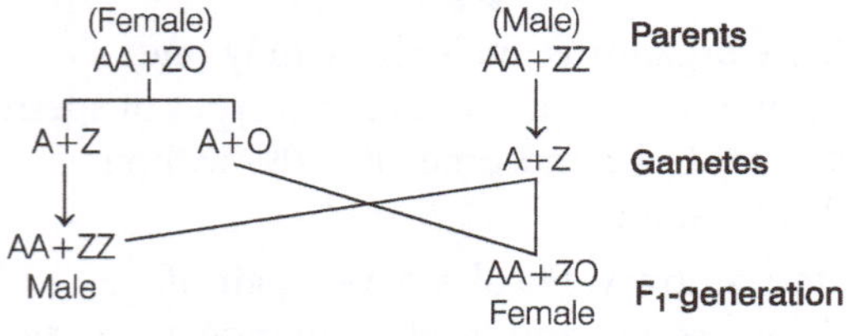

Fig. 4.12 Determination of sex in moths

Sex-Determination in Humans

- It has been already mentioned that the sex determining mechanism in humans is XX-XY type.
- In humans, out of 23 pairs of chromosomes, 22 pairs are exactly same in both males and females and are known as **autosomes**.
- The 23rd pair of chromosomes is the sex chromosome, i.e. a pair of X-chromosome (XX) is present in females and males possess one X and one Y-chromosome (XY).
- During spermatogenesis in males, two types of gametes are produced.
- Out of total sperms produced, 50% carry X-chromosomes and the rest 50% carry Y-chromosomes besides autosomes.
- Females produce only one type of ovum with an X-chromosome besides autosomes.
- If an ovum fertilises with a sperm carrying X-chromosome, the zygote develops into a female (XX). However, if an ovum is fertilised with sperm carrying Y-chromosome, zygote thus formed will be a male (XY).

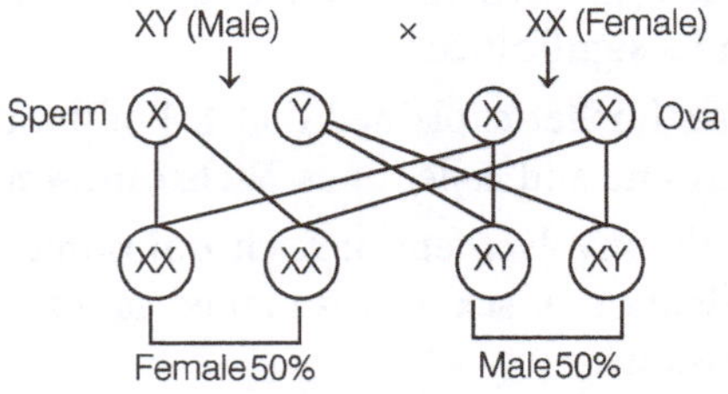

Fig. 4.13 Sex-determination in human

- Hence, the genetic make up of a sperm, which fertilises the ovum determines the sex of a child. There are 50% chances of having either a male or female in each pregnancy. Thus, it is a chance phenomenon.
- So, women should not be blamed for giving birth to a girl child.

Sex- Determination in Honeybee (Haploid-Diploid Method)

- In insects like honeybees and ants, sex chromosomes are not differentiated and sex is determined on the basis of ploidy number of sets of chromosomes of the individual.
- An offspring formed from the union of a sperm and egg develops as a female (queen or worker), which is diploid and have 32 chromosomes.

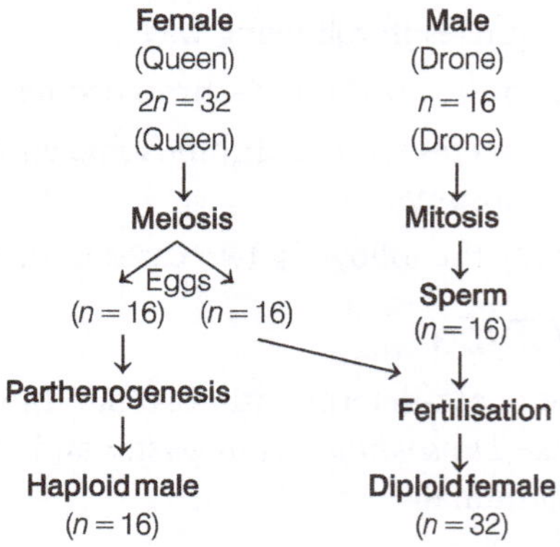

Fig. 4.14 Sex-determination in honeybees

- The unfertilised egg develops as male (drone) by the process of parthenogenesis. The males are haploid and have 16 chromosomes.
- Therefore, in honeybees, sex-determination is referred to as **haploid-diploid method**.
- They have special characteristic features in which male produces sperms by mitosis.
- In honeybees males neither have father nor sons, but they can have grandfather and grandsons.

4.7 Mutation

- It is a sudden, stable and inheritable change in genetic material or DNA sequences of an organism.
- It is a phenomenon which results in alteration of DNA sequence which further results, change in genotype and phenotype of an organisms.
- The organism, which undergoes mutation is called **mutant**.
- The chemical and physical factors that induce mutations are referred to as **mutagens**, e.g. UV radiations, etc.
- The mutations are of following types

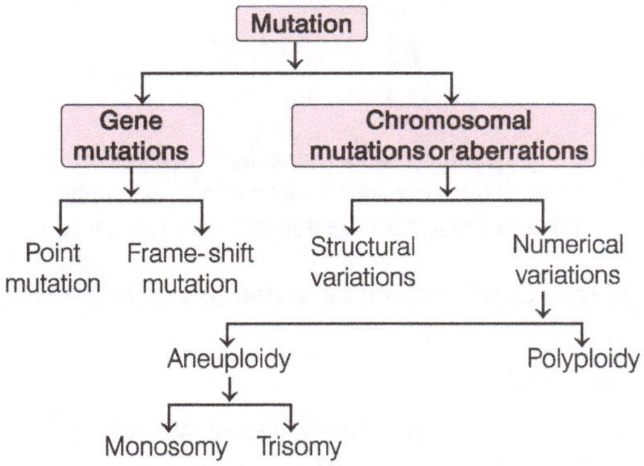

Types of Mutations

Mutations could be of various types which are discussed below

- **Point Mutation** This type of mutation occur due to change in a single base pair of DNA, e.g. sickle-cell anaemia.
- **Frame-shift Mutation** Deletions and insertions of base pairs of DNA cause frame-shift mutation.
- **Structural Variations** The loss or gain of a segment of DNA, results in structural alteration in chromosomes because genes are located on the chromosomes. This alteration in chromosomes results in abnormalities and it is common in cancerous cells.
- **Aneuploidy** When members of a homologous pair of chromosomes fail to segregate during meiosis, aneuploidy occurs. It means, there is loss or gain of one or more chromosomes.
  - **Monosomy**, i.e. lack of one chromosome from a normal complement.
  - **Trisomy**, i.e. presence of three chromosomes instead of normal two chromosomes.
- **Polyploidy** It occurs due to the failure of cytokinesis after telophase stage of cell division. It result in an increase in a whole set of chromosomes in an organism. This condition is often seen in plants.

Quick Test 6

1. In Drosophila, which parent is responsible for determining the sex of the offspring?
2. **State True or False.**
   In grasshoppers, only 50% of the sperms contain X chromosomes.
3. Mention the type of chromosomes other than sex chromosomes in birds.
4. **State True or False.**
   Point mutations involve the insertion or deletion of base-pairs of DNA.
5. Identify the condition when a person has 47 chromosomes instead of the normal 46?

4.8 Pedigree Analysis

- The analysis of traits in several generations of a human family in the form of a family tree or diagram is called **pedigree analysis**.
- It serves as a strong tool, which is utilised to trace the inheritance of a specific trait, abnormality or disease.
- Inheritance pattern of traits in human beings cannot be studied by crosses as in case of other organisms due to following reasons
  - The produced progeny is very small (usually one) and takes long time in development.
  - Controlled crosses cannot be performed.

- The standard symbols used in pedigree analysis are given below

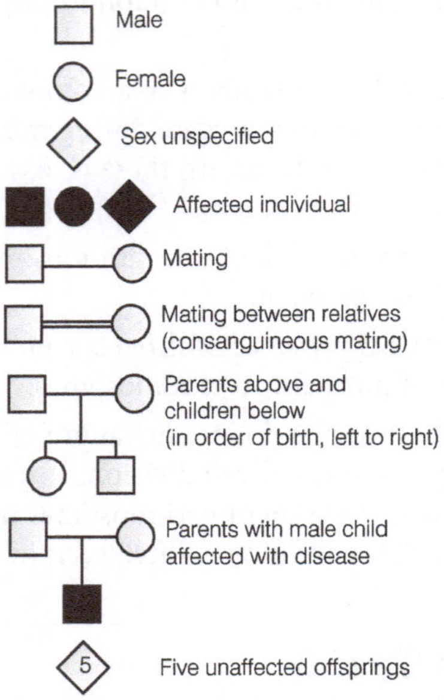

Fig. 4.15 Symbols used in the human pedigree analysis

> **TEACHER'S TIP**
>
> To study pedigree charts, recognise key inheritance patterns. In **autosomal dominant traits**, affected individuals have at least one affected parent, and the trait appears in every generation. **Autosomal recessive traits** may skip generations, with two unaffected parents potentially having affected offspring if both are carriers.

4.9 Genetic Disorders

- These are disorders or illness caused by one or more abnormalities in the autosomes or sex chromosomes of the person. Thus, these are referred to as **autosomal disorders** or **sex-linked disorders,** respectively.
- The genetic disorders are divided into following

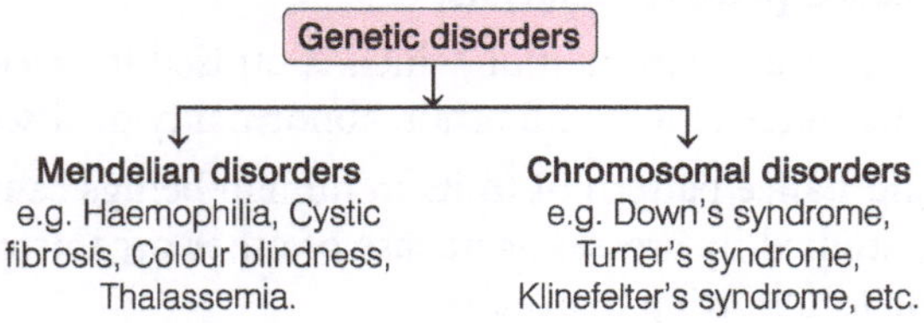

1. Mendelian Disorders

- These are mainly determined by alteration or mutation in a single gene.
- These are transmitted to next generation according to the principle of inheritance and can be studied with the help of pedigree analysis. These can be dominant or recessive as follows
  - **Autosomal dominant,** e.g. Huntington disease, myotonic dystrophy, etc.
  - **Autosomal recessive,** e.g. cystic fibrosis, thalassemia.
  - **Sex-linked recessive,** e.g. colour blindness, haemophilia.
- The pattern of inheritance of autosomal dominant and recessive trait is shown in pedigree charts given below

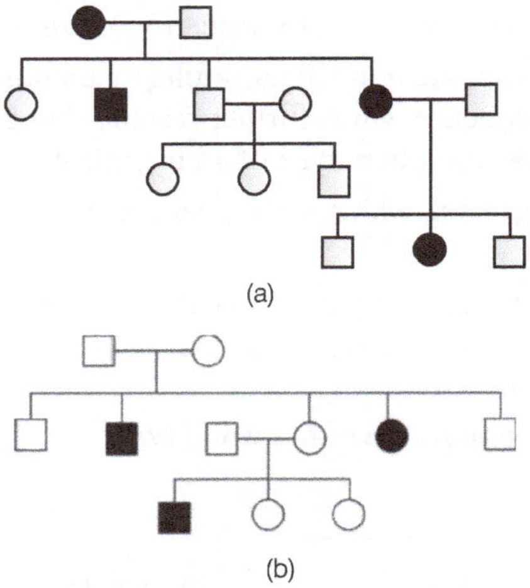

Fig. 4.16 Representative pedigree analysis of :
(a) Autosomal dominant trait (myotonic dystrophy)
(b) Autosomal recessive trait (sickle-cell anaemia)

Some Mendelian disorders are discussed below

Haemophilia

- It is a sex-linked recessive disease, which is transmitted from an unaffected carrier heterozygous female to some of the male offspring.
- The gene for haemophilia is located on **X-chromosome.**
- In this disease, a single protein that is a part of cascade of proteins involved in blood clotting is affected.
- Due to this, patient continues to bleed even in a minor injury because of defective blood coagulation, Thus, it is also called **bleeder's disease.**
- The possibility of a female becoming a haemophilic is extremely rare because mother of such a female has to

be atleast carrier and father should be haemophilic. Thus, females suffer from this disease only in homozygous condition, i.e. X^hX^h.

- The family pedigree of **Queen Victoria** (who was a carrier of haemophilia) shows a number of haemophilic individuals as she was the carrier of the disease.

Colour Blindness

- It is a sex-linked recessive disorder, caused by a defect in either red or green cone cells of eye.
- This defect leads to the failure in discrimination between **red** and **green colour**.
- The gene for colour blindness is present on X-chromosome. This disease is observed mostly in males (X^CY) because of the presence of only one X-chromosome as compared to two X-chromosomes in females.
- It occurs in about 8 per cent of males and only about 0.4 per cent of females.
- A heterozygous female (XX^C) has normal vision, but is a carrier and passes on the disorder to some of her sons.
- A daughter will not normally be colourblind, unless her mother is a carrier and her father is colourblind.

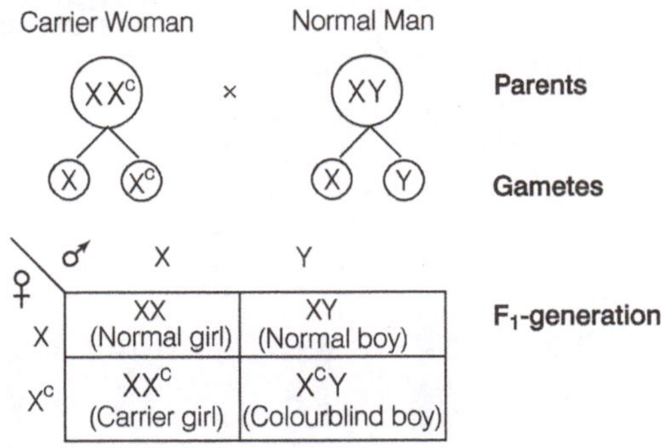

> **Criss-cross Inheritance**
>
> Haemophilia and colour blindness show *criss-cross* inheritance pattern, where inheritance of sex-linked character is transmitted from father to daughter or from mother to son.

Sickle-Cell Anaemia

- It is an autosomal linked recessive trait that can be transmitted from parents to the offspring, when both the partners are carrier for the gene (heterozygous).
- This disease is controlled by a single pair of allele Hb^A and Hb^S, where Hb stands for haemoglobin.
- Only homozygous individuals for Hb^S (Hb^S Hb^S) show the diseased phenotype.
- The heterozygous individuals are carriers (Hb^A Hb^S).
- Sickle-cell anaemia is caused by the substitution of **Glutamic acid** (Glu) by **Valine** (Val) at the sixth position of the β-globin chain of the haemoglobin molecule.
- The substitution of amino acid in the globin protein results due to single base substitution at the sixth codon from GAG to GUG (which is also an example of point mutation).
- The mutant haemoglobin molecule undergoes polymerisation under low oxygen tension.
- It leads to the change in the shape of the RBCs from biconcave disc to the elongated sickle-like structure.
- This defect is beneficial to people (in heterozygous condition) living in malarial prone areas because malarial parasite could not survive in sickle-shaped RBCs.

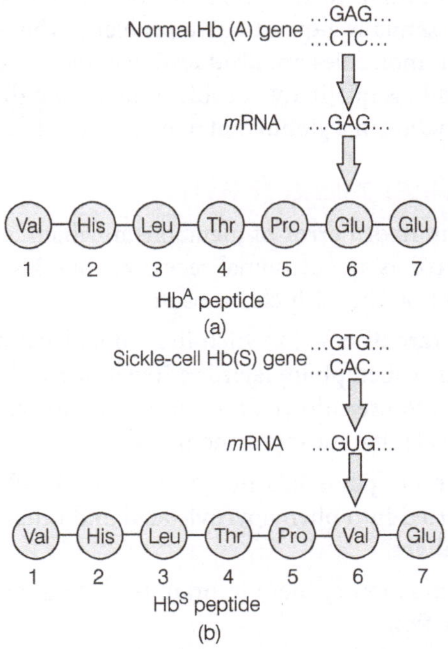

Fig. 4.17 The amino acid composition of the relevant portion of β-chain of haemoglobin : (a) From a normal individual; (b) From an individual with sickle-cell anaemia.

Thalassemia

- It is an autosomal recessive disease that can be transmitted from parents to offsprings when both the partners are unaffected carrier for the gene (or heterozygous).

- It occurs due to either mutation or deletion of genes, resulting in reduced rate of synthesis of one of the globin chains of haemoglobin.
- **Anaemia** is the main feature of this disease. There are two forms of thalassemia.

(i) α-thalassemia

- In this, the production of α-globin chain is affected, which is governed by two closely linked genes HBA1 and HBA2 on chromosome 16.
  - It occurs due to mutation or deletion of one or more of the four genes.
  - The more genes are affected, the less alpha globin molecule is produce.

(ii) β -thalassemia

- In this production of β -chain is affected which is governed by a single gene HBB present on 11th chromosome.
- It occurs due to mutation of one or both the genes. Thalassemia is a quantitative problem, where too few globin molecules are produced, whereas sickle-cell anaemia is qualitative problem, involving the production of a globin that does not function properly.

Phenylketonuria (PKU)

- It is an inborn error of metabolism, which is inherited as an autosomal recessive trait. Its gene is present on the 12th chromosome.
- It is a rare disease in which individual lacks an enzyme called **phenylalanine hydroxylase**. It is needed to breakdown an essential amino acid, phenylalanine into tyrosine in liver.
- As a result, **phenylalanine** gets accumulated and converted into phenylpyruvic acid and other derivatives.
- Accumulation of these in brain leads to mental retardation.
- These are also excreted through urine because of its poor absorption by kidney.

2. Chromosomal Disorders

- These are caused by the absence or excess or abnormal arrangement of one or more chromosomes.
- The chromosomal disorders can be studied by the analysis of karyotypes.
- A **karyotype** is an organised profile of a person's chromosomes according to their shape, size and number.
- Some chromosomal disorders are discussed below

Down's Syndrome

- It was described by **Langdon Down** in 1866.
- It occurs due to the presence of an additional copy of a chromosome **(trisomy of 21st chromosome)** in humans.
- **Symptoms** of this syndrome are as follows
  - Individuals are short statured with small, round head and furrowed tongue and partially open mouth.
  - Palm is broad with characteristic palm crease.
  - Mental, physical and psychomotor development is retarded.

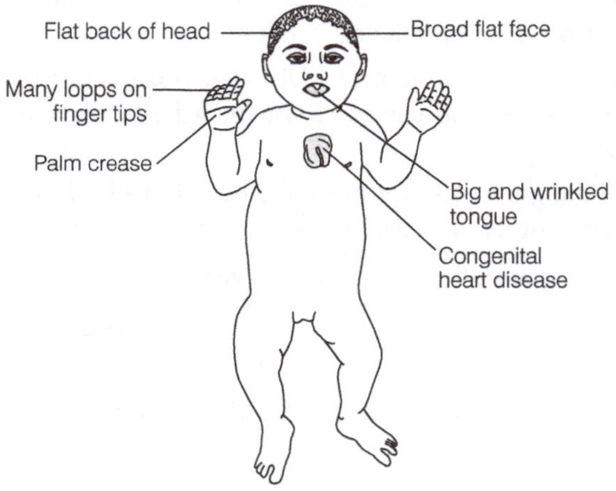

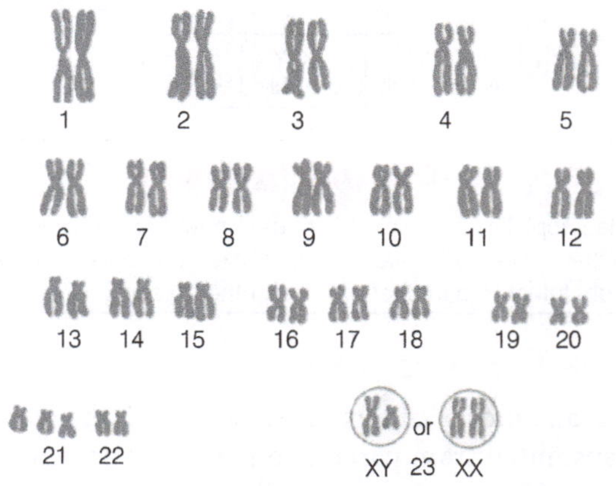

Fig. 4.18 A representative figure showing an individual inflicted with Down's syndrome and the corresponding chromosomes of the individual

Turner's Syndrome

- It is a disorder which is caused due to the absence of one of the X-chromosome, i.e. **45 with XO.**
- **Symptoms** of this syndrome include
  - Affected females are sterile as ovaries are rudimentary.
  - Lack of secondary sexual characters and poor breast development.

Klinefelter's Syndrome

- It occurs due to the presence of an additional copy of X-chromosome resulting in the karyotype of **47, XXY males.**
- **Symptoms** of this syndrome include
  - Individuals have masculine development, however feminine characters like development of breasts (gynaecomastia) also expressed.
  - Such individuals are sterile.

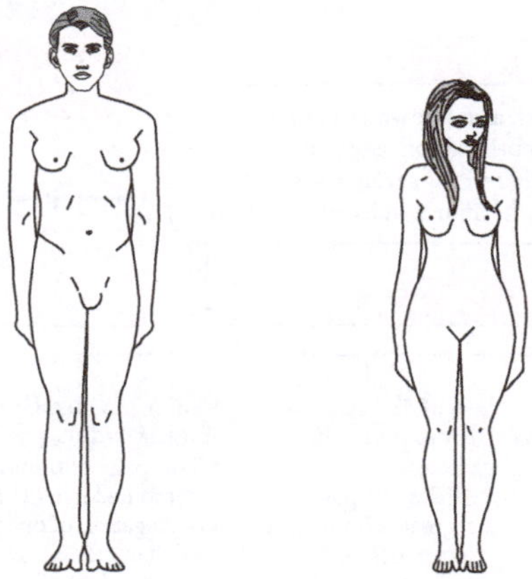

Fig. 4.19 Diagrammatic representation of genetic disorders due to sex-chromosome composition in humans : (A) Klinefelter's syndrome ; (B) Turner's syndrome

Quick Test 7

1. If a woman is suffering from haemophilia, what are the chances of her transmitting it to her daughter?
2. **State True or False.**
   In criss-cross inheritance, a father can pass a sex-linked recessive trait to his son.
3. What is the probability of a child inheriting sickle-cell anaemia if both parents are carriers?
4. Name the coudition which is caused by abnormal haemoglobin production.
5. A female patient exhibits short stature and infertility. What genetic disorder could be responsible for these symptoms?

Mind Map

Principles of Inheritance and Variation

Mendel's Experiment

Gregor Johann Mendel, also known as Father of Genetics conducted hybridisation experiments on garden pea (*Pisum sativum*) for seven years and proposed the laws of inheritance in living organisms.

Mendel's Laws

Law of Dominance
- Expression of only one of parental character in F_1 progeny.
- Occurrence of 3 : 1 ratio in F_2 individual.

Law of Segregation
(Law of purity of gametes)
- Alleles of a pair segregate from each other such that gamete receives only one of the two factors.

Law of Independent Assortment
- Two pairs of traits are combined in a hybrid.
- Segregation of one pair of character is independent of the other pair of characters.

Few Exceptions to the Mendel's Law

Incomplete Dominance
- Both alleles are partially expressed, resulting in intermediate or distinct phenotype; dog flower (snapdragon or *Antirrhinum* sp).
- 1:2:1 for Red : Pink : White.

Co-dominance
- Both alleles express simultaneously, i.e. AB blood group.
- I gene controls sugar polymer of RBCs.
- Multiple alleles : ABO blood grouping.

Pleiotropy
- A single gene can exhibit multiple phenotypic expression.
- In garden pea pleiotropic gene controls; flower colour, seed coat.

Chromosomal Theory

- **Sutton and Boveri** noted that the behaviour of chromosome was parallel to the behaviour of genes.
- **Chromosomal segregation + Mendelian principle**
- Verification of theory done by **Thomas Hunt Morgan** and his colleague
- Morgan worked on fruitflies, *Drosophila melanogaster*.

Chromosomes	Genes
Occur in pairs.	Occur in pairs.
Segregate at the time of gamete formation such that only one of each pair is transmitted to a gamete.	Segregate at gamete formation and only one of each pair is transmitted to a gamete.
Independent pairs segregate independently of each other.	One pair segregates independently of another pair.

Linkage and Recombination

- **Linkage** Tendency of genes staying together (parental combination)
- **Recombination/ Crossing over** Non- parental combination
- **Alfred Sturtevant** used frequency of recombination
  1 map unit = 1% of crossing over
- **1 map** unit is now referred as cM (**centiMorgan**)

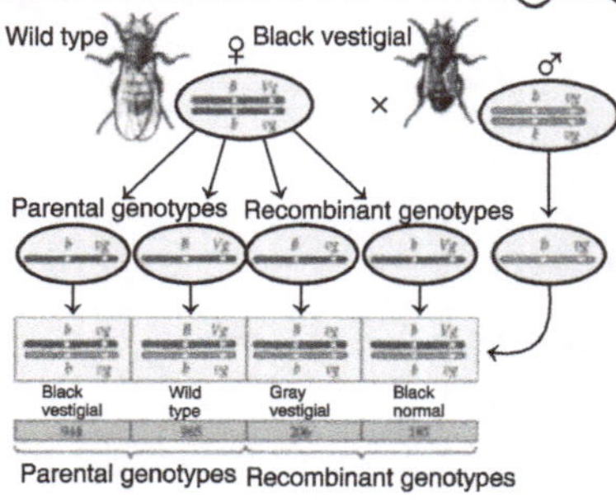

Sex Determination

- Mechanism by which sex of an individual is determined.
  - **Genetic Mechanism** XX-XY type (humans and *Drosophila)* XX-XO (insects) and ZW-ZZ (birds).
  - **Haplodiploidy Method** Honeybee.

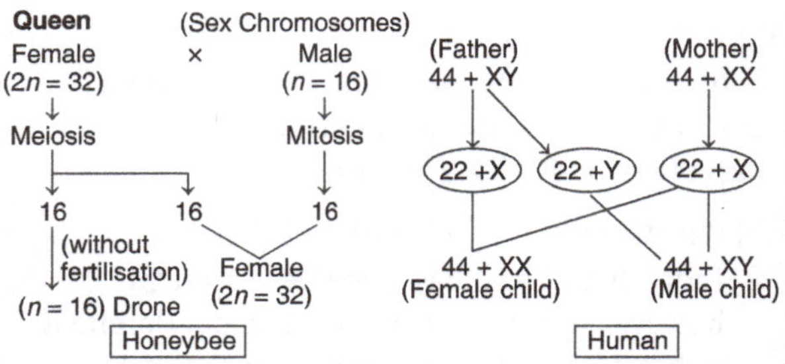

Mutation

Alternation of DNA sequence : results change in genotype and phenotype

Chromosomal mutation
- addition
- deletion

Gene mutation
- **Point mutation** (Change in nucleotide sequence)
- **Frameshift mutation** (Shift in reading frame)

Pedigree Analysis

- It is the analysis of traits in several generations of a human family in the form of a family tree or diagram.
- It provides a strong tool, which is utilised to trace the inheritance of a specific trait, abnormality or disease.

Genetic Disorders

- These are caused by one or more abnormalities in the genome, especially a condition that is present from birth.

Mendelian disorders
- Alteration or mutation in the single gene.
- Transmitted to the offspring.
- Can be traced in a family by the pedigree analysis.
- **Examples** Haemophilia, cystic fibrosis, sickle-cell anaemia, colour blindness, phenylketonuria, thalassemia.

Chromosomal disorders
- Due to absence/excess/abnormal arrangement of one or more chromosomes.
- Failure of segregation of chromatids in cell division cycle results in the gain/loss of a chromosome (s) called aneuploidy.
- **Examples** Down's syndrome, Klinefelter's syndrome.

EXAM PATTERN QUESTIONS

Objective Type Questions

Multiple Choice Questions

1. Given below are the pairs of contrasting traits in *Pisum sativum* as studied by Mendel. Identify the incorrect pair of traits. **CBSE 2021 Term-I**

	Characters	Dominant	Recessive
(a)	Stem height	Tall	Dwarf
(b)	Seed shape	Round	Wrinkled
(c)	Pod colour	Yellow	Green
(d)	Flower position	Axial	Terminal

Ans. (*c*)

2. During a monohybrid cross involving a tall pea plant with a dwarf pea plant, the offspring populations were tall and dwarf in equal ratio. **CBSE 2025**

Find out the genotype of parent pea plants.

(a) Tt x tt (b) TT x Tt
(c) tt x tt (d) Tt x Tt

Ans. (*a*) A monohybrid cross between a tall pea plant and a dwarf pea plant produced offspring in a 1:1 ratio of tall and dwarf.

This occurs when a heterozygous tall (Tt) plant is crossed with a homozygous recessive dwarf (tt) plant.

Tt × tt produces 50% Tt (tall) and 50% tt (dwarf).

3. In *Pisum sativum*, the flower position may be axial (allele A) or terminal (allele a). What would be the percentage of the offspring with respect to axial flower position, if a cross is made between parents Aa × aa? **CBSE 2021 Term-I**

(a) 25% (b) 50% (c) 75% (d) 100%

Ans. (*b*)

4. In a pea plant (*Pisum sativum*), green pod colour is dominant over yellow pod colour. The expected ratio of the phenotypes of the offsprings (F_1) in a cross between parents with heterozygous green pod colour and homozygous yellow pod will be **CBSE 2025**

(a) 1 : 1 (b) 2 : 1 (c) 3 : 1 (d) 4 : 1

Ans. (*a*) 1:1 – Gg × gg cross yields 50% Green, 50% Yellow.

5. Genotypic ratio of 1 : 2 : 1 is obtained in a cross between **CBSE SQP 2021 Term-I**

(a) AB × AB (b) Ab × Ab
(c) Ab × ab (d) ab × ab

Ans. (*b*)

6. According to Mendel, the nature of the unit factors that control the expression of traits were **CBSE 2021 Term-I**

(a) stable (b) blending
(c) stable and discrete (d) discrete

Ans. (*c*)

7. In mice, brown fur is dominant and white fur is recessive. A biologist crossed a brown fur male with a white fur female and obtained two brown fur and two white fur offspring. Which of the following statement is most likely to be true?

(a) Both parents are heterozygous
(b) Only the male parent is homozygous
(c) Only the male parent is heterozygous
(d) Only the female parent is heterozygous.

Ans. (*c*)

8. In a dihybrid cross, if you get 9 : 3 : 3 : 1 ratio it denotes that **NCERT Exemplar**

(a) the alleles of two genes are interacting with each other
(b) it is a multigenic inheritance
(c) it is a case of multiple allelism
(d) the alleles of two genes are segregating independently

Ans. (*d*)

9. A plant breeder crossed a pure breed tall plant having white flowers with a pure breed dwarf plant having blue flowers. He obtained 202 F_1 progeny and found that they are all tall having blue flowers. Upon selfing these F_1 plants he obtained a progeny of 2160 plants. Approximately how many of these are likely to be short having blue flowers? **CBSE 2021 Term-I**

(a) 1215 (b) 405
(c) 540 (d) 135

Ans. (*b*)

10. Mendel's law of independent assortment holds good for genes situated on the **Diksha**

(a) non-homologous chromosomes
(b) homologous chromosomes
(c) extra nuclear genetic element
(d) same chromosomes

Ans. (*a*)

11. In *Antirrhinum*, RR is phenotypically red flowers, rr is white and Rr is pink. Select the correct phenotypic ratio in F_1-generation, when a cross is performed between RR × Rr. **CBSE 2021 Term-I**

(a) 1 red : 1 pink : 1 white (b) 2 pink : 1 white
(c) 2 red : 2 pink (d) All pink

Ans. (c)

12. The gene that controls the ABO blood group system in human beings has three alleles; I^A, I^B and i. A child has blood group O. His father has blood group A and mother has blood group B. Genotypes of other offsprings can be **CBSE SQP 2021 Term-I**

I. I^BI^B II. I^Ai
III. I^Bi IV. I^AI^B
V. ii

(a) I, II, III and V (b) II, III, IV and V
(c) III, IV and V (d) I, III and IV

Ans. (b)

13. Match the terms in Column I with their description in Column II and choose the correct option.

Column I (Terms)		Column II (Description)
A.	Dominance	1. Many genes govern a single character
B.	Codominance	2. In a heterozygous organism only one allele expresses itself
C.	Pleiotropy	3. In a heterozygous organism both alleles express themselves fully
D.	Polygenic inheritance	4. A single gene influences many characters

Codes

	A	B	C	D		A	B	C	D
(a)	4	1	2	3	(b)	2	3	4	1
(c)	4	3	1	2	(d)	2	1	4	3

Ans. (b)

14. Which of the following statements indicates parallelism in genes and chromosomes?

I. They occur in pairs.
II. They segregate during gamete formation.
III. They show linkage.
IV. Independent pairs segregate independently. **CBSE 2021 Term-I**

(a) I and III (b) II and III
(c) I, II and III (d) I, II and IV

Ans. (d)

15. Given below is a dihybrid cross performed on *Drosophila*. **CBSE SQP 2021 Term-I**

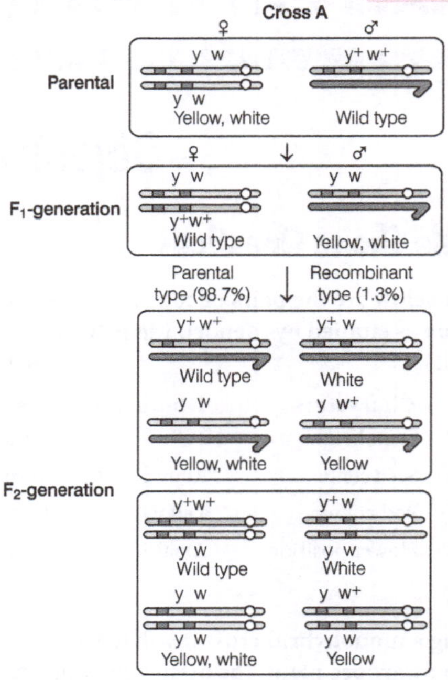

Which of the following conclusions can be drawn on the basis of the cross?
When yellow bodied (y), white eyed (w) *Drosophila* females were hybridised with brown bodied (y^+), red eyed males (w^+) and F_1 progenies were intercrossed, F_2-generation would have shown the following ratio.

(a) 1 : 2 : 1 because of linkage of genes
(b) 9 : 3 : 3 : 1 because of recombination of genes
(c) Deviation from 9 : 3 : 3 : 1 ratio because of segregation of genes
(d) Deviation from 9 : 3 : 3 : 1 ratio because of linkage of genes

Ans. (d)

16. In the dihybrid cross that was conducted by Morgan involving mating between parental generation for genes yellow bodied, white eyed female *Drosophila* and wild type male *Drosophila*, upto F_2-generation is given below. **CBSE 2021 Term-I**

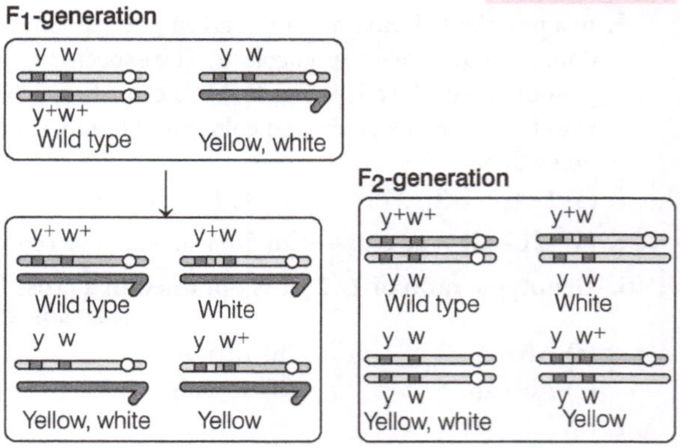

Study the result obtained from the F_2 progeny. Select the correct option from the given choices for the F_2 progeny.

(a) Parental type, 1.3% : Strength of linkage high
(b) Recombinant types, 1.3% : Strength of linkage low
(c) Parental type, 98.7% : Strength of linkage high
(d) Recombinant types, 98.7% : Strength of linkage low

Ans. (c)

17. The probability of all possible genotypes of offspring in a genetic cross can be obtained with the help of CBSE 2021 Term-I

(a) test cross (b) back cross
(c) Punnett square (d) linkage cross

Ans. (*c*)

18. Distance between the genes and percentage of recombination shows

(a) a direct relationship (b) an inverse relationship
(c) a parallel relationship (d) no relationship

Ans. (*a*) Crossing over separates genes away from each other. So, the distance between the genes and percentage of recombination shows an direct relationship, *i.e.*, when genes are close together they have high linkage and exhibit low recombination frequencies.

Thus, the other option are wrong as it does not show parallel or inverse relationship.

19. Which of the following animals exhibit male heterogamety? CBSE 2021 Term-I

(i) Fruit fly (ii) Fowl
(iii) Human (iv) Honeybee

(a) (i) and (iii) (b) (ii) and (iv)
(c) (ii) and (iii) (d) (i) and (iv)

Ans. (*a*)

20. A couple has two daughters. What is the probability that the third child will also be a female? CBSE SQP 2021 Term-I

(a) 25% (b) 50% (c) 75% (d) 100%

Ans. (*b*)

21. Point mutation arises due to the change in

(a) single nucleoside (b) single base pair of DNA
(c) segment of DNA (d) double base pair of DNA

Ans. (*b*) Point mutations refer to those mutations which arise due to change in single base pair of DNA. This change may either be deletion or addition of one or more bases or it may be due to substitution of one base by another.

22. In humans rolling of tongue is an autosomal dominant trait (R). In a family both the parents have the trait of rolling tongue, but their daughter does not show the trait, whereas the sons have the trait of rolling of tongue.

The genotypes of the family would be CBSE 2021 Term-I

	Mother	Father	Daughter	Son
(a)	Rr	Rr	rr	rr
(b)	Rr	Rr	rr	RR
(c)	rr	Rr	RR	rr
(d)	RR	rr	Rr	Rr

Ans. (*b*)

23. Study the pedigree chart of a family showing the inheritance of myotonic dystrophy. CBSE 2025

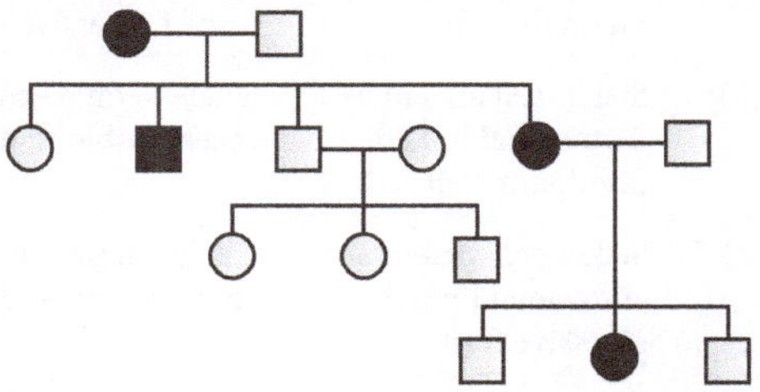

The trait under study is
(a) dominant X-linked trait
(b) recessive X-linked trait
(c) autosomal dominant trait
(d) autosomal recessive trait

Ans. (*c*) The pedigree chart indicates autosomal dominant inheritance of myotonic dystrophy, as the trait appears in every generation and affects both males and females equally. Affected individuals have at least one affected parent, ruling out recessive inheritance. The absence of direct father-to-daughter transmission excludes X-linked dominance.

24. The figure below shows the normal haemoglobin at genetic level. Competency Based Que.

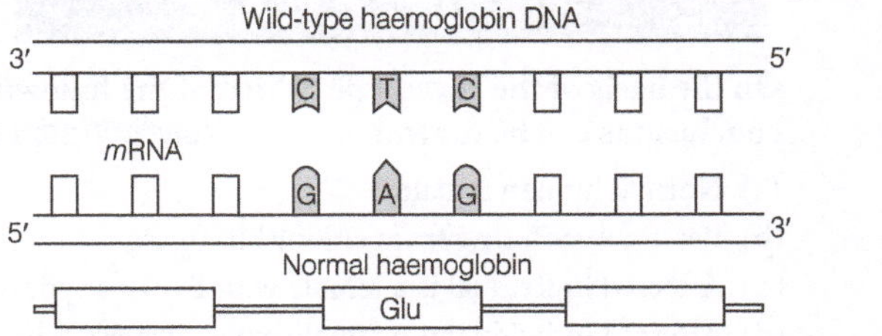

In sickle-cell anaemia, the DNA sequence changes from GAG to GTG on the non-transcribed strand of haemoglobin.

Choose the correct result for the given mutation from the given table.

	Resultant *m*RNA	Resultant Polypeptide
(a)	CAC	Glycine
(b)	GAC	Alanine
(c)	GUG	Valine
(d)	GUG	Lysine

Ans. (*c*)

25. **Suresh and Rajesh have defective haemoglobin due to genetic disorders. In Suresh, the problem is qualitative as he is having incorrectly functioning globin molecules, while in Rajesh the problem is quantitative as he is having very few globin molecules. Identify the disorder they are suffering from.**

	Suresh	Rajesh
(a)	Thalassemia-Autosomal dominant blood disorder	Sickle-cell anaemia-Autosomal linked recessive trait.
(b)	Sickle-cell anaemia-Autosomal linked dominant trait	Thalassemia-Autosomal recessive blood disorder.
(c)	Sickel-cell anaemia-autosomal linked recessive trait	Thalassemia-Autosomal recessive blood disorder.
(d)	Thalassemia-Autosomal dominant blood disorder	Sickle-cell anaemia-Autosomal linked dominant trait.

Ans. (*c*)

26. **Placed below is a karyotype of a human being.**

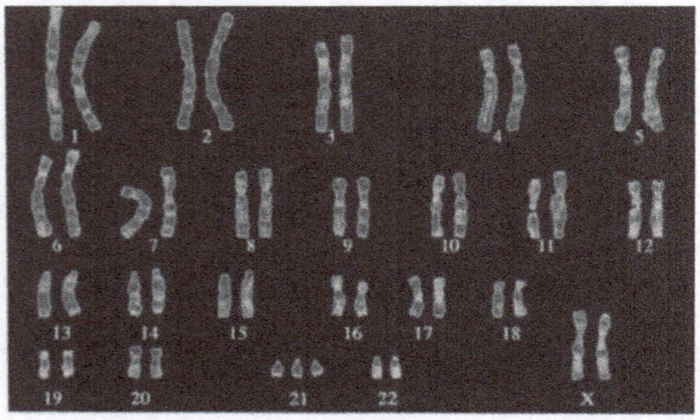

On the basis of the karyotype, which of the following conclusions can be drawn? **CBSE SQP 2021 Term-I**

(a) Normal human female
(b) Person is suffering from colour blindness
(c) Affected individual is a female with Down's syndrome
(d) Affected individual is a female with Turner's syndrome

Ans. (*c*)

27. **A person with trisomy of 21st chromosome shows** **CBSE 2024**

I. furrowed tongue
II. characteristic palm crease
III. rudimentary ovaries
IV. gynecomastia

Select the correct answer from the options given below

(a) II and IV
(b) I, II and IV
(c) II and III
(d) I and II

Ans. (*d*)

28. **In humans , non-disjunction of the 21st pair of chromosomes leads to** **CBSE 2024 C**

(a) Acquired Immune Deficiency Syndrome (AIDS)
(b) Klinefelter's syndrome
(c) Turner's syndrome
(d) Down's syndrome

Ans. (*d*)

29. **Given below is a karyotype of a human foetus obtained for screening to find any probable genetic disorder.**

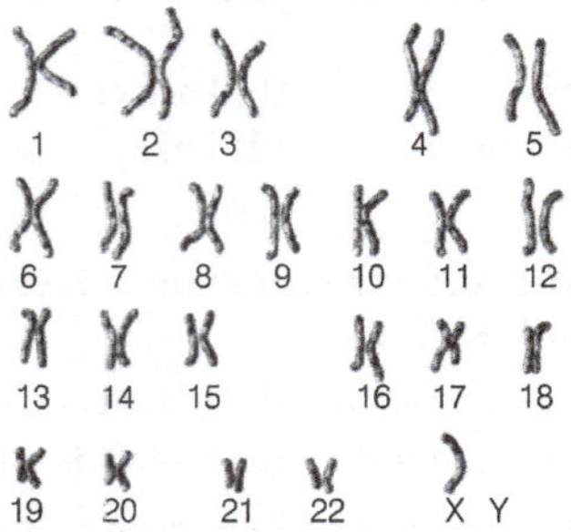

Based on the karyotype, the chromosomal disorder detected in unborn foetus and the consequent symptoms the child may suffer from are **CBSE 2021 Term-I**

(a) Turner's syndrome : Sterile ovaries, short stature
(b) Down's syndrome : Gynecomastia, overall masculine stature
(c) Turner's syndrome : Small round head, flat back of head
(d) Down's syndrome : Furrowed tongue, short stature

Ans. (*a*)

30. **Match the Column I with Column II and choose the correct answer from the codes given below.**

Column I	Column II
A. Phenylketonuria	1. Failure of cytokinesis at telophase
B. Thalassemia	2. Deletion
C. Polyploidy	3. Base pairs substitution
D. Sickle-cell anaemia	4. Autosomal recessive trait

Codes

	A	B	C	D
(a)	2	1	4	3
(b)	2	3	4	1
(c)	4	1	2	3
(d)	4	2	1	3

Ans. (*d*)

31. **Which of the following is not an example of aneuploidy?** **CBSE 2025**

(a) Turner's syndrome (b) Down's syndrome
(c) Phenylketonuria (d) Klinefelter's syndrome

Ans. (*c*) Phenylketonuria (PKU) is not an aneuploidy but a genetic metabolic disorder.

32. **Select the incorrect match from the following.**

	Human Karyotype		Characters
(a)	45 + XX	1.	Broad palm with characteristic palm crease
(b)	44 + XXY	2.	Overall feminine development
(c)	43 + XO	3.	Sterile females as ovaries are rudimentary
(d)	44 + XY	4.	Normal male

Ans. (*c*)

Assertion-Reason Questions

Direction (Q. Nos. 1-10) *In each of the following questions, a statement of Assertion (A) is given followed by corresponding statement of Reason (R). Of the statements, mark the correct answer*

(a) Both A and R are true and R is the correct explanation of A
(b) Both A and R are true, but R is not the correct explanation of A
(c) A is true, but R is false
(d) A is false, but R is true

1. **Assertion** (A) Genes are not passed on from one generation to the next.

Reason (R) Genes serves as the units of inheritance.

Ans. (*d*)

2. **Assertion** (A) When the two genes in a dihybrid cross are situated on the same chromosome, the proportion of parental gene combinations is much higher than non-parental type.

Reason (R) Higher parental gene combination can be attributed to crossing over between two genes.

Ans. (*c*) A is true, but R is false. R can be corrected as

Higher parental gene combination can be attributed to the linkage between the two genes.

3. **Assertion** (A) In incomplete dominance, the phenotype of the heterozygous individual is different from both homozygous parents.

Reason (R) In incomplete dominance, the alleles do not show complete dominance over one another, resulting in an intermediate phenotype.

Ans. (*a*)

4. **Given below is the pedigree chart of a non-Mendelian inheritance in human. The square represents male and the circle represents female. I^A, I^B, i represents the alleles of gene I which determines blood group in humans.**

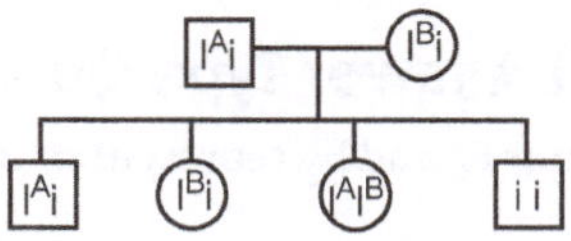

Assertion (A) The given pedigree chart represents codominance.

Reason (R) In codominance, the F_1-generation resembles both the parents.

Ans. (*a*)

5. **Assertion** (A) Pleiotropy occurs when a single gene affects multiple traits in an organism.

Reason (R) In pleiotropy, a single gene produces a mutation that causes an organism to have more than one type of gene.

Ans. (c) A is true, but R is false. R can be corrected as Pleiotropy involves one gene influencing multiple traits.

6. **Assertion** (A) Gene pairs present on the same chromosome may be tightly linked or loosely linked.

Reason (R) Frequency of recombination between gene pairs on different chromosomes as a measure of the distance between genes can be used for 'mapping' their position on the chromosomes. **CBSE 2025**

Ans. (*c*) A is true, but R is false. R can be corrected as

The frequency of recombination between gene pairs on the same chromosome can be used as a measure of the distance between them for mapping their position.

7. **Assertion** (A) Linked genes do not show dihybrid F_2 ratio 9 : 3 : 3 : 1.

Reason (R) Linked genes do not undergo independent assortment. **CBSE 2024**

Ans. (*a*)

8. **Assertion** (A) *Drosophila* shows female heterogamety.

Reason (R) In female heterogamety female produces two different type of sex chromosomes, while male produces two identical sex chromosomes.

Ans. (*d*)

9. **Assertion** (A) Down's syndrome, Klinefelter's syndrome and Turner's syndrome are chromosomal disorders.

Reason (R) In Klinefelter's syndrome females are sterile.

Ans. (*c*)

10. **Assertion** (A) Down's syndrome is a Mendelian disorder.

Reason (R) Down's syndrome is caused due to the presence of an additional copy of chromosome 21.

Ans. (*d*)

Subjective Questions

Very Short Answer Type Questions

1. What do letter F_1 and F_2 represent in heredity studies?

Ans. F_1 – First filial progeny, F_2 – Second filial progeny. (½ + ½)

2. Mention the type of allele that expresses itself only in homozygous state in an organism.

Ans. Recessive allele

3. Name the type of cross that would help to find the genotype of a pea plant bearing violet flowers.

Ans. Test cross

4. List any two characters of pea plants used by Mendel in his experiments other than height of the plant and the colour of the seed.

Ans. The two characters of pea plant used by Mendel in his hybridisation experiment other than height of the plant and the colour of the seed are

(i) Flower colour – Violet and white

(ii) Pod colour – Green and yellow (½ + ½)

5. A garden pea plant (*A*) produced inflated yellow pod and another plant (*B*) of the same species produced constricted green pods. Identify the dominant traits.

Ans. The dominant traits are

(i) For pod shape – Inflated (or full)

(ii) For pod colour – Green (½ + ½)

6. AaBb was crossed with aabb. What would be the phenotypic ratio of the progeny? Mention the term to denote this kind of cross.

Ans. 1 AaBb : 1 Aabb : 1 aaBb : 1 aabb.

It is a test cross. (½ + ½)

7. How many types of gametes would be produced if the genotype of a parent is AaBB?

Ans. 2 (AB, aB).

8. Write the percentage of F_2 homozygous and heterozygous populations in a typical monohybrid cross.

Ans. In a typical monohybrid cross, the percentage of homozygous and heterozygous population is 50% each.

9. Why are gametes said to be pure for a character?

Ans. Gametes are pure for a character because they are always haploid (*n*). During gamete formation, alleles of a gene segregate in such a way that a gamete receives only one allele for a character.

10. Write an example where Punnett square can be effectively used.

Ans. Punnett square can be effectively used to understand the independent segregation of the two pairs of genes during meiosis.

11. Law of independent assortment was based on which observations of Mendel?

Ans. It is based on the observations of dihybrid crosses (crosses between plants differing in two traits).

12. Name the respective pattern of inheritance where F_1-phenotype

(i) does not resemble either of the two parents and is in between the two.

(ii) resembles only one of the two parents.

Ans. (i) Incomplete dominance

(ii) Dominance (½ + ½)

13. Multiple allelism can be investigated only in population. Justify.

Ans. A gene exists in more than two allelic forms in multiple allelism. As a person can have only two of those alleles, so multiple allelism can be studied only in a population.

14. The gene I that controls the ABO blood grouping in human beings has three alleles I^A, I^B and i.

(i) How many different genotypes are likely to be present in the human population?

(ii) Also, how many phenotypes are possibly present?

Ans. (i) Six, (ii) Four (½ + ½)

15. Complete the sentence.
Pleiotropy is said to occur when a gene has

(i) smaller effects on phenotype.

(ii) multiple effects on the phenotype.

Ans. Pleiotropy occur when a gene influence two or more different phenotypes.

16. Give an example of polygenic trait in humans.

Ans. An example of polygenic trait in human is skin colour.

17. Who had proposed the chromosomal theory of the inheritance? NCERT

Ans. Walter Sutton and Theodor Boveri proposed the chromosome theory of inheritance.

18. Who experimentally verified the chromosomal theory of inheritance proposed by Sutton and Theodor Boveri?

Ans. Thomas Hunt Morgan

19. Why do certain genes tend to be inherited together in a cell at the time of cell division?

Ans. They show a phenomenon called linkage.

20. Identify the sex-determination mechanism in following. (½ + ½)

(i) Mammals **(ii) Birds**

Ans. (i) Mammals–XX-XY type. (ii) Birds–ZZ-ZW type.

21. Give one example of organism exhibiting female heterogamety.

Ans. Birds show female heterogamety.

22. Give an example each of the following cases, where
(i) the sperm is responsible and
(ii) ovum is responsible for the sex-determination.

Ans. (i) Human beings/*Drosophila* (ii) Birds (fowls) (½ + ½)

23. Why is X-chromosome called sex-chromosome?

Ans. X-chromosome is involved in the determination of sex of an individual, hence it is called sex-chromosome.

24. How many X-chromosomes and how many autosomes are present in a human ovum?

Ans. One X-chromosome and 22 autosomes.

25. A recessive mutation will be expressed in what condition?

Ans. A recessive mutation will express itself when it is present in homozygous condition.

26. What is point mutation? Give one example. **NCERT**

Ans. Refer to text on page 101.

27. Due to insertion or deletion of the nucleotides the reading frame in the DNA sequence gets changed. What is this type of mutation called as?

Ans. Frame shift mutation

28. The pedigree chart given below shows a particular trait which is absent in parents, but present in the next generation irrespective of sexes. Draw your conclusion on the basis of the pedigree.

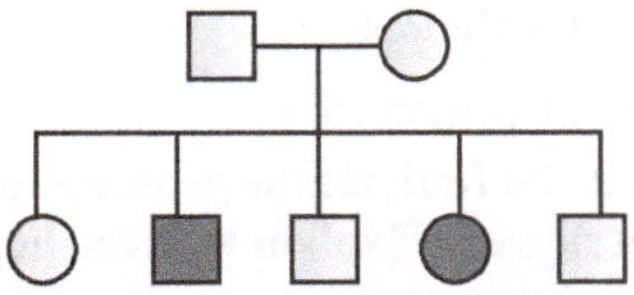

Ans. It is an autosomal recessive trait that is not found in the parents, but has appeared, irrespective of sex, in the offspring. In this case, both the parents are heterozygous for the trait.

29. The diagram below depict the inheritance of a genetic disorder across a few generations in a family.

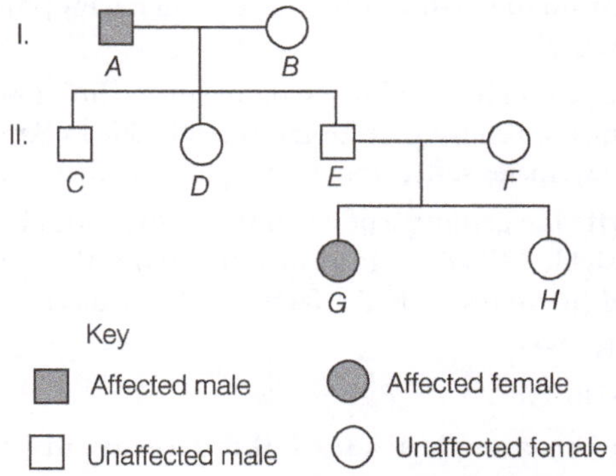

What conclusion can you draw from this pedigree chart?

Ans. The offspring of affected individual *A* and unaffected individual *B* remain unaffected in generation II. This indicates that the allele for this particular disease is recessive.

30. Given below is a pedigree chart showing the inheritance of a certain sex-linked trait in humans.

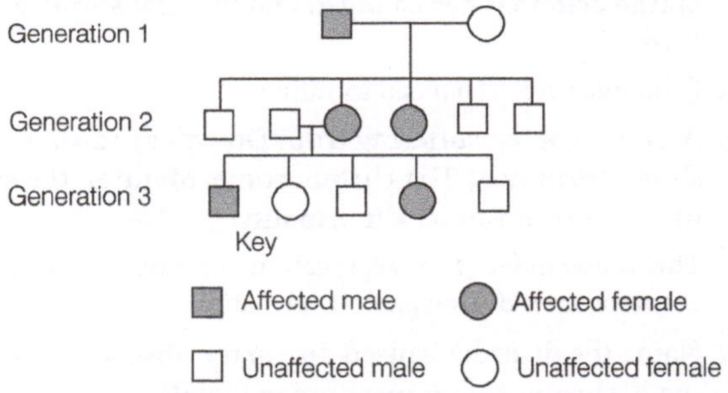

What will the trait traced in the above pedigree chart be called as?

Ans. The trait traced in the given pedigree chart will be called as X-linked dominant because it equally affect both males and females and does not skip generations.

31. Individual A who does not have a genetic disorder, but is still identified as the carriers of the particular disorder. Give reason.

Ans. Individual A is a heterozygote for the gene that can cause this disorder. Thus, he is identified as carrier of the disease.

32. Name one autosomal dominant and one autosomal recessive Mendelian disorder in humans.

Ans. Autosomal dominant disorder – Myotonic dystrophy disease

Autosomal recessive disorder – Thalassemia

33. The son of a haemophilic man may not get this genetic disorder. Mention the reason.

Ans. Refer to text on page no. 102-103.

34. Why do the males suffer more from haemophilia than females?

Ans. The gene of haemophilia is located on X-chromosome. So in males, a single gene for the defect is able to express, that is why, males suffer from haemophilia more than female.

35. Write the genotype of (i) an individual, who is carrier of sickle-cell anaemia gene, but apparently unaffected and (ii) an individual affected with the disease.

Ans. (i) $Hb^{A}Hb^{S}$

(ii) $Hb^{S}Hb^{S}$. (½ + ½)

36. Give an example of a sex-linked recessive disorder in humans.

Ans. Haemophilia is sex-linked recessive disorder in humans.

37. Give an example of a human disorder that is caused due to a single gene mutation.

Ans. Sickle-cell anaemia is an example of human disorder that is caused due to single gene mutation.

38. A change in the amino acid at the sixth position in the beta globin chain leads to sickle-cell anaemia. Name the amino acid that has changed and the new amino acid formed.

Ans. Glutamic acid is changed to valine.

39. A human being suffering from Down's syndrome shows trisomy of 21st chromosome. Mention the cause of this chromosomal abnormality.

Ans. This is due to failure of segregation of homologous chromosomes during gamete formation.

40. Name the disorder caused due to the absence of one of the X-chromosomes in a human female.

Ans. Turner's syndrome is 45, XO.

41. An individual with the chromosomal description 45 + X would be identified having which disorder?

Ans. Turner's syndrome

Short Answer Type Questions

1. State a difference between a gene and an allele.

Ans. A factor which is passed down from parent to offspring through gametes over successive generation is called a gene.

Genes contain a pair of constrasting forms known as alleles Alleles are slightly different forms (contrasting forms) of the same gene.

2. How are alleles of particular gene differ from each other? Explain its significance. NCERT Exemplar

Ans. Alleles are polymorphs that differ in their nucleotide sequence resulting in contrasting phenotypic expression.

These are the alternative forms of a same gene, e.g. genes for height have two alleles, one for dwarfness (t) and one for tallness (T).

Significance of alleles are as follows (2)

(i) A character may have two or more contrasting phenotypic expression, thus resulting in variation in a population.

(ii) These are used in the studies of inheritance. (1)

3. Mendel published his work on inheritance of characters in 1865, but it remained unrecognised till 1900. Give three reasons for the delay in accepting his work.

Ans. Refer to text on page no. 89 (Rediscovery of Mendel's law).

4. Using a Punnett square, work out the distribution of phenotypic features in the first (F_1) filial generation after a cross between a homozygous female and a heterozygous male for a single locus. NCERT

Ans. Homozygous female–WW

Heterozygous male–Ww

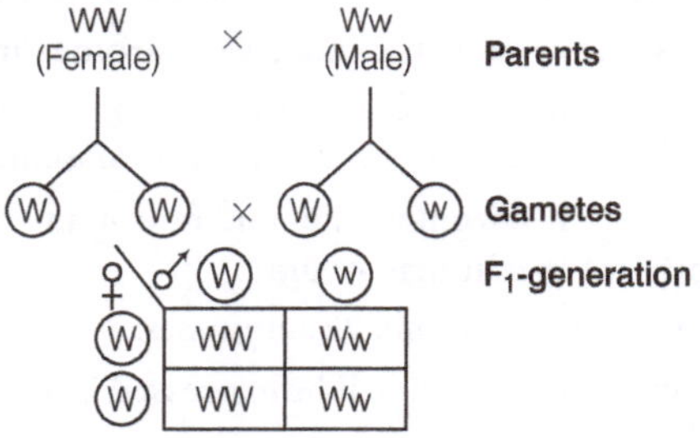

In this case, all individuals of F_1-generation would possess dominant trait. 50% are homozygous dominant and 50% are heterozygous dominant.

5. How many different types of gametes could result from each of the following genotypes? What will be their genotypes?

(i) Aa (ii) AABB (iii) AaBb (iv) EeCc

Ans. The number of different types of gametes and their genotypes are

(i) Aa : 2 (A, a)

(ii) AABB : 1 (AB)

(iii) AaBb : 4 (AB, Ab, aB, ab)

(iv) EeCc : 4 (EC, Ec, eC, ec) (½ × 4)

6. Mention the advantages of selecting pea plant for experiment by Mendel. NCERT

Ans. Refer to text on page no. 91.

7. How would you find out the genotype of a pea plant with violet flowers? Explain with the help of Punnett square showing crosses. CBSE SQP 2023

Ans. Genotype of violet flower can be found out with the help of test cross. This method was devised by Mendel to determine whether the dominant phenotype is homozygous or heterozygous. (1)

There can be two possible genotypes of an unknown dominant phenotype as illustrated below.

(i) If the unknown is homozygous violet (WW) then crossing with white recessive (ww) gives all violet offspring (i.e. all Ww).

(ii) If the unknown is heterozygous (Ww) then crossing with white recessive results in violet (Ww) and white (ww) progeny in 1 : 1 ratio.

Refer to fig. no. 4.3 on page no. 93. (2)

8. What is a test cross? How can it decipher the heterozygosity of a plant?

Or **Define and design a test cross.** **NCERT**

Or

A teacher wants his/her students to find the genotype of pea plants bearing purple coloured flowers in their school garden. Name and explain the cross that will make it possible.

Ans. **Test cross** is a method devised by Mendel to determine the genotype of plant with dominant phenotype (purple flower in his experiment). In a test cross, the unknown dominant genotype is crossed with recessive parent.

Refer to text on page no. 93.

9. By using Punnett square depict the genotypes and phenotypes of test crosses [where green pod colour (G) is dominant over yellow pod colour (g)] in garden pea with unknown genotype. **CBSE 2023**

Ans. Test cross is a type of genetic cross which is used to know the genotype of an organism. In this type of cross, unknown parent is crossed with a homozygous recessive parent.

As given in the question,

Dominant allele: G

Dominant trait: Green pod colour

Recessive allele: g

Recessive trait: Yellow pod colour

Condition 1.

gg

GG	g	g
G	Gg	Gg
G	Gg	Gg

Genotypic ratio: 100% heterozygous dominant

Phenotypic ratio: All green

Conculsion: Unknown is homozygous dominant. (1)

Condition 2:

gg

Gg	g	g
G	Gg	Gg
G	gg	gg

Genotypic ratio: 50% heterozygous dominant and 50% homozygous recessive, i.e. 1:1 ratio

Phenotypic ratio: 50% Green: 50% Yellow

Conculsion: Unknown is heterozygous dominant. (1)

10. Name and state the law of Mendel, which explains the expression of only one of the parental characters in the F_1-generation of a monohybrid cross.

Ans. Law of dominance states that when two individuals of a species, differing in a pair of contrasting characters are crossed, the parental character which appears in the F_1-hybrid is said to be dominant over the trait that remains hidden (recessive).

11. A cross was carried out between two pea plants showing contrasting traits of height of the plants. The result of the cross showed 50% parental characters.

(i) Work out the cross with the help of a Punnett square.

(ii) Name the type of the cross carried out.

Ans. (i) A Punnett square representing the cross given in the question is represented below.

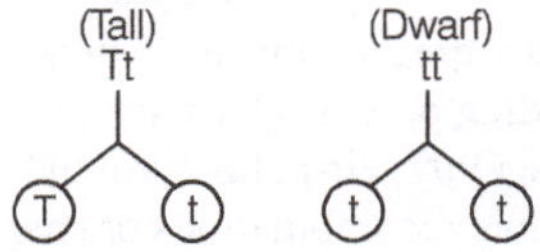

♀ \ ♂	T	t
t	Tt (Tall)	tt (Dwarf)
t	Tt (Tall)	tt (Dwarf)

(2)

(ii) The type of cross carried out here is a test cross (in which an individual with an unknown dominant phenotype is crossed with a homozygous recessive for that trait). (1)

12. Explain the law of dominance using a monohybrid cross. **NCERT**

Or **State Mendel's law of dominance. How did he deduce the law? Explain with the help of a suitable example.** **CBSE 2020**

Ans. Refer to text on page no. 93.

13. During a monohybrid cross involving a tall pea plant with a dwarf pea plant, the offspring populations were tall and dwarf in equal ratio. Workout a cross to show how is it possible?

Ans. In a monohybrid test cross, involving a heterozygous tall plant (Tt) and a pure dwarf plant (tt), the progeny consists of tall and dwarf plants in the ratio of 1 : 1.

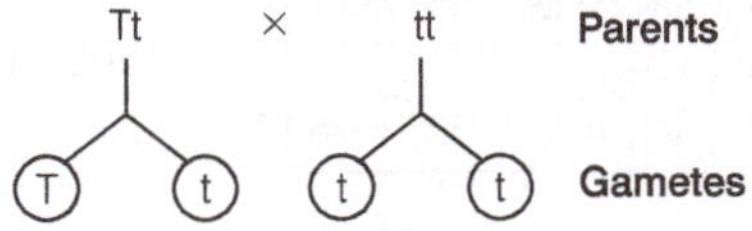

	t	t
T	Tt	Tt
t	tt	tt

F_1-generation

Genotypic ratio : 50% heterozygous dominant and 50% homozygous recessive.

14. Explain the laws that Mendel derived from his monohybrid crosses.

Ans. Mendel derived law of dominance and law of segregation from his monohybrid crosses.

Refer to text on page no 93.

15. Which law of inheritance of Mendel is universally acceptable and without any exception? State the law.

Ans. Law of segregation states that the members of the allelic pair that remained together in the hybrid, segregate or separate during gametogenesis and enter in different gametes.

16. In order to obtain the F_1-generation, Mendel pollinated a pure-breeding tall plant with a pure-breeding dwarf plant. But for getting the F_2-generation, he simply self-pollinated the tall F_1-plants. Why? **NCERT Exemplar**

Ans. Characters segregate during gamete formation. Pure-breeding parents give rise to F_1 with heterozygous conditions. Only self-pollination of heterozygous can result in all possible recombinations of characters in progeny since the mating is random.

17. Work out a typical Mendelian dihybrid cross and state the law that he derived from it.

Or

State and explain the law of independent assortment in a typical Mendelian dihybrid cross.

Ans. Refer to text on dihybrid cross on page no. 93-94.

18. How would you find genotype of a tall pea plant bearing white flowers? Explain with the help of a cross. Name the type of cross you would use.

Ans. Genotype of a tall pea plant bearing white flowers can be found out with the help of test cross.

Case I Tall (homozygous) pea plant with white flowers crossed with dwarf pea plant with white flowers.

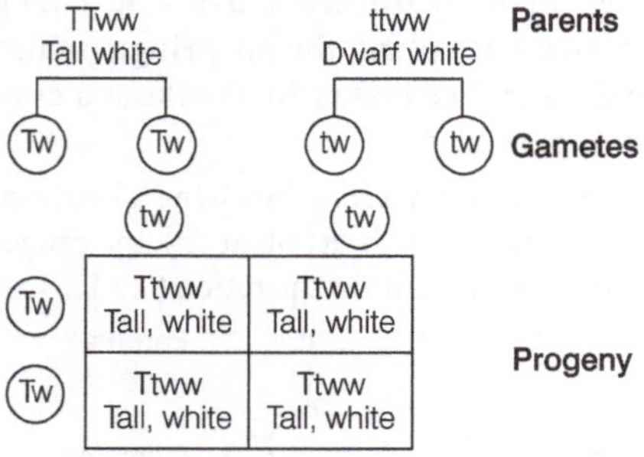

If 100% plants are tall with white flowers then the genotype is TT ww. (1½)

Case II Tall (heterozygous) pea plant with white flowers is crossed with dwarf pea plant with white flowers.

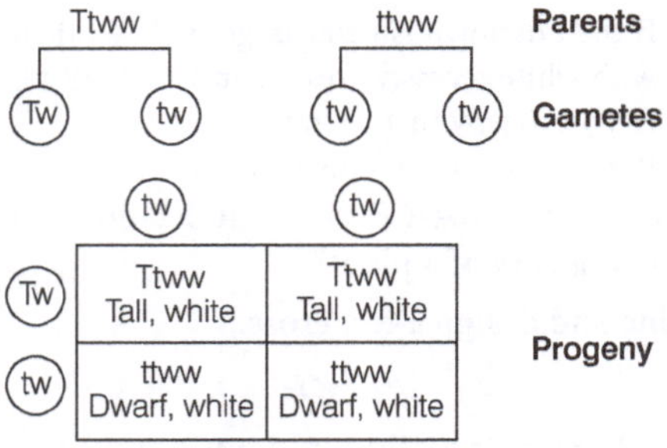

If 50% plants are tall with white flowers and 50% are dwarf with white flower then the genotype is Ttww. (1½)

19. When a cross is made between tall plant with yellow seeds (TtYy) and tall plant with green seed (Ttyy), what proportions of phenotype in the offspring could expected to be?

(i) Tall and green **(ii) Dwarf and green** **NCERT**

Ans.

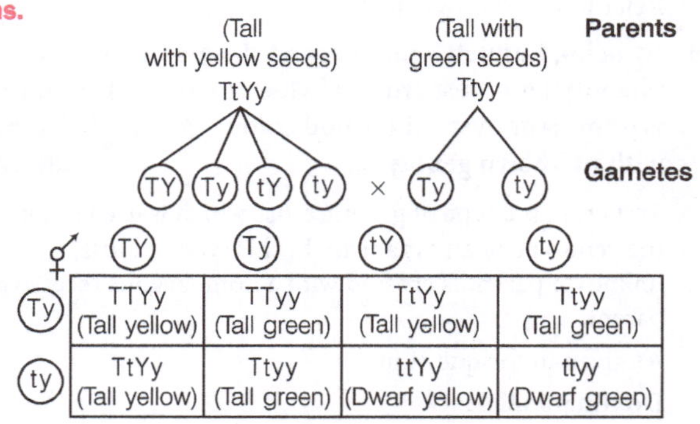

(i) Tall green – 3/8 or 6/16

(ii) Dwarf green – 1/8 or 2/16

20. A diploid organism is heterozygous for 4 loci, how many types of gametes can be produce? **NCERT**

Ans. The formula 2^n is applied here

where, n = Number of heterozygous loci

The organism is heterozygous for 4 loci, $n = 4$

So, $2^n = 2^4 = 2 \times 2 \times 2 \times 2 = 16$

21. A, B, D are three independently assorting genes with their recessive alleles a, b, d, respectively. A cross was made between individual of AabbDD genotype with aabbdd. Find out the type of genotypes of the offspring produced. **NCERT Exemplar**

Ans.

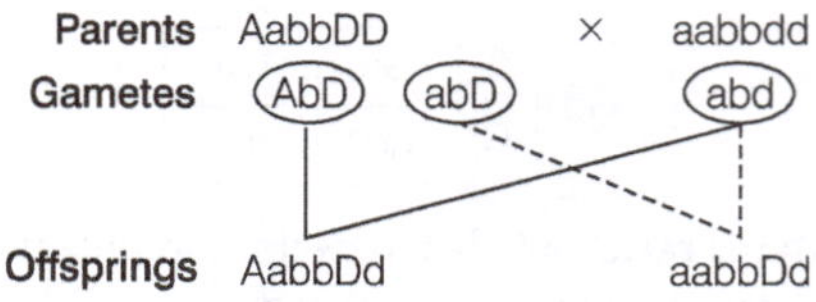

The genotypes of the offsprings are AabbDd and aabbDd.

22. A snapdragon plant with violet flowers was crossed with another such plant with white flowers. The F_1 progeny obtained had pink flowers. Explain, in brief, the inheritance pattern seen in offspring of F_1-generation. **CBSE SQP 2023**

Ans. The inheritance pattern seen in offspring of F_1-generation in the question is incomplete dominance. In such inheritance pattern, new intermediate phenotype of two parental phenotypes is obtained because one allele for a specific trait do not express completely over the other allele.

23. In snapdragon, a cross between true-breeding red flowered (RR) plants and true-breeding white flowered (rr) plants showed a progeny of plants with all pink flowers.

(i) The appearance of pink flowers is not known as blending. Why?

(ii) What is this phenomenon known as?

Ans. (i) Blending is the mixing of two colours, but in this example red and white colours are appearing independently at cellular level. Thus, no blending of characters occurs in this case. Also, red and white colours reappear in F_2-generation. (2)

(ii) This phenomenon is known as incomplete dominance. (1)

24. With the help of one example, explain the phenomenon of codominance and multiple allelism in human population.

Ans. Inheritance pattern of ABO blood groups in human population.

(i) **Codominance** Codominance is a phenomenon where both allaeles of a gene are fully expressed in a heterozygous organism. I^A and I^B both are codominant as both of them express themselves independently in blood group AB (I^AI^B). (1)

(ii) **Multiple Allelism** A phenomenon in which genes exist in more than two allelic forms or combinations. For example, the gene for blood group exists in three allelic forms I^A, I^B and i. (1)

25.

Genotypes	RBCs	Phenotypes
I^AI^A	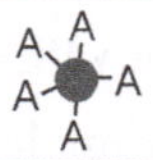	A
I^Ai		A
I^BI^B	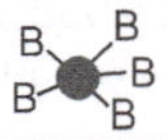	B
I^Bi	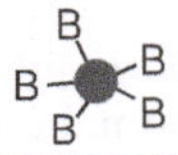	B
I^AI^B	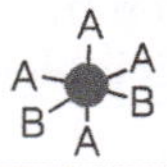	AB
ii		O

Study the diagram above and answer the following questions. **CBSE 2025**

(i) How many alleles are involved in blood grouping?

(ii) A person having 'AB' blood group has both dominant alleles. What is this inheritance type called?

(iii) A man with 'A' blood group marries a woman with 'B' blood group. Can they have a child with 'O' blood group? Explain with the help of a cross.

Ans. (i) Three alleles (I^A, I^B, i) are involved in blood grouping.

(ii) The inheritance type is codominance, as both I^A and I^B alleles are expressed equally in AB blood group individuals.

(iii) Yes, they can have a child with O blood group if the father has genotype I^Ai and the mother has I^Bi. The possible cross is

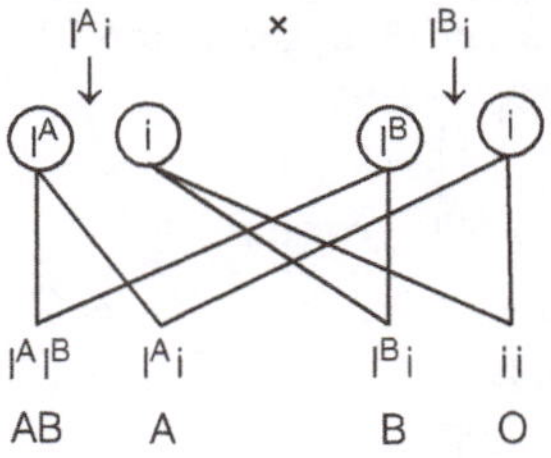

(1 × 3)

26. Two children one with blood group 'AB' and other with blood group 'O' are born to parents, where the father has blood group 'A' and the mother has blood group 'B'. Work out a cross to show how is it possible? **CBSE 2020**

Ans. Parents must be heterozygous, since blood group 'O' appears in progeny.

There are three alleles of the gene controlling blood group character, i.e. I^A, I^B and i. I^A and I^B are dominant over 'i' and together they are codominant to each other.

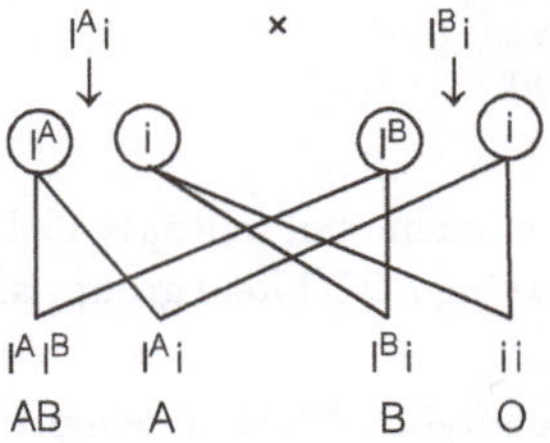

27. Given below is the pedigree chart up to 3 generations (Generation I, Generation II, Generation III) of a family with respect to their blood groups. CBSE 2024 C

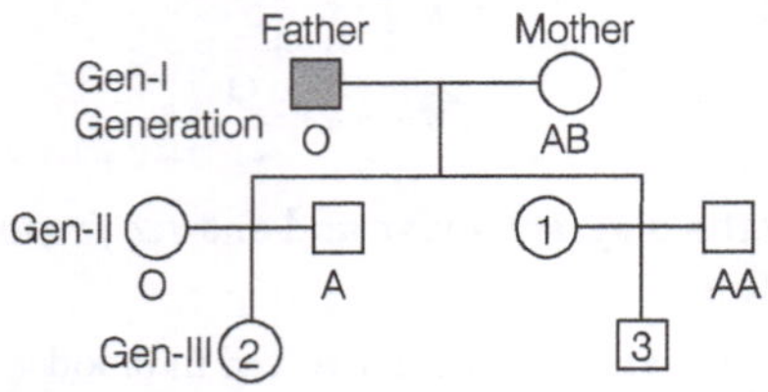

(i) **Mention the blood group along with the genotype of the offspring numbered '1' in generation II.**

(ii) **Write the possible blood groups along with their genotypes of the offsprings numbered '2' and '3' in generation III.**

Ans. (i) Blood group of number 1 in generation II

	I^O	I^O
I^A	I^OI^A	I^OI^A
I^B	I^OI^B	I^OI^B

Genotype of number 1 is → I^OI^A, I^OI^B
Blood group →A or B (2)

(ii) Possible blood group along with their genotype of offsprings no '2' and '3' in generation III.

$I^OI^O \times I^AI^A$
↓
I^OI^A (Genotype)

Blood group is A.
If the genotype is

$I^OI^O \times I^AI^O$
I^AI^O I^OI^O

Blood group → O or A/ Genotype - I^OI^A
For No. '3', if the genotype is

$I^AI^O \times I^AI^A$
↓
I^AI^O

Blood group → 'A',Genotype -I^OI^A
If the genotype is $I^OI^A \times I^OI^B$

I^OI^B I^OI^A I^AI^B

Blood group → 'A' 'AB' or 'B'
Genotype → I^OI^B, I^OI^A, I^AI^B (1)

28. (i) Explain the phenomenon of multiple allelism and codominance taking ABO blood groups as an example.

(ii) What is the phenotype of the following?

(a) I^Ai (b) ii

Ans. (i) Refer to text on page no. 96. (2)

(ii) (a) I^Ai–'A' blood group (b) ii–'O' blood group (1)

29. Can a child have blood group 'O' if his/her parents have blood group 'A' and 'B'? Explain. NCERT Exemplar

Ans. Yes, a child can have blood group 'O', if his/her parents have blood group A. As the child with blood group O will have homozygous recessive alleles. Therefore, both the parents should be heterozygous, i.e. genotype of father will be I^A i or I^B i and of mother will be I^A i or I^B i.

30. A child has blood group O. If the father has blood group A and mother's blood group is B, workout the genotypes of the parents and the possible genotypes of the other offsprings. NCERT

Ans. The child with blood group O will have homozygous recessive alleles. Therefore, both the parents should be heterozygous, i.e. the genotype of father will be I^Ai and the mother will be I^Bi.

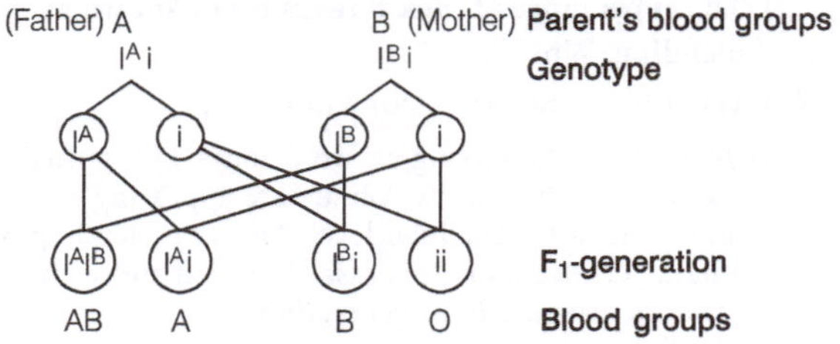

The other possible genotypes of offsprings will be A, B and AB blood groups.

31. Expression of different genes for different traits may show dominance, incomplete dominance or codominance. Write about expression of such genes with the help of one example each.

Ans. Expression of different genes for different traits may show dominance, incomplete dominance or codominance based on expression of genes.

(i) **Dominance** In this one allele of a gene dominates (dominant) the other (recessive) and is able to express itself in the heterozygous condition also, e.g. a pea plant with two alleles, of stem height. T (tall; dominant) and t (short; recessive). For cross see page no. 92. (1)

(ii) **Incomplete dominance** Refer to text on page no. 94-95. (1)

(iii) **Codominance** Refer to text on page no. 95. (1)

32. Explain the follwing terms with example NCERT

(i) Co-dominance (ii) Incomplete dominance

Ans. Refer to the text on page 95 and 94. (2 × 1)

33. Compare in any three ways the chromosomal theory of inheritance as proposed by Sutton and Bovery with that of experimental results on pea plant presented by Mendel. CBSE 2019

Ans. Through any of the given ways, the chromosomal theory of inheritance given by Sutton and Boveri and experimental results presented by Mendel can be compared

(i) In a diploid organism, the factors (genes) and chromosomes occur in pairs.

(ii) Both chromosomes as well as genes segregate at the time of gamete formation such that only one of each pair is transmitted to a gamete.
(iii) A gamete contains only one chromosome of a type and only one of the two allele of a trait.
(iv) The paired condition of both chromosomes as well as Mendelian factors is restored during fertilisation. (Any three)

34. Briefly mention the contribution of TH Morgan in genetics. **NCERT**

Ans. Refer to text on page no. 97.

35. Write the scientific name of the fruitfly. Why did Morgan prefer to work with fruitflies for his experiments? State any three reasons. **CBSE 2014**

Ans. Refer to text on page no. 97.

36. In a dihybrid cross, white eyed, yellow-bodied female *Drosophila* was crossed with red eyed, brown-bodied male *Drosophila*, produced in F_2-generation are 1.3% recombinants and 98.7% progeny with parental type combinations.
This observation of Morgan deviated from Mendelian F_2 phenotypic dihybrid ratio. Explain giving reasons, Morgan's observations.

Ans. Morgan observed that when the two genes in dihybrid cross were situated on same chromosome, the proportion of parental gene combinations were higher than non-parental type. This is due to physical association of genes on a chromosome or linkage. In Morgan's experiment, the genes for eye and body colour show linkage and do not always allow crossing over during gamete formation. Hence, parental type progeny is in greater ratio than that of recombinants.

37. During his studies on genes in *Drosophila* that were sex-linked, TH Morgan found F_2 population phenotypic ratio to be deviated from expected 9 : 3 : 3 : 1 . Explain the conclusion he arrived at.

Or **When Morgan conducted dihybrid cross on *Drosophila* like Mendel did with pea plants, the F_2 ratio deviated significantly from that of Mendel's F_2 ratio. Write the explanation Morgan and his group gave to the observations they obtained from their experiment.**

Ans. Conclusion of Morgan's experiments are
(i) Genes were located on the X-chromosome. (1)
(ii) When the two genes in a dihybrid cross were studied on the same chromosome, the proportion of parental gene combinations were much higher than the non-parental type.
Morgan stated this association as 'linkage' to describe the physical association of genes on a chromosome. (1)
(iii) Morgan and his group also found that even when genes were grouped on the same chromosome, some genes were tightly linked (low recombination) and others were loosely linked (high recombination). (1)

38. Linkage and crossing over of genes are alternatives of each other. Justify with the help of an example.

Ans. Linkage is the tendency of certain loci or alleles (genes) to be inherited together. Crossing over is the segregation of genes. The genes on a chromosome either follow linkage path or cross over to form the gametes during gametogenesis in human.

39. Two heterozygous parents are crossed. If the two loci are linked, what would be the distribution of phenotypic features in F_1-generation for a dihybrid cross? **NCERT**

Ans. If the two loci in parents are completely linked, there would be no segregation. The F_1-generation will exhibit parental characters only. But, if the two loci are incompletely linked, then segregation would occur partly and the F_1-generation will exhibit both parental and recombinant characteristics, but the recombinants will be in a very small proportion.

40. What are linked genes? How can a pair of linked gene be identified?

Ans. The two genes that are present close together on a same chromosome and did not assort independently are said to be linked. Linked genes can be identified through combination of genetic mapping technique and by observing the inheritance pattern of traits in offsprings.

41. State the fate of a pair of autosome during gamete formation.

Ans. During gamete formation, the homologous pair of autosomes gets separated from each other and moves to different gametes. Hence, each gamete receives haploid set of chromosomes.

42. Give an example of each type.
(i) Female XX with male XO
(ii) Female ZW with male ZZ

Ans. (i) The type of sex-determination mechanism in which female XX with male XO is male heterogamety, e.g. grasshopper. (1)
(ii) The type of sex-determination mechanism shown in female ZW with male ZZ is female heterogamety, e.g. birds. (1)

43. Differentiate between male and female heterogamety.

Ans. Refer to text on page no. 99.

44. Explain the mechanism of 'sex-determination' in birds. How does it differ from that of human beings?

Ans. Refer to text on page no. 100.

45. A male is accountable for the sex of the foetus. Using your knowledge of sex determining mechanism in humans, provide a valid explanation for the above statement.

Ans. Refer to text on page no. 100.

46. How is the sex-determined in humans? **NCERT**

Ans. Refer to text on page no. 100.

47. How many chromosomes do drones of honeybee possess? Name the type of cell division involved in the production of sperms by them.

Ans. Drones of honeybee possess 16 chromosomes (haploid). They produce sperms by a mitosis like division, rather than by meiosis.

48. Aneuloidy is which type of mutation? How is it different from polyploidy?

Ans. Aneuploidy is the condition used to describe a chromosomal aberration or alteration that is caused by an addition or deletion of one or more chromosomes. It results in genetic disorders. It differs from polyploidy which is the addition of one or more complete sets of chromosome in the genome.

49. What happens when chromatids fail to segregate during cell division cycle? Explain your answer with an example.

Ans. When chromatids fail to segregate during cell division, mutation or aneuploidy occurs. This can cause chromosomal disorder in humans. For example, Down's syndrome (trisomy of 21st chromosome) and Klinefelter's syndrome (presence of an additional copy of X-chromosome resulting in the karyotype of 47, XXY in males).

50. Why does deletion or insertion of a segment of DNA result in alteration of chromosomes?

Ans. Refer to text on page no. 101.

51. What is pedigree analysis? Suggest how such an analysis can be useful? **NCERT**

Ans. Pedigree analysis is the study of transmission of particular traits over the generations for finding out the possibility of their occurrence in the future generations. (1)

Importance of pedigree analysis are as follows

(i) It is used to know the possibility of expressive or recessive allele, which may cause genetic disorders. (1)

(ii) It shows the origin of a trait and inheritance pattern of that trait in a family. (1)

52. Why is pedigree analysis done in humans? List two reasons why the Mendelian experiments cannot be carried out in human beings.

Ans. (i) Pedigree analysis is carried out for studying inheritance of human traits. It is also useful when studying species with a long generation time. (1)

(ii) The common Mendelian experiments are not possible in humans because

(a) Developnental period is long.

(b) Progeny is small in number. (1)

53. Is haemophilia in humans a sex-linked or autosomal disorder? Work out a cross in support of your answer.

Ans. Haemophilia is a sex- linked recessive disease. The gene responsible for haemophilia is located on X-chromosome and males have only single copy of X-chromosome with no alternate normal allele. Therefore, it is quite common in males

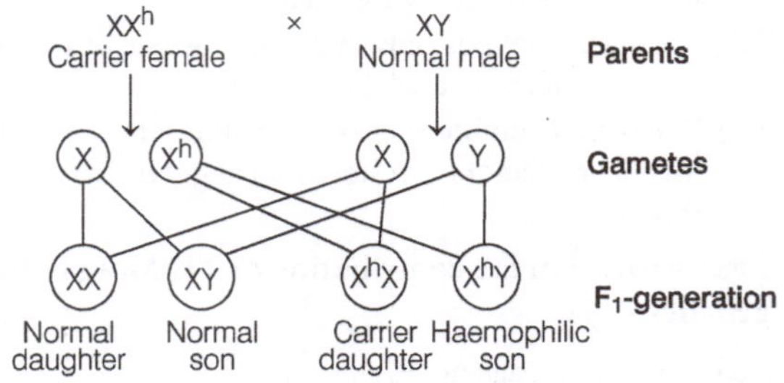

54. Haemophilia is a sex-linked inheritance condition in humans where a simple cut causes non-stop bleeding. Study the pedigree chart showing the inheritance of haemophilia in a family.

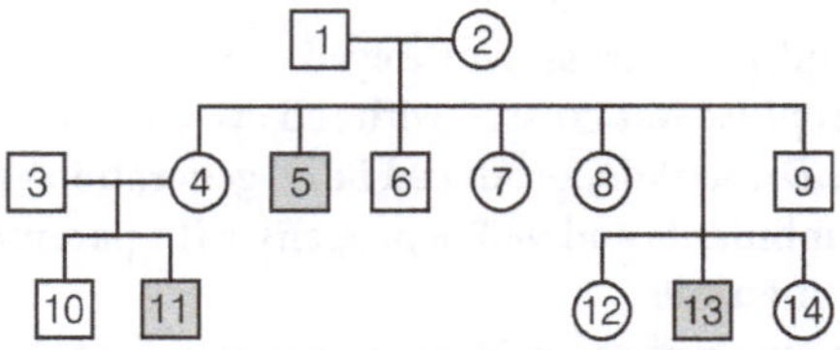

Give reasons, which explain that haemophilia is (i) sex-linked, (ii) caused by X-linked gene.

Ans. (i) Haemophilia is sex-linked because

(a) It is transmitted from an unaffected carrier female to some of the male offspring.

(b) Female rarely becomes haemophilic as her mother has to be atleast a carrier and father should be haemophilic. (2)

(ii) Gene for haemophilia is present on X-chromosome, therefore the heterozygous female for haemophilia may transmit the disease to sons. (1)

55. A cross between a normal couple resulted in a son who was haemophilic and a normal daughter. In course of time, when the daughter was married to a normal man, to their surprise, the grandson was also haemophilic.

(i) Represent this cross in the form of a pedigree chart. Give the genotypes of the daughter and her husband.

(ii) Write the conclusion you draw of the inheritance pattern of this disease.

Ans. (i)

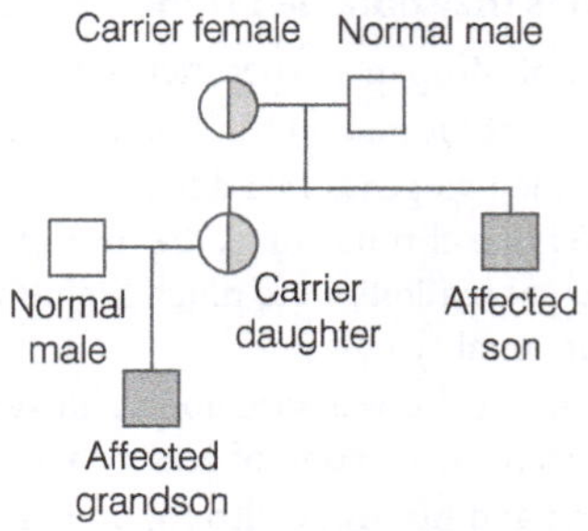

Genotype of daughter and her husband are X^hX and XY, respectively. (1)

(ii) Haemophilia is a sex-linked recessive disease. It is transmitted from the carrier female to some of her sons. From the above pedigree chart, it can be observed that the disease is being transmitted from the carrier female to her daughter (carrier) and son (affected). The carrier daughter transmits this disease to the grandson. This pattern of inheritance is called *criss-cross* inheritance. (2)

56. A colourblind boy is born to a couple with a normal colour vision. Write the genotype of the parents.

Ans. X^CY (colourblind boy)

Its parent could be XX^C (carrier mother) and XY (normal father).

57. A couple with normal vision bears a colourblind child. Work out the cross to show how it is possible and mention the sex of the affected child?

Ans. Colour blindness is a sex-linked disease. The gene for this disorder is present on the X-chromosome. Hence, it is carried by normal females not expressing the disease. If a colourblind child is born to a normal couple, then the mother could be the carrier of the disease.

The inheritance of the disorder is shown by cross. Refer to text on page no. 103 (For cross).

58. Given below is the representation of a relevant part of amino acid composition of the β-chain of haemoglobin, related to the shape of human red blood cells.

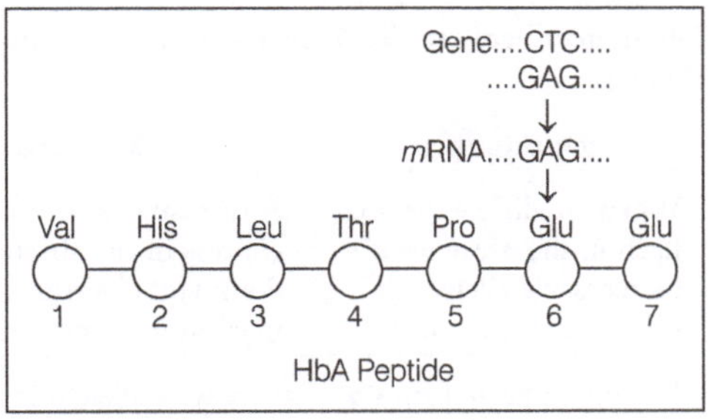

(i) Is this representation of the sequence of amino acids indicating a normal human or a sufferer from a certain blood related genetic disease? Give reason in support of your answer.

(ii) Why is the disease referred to as a Mendelian disorder? Explain. **CBSE 2019**

Ans. (i) The sequence of amino acids indicates a normal human. Refer to text on page no. 103 (Sickle-cell anaemia). (1)

(ii) The disease transmission follows Mendelian principles, therefore it is called Mendelian disorder.

It is transmitted from parents to the offspring, when both the partners are carriers (heterozygous) of the disease. In this disease, RBCs become sickle-shaped. (1)

59. Given below is a picture that shows the magnified blood smear of a patient under a microscope.

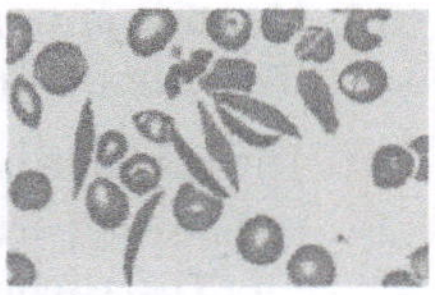

(i) Name the disease the blood smear is indicative of. Write the symptoms of the disease and its cause.

(ii) Explain the inheritance pattern of the disease with the help of a suitable cross.

Ans. (i) The given blood smear shows sickle-shaped RBCs and thus, is indicative of diseases called sickle-cell anaemia.

Symptoms Biconcave disc to elongated sickle like RBC, severe anaemia, shortness of breath, etc.

Cause It is caused by substitution of glutamic acid (Glu) by valine (Val) at sixth position of beta globin chain of haemoglobin molecule. (1½)

(ii) Sickle-cell anaemia is an autosomal recessive trait that can be transmitted from parent to the offspring, when both partners are carrier for the gene (heterozygous). This disease is controlled by a single pair of allele Hb^A and Hb^s, where Hb stands for haemoglobin Hb^s represents the diseased genotype of blood. Only homozygous individual for Hb^s ($Hb^S Hb^S$) show the diseased phenotype. The heterozygous individuals are carriers ($Hb^A Hb^S$).

(Carrier mother) $Hb^S Hb^A$ ↓ (Hb^S) (Hb^A)

(Carrier father) $Hb^S Hb^A$ ↓ (Hb^S) (Hb^A)

♀ \ ♂	Hb^S	Hb^A
Hb^S	$Hb^S Hb^S$ (Affected)	$Hb^S Hb^A$ (Carrier)
Hb^A	$Hb^S Hb^A$ (Carrier)	$Hb^A Hb^A$ (Normal)

Outcome : 1 Affected : 2 Carriers : 1 Normal (1½)

60. (i) Sickle-cell anaemia in humans is a result of point mutation. Explain.

(ii) Write the genotypes of both the parents, who have produced a sickle-celled anaemic offspring.

Ans. . (i) Refer to text on page no. 103. (1)

(ii) The genotypes of parents must be Hb^AHb^S and Hb^AHb^S. (1)

61. How thalassemia-α differs from thalassemia-β?

Ans. Refer to text on page no. 104.

62. Both haemophilia and thalassemia are blood related disorders in humans. Write their causes and name the category of genetic disorder they both come under.

Ans. Refer to text on page no. 102 and 104. (for causes). **(2)**

Category of genetic disorder

Haemophilia – Sex-linked disease.

Thalassemia – Autosomal recessive disease. (1)

63. Mention any two autosomal genetic disorders with their symptoms. NCERT

Ans. The autosomal genetic disorders are

(i) **Down's syndrome** Refer to text on page no. 104. (1)

(ii) **Thalassemia** Refer to text on page no. 103-104. (1)

64. A woman of 47 years delivered an abnormal child with a flattened nasal bridge and mouth partially open with a large protruding tongue. Name this genetic abnormality. What causes this condition?

Ans. (i) This genetic disorder is called Down's syndrome. (1)

(ii) This condition is caused due to trisomy of chromosome number 21 (an additional copy of chromosome 21). (1)

65. During a medical investigation, an infant was found to possess an extra copy of chromosome no. 21. Identify the disorder the child is suffering from. Describe the symptoms the child is likely to develop later in life. CBSE 2025

Ans. An additional copy of chromosome number 21 (trisomy of chromosome number 21) in humans results in Down's syndrome. (1)

Following characteristic symptoms are likely to develop in the child due to the above mentioned conditions

(i) Short statured with small, round head.

(ii) Furrowed tongue and partially open mouth.

(iii) Broad palm with characteristics palm crease.

(iv) Slow mental, physical and psychomotor development. (2)

66. Name one commonly occurring genetic disorder in humans which is caused due to monosomy (one chromosome less than the normal number of chromosomes) of sex chromosome. Give its two symptoms. CBSE 2025

Ans. Turner's syndrome is a commonly occurring genetic disorder in humans caused by monosomy of the sex chromosome (45, XO). (1)

Two symptoms of this disorder are as follows

(i) Individuals are shorter than average.

(ii) Underdeveloped ovaries lead to the absence of menstruation and infertility. (2)

67. Name a disorder, give the karyotype and write the symptoms, where a human male suffers as a result of an additional X-chromosome.

Ans. The disorder is Klinefelter's syndrome. It is a chromosomal disorder, which occurs in males.

The presence of an additional copy of X-chromosome results in karyotype 44+XXY.

For symptoms, refer to text on page no. 105. (1 × 3)

68. Identify (i), (ii), (iii), (iv), (v) and (vi) in the table given below.

Syndrome	Causes	Characteristics of Affected Individual	Sex male /Female /Both
Down's	Trisomy of 21	(i) (a) (b)	(ii)
(iii)	XXY	Overall masculine development	(iv)
Turner's	45 with XO	(v) (a) (b)	(vi)

Ans. (i) (a) Short stature individuals with round head and furrowed tongue.

(b) Slow mental development.

(ii) Both (iii) Klinefelter's syndrome

(iv) Male

(v) (a) Rudimentary ovaries

(b) Lack of secondary sexual characters

(vi) Females.

Long Answer Type Questions

1. Differentiate between the following.

(i) Dominance and recessive

(ii) Homozygous and heterozygous

(iii) Monohybrid and dihybrid NCERT

Ans. (i) Differences between dominance and recessive are as follows

Dominance	Recessive
When an allele expresses itself in the presence of its recessive allele, it is called dominant trait.	A recessive allele can only express in the absence of its dominant allele and remain masked in its presence.
Dominant allele forms a complete functional enzyme due to which complete polypeptide is formed to express.	Recessive allele forms incomplete polypeptide enzyme due to which non-functional polypeptide is formed that fails to express completely.

(2)

(ii) Differences between homozygous and heterozygous are as follows

Homozygous	Heterozygous
It is a condition when both alleles of a gene are similar.	It is a condition when both alleles of a gene are dissimilar.
The genotype is expressed as TT or tt.	The genotype is expressed as Tt.

Homozygous	Heterozygous
They are true breeding. Thus, leading to pure lines.	They are not true breeding.
The gametes produced by them are similar in genotype.	The gametes produced by them are of two types, one with dominant allele and other with recessive allele.

(2)

(iii) Differences between monohybrid and dihybrid are as follows

Monohybrid	Dihybrid
It is a genetic cross that involve inheritance of a single trait or gene.	It is a genetic cross that involves the inheritance of two traits each with two alleles
Typical phenotypic ratio is 3 :1 .	Typical phenotypic ratio is 9 : 3 : 3 : 1

(1)

2. **(i) Explain a monohybrid cross taking seed coat colour as a trait in *Pisum sativum*. Work out the cross upto F_2 -generation.**

(ii) State the laws of inheritance that can be derived from such a cross.

(iii) How is the phenotypic ratio of F_2-generation different in a dihybrid cross?

Ans. . (i) In a monohybrid cross, when homozygous dominant and homozygous recessive parents are crossed, F_1-hybrid would be heterozygous for the trait and would express the dominant allele.

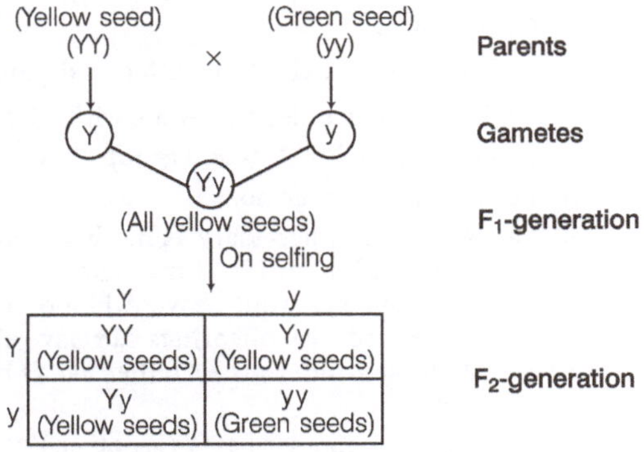

(2)

(ii) The hybrid is heterozygous containing both alternative alleles (Y and y) but only one trait, i.e. yellow colour appeared and green colour trait is suppressed in F_1-generation. This shows that yellow seed colour is dominant over the green seed colour trait. This explains Mendel's law of dominance. (2)

(iii) Phenotypic ratio in F_2-generation in monohybrid cross is 3 : 1 and in dihybrid cross is 9 : 3 : 3 : 1. (1)

3. **A cross was carried out between two pea plants homozygous dominant for yellow and round seeds with homozygous recessive for the same trait. The F_2 progeny of such a cross showed phenotypic ratio of 9: 3 : 3 : 1.**

(i) State the different laws of Mendel that could be derived from such a cross.

(ii) Write the possible genotypes for the progeny for such a cross having

(a) yellow and wrinkled seeds

(b) green and round seeds **CBSE 2020**

Ans. (i) The given cross in the question is a dihybrid cross. Based upon this, Mendel proposed a law of independent assortment.

For detail see page no. 93-94. (3)

(ii) The possible genotype of the progeny in the above given dihybrid cross is

(a) yellow and wrinkled seeds – YYrr, Yyrr

(b) green and round seed – yyRR, yyRr. (2)

4. **(i) By taking two suitable traits in a pea plant, work out a dihybrid cross up to F_2 generation.**

(ii) State the Mendel's law derived from such a cross only.

Ans. Refer to text on page no. 93-94.

5. **Describe the dihybrid cross upto F_2-generation as conducted by Gregor Mendel using pure lines of garden pea for characters; seed shape and seed colour.** **CBSE 2023**

Ans. In a dihybrid cross, Mendel took a pair of contrasting traits together for crossing; For example, colour and the shape of seeds at a time. He picked the wrinkled-green seed and round-yellow seed and crossed them. From the cross, he obtained only round-yellow seeds in the F_1-generation. This indicated that round shape and yellow colour of seeds are dominant in nature. While the wrinkled shape and green colour of seeds are recessive traits.

Following the first cross, F_1 progeny was self-pollinated. This resulted in four different combinations of seeds in F_2-generation. They were round-yellow, round-green, wrinkled-yellow seeds and wrinkled-green in the phenotypic ratio of 9:3:3:1.

For figure refer to fig. no. 4.4.

6. **It is sometimes observed that the F_1 progeny has a phenotype that does not resemble either of the two parents and has intermediate phenotype. Explain by taking a suitable example and working out the cross upto F_2 progeny.** **CBSE 2023**

Ans. Refer to text on page no. 94-95 (Incomplete dominance).

7. **Inheritance pattern of flower colour in garden pea plant and snapdragon differs? Why is this difference observed? Explain showing the crosses upto F_2 -generation.**

Ans. (i) Inheritance pattern of flower colour in garden pea plant.

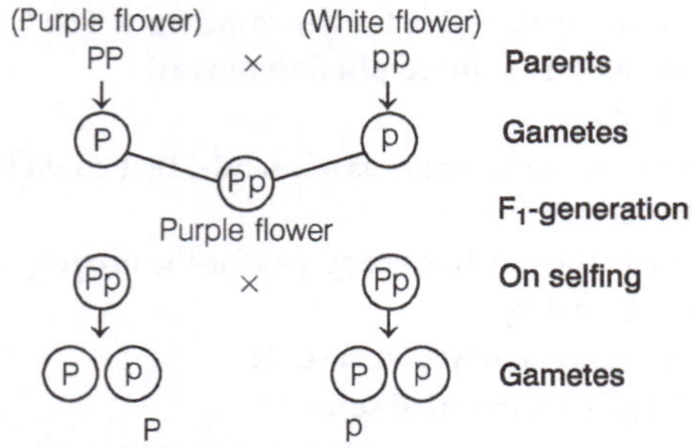

	P	p
P	PP (Purple flower)	Pp (Purple flower)
p	Pp (Purple flower)	pp (White flower)

F_2-generation

Phenotypic ratio Purple : White
3 : 1

Genotypic ratio PP : Pp : pp
1 : 2 : 1

Inheritance of flower colour in garden pea shows true dominance. In F_1-generation, dominant colour purple is expressed and in F_2-generation both dominant (purple) and recessive (white) colour are expressed in the ratio of 3 : 1. (2½)

(ii) Inheritance pattern of flower colour in snapdragon is given below

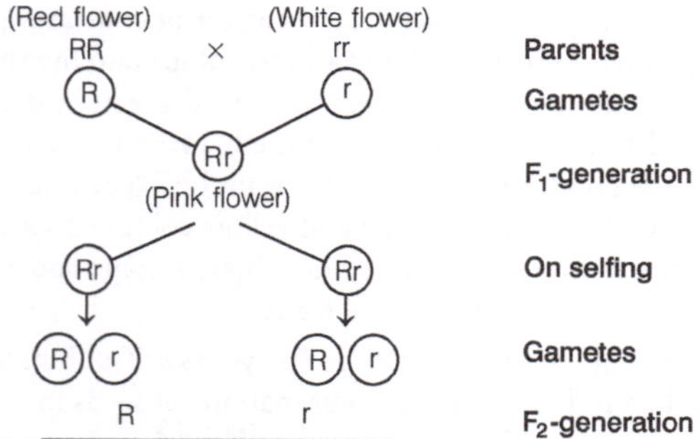

	R	r
R	RR (Red flower)	Rr (Pink flower)
r	Rr (Pink flower)	rr (White flower)

Phenotypic ratio Red : Pink : White
1 : 2 : 1

Genotypic ratio RR : Rr : rr
1 : 2 : 1

Inheritance in snapdragon flower colour shows incomplete dominance. In this phenomenon, neither of the two alleles are completely dominant over the other and the hybrid is intermediate between the two. Hence, red is a homozygous dominant, white is a homozygous recessive, while hybrid is an intermediate, i.e. pink. (2½)

8. What is the inheritance pattern observed in the size of starch grains and seed shape in *Pisum sativum*?

Workout the monohybrid cross showing the above traits. How does this pattern of inheritance deviate from that of Mendelian law of dominance?

Ans. Seed shape shows complete dominance. Heterozygotes produce the round seeds. (1)

Size of starch grains shows incomplete dominance. Heterozygotes produce intermediate sized starch grains in seeds. (2)

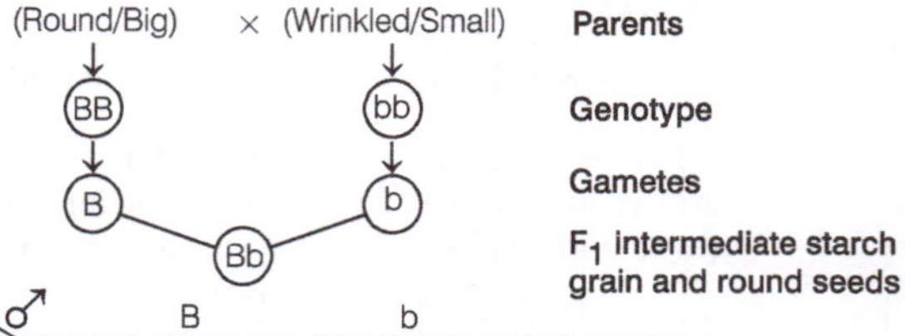

♀ \ ♂	B	b
B	BB (Big starch grain and round seed)	Bb (Intermediate starch grain and round seed)
b	Bb (Intermediate starch grain and round seed)	bb (Wrinkled seed with small starch grain)

Size of starch grain is an example of incomplete dominance, whereas in Mendelian inheritance, seed shape shows complete dominance. (4)

9. (i) List three different allelic forms of gene 'I' in human. Explain the different phenotypic expression, controlled by these three forms.

(ii) A woman with blood group 'A' marries a man with blood group 'O'.

Discuss the possibilities of the inheritance of the blood group in the following starting with 'Yes' or 'No' for each.

(a) They produce children with blood group 'A' only.

(b) They produce children some with 'O' blood group and some with 'A' blood group.

Ans. . (i) Refer to text on page no. 95. (3)

(ii) (a) No, it is not necessary as mother could have a genotype I^AI^A or I^Ai. If the genotype is I^AI^A, all the offsprings would have A blood group, but in the second case offsprings can have either A or O blood group as their father has O blood group. (1)

(b) Yes, if the mother has A (genotype I^Ai) and father has O (genotype ii) blood group, then the blood group of children can be O and be with blood group or A. (1)

10. It is sometimes observed that the F_1 progeny shows a phenotype that resembles both the parents. Explain this type of inheritance using the example of ABO blood groups in human. **CBSE 2023**

Ans. Refer to text on page no. 95 (Codominance).

11. (i) **What is polygenic inheritance? Explain with the help of a suitable example.**

(ii) **How are pleiotrophy and Mendelian pattern of inheritance different from polygenic pattern of inheritance?**

Ans. (i) **Polygenic inheritance** Refer to text on page no. 96. (2)

(ii) Diffference between Mendelian inheritance, polygenic inheritance and pleiotropy is given below

Mendelian Inheritance	Polygenic Inheritance	Pleiotropy
One gene controls one trait or character or phenotype.	Two or more genes influence the expression of one trait or character or phenotype.	One gene controls expression of more than one trait or one character or phenotype.

(3)

12. Many patterns of inheritance deviate considerably form the pattern of inheritance as explained by Mendel. List any four such inheritance patterns and explain any three with the help of an example each.

Ans. Many patterns of inheritance deviated considerably from the pattern of inheritance as explained by Mendel. These deviation were due to different reasons and phenomena. Four such inheritance patterns are

1. Incomplete dominance 2. Codominance
3. Pleiotropy
4. Linkage and recombination (2)

For detail refer to text on page no. 95-97. (3)

13. (i) **Write the scientific name of the organism Thomas Hunt Morgan and his colleagues worked with for their experiments. Explain the correlation between linkage and recombination with respect to genes as studied by them.**

(ii) **How did Sturtevant explain gene mapping, while working with Morgan?**

Ans. (i) Refer to text on page no. 97. (3)

(ii) Refer to text on page. no. 98 (2)

14. (i) **Why are grasshopper and *Drosophila* said to show male heterogamety? Explain.**

(ii) **Explain female heterogamety with the help of examples.**

Ans. (i) Refer to text on page no. 99. (2½)

(ii) Refer to text on page no. 100. (2½)

15. Describe sex-determination in birds with example.

Ans. Refer to text on page no. 100.

16. (i) **In humans, males are heterogametic and females are homogametic, explain. Are there any examples where males are homogametic and females heterogametic?**

(ii) **Also describe as to, who determines the sex of an unborn child?**

Mention whether temperature has a role in sex-determination. **NCERT Exemplar**

Ans. (i) Refer to text on page no. 99-100. (2½)

(ii) As a rule, the heterogametic organism determines the sex of the unborn child. In case of humans, since males are heterogametic, it is the father and not the mother who decides the sex of the child.

In some animals like crocodiles, lower temperature favours the hatching of female offspring and higher temperatures lead to hatching of male offspring. (2½)

17. Explain the causes, inheritance pattern, symptoms of two Mendelian genetic disorders.

Ans. Refer to text on page no. 102-103. (2½ × 2)

18. (i) **How does a chromosomal disorder differ from a Mendelian disorder?**

(ii) **Name any two chromosomal aberration - associated disorders. Also explain them.**

Ans. (i) Differences between chromosomal and Mendelian disorders are as follows

Chromosomal Disorders	Mendelian Disorders
They are caused by alteration in chromosome number or structure.	These disorders are caused by mutation in a single gene.
Chromosomal abnormalities develop due to defective synapsis and non-disjunction phenomenon.	Mutation at random place, create allelic abnormalities.
These disorders are rarely transmitted.	The Mendelian disorders follow Mendel's inheritance pattern and get transmitted to the progeny.

(3)

(ii) Refer to text on page no. 104 and 105. (2)

19. With reference to the below schematic representation of pedigree analysis and answer the questions that follows

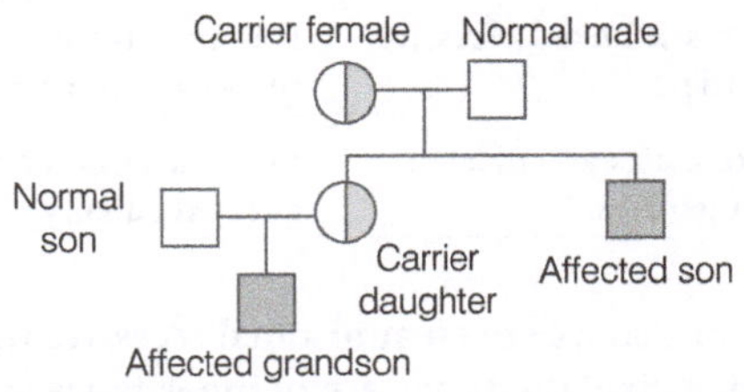

(i) **What are the genotypes of carrier female and normal male?**

(ii) **Write the conclusion of the inheritance pattern if the trait transmitted is haemophilic.**

Ans. (i) Genotypes of carrier female and normal male are XX^h and XY, respectively. (2)

(ii) Haemophilia is a sex-linked recessive disease. The allele of disease is being transmitted from the carrier female to her daughter (carrier) and son (affected).
The carrier daughter transmits this disease to the grandson. This pattern of inheritance is called *criss-cross* inheritance. (3)

20. Study the given pedigree chart showing inheritance of sickle-cell anaemia and answer the questions that follows

(i) Is the trait recessive or dominant?

(ii) Is the trait sex-linked or autosomal?

(iii) Give the genotype of the parents.

Ans. (i) Sickle-cell anaemia is controlled by a single pair of allele Hb^A and Hb^s. Only homozygous individuals for Hb^s, i.e. Hb^s Hb^s show the diseased phenotype, while the heterozygous individuals are carriers (Hb^A Hb^S). Thus, it is a recessive trait. (1)

(ii) This trait is autosomal in nature because its gene is present on autosomes.

The disease can be transmitted from the parents to the offspring only if both the parents are heterozygous (i.e. carrier for the gene). (2)

(iii) The parents are heterozygous for the trait as only two of their offspring have diseased phenotypes. The genotypes of parents would be Hb^A Hb^S and Hb^A Hb^S. (2)

21. Write the symptoms of haemophilia and sickle-cell anaemia in humans. Explain how the inheritance pattern of the two diseases differs from each other?

Ans. For symptoms, refer to text on page no. 102-103. (2)

Differences between inheritance pattern of haemophilia and sickle-cell anaemia are as follows

Haemophilia	Sickle-cell Aanaemia
It occurs due to a defective recessive allele present on the X-chromosomes.	It occurs due to point mutation, i.e. a single base pair change leads to a change in amino acid.
It is a sex-linked recessive disorder.	It is an autosomal linked recessive disorder.
More males are affected than females.	Both males and females are affected equally.

(3)

22. Give an example of an autosomal recessive trait in humans. Explain its pattern of inheritance with the help of a cross.

Ans. Refer to text on page no. 103-104 (Thalassemia).

23. (i) Why are thalassemia and haemophilia categorised as Mendelian disorders? Write the symptoms of these diseases. Explain their pattern of inheritance in humans.

(ii) Write the genotypes of the normal parents producing a haemophilic son.

Ans. (i) Haemophilia is categorised as Mendelian disorders because these disorders occurs due to alteration in a single gene. Also, they are transmitted to offspring through Mendelian principles of inheritance.
Symptoms and pattern of inheritance are given below (1)

(a) **Thalassemia** Refer to text on page no. 103-104.

(b) **Haemophilia** Refer to text on page no. 102-103. (2)

(ii) Genotypes of the normal parents producing a haemophilic son are X^hX (carrier mother) and XY (father).

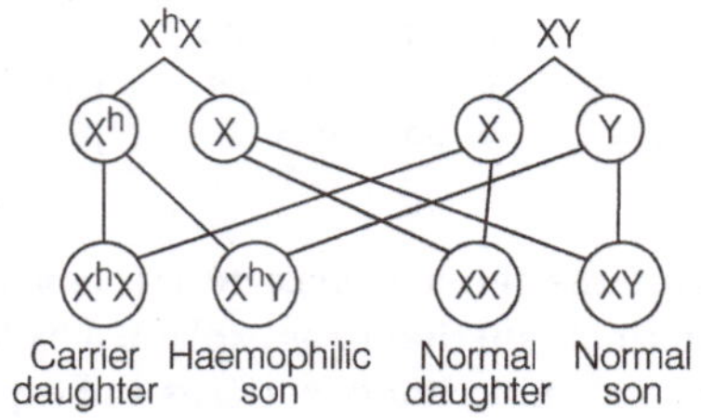

(2)

24. Describe the individuals having the following chromosomal abnormalities.

(i) Trisomy of 21st chromosome (ii) XXX

(iii) XO NCERT Exemplar

Ans. Individuals having following chromosomal abnormalities are described as

(i) **Trisomy of 21st chromosome** It is also known as Down's syndrome. In this, a person is born with three chromosomes at 21st position rather than normal pair.
Symptoms– Refer to text on page no. 104. (1)

(ii) **XXX** It is also known as triple X-syndrome. This condition can occur only in females where they have three X-chromosomes instead of two. (2)

(iii) **XO** It is also known as Turner's syndrome. It always affects the females in which one of the two chromosomes are defective or completely absent. The individuals with this syndrome are born with 45 chromosomes in each cell rather than 46.
Symptoms– Refer to text on page no. 105. (2)

Source Based/Case Based/Passage Based Questions

1. Kernel colour in wheat ranges from dark red to white depending on the number of dominant alleles in the genotype of the plant as shown below.

Kernel Colour	No. of Dominant Alleles
Dark red	4
Medium red	3
Intermediate red	2
Light red	1
White	0

Assuming that a cross is performed between a homozygous dominant male and a homozygous recessive female, answer the questions that follows.

(i) **What will be the kernel colour of offspring in the F_1-generation?**

(ii) **How many genes code for kernel colour in wheat?**

(iii) **What phenomenon is indicated by the presence of medium red colour in wheat?**

Ans. (i) On crossing the two pure breeding wheat varieties, i.e. dark red and a white, medium red coloured kernels will be obtained in the F_1-generation. (1)

(ii) Kernel colour is determined by two genes, each having two alleles, where the allele for red kernel colour is dominant over the allele for white. (1)

(iii) The presence of medium red colour in wheat indicates **incomplete dominance** (where heterozygous plants show an intermediate colour) and **polygenic inheritance** (where multiple genes contribute to the final colour). (2)

2. Observe the following schematic representation of determination of sex (XX-XY type mechanism) and answer the questions that follows.

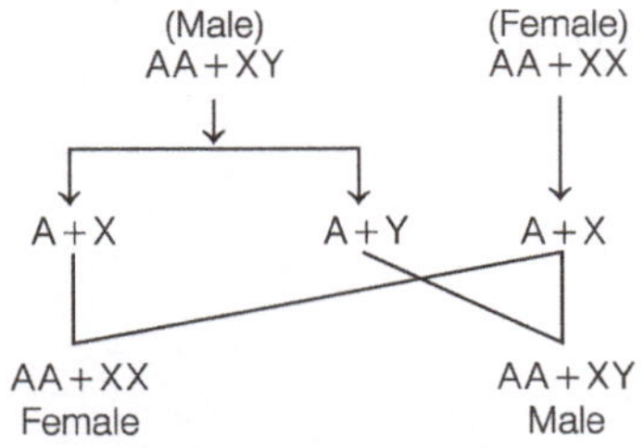

(i) **The given method of sex-determination is an example of male heterogamety or female heterogamety? Justify your answer.**

(ii) **Name two organisms in which this type of sex-determination method is seen.**

Ans. (i) XX-YY type of sex-determination is an example of male heterogamety. This is because it is the mechanism in which male produces two different types of gametes, some gametes with X-chromosome and some with Y-chromosome. (2)

(ii) This type of sex-determination method is seen in certain insects like *Drosophila melanogaster* and mammals including human. (2)

3. ACHOO syndrome is characterised by uncontrollable sneezing in response to the sudden exposure to bright light, typically intense sunlight. It is inherited as an autosomal dominant condition.

(i) **Draw a Punnett grid to determine the probability of producing an unaffected child by a heterozygous father and an unaffected mother.**

(ii) **Depict the inheritance using a pedigree.**

(iii) **If a mother is diseased (heterozygous) and the father is unaffected, what is the probability that their offspring will inherit the disease?**

Ans. (i) Suppose A represent the dominant allele and a represent the recessive allele. Then the punnet grid of a heterozygous father and an unaffected mother is as follows

(Father) Aa × aa(Mother) **Parents**

A a a **Genotype**

	A	a
a	Aa	aa
a	Aa	aa

(2)

(ii) The pedigree of the of the given disease is as follows

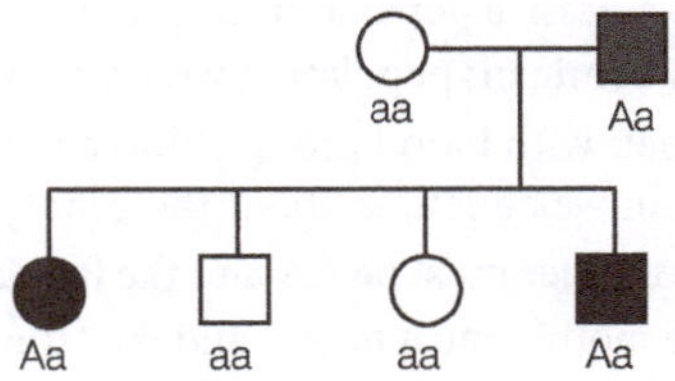

(1)

(iii) The mother is heterozygous (Aa), and the father is homozygous recessive (aa). Each child has a 50% chance of inheriting the dominant allele (A) from the mother and being affected. (1)

4. Cystic fibrosis is a condition in which a defective gene (consider allele c) produces faulty transport channels that causes mucus to build up in the ducts of different organs leading to vitamin deficiency diseases, respiratory infections and excessive loss of salt through sweat.

Given below is a pedigree chart for a family. The great-grandmother, represented as I- 1, suffers from cystic fibrosis.

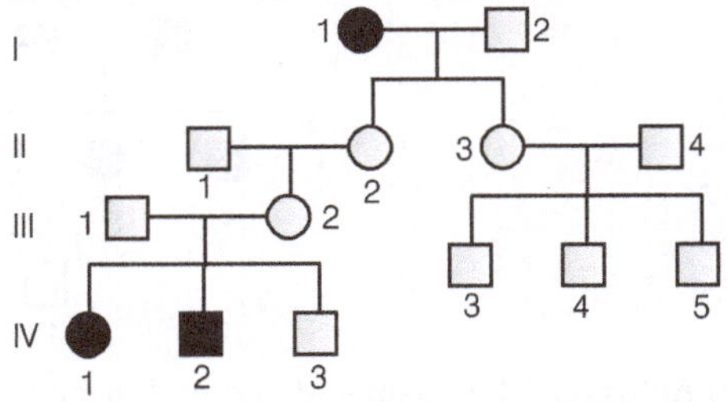

(i) **Identify the type of expression of the cystic fibrosis gene. Give a reason to support your answer.**

(ii) **From the pedigree, deduce the pattern of inheritance exhibited by the gene. Justify your answer.**

(iii) **Identify the genotypes of II-2 and III-2.** CBSE CFPQ

Ans. (i) The cystic fibrosis gene exhibits pleiotropy as one gene is affecting multiple organs and therefore contributing to multiple phenotypes. (2)

(ii) Recessive disorder expression as the trait is skipping generations so it cannot be dominant. (1)

(iii) II-2 - Cc III-2 - Cc (1)

SELF ASSESSMENT TEST

Multiple Choice Questions

1. The number and type of gametes produced when a homozygous dominant (AABB) male is crosses with homozygous recessive (aabb) female.
   (a) Four; AB, Ab, aB and Ab
   (b) Four; AABB, AABb, AaBB, and aabb
   (c) Three; AABB, AaBb and aabb
   (d) Two; AB and ab
2. A cross between two hybrids result in the formation of
   (a) 50% recessive population with genotype tt
   (b) 50% dominant population with genotype Tt
   (c) 75% dominant population with genotype TT
   (d) 50% recessive population with genotype tt
3. A woman with blood group A has a child with blood group O. The father of the child has blood group B. What can we conclude about the genotypes of the mother and father?
   (a) The mother must be AA and the father must be BB.
   (b) The mother must be AO and the father must be BO.
   (c) The mother must be AO and the father must be AB.
   (d) The mother must be AA and the father can be either BO or BB.
4. Choose the incorrect match-pair with respect to the sex-determination in different animals.
   (a) Human – XX-XY type
   (b) Grasshopper – XO type
   (c) Drosophila – XX-XO type
   (d) Chicken – ZW-ZZ type
5. Select the incorrect pair.

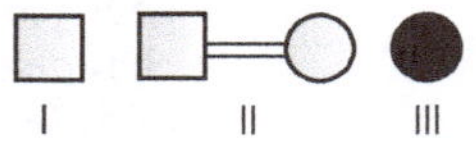

   (a) Normal female, heterozygous female and affected male, respectively.
   (b) Affected female, carrier male and normal male, respectively.
   (c) Affected male, homozygous female and normal female, respectively.
   (d) Normal male, mating between relatives and affected female, respectively.
6. Analyse the given pedigree and choose the correct option.

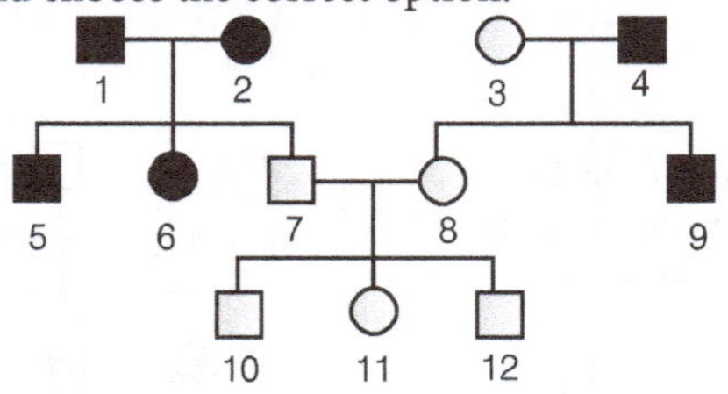

   (a) Autosomal dominant – Myotonic dystrophy
   (b) Autosomal recessive – Sickle-cell anaemia
   (c) X-linked dominant – Haemophilia
   (d) X-linked recessive – Colour blindness
7. If a colourblind man has a child with a colourblind woman, what is the probability that their male child will be colourblind?
   (a) 50%
   (b) 75%
   (c) 25%
   (d) 100%

Assertion-Reason Questions

Direction *(Q. Nos. 8-11) In each of the following questions, a statement of Assertion (A) is given followed by corresponding statement of Reason (R). Of the statements, mark the correct answer If*

(a) Both A and R are true and R is the correct explanation of A.
(b) Both A and R are true, but R is not the correct explanation of A.
(c) A is true, but R is false.
(d) A is false, but R is true.

8. **Assertion** (A) Gametes receive only one allele of a gene.

Reason (R) Alleles segregate independent of each other at the time of gamete formation.

9. **Assertion** (A) Human skin colour is determined by three distinct pairs of alleles that collectively influence pigmentation.

Reason (R) Skin colour in humans exhibits pleiotropic inheritance, where multiple genes interact to affect various traits.

10. **Assertion** (A) In birds, females are responsible for determining the sex of the baby.

Reason (R) In birds, male possess two different types of sex chromosomes.

11. **Assertion** (A) Sickle-cell anaemia can transmit from unaffected parents to offspring.

Reason (R) Sickle-cell anaemia is an autosome linked recessive disorder.

Very Short Answer Type Questions

12. Differentiate between test cross and back cross.
13. What are linked genes?
14. What are the characteristics of a person having Klinefelter's syndrome?
15. In a cross between pea plants having round green seeds (RRGG) and wrinkled yellow seds (rrgg) what percentage of eggs will carry both the round and green alleles for the F_2 generation?

Short Answer Type Questions

16. How sex-determination in humans differ from that of sex-determination in birds?
17. Write a short note on haplo-diploid type of sex-determination in honeybee.
18. Explain how a couple with normal vision can have colourblind son.

Long Answer Type Questions

19. (i) Explain incomplete dominance with the help of a cross, upto F_2-generation.

(ii) Differentiate between incomplete dominance and codominance.

20. How pleiotropy is different from polygenic inheritance. Explain with the help of example.
21. (i) Elaborate the process of sex determination in honey bee.

(ii) How sex of the offspring is determined in case of birds.

Case Based Question

22. Given below is the pedigree of a family for a trait.

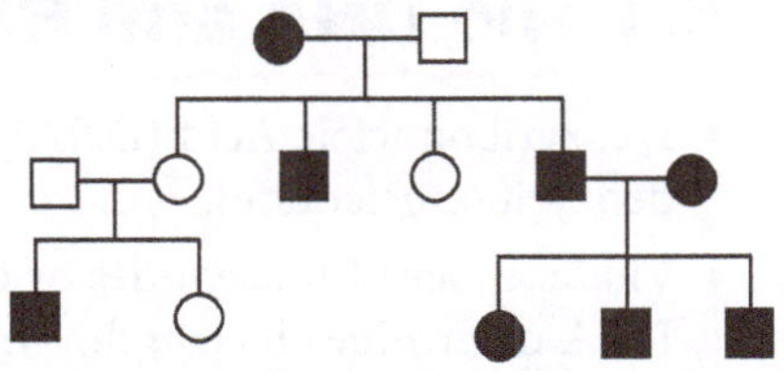

(i) Identify the mode of inheritance of the trait. Give a reason(s) to support your answer.

(ii) Give two examples for the same.

(iii) What is the probability of first son being diseased if mother is diseased, while father is normal?

Answers

1. (d) 2. (b) 3. (b) 4. (c) 5. (d) 6. (a) 7. (d)
8. (a) 9. (c) 10. (c) 11. (a)

05

CHAPTER

Molecular Basis of Inheritance

The cells of all living organisms have two types of nucleic acids. These are **Deoxyribonucleic Acid** (DNA) and **Ribonucleic Acid** (RNA).
DNA is the genetic material in majority of organisms as it carries hereditary information from one generation to another.

YOUR STUDY GOALS

5.1 The DNA and RNA World
5.2 Packaging of DNA Helix
5.3 The Search for Genetic Material
5.4 Central Dogma
5.5 Replication of DNA
5.6 Transcription
5.7 Genetic Code
5.8 Translation
5.9 Regulation of Gene Expression
5.10 Human Genome Project (HGP)
5.11 DNA Fingerprinting

YOUR PRACTICE GOAL

- Objective Type Questions (41 Qs ; MCQs, A-R) Case Based Questions (5)
- Subjective Type Questions
- (30 VSAs, 81 SAs, 36 LAs)

- In this chapter, we will discuss the structure of DNA, its replication and the transcription process (i.e. making RNA from DNA).
- Then, we will study about the role of genetic code in determining the sequences of amino acids in proteins, translation process (i.e. protein synthesis) and their regulation.
- In the last section, the genomics and the essentiality of human genome sequencing and its consequences will also be discussed.

5.1 The DNA and RNA World

- Deoxyribonucleic Acid (DNA) is a long polymer of deoxyribonucleotides.
- The number of nucleotides or base pairs (bp) present in the DNA determines its length. This length is also the characteristic of an organism, e.g.
  - ***Escherichia coli*** — 4.6×10^6 bp
  - **Bacteriophage** $\phi \times 174$ — 5,386 bp
  - **Lambda phage** — 48,502 bp
  - **Human beings** — 3.3×10^9 bp (haploid content)

Structure of a Polynucleotide Chain (DNA/RNA)

- A nucleotide is composed of a nitrogenous base, pentose sugar and a phosphate group.
- The detailed structure of a nucleotide components are given below.

A Pentose Sugar

Two types of sugars or carbohydrates (monosaccharides) having 5 carbon atoms are present in nucleic acids as given below.

- **Ribose** (in case of RNA)
- **Deoxyribose** (in case of DNA)

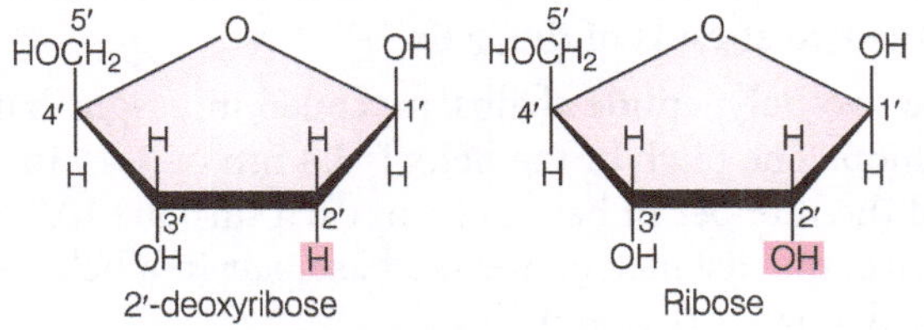

Fig 5.1 Pentose sugar

A Nitrogenous Base

- It is a nitrogen containing heterocyclic organic molecule having similar physical properties of a base.
- There are two types of nitrogenous bases
    - **Purines** These are nitrogen bases with double ring structure, e.g. adenine and guanine.
    - **Pyrimidines** These are nitrogen bases with single ring structure, e.g. cytosine, uracil and thymine.
- Out of pyrimidines, cytosine is common for both DNA and RNA, while thymine is present in DNA and uracil is present in RNA at the place of thymine.
- These nitrogenous bases when linked to the OH of 1'C of pentose sugar through N-glycosidic bonds form **nucleoside**.

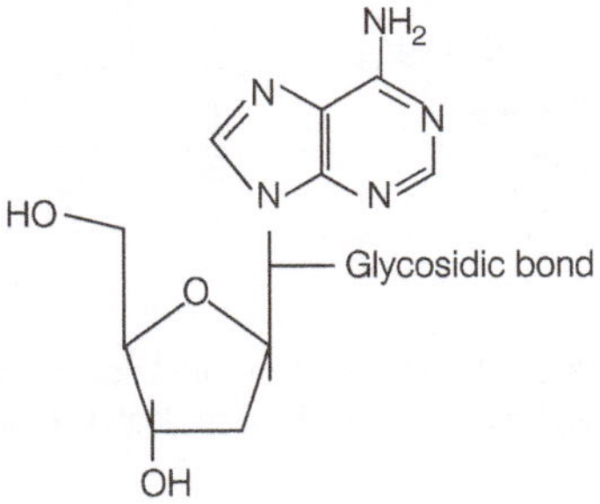

Fig. 5.2 Nucleoside

- For example, Adenosine or deoxyadenosine, guanosine or deoxyguanosine, cytidine or deoxycytidine and uridine or deoxythymidine

A Phosphate Group

- It plays a crucial role in the formation of structure of DNA.
- Phosphate group is attached to the OH of 5' carbon of the sugar (deoxyribose in DNA or ribose in RNA) of the nucleoside, forming a **phosphoester bond** and transforming it into a **nucleotide.**

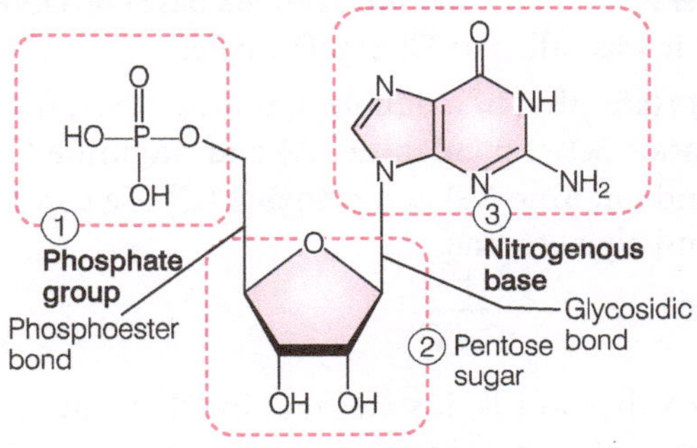

Fig 5.3 Nucleotide

- This nucleotide then links with other nucleotides through **phosphodiester bonds.**
- Two nucleotides when linked through a 3'–5' phosphodiester linkage (– C– O– P–O –C –) form a dinucleotide.
- In a similar fashion, more nucleotides may join to form a **polynucleotide chain.**
- The polymer chain, thus formed has
    - one end with a free phosphate moiety at 5′-end of sugar. This is marked as 5′ end of polynucleotide chain.
    - the other end with a free hydroxyl group which is marked as 3′ end of the polynucleotide chain.
- Thus, the sugar and phosphates form the backbone in a polymer chain.
- The nitrogenous bases linked to sugar moiety project from this backbone.

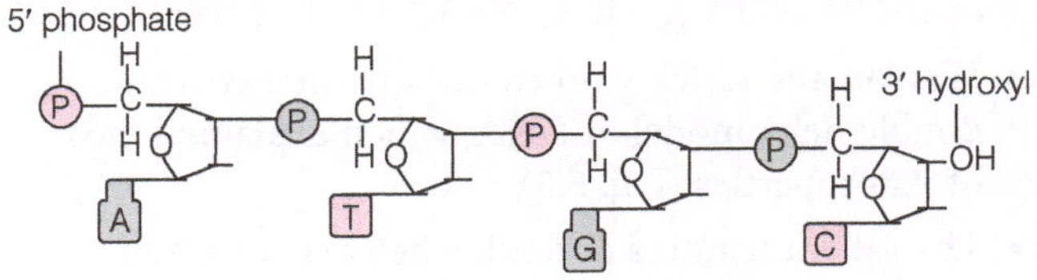

Fig. 5.4 A polynucleotide chain

- In RNA, there is an additional hydroxyl (OH) group at 2′ position in the ribose of every nucleotide residue.

Discoveries Related to Structure and Composition of DNA

- **Friedrich Meischer** (in 1869) first identified DNA as an acidic substance present in nucleus. He termed it as **'nuclein'**.
- **Erwin Chargaff** (in 1950) formulated important generalisation on the nitrogenous bases of DNA and it was called as **Chargaff's rule**.
  - It states that in a double-stranded DNA, the ratios between **adenine** (A) and **thymine** (T) and **guanine** (G) and **cytosine** (C) are constant and equal to one.

    i.e. $$\frac{A+G}{T+C}=1$$
  - In other words, it states that in DNA, the amount of guanine should be equal to cytosine.
  - Similarly, the amount of adenine should be equal to thymine.

    i.e. $A+G=T+C$
- **James Watson** and **Francis Crick** (in 1953) proposed the **double helix** model for the DNA structure on the basis of X-ray diffraction data, produced by **Maurice Wilkins** and **Rosalind Franklin** in the same year.
  - One of the important features of this model was the complementary base pairing.
  - It means if the sequence of bases in one strand is known, the sequence in other strand can be easily predicted.
  - Also, if each strand from a DNA acts as a template for synthesis of a new strand, the daughter DNA thus produced would be identical to the parental DNA molecule.

Watson and Crick Model of DNA

- Watson and Crick worked out the first correct double helix model of DNA, which explained most of its properties (Fig. 5.5).
- The salient features of double helix structure of DNA are as follows.
- DNA is made up of two polynucleotide chains. The backbone is constituted by sugar-phosphate, while the nitrogenous bases project inwards.
- The two chains have anti-parallel polarity, i.e. when one chain has $3' \rightarrow 5'$ polarity, the other has $5' \rightarrow 3'$ polarity.
- The bases in two strands are paired through hydrogen bonds (H-bonds) to form base pairs.
  - **Adenine** (A) is bonded with thymine (T) of the opposite strand with the help of **two hydrogen bonds**.
  - **Guanine** (G) is bonded with cytosine (C) of the opposite strand with the help of **three hydrogen bonds**.
  - As a result, a purine always bonds with a pyrimidine. It helps in maintaining a uniform distance between the two strands of the helix.
- The two polypeptide chains are coiled in a right-handed fashion. The pitch of the helix is 3.4 nm or 3.4×10^{-9} m and the number of base pairs in each turn are 10. Hence, the distance between a base pair in a helix is approximately 0.34 nm.

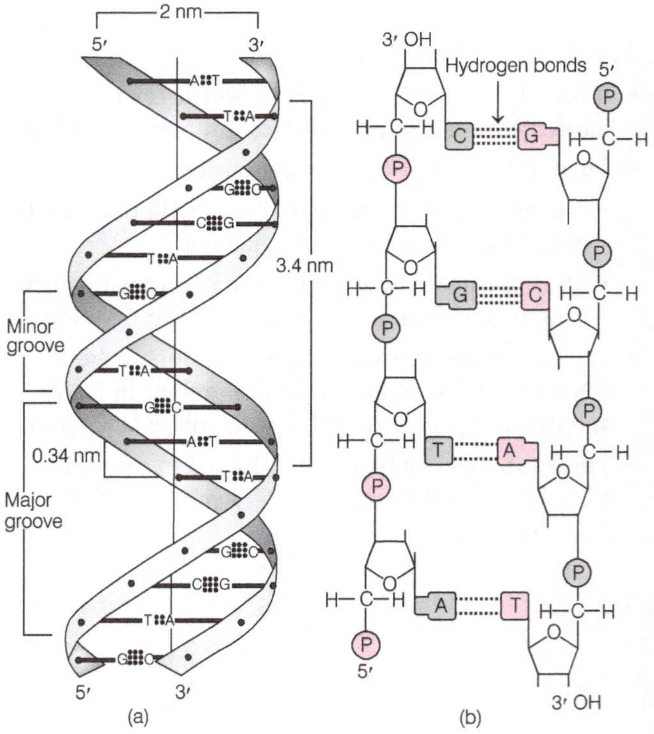

Fig. 5.5 Structure of a DNA : (a) Watson and Crick model of double helix (b) Double-stranded polynucleotide chain

- The plane of one base pair stacks over the other in double helix. This provides the stability to the helical structure, in addition to H-bond.

> **Quick Test 1**
>
> 1. An organism has 4.6×10^6 base pairs in its genome. Identify the organism.
> 2. A structure is composed of a pentose sugar and a nitrogenous base. Mention the type of linkage present between them.
> 3. Among phosphate group adenine and deoxyribose sugar, which one does not form the backbone of the polynucleotide chain.
> 4. Given a double-helix DNA with 260 base pairs, of which 80 are adenine bases, determine the total number of guanine and cytosine bases.
> 5. A DNA double helix has 80 adenine and 60 cytosine bases. How many nitrogenous bases have double hydrogen bonds between them?

5.2 Packaging of DNA Helix

The length of DNA in humans can be calculated as

- Distance between two consecutive base pairs is
$$0.34 \text{ nm} = 0.34 \times 10^{-9} \text{ m}$$
- Total number of base pairs in a DNA helix in a typical mammalian cell $= 6.6 \times 10^9$ bp

  $\therefore$ Length of the DNA double helix = Total number of base pairs $\times$ distance between two consecutive base pairs.
$$= 6.6 \times 10^9 \text{ bp} \times 0.34 \times 10^{-9} \text{ m/bp}$$
$$= 2.2 \text{ m (approximately)}$$
- This length of DNA is far greater than the dimension of a typical nucleus, which is approximately 10^{-6}m in diameter.
- Therefore, DNA need to be packed to accommodate such a long polymer in a cell of both prokaryotes and eukaryotes.

In Prokaryotes

- In prokaryotes, such as *E. coli*, a well defined nucleus is absent.
- DNA (carrying negative charge) is held together with some proteins (that have positive charge) in a region known as **nucleoid**.
- The DNA in nucleoid is organised in large loops held by proteins.

In Eukaryotes

- The organisation of DNA is much more complex in eukaryotes.
- DNA packaging in eukaryotes is mediated by histone proteins.
- Histones are the proteins that are rich in basic amino acids namely lysine and arginine.
- Depending upon the abundance of amino acid residues with charged side chains, a protein acquires its charge.
- Both lysine and arginine carry positive charges on their side chains. So, histones are a set of positively charged, basic proteins.
- These histones organise themselves to make a unit of eight molecules known as **histone octamer**.
- The negatively charged DNA is wrapped around the positively charged histone octamer to form a structure known as **nucleosome.**

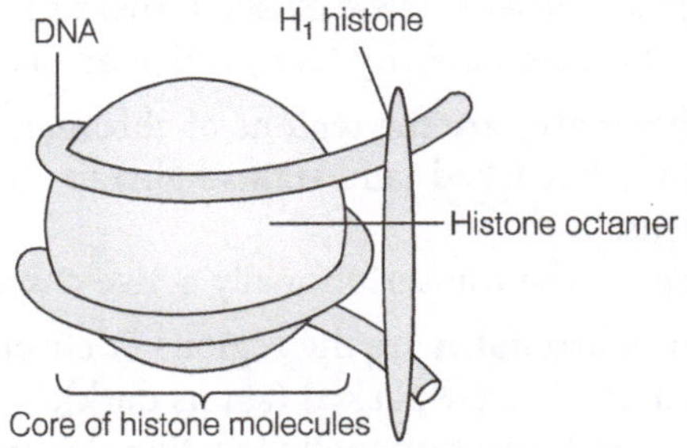

Fig. 5.6 A nucleosome

- There are five types of **histone proteins**, i.e. H_1, H_2A, H_2B, H_3 and H_4.
- Four of these types (H_2A, H_2B, H_3 and H_4) forms the core of nucleosome.
- While the H_1 histone binds to the linker DNA and helps to stabilise the structure, facilitating the compaction of chromatin.
- DNA connecting the two adjacent nucleosome is called **linker DNA.**
- A typical nucleosome contains approximately 200 base pairs of DNA helix.
- Nucleosomes are the repeating units of chromatin, which are thread-like stained (coloured) bodies present in nucleus.
- The nucleosomes in chromatin look like a 'beads-on-string' structure when observed under an Electron Microscope (EM).

- The chromatin is packed to form a **solenoid structure** of 30 nm diameter.
- It further undergoes supercoiling to form a looped structure called **chromatin fibre**.
- This further coils and condenses at metaphase stage of cell division to form the **chromosomes**.

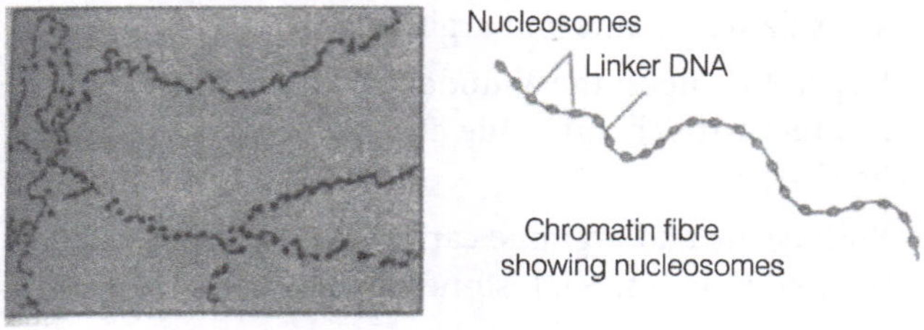

Fig. 5.7 EM Picture-Beads on string

Non-Histone Chromosomal (NHC) Proteins

- These are additional sets of proteins that contribute to the packaging of chromatin at a higher level.
- In a typical nucleus, DNA exists in two forms that reflects the cells's activity level, which are as follows
  - **Euchromatin** are the regions of chromatin, which are loosely packed (and stains light) in a typical nucleus.
    These are the transcriptionally active chromatin.
  - **Heterochromatin** are the regions of chromatin, which are densely packed (stains dark).
    These are transcriptionally inactive chromatin.

Quick Test 2

1. If the distance between two consecutive base pairs decreases by 0.02 nm, will there be any change in the length of human DNA?
2. A cell has 25 nucleosomes. How many base pairs are likely to be present in this structure ?
3. **State True or False.**
   The 'beads on a string' structure is likely to be observed in prokaryotes.
4. Mention the term given to the set of proteins that are associated with chromatin packaging at the higher level.
5. In electron micrographs of two cell nuclei, cell *A* shows more darkly stained regions, while cell *B* shows more lightly stained regions. Which cell is likely to be more transcriptionally active ?

5.3 The Search for Genetic Material

- The discovery of nuclein by **Meischer** and the proposition of principle of inheritance by **Mendel** were almost at the same time, i.e. 1869 and 1866, respectively.
- But the fact that DNA acts as a genetic material took a long time to be discovered and proven.
- By 1926, the quest to determine the mechanism for genetic inheritance had reached the molecular level.
- Previous discoveries by Gregor Mendel, Walter Sutton, Thomas Hunt Morgan and numerous other scientists has narrowed the focus to the chromosomes located in the nucleus of most cells.
- However, the question of which molecule actually serves as the genetic material remain unassured.

Transforming Principle

- **Frederick Griffith** in 1928, carried out a series of experiments with *Streptococcus pneumoniae* (a bacterium that causes pneumonia).
- He observed that when these bacteria (*Streptococcus pneumoniae*) were grown on a culture plate, some of them produced **smooth, shiny colonies** (S-type), whereas the others produced **rough colonies** (R-type).
- This difference in appearance of colonies (smooth/ rough) is due to the presence of mucus (polysaccharide) coat on S-strains, but not on R-strains.
- Griffith carried out following four major steps in his experiment
  - He first infected two separate groups of mice. The mice that were injected with the S-strain died from pneumonia as S-strains are the virulent strains causing **pneumonia.**
  - The mice that were injected with the R-strain did not develop pneumonia and survived.
  - In the next set of experiments, Griffith killed the bacteria by heating them. The mice that were injected with heat killed, S-strain bacteria did not die and survived.

- On injecting a mixture of heat killed, S-strain and live R-strain bacteria, the mice died. Moreover, living S-strain bacteria was recovered from the dead mice.

- From all these observations Griffith concluded that the live R-strain bacteria, had been transformed by the heat-killed S-strain bacteria.

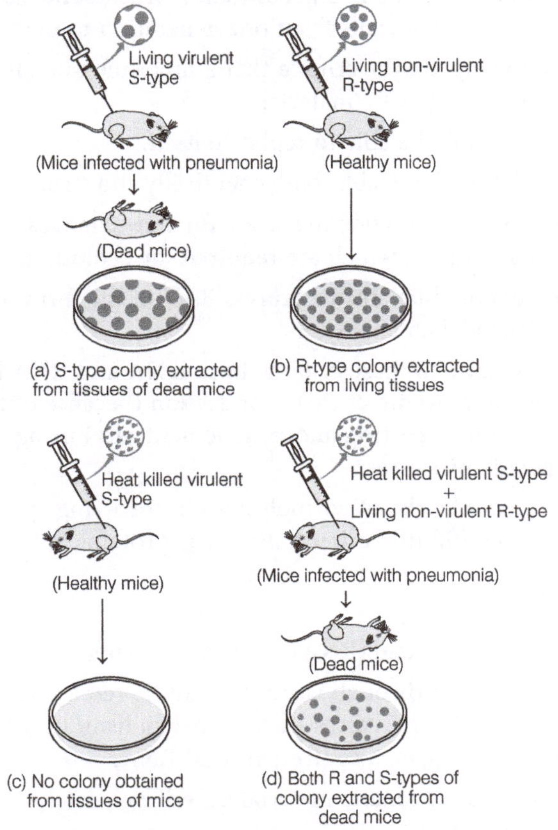

Fig. 5.8 Summary of Griffith's experiments on transformation in *Streptococcus pneumoniae*

- It mean some 'transforming principle, had transferred from the heat-killed S-strain, which helped the R-strain bacteria to synthesise a smooth polysaccharide coat and thus become virulent.
- This transforming principle was detected to be the **genetic material**. However, he was not able to define the biochemical nature of genetic material from his experiments.

Biochemical Characterisation of Transforming Principle

- **Oswald Avery**, **Colin MacLeod** and **Maclyn McCarty** (1933-44) worked to determine the biochemical nature of 'transforming principle' in Griffith's experiment in an *in vitro* system.
- Prior to this experiment, the genetic material was thought to be a protein.
- During this experiment, purified biochemicals (i.e. proteins, DNA, RNA, etc.) from the heat-killed S-cells were taken, to observe which biochemicals could transform live R-cells into S-cells.
- They discovered that DNA alone from heat-killed S-type bacteria caused the transformation of non-virulent R-type bacteria into S-type virulent bacteria.
- They also discovered that **protein-digesting enzymes** (protease) and **RNA digesting enzymes** (RNAse) did not inhibit this transformation.
- This proved that the 'transforming substance' was neither protein nor RNA.
- However, DNA-digesting enzyme (DNAse) caused the inhibition of transformation, which suggested that the DNA caused the transformation.
- Thus, these scientists came to the conclusion that DNA is the hereditary material. But still, not all the biologists were convinced.

The Genetic Material is DNA (Hershey-Chase Experiment)

- The unequivocal proof that DNA is the genetic material came from the experiments of **Alfred Hershey** and **Martha Chase** (1952).
- They carried out some experiments with viruses that infect bacteria called **bacteriophages**.
- The genetic material of bacteriophage enters the bacterial cell after the bacteriophage gets attached to the bacteria.
- The bacterial cell treats the genetic material of the virus (bacteriophage) like its own and then produces more virus particles.
- **Hershey** and **Chase** experimented to find out whether it was protein or DNA from the viruses that entered into the bacteria (Fig. 5.9).
- They took two separate media for growing the bacteriophages.
- Out of the two, one medium contained radioactive phosphorus and the other medium contained radioactive sulphur.

- Bacteriophages (Viruses) were then grown on each medium.
  - The viruses grown in the presence of radioactive phosphorus (^{32}P) contained radioactive DNA (but not radioactive protein). This is because DNA contains phosphorus, but protein does not.
  - In the same way, the viruses grown in the medium containing radioactive sulphur (^{35}S) contained radioactive protein (not radioactive DNA). This is because DNA does not contain sulphur.
- These radioactive viruses (bacteriophages) were then allowed to attach and infect bacteria (*E. coli*).
- As the process of infection with virus continued, the bacteria were agitated in a blender and the viral coats were removed from the bacteria.
- When they were spinned in a centrifuge, the virus particles were separated from the bacteria.

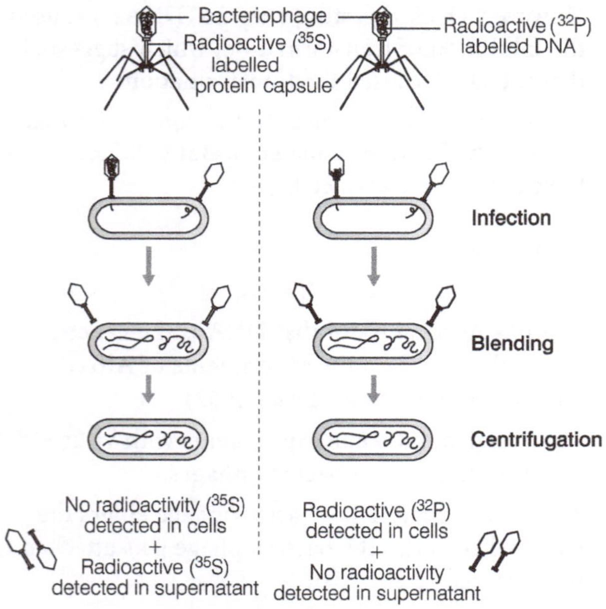

Fig. 5.9 Hershey and Chase experiment

- They observed that the bacteria that were infected with viruses containing radioactive DNA were radioactive, while the bacteria that were infected with radioactive proteins were not radioactive.
- This indicated that only DNA (and not the protein coat) entered the bacterial cell from the viruses. Thus, the genetic material that is passed from virus to bacteria was DNA.
- From the Hershey and Chase experiment, the fact was established that DNA acts as genetic material.

> Experimentations by different scientists lead to the establishment of the fact that DNA is a genetic material. However, later studies also revealed that in some viruses (e.g. Tobacco Mosaic Viruses, QB bacteriophage, etc.), RNA is the genetic material.

Properties of Genetic Material

- Genetic material is that substance which controls the inheritance of traits from one generation to next.
- Following are the criteria that a molecule must fulfill to act as a genetic material
  - It should be able to replicate itself.
  - It should be stable, both chemically and structurally.
  - It should provide the scope for slow changes (mutation), which are required for evolution.
  - It should be able to express itself in the form of 'Mendelian characters'.
- According to these criteria, both DNA and RNA have the ability to direct their duplication (because of the rule of base pairing and complementarity) using specific processes.
- Conversely, the other molecules in the living system fail to fulfill first criteria itself, e.g. proteins.

RNA World

- Ribonucleic Acid (RNA) was the first genetic material.
- It is evident through various scientific researches that essential life processes such as metabolism, translation and splicing, etc., evolved around RNA.
- RNA act as genetic material as well as a catalyst.
- But RNA being a catalyst was reactive and hence unstable.
- Therefore, DNA has evolved from RNA with chemical modifications that makes it more stable.
- DNA being double-stranded and having complementary strand further resists changes by evolving a process of repair.

DNA *versus* RNA

- It is evident from Griffith's transforming principle that the heat, which killed the bacteria, did not destroy some of the properties of the genetic material.
- This can be explained by the two complementary strands of DNA, which when separated by heating, again come together, when favourable conditions are provided.

- Stability is the main property of the genetic material as it should not change with the different stages of life cycle, age or with change in the physiology of an organism.
- In the structure of RNA, the 2′–OH group present at every nucleotide is a reactive group.
- This 2′–OH group makes RNA labile and easily degradable.
- RNA is also catalytic, so it is reactive, whereas DNA is structurally more stable and chemically less reactive. This is due to the presence of thymine at the place of uracil in DNA.

TEACHER'S TIP

The presence of thymine in DNA makes it more stable due to presence of methyl in its structure. The methyl group prevents deamination (a major source of mutations) and makes thymine more resistant to chemical changes.

- Both DNA and RNA have the ability to mutate. Since, RNA is unstable, it mutates at a faster rate.
- That is why, those viruses, which have RNA genome and a shorter lifespan, undergo mutation and thus evolve rapidly.
- DNA is dependent on RNA for protein synthesis, whereas RNA directly codes for protein synthesis.
- This proves that both RNA and DNA act as genetic material, but DNA being more stable is preferred for the storage of genetic information.
- RNA is more suitable for the transmission of genetic information.

Differences Between DNA and RNA

DNA	RNA
It is double-stranded with exception of some viruses.	It is generally single-stranded.
It is the genetic material in majority of living organisms.	It is the genetic material in some viruses only.
The sugar is deoxyribose.	The sugar is ribose.
Nitrogenous bases are adenine, guanine, thymine and cytosine.	Nitrogenous bases are adenine, guanine, cytosine and uracil.
It is less reactive, chemically and structurally more stable.	It is more reactive chemically and structurally less stable.
It usually occurs inside the nucleus and in some cell organelles.	Very little RNA occurs inside the nucleus. Most of it is found in the cytoplasm.

Quick Test 3

1. State one characteristic of the bacterial colony that killed the mouse in the Griffith's experiment.
2. A mouse was injected with a mixture of RNAse, heat-killed S-strain bacteria and live R-strain bacteria. Will this mouse survive or not?
3. A biochemical molecule is both structurally and chemically stable but is unable to replicate itself. Can this be considered genetic material with some exceptions?
4. Out of DNA and RNA, which one has the presence of a more reactive group?
5. Organism *A* has RNA as its genetic material, while Organism *B* has DNA as its genetic material. Which one is able to evolve faster?

5.4 Central Dogma

- Central dogma (proposed by Francis Crick in 1958) states that there is one way or unidirectional flow of information from master copy DNA to RNA (transcription) and from RNA to polypeptide (translation). It is also written as follows

Replication

$$\circlearrowleft \text{DNA} \xrightarrow{\text{Transcription}} m\text{RNA} \xrightarrow{\text{Translation}} \text{Protein}$$

- Transcription or RNA synthesis occurs on DNA and translation or protein synthesis occurs on *m*RNA.

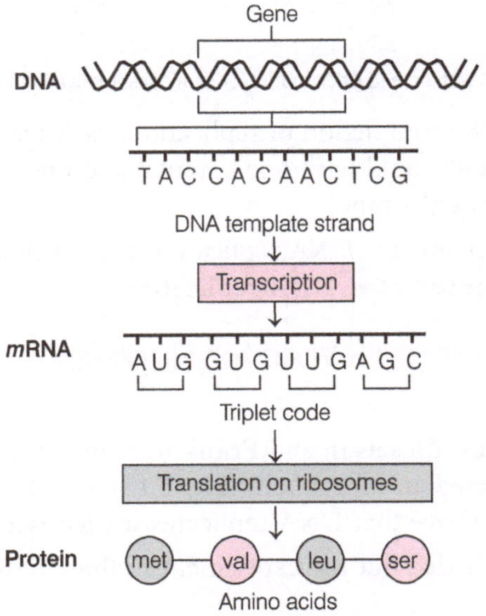

Fig. 5.10 Transfer of information from DNA to protein (an outline view)

- Later it was also found that retroviruses perform central dogma in reverse and it is called as reverse transcription (formation of DNA from RNA), e.g. HIV.

5.5 Replication of DNA

- In addition to the double helical structure of DNA, **Watson** and **Crick** also proposed a scheme for DNA replication.
- According to this model, the two strands of double helix would separate and act as a template for the synthesis of new complementary strands.

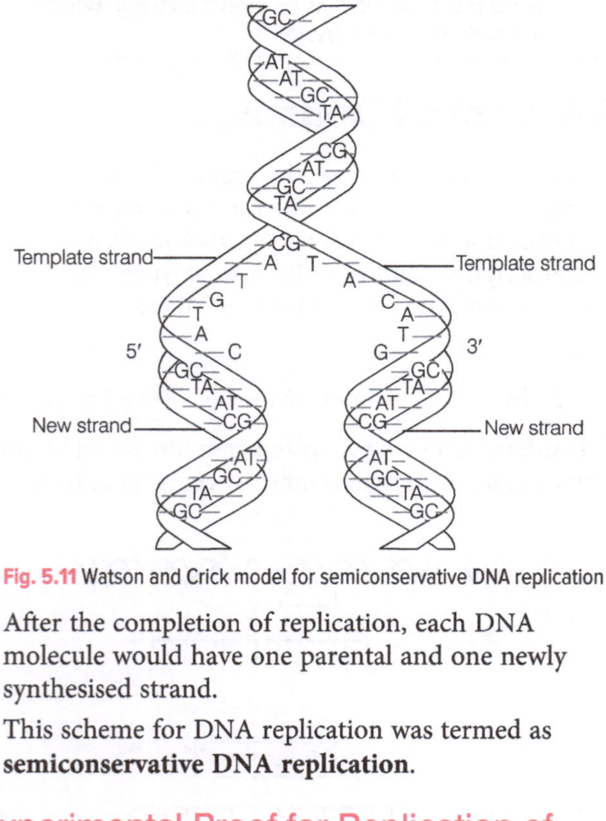

Fig. 5.11 Watson and Crick model for semiconservative DNA replication

- After the completion of replication, each DNA molecule would have one parental and one newly synthesised strand.
- This scheme for DNA replication was termed as **semiconservative DNA replication.**

Experimental Proof for Replication of DNA

- **Matthew Meselson** and **Franklin Stahl** (in 1958) conducted an experiment (Fig. 5.12) with *Escherichia coli* to prove that DNA replicates semiconservatively.
- They carried out the experiment in the following steps.
  - They grew many generations of *E. coli* in a medium that contained $^{15}NH_4Cl$ (^{15}N is the heavy isotope of nitrogen) as the only source of nitrogen.
    As a result, ^{15}N got incorporated into the newly synthesised DNA.
    By centrifugation in a cesium chloride (CsCl) density gradient, this heavy DNA molecule could be distinguished from the normal DNA.
  - The cells were then transferred into a medium containing normal $^{14}NH_4$ Cl.
  - At definite time intervals, as the cells multiplied, samples were taken and the DNA which remained as double-stranded helices was extracted.
  - The samples were separated independently on CsCl gradient to measure the densities of DNA.
  - The DNA obtained from the culture, one generation after the transfer from ^{15}N to ^{14}N medium (i.e. after 20 minutes because *E. coli* divides in 20 minutes) had a hybrid or intermediate density.
  - The DNA obtained from the culture after another generation (i.e. after 40 minutes, II generation) was composed of equal amounts of hybrid DNA and ^{14}N (light) DNA.

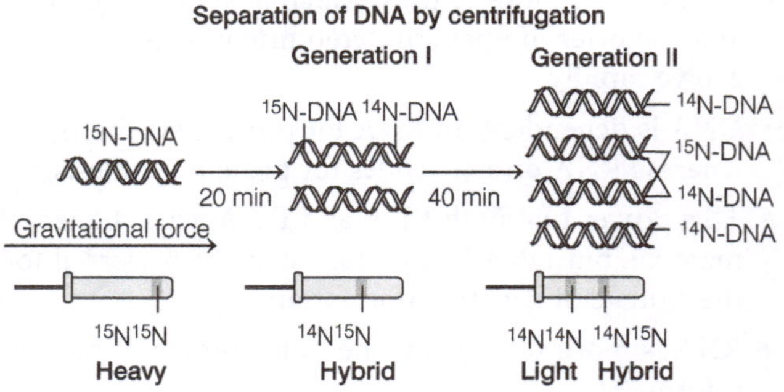

Fig. 5.12 Meselson and Stahl's experiment

- Similar experiments on '*Vicia faba*' (faba beans) were conducted by **Taylor** and colleagues in 1958, involving the use of radioactive thymidine.
- The results of this experiment demonstrated that the DNA in chromosomes also replicate semiconservatively.

Enzymes for DNA Replication

- The process of replication requires a set of catalysts (enzymes) as given below

DNA-Dependent DNA Polymerase

- It is the main enzyme which uses a DNA template to catalyse the polymerisation of deoxynucleotides.

- *E. coli* has about 4.6×10^6bp in its DNA and DNA polymerase takes approximately 18 minutes to completely replicate its genome.
- The average rate of polymerisation is 2000 bp (base pairs) per second.
- This enzyme is highly efficient as it have to catalyse the polymerisation of a large number of nucleotides in a very short time with high degree of accuracy, as any mistake would result in mutations.

Helicase

It unwinds the DNA strand, i.e. separates the two strands from one point, for the formation of a **replication fork.**

Topoisomerase

The unwinding of double helix of the DNA creates a tension in the strands, which is released by the enzyme topoisomerase.

DNA Ligase

- It facilitates the joining of DNA strands together by catalysing the formation of phosphodiester bond.
- It plays a role in repairing single-strand breaks in duplex DNA.

Process of DNA Replication

- Replication is an energy expensive process. Therefore, **Deoxyribonucleoside triphosphates** (*d*NTPs) serve the dual purpose of
  - acting as a substrate
  - providing energy for polymerisation reaction (from two terminal phosphates)
- In a long DNA molecule, replication takes place within a small opening of the DNA helix, known as **replication fork** (fig. 5.13).
- DNA-dependent DNA polymerases catalyse polymerisation only in one direction, i.e. 5′→3′. This creates some complications at the replication fork.
- Due to this, on one strand (template with polarity 3′→5′), replication is **continuous**. This DNA strand is called **leading strand.**
- While on the 5′ → 3′ strand, replication is **discontinuous**, i.e. in small fragments called **Okazaki fragments**, thereby forming **lagging strand.**
- These fragments synthesised are later joined by the enzyme DNA ligase.
- The DNA polymerases cannot initiate replication process on their own. Also, replication does not initiate randomly anywhere in DNA.
- It begins at definite regions in a *E. coli* DNA molecule known as **origin of replication** *(ori)* which has recognition site for DNA polymerase and which also provides site for attachment of **RNA primer.**
- In the absence of RNA primer, DNA polymerase cannot add nucleotides.

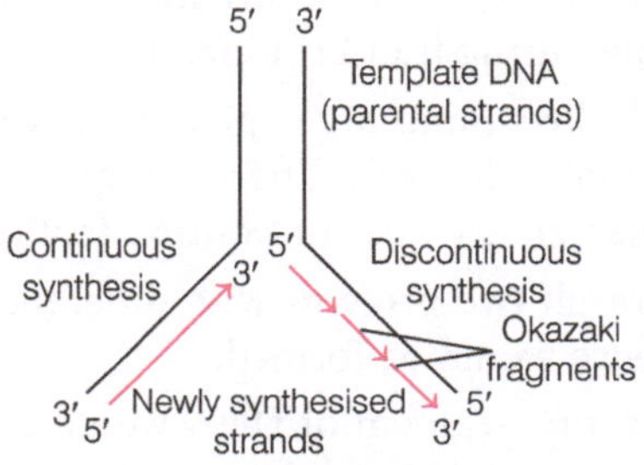

Fig. 5.13 Replicating fork of DNA

- Due to the requirement of the origin of replication, if a piece of DNA needs to be propagated during recombination, a vector is required.
- The vectors provide the origin of replication.
- In eukaryotes, the replication of DNA takes place at S-phase of the cell cycle.
- After DNA replication, if cell division fails to take place, it results in polyploidy (a chromosomal anomaly).

Quick Test 4

1. If a virus has RNA as its genetic material, which step of the central dogma is altered from the usual process?
2. After DNA replication, each strand consists of one parental strand and one newly synthesised strand. What property of DNA can be concluded from this?
3. In the Meselson and Stahl's experiment, after how many generations will there be a 2:6 ratio of light to hybrid DNA?
4. A cell is unable to join the Okazaki fragments after replication. A defect in which enzyme is responsible for this?
5. If the S-phase of the cell cycle is halted, which process will be affected?

5.6 Transcription

- It is the process of copying genetic information from one strand of the DNA into RNA.
- The process of transcription is also governed by the principle of complementarity, except the adenosine (A) forms base pair with uracil (U) instead of thymine (T).
- Unlike in replication, where the total DNA of an organism gets duplicated, in transcription, only a segment of DNA or only one of the two strands is copied into RNA.
- The reasons why both the strands are not copied at the same time during transcription are
  - If both the strands are copied, they would code for RNA molecules with different sequences (because complementary does not mean identical).

    As a result two proteins with different amino acid sequence would be formed.

    Hence, one segment of DNA would code for two different proteins and the genetic information transfer machinery would become much more complicated.
  - The two RNA molecules produced simultaneously would be complementary to each other.

    Hence, they would bind together to form a double-stranded RNA.

    This would prevent RNA from being translated into protein and the exercise of transcription would become a futile one.

Transcription Unit

- A transcription unit of DNA is defined primarily by three regions in the DNA. These are as follows
  - **A promoter** is a DNA sequence that provides binding site for RNA polymerase.
    It is located at 5′ end (upstream) of the structural gene.
    Its presence also defines the template and coding strands.
    The definition of coding strand and template strand could be reversed by switching the position of promoter with terminator.
  - **The structural gene** in a transcription unit is flanked by the promoter and terminator.
  - A **terminator** is located towards the 3′ end (downstream) of the coding strand. It usually defines the end of transcription process.

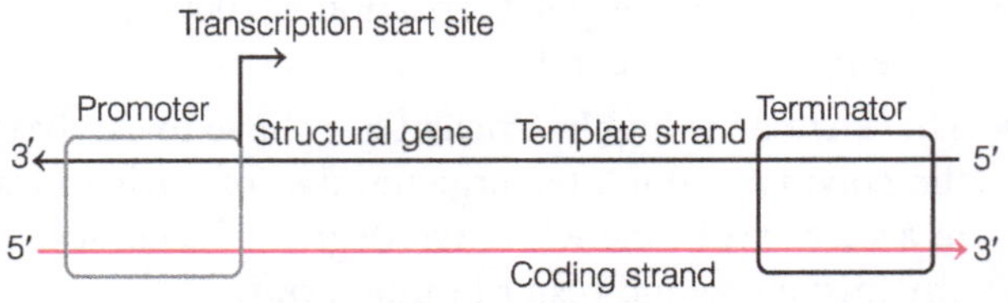

Fig. 5.14 Schematic structure of a transcription unit

- The two strands of DNA have opposite polarity and the enzyme **DNA-dependent RNA polymerase** catalyses the polymerisation in only one direction (i.e. 5′ → 3′ direction).
- Therefore, the strand with 3′ → 5′ polarity acts as a template and is known as **template strand**.
- The strand with 5′ → 3′ polarity and same sequence as that of RNA (except thymine at the place of uracil) is displaced during transcription and is known as **coding strand**.

Transcription Unit and The Gene

- **Gene** is the functional unit of inheritance. The DNA sequence coding for *t*RNA or *r*RNA molecule also define a gene.
- **Cistron** is a segment of DNA that codes for a polypeptide.
- In a transcription unit, the structural gene could be
  - **Monocistronic** (mostly in eukaryotes).
  - **Polycistronic** (mostly in bacteria or prokaryotes).
- The monocistronic structural genes in eukaryotes have interrupted coding sequences.
  These include
  - **Exons** These are coding sequences or expressed sequences that appear in mature or processed RNA.
  - **Introns** These are intervening sequences which do not appear in mature or processed RNA. They only interrupt exons. The genes in eukaryotes are **split**. It is the gene with both exons and introns.
- The **promoter** and **regulatory sequences** of a structural gene also affect the inheritance of a character.

That is why, sometimes the regulatory sequences are defined as **regulatory genes**, even though these sequences do not code for any RNA or protein.

Types of RNA and Process of Transcription

Three major types of RNAs found in bacteria are

- ***m*RNA** (messenger RNA) which provides the template for translation.
- ***t*RNA** (transfer RNA) which brings amino acids and reads the genetic code.
- ***r*RNA** (ribosomal RNA) which plays structural and catalytic role during translation.

All three RNAs are needed for the synthesis of a protein in a cell.

Transcription in Prokaryotes

- In prokaryotes, the transcription of all three types of RNA (*m*RNA, *t*RNA and *r*RNA) is catalysed by single DNA dependent RNA polymerase. It takes place in three steps which are as follows.

1. Initiation

- RNA polymerase binds to promoter and initiates transcription by associating transiently with **initiation factor** (σ).
- It uses nucleoside triphosphates as substrate and polymerises in a template depended fashion by obeying the rule of complementarity.

2. Elongation

- Chain elongation proceeds in the $5' \rightarrow 3'$ direction.
- RNA polymerase also facilitates the opening of DNA helix and continues the process of elongation [Fig. 5.15].
- The RNA polymerase after initiation of transcription loses the σ factor.
- However, it continues the polymerisation of ribonucleotides to form RNA.

3. Termination

- Once the RNA polymerase reaches the terminator region of DNA, the nascent RNA gets separated and the RNA polymerase falls off. This result in the termination of transcription.

- In the whole process RNA polymerase perform following functions
  - It catalyses the process of elongation.
  - It associates transiently with initiation factor (σ) and termination factor (ρ) to alter its own specificity to initiate and terminate the transcription, respectively.

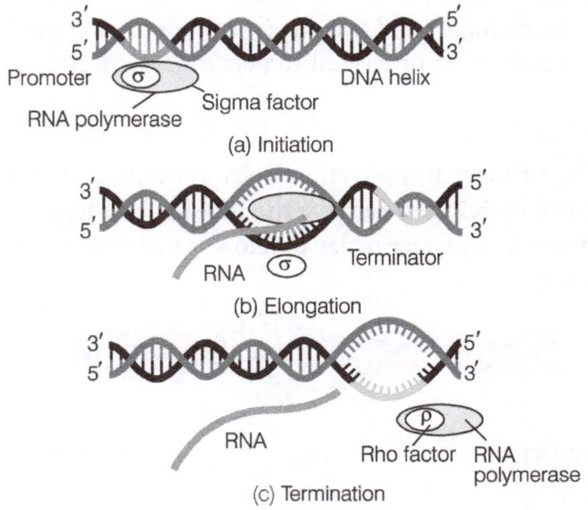

Fig. 5.15 Process of transcription in prokaryotes (bacteria)

- In prokaryotes (bacteria), *m*RNA does not require any processing to become active.
- Also, both the processes transcription and translation occurs in same compartment (as there is no separation of nucleus and cytosol in bacteria).
- Therefore, many times translation can start much before the *m*RNA is fully transcribed, i.e. transcription and translation can be coupled in prokaryotes.

Transcription in Eukaryotes

- The process of transcription in eukaryotes is similar to that in prokaryotes.
- Structural genes are monocistronic in eukaryotes.
- Although, two additional complexities are present in eukaryotes which are given below
  - In nucleus, there are atleast three **RNA polymerases** in addition to RNA polymerase found in organelles.

    It indicates a clear cut division of labour as described below

- **RNA Polymerase-I** Transcribes *r*RNAs (28S, 18S, 5.8S).
- **RNA Polymerase-II** Transcribes precursor of *m*RNA, which is called **heterogeneous nuclear RNA** (*hn*RNA).
- **RNA Polymerase-III** Transcribes *t*RNA, 5*sr*RNA and *sn*RNAs **(small nuclear RNAs)**.
- The primary transcript contains both the exons (functional) and introns (non-functional) and it needs to be processed to become functional.

Post transcriptional Modifications

- The primary transcript, *hn*RNA undergo a process called **splicing** to remove the **introns** and to join the **exons** in a proper order to allow translation to take place.

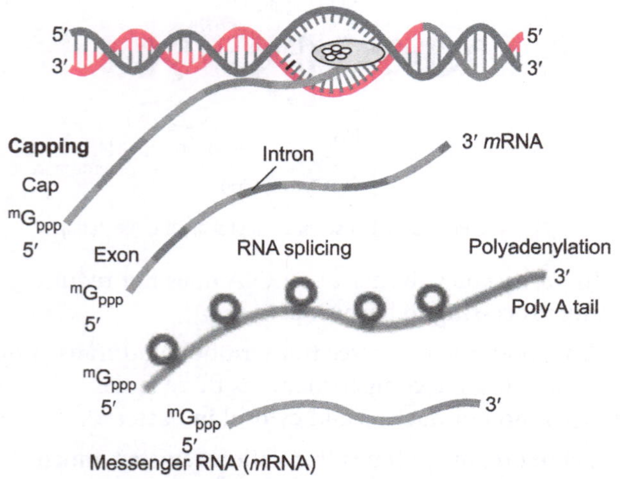

Fig. 5.16 Process of transcription in eukaryotes

- It also undergoes two additional processes which are as follows
  - **Capping** In capping, methyl guanosine triphosphate, an unusual nucleotide is added to the 5′ end of *hn*RNA.
  - **Tailing** In tailing, adenylate residues (200-300) are added at 3′ end in a template independent manner. The fully processed *hn*RNA, is called **mRNA.** The *m*RNA gets transported out of the nucleus into the cytoplasm for translation.

Note The presence of introns is reminiscent of antiquity and the process of splicing represents the dominance of **RNA world.**

Quick Test 5

1. Name one nitrogenous base that is not found in *m*RNA.
2. If one strand of DNA has the nitrogenous base sequence as ATCTG. What would be the complementary RNA strand sequence?
3. **State True or False**
   A segment of DNA that contains multiple coding regions for different proteins is called monocistronic.
4. Name the enzyme that catalyses the transcription of *hn*RNA and *t*RNA respectively.
5. If a mutation occurs in the intron regions of a gene, will it affect the protein production?

5.7 Genetic Code

- It is the relationship between the sequence of nucleotides on *m*RNA and the sequence of amino acids in the polypeptide which is interpreted during the process of translation.
- The process of translation (i.e. synthesis of proteins) requires transfer of information in *m*RNA to amino acid sequences in the polypeptides.
- These sequences are specified by genetic code.
- In 1954, **George Gamow**, a physicist proposed that in order to code for all the 20 amino acids, the code should be made up of three nucleotides (**triplet code**).
- This can be explained as, if one base code for one amino acid, only four amino acids could be specified.
- It means the proteins could contain only four amino acids, which is inadequate.
- If a sequence of two bases code for one amino acid, the four bases could specify only 16 (4×4) amino acids, which is also inadequate.
- But if a sequence of three bases code for one amino acid, the four bases would specify 64 (4×4×4) amino acids.
- But this generated many more codons than required.
- The proof that genetic codes are infact triplets, came from the researches of the following scientists.
  - **Har Gobind Khorana** developed a chemical method for the synthesis of RNA molecule with defined base combinations (homopolymers and copolymers).

Homopolymers are made from one type of monomers, while copolymers are made from two or more different types of monomers.

- **Marshall Nirenberg** developed a cell-free system for protein synthesis that helped in deciphering the code. Hence, he decoded the first triplet.
- **Severo Ochoa** showed that the polynucleotide phosphorylase (Severo Ochoa enzyme) also helped in polymerising RNA with defined sequences in a template independent manner (enzymatic RNA synthesis).

- On the basis of above discoveries, the sequences of the genetic code were put together in a checker-board as given in fig. 5.17.

First position ↓	Second position: U	C	A	G	Third position ↓
U	UUU Phe	UCU Ser	UAU Tyr	UGU Cys	U
	UUC Phe	UCC Ser	UAC Tyr	UGC Cys	C
	UUA Leu	UCA Ser	UAA Stop	UGA Stop	A
	UUG Leu	UCG Ser	UAG Stop	UGG Trp	G
C	CUU Leu	CCU Pro	CAU His	CGU Arg	U
	CUC Leu	CCC Pro	CAC His	CGC Arg	C
	CUA Leu	CCA Pro	CAA Gln	CGA Arg	A
	CUG Leu	CCG Pro	CAG Gln	CGG Arg	G
A	AUU Ile	ACU Thr	AAU Asn	AGU Ser	U
	AUC Ile	ACC Thr	AAC Asn	AGC Ser	C
	AUA Ile	ACA Thr	AAA Lys	AGA Arg	A
	AUG Met	ACG Thr	AAG Lys	AGG Arg	G
G	GUU Val	GCU Ala	GAU Asp	GGU Gly	U
	GUC Val	GCC Ala	GAC Asp	GGC Gly	C
	GUA Val	GCA Ala	GAA Glu	GGA Gly	A
	GUG Val	GCG Ala	GAG Glu	GGG Gly	G

Fig. 5.17 The codons for the various amino acids

Features of Genetic Code

The various features of genetic code which can be explained by using the given checker board are as follows.

- The codon is a **triplet**. Out of 64 codons, 61 code for 20 amino acids and 3 codons (UAA, UGA and UAG) do not code for any amino acids. Thus, they function as **terminating** or **stop codons**.
- Genetic code is **unambiguous** and **specific**. Thus, one codon codes for only one amino acid. For example, CCU codes only for proline and not for any other amino acid.
- Since, the number of codons is greater, all of the amino acids, with exceptions of methionine (AUG) and tryptophan (UGG), are coded by more than one codon. This feature is referred to as the **degeneracy of genetic code**. For example, GGU, GGC, GGA and GGG, all specify the same amino acid, i.e. glycine.
- The codon is read in *m*RNA in a contiguous fashion, i.e. without punctuation. Thus, the code is **commaless**.
- The genetic code is nearly universal, i.e. particular codon codes for the same amino acid in all organisms. For example, phenylalanine is coded by UUU in bacteria to humans, except in mitochondria and few protozoans.
- AUG is a codon with dual functions. It codes for the amino acid, methionine (met) and it also acts as an **initiator codon**.

The Genetic Code and Mutation

- The sudden inheritable change in the genetic material is defined as **mutation**. It is of the following types

1. Point Mutation

- Mutation in a single base pair, which is replaced by another base pair.
- For example, in sickle-cell anaemia, a point mutation in β-globin chain results in the change of amino acid residue glutamate to valine.

2. Frameshift Mutation

- It is a change in the reading frame because of insertion or deletion of base pairs.
- It is of the following types
  - **Insertion** If one or more nucleotides are added in the DNA segment, it is called insertion. It leads to the change in the reading frame.

    If three or its multiple bases are added, they will not change the reading frame. Infact, they will form a protein with new amino acids.
  - **Deletion** If one or more nucleotides are removed from the DNA segment, it is called deletion. Here also, if three or its multiple bases are removed, it will not change the reading frame, but it will remove one or more amino acid from the polypeptide.

*t*RNA : The Adapter Molecule

- Francis Crick proposed the presence of an adapter molecule (*t*RNA), which could read the code on one hand and on other hand would bind to specific amino acids during translation.
- *t*RNA was known before genetic code and was called ***s*RNA (soluble RNA)**, but its role as an adapter molecule was reported later.

Structure of *t*RNA

- The secondary structure of *t*RNA is a like a **clover leaf.**
- But its three dimensional structure depicts it as an inverted **L-shaped molecule.**
- *t*RNA has five arms or loops which as follows
  - **Anticodon Loop** It has bases complementary to the code. *t*RNAs are specific for specific amino acid.

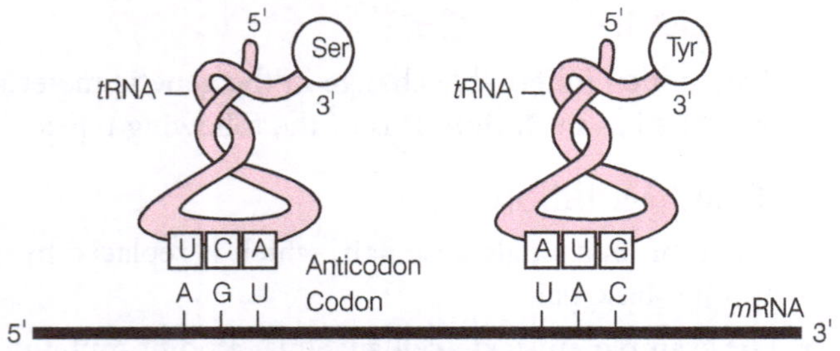

Fig. 5.18 *t*RNA-the adapter molecule

  - **Amino Acid Acceptor End** At this end, amino acids binds to the *t*RNA
  - **T-loop** It helps in the binding to ribosome.
  - **D-loop** It helps in the binding of aminoacyl synthetase.
  - **Variable Loop** It is variable in both nucleotide composition and in length.

Quick Test 6

1. Name the scientist who proposed that the codon is triplet in nature.
2. Give an example of codon having dual functions.
3. How many amino acids will be transcribed from the given *m*RNA sequence?
   5' AUGGGGUUUAGGUAAUUU 3'
4. Mention the type of mutation that causes a change in the reading frame of the *m*RNA, altering the polypeptide sequence.
5. If an adapter molecule has a defect in its amino acid acceptor end, will this cause any difficulty in protein synthesis?

5.8 Translation

- It is the process of synthesis of proteins from RNA.
- The sequence and order of amino acids are defined by the sequence of bases in the *m*RNA.

Translation Machinery

- Translation requires a machinery which consists of ribosome, *m*RNA, *t*RNAs, aminoacyl *t*RNA synthetase (enzyme that helps in combining amino acid to particular *t*RNA) and amino acids.

Initiator *t*RNA

- It is a specific *t*RNA for the process of initiation and there are no *t*RNAs for stop codons.

Ribosome

- It is responsible for protein synthesis. It consists of structural RNAs and approximately 80 different proteins.
- Ribosome exists as two subunits in its inactive stage.
  - **Small Subunit** When the small subunit encounters an *m*RNA, translation of *m*RNA to protein begins.
  - **Large Subunit** It consists of two sites where amino acids can bind and when two amino acids come close to each other, the formation of a **peptide bond** occurs.
- Ribosome also acts as a catalyst (23S *r*RNA in bacteria is the enzyme- **ribozyme**) for peptide bond formation.

Translational Unit

- It is the sequence of *m*RNA flanked by the start codon (AUG) and the stop codon.
- It codes for a polypeptide that has to be synthesised.

Untranslated Regions (UTRs)

- These are some additional sequences in an *m*RNA that are not translated.
- They are present at both the ends, i.e. at 5′ end (before start codon) and at 3′ end (after stop codon).
- They improve the efficiency of translation process.

Process of Translation

Synthesis of proteins takes place through the three stages, i.e. initiation, elongation and termination.

Initiation

- In prokaryotes, initiation requires ribosome (large and small subunits), *m*RNA, initiation *t*RNA and three Initiation Factors (IFs).
- For initiation to take place, the ribosome first binds to *m*RNA at the start codon (AUG).
- It is recognised only by the initiator *t*RNA.

Activation of Amino Acid

- The formation of peptide bond requires energy.
- Hence, in first phase, the amino acids are activated in the presence of ATP and linked to their cognate *t*RNA. This process is known as **charging of *t*RNA** or **aminoacylation of *t*RNA**.
- In the presence of ATP and Mg^{2+}, amino acids become activated by binding with aminoacyl *t*RNA synthetase enzyme.

$$\underset{\text{(AA)}}{\text{Amino acid}} + \text{ATP} \xrightarrow[\text{synthetases, } Mg^{2+}]{\text{Aminoacyl } t\text{RNA}} \text{AA} - \text{AMP} - \text{Enzyme complex} + \text{PPi}$$

- The amino acids – AMP– enzyme or AA–AMP– enzyme complex is called an **activated amino acid**.
- The steps of chain initiation are
  - The smaller ribosomal subunit attaches to 5′ end of *m*RNA to form a complex.
  - Downstream to this *m*RNA, AUG initiator codon is present, which initiates the translation process.
  - The *t*RNA joins the initiation codon by its anticodon through H-bonds.
  - Now the binding of large subunit of ribosome with its smaller subunit completes forms the complete translation-initiation- complex.
  - At this stage, the initiator *t*RNA lies at the P-site (peptidyl site) of the ribosome and the A- site (aminoacyl site) is vacant to let another charged *t*RNA to enter.

Elongation of Polypeptide Chain

- In this step, another charged aminoacyl *t*RNA complex binds to the A-site of the ribosome.
- A peptide bond forms between carboxyl group (—COOH) of amino acid at P-site and amino group (—NH_3) of amino acid at A-site by the enzyme **peptidyl transferase** (Fig. 5.19).
- During this stage, ribosome moves from one codon to another codon along the *m*RNA in the 5′⟶3′ direction.
- Amino acids are then added one-by-one in the sequence of codons and translated into a polypeptide sequences, dictated by DNA and represented by *m*RNA.

Termination of Polypeptide

- When the A-site of ribosome receives a termination codon, then no *t*RNA binds to the A-site of ribosome.
- At the end, a release factor binds to the stop codon and translation is terminated.
- Following this, release of the polypeptide completely occurs from the ribosome.

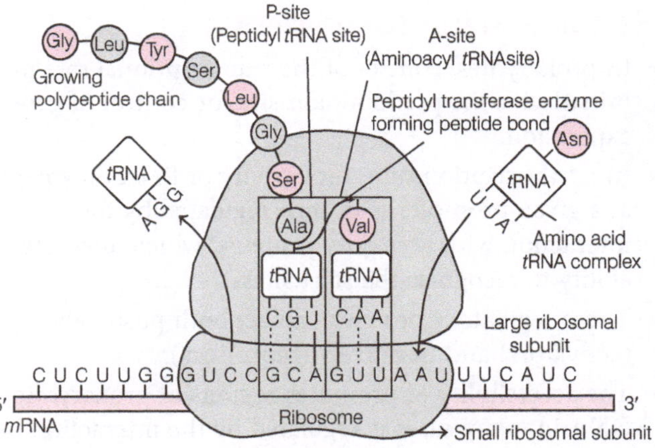

Fig. 5.19 Translation

5.9 Regulation of Gene Expression

- Gene expression results in the formation of a polypeptide.
- Gene regulation is the mechanism of switching 'off' and switching 'on' of the genes, depending upon the requirement of the cells and the stage of development.
- The regulation of gene expression may occur at various levels.
- The mechanism of regulation in eukaryotes and prokaryotes is discussed as follows

Regulation in Eukaryotes

- In eukaryotes, regulation of gene expression takes place at the following levels
  - **Transcriptional Level** A primary transcript is formed.
  - **Processing Level** Regulation of splicing.
  - **Transport of *m*RNA** from nucleus to the cytoplasm.
  - **Translational Level** occurs in cytoplasm and result in protein synthesis.
- Genes in a cell are expressed to perform a particular function or a set of functions.
- The metabolic, physiological or environmental conditions regulate the expression of genes.
- For example the development and differentiation of embryo into adult organism is also a result of the coordinated regulation of expression of several sets of genes.

Regulation in Prokaryotes

- In prokaryotes, control of the transcriptional rate of initiation is the predominant site for control of gene expression.
- In a transcription unit, the activity of RNA polymerase at a given promoter is in turn regulated by the interaction with accessory proteins, which affect its ability to recognise the start sites.
- These regulatory proteins can act both positively (activators) and negatively (repressors).
- The accessibility of promoter regions of prokaryotic DNA in many cases is regulated by the interaction of proteins with sequences termed as **operators**.
- The operator region is adjacent to the **promoter** elements in most operons and in most cases, the sequences of the operator bind a **repressor** protein.
- Each operon has its specific operator and specific repressor, e.g. *lac* operator is present only in the *lac* operon and it interacts with *lac* repressor only.

Lac Operon

- **Francois Jacob** and **Jacques Monod** in 1961 were the first to propose the concept of a transcriptionally regulated system.
- In this system, a polycistronic structural gene is regulated by a common promoter and regulatory genes.
- Such an arrangement is referred as an **operon**, e.g. *lac* (lactose) operon, *trp* (tryptophan) operon, *ara* (arabinose) operon, *his* (histidine) operon and *val* (valine) operon, etc.

Structure of *Lac* Operon

It consists of various genes as shown in fig. 5.20 and is discussed below

- One **regulatory gene** (the *i* gene), which codes for the repressor of the *lac* operon.
  The term *i* does not refer to an inducer, rather it is derived from the word inhibitor.
- Three **structural genes** are
  - **z gene** codes for enzyme β-galactosidase (β-gal), that helps in the hydrolysis of disaccharide into its monomeric units, e.g. lactose into galactose and glucose.
  - ***y* gene** codes for enzyme permease, that increases the permeability of the cell to β-galactosides.
  - ***a* gene** codes for enzyme transacetylase.

Mechanism of *Lac* Operon

- Lactose is known to be the **inducer** and the substrate for the enzyme is **β-galactosidase**. If lactose is provided as the carbon source in the growth medium, in the absence of the preferred carbon source such as glucose, the lactose is transported into the cells by the action of enzyme permease.
- The lactose then induces the operon.
- The *i* gene synthesises the repressor of the operon.
- Repressor protein binds to the operator region of the operon and prevent RNA polymerase from transcribing the operon. Thus, the operon gets inactivated.
- By interaction with the inducer such as lactose or allolactose, the repressor gets inactivated.
- As a result, RNA polymerase is allowed access to the promoter and transcription proceeds (Fig. 5.20).
- Regulation of *lac* operon by repressor is referred to as **negative regulation**. *Lac* operon can work under the control of **positive regulation** also.
- **When Lactose is Absent** '*i*' gene regulates and produces repressor *m*RNA, which blocks transcription.

- The repressor protein binds to the operator region of the operon and as a result prevents RNA polymerase from binding to the operon.

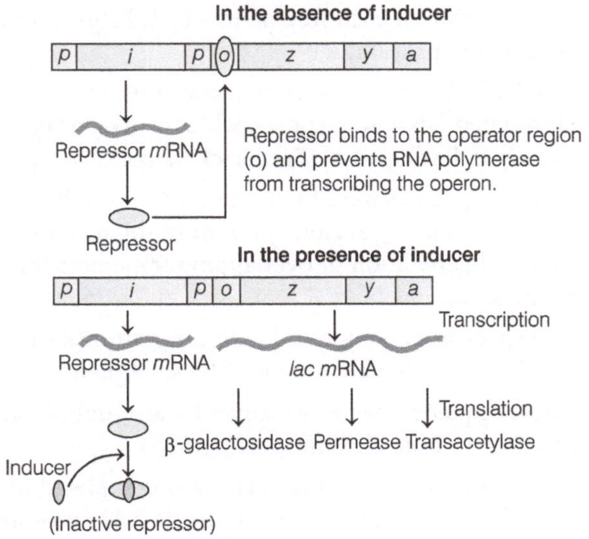

Fig. 5.20 The *lac* operon

- The operon is switched off in this situation.
- **When Lactose is Present** Lactose acts as an inducer and binds to the repressor.
- Thus, it inactivates the repressor and the repressor fails to bind to the operator region.
- The RNA polymerase binds to the operator and transcripts *lac* *m*RNA.
- *Lac* *m*RNA is known to be polycistronic, which produces all three enzymes– β-galactosidase, permease and transacetylase.
- In this situation, operon is switched on.

Quick Test 7

1. Name an organelle where protein synthesis occurs in bacteria.
2. Mention the name of the enzyme that catalyses the formation of a bond between the carboxyl and amino group during protein synthesis.
3. **State True or False.**
   In a eukaryotic cell, after *m*RNA is transported to the cytoplasm, gene expression can be regulated.
4. In the culture medium, where both lactose and glucose are substrates, which one is less likely to be used by bacteria?
5. **State True or False.**
   In the *lac* operon, the repressor protein is unable to bind to the operator in the presence of an inducer.

5.10 Human Genome Project (HGP)

- The genetic make up of an organism lies in its DNA sequence.
- If any two individuals differ from each other, then their should also be difference in their DNA, atleast at some places.
- These assumptions led to the idea of determining the complete DNA sequence of human genome and consequently of human genome project.
- It was a mega project which took 13 years for its completion, i.e. from 1990 to 2003.
- It was coordinated by the **US Department of Energy** and the **National Institute of Health.**
- The two main factors that contributed in the completion of this project were
  - Availability of simple and fast techniques for the determination of DNA sequences.
  - Genetic engineering techniques, which help to isolate and clone any segment of DNA.

HGP : A Mega Project

Human genome project was called a **mega project,** because of the following reasons

- The human genome is said to have approximately 3×10^9 bp and if the cost of sequencing is **US $ 3 per bp**, then total cost would be about **US $ 9 billion** approximately.
- If the sequence were to be stored in a typed form in books and it each page of the book contained 1000 letters and each book contained 1000 pages, then approximately 3300 books would be needed to store the complete information of DNA sequence from a single human cell.
- The large and enormous amount of data that was expected to be generated also necessitated the use of high speed computational devices for the data storage, retrieval and analysis.
- Human genome project was in close association with the new and rapidly developing area of biology known as **bioinformatics.**
- Bioinformatics is a scientific discipline that encompasses the application of computing science and technology to analyse and manage the biological data.

Goals of HGP

Some of the important goals of HGP are as follows.

- To identify all the genes (approximately 20,000-25,000) in human DNA.
- To determine the sequences of the 3 billion chemical base pairs that constitute human DNA.
- To store this information in databases in digital format.
- To improve the tools required for data analysis.
- To transfer the related technologies to other sectors (like industries).
- To address the Ethical, Legal and Social Issues (ELSI) that could arise from the project.

Benefits of HGP

- The knowledge about effects of the DNA variations among individuals can lead to the discovery of new ways in diagnosis, treatment and prevention of various diseases affecting mankind.
- It can help in learning about DNA sequences of non-human organisms that can lead to an understanding of their natural capabilities.
- This can be applied to solve challenges in healthcare, agriculture, energy production, environmental remediation, etc.
- Bacteria, yeast, *Caenorhabditis elegans* (a free-living non-pathogenic nematode), *Drosophila* (fruit-fly), plants (rice and *Arabidopsis*), have also been sequenced.

Methodologies of HGP

Two major approaches involved in HGP are as follows

- **Expressed Sequence Tags** (ESTs) This method focuses on identifying all the genes that are expressed as RNA.
- **Sequence Annotation** This method involves the sequencing of whole set of genome (that contained all coding and non-coding sequence) and then assigning functions to the different regions in the sequence.

Sequencing of Genome

The steps of genome sequencing are as follows.

- First the total DNA from a cell is isolated and converted into random fragments of smaller sizes.
- Then these fragments are cloned in a suitable host, (such as bacteria and yeast) using specialised vectors such as **BAC** (Bacterial Artificial Chromosome) and **YAC** (Yeast Artificial Chromosome).
- The cloning of DNA fragments lead to the amplification of each fragment, which helps in easy sequencing process.
- The DNA fragments were sequenced using automated DNA sequencers, which work on the principle developed by **Frederick Sanger.**
- These sequences were then arranged on the basis of some overlapping regions present in them. This required generation of overlapping fragments for sequencing.
- The specialised computer based programmes were developed for the alignment of these sequences.
- These sequences were subsequently **annotated** and assigned to each chromosome.
- The sequence of chromosome 1 was completed in May, 2006 [this was the last of the 24 (22 autosomes, X and Y) human chromosomes to be sequenced].
- Finally, the genetic and physical maps of the genome were constructed by collecting information on polymorphism of restriction endonuclease recognition sites and certain repetitive DNA sequences called **microsatellite**.

Salient Features of Human Genome

Some of the salient observations drawn from human genome project are as follows.

- There are 3164.7 million nucleotide bases in the human genome.
- In an average gene, there are 3000 bases. The largest known human gene is **dystrophin** (2.4 million bases).
- Total number of genes in human genome are estimated to be 30,000. Almost, all (99.9%) of the nucleotide bases are exactly same in every human individual.
- For over 50% of the discovered genes, their functions are unknown.
- Less than 2% of the genome codes for proteins.
- Repeated sequences make up very large portion of human genome. These are the stretches of DNA sequences, which are repeated many times (sometimes 100-1000 times). They have no direct coding functions, but help in understanding chromosome structure, dynamics and evolution.

- **Chromosome 1** has the maximum number of genes (2968) and **chromosome-Y** has the least number of genes (231).
- There are about 1.4 million locations in human genome, where single-base DNA differences occur (**SNPs– Single Nucleotide Polymorphisms**).

  This information is helpful in finding chromosomal locations for disease-associated sequences and tracing human history.

Applications and Future Challenges

- Its knowledge is helpful in research involving biological systems including human biology.
- With the whole genome sequences and newer technologies, we can be systematic in our approach to various medical questions on a broader scale.
- All the genes in a genome such as all the transcripts in a particular tissue/organ/tumour can be studied.

Rice Genome Project

- Rice (*Oryza sativa*) is one of the most important crop in the world.
- The rice genome is well mapped and it is the smallest of the major cereal crop genomes (400-430 Mb) that consists of 12 chromosomes.
- The **International Rice Genome Sequencing Project** (IRGSP) started in September 1997. The IRGSP has evolved to include 11 nations.
- The recent interim IRGSP meeting at Clemson University in South Carolina was held on September 19 and 20, 2000.
- It was the longest rice genome meeting till today.
- It was attended by more than 70 scientists and administrators from India, USA, Japan, China, Thailand, Korea, Taiwan, Brazil, France and Canada.
- Till date, 98 PACs/BACs corresponding to 12 Mb of sequence have been completed and released to **DNA Data Bank of Japan.**

5.11 DNA Fingerprinting

- It is a very quick way to analyse the differences in the DNA sequences of two individuals.
- It involves the identification of differences in repetitive DNA.
- The **repetitive DNA** is a specific region in DNA in which a small stretch of DNA is repeated many times.
- Through density gradient centrifugation, these repetitive DNA are separated from the bulk genomic DNA.
- The bulk DNA forms a major peak during centrifugation and the other small peaks are known as **satellite DNA**.
- The satellite DNA is classified into many categories such as microsatellites, minisatellites, etc., on the basis of length of segment, number of repetitive units, the base composition (A : T-rich or G : C-rich), etc.
- The satellite DNA sequences also show high degree of polymorphism and forms the basis of DNA fingerprinting.
- These sequences do not code for any proteins normally, but they constitute a large portion of human genome.

Polymorphism

- It is the variation in individuals at genetic level.
- Polymorphism arises due to mutations.
- Polymorphism plays an important role in evolution and speciation.
- In a population, if an **inheritable mutation** is observed at high frequency, it is referred to as **DNA polymorphism**.
- There are different types of polymorphism, from single nucleotide change to large scale changes.
- In an individual, DNA from every tissue (e.g. blood, hair follicle, skin, bone, saliva, etc.) shows the same degree of polymorphism.
- Thus, these tissues become very essential identification tool in forensic applications.
- As polymorphisms are inherited from parents to children, so it is useful in paternity testing.

Technique of DNA Fingerprinting

- **Alec Jeffreys** initially developed DNA fingerprinting, also known as **DNA typing** or **DNA profiling**, to find out markers for the inherited diseases.
- He used a satellite DNA as a probe that shows very high degree of polymorphism and was called as **Variable Number of Tandem Repeats** (VNTRs). The technique involved Southern blot hybridisation using radiolabelled VNTR as a probe.

- The technique is carried out in following steps
    1. **DNA Isolation** DNA is separated from the cellular components using in a high speed centrifuge.
    2. **Digestion of DNA** Restriction endonucleases helps in the digestion of DNA which result in the generation of DNA fragments.
    3. **Separation** DNA fragments are separated by gel electrophoresis.
    4. **Southern Blotting** Transfer of separated DNA fragments to synthetic membranes (like nylon or nitrocellulose).
    5. **Hybridisation** The radiolabelled VNTR probe (small segments of DNA which help to detect the presence of a gene in a long DNA sequence) gets attached to single-stranded VNTRs having complementary nucleotide sequences.
    6. **Autoradiographic Exposure to X-ray Films** Detection of hybridised DNA fragments by autoradiography. This shows many dark bands of different sizes.

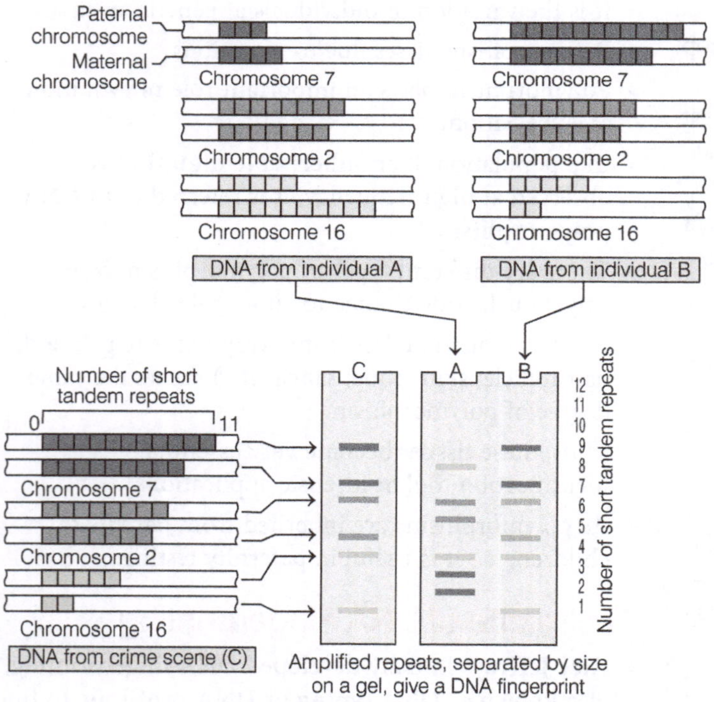

Fig. 5.21 Schematic representation of DNA fingerprinting

- A small DNA sequence is arranged tandemly in many copy numbers, which varies from chromosome to chromosome in an individual.
- The number of repeats show very high degree of polymorphism.
- The size of VNTR varies from 0.1-20 kb. Consequently, after the hybridisation with VNTR probe, the autoradiogram gives many bands of different sizes.
- Thus, these bands give a characteristic pattern for an individual DNA.
- Therefore, it differs from person to person in a population except in the case of monozygotic (identical) twins.
- The VNTR belong to a class of satellite DNA known as **minisatellite** and are essential for DNA fingerprinting.
- The sensitivity of this technique has been increased by using PCR (Polymerase Chain Reaction).

Applications of DNA Fingerprinting

- Used as a tool in forensic investigations.
- To settle paternity disputes.
- To study evolution by determining the genetic diversities among population.

Quick Test 8

1. Mention the scientific discipline developed significantly as a result of the Human Genome Project.
2. Name any non-human model organism whose genome has been completely sequenced.
3. **State True or False.**
   The number of repeats in VNTRs is constant across individuals and they do not contribute to genetic variation.
4. Name the technique that can be used to detect suspects at crime scenes.
5. Can DNA fingerprinting be performed in the absence of restriction endonucleases?

Mind Map

Molecular Basis of Inheritance

Search for Genetic Material

- Genetic materials is that substance which controls the inheritance of traits from one generation to next. Nucleic acids are the building blocks of genetic material.
- Frederick Griffith, carried out a series of experiments with *Streptococcus pneumoniae* and discovered the genetic material as transforming principle.
- Avery, MacLeod and McCarty worked to determine the biochemical nature of Griffith's transforming principle. They proved that DNA is the hereditary material.
- Hershey-Chase experiment with bacteriophage gave a proof that DNA is the genetic material that is passed.

DNA (Deoxyribonucleic Acid)

- It is a double-helical structure composed of two strands made of nucleotides, with a sugar-phosphate backbone and nitrogenous bases.

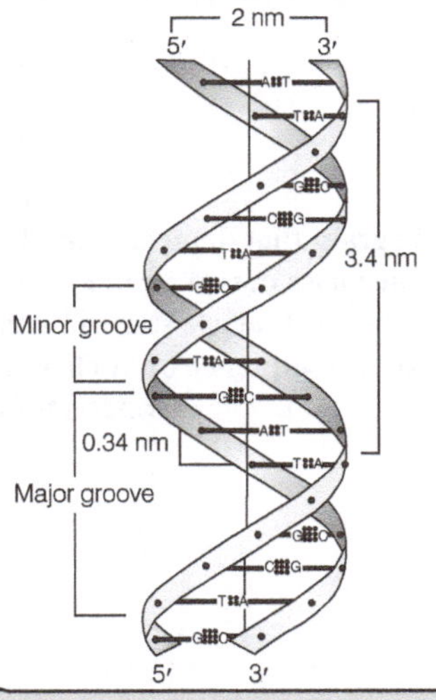

Replication

The process of producing two identical copies from a single original DNA molecule.

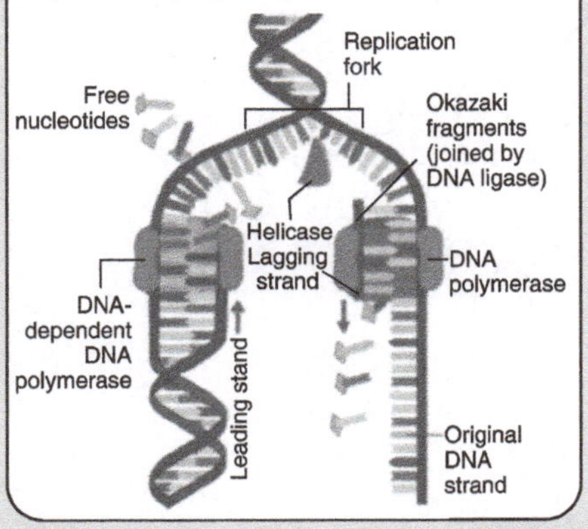

RNA (Ribonucleic Acid)

- First genetic material to be discovered.
- Same composition as DNA except it has ribose sugar and U (Uracil) in place of T (Thymine).

Central Dogma

- Francis Crick proposed it.

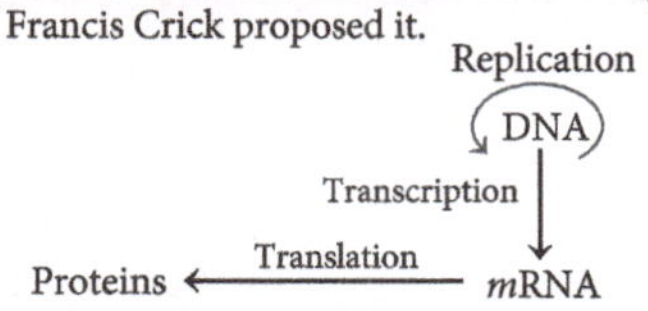

Transcription

- The process of copying genetic information from one strand of DNA to *m*RNA.
- Transcription unit has three regions, i.e. a promoter, the structural gene and a terminator.

DNA Fingerprinting

- It was developed by Alec Jeffreys, involves identification of differences in repetitive DNA.
- Steps involved are DNA isolation, amplification, digestion, separation, blotting, hybridisation and auto-radiography.
- Used in forensic investigation, paternity disputes and to study evolution.

Genetic Code

- It is the relationship between the sequence of nucleotides on *m*RNA and the sequence of amino acids in the polypeptide.
- Features of genetic code are; triplet in nature, unambiguous, specific, commaless, universal and degenerative.

Mutation

- It is the sudden inheritable change in the genetic material.
- It is of two types, i.e. point mutation and frame-shift mutation.

Human Genome Project

- Its goal was to identify all human genes to store this information.
- ESTs and sequence annotations were methodologies of HGP.

Regulation of Gene Expression

- It means to control the amount of time of formation of gene products, according to the requirement of the cell.
- **In eukaryotes** It takes place at four levels, i.e. transcriptional, processing, transport of *m*RNA and translational.
- **In prokaryotes** It takes place through operon system in bacteria. First given by Jacob-Monod in *E. coli-lac* operon, it is induced by lactose.

Translation

- It is the process of polymerisation of amino acids to form a polypeptide, i.e. protein synthesis.
- Synthesis of proteins takes place, through the three stages, i.e. initiation, elongation and termination.

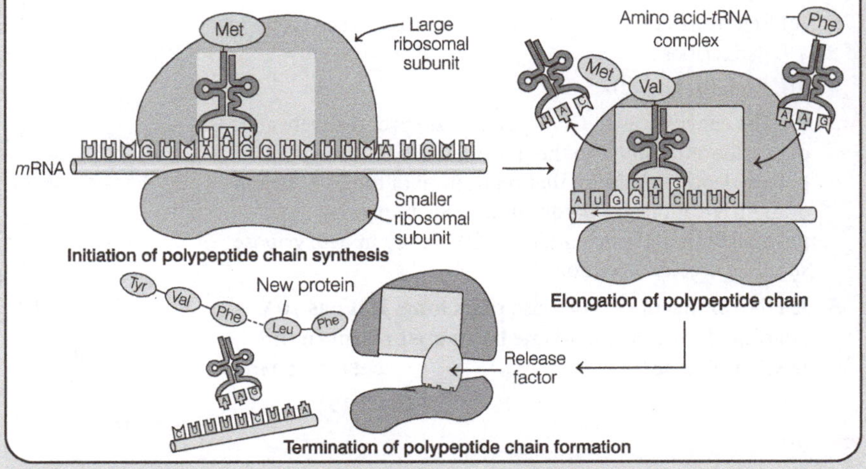

EXAM PATTERN QUESTIONS

Objective Type Questions

Multiple Choice Questions

1. Observe structures *A* and *B* given below. Which of the following statements are correct? **CBSE SQP 2021 Term-I**

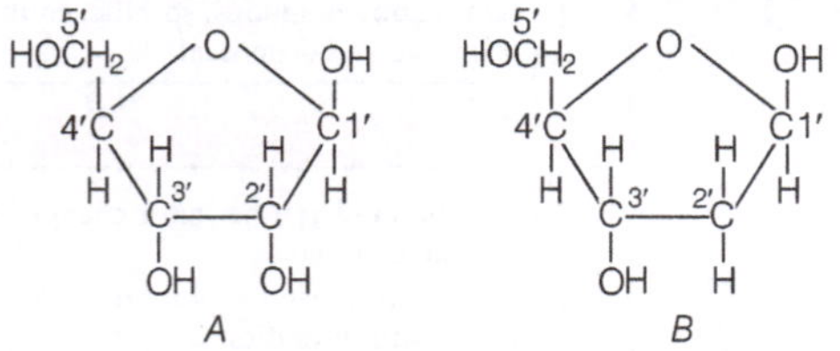

(a) *A* is having 2′—OH group which makes it less reactive and structurally stable, whereas *B* is having 2′—H group which makes it more reactive and unstable

(b) *A* is having 2′—OH group which makes it more reactive and structurally unstable, whereas *B* is having 2′—H group which makes it less reactive and structurally stable

(c) *A* and *B* both have —OH groups which make it more reactive and structurally stable

(d) *A* and *B* both are having —OH groups which make it less reactive and structurally stable

Ans. (*b*)

2. DNA is a polymer of nucleotides which are linked to each other by 3'–5' phosphodiester bond. To prevent polymerisation of nucleotides, which of the following modifications would you choose? **Competency Based Que.**

(a) Replace purine with pyrimidines

(b) Remove/Replace 3' OH group in deoxyribose

(c) Remove/Replace 2' OH group with some other group in deoxyribose

(d) Both (b) and (c)

Ans. (*b*) The enzyme called DNA polymerase progressively adds deoxyribonucleotides to the free 3'-end of the growing polynucleotide chain so, that replication of the 3'–5' strand of the DNA molecule is continuous. So, to prevent polymerisation of nucleotides, 3' OH group in deoxyribose should be replaced/removed.

3. A DNA molecule is 160 base pairs long. If it has 20% adenine, how many cytosine bases are present in this DNA molecule? **CBSE 2021 Term-I**

(a) 48 (b) 64 (c) 96 (d) 192

Ans. (*a*)

4. A sample of normal double-stranded DNA was found to have thymine content of 27%. What will be the expected proportion of guanine in this strand? **CBSE SQP 2024**

(a) 23% (b) 32%
(c) 36% (d) 73%

Ans. (*a*) According to Chargaff's rules, A = T and G = C

Thus, A + T + G + C = 100

Given T = 27%, So A = T = 27%

Thus, A + T = 27 + 27 = 54%

Thus, G + C = 100 − 54 = 46%

Since, G = C,

So, $G = \frac{46}{2} = 23\%$

5. Observe the schematic diagram that depicts a small section of nucleic acid. The bases in two strands are paired through hydrogen bonds that are shown by the dark lines. Identify the correct sequence of nucleotide in the 5'-3' direction. **CBSE SQP 2024**

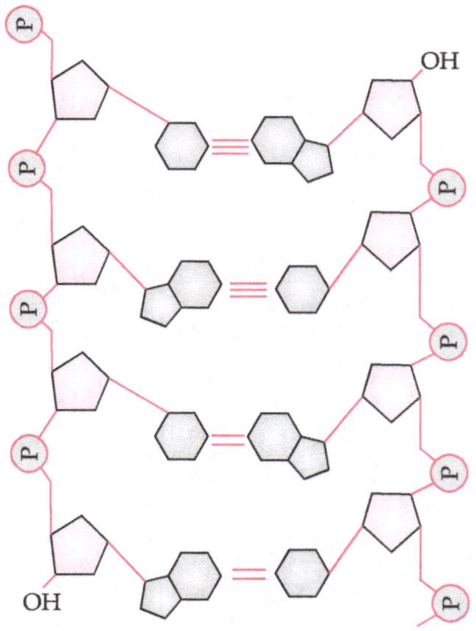

(a) GCAT (b) CGTA
(c) TAGC (d) ATCG

Ans. (*b*)

6. The correct feature of double-helical structure of DNA as given by Watson and Crick is **CBSE 2021 Term-I**

(a) right-handed helix, pitch is 3.4 nm
(b) left-handed helix, pitch is 3.8 nm
(c) right-handed helix, pitch is 3.8 nm
(d) left-handed helix, pitch is 3.4 nm

Ans. (*a*)

7. The histone core in a nucleosome of chromatin thread is a/an **CBSE 2025**

(a) pentamer (b) hexamer (c) heptomer (d) octamer

Ans. (*d*) The histone core in a nucleosome is an octamer, made of eight histone proteins (two each of H2A, H2B, H3 and H4). DNA wraps around this octamer to form the basic unit of chromatin.

8. Study the given diagrammatic representation of Griffith's experiment to demonstrate transformation in bacteria. **Competency Based Que.**

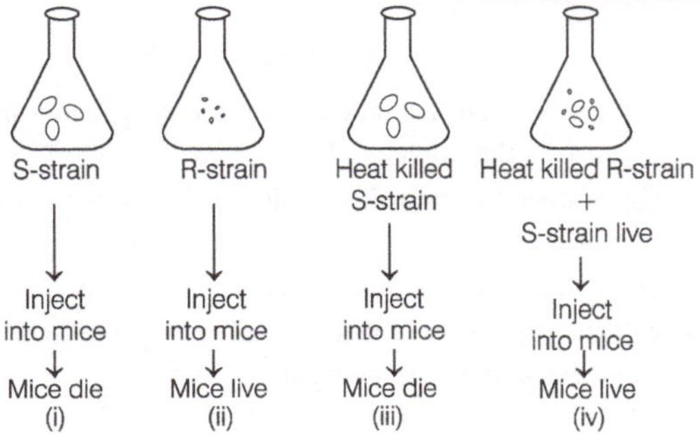

Select the option which is incorrectly representing the experiment. **CBSE 2021 Term-I**

(a) (i) and (iii) (b) (ii) and (iii)
(c) (iii) and (iv) (d) (ii) and (iv)

Ans. (*c*)

9. The correct depiction of the centrifugation step of the experiment conducted by Alfred Hershey and Martha Chase on using radioactive labelled phages to prove that DNA is the genetic material is **CBSE 2025**

(a)

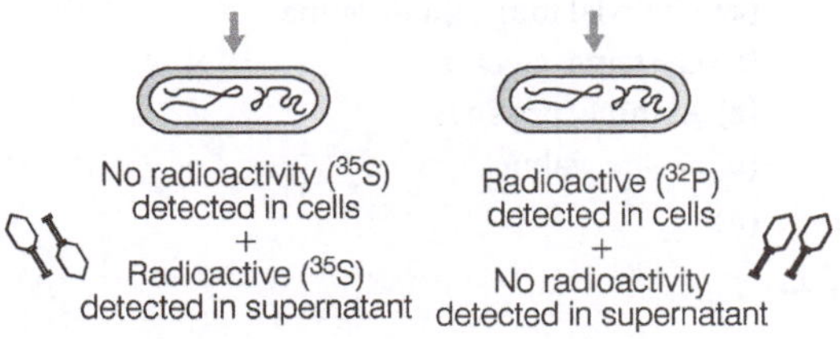

(b)

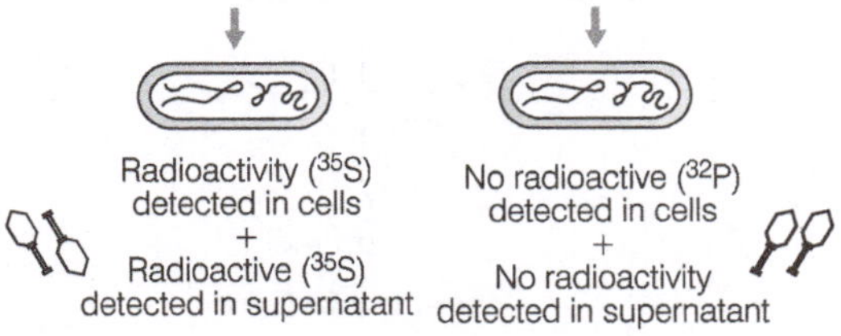

(c)

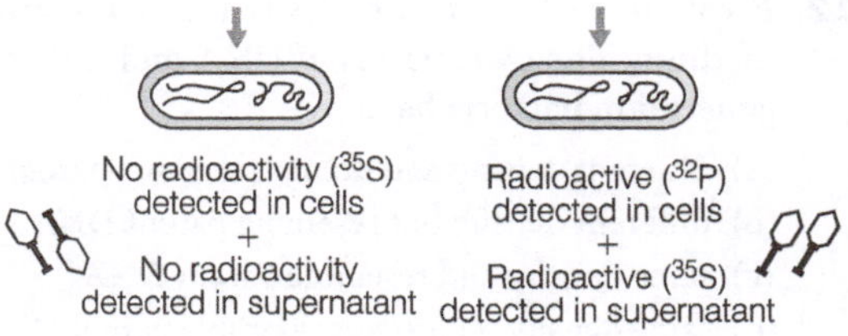

(d)

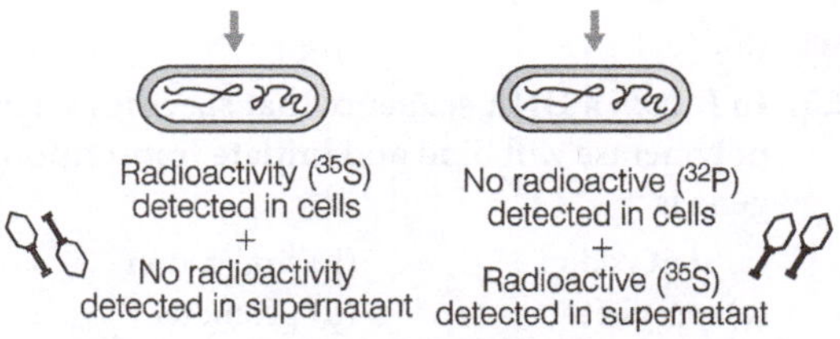

Ans. (*a*) In the Hershey and Chase experiment, P^{32}-labelled DNA was found inside the bacterial cells, while S^{35}-labelled protein remained in the supernatant, proving that DNA is the genetic material.

10. If *E. coli* were allowed to grow in the culture medium for 80 minutes by Matthew Meselson and Franklin Stahl in their experiments, the proportion of light and hybrid density DNA molecule would have been **CBSE 2021 Term-I**

(a) 87.5% of light density DNA and 12.5% of hybrid density DNA
(b) 75.0% of light density DNA and 25% of hybrid density DNA
(c) 50% of light density DNA and 50% of hybrid density DNA
(d) 12.5% of light density DNA and 87.5% of hybrid density DNA

Ans. (*a*)

11. Which one of the following diagram correctly represents DNA replication in eukaryotes? **CBSE 2021 Term-I**

(a)

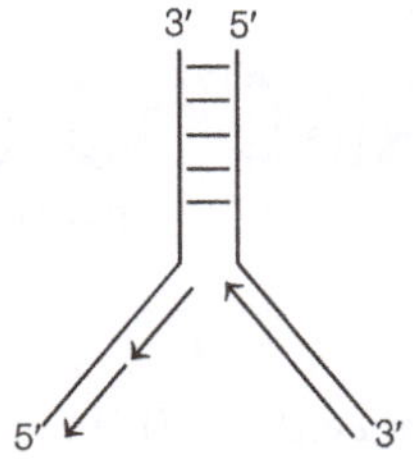

(b)

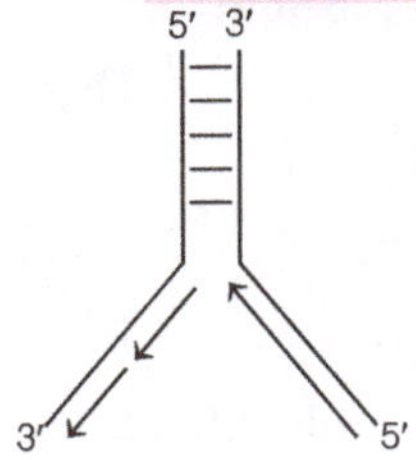

(c)

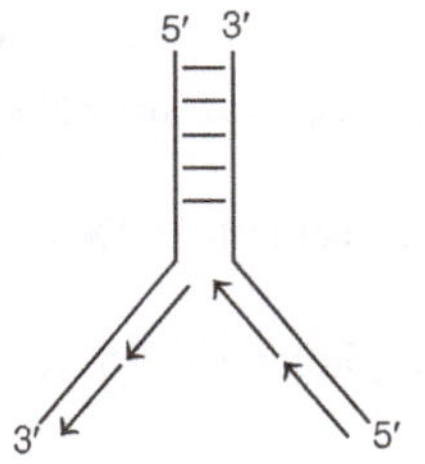

(d)

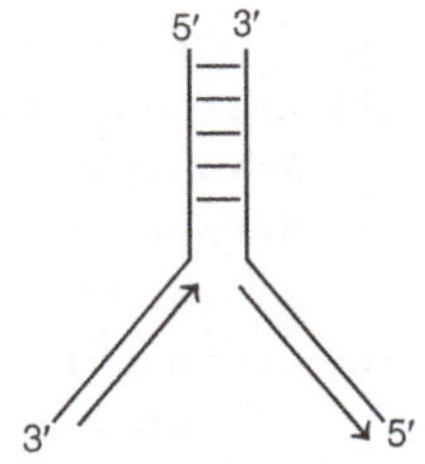

Ans. (*a*)

12. *E. coli* fully labelled with ^{15}N is allowed to grow in ^{14}N medium. The two strands of DNA molecule of the first generation bacteria have **Diksha**

(a) different density and do not resembel parent DNA
(b) different density but resemble parent DNA
(c) same density and resemble parent DNA
(d) same density but do not resemble parent DNA

Ans. (*b*)

13. In *E. coli*, a DNA sequence that specifies where RNA polymerase will bind and initiate transcription of a gene is **CBSE 2025**

(a) start codon (b) stop codon
(c) terminator (d) promoter

Ans. (*d*) The promoter is a specific DNA sequence in *E. coli*, where RNA polymerase binds to initiate transcription.

14. During the process of transcription, after binding to a promoter, RNA polymerase catalyses and makes the bases in the template strand of DNA available for base pairing, with the bases of **CBSE 2025**

(a) deoxyribonucleotide triphosphate
(b) deoxyribonucleoside triphosphate
(c) ribonucleotide triphosphate
(d) ribonucleoside triphosphate

Ans. (*c*) During transcription, RNA polymerase catalyses the addition of ribonucleotide triphosphates (*r*NTPs) to synthesise RNA using the DNA template strand.

15. 'AGGTATCGCAT' is a sequence from the coding strand of a gene. What will be the corresponding sequence of the transcribed *m*RNA? **CBSE 2025**

(a) AGGUAUCGCAU (b) ACCUAUGCGAU
(c) UGGTUTCGCAT (d) UCCAUAGCGUA

Ans. (*a*)

16. Transcription unit is represented in the diagram given below.

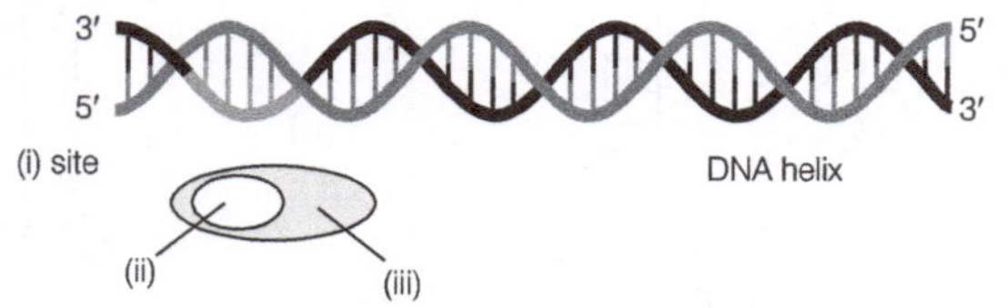

Identify site (i), factor (ii) and enzyme (iii) responsible for carrying out the process. **CBSE SQP 2021 Term-I**

(a) (i) Promoter site, (ii) Rho factor, (iii) RNA polymerase
(b) (i) Terminator site, (ii) Sigma factor, (iii) RNA polymerase
(c) (i) Promoter site, (ii) Sigma factor, (iii) RNA polymerase
(d) (i) Promoter site, (ii) Sigma factor, (iii) DNA polymerase

Ans. (*c*)

17. Removal of RNA polymerase-III from nucleoplasm of a eukaryotic cell will affect the transcription of which of the following? **CBSE 2025**

(a) *t*RNA (b) *hn*RNA (c) *m*RNA (d) *r*RNA

Ans. (*a*) *t*RNA - RNA polymerase-III transcribes *t*RNA, not *m*RNA or *r*RNA.

18. A diagrammatic illustration of the process of transcription by RNA polymerase-II in eukaryote is given below. Choose the most appropriate statement with respect to the fate of the precursor of *m*RNA transcribed that will be **CBSE 2021 Term-I**

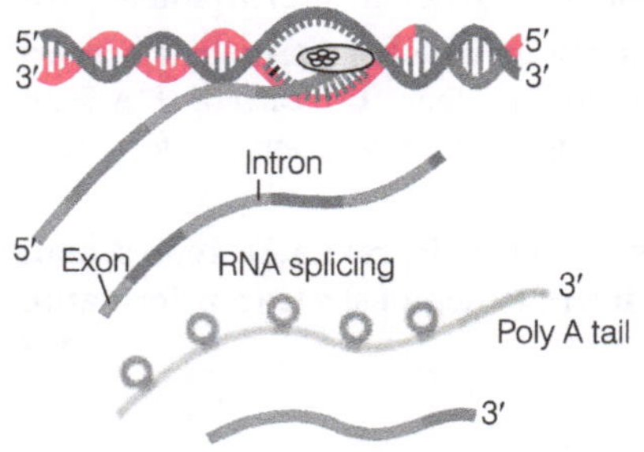

(a) translation will take place once the precursor of *m*RNA leaves the nucleus
(b) translation on *m*RNA will not take place once the precursor of *m*RNA leaves the nucleus
(c) translation will take place in the nucleus
(d) the precursor of *m*RNA has to be processed further in next step before being translated

Ans. (*d*)

19. Which one of the following codons has dual function ? **CBSE 2024 C**

(a) AUG (b) AUC (c) ACU (d) ACA

Ans. (*a*)

20. Given below is a sequence of bases in *m*RNA of a bacterial cell. Identify the amino acid that would be incorporated at codon position 3 and codon position 5 during the process of its translation.

3′ AUCAGGUUUGUGAUGGUACGA 5′

(a) Phenylalanine, methionine **CBSE 2023**
(b) Cysteine, glycine
(c) Alanine, proline
(d) Serine, valine

Ans. (*a*)

21.

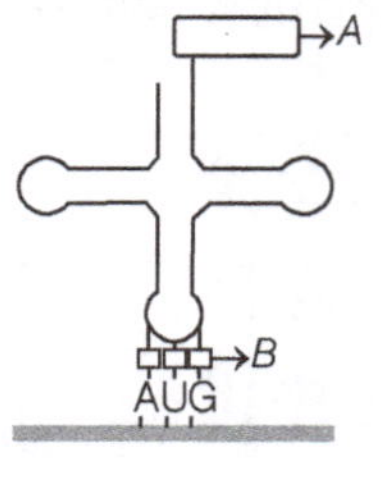

AUG on the *m*RNA will result in the activation of which of the following RNA having correct combination of amino acids? **CBSE SQP 2021 Term-I**

	Site *A*	Site *B*
(a)	UAC	Methionine
(b)	Methionine	UAC
(c)	Methionine	AUG
(d)	AUG	Methionine

Ans. (*b*)

22. **A eukaryotic cell, post-transcription prepares itself for synthesis of proteins, so as to meet its metabolic needs. The modified *m*RNA translates into proteins through a sequential stepwise process. Identify the correct sequence of steps in translation and select the correct option.** **Competency Based Que.**

I. **Aminoacylation of *t*RNA.**
II. **Attachment of larger subunit of ribosome to *m*RNA-*t*RNA met complex.**
III. **Linking of adjacent amino acids to form a polypeptide.**
IV. **Codon-anticodon reaction between RNA and amino acyl *t*RNA complex.**
V. **Attachment of *m*RNA with smaller subunit of ribosome.**

(a) I → II → V → IV → III
(b) II → III → I → IV → V
(c) I → V → IV → II → III
(d) II → IV → V → I → III

Ans. (*c*)

23. **In the given figure of translation machinery of eukaryotes, select the correct labellings for (i), (ii), (iii) and (iv).** **CBSE 2021 Term-I**

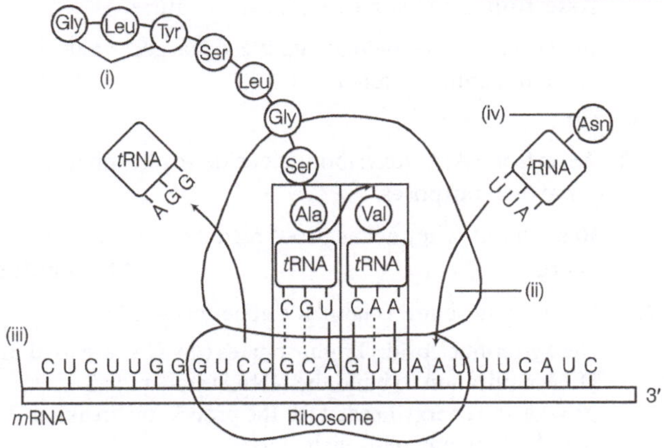

(a) (i) Codon, (ii) Anticodon, (iii) *t*RNA, (iv) 3′ end of *m*RNA
(b) (i) Anticodon, (ii) Codon, (iii) 3′ end of *m*RNA, (iv) 5′ end of *m*RNA
(c) (i) Polypeptide chain, (ii) Large subunit of ribosome, (iii) 5′ end of *m*RNA, (iv) *t*RNA
(d) (i) Ribozyme, (ii) Polypeptide chain, (iii) *t*RNA, (iv) 5′ end of *t*RNA

Ans. (*c*)

24. **What would happen if a gene encoding a polypeptide of 50 amino acids, 25th codon (UAU) is mutated to "UAA"?** **CBSE 2025**

(a) A polypeptide of 49 amino acids will be formed.
(b) A polypeptide of 25 amino acids will be formed.
(c) A polypeptide of 24 amino acids will be formed.
(d) A polypeptide of 50 amino acids will be formed.

Ans. (*c*) If a gene encoding a polypeptide of 50 amino acids undergoes a mutation where the 25th codon (UAU), which codes for tyrosine, is changed to UAA, a stop codon. This premature stop codon causes early termination of translation, leading to the formation of a shorter polypeptide. Instead of the full-length 50 amino acid polypeptide, only the first 24 amino acids are synthesised before translation stops.

25. **The figure given below shows the functioning of *lac* operon.**

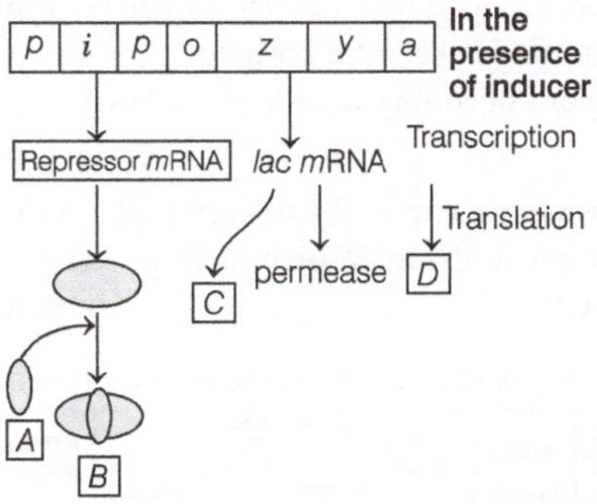

Identify the components and select the correct codes. A prokaryotic bacterial cell, regulates the expression of genes and switches on the *lac* operon in the presence of inducer, i.e. lactose.

(a) *A*–Promoter , *B*–Inactive repressor, *C*–β-galactosidase, *D*–Transacetylase
(b) *A*–Transacetylase, *B*–Inducer, *C*–Inactive repressor, *D*–β-galactosidase
(c) *A*–Inducer, *B*–Inactive repressor, *C*–β-galactosidase, *D*–Transacetylase
(d) *A*–Inactive repressor, *B*–Transacetylase, *C*–Promoter, *D*–β-galactosidase

Ans. (*c*)

26. **Select the important goals of HGP from the given options.**

(i) **Store the information for data analysis.**

(ii) **Cloning and amplification of human DNA.**

(iii) **Identify all the genes present in human DNA.**

(iv) **Use of DNA information to trace human history.** CBSE 2021 Term-I

(a) (i) and (ii) (b) (ii) and (iii)

(c) (i) and (iii) (d) (ii) and (v)

Ans. (*c*)

27. **The approach used in HGP of identifying all the genes that are expressed as RNA is referred to as** CBSE 2025

(a) SNPs (b) YACs

(c) ESTs (d) BACs

Ans. (*c*) In the Human Genome Project (HGP), one approach to gene identification was to analyse only the genes that are actively expressed as RNA. This method involves sequencing short fragments of *c*DNA (complementary DNA), which are derived from *m*RNA transcripts and these short sequences are called Expressed Sequence Tags (ESTs).

28. **What are minisatellites?** CBSE 2021 Term-I

(a) 10-40 bp sized small sequences within the genes

(b) Short coding repetitive region on the eukaryotic genome

(c) Short non-coding repetitive sequence forming large portion of eukaryotic genome

(d) Regions of coding strands of the DNA

Ans. (*c*)

29. **There was a mixup at the hospital after a fire accident in the nursery division. Which of these children belong to the parents?** CBSE SQP 2021 Term-I

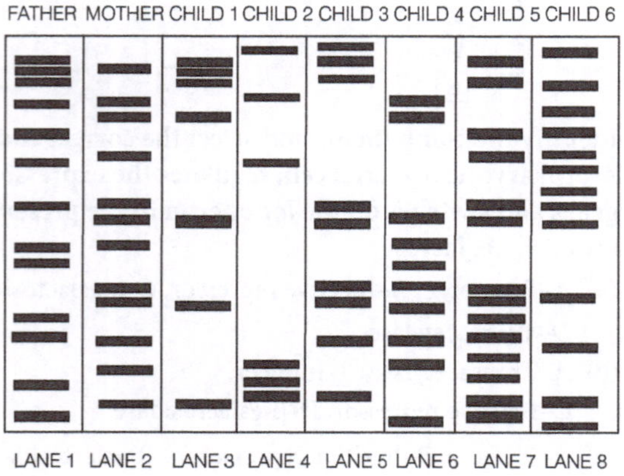

(a) All of the children (b) Children 2, 3 and 6

(c) Children 1 and 3 (d) Children 2 and 4

Ans. (*c*)

Assertion-Reason Questions

Directions (Q. Nos. 1-12) In each of the following questions, a statement of Assertion (A) is given by corresponding statement of Reason (R). Of the statements, mark the correct answer as

(a) Both A and R are true and R is the correct explanation of A

(b) Both A and R are true, but R is not the correct explanation of A

(c) A is true, but R is false

(d) A is false, but R is true

1. **Assertion** (A) Cytidine is a nucleoside.

Reason (R) A nucleoside is formed by the combination of sugar and phosphate group.

Ans. (*c*)

2. **Assertion** (A) DNA has two chains having antiparallel polarity.

Reason (R) One end of DNA has a free phosphate moiety at 5′ end of sugar and at other end the sugar has a free 3′ OH group.

Ans. (*a*)

3. **Given below is the nucleosome model in which the histone proteins are bounded by DNA. One nucleosome contains about 200 base pairs of DNA helix. Study the structure and comment upon the appropriateness of the Assertion and the Reason.** Competency Based Que.

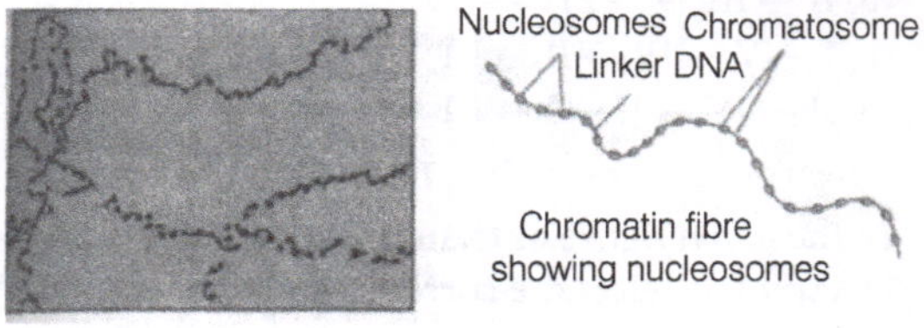

Assertion (A) Histones are basic in nature.

Reason (R) DNA being negatively charged, wrap around histone octamer.

Ans. (*b*)

4. **Assertion** (A) Deoxyribonucleoside triphosphates serve dual purposes.

Reason (R) They act as proof readers and provide energy. CBSE SQP 2024

Ans. (*c*) A is true, but R is false. R can be corrected as Deoxyribonucleoside Triphosphates (*d*NTPs) are used in DNA replication to build the DNA strand and also provide the energy needed for the process by breaking their high-energy phosphate bonds.

5. Assertion (A) Replication on one strand of DNA is continuous and on another it is discontinuous.

Reason (R) The DNA polymerase works in $3' \rightarrow 5'$ direction.

Ans. (*c*)

6. Assertion (A) In transcription, the strand with $5' \rightarrow 3'$ polarity acts as the template strand.

Reason (R) The enzyme RNA polymerase catalyses the polymerisation in only one direction, i.e. $5' \rightarrow 3'$.

Ans. (*d*) A is false, but R is true. A can be corrected as

In transcription, the strand with $3' \rightarrow 5'$ polarity acts as the template strand .

7. Assertion (A) DNA-dependent RNA polymerase catalyses polymerisation in the 5' to 3' direction.

Reason (R) The strand with 5' to 3' polarity is called the coding strand. **Competency Based Que.**

Ans. (*b*)

8. Assertion (A) A fully processed *hn*RNA is called *m*RNA.

Reason (R) *hn*RNA undergoes splicing and other post-transcriptional modifications like capping and tailing.

Ans. (*a*)

9. Given below picture represents heterogenous nuclear RNA (*hn* RNA) that refers to the bulk of transcribed RNA. *hn*RNA undergoes processing to *m*RNA. Based on the above information and given picture comment upon the appropriateness of Assertion and Reason. **Competency Based Que.**

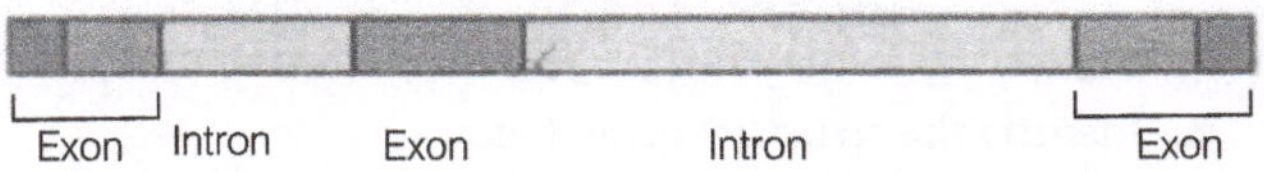

Assertion (A) *hn*RNA is larger than *m*RNA.

Reason (R) *hn*RNA has non-coding introns which are not required for translation.

Ans. (*a*)

10. Assertion (A) Most of the amino acids are represented by more than one codon.

Reason (R) The genetic code is non-ambiguous.

Ans. (*b*)

11. Assertion (A) During protein synthesis the correct amino acid is brought to the ribosome and inserted at its place in the growing polypeptide chain.

Reason (R) This insertion is facilitated by the interaction between the *m*RNA anticodons and codons on *t*RNA.

Ans. (*c*) A is true, but R is false. R can be corrected as

The insertion of amino acids during the protein synthesis is facilitated by the interaction between the *m*RNA codon and anticodons on *t*RNA.

12. Assertion (A) In *E. coli*, the *lac* operon gets switched on in presence of lactose.

Reason (R) Lactose binds to the repressor.

Ans. (*a*)

Subjective Questions

Very Short Answer Type Questions

1. Identify the structure given below.

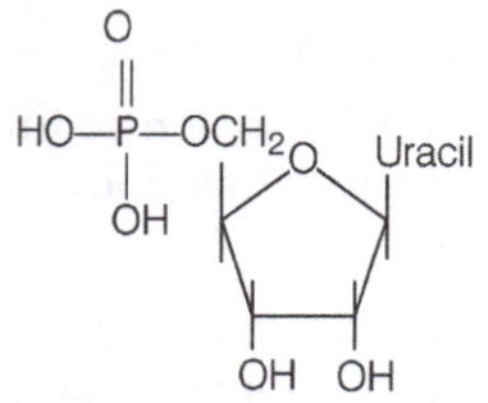

Ans. The given structure represents a nucleotide called uridylic acid.

2. Name the specific components and the linkage between these component that form a deoxyadenosine.

Ans. Adenine (N-glycosidic linkage) + Deoxyribose → Deoxyadenosine

3. What is the base pairing pattern of DNA?

Ans. Guanine pair with cytosine and adenine pair with thymine.

4. If a double-stranded DNA has 20% of cytosine, calculate the percentage of adenine in the DNA. **NCERT, Competency Based Que.**

Ans. Given cytosine = 20%

∴Percentage of guanine = 20%

Now according to Chargaff's rule

$A + T = 100 - (G + C)$

$\Rightarrow A + T = 100 - 40$

∴Percentage of thymine = Percentage of adenine

$$\frac{60\%}{2} = 30\%$$

5. If the base adenine constitutes 31 percent of an isolated DNA fragment, then what is the expected percentage of the base cytosine in it? **CBSE 2011C**

Ans. According to Chargaff's rule

$A + G + C + T = 100$

∴ If $A = 31\%$ then, $T = 31\%$

Thus, $A + T = 31 + 31 = 62\%$

Thus, $G + C = 100 - 62 = 38\%$

Since, $G = C$

So, $C = \frac{38}{2} = 19\%$

6. Why does the distance between the two polynucleotide strands of DNA remain almost constant?

Ans. In a DNA molecule, a large sized purine (A, G) always positioned opposite and pairs with pyrimidines (T, C). This generates a uniform distance between the two strands of a DNA helix

7. Name the two basic amino acids that provide positive charge to histone proteins.

Ans. Lysine and arginine

8. Name the negatively charged and positively charged components of a nucleosome.

Ans. A histone octamer is the positively charged component and the DNA helix is the negatively charged component of nucleosome.

9. Name the transcriptionally active region of chromatin in a nucleus.

Ans. Euchromatin.

10. Why is RNA more reactive in comparison to DNA?

Ans. The OH-group in the ribose sugar of RNA makes the molecule more reactive as compared to the DNA.

11. Why were protein discarded from being the genetic material?

Ans. Proteins were discarded from being the genetic material because they are not able to replicate itself.

12. If the sequence of one strand of DNA is written as follows;

5'–ATGCATGCATGCATGCATGCATGCATGC– 3'

Write down the sequence of complementary strand in $3' \rightarrow 5'$ direction. **NCERT, Competency Based Que.**

Ans. The sequence of strand in 3 → '5 direction

3'–TACGTACGTACGTACGTACGTACGTACG –5'

13. Name the enzyme involved in continuous replication of DNA strand. Mention the polarity of the template strand.

Ans. Enzyme involved in continuous replication of DNA strand is DNA-dependent DNA polymerase. Template strand has 3' → 5' polarity. (½ + ½)

14. Mention the polarity of the DNA strands *A—B* and *C—D* shown in the replicating fork given below

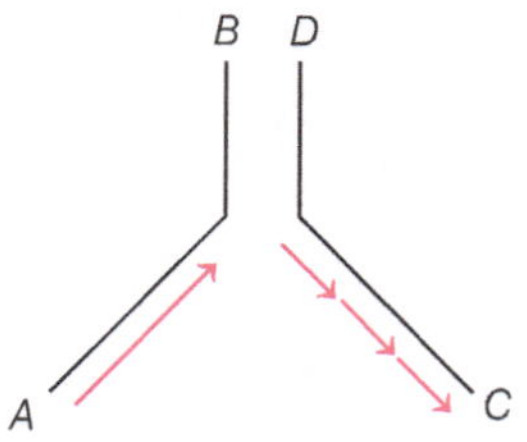

Ans. $A \rightarrow B$ is 3' → 5' and $C \rightarrow D$ is 5' → 3'

15. Name the property of DNA that governs transcription.

Ans. Principle of complementarity

16. If the sequence of the coding strand in a transcription unit is written as follows
5'—ATGCATGCATGCATGCATGCATGCATGC —3'
Write down the sequence of *m*RNA. NCERT, Competency Based Que.

Ans. 5'—AUGCAUGCAUGCAUGCAUGCAUGCAUGC —3'

17. Which one out of rho factor and sigma factor act as an initiation factor during transcription in a prokaryote?

Ans. Sigma factor acts as an initiation factor and it binds to the promoter site during transcription in prokaryotes.

18. Name the enzyme that transcribes *hn*RNA in eukaryotes.

Ans. The RNA polymerase-II transcribes the precursor of *m*RNA, i.e. the heterogeneous nuclear RNA (*hn*RNA) in eukaryotes.

19. Why does *hn*RNA undergo splicing? Where does splicing occur in the cell?

Ans. *hn*RNA undergoes splicing to remove introns and join exons. Splicing occurs in the nucleus of the cell. (½ + ½)

20. Given below is a sequence of steps of transcription in an eukaryotic cell. Identify *A* and *B* in it.

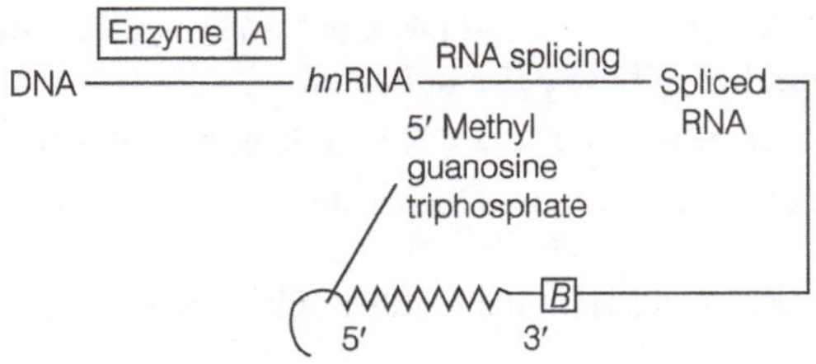

Ans. *A* – DNA polymerase, *B* – *m*RNA

21. Which one out of an intron and an exon is the reminiscent of antiquity?

Ans. Intron is considered to be the reminiscent of antiquity because they were present even before splicing event. They might had important information to form RNA, but they do not serve any function.

22. Predict the effect, if the codon UAU coding for an amino acid at the 25th position of a polypeptide of 50 amino acids is mutated to UAA. CBSE SQP 2023

Ans. If the codon at 25th position is mutated to UAA, a polypeptide of 24 amino acids will be formed as UAA is a stop codon.

23. Give an example of codon having dual function.

Ans. AUG codes for amino acid methionine (met) and also acts as an initiation codon.

24. Mention the role of the codons AUG during protein synthesis.

Ans. AUG acts as initiation codon and also codes for amino acid methionine.

25. All terminater codons begin with nucleotide of which base?

Ans. Uracil 'U'

26. Write any one function of *t*RNA.

Ans. *t*RNA acts as an adapter molecule. It reads the genetic code and binds to specific amino acids from the cellular pool to the site of *m*RNA, where these amino acids get incorporated into the polypeptide chain.

27. Where does transcription and translation occur in eukaryotes?

Ans. In eukaryotes, transcription occurs in nucleus, while translation occurs in the cytoplasm.

28. Given below is a schematic representation of a *lac* operon in the absence of an inducer.
Identify *A* and *B* in it.

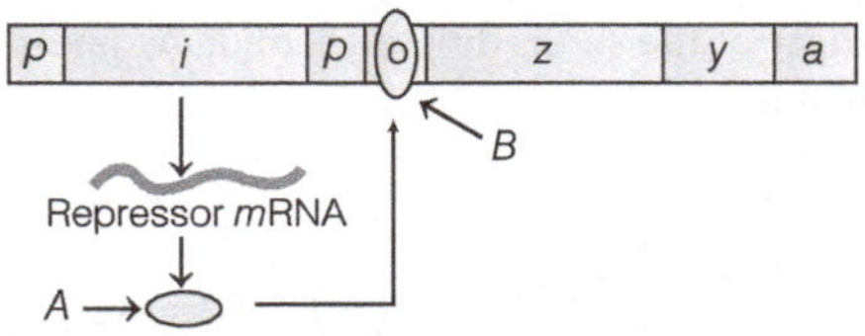

Ans. *A*—Repressor protein
B—Repressor bound to the operator and it prevents transcription of structural genes (½ + ½)

29. Name the last human chromosome to be completely sequenced?

Ans. Chromosome-1.

30. When did rice genome project was started?

Ans. The rice genome project was started in September 1997.

Short Answer Type Questions

1. Group the following as nitrogenous bases and nucleosides.
Adenine, guanosine, cytosine, cytidine, thymine, uracil NCERT

Ans. Nitrogenous bases are adenine, cytosine, thymine and uracil. Nucleosides are guanosine and cytidine.

2. Study the diagram given below

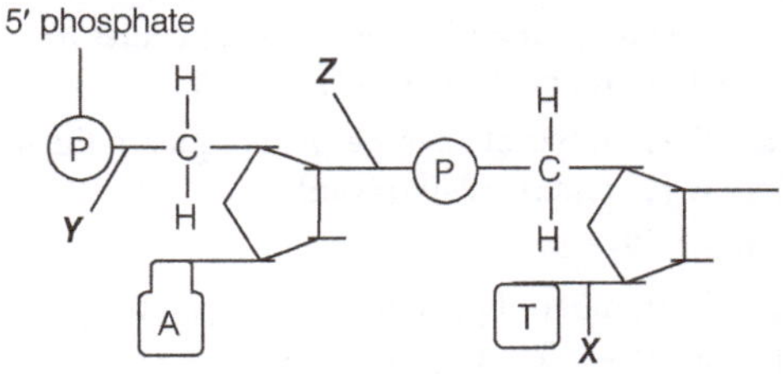

Name the linkage *X*, *Y*, *Z* and the molecules formed by *X*.

Ans. *X* : N-glycosidic linkage.

Y : Phosphoester linkage.

Z : 3′–5′ phosphodiester linkage.

X forms nucleoside. (½ × 4)

3. Describe the structure of a RNA polynucleotide chain having four different types of nucleotides.

Ans.
- RNA is a single stranded polynucleotide structure composed of ribose sugar, phosphate and nitrogenous bases (adenine, guanine, cytosine and uracil)
- The nitrogenous base molecule is joined to the sugar molecule by a glycosidic bond and forms a structure called nucleoside.
- The nucleoside combines with a phosphate group by a phosphoester bond to form a nucleotide.
- In a nucleic acid a phosphate moiety (moiety is a part of a larger molecule or structure) links the 3' carbon of one sugar of one nucleotide to the 5' carbon of the sugar of the succeeding nucleotide by phosphodiester bond.

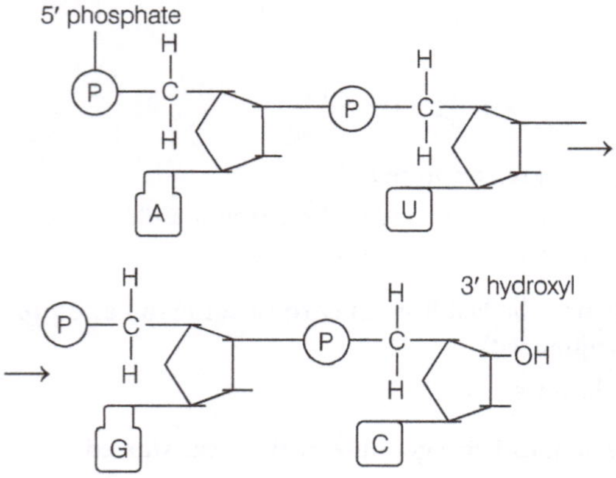

4. Mention the two factors responsible for conferring stability to double helix structure of DNA.

Ans. The factors responsible for conferring stability of double helix structure of DNA are as follows

(i) Stacking of one base pair over other. (1)

(ii) H-bond between nitrogenous bases. (1)

5. A DNA segment has a total of 1000 nucleotides, out of which 240 of them are adenine containing nucleotides. How many pyrimidine bases this DNA segment possesses?

Ans. According to Chargaff's rule, ratio of purines to pyrimidines is equal, i.e. $A + G = C + T$

Since, the number of adenine (A) is equal to the number of thymine (T) and $A = 240$ (given)

Therefore, $T = 240$

Also, the number of guanine (G) is equal to cytosine (C). Thus, $G + C = 1000 - (A + T)$

$G + C = 1000 - 480 = 520$

Hence, $G = 260, C = 260$

The number of pyrimidine bases, i.e. $C + T$

$= 240 + 260 = 500$

6. The base sequence in one of the strands of DNA is TAGCATGAT.

(i) Give the base sequence of the complementary strand.

(ii) How are these base pairs held together in a DNA molecule?

(iii) Explain the base complementarity rule. Give the name of the scientist who framed this rule.

Ans. (i) ATCGTACTA (½)

(ii) Base pairs are held together by weak hydrogen bonds in a DNA molecule. Adenine pairs with thymine by two H-bonds and guanine pairs with cytosine by three H-bonds. (1)

(iii) According to base complementarity rule proposed by Erwin Chargaff for a double-stranded DNA, the ratios between adenine-thymine and guanine-cytosine are constant and equal to one. (1½)

7. The length of a DNA molecule in a typical mammalian cell is calculated to be approximately 2.2 m. How is the packaging of this long molecule done to accommodate it within the nucleus of the cell? **Competency Based Que.**

Ans. Refer to text on page no. 133, 134.

8. If the length of *E. coli* DNA is 1.36 mm, calculate the number of base pairs in *E. coli*.

Ans. Given, length of *E. coli* DNA $= 1.36 \text{ mm} = 1.36 \times 10^{-3}$ m.

Distance between two consecutive base pairs $= 0.34$ nm $= 0.34 \times 10^{-9}$ m.

Hence, for *E. coli* total number of base pairs

$$= \frac{1.36 \times 10^{-3}}{0.34 \times 10^{-9}} = 4 \times 10^6 \text{ bp}$$

9. Draw a labelled diagram of a nucleosome. Where is it found in a cell?

Ans. Structure of a nucleosome

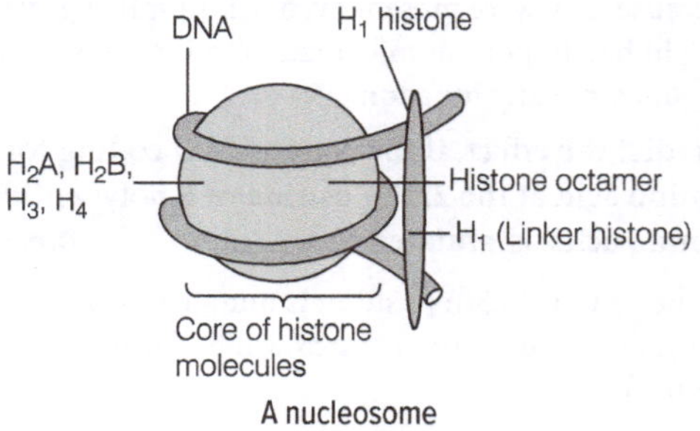

A nucleosome (2)

A nucleosome is found in the nucleus of the cell. (1)

10. How do histones acquire positive charge?

Ans. A protein acquires positive charge depending upon the abundance of amino acids residues that have positively charged groups in their side chains. Histones are rich in the basic amino acid residues–lysines and arginines.

Both of these amino acids carry positive charge in their side chains. Hence, histones are positively charged molecules.

11. Packaging of eukaryotic DNA is a complex process commment. **Diksha**

Ans. The packaging of eukaryotic DNA is a complex process as it involves multiple levels of organisation. In eukaryotic organisms the DNA wraps around histone proteins to form nucleosomes, which are then packed into more compact structures called chromatin. This packaging allows for efficient storage of genetic material, regulation of gene expression and proper segregation during cell division.

12. A DNA molecule is much longer than the length of nucleus of a cell. Describe the organisation of DNA inside a nucleus. **Competency Based Que.**

Ans. DNA in a eukaryotic cell is indeed much longer than the actual size of the nucleus. To fit inside the nucleus, which is only about 6-10 micrometres in diameter, the DNA must be highly organised and compact. DNA is wrapped around the histone octamer to form a nucleosome. Many such nucleosomes repeat to form a bead-in-a-string structure called the chromatin which are thread-like bodies.

The chromatin is further packaged with the help of non-histone chromosomal proteins to fit into the nucleus.

13. What are chromatin ? Why are they seen as 'beads on string' structure under electron microscope?

Ans. Refer to text on page no. 133 and 134.

14. In a typical nucleus, some regions of chromatin are stained light and others dark. Explain why is it so and what is its significance? **All India 2016 C**

Ans. In a typical nucleus, some regions of chromatin are stained light because of loose packing of chromatin and some regions of chromatin are stained dark because the chromatin is densely packed. Euchromatin is transcriptionally active chromatin (lightly stained), while heterochromatin (darkly stained) is transcriptionally inactive chromatin.

15. Explain the discovery made by Hershey and Chase using radioactive sulphur and phosphorus in their experiment. **CBSE 2020**

Ans. Refer to text on page no. 135 and 136.

16. Answer the following questions based on Meselson and Stahl's experiment.

(i) Write the name of the chemical substance used as a source of nitrogen in the experiment by them.

(ii) Why did the scientists synthesise the light and the heavy DNA molecules in the organism in this experiment?

(iii) How did the scientists make it possible to distinguish the heavy DNA molecule from the light DNA molecule? Explain.

(iv) Write the conclusion the scientists arrived at after completing the experiment. **CBSE 2019**

Ans. (i) NH_4Cl (ammonium chloride). (½)

(ii) The scientists synthesise the light and heavy DNA molecules to check the semiconservative mode of DNA replication. (1)

(iii) The heavy and light DNA molecules can be differentiated by centrifugation in a cesium chloride (CsCl) density gradient. The ^{15}N-DNA was heavier than ^{14}N-DNA and the hybrid $^{15}N-^{14}N$-DNA had density intermediate of the two. (1)

(iv) Scientists concluded that the DNA replication is semiconservative, i.e. out of two strands of DNA, one is the parental strand, while another is newly synthesised. (½)

17. It is established that RNA is the first genetic material. Explain giving four reasons.

Ans. RNA is the first genetic material because

(i) It is capable of both storing genetic information and catalysing chemical reactions.

(ii) Essential life processes such as metabolism, translation, splicing, etc., have evolved around RNA.

(iii) It can directly code for protein synthesis and hence can easily express the character.

(iv) It has ability to replicate under certain conditions.

18. The schematic representation given below shows the concept of central dogma.

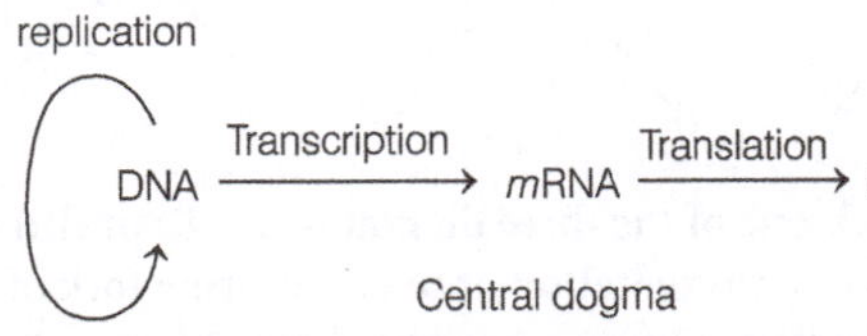

A. During the process of replication and transcription the pairing of nitrogenous bases is not similar. Explain.

B. How is the above process modified in a retrovirus? Name the process.

C. Justify why during the process of transcription only a segment of DNA is copied into RNA.

CBSE SQP 2024, Competency Based Que.

Ans. A. During the process of replication and transcription the pairing of nitrogenous bases is not similar as in replication, adenine pairs with thymine in DNA but during the transcription, adenine pairs with uracil in RNA. (1)

B. In retrovirus the nucleic acid is RNA and it is used to synthesise DNA; the process is called reverse transcription. (1)

C. During transcription, only a segment of DNA is copied into RNA because cells need to regulate gene expression.

Not all genes are needed at the same time, so only specific segments of DNA (genes) are transcribed to produce RNA. This ensures efficiency and energy conservation, allowing the cell to produce only the necessary proteins or functional RNAs. (1)

19. (i) Given below is a representation of the "central dogma"

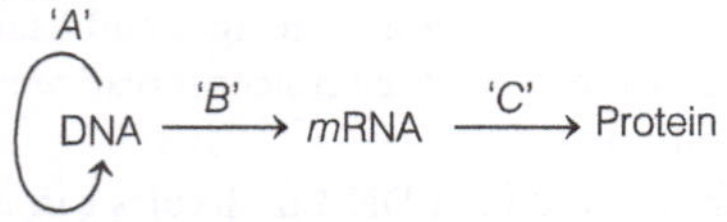

Identify 'A', 'B' and 'C' in the above representation.

(ii) What does the central dogma state in molecular biology ? Write an example where it is not applicable.

Ans. (i) A – Replication
B – Transcription
C – Translation

(ii) The Central Dogma of Molecular Biology states that genetic information flows from DNA to RNA to protein. This means:
- DNA is transcribed into *m*RNA.
- *m*RNA is then translated into a protein.

20. Given below are the diagrammatic representations of the replicating fork of DNA in *E. coli*. Study the diagrams and answer the questions that follows **CBSE 2025**

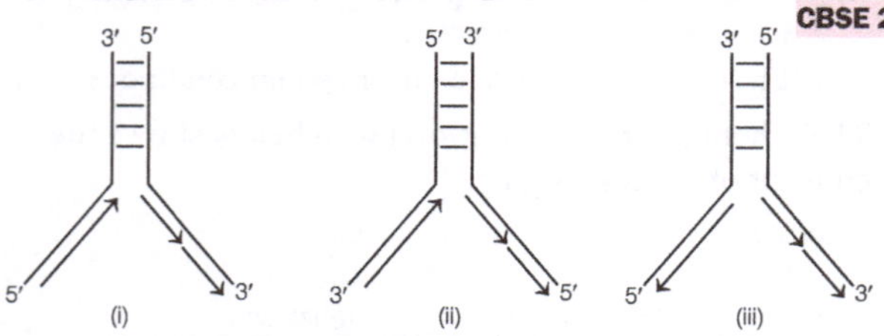

(a) Which one of the three diagrams (i), (ii) or (iii) is the correct representation of the replicating fork of DNA replication? Explain your answer.

(b) Name the enzyme used in *E. coli* to join the newly synthesised fragments of DNA.

Ans. (a) The correct diagram is (iii).
In DNA replication, the new DNA strands are synthesised in the 5' to 3' direction.
The leading strand is synthesised continuously towards the replication fork.
The lagging strand is synthesised away from the replication fork in short Okazaki fragments.
In diagram (iii), the replication fork correctly shows the leading strand in the 5' $\rightarrow$ 3' direction and the lagging strand with Okazaki fragments.

(b) The enzyme used in *E. coli* to join the newly synthesised fragments of DNA is DNA ligase.

21. Name a few enzymes involved in DNA replication other than DNA polymerase and ligase. Name the key functions for each of them. **NCERT Exemplar**

Ans. The enzymes involved in DNA replication other than DNA polymerase and ligase are listed below with their functions.
(i) Helicase — Unwinds the double-stranded helix (1)
(ii) Topoisomerases — Removes the tension in the opened strands (1)

22. Explain the mechanism of DNA replication with the help of a replication fork. What role does the enzyme DNA-ligase play in a replication fork? **CBSE 2019**

Ans. Refer to text on page no 139.

23. Discuss the role of enzyme DNA ligase plays during DNA replication.

Ans. DNA ligase facilitates the joining of Okazaki fragments in lagging DNA strands together by catalysing the formation of phosphodiester bond. It also play a role in repairing single-strand breaks in duplex DNA.

24. State the dual role of deoxyribonucleoside triphosphates during DNA replication.

Ans. (i) The deoxyribonucleoside triphosphates are the building blocks for the DNA strand (polynucleotide chain), as substrate. (1)
(ii) These also serve as energy source in the form of ATP and GTP from there two terminal phosphates. (1)

25. Name the enzyme and state its property that is responsible for continuous and discontinuous replication of the two strands of a DNA molecule.

Ans. DNA-dependent DNA polymerase enzyme can polymerise deoxynucleotides in $5' \rightarrow 3'$ direction only. Due to this, replication of DNA is continuous in template strand with polarity $3' \rightarrow 5'$ while discontinuous in another strand with polarity $5' \rightarrow 3'$.

26. Differentiate between leading strand and lagging strand.

Ans. Refer to text on page no. 139.

27. Why is it not possible for an alien DNA to become part of chromosome anywhere along its length and replicate normally?

Ans. An alien DNA cannot become a part of chromosome anywhere until its attaches to the origin of replication (*ori*), the site where the replication process is initiated. This site contains specific sequence of bases which aids in starting replication within host cell.

28. What will happen if DNA replication is not followed by cell division in a eukaryotic cell? **Competency Based Que.**

Ans. If cell division is not followed after DNA replication then replicated chromosomes (DNA) would not be distributed to daughter nuclei. This will results in the accumulation of DNA inside the cell causing polyploidy.

29. Why is it essential to have an RNA primer when DNA is getting replicated?

Ans. Refer to text on page no. 139.

30. Show DNA replication with the help of a diagram only.

Ans. Refer to fig 5.13 on page no. 139.

31. Why both the strands of DNA are not copied during transcription? Explain.

Ans. Refer to text on page no. 140.

32. With the help of a schematic diagram, explain the location and role of the following in a transcription unit.
Promoter, structural gene, terminator. **CBSE 2014 C**

Ans. Refer to text on page no. 140.

33. State the difference between the structural genes in a transcription unit of prokaryotes and eukaryotes.

Ans. Prokaryotic structural genes are found in continuity without any non-coding region. In contrast, eukaryotic structural genes are divided into exons (coding DNA) and introns (non-coding DNA).

34. Differentiate between a template strand and a coding strand of DNA. **NCERT**

Ans. The differences between coding strand and template strands are given below.

Coding strand	Template strands
The coding strand is the DNA strand whose base sequence is similar to its primary transcript (RNA).	The template strand is the DNA strand that is being transcribed during *m*RNA synthesis.
The coding strand is directed in the 5' to 3' direction.	The template strand is directed in the 3' to 5' direction.
It is also known as sense strand.	It is the antisense strand or a non-coding strand.

35. Construct and label a transcription unit from which the RNA segment given below has been transcribed.
Write the complete name of the enzyme that transcribed this RNA. **CBSE 2019, Competency Based Que.**

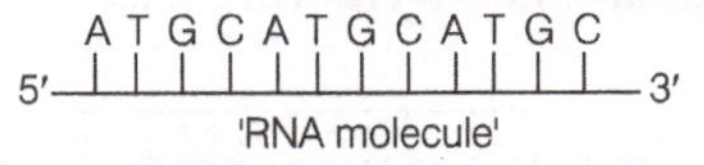

Ans. The RNA molecule given in question should be

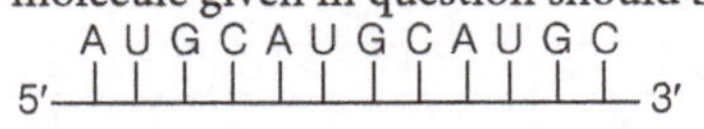

As RNA have uracil in the place of thymine, for given RNA, the transcription unit will be

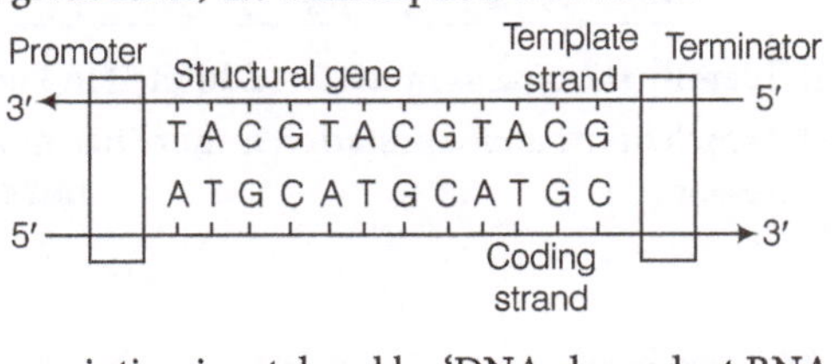

(2)

Transcription is catalysed by 'DNA-dependent RNA polymerase'. (1)

36. Which of the two–the coding strand or the template strand of DNA, will the transcribed RNA resemble more? Why? How will they differ from each other?

Ans. Refer to text on page no. 140.

37. Describe the initiation process of transcription in bacteria. **CBSE 2010**

Ans. Refer to text on page no. 141.

38. DNA is unzipped twice in a cell. Mention the two events and the enzymes responsible for it.

Ans. DNA is unzipped twice in a cell, once during transcription and once during DNA replication.

The enzymes that are responsible for unzipping of DNA during these processes are.

Helicase unwinds the DNA double-helix during replication.

RNA polymerase also facilitates the opening of DNA helix during transcription.

39. Depending upon the chemical nature of the template (DNA or RNA) and the nature of nucleic acids synthesised from it (DNA or RNA), list the types of nucleic acid polymerases. **NCERT**

Ans. The type of nucleic acid polymerases are as follows

(i) **DNA-dependent DNA polymerase** uses DNA template to catalyse the polymerisation of deoxynucleotides. (1)

(ii) **DNA-dependent RNA polymerase** catalyses transcription of all types of RNAs in bacteria. (1)

(iii) In eukaryotes, there are three types of DNA-dependent RNA polymerase which are as follows

(a) **RNA Polymerase-I** Transcribes *r*RNAs.

(b) **RNA Polymerase-II** Transcribes precursor of *m*RNA, i.e. *hn*RNA.

(c) **RNA Polymerase-III** Transcribes *t*RNA,5 *sr*RNA and *sn*RNAs. (1)

40. Why *hn*RNA is required to undergo splicing?

Ans. *hn*RNA is required to undergo splicing because of the presence of introns (the non-coding sequences) in it. These need to be removed and the exons (the coding sequences) have to be joined in a specific sequence for translation to take place.

41. (i) Name the scientist who suggested that the genetic code should be made of a combination of three nucleotides.
(ii) Explain the basis on which he arrived at this conclusion.

Ans. (i) **George Gamow** suggested that the genetic code should be made up of a combination of three nucleotides. (1)

(ii) He proposed that there are four bases and 20 amino acids. So, there should be atleast 20 different genetic codes for these 20 amino acids. The only possible combinations that would meet the requirement is combinations of 3 bases that will give 64 codons. (2)

42. **Unambiguous, universal and degenerate are some of the terms used for the genetic code. Explain the salient features of each of them.**

Or **Explain when is a genetic code said to be**
 (i) Degenerate
 (ii) Universal **CBSE 2020**

Ans. Unambiguous code means that one codon codes for only one amino acid, i.e. AUG codes only for methionine.

Genetic code is **universal**, as particular codon codes for the same amino acid in all organisms. It is **degenerate** because some amino acids are coded by more than one codon, e.g. UUU and UUC, both code for phenylalanine.

43. **A genetic code is specific and nearly universal. Justify.**

Ans. Refer to text on page no. 143.

44. **(i) How many codons code for amino acids and how many are unable to do so?**
 (ii) Why are codes said to be
 (a) degenerate
 (b) unambiguous

Ans. (i) Out of 64 codons, 61 code for amino acids and rest 3 codons do not code for any amino acids. These function as stop codons. (1)

(ii) Refer to text on page no. 143. (2)

45. **(i) Differentiate between unambiguous and degenerate codons.**
 (ii) Write two functions of the codon AUG.

Ans. (i) Differences between unambiguous and degenerate codons are as follows

Unambiguous codon	Degenerate codon
A particular codon will always code for the same amino acid.	One amino acid often has more than one codon.
e.g. GGA is an unambiguous codon, it codes only for glycine and no other amino acid.	e.g. Phenylalanine has two codons, i.e. UUU and UUC.

(2)

(ii) Functions of codon AUG are as follows
 (a) Codes for amino acid methionine.
 (b) Initiate protein synthesis (initiator codon).

46. **Identify by giving reasons, the salient features of genetic code by studying the following nucleotide sequence of *m*RNA strand and the polypeptide translated from it.**

(AUG UUU UCU UUU UUU UCU UAG)
(Met - Phe - Ser - Phe - Phe - Ser) **Competency Based Que.**

Ans.

Salient features of genetic code	Reason
The codon is triplet.	AUG, UCU, etc., are triplets.
One codon codes for only one amino acid, so it is unambiguous and specific.	UCU codes for serine, AUG codes for methionine, etc.
AUG has dual function as it codes for methionine and it also acts as initiator codon.	AUG is found at the beginning of the polypeptide chain.
UAG act as a stop codon.	No amino acid is coded by UAG in the polypeptide chain.

47. **Following are the features of genetic codes. What does each one indicate?**
Stop codon, unambiguous codon, degenerate codon, universal codon.

Ans. Refer to text on page no. 143.

48. **What is mutation? Explain with the help of an example how does a point mutation affect the genetic code.**
Name another type of mutation. **CBSE 2016 C**

Ans. A mutation is a sudden, inheritable change in genetic material. A classical example of point mutation is a change of single base pair in the gene for β-globin chain that results in the change of amino acid residue glutamate to valine. It results into a diseased condition called sickle-cell anaemia. (2)

The insertion or deletion of one or two bases may change the reading frame from the point of insertion or deletion. Insertion or deletion of three or its multiple bases insert or delete one or multiple codon, hence one or multiple amino acid may be formed in polypeptide. The other type of mutation is frameshift mutation. (1)

49. **The schematic representation given below shows a DNA strand and two types of mutations in the DNA strand.**

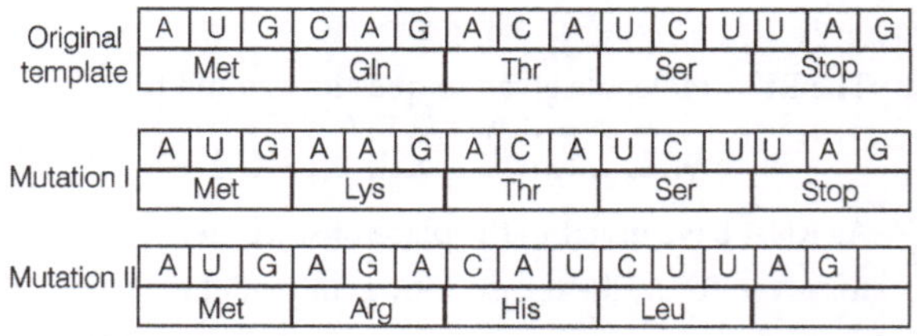

(i) Identify the type of mutation exhibited in I and II.
(ii) Which of the above mutation is more harmful? Given reason. **CBSE SQP 2024**

Ans. (i) The type of mutation exhibited in I is point mutation and in II is frameshift mutation. (1)

(ii) A frameshift mutation is generally more harmful than a point mutation because it alters the reading frame of the entire gene, leading to a completely different sequence of amino acids. This often results in a non-functional or severely altered protein. (2)

50. **(i) Name the scientist who called *t*RNA an adapter molecule.**

(ii) Draw a clover leaf structure of *t*RNA showing the following

(a) Tyrosine attached to its *t*RNA

(b) Anticodon for this amino acid in its correct site (codon for tyrosine is UAC).

(iii) What does the actual structure of *t*RNA look like?

Ans. (i) Francis Crick. (1)

(ii)

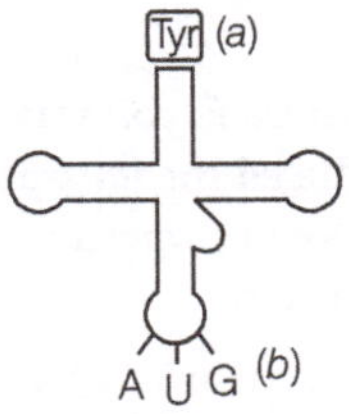

(1)

(iii) *t*RNA looks like an inverted L structure. (1)

51. **(i) Name the enzyme responsible for the transcription of *t*RNA.**

(ii) Draw a labelled diagram of an *t*RNA charged with its respective amino acid.

(iii) Explain the role of the initiator *t*RNA in initiation of protein synthesis.

Ans. (i) In prokaryotes, RNA polymerase is responsible for the transcription of *t*RNA, while in eukaryotes, RNA polymerase III carries out this function. The initiator *t*RNA is charged with methionine in eukaryotes and formylmethionine in prokaryotes.

(ii)

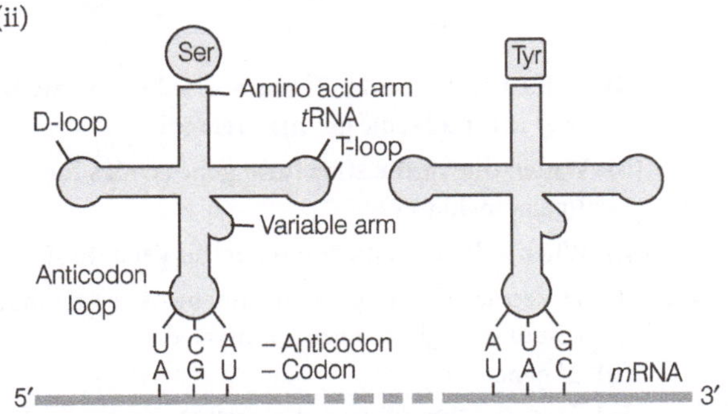

(iii) The initiator *t*RNA, carrying the amino acid methionine, binds to the small ribosomal subunit. Its anticodon (UAC) recognises and pairs with the start codon (AUG) on the *m*RNA through complementary base pairing. Once this binding occurs, the large ribosomal subunit joins the small subunit, and translation is initiated.

52. **Study the *m*RNA segment given below, which is complete and to be translated into a polypeptide chain.**

(i) Write the codons '*A*' and '*B*'.

(ii) What do they code for?

(iii) How is peptide bond formed between two amino acids in the ribosome? Competency Based Que.

Ans. (i) *A*–AUG, *B*–UAA/UAG/UGA (1)

(ii) AUG codes for methionine. UAA/UAG/UGA does not code for any amino acid, but brings about the termination of polypeptide synthesis. (1)

(iii) In the large subunit of ribosome, there are two sites on which subsequent amino acids bind to and come close enough for the formation of peptide bond. It is catalysed by the enzyme called peptidyltransferase. (1)

53. **List two essential roles of ribosomes during translation.** NCERT

Ans. Two essential roles played by ribosomes during translation are as follows

(i) Ribosomes acts as a catalyst for the formation of peptide bonds.

(ii) They also acts as a site of protein synthesis. The larger subunit of ribosomes acts as on amino acid binding site, while small subunit attaches to the *m*RNA. (1 × 2)

54. **Identify the untranslated regions for the following mRNA and mention their location.**

5'—ACGUCGAUGGCGUUUUAGGAGGAA—3'

Ans. ACGUCG at the 5' end before the initiation codon. (1)

GAGGAA at the 3' end after the termination codon. (1)

They are normally located before the initiation codon at the 5' end and after termination codon at the 3' end of the coding strand of DNA. (1)

55. **Given below is a schematic representation of a *m*RNA strand**

*m*RNA

5′ ———————————————— 3′

AGGAGGUAUGAUCUCGUAAAU A A A

(i) In the above sequence identify the translational unit in *m*RNA.

(ii) Where are UTRs found and what is their significance? CBSE SQP 2024

Ans. (i) Translational unit in *m*RNA is the sequence of RNA that is flanked by the start codon (AUG) and the stop codon (UAA) and codes for a polypeptide. In the given sequence the translational unit is AUG AUC UCG UAA. (1)

(ii) The Untranslated Regions (UTRs) are present at both 5' -end (before start codon) and at 3' -end (after stop codon). They are required for an efficient translation process. (2)

56. What is aminoacylation? State its significance.

Ans. Refer to text on page 145.

57.

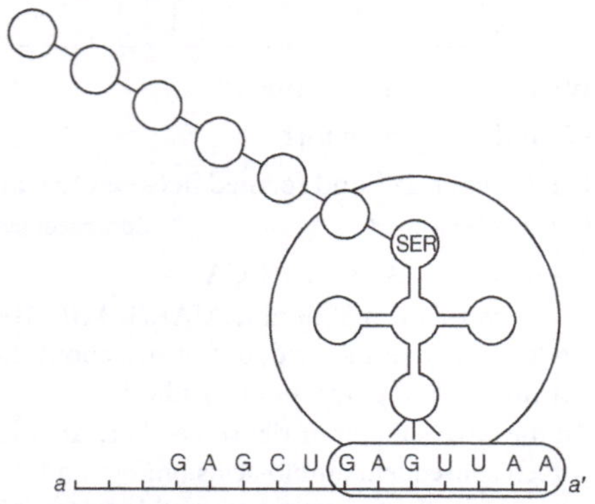

(i) Identify the polarity of strand in the diagram from *a* to *a*', and mention how many more amino acids can be expected to be added to this polypeptide chain.

(ii) Mention the DNA sequence coding for serine and the anticodon of *t*RNA for the same amino acid.

(iii) Why are some untranslated sequence of bases seen in *m*RNA coding for a polypeptide? Where exactly are they present on *m*RNA? **Competency Based Que.**

Ans. (i) *a* to *a*' is 5'⟶ 3'. (1)

No more amino acid will be added.

(ii) TCA; anticodon is UCA. (1)

(iii) The untranslated regions are required for efficient translation process.

They are present before the initiation codon at the 5' end and after the stop/termination codon, at the 3' end. (1)

58. Write down the possible levels of regulation of gene expression in eukaryotes.

Ans. The possible regulation of gene expression can occur at following levels

(i) Transcriptional level, i.e. during the formation of primary transcript.

(ii) Processing level (during splicing).

(iii) During transport of *m*RNA from the nucleus to the cytoplasm.

(iv) Translational level. (2)

59. Given below is a schematic representation of a *lac* operon.

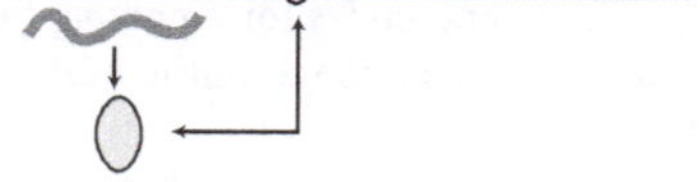

(i) Identify *i* and *p*.

(ii) Name the inducer for this operon and explain its function.

Ans. (i) *i*–Regulatory gene, *p*–Promoter gene. (½)

(ii) Inducer is lactose. (½)

Functions

(a) Enters the cell and binds to the repressor and inactivates it.

(b) As a result, repressor cannot bind to the operator. This allows RNA polymerase to access the promoter and thus, transcription proceeds. (1 × 2)

60. A low level expression of *lac* operon occurs at all the time in a cell. Can you explain the logic behind this phenomenon?

Ans. In the complete absence of expression of *lac* operon, permease will not be synthesised which is essential for the transport of lactose from the medium into the cells. If lactose cannot be transported into the cell, then it cannot act as an inducer and cannot relieve the *lac* operon from its repressed state.

61. In the medium where *E. coli* was growing, lactose was added, which induced the *lac* operon. Then, why does *lac* operon shut down sometimes after addition of lactose in the medium? **NCERT**

Ans. *Lac* operon is switched on by adding lactose in the medium, as lactose acts as inducer and makes the repressor inactive.

Due to this, β-galactosidase is formed which converts lactose into glucose and galactose. As soon as lactose is consumed, repressor again becomes active and causes the system to switch off. (2)

62. Study the figure given below and answer the following questions.

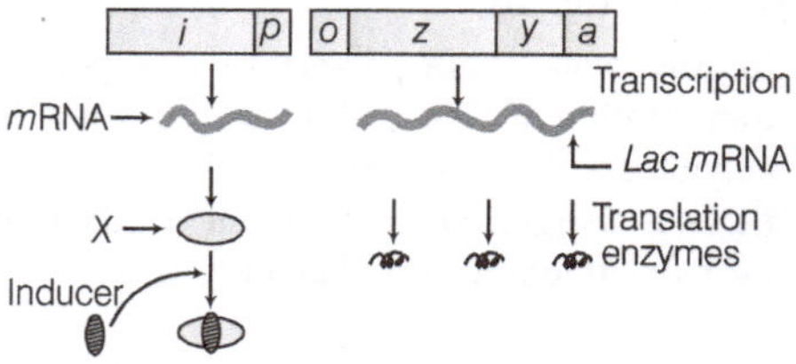

(i) Name the molecule 'X' synthesised by *i* gene. How does this molecule get inactivated?

(ii) Which one of the structural genes codes for β-galactosidase?

(iii) When will the transcription of this gene stop?

Ans. (i) Molecule 'X' is a repressor protein. When an inducer combines with it, it gets inactivated. (1)

(ii) 'z' gene. (1)

(iii) Transcription of gene stops when

(a) Substrate (lactose) is not available.

(b) Energy source (glucose) is available to the cells. (1)

63. Why is the human genome project called a mega project? **NCERT**

Ans. Refer to text on page no. 147.

64. Briefly describe the following
(i) Polymorphism (ii) Translation
(iii) Bioinformatics

Ans. (i) Refer to text on page no. 149.
(ii) Refer to text on page no. 144.
(iii) Refer to text on page no. 147. (3 × 1)

65. Write any three goals of human genome project.

Ans. Refer to text on page no. 148.

66. (i) List the two methodologies which were involved in human genome project. Mention how they were used?
(ii) Expand 'YAC' and mention what was it used for.

Ans. (i) Refer to text for methodologies of HGP on page no. 148.
(ii) YAC stands for Yeast Artificial Chromosome. These were used as vectors in which fragments of whole DNA of human were inserted and cloned. (1½ + 1½)

67. (i) What do 'Y' and 'B' stand for in 'YAC' and 'BAC' used in Human Genome Project (HGP)? Mention their role in the project.
(ii) Write the percentage of the total human genome that codes for proteins and the percentage of discovered genes whose functions are known as observed during HGP.
(iii) Expand SNPs identified by scientists in HGP.

Ans. (i) Y stands for yeast in the word YAC (Yeast Artificial Chromosomes) and B stands for bacteria in the word BAC (Bacterial Artificial Chromosomes). These are vectors used in cloning of DNA. (½ + ½)
(ii) Less than 2% of the total human genome codes for protein, 50% of discovered genes are not known for their functions. (½ + ½)
(iii) SNPs stands for Single Nucleotide Polymorphisms. (1)

68. Name the two most commonly employed hosts and the vectors for human gene cloning.

Ans. Bacteria and yeast are the hosts.
Bacterial Artificial Chromosomes (BACs) and Yeast Artificial Chromosomes (YACs) are the vectors.

69. Human Genome Project (HGP) was a mega project launched in the year 1990 with some important goals.
(i) Enlist any four prime goals of HGP.
(ii) Name any one common non-human animal model organism which has also been sequenced thereafter. **CBSE 2023**

Ans. . (i) Four major goals of HGP are given below
(a) Identify all the (approximately 20,000-25,000) genes in human DNA.
(b) Determine the sequences of the 3 billion chemical base pairs that make up human DNA.
(c) Store this information in databases.
(d) Improve tools for data analysis. (2)

(ii) One common non-human animal model organism which has also been sequenced thereafter is *Caenorhabditis elegans* (a free-living, non-pathogenic nematode). (2)

70. Mention three applications and future challenges of human genome project. (3)

Ans. Refer to text on page no. 149.

71. List the name of the countries whose scientists and administrators attended rice genome meeting in South Carolina.

Ans. The rice genome meeting was the longest meeting till today. It was held in Clemson University in South Carolina on September 19 and 20, 2000. More than 70 scientists and administrators from India, China, Japan, Thailand, Korea, France, Canada, Brazil had attended it.

72. Explain (in one or two line) the function of the followings **NCERT**
(i) Promoter (ii) *t*RNA (iii) Exons

Ans. Refer to text on page no. 140, 141, 140.

73. (i) Explain DNA polymorphism as the basis of genetic mapping of human genome.
(ii) State the role of VNTR in DNA fingerprinting.

Ans. (i) Polymorphism is inherited from parents to children. So, it is useful in the identification (forensic application) and paternity testing. It arises due to mutations and also plays an important role in evolution and speciation. These mutations in the non-coding sequences piles up with time and forms the basis of DNA polymorphism. It is the basis of genetic mapping of human genome as well as DNA fingerprinting. (2)
(ii) Variable Number of Tandem Repeats (VNTRs) belong to a class of satellite DNA called as minisatellite. VNTR are used as probes in DNA fingerprinting. (1)

74. Write the full form of VNTR. How is VNTR different from 'probe'? **CBSE 2011**

Ans. Variable Number of Tandem Repeats (VNTR). (1)
Difference between VNTR and probe are as follows

VNTR	Probe
It is a class of satellite DNA, where a small sequence is arranged tandemly in many copy numbers.	It is a radioactily labelled VNTR, used for hybridisation with DNA segments.

(1)

75. What is DNA fingerprinting? Mention its applications. **NCERT**

Or

(i) Expand VNTR and describe its role in DNA fingerprinting.

(ii) **List any two applications of DNA fingerprinting technique.**

Ans. Refer to text on page no. 149-150

76. Explain the significance of satellite DNA in DNA fingerprinting technique.

Ans. Significance of Satellite DNA in DNA Fingerprinting
A satellite DNA is a short, non-coding region that consists of short DNA sequences repeated many times. The variation between individuals in the lengths of their DNA satellites forms the basis of DNA fingerprinting.

77. The following is the flowchart highlighting the steps in DNA fingerprinting technique. Identify *A, B, C, D, E* and *F*.

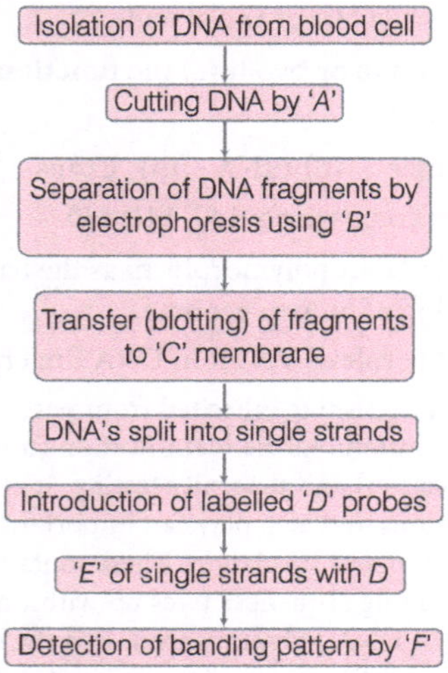

Ans. A–Restriction endonuclease,
B–Agarose gel, *C*–Nylon/Nitrocellulose, *D*–VNTR
E–Hybridisation, *F*–Autoradiography (½ × 6)

78. Describe the steps involved in Southern blot hybridisation using radiolabelled VNTR as a probe.

Ans. The steps involved in Southern blot hybridisation are using radio labelled VNTR as a probe. These steps include
(i) Isolation of DNA
(ii) Digestion of DNA by restriction endonucleases,
(iii) Separation of DNA fragments by electrophoresis,
(iv) Transferring (blotting) of separated DNA fragments to synthetic membranes, such as nitrocellulose or nylon,
(v) Hybridisation using labelled VNTR probe, and
(vi) Detection of hybridised DNA fragments by autoradiography. (½ × 6)

79. A number of passengers were severely burnt beyond recognition during a train accident. Name and describe a modern technique that can help hand over the dead to their relatives. **Competency Based Que.**

Or **Following the collision of two trains a large number of passengers are killed. A majority of them are beyond recognition. Authorities want to hand over the dead to their relatives. Name a modern scientific method and write the procedure that would help in the identification of kinship.**

Ans. The technique that can help in the identification of victims is DNA fingerprinting. It distinguishes between individuals of same species by using their DNA as sample. The chemical structure of DNA is same in everyone (99.9%) except the order of base pairs, i.e. only 0.1% of DNA makes every individual unique. DNA fingerprinting exploits the highly variable repeating sequences, i.e. VNTRs for profiling. These VNTRs are highly conserved among members of the same species.

Procedure Refer to text on page no. 150. (2)

The presence of similarities between the victims and their relatives determines their association on the basis of which dead bodies can be identified and handed over to their families. (1)

80. 'A very small sample of tissue or even a drop of blood can help to determine paternity'. Provide a scientific explanation to substantiate the statement.

Or **There is a paternity dispute for a child. Which technique can solve the problem? Discuss the principle involved.** **NCERT Exemplar**

Ans. Refer to text DNA Fingerprinting on page no. 149-150.

81. (i) **Name and write two characteristics of the type of DNA that forms the basis of DNA fingerprinting technique.**
(ii) **Mention any two applications of this technique.** **CBSE 2024**

Ans. (i) Satellite DNA forms the basis of DNA fingerprinting technique. The two characteristics of the satellite DNA are
(a) Do not code for any protein
(b) Form a large portion of human genome, show high degree of polymorphism. (2)

(ii) The two applications of this technique are follows
(a) It is useful in forensic applications.
(b) It helps in determining genetic diversities among population. (1)

Long Answer Type Questions

1. (i) **How are the following formed and involved in DNA packaging in a nucleus of a cell?**
(a) **Histone octamer** (b) **Nucleosome**
(c) **Chromatin**

(ii) **Differentiate between heterochromatin and euchromatin.** **CBSE 2016**

Ans. (i) Refer to text on page no. 132-133. (3)

(ii) Differences between heterochromatin and euchromatin are as follows

Heterochromatin	Euchromatin
It is darkly stained region of the chromatin (chromosome).	It is lightly stained region.
It is the compactly coiled region and thus has more DNA.	It is loosely coiled region and thus has less DNA.
It is transcriptionally inactive and cannot be transcribed into *m*RNA due to very tight coiling.	It is transcriptionally active and is transcribed into *m*RNA.

(2)

2. The 'beads on string', this description is used for which component of cell. Also discuss its formation.

Ans. Refer to text on page no. 132-133.

3. Stability, as one of the properties of genetic material, was very evident in one of the very early experiments in genetics. Name the scientist and describe his experiment. State the conclusion he arrived at. **CBSE 2024**

Ans. Frederick Griffith showed the stability as one of the properties of genetic material in the genetics. (1)

He took two strains of *Streptococcus pneumoniae* bacteria i.e. R-strain and S-strain and inject them into mice.

S-strain ⟶ Inject into mice ⟶ Mice die

R-strain ⟶ Inject into mice ⟶ Mice live

S-strain (heat-killed) ⟶ Inject into mice ⟶ Mice live

S strain (heat -killed) + R-strain (live) ⟶ Inject into mice ⟶Mice die (2)

Conclusion

(i) R–strain bacteria had been transformed by heat-killed S – strain.

(ii) 'Transforming principle' transferred from heat-killed S-Strain and enabled R– strain to synthesise a smooth polysaccharide coat. This must be due to the transfer of the genetic material.

(iii) Heat which killed bacteria did not destroy some of the properties of genetic material which shows stability of genetic material. (2)

4. Study the flowchart given below and answer the questions that follows

(a) S-strain → into mice → mice die.

(b) R-strain → into mice → mice live.

(c) Heat-killed S-strain + live R-strain → into mice → *A*.

(d) Heat-killed S-strain + DNAse + live R-strain → into mice → *B*.

(i) Name the organism and differentiate between its two strains, R and S, respectively.

(ii) Write the results *A* and *B* obtained in steps (c) and (d), respectively.

(iii) Name the scientist who performed the steps (a), (b) and (c).

(iv) Write the specific conclusion drawn from the step (d). **Competency Based Que.**

Ans. Refer to text on page no. 133-134 for (i), (iii) and (iv).

(ii) In step (c) the mice will die and in step (d), the mice will will live.

5. (i) Describe the various steps of Griffith's experiment that led to the conclusion of the 'transforming principle'.

(ii) How did the chemical nature of the 'transforming principle' get established? **CBSE 2014**

Ans. (i) Refer to text on page no. 133-134 (3)

(ii) Griffith was not able to find the chemical nature of transforming agent. It was Hershey and Chase who proved that DNA is the genetic material. They proved it by using radiolabelled elements, such as ^{35}S and ^{32}P. Radioactivity was detected in the cell, which was due to the presence of ^{32}P in DNA. (2)

6. How did Hershey and Chase differentiate between DNA and protein in their experiment, while proving that DNA is the genetic material? **NCERT**

Ans. Refer to text on page no. 134-135.

7. Answer the following questions based on Hershey and Chase's experiments.

(i) Name the kind of virus they worked with and why?

(ii) Why did they use two types of culture media to grow viruses in? Explain.

(iii) What was the need for using a blender and later a centrifuge during their experiments?

(iv) State the conclusion drawn by them after the experiments. **CBSE 2016**

Ans. (i) They worked with bacteriophage, i.e. viruses that infect bacteria. These viruses were used because during infection, they transfer their genetic material into bacteria. (1)

(ii) They used two types of culture media, so as to compare that which one out of DNA and proteins gets transformed from virus to bacteria and act as genetic material. (1)

(iii) The blender was used to physically separate the bacteriophages (viruses that infect bacteria) from the surface of the bacterial cells after the viruses had injected their genetic material.

After blending the mixture was centrifuged to separate the heavier bacterial cells (which settled at the bottom) from the lighter viral particles that remained in the liquid (supernatant). (2)

(iv) After the experiment, it was concluded that the genetic material that is passed from virus to bacteria was DNA. (1)

8. List the criteria of a molecule that can act as genetic material must fulfill. Which one of the criteria is best fulfilled by DNA or by RNA thus making one of them a better genetic material than the other? Explain. CBSE 2016

Ans. The criteria that a molecule must fulfill to act as a genetic material are as follows.

Refer to text on page no. 136. (2)

According to these criteria, both DNA and RNA have the ability to direct their duplications (because of the rule of base pairing and complementarity). The other molecules in the living system, fail to fulfill first criteria itself, e.g. protein. The most important criteria of genetic material is the stability, as the genetic material should not change with the different stages of life cycle, age or with change in the physiology of an organism.

Both DNA and RNA have the ability to mutate. Since, RNA is unstable, it mutates at a faster rate. That is why, those viruses, which have RNA genome and a shorter lifespan, undergo mutation and thus, evolve rapidly.

DNA is dependant on RNA for protein synthesis, whereas RNA directly codes for protein synthesis.

This proves that both RNA and DNA act as genetic material, but DNA being more stable is preferred for the storage of genetic information. (3)

9. For a molecule, to act as the genetic material it must fulfill certain traits. Among these traits one is that it should be structurally and chemically stable. Why is this stability such an essential criteria ?

Ans. Refer to text on page no. 136-137 (5)

10. During the course of evolution why DNA was chosen over RNA as genetic material. Give reasons by first discussing the desired criteria in a molecule that can act as genetic material and in the light of biochemical differences between DNA and RNA. NCERT Exemplar

Ans. For properties of genetic material refer to text on page no. 136. (3)

For biochemical differences between DNA and RNA, refer to text on page no. 136-137. (2)

11. (i) State the 'central dogma' as proposed by Francis Crick.

(ii) Explain how the biochemical characterisation (nature) of 'Transforming Principle' was determined, which was not defined from Griffith's experiments.

Ans. (i) **Central Dogma** It states that there is one way or unidirectional flow of information from master copy DNA to working copy RNA (transcription) and from working copy RNA to building plan of polypeptide chain (translation).

$$\text{DNA} \xrightarrow{\text{Transcription}} m\text{RNA} \xrightarrow{\text{Translation}} \text{Polypeptide Chain (protein)}$$

Central dogma of molecular biology was proposed by **Crick** (1958). It can also written as follows

$$\text{DNA} \xrightarrow{\text{Replication}} \text{DNA} \xrightarrow{\text{Transcription}} m\text{RNA} \xrightarrow{\text{Translation}} \text{Polypeptide}$$ (2)

(ii) Griffith concluded that some substance caused transformation but he could not identify the transforming agents.

Biochemical Characterisation of Transforming Principle

Three scientists Avery, MacLeod and McCarty revealed that the chemical nature of the transforming substance was DNA.

The outline of the experiment is given below

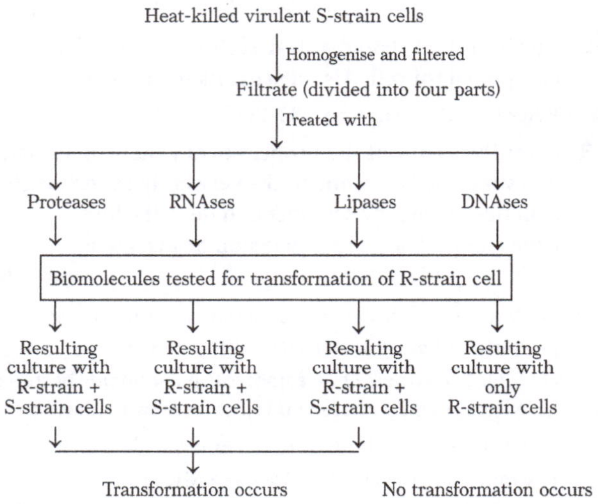

Summary of Avery, MacLeod and McCarty experiment, which demonstrates that DNA is the transforming material

Thus, on the basis of their experiment, they concluded that DNA is the hereditary material. (3)

12. State the aim and describe Meselson and Stahl's experiment. CBSE 2012

Or **Discuss the significance of heavy isotope of nitrogen in the Meselson and Stahl's experiment.** NCERT Exemplar

Ans. Meselson and Stahl in 1958, aimed to prove that DNA replicates in a semiconservative manner. The semiconservative DNA replication suggests that, after the completion of replication, each DNA molecule contain one parental and one newly synthesised strand. (2)

Refer to text on page no. 138. (3)

13. (i) Draw a labelled diagram of a 'replication fork' showing the polarity. Why does DNA replication occur within such 'forks'?

(ii) Name two enzymes involved in the process of DNA replication, along with their properties.

Ans. (i) For figure of replication fork refer to fig. 5.13 on page no. 139.

The replication does not initiate randomly at any place in DNA. Replication begins at definite region of DNA called **origin of replication** wherein lies the replication fork. It is site where the doube-helix unwinds, creating single-stranded templates. This allows DNA polymerases to synthesise new strands in the 5' to 3' direction, efficiently enabling the simultaneous replication of both leading and lagging strands. The fork provides the necessary access for enzymes and nucleotides to perfrom accurate replication. (3)

(ii) For enzymes involved in the process of DNA replication. Refer to text on page no. 138-139. (2)

14. (i) Explain the process of DNA replication with the help of a schematic diagram.

(ii) In which phase of the cell cycle does replication occur in eukaryotes? What would happen if cell division is not followed after DNA replication?

Or **(i) Name the stage in the cell cycle where DNA replication occurs.**

(ii) Explain the mechanism of DNA replication, highlight the role of enzymes in the process.

(iii) Why is DNA replication said to be semiconservative?

Or **Explain the mechanism of DNA replication as suggested by Watson and Crick.** **CBSE SQP 2023**

Ans. (i) Refer to text on page no. 139. (3)

(ii) Refer to text on page no. 139. (2)

Or (i) Cell cycle phase in which DNA replication occurs is S-phase. (1)

(ii) Refer to text on page no. 138 and 139. (3)

(iii) Refer to text on page no. 138. (1)

Or Refer to text on page no. 138.

15. During DNA replication, why is it that the entire molecule does not open in one go? Explain replication fork. What are the two functions that the monomers (*d*NTPs) play? **NCERT Exemplar**

Ans. While replicating, the entire DNA molecule does not open in one go in order to keep the whole molecule stabilised moreover, it would be a highly expensive process energetically. (1)

The unwinding of DNA creates tension in the double helix ahead of the uncoiled part of DNA. The tension leads to supercoiling which occurs when the DNA twists upon itself in response to the strain. To manage this supercoiling and relieve the tensions. Enzymes like topoisomerase cut and re-join the DNA strands, allowing them to unwind slightly.

Slowly, with the help of enzymes, exposed strands are copied as the point of unwinding moves ahead in both directions. It gives an appearance of Y-shaped structure which is called replication fork. (2)

For the two functions of *d*NTPs, refer to process of DNA replication on page no. 139. (2)

16. Explain the process of transcription in prokaryotes. How is the process different in eukaryotes?

Ans. Refer to text on page no. 141-142.

17. (i) Describe the process of trancription in bacteria.

(ii) Explain the processing the *hn*RNA needs to undergo before becoming functional *m*RNA in eukaryotes. **CBSE 2016**

Ans. (i) The process of transcription in prokaryotes consists of three steps

(a) **Initiation** Refer to text on page no. 141.

(b) **Elongation** Refer to text on page no. 141.

(c) **Termination** Refer to text on page no. 141. (2½)

(ii) Refer to text on page no. 142. (2½)

18. State two points of similarity between the process of replication and transcription in humans. Describe the fate of the products of replication and transcription with respect to the following

(i) location of the product(s)

(ii) lifespan of the product(s)

(iii) In which phase/s of the cell cycle do these processes occur? **Competency Based Que.**

Ans. Both processes involve the copying of a DNA molecule.

Both processes take place in the nucleus of the cell. (2)

(i) **Location** DNA strands formed after replication continue to stay in the nucleus whereas *m*RNA formed after transcription is exported to the cytoplasm.

(ii) **Lifespan** DNA strands formed after replication continue to remain in the nucleus as long as the cell is living whereas *m*RNA is degraded after translation. (1)

(iii) DNA replication takes place in the S-phase of cell cycle whereas DNA transcription occurs throughout the cell cycle. (1)

19. (i) Write the contributions of the following scientists in deciphering the genetic code.

George Gamow; Har Gobind Khorana; Marshall Nirenberg; Severo Ochoa

(ii) State the importance of genetic code in protein biosynthesis. **CBSE 2019**

Ans. (i) Refer to text on page no. 142-143. (4)

(ii) Refer to text on page no. 142. (1)

20. There are 64 codons in the genetic code dictionary.

(i) How many of them code for amino acids?

(ii) How many amino acids are coded?

(iii) What term would you give to those codons, which do not code for amino acids?

(vi) State some features of genetic code.

Ans. Refer to text on page no. 143. (1+1+1+2)

21. **(i) Describe the structure and function of a tRNA molecule. Why is it referred to as an adapter molecule?**

(ii) Explain the process of splicing of *hn*RNA in a eukaryotic cell. **CBSE 2017**

Ans. (i) **Structure of *t*RNA**-Refer to fig. 5.18 and text on page no. 144. (1½)

Function of *t*RNA The function of *t*RNA is to align the required amino acids according to the nucleotide sequences of *m*RNA.

*t*RNA is also called the **adapter molecule** because on one hand, it can read the code and on the other, it can bind to specific amino acid. It acts as an intermediate molecule between triplet code of *m*RNA and amino acid sequence of polypeptide chain. (1½)

(ii) **Splicing of *hn*RNA**

Eukaryotic transcription possess extra segments called introns or intervening sequence or non-coding sequence. They do not appear in mature or processed RNA. The functional coding sequences are called exons. Splicing is the removal of introns and fusion of exons to form functional RNAs. (2)

22. **Explain the relationship of ribosomes, *t*RNA and *m*RNA during the process of translation in prokaryotes.** **CBSE 2020**

Ans. Refer to text on page no. 144-145.

23. **(i) How and why is charging of tRNA essential in the process of translation?**

(ii) State the function of ribosome as a catalyst in bacteria during the process of translation.

(iii) Explain the process of binding of ribosomal units to mRNA during protein synthesis. **CBSE 2023**

Ans. . (i) Transfer RNA (*t*RNA) is an essential link between the genetic code and amino acid sequence of proteins. During the process of translation, *t*RNA is charged with its cognate amino acid and delivers it to the ribosome, thus serving as a substrate for protein synthesis. (2)

(ii) Ribosome acts as the site where protein synthesis takes place from individual amino acids. It is made up of two subunits. The smaller subunit comes in contact with *m*RNA and forms a protein synthesising complex whereas the larger subunit acts as an amino acid binding site. It also acts as a catalyst for forming peptide bond. For example, 23s *r*RNA in bacteria acts as a ribozyme. (2)

(iii) Initiation of protein synthesis includes binding of *m*RNA to the smaller of two ribosomal subunits and to the initiating aminoacyl-*t*RNA. The large ribosomal subunit then binds to form an initiation complex to facilitate binding of charged *t*RNA during elongation of polypeptide chain. (1)

24. **(i) Explain the process of aminoacylation of tRNA and its role in the process of translation.**

(ii) How does initiation of the translation process occur in prokaryotes? Explain.

(iii) Where are the untranslated regions located on *m*RNA and why? **Delhi 2023**

Ans. (i) Activation of amino acids and formation of AA-*t*RNA complex is the first step of translation. In presence of an enzyme *t*RNA synthetase, the amino acid (AA) molecule is activated and then each amino acid is attached to the specific *t*RNA molecule at 3' end to form aminoacyl- *t*RNA complex. The reaction needs ATP. This process is called charging of *t*RNA or aminoacylation of *t*RNA.

This process is essential to initiate translation. (2)

(ii) During initiation of translation process, the smaller ribosomal subunit attaches to the 5'end of *m*RNA to form a complex.

Downstream to this *m*RNA lies the AUG initiator codon, which initiates the process of translation. The initiator *t*RNA joins the initiation codon by its anticodon through H-bonds. Now the binding of large subunit of ribosome with its smaller subunit completes the translation -initiation -complex. At this stage, the initiator *t*RNA lies at the P-site of the ribosome and the A-site is vacant to let another charged *t*RNA to enter. (2)

(iii) *m*RNA has some additional sequences that are not translated and are referred as Untranslated Regions (UTRs). The UTRs are present at both the 5'-end (before the start codon) and the 3'-end (after the stop codon). They are required for an efficient translation process. (1)

25. **(i) Write any two different levels at which regulation of gene expression could be exerted in eukaryotes.**

(ii) Give a labelled schematic representation of '*lac* operon' in its 'switched off' position.

Ans. (i) Refer to text on page no. 146. (2)

(ii) Refer to fig 5.20 on page no. 147 (In the absence of inducer). (1)

26. **(i) Explain the role of regulatory gene, operator, promoter and structural genes in *lac* operon when E. *coli* is growing in a culture medium with the source of energy as lactose.**

(ii) Mention what would happen if lactose is withdrawn from the culture medium.

Ans. . (i) Refer to text on page no. 146.

(ii) Refer to text on page no. 146-147

27. **Describe how the *lac* operon operates, both in the presence and absence of an inducer in *E. coli*.**

Ans. Refer to text on page no. 146-147.

28. Study the schematic representation of the genes involved in the *lac* operon given below and answer the questions that follows.

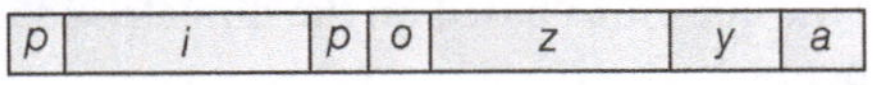

(i) Identify and name the regulatory gene in this operon. Explain its role in 'switching off' the operon.

(ii) Why is *lac* operon's regulation referred to as negative regulation?

(iii) Name the inducer molecule and the products of the genes 'z' and 'y' of the operon. Write the function of these gene products.

CBSE 2019, Competency Based Que.

Ans. (i) Regulatory gene in this operon is *i* gene.

Role of regulatory gene in switching off the operon are as follows

(a) It codes for the repressor protein of the operon, which is synthesised constitutively.

(b) The repressor has affinity for the operator gene. It binds to operator and prevents the RNA polymerase from transcribing the structural genes. (2)

(ii) When repressor binds to the operator, the operon is switched off and transcription is stopped. So, it is called negative regulation. (1½)

(iii) Lactose is an inducer molecule.

Refer to text on page no. 146 (For structural genes). (1½)

29. Observe the representation of genes involved in the *lac* operon given below.

(i) Identify the region where the repressor protein will attach normally.

(ii) Under certain conditions repressor is unable to attach at this site. Explain.

(iii) If repressor fails to attach to the site what products will be formed by *z*, *y* and *a*?

(iv) Analyse why this kind of regulation is called negative regulation.

Ans. (i) Repressor will attach at the operator (*o*) region. (1)

(ii) If an inducer (like lactose) binds to the repressor and inactivates it, it cannot bind to the operator. (1)

(iii) If repressor is not bound to the operator, the operon is 'on' and transcription begins. It leads to the formation of β-galactosidase, permease and transacetylase. (1)

(iv) In the absence of an inducer molecule the repressor protein binds to the operator gene. This causes switching off the operon. Hence it is called negative regulation. (2)

30. (i) Absence of lactose in the culture medium affects the expression of *lac* operon in *E. coli*. Why and how ? Explain. **CBSE 2024 C**

(ii) Write any two ways in which the gene expression is regulated in eukaryotes.

Ans. (i) When lactose is absent, the I gene produces repressor *m*RNA, which is then translated into a repressor protein. This protein binds to the operator region of the *lac* operon, blocking RNA polymerase from attaching to the operon. As a result, the operon is turned off, and the genes for lactose metabolism are not expressed.

(ii) Two ways in which gene expression is regulated in eukaryotes are:

1. **Transcriptional Regulation** The initiation of transcription can be controlled by transcription factors and enhancers. These regulatory proteins bind to specific DNA sequences, either promoting or inhibiting the binding of RNA polymerase to the gene's promoter, thus controlling whether a gene is transcribed or not.
2. **Post-transcriptional Regulation** After transcription, gene expression can be regulated at the level of RNA processing, including splicing of introns, *m*RNA stability and RNA editing.

31. (i) List any four major goals of human genome project.

(ii) Write any four ways the knowledge from HGP is of significance for humans.

(iii) Expand BAC and mention its importance. **CBSE 2020**

Ans. For (i), (ii) refer to text on page no. 148. (2 + 2 +1)

For (iii) refer to text on page no. 148

32. Write the sequence of steps involved in the sequencing of genome of an organism.

Ans. Refer to text on page no. 148.

33. According to the human genome project, almost 99.9% nucleotide bases are exactly the same in all people. Reading this, Samya was confused about why people are discriminated on various issues if all of them are so similar. She asked about it to her biology teacher who explained that it is due to human thinking and behaviour that this difference has risen.

(i) What percentage of the human genome codes for proteins?

(ii) Which chromosome has most genes on it?

(iii) When was HGP started? What is its aim?

(iv) List two major approaches that are involved in HGP.

Ans. Refer to text on page no. 147-149. (5)

34. **Differentiate between the following**

(i) **Repetitive DNA and Satellite DNA**

(ii) ***m*RNA and *t*RNA** NCERT

Ans. (i) Differences between repetitive DNA and satellite DNA are as follows

Repetitive DNA	Satellite DNA
It is the non-coding DNA with multiple copies of identical sequences, which may lie in tandem repeats or interspersed.	It is non-coding tandem repeat sequence.
These can be few base pairs to hundreds or thousands of base pairs long.	These are generally 100 base pairs to several thousand base pairs long).
In CsCl density gradient analysis, it appear as light bands.	It appear as small dark bands in CsCL density gradient analysis.

(2½)

(ii) Differences between *m*RNA and *t*RNA are as follows

*m*RNA	*t*RNA
It is called messenger RNA and carries the codes for amino acid sequence.	It is called transfer RNA as it carries amino acids to the site of protein synthesis.
It is a long chain of bases with high molecular weight.	It is a clover-leaf like structure, with low molecular weight.
It is synthesised by RNA polymerase-II.	It is synthesised by RNA polymerase-III.

(2½)

35. **A DNA testing laboratory was given three blood samples. Mention the steps involved the procedure performed to get the DNA fingerprinting done for the above samples.**

Ans. Refer to text on page no. 150.

36. **Name and describe the steps involved in the technique widely used in forensics that serves as the basis of paternity testing in case of disputes.** CBSE 2023

Ans. Refer to text on page no. 149 and 150.

Source Based/Case Based/Passage Based Question

1. **Answer the questions based on the dinucleotide structure shown below.**

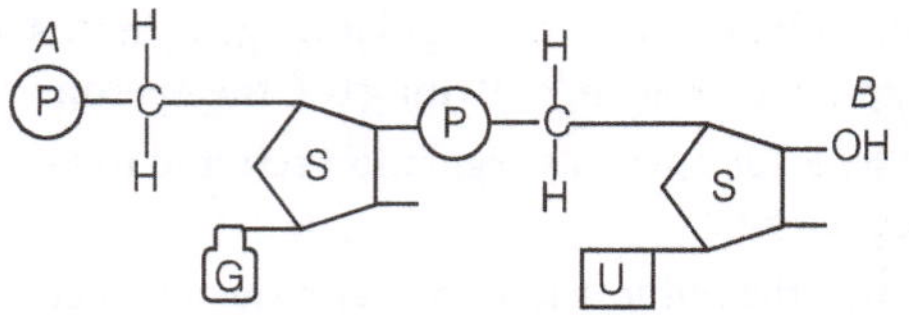

(i) **Name the type of sugar guanine base is attached to.**

(ii) **Name the linkage connecting the two nucleotides.**

(iii) **Identify the 3′ end of the dinucleotide. Give a reason for your answer.**

(iv) **Name the linkage connecting the nitrogenous base.**

Ans. (i) Ribose sugar. (1)

(ii) Two nucleotides are linked through $3' \rightarrow 5'$ phosphodiester linkage to form a dinucleotide. (1)

(iii) *B* is 3′ end, here the sugar has a free 3′ OH group. (1)

(iv) Hydrogen bond (1)

2. **Refer to the below mentioned flow diagram and answer the questions that follows**

(i) **What information is derived from the above mentioned flow diagram?**

(ii) **Who proposed this concept?**

(iii) **Is there any exception to this concept? If yes, describe it.**

Ans. (i) The given flow diagram depicts the central dogma of molecular biology. It states that there is only one way of flow of information from master copy, i.e. DNA to the working copy, i.e. RNA (transcription) and from working copy (RNA) to building polypeptides (translation). (2)

(ii) The concept of central dogma of molecular biology was proposed by **Francis Crick** in 1958. (1)

(iii) **Yes, Temin** and **Baltimore** (1970) independently found that retroviruses perform central dogma in reverse, which involves reverse transcription (formation of DNA from RNA). (1)

3. **Given below is the sequence of an mRNA the image of the genetic code. Assume that this sequence begins with a start codon.**

5’ - GCUAUCAAGUACCUA - 3’

	U	C	A	G	
U	UUU Phe	UCU Ser	UAU Tyr	UGU Cys	U
	UUC Phe	UCC Ser	UAC Tyr	UGC Cys	C
	UUA Leu	UCA Ser	UAA Stop	UGA Stop	A
	UUG Leu	UCG Ser	UAG Stop	UGG Trp	G
C	CUU Leu	CCU Pro	CAU His	CGU Arg	U
	CUC Leu	CCC Pro	CAC His	CGC Arg	C
	CUA Leu	CCA Pro	CAA Gln	CGA Arg	A
	CUG Leu	CCG Pro	CAG Gln	CGG Arg	G
A	AUU Ile	ACU Thr	AAU Asn	AGU Ser	U
	AUC Ile	ACC Thr	AAC Asn	AGC Ser	C
	AUA Ile	ACA Thr	AAA Lys	AGA Arg	A
	AUG Met	ACG Thr	AAG Lys	AGG Arg	G
G	GUU Val	GCU Ala	GAU Asp	GGU Gly	U
	GUC Val	GCC Ala	GAC Asp	GGC Gly	C
	GUA Val	GCA Ala	GAA Glu	GGA Gly	A
	GUG Val	GCG Ala	GAG Glu	GGG Gly	G

(a) Identify the amino acid sequence to which this *m*RNA will get translated.

(b) Identify the type of mutation and the change in the protein sequence in the following:

(i) Cytosine in codon 4 gets modified to uracil

(ii) GCU gets added after the second cytosine in the sequence

Ans. (a) The amino acid sequence of given *m*RNA will be Ala Ile Lys Tyr Leu (1)

(b) (i) If cytosin in codon 4 gets modified to the uracil it will be the example of point mutation. There will be no change in the protein sequence.

(ii) If GCU gets added after the second cytosine in the sequence, then it will cause frameshift mutation which will result in the addition of alanine in between the between isoleucine and lysine. (2)

4. An organism is able to survive on a culture medium, containing nutrient *A*, by the enzyme catalysed reaction.

$$A \xrightarrow{p} B \xrightarrow{q} C \xrightarrow{r} D$$

A mutant organism failed to survive on this medium, but grew well when nutrient *B* was added to it.

(i) Which gene of this mutant organism is defective?

(ii) What does such a condition indicate ?

(iii) Mention the major components in an operon.

Ans. (i) In the given question, the gene *p* is defective. (1)

(ii) This indicates that one gene controls the synthesis of one enzyme. (1)

(iii) An operon has the following components

(a) Structural gene (*s*), which transcribes the *m*RNA for the protein synthesis.

(b) An operator gene, which controls the structural gene (*s*) as a unit.

(c) A promoter, where the RNA polymerase binds for transcription. (2)

5. The graph given below shows the growth of bacteria over time in the presence of two sugars namely, glucose and lactose.

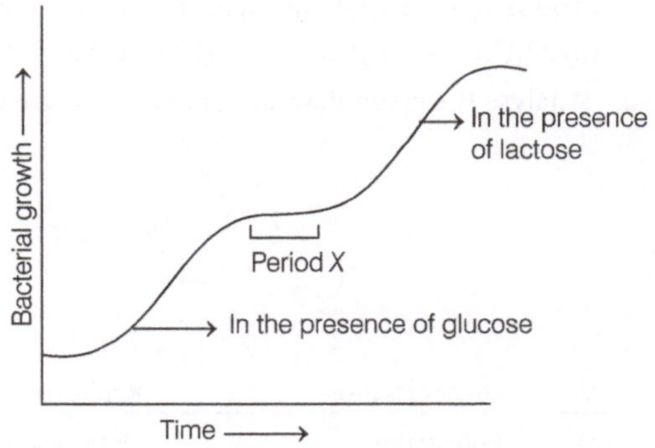

(i) What is the preferred substrate of bacterial growth?

(ii) What does period *X* represents in graph?

(iii) Why does the growth curve is less steep in case of lactose as compared to glucose?

Or

(iii) What would be the consequence of high glucose concentration in the system throughout the regulation of *lac* operon?

Ans. (i) The preferred substrate for bacterial growth is glucose. Bacteria use alternative substrates only when glucose has been depleted. (1)

(ii) The phase *X* represents the period of slow growth when glucose levels are depleted. (1)

(iii) Bacteria have the ability to use a variety of substrates as carbon sources.

However, glucose is preferred source and in the presence of other substrates like lactose, the growth rate slows down. It is indicated by the lower steepness of growth curve. (2)

Or

(iii) In the presence of high glucose concentration the repressor protein remain bound to the operator region, thus preventing the gene expression in *lac* operon. (2)

SELF ASSESSMENT TEST

Multiple Choice Questions

1. If 34% bases of DNA are adenine. Then the percent of guanine, cytosine and thymine would be
   (a) 16%, 16% and 34% respectively
   (b) 34%, 16% and 16% respectively
   (c) 12%, 27% and 27% respectively
   (d) 22%, 22% and 17% respectively
2. In Meselson and Stahl's experiment, if *E.coli* was allowed to grow for 60 minutes then what would be the proportions of light and hybrid density DNA molecule?
   (a) 2 light and 4 hybrid
   (b) 2 light and 2 hybrid
   (c) 6 light and 2 hybrid
   (d) 2 light and 6 hybrid
3. Analyse the given diagram of central dogma and choose the correct answer

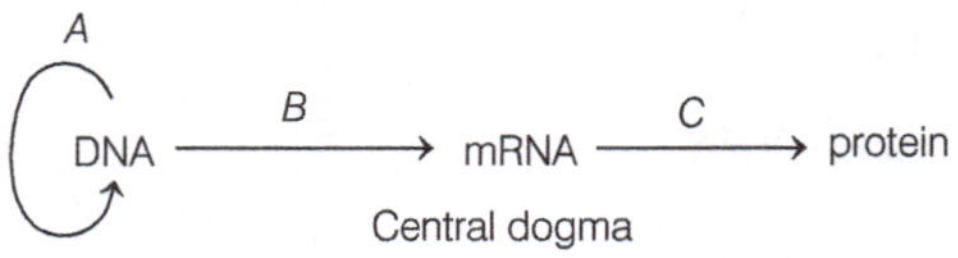

Central dogma

	A	B	C
(a)	Polymerisation	Replication	Hybridisation
(b)	Translation	Hybridisation	Transcription
(c)	Hybridisation	Translation	Transcription
(d)	Replication	Transcription	Translation

4. A hypothetical sequence from a transcription unit is given below.
   3'-ATGCATGCATGCATGCATGC-5' – Template strand
   Which of the following option is correct with respect to the sequence of RNA transcribed from this DNA?
   (a) 3'- GCAUGCAUGCAUGCAUGCAU-5'
   (b) 5'- GCAUGCAUGCAUGCAUGCAU-3'
   (c) 3'-AUGCAUGCAUGCAUGCAUGC-5'
   (d) 5'- AUGCAUGCAUGCAUGCAUGC-3'
5. RNA polymerase-III is responsible for the transcription of
   (a) 5s*r*RNA, *hn*RNA and *r*RNA
   (b) 28S RNA, *sn*RNA and *m*RNA
   (c) *t*RNA, 5s*r*RNA and *sn*RNA
   (d) S RNA, *hn*RNA and *m*RNA
6. Analyse the given sequence of *m*RNA and select the correct option with respect to the sequence of polypeptide chain.
   *m*RNA – 5'-UUU CGU AUG CGU UAG AGC GGG-3'
   (a) Meth Arg
   (b) Phe Arg Meth Arg Ser Gly
   (c) Meth Arg Ser Gly
   (d) Phe Arg Meth Arg
7. In case of a *lac* operon, what happens when lactose is present but glucose is absent?
   (a) The *lac* operon is turned off
   (b) The *lac* operon is expressed at low levels
   (c) The *lac* operon is fully activated
   (d) The *lac* repressor is able to bind to the operator.
8. The maximum and minimum number of genes are present on
   (a) chromosome 1 and chromosome 23 respectively
   (b) X-chromosome and Y-chromosome respectively
   (c) Y-chromosome and X-chromosome respectively
   (d) chromosome 1 and Y-chromosome respectively
9. Alec Jeffrey used a satellite DNA as probe that shows very high degree of polymorphism. This is known as
   (a) short number of tandem repeats
   (b) variable number of tandem repeats
   (c) long number of tandem repeats
   (d) sequential number of tandem repeats

Assertion-Reason Questions

Direction (Q. Nos. 10-13) *In each of the following questions, a statement of Assertion (A) is given followed by corresponding statement of Reason (R). Of the statements, mark the correct answer as .*

(a) Both A and R are true and R is the correct explanation of the A.

(b) Both A and R are true, but R is not the correct explanation of the A.

(c) A is true, but R is false.

(d) A is false, but R is true.

10. **Assertion** (A) Histones are rich in the basic amino acid residues like lysine and arginine.

    Reason (R) Lysine and arginine carry positive charges that promote strong interactions with negatively charged DNA.

11. **Assertion** (A) RNA is a labile and easily degradable molecule.

    Reason (R) The 4'-OH group present at every nucleotide in RNA is a reactive group.

12. **Assertion** (A) The heterogeneous RNA is usually shorter than *m*RNA.

    Reason (R) The *hn*RNA includes both exons and introns, while *m*RNA consists of the only exons.

13. **Assertion** (A) *Lac* operon is switched off when repressor protein binds to operator gene.

    Reason (R) Regulation of *lac* operon by repressor is referred to as negative regulation.

Very Short Answer Type Questions

14. Why DNA replication is termed semi conservative?
15. *E. coli* has only 4.6 X 10^6 base pairs and complete the process of replication within 18 minutes. Calculate approximate value of the average rate of polymerisation.
16. At what end does capping and tailing of *hn*RNA takes place?
17. What is charging of *t*RNA?

Short Answer Type Questions

18. Write a short note on central dogma of molecular biology.
19. Differentiate between transcription and translation.
20. What are the key steps involved in the DNA fingerprinting process?

Long Answer Type Questions

21. Explain Hershey and Chase experiment with suitable diagram.
22. Describe the following terms

    (a) Linker DNA (b) Heterochromatin (c) Nucleoside (d) Cistron (e) Mutation

23. What are the salient features of human genome project?

Case Based Question

24. Given below is a representation of the structure of the *t*RNA with two of its parts marked *P* and *Q*. *Q* is the amino acid acceptor end of the *t*RNA.

    (a) What is loop *P* called?

    (b) How can the polarity of the *t*RNA molecule be identified from the image?

    (c) What does an actual structure of *t*RNA looks like?

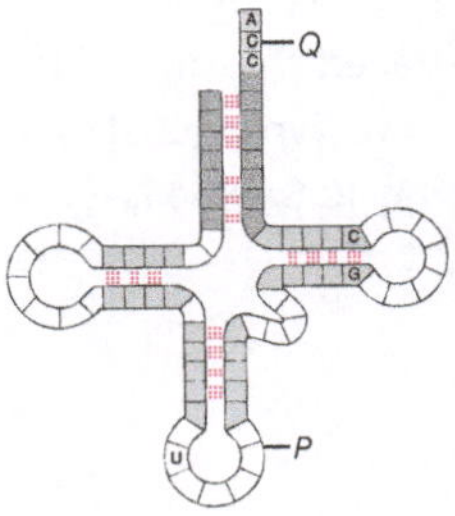

Answers

1. (a)	2. (c)	3. (d)	4. (a)	5. (c)	6. (a)	7. (c)
8. (d)	9. (b)	10. (b)	11. (c)	12. (d)	13. (b)	

06

CHAPTER

Evolution is the sequence of gradual changes from simple life to complex life forms, i.e. from primitive organisms that lived over millions of years ago to new organisms that exist today. Human beings are the most recent and highly evolved among these organisms.

▼ YOUR STUDY GOALS

6.1 Origin of Life
6.2 Evidences of Evolution
6.3 Theories of Evolution
6.4 Account of Evolution
6.5 Origin and Evolution of Human

▼ YOUR PRACTICE GOAL

- Objective Type Questions (37 Qs ; MCQs, A-R) Case Based Questions (4)
- Subjective Type Questions
- (33 VSA, 40 SAs, 14 LAs)

Evolution

In this chapter, we will study various theories of evolution, their evidences biological evolution, speciation, Darwinian ideas of organic evolution by natural selection and most importantly, the origin and evolution of human.

6.1 Origin of Life

- The origin of life on the earth took place million of years ago and the study of history of life forms on earth is called **evolutionary biology**.
- The history of life actually comprises of two events, i.e. firstly, origin of life and secondly, the mechanism involved in the changes of living organisms through time or evolution of life.
- The origin of life is considered a unique event in the history of universe.

Origin of Universe

- The universe is about 15-20 billion years old.
- It comprises of huge clusters of galaxies, which contains stars, clouds of gas and dust.

- According to the **Big Bang theory**, the universe arose from a singular, huge explosion (unimaginable in physical terms).
- As the universe expanded, the temperature lowered and the gases like hydrogen and helium were formed later.
- The gases condensed by the force of gravitation and galaxies were formed.

Origin of Earth

- Earth was supposed to have been formed about 4.5 billion years back in the solar system of the milky way galaxy.
- The early earth has no atmosphere, the surface was covered with water vapour, methane, carbon dioxide and ammonia released from molten mass.
- Later on, the water molecules were broken down into hydrogen and oxygen by UV rays of the sun.
- The lighter hydrogen gas escaped from the surface, while oxygen combined with ammonia and methane to form water, CO_2 and other substances.
- Subsequently, the ozone layer was formed. As the earth cooled, the water vapour fell as rain and filled all depressions to form oceans and other water bodies.

Theories of Origin of Life

- Life on earth appeared 500 million years after its formation, about 4 billion years ago.
- In order to explain origin of life on the earth, different theories were given by different thinkers and scientists. These are discussed below.

1. Theory of Special Creation

- This theory states that God has created life by the divine act of creation, i.e. the earth, light, plants and animals are all being created by the supernatural power.
- This theory has **three connotations**
  - All living organisms or species that we see today were created as such.
  - Diversity was always the same since creation and will remain same in future also.
  - Earth is about 4000 years old.

2. Theory of Panspermia

- It states that the life on earth arose from the **spores** or **panspermia**, which came from outer space and developed into different living forms.

3. Theory of Spontaneous Generation

- It states that life originated from non-living matter simultaneously.
- This theory is also known as **theory of abiogenesis** or **autobiogenesis**.
- According to this theory, life originated from decaying and rotting matter like straw, mud, etc.
- **Louis Pasteur** rejected the theory of spontaneous generation.
- He demonstrated that life came from pre-existing life through his swan necked flask experiment.
- In this experiment, life did not appear in pre-sterilised flask containing killed yeast, while in another flask exposed to air, microbial growth was observed.

4. Theory of Chemical Evolution

- This theory was given by **Oparin** and **Haldane.**
- According to them, the first form of life came from pre-existing, non-living organic molecules (e.g. RNA, protein, etc.) and chemical evolution followed the formation of life.
- The conditions on the earth, favouring chemical evolution, were high temperature, volcanic storms and reducing atmosphere (absence of oxygen) containing CH_4, NH_3, etc.

Experimental Evidence of Chemical Evolution (Miller-Urey's Experiment)

- Evidence for chemical evolution is provided by the experiment conducted by **Stanley Miller** and **Harold Urey** in 1953.
- It demonstrate that ultraviolet radiations or electrical discharges or a combination of these can produce complex organic compounds from a mixture of CH_4, NH_3, H_2 and water vapour (H_2O) at 800° C (as shown in fig 6.1).

- The conditions were set similar to those of the primitive atmosphere in the laboratory.

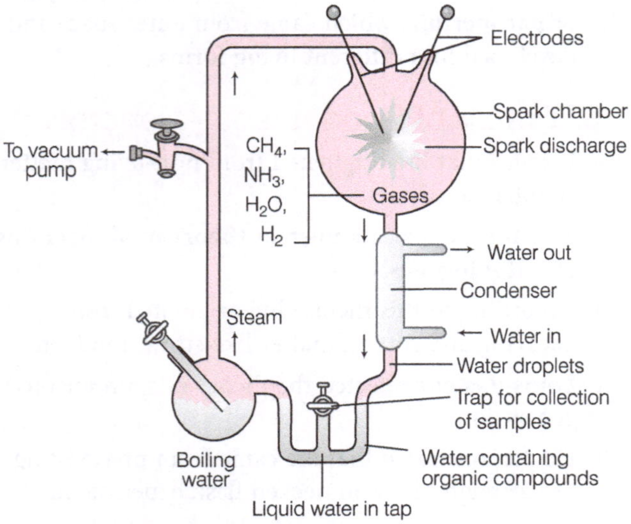

Fig. 6.1 Diagrammatic representation of Miller and Urey's experiment

Observation

- Miller and Urey observed the formation of amino acids.
- In similar experiments performed by other scientists, the presence of complex molecules like sugars, pigments, nitrogen bases and fats were also observed.

Conclusion

- Miller-Urey's experiment supported the theory of chemical evolution.
- Analysis of meteorite content also revealed similar compounds indicating that similar processes are occurring elsewhere in space.
- Thus, with these limited evidences, the idea of chemical evolution was more or less accepted.

Formation of First Cell

- The first non-cellular life forms must have been originated 3 billion years ago in the form of giant molecules like RNA, protein and polysaccharides inside a self-replicating metabolic capsule.
- These capsules must have later reproduced their molecules.
- The first cellular form of life originated about 2000 million years ago (mya).
- These might have been single cells formed in aquatic environment only.
- This theory of biogenesis, i.e. the formation of first form of life rising slowly through the evolutionary forces acting on non-living molecules, was accepted by a great majority.
- However, once formed the first cellular forms evolved into complex biodiversity of today.

Quick Test 1

1. Name the theory that suggests life originated from non-living matter on primitive earth ?
2. Which theory suggests that life on earth may have originated from spores from space?
3. According to the theory of chemical evolution, what were the primary components in earth's early atmosphere that helped to form organic molecules?
4. **State True or False.**
   According to the theory of chemical evolution, oxygen was a major component in earth's early atmosphere.
5. Name two scientists who conducted a special experiment to prove Oparin theory of origin of life.

6.2 Evidences of Evolution

Evidences that the evolution of life forms took place on earth came from palaeontology, comparative anatomy and morphology, as well as biochemical and biogeographical evidences.

Palaeontological Evidences

- Palaeontology is the study of **fossils** (i.e. remains of hard parts of life forms found in rocks).
- Rocks form sediments and a cross-section of the earth's crust depicts the arrangement of these sediments one over the other, during the long history of earth.
- Sediments of different aged rocks contain fossils of the variety of life forms that lived and died during the formation of a particular sediment.
- Some of them appear similar to modern organisms. For example, many modern day organisms like crocodile appear similar to extinct organisms, like dinosaurs (fig 6.2).
- The study of fossil in different sedimentary layers indicates the geological period in which they existed.

- It demonstrates that life forms varied over time, with specific organisms being restricted to certain geological time scale.
- Hence, new forms of life have evolved at different times in the history of earth.
- All these forms constitutes the palaeontological evidences.
- The age of these fossils is estimated by using methods like radioactive dating.

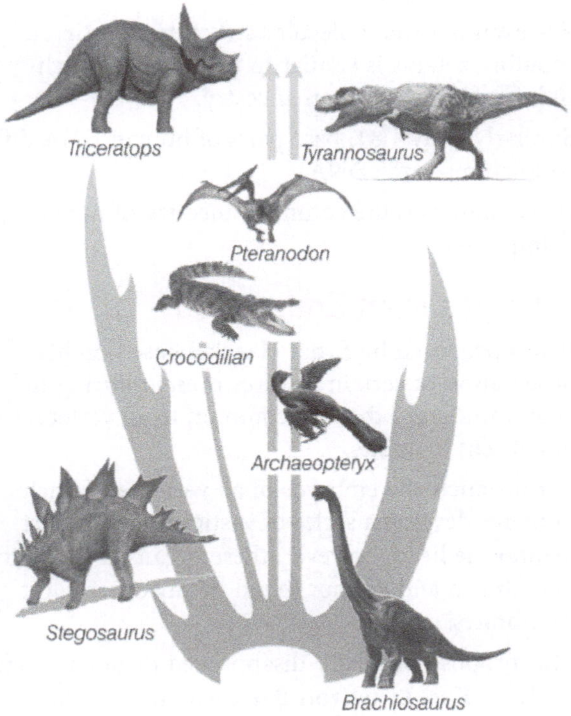

Fig. 6.2 A family tree of dinosaurs and their living modern day counterpart organisms like crocodiles and birds

- The *Archaeopteryx* shown in above picture is considered as a **connecting link** between reptiles and birds.

> **TEACHER'S TIP**
>
> Scientists determine fossil ages using radiometric dating. This method relies on radioactive decay, where unstable isotopes act like timers starting when an organism dies. For recent fossils, we use carbon-14 dating to measure the decay of carbon-14, estimating ages up to about 50,000 years. For older fossils, uranium-lead dating tracks the decay of uranium into lead, revealing ages in millions or billions of years.

Comparative Anatomical and Morphological Evidences

- These show the similarities and differences among organisms of today and those that existed years ago.
- These evidences came from the comparative study of external and internal structures. They reveals shared ancestory among organisms.
- These can be determined by the following types.

1. Homologous Organs and Homology

- The organs which have the same fundamental structures, but perform different functions are called **homologous organs**.
- Homology in organs indicates **common ancestry**.
- It is based on **divergent evolution**, which leads to the formation of homologous organs.
- In divergent evolution, a same basic organ gets specialised to perform different functions in various animals, in order to adapt to the different environmental conditions prevailing in the habitat.

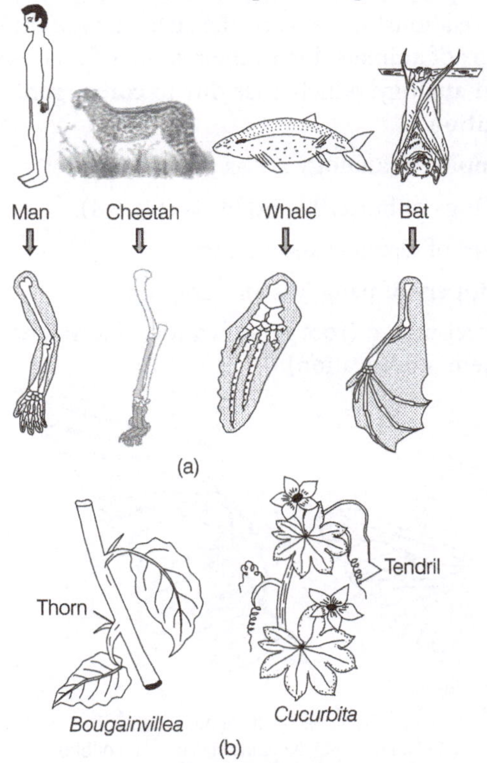

Fig. 6.3 Examples of homologous organs in (a) Animals and (b) Plants

- **Examples of homology** are as follows
  - **Forelimbs** of man, cheetah, whale and bat share similarities in the pattern of bones of forelimbs, (all of them have humerus, radius, ulna, carpals, metacarpals and phalanges) but perform different functions [Fig. 6.3 (a)].
  - **Thorns** of *Bougainvillea* and tendrils of *Cucurbita* both arise in axillary position [Fig. 6.3 (b)], but perform different functions.
  - Structural homology is seen in vertebrates' heart and brain.

2. Analogous Organs and Analogy

- In contrast to homologous organs, the analogous organs are different in their basic structure and developmental origin, but appear same and perform similar functions.
- It can be said that similar habitats have led to the developement of comparable adaptive traits in different group of organisms, all serving the same function.
- This relationship between the structures of different groups of animals due to their similar functions is called **analogy**, which arise due to **convergent evolution.**
- **Examples of analogy** are as follows
  - **Wings** of butterfly and birds (Fig 6.4).
  - **Eyes** of *Octopus* and mammals.
  - **Flippers** of penguins and dolphins.
  - Sweet potato (root modification) and potato (stem modification).

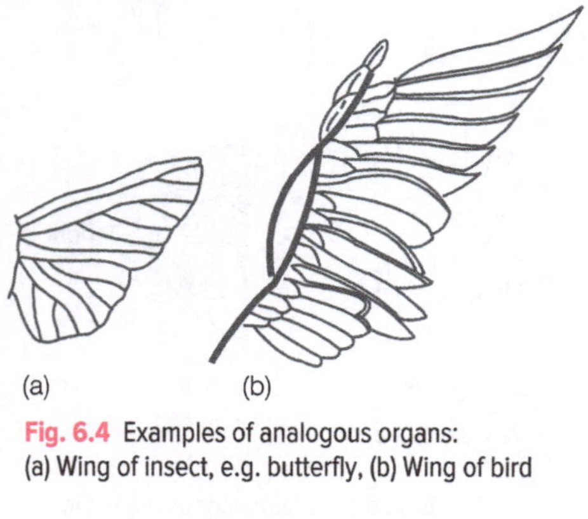

Fig. 6.4 Examples of analogous organs: (a) Wing of insect, e.g. butterfly, (b) Wing of bird

Biochemical or Molecular Evidences

- Among diverse organisms, the similarities in proteins and genes performing a common function indicates common ancestry.
- The metabolic processes in different organisms are also similar, which also points toward shared ancestry.
- Molecular evidences are also indicated by the degree of similarity in the base sequence of nucleic acids and amino acid sequence in the proteins.
- For example, the molecular structure of actin and tubulin proteins is similar in all animals, which indicates their common ancestry.
- Similarly, only 1.8% base pairs of human DNA differs from chimpanzee DNA.
- It also indicates the common ancestry of human and chimpanzee.

Evidences from Embryology

- It was proposed by **Ernst Haeckel** based on his observation of certain features present during the embryonic stage that are common to all vertebrates but absent in adults.
- For instance, the embryos of all vertebrates, including humans, develop a series of vestigial gill slits just behind the head; however, these organs are functional only in fish and are not found in any other adult vertebrates.
- This proposal was later disapproved through careful study by **Karl Ernst von Baer**, who noted that embryos do not actually pass through the adult stages of other species.

Biogeographical Evidences

- Biogeography is the study of distribution of animals and plants on the earth.
- The evidence of evolution based on biogeography are called **biogeographical evidences**.
- It suggests that the species restricted to a region, develop unique features.
- Also, species present in widely separated regions show similarity in ancestry.

- Habitat isolation had probably restricted these organisms to a particular geography on the earth.
- This can be explained with the help of following processes.

1. Adaptive Radiation

- The process of evolution of different species starting from a point in a geographical area and finally radiating to other areas of geography (habitats) is called **adaptive radiation.**
- **Examples of adaptive radiation** are discussed below.

(i) Darwin's Finches

- Darwin observed an amazing diversity of creatures in **Galapagos Islands.**
- There he saw the small black birds, that amazed him the most. Later these birds were called **Darwin finches.**
- Darwin observed that there were many varieties of finches in the same island and all the varieties had evolved on the island itself from original seed-eating finches.
- He explained that after originating from a common ancestral seed-eating stock, the finches must have radiated to different geographical areas and undergone adaptive changes, especially in the type of beaks.

Fig. 6.5 Different types of beaks of finches observed by Darwin in Galapagos Island

- Hence, due to the alternation in beaks, some finches gradually became insectivorous and some became vegetarian.
- As they were living in isolation for long, the new kinds of finches emerged that could function and survive in the new habitat.

(ii) Marsupials of Australia

- These are another examples of adaptive radiation.
- A variety of marsupials (pouched mammals) each different from the other, evolved from an ancestral stock, but all within the Australian island continent.

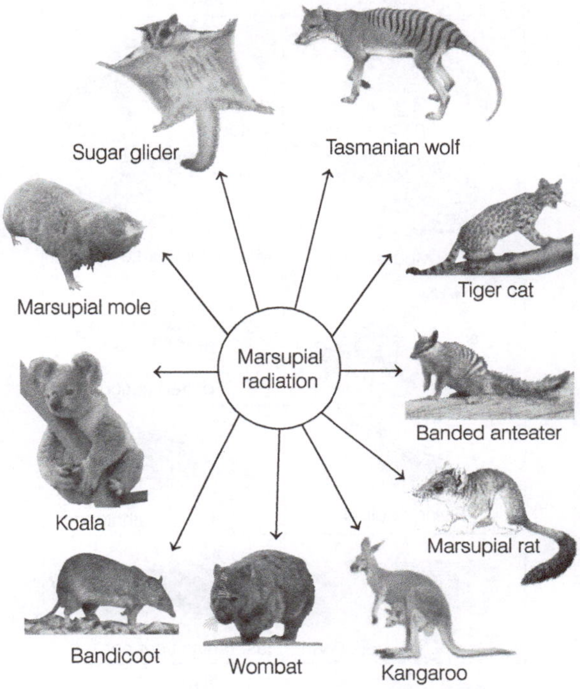

Fig. 6.6 Adaptive radiation of marsupials of Australia

2. Adaptive Convergence/Convergent Evolution

- When more than one adaptive radiation appears to have occurred in an isolated geographical area (representing different habitats) and the development of similar adaptive functional structures occurs in unrelated groups of organisms, this is called **adaptive convergence.**
- **Examples of adaptive convergence** is Australian marsupials and placental mammals in North America.
- Despite the temporal and geographical separation, marsupials in Australia and placental mammals in North America have produced varieties of species living in similar habitat with similar ways of living.

- They are not related, but resemble each other because they occupy similar niches in each continent.

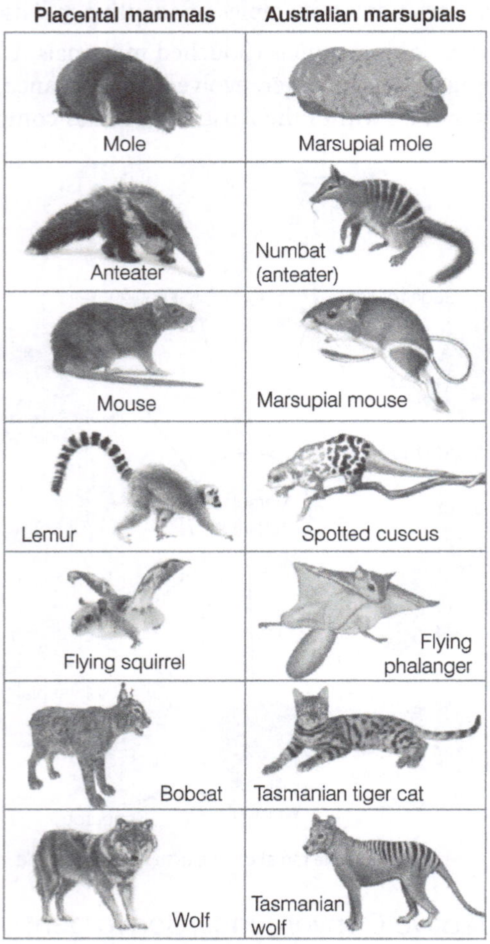

Fig. 6.7 Picture showing convergent evolution of Australian marsupials and placental mammals

Quick Test 2

1. Mention the connecting link between reptiles and birds that has been discovered through palaeontology.
2. A fossil was found at a historical site and it is assumed to be around 500 years old. How can its age be determined?
3. The stem of *Opuntia* and the leaves of peepal perform the same function, i.e., photosynthesis, but have different origins. Can they be considered as homologous structures?
4. Name the scientist who discarded the idea that embryonic development directly reflects evolutionary history.
5. **State True or False.**
   Darwin's finches and Australian marsupials show convergent evolution.

6.3 Theories of Evolution

- Various theories regarding evolution of species, i.e. biological evolution have been postulated by different evolutionists.
- Some of them are as follows

Theory of Natural Selection-Darwinism

- **Charles Darwin** made a sea voyage around the world between 1831-1836 in a sail ship named **HMS Beagle**.
- During that period, Darwin explored the fauna and flora of a number of continents and Islands.
- Based on his observations, he formulated following conclusions
  - There has been gradual evolution of life forms with new forms arising at different periods of history of earth.
  - The rate of appearance of new forms is linked to the life cycle or life span. For instance, microbes that divide fast have the ability to multiply and become millions of individuals within hours, while fish or fowl would take millions of years as life span of these animals are in years.
  - Varying degrees of similarities can be observed between existing life forms and those which existed million of years ago.
  - Population of all organisms have variations in characteristics, which make them adapt to a better environment.
  - The characteristics which enable some population or individuals to survive better in natural conditions (foods, climate, physical factors) would outbreed others (survival of the fittest).
- The fitness of the individual, according to Darwin, refers ultimately to the reproductive fitness.
- Reproductively fit individuals leave more progeny than others.
- Thus, those organisms, which are better fit or adapt well, survive and get selected by nature and further undergoes evolution. This is called **natural selection**.
- **Branching descent** (e.g. Darwin finches) and **natural selection** are the two key concepts of Darwinian theory of evolution.
- **Alfred Wallace**, a naturalist, worked in Malay Archipelago and came to a similar conclusions like Darwin.

- Later Darwin, who may also be influenced by work of Thomas Malthus proposed the '**Theory of natural selection**'.
- It is based on following observations, which are factual.
  - There are limited natural resources.
  - Populations remain stable in size except for seasonal fluctuations.
  - Varying characteristics in members of a population, i.e. no two members of a population are identical even though they look superficially similar.
  - Variations are generally inherited.
  - Theoretically, the population would grows exponentially if everybody reproduced maximally.
  - However, in reality, population size is limited, due to the competition among the individual for resources. Those, which are better adapted could survive and reproduce at the cost of others, i.e. who are less adapted in the environment.

Examples of Natural Selection

Some of the examples given below explain the mechanism of natural selection.

Industrial Melanism

- Industrial melanism in peppered moth (*Biston betularia*) is an example of natural selection.
- In England, 1850s before industrialisation, there were more **white-winged moths** on trees than **dark-winged** or **melanic forms**.
- But after industrialisation, i.e. in 1920, the number of dark-winged moths became more than white-winged moths.
- This is because during industrialisation, the tree trunks covered by white lichens became dark due to air pollution (dust and soot particles).
- Due to this, white-winged moths could be easily seen and eaten by the predators as they failed in **camouflaging** (hide or disguise the presence of a person, animal or object in the background).
- Moreover, in areas where industrialisation did not occur, i.e. rural area, the count of melanic moths were low.
- This shows that in a mixed population, those that can adapt are able to survive better and increase their population size.

(a)

(b)

Fig 6.8 Representation of white-winged moth and dark-winged moth (melanised) on a tree trunk, (a) In unpolluted area, (b) In polluted area

Nate Lichens can be used as industrial pollution indicator as they do not grow in polluted areas.

Chemical Resistance

- It is another example of natural selection.
- The excess use of herbicides and pesticides leads to the selection of resistant varieties of microbes in very less time.
- Likewise, due to these anthropogenic actions, antibiotic resistant bacteria are also appearing now-a-days.
- The above discussed industrial melanism and chemical resistance are also examples of evolution by anthropogenic (man made) action.
- This tells us that evolution is a stochastic process, based on chance events in nature and chance mutation in the organisms.

Artificial Selection

- Artificial selection is the process of selecting genetically improved and domesticated plants and animals by man and interbreeding them to get individuals of desired genetic traits .
- If it is repeated for many generations, it produces a new breed with desired characters.
- For example, if cows with high milk yield are desired, then the animal breeders select those cows which produce a large quantity of milk.

Theory of Inheritance of Acquired Characters-Lamarckism

- Even before the Darwin, a french naturalist Lamarck had proposed that the evolution of life forms had occurred by the use and disuse of organs.
- He gave the example of Giraffes, which initially did not have long necks.
- But, due to sudden disappearance of surface vegetation, they had to stretch their neck in order to reach the leaves on tall trees.
- So, they got adapted to their surroundings by elongating their necks.
- By passing this acquired character to succeeding generations, over the years, they came to acquire long necks.
- This theory, also called as **Lamarckism**, is no more accepted.

Mutation Theory of Evolution (Mechanism of Evolution)

- In 1901, **Hugo de Vries** carried out experiments on evening primrose plant (*Oenothera lamarckiana*) and proposed the mutation theory of evolution.
- This theory states that the evolution occurs by the appearance of sudden large differences in the population.
- He believed that mutation is the only cause of evolution and not the minor heritable variations that Darwin talked about.
- He stated that the mutation caused speciation and named it **saltation** (single step large mutation).
- The mutations are random and without directions, while Darwinian variations were small and directional.

Modern Synthetic Theory of Evolution

- With progress in genetics, the sources of variation were explained and Darwin's theory was modified.
- Now, the most accepted theory of evolution is known as **modern synthetic theory of evolution**, designated by **Huxley** in 1942.
- In this theory, the origin of species is based on the interaction of genetic variation in a population, natural selection and reproductive isolation by various means such as migration, hybridisation, chance, etc.

Hardy-Weinberg Principle

- Mutation introduce new genes into a species resulting in change in gene frequencies.
- In 1908, **GH Hardy** and **W Weinberg** established a simple mathematical relationship to study these gene frequencies and gave **Hardy-Weinberg principle.**
- This principle states that the allele frequency in a population is stable and is constant from generation to generation, i.e. gene pool remains constant. This is called **genetic equilibrium** or **Hardy-Weinberg equilibrium**.
- Sum total of all the allelic frequencies is equal to 1, e.g. in a diploid organism, if p and q represent the frequency of an allele A and allele a, the frequency of AA individuals in a population is p^2, similarly of aa is q^2 and of Aa is $2pq$.
- Hence, it can be expressed by the following reaction

$$p^2 + 2pq + q^2 = 1$$

- This is called **binomial expansion** of $(p+q)^2$.
- The extent of evolutionary change is the difference between the value of frequency measured and the value expected (frequency obtained)
- The disturbance in genetic equilibrium (Hardy-Weinberg equilibrium) would result in evolution.

Factors Affecting Hardy-Weinberg Equilibrium

Certain factors that affect Hardy-Weinberg equilibrium and leads to evolution are as follows.

1. Gene Migration or Gene Flow

- When individuals migrate to another place or population. New genes or alleles are added to new population and are lost from old population, inturn changing the gene frequencies. This is called **gene migration.**
- When gene migration occurs multiple times, it is called **gene flow**.

2. Genetic Drift

- It refers to a random gene frequency change and occurs only by chance.
- At times, the change in allele frequency is so different in the new sample of population that they become a different species.

- The original drifted population becomes the founder and the effect is called **founder effect.**

3. Mutation

- The sudden appearance of variations in an individual or a population are called **mutations.**
- They lead to development the new phenotypes.
- Though mutations are random and occur at very slow rates, they are sufficient to create considerable genetic variations for speciation to occur.

4. Genetic Recombination

- When the alleles of parental linkage groups separate and new associations of alleles are formed due to crossing over during gametogenesis, the process is known as **genetic recombination.**

5. Natural Selection

- It occurs due to the inheritance of variations.
- It leads to the survival of those who best fit in an environment, reproduce well and survive.
- Hence, gets selected by the nature (survival of the fittest).
- Depending upon the traits favoured, natural selection can have following three effects

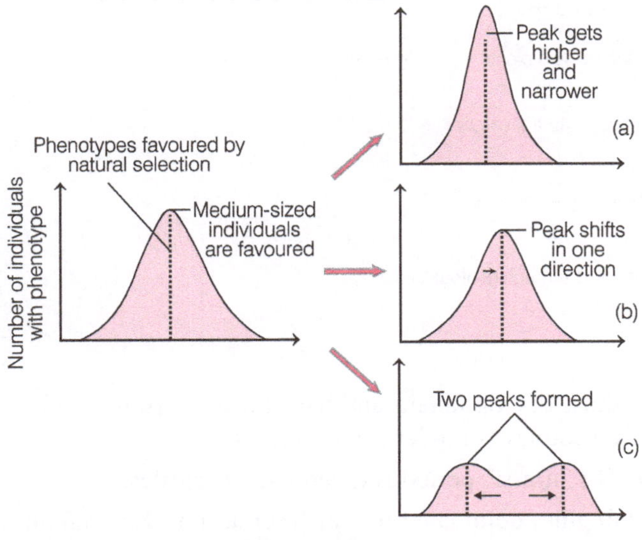

Fig. 6.9 Diagrammatic representation of the operation of natural selection on different traits, (a) Stabilising, (b) Directional, (c) Disruptive

- **Stabilisation** Large number of individuals acquire mean character value, i.e. variation is much reduced [Fig. 6.8 (a)]. This operates in optimal environmental conditions where competition is not severe.
- **Directional Change** Large number of individuals acquire value other than mean character value [Fig. 6.8 (b)]. This operates in response to gradual changes in environmental conditions like during industrial revolution in peppered moths.
- **Disruption** Large number of individuals acquire peripheral character value at both ends of the distribution curve [Fig. 6.8 (c)]. It is rare in occurrence, but important for evolutionary changes. Fluctuating conditions within environment may favour this type of natural selection.

Quick Test 3

1. Name the scientist who concluded that fitness of an individual refers to reproductive fitness.
2. If pollution had been controlled after industrialisation, would it have had any impact on the population of white-winged moths?
3. Mention the term given to a single step large mutation.
4. **State True or False.**

   Genetic recombination and genetic drift affects the Hardy-Weinberg equilibrium.
5. In a population, the number of heterozygous individuals increases. What kind of natural selection does this suggest?

6.4 Account of Evolution

- The cellular forms of life first appeared on earth around 2000 million years ago (mya).
- Some of these cells had the ability to release O_2 by splitting water molecule with the help of solar energy.
- This reaction could have been similar to the light reaction in photosynthesis where water is split with the help of solar energy captured and channelised by appropriate light harvesting pigments.
- Slowly, single-celled organisms became multicellular life forms.

Evolution in Plants

- The first organism that existed on land were plants. A rough sketch of evolution of plants through time, is discussed as follows.
- Vascular plants first originated in Silurian period.
- Existence of sea weeds and few plants were reported around 320 mya.
- Herbaceous lycopods were first appeared in Mesozoic era.
- Arborescent lycopods evolved from *Zosterophyllum* of Paleozoic era.
- *Psilophyton* is evolved during Paleozoic era and it is the common ancestor for horsetails, ferns and gymnosperms.

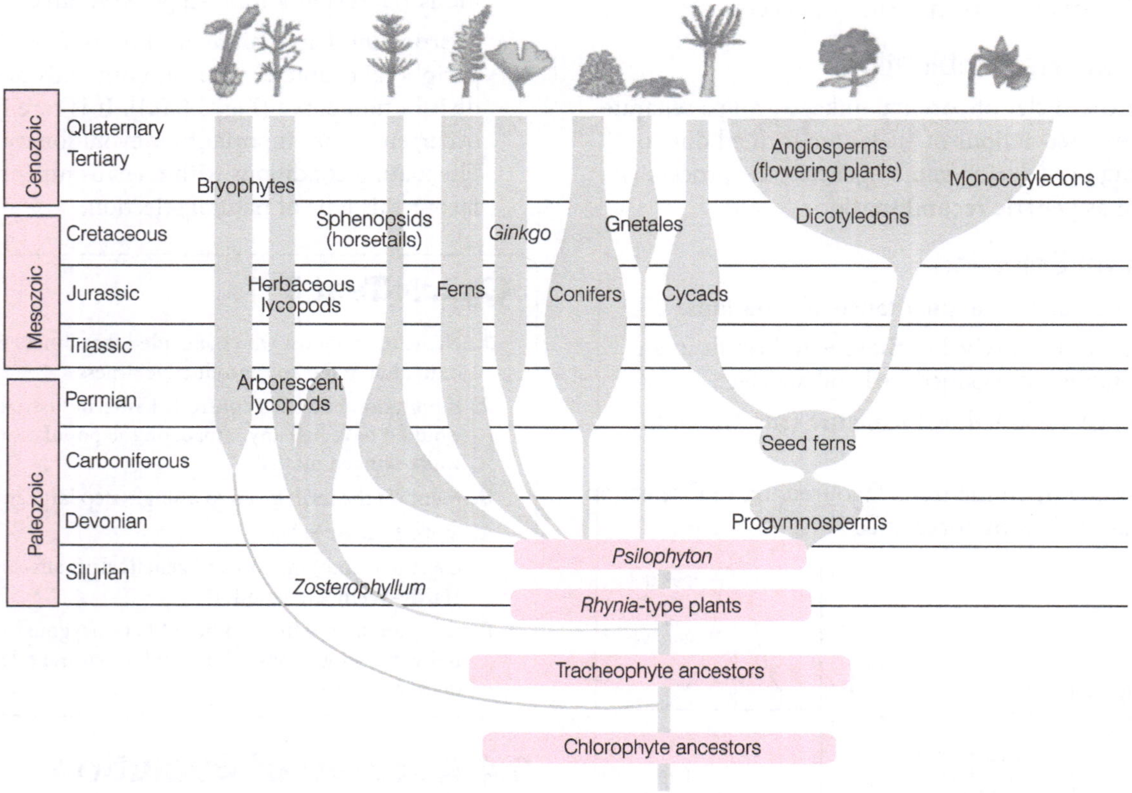

Fig. 6.10 Sketch of the evolution of plant forms through geological periods

Evolution in Animals

- Evolution of animals occurred around 500 mya and first animals were invertebrates.
- Jawless fish and amphibious fish with stout and strong fins originated around 350 mya.
- The first ancestors of amphibians and modern day frogs and salamander were lobefins (Coelacanth).
- The amphibians evolved into reptiles. Reptiles lay thick shelled eggs which do not dry up in sun, unlike those of amphibians and have turtles, tortoises and crocodiles as modern descendants.
- The Jurassic period is called **age of reptiles**.
- Reptiles dominated the earth for around 200 million years. Some of the land reptiles went back into water to evolve into fish-like reptiles probably 200 mya, e.g. *Ihcthyosaurus*.
- Land reptiles include dinosaurs of which *Tyrannosaurus rex* (about 20 feet in height) was biggest.

- *Tyrannosaurus rex* was about 20 feet in height and had huge fearsome dagger like teeth.
- Dinosaurs suddenly disappeared from earth around 65 mya and the exact cause remains uncertain.
- Some theories suggest climate changes led to their extinction, while others propose that many evolved into birds.
- The truth may lie somewhere in between. Small reptiles from that era still exist today.
- When reptiles came down, mammals took over the earth.
- Mammals appeared in Triassic period and the first mammals were like shrews. Their fossils are small sized. These mammals were viviparous.
- They protected their unborn young ones inside the mother's body and they were the more intelligent in sensing and avoiding danger.

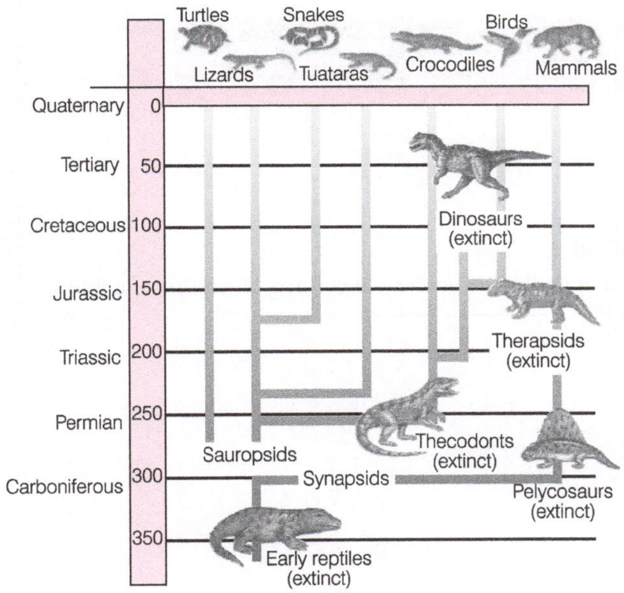

Fig. 6.11 Representative evolutionary history of vertebrates through geological period

- Before continental drift, horse, *Hippopotamus*, bear, rabbit, etc., were present in South America, but afterward when South America joined North America, these animals were over ridden by North American fauna.
- Due to the same continental drift pouched mammals of Australia survived because of lack of competition from any other mammals.

6.5 Origin and Evolution of Human

- About 15 mya, primates called *Dryopithecus* and *Ramapithecus* were existing.
- Thus, the common ancestor of apes and man was *Dryopithecus*.
- The next stage was *Ramapithecus* in the hominid evolution.
- Both *Ramapithecus* and *Dryopithecus* were hairy and walked like gorillas and chimpanzees.
- Few fossils of human-like bones have been discovered in Ethiopia and Tanzania (Fig 6.11).
- These revealed hominid features leading to the belief that around 3-4 mya, human-like primates walked in Eastern Africa. They were probably not taller than 4 feet but walked upright.

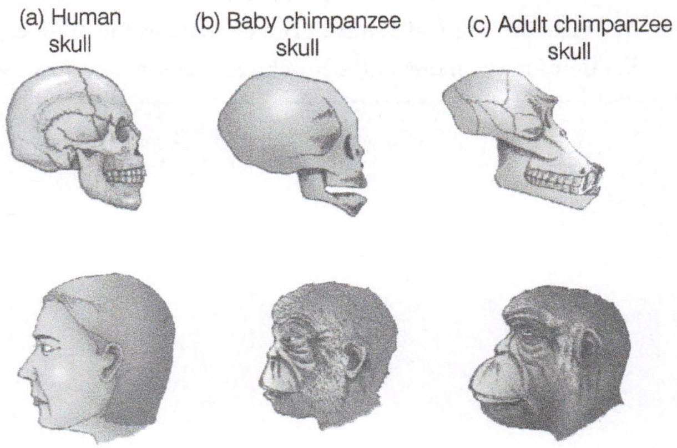

Fig. 6.12 A comparison of the skulls; (a) adult modern human being, (b) baby chimpanzee and (c) adult chimpanzee. The skull of baby chimpanzee is more like adult human skull than adult chimpanzee skull.

The human evolution took place as follows

Human ancestors	Time of origin	General features
Dryopithecus	20-25 mya	Ape-like, hairy, ate soft fruits and leaves.
Ramapithecus	14-15 mya	More man-like, walked more erect, teeth resemble modern man.
Australopithecines (The first ape man)	2 mya	Probably lived in East African grasslands and ate fruits, hunted with stones weapons.
Homo habilis (Handy man)	1.6-2.3 mya	Fossils found in East Africa, first hominid, i.e. human-being like, brain capacity 650-800 cc, did not eat meat.
Homo erectus (Java man)	1.5 mya	Fossils found in Java in 1891, brain capacity 900 cc, probably ate meat.
Homo sapiens neanderthalensis (Primitive man)	1,00,000-40,000 years ago	Known as Neanderthal man. Fossils found in East and Central Asia, brain size 1400 cc, use hides to protect body, buried their dead.
Homo sapiens (Modern man)	75,000-10,000 years ago (ice age)	Arose in Africa, developed cave art around 18,000 years ago, agriculture started around 10,000 years back and thus, human settlement and civilisation started.

Quick Test 4

1. State the geographical period in which origin of *Psilophyton occured.*
2. Rearrange the following in the increasing order of their origin.
   Therapsida, Pelycosaurs, Mammals
3. **State True or False.**
   Tharapsids appear in Jurassic period.
4. Write the name of 1.5mya primate that has the brain capacity of 900cc.
5. Mention the name of the human ancestor whose fossil was found in East Africa and who is considered the first hominid.

Mind Map

Evolution

Origin of Life

- Evolutionary biology deals with the two important aspects of life, i.e. its origin and evolution.
- Origin of universe 15-20 bya, arose as cataclysmic eruption (Big-Bang Theory).
- Origin of earth 4.5 bya.

Theories of Origin of Life

- **Theory of special creation**— God created life.
- **Theory of panspermia**— By early Greek thinkers, life came from spores.
- **Theory of spontaneous generation**— Life originated from non-living matter automatically. Rejected by Louis Pasteur who demonstrated that life came from pre-existing cells.
- **Theory of chemical evolution**— Formation of diverse organic molecules from inorganic constituents.
- **Miller and Urey** gave the experimental evidence of chemical evolution.

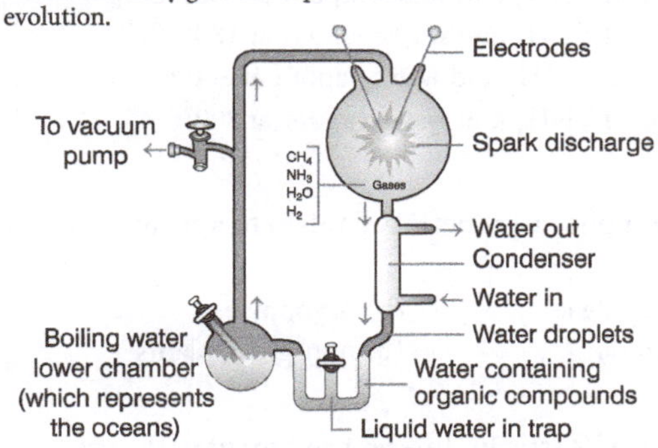

Urey and Miller's Experiment

Evidences of Evolution

- **Palaeontological evidences** takes fossils into account.
- **Comparative anatomy** and **morphological evidences.**

Homology, e.g. vertebrate's hearts and brains

Analogy, e.g. wings of butterfly and birds.

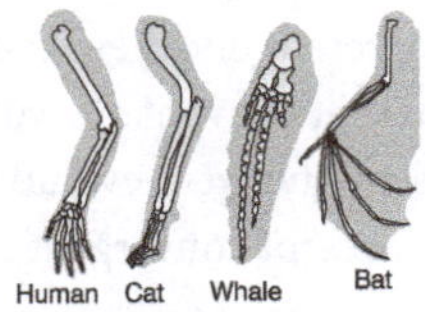

Homologous Organs

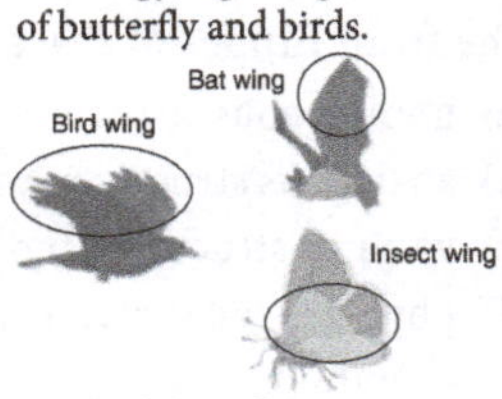

Analogous Organs

- **Biochemical evidences,** e.g. same metabolic processes in different organisms.
- **Embryological evidences** by Ernst Haeckel *Ontogeny Recapitulates Phylogeny*, e.g. fish-like characters in frog larva.
- **Biogeographical evidences** — Species restricted to a region develop unique features. Also, species in widely different region show similarity of ancestry. They are
  - **Adaptive Radiation** The process of evolution of different species starting from a point in an area and radiating to other areas, e.g. Darwin's finches, marsupial in Australia.
  - **Adaptive Convergence** Two or more groups of unrelated or distantly related species evolve similar mode of life. More than one adaptive radiation have occurred, e.g. placental mammals in North America and marsupial in Australia.

Theories of Evolution

- **Lamarck's theory** It states that the evolution of life forms occurred by use and disuse of organs, e.g. long neck of giraffe.
- **Darwin's theory** It states that useful variations from the organisms are selected by nature, i.e. natural selection and gets accumulated in the organism. This causes evolution, e.g. industrial melanism, chemical resistance.
- **Mutation theory** by Hugo de Vries, it states that evolution occurs by a single step large mutations (saltation) that are random and directionless.
- **Modern synthetic theory** It is most accepted theory. Origin of species is based on interaction of genetic variation and natural selection.

Hardy-Weinberg Principle

- It states that allele frequencies in a population are stable and remain constant from generation to generation.

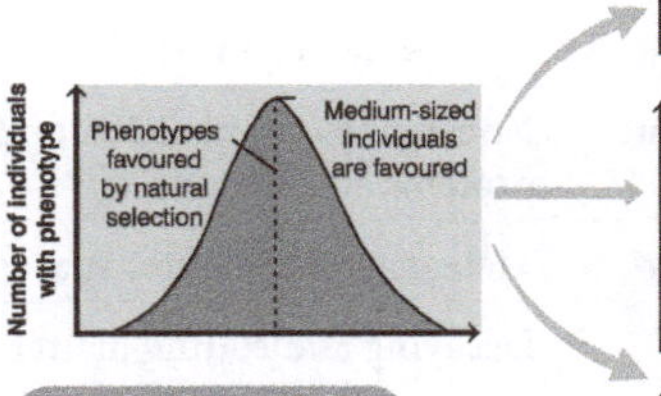

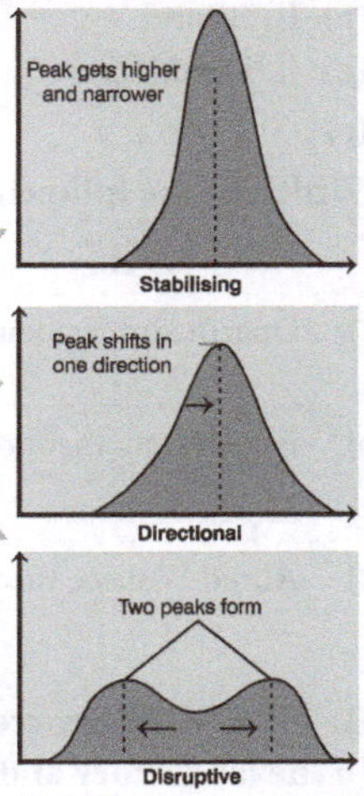

$(p+q)^2=p^2+2pq+q^2=1$

Frequency of allele 'A' = p
Frequency of allele 'a' = q
Frequency of population with 'AA' = p^2
Frequency of population with 'Aa' = $2pq$
Frequency of population with 'aa' = q^2

- Factors affecting are : gene migration, genetic drift, mutation, genetic recombination and natural selection (which leads to stabilisation, directional change and disruption).

Brief Account of Evolution

1st cellular life : 2 bya
Invertebrates : 500 mya
Jawless fishes : 350 mya
Sea weeds and few plants : 320 mya
Reptiles : 200 mya (*Ichthyosaurus*)

- Lobe fins evolved into first amphibians
- Amphibians evolved into reptiles, giant ferns form coal deposits slowly
- *Tyrannosaurus rex* : 20 feet height and dagger-like teeth
- First mammals were like shrews
- Mammals were viviparous.

Origin and Evolution of Man

- Occurred in Central Asia, China, Java and India.
- It took place in sequence as : *Dryopithecus* → *Ramapithecus* → *Australopitheus* → *Homo habilis* → *Homo erectus* → *Homo sapiens neanderthalensis* → *Homo sapiens.*

EXAM PATTERN QUESTIONS

Objective Type Questions

Multiple Choice Questions

1. Which of the following statements are related with the concept of the Big-Bang theory?

I. A single huge explosion led to the expansion of universe.

II. Huge clusters of galaxies comprising stars and clouds of dust were formed.

III. The earth was formed about 4.5 billion years ago on milky way galaxy.

IV. Considering the size of earth, universe is indeed a speck.

V. The universe is about 20 million years old.

(a) II, III and V (b) I, II, III and V
(c) I, II and III (d) II, IV and V

Ans. (*c*)

2. Which of the following pairs is incorrectly matched?

	Theory	Life origin from
(a)	Oparin and Haldane	Non-living organic RNA and protein molecules
(b)	Panspermia theory	Meteorites from outer space
(c)	SL Miller theory	Decaying and rotting matter
(d)	Alfred Wallace theory	Similar to natural selection

Ans. (*c*)

3. In 1953, SL Miller created primitive earth conditions in the laboratory and gave experimental evidence for origin of first form of life from pre-existing non-living organic molecules. The primitive earth conditions created include **NCERT Exemplar**

(a) low temperature, volcanic storms, atmosphere rich in oxygen
(b) low temperature, volcanic storms, reducing atmosphere
(c) high temperature, volcanic storms, non-reducing atmosphere
(d) high temperature, volcanic storms, reducing atmosphere containing CH_4, NH_3, etc.

Ans. (*d*) The Millers experiment tested for the occurrence of chemical evolution by stimulating hypothetical conditions present on early earth.

These primitive earth conditions include high temperature, volcanic storms and reducing environment containing methane (CH_4), ammonia (NH_3), hydrogen (H_2) and water (H_2O).

4. Which one of the following options gives the correct temperature condition and the mixture of the gaseous components that were used by S.L. Miller in 1953 to prove abiogenesis of life?

(a) CH_4, H_2, NO_2 and water vapour at 1800°C
(b) CH_4, H_2, NH_3 and water vapour at 1800°C
(c) CO_2, H_2, NH_3 and water vapour at 800°C
(d) CH_4, H_2, NH_3 and water vapour at 800°C

Ans. (*d*)

5. The first photosynthetic organism to appear on the earth was

(a) green algae (b) bryophytes
(c) bacteria (d) non-green plants

Ans. (*c*)

6. A study of fossils in different sedimentary layers indicates

(a) physiological period in which they existed
(b) geological period in which they existed
(c) conditions in which they were living
(d) conditions in which they reproduce

Ans. (*b*)

7. The front flipper of seal and a bat's wings are

(a) homologous structures and represent divergent evolution
(b) analogous structures and represent convergent evolution
(c) vestigial structures and represent divergent evolution
(d) phylogenetic structures and represent convergent evolution

Ans. (*a*)

8. Which of the following sets contain only analogous organs?

(a) Wisdom tooth of human and chimpanzee
(b) Sepals of brinjal and potato
(c) Flipper of penguin and dolphin wings of bird and bat
(d) Sweet potato and potato, tendrils of pea and thorn of *cucurbita*

Ans. (*c*)

9. Which of the following combinations is a correct example of convergent evolution in Australian marsupials and placental mammals? CBSE 2025

	Australian Marsupials	Placental Mammals
(a)	Lemur	Spotted cuscus
(b)	Tasmanian tiger cat	Anteater
(c)	Bobcat	Lemur
(d)	Numbat	Anteater

Ans. (*d*) The numbat (marsupial) and the anteater (placental mammal) show convergent evolution as both are adapted for ant and termite feeding, despite their different evolutionary origins.

10. Which of the following combinations is a correct example of convergent evolution in Australian marsupials and placental mammals? CBSE 2025

	Australian Marsupials	Placental Mammals
(a)	Tasmanian tiger cat	Lemur
(b)	Tasmanian tiger cat	Numbat
(c)	Spotted cuscus	Lemur
(d)	Spotted cuscus	Numbat

Ans. (*c*) Convergent evolution occurs when unrelated organisms develop similar traits due to similar environments. The spotted cuscus (marsupial) and lemur (placental mammal) share body structure and ecological roles.

11. Adaptive radiation leads to which of the following?

(a) Increased competition among species
(b) Decreased speciation rates
(c) Limited morphological diversity among species
(d) Rapid divergence of traits among populations inhabiting a given geographical area

Ans. (*d*)

12. Which of the following are the two key concepts of Darwinian theory of evolution?

(a) Genetic drift and mutation
(b) Adaptive radiation and homology
(c) Mutation and natural selection
(d) Branching descent and natural selection

Ans. (*d*)

13. Select the correct statement from the following. Diksha

(a) Fitness is the end result of the ability to adapt and gets selected by nature
(b) Darwinian variations are small and directionless
(c) Mutations are random and directional
(d) All mammals except whales and camels have seven cervical vertebrae

Ans. (*a*)

14. The phenomenon of industrial melanism in the peppered moth in England highlights that

(a) melanism was caused by industrial pollution
(b) light coloured moths had selective advantage in polluted areas
(c) dark coloured moths arose by recurring random mutations
(d) None of the above

Ans. (*d*)

15. Among the examples listed below, which of the following does support the Lamarck's theory of evolution?

(a) Giraffes with long necks for foraging on tall trees
(b) Pierced ears in mothers are not inherited by their babies
(c) Loss of vision in cave dwelling mammals
(d) Loss of hindlimbs in whales

Ans. (*a*)

16. Variations during mutations of meiotic recombinations are NCERT Exemplar

(a) random and directionless
(b) random and directional
(c) random and small
(d) random, small and directional

Ans. (*a*) Variations during mutations of meiotic recombinations are random and directionless.

Hugo de Vries based on his work on evening primrose stated that mutations are sudden, heritable and persistent in successive generation. He contradicted Darwinian variations that are small and directional.

17. Match the Column I with Column II and select the correct option from the codes given below.

	Column I (Scientists)		Column II (Related to)
A.	Darwin	1.	Natural selection
B.	Lamarck	2.	Inheritance of acquired character
C.	Pasteur	3.	Swan-necked experiment
D.	de Vries	4.	Mutational theory of inheritance

Codes

	A	B	C	D
(a)	2	3	4	1
(b)	1	3	4	2
(c)	1	2	3	4
(d)	1	2	4	3

Ans. (*c*)

18. **For the MN-blood group system, the frequencies of M and N alleles are 0.7 and 0.3, respectively. The expected frequency of MN-blood group bearing organisms is likely to be** Competency Based Que., NCERT Exemplar

(a) 42% (b) 49%
(c) 9% (d) 58%

Ans. (*a*) The expected frequency of MN-blood group bearings organisms is likely to be 42%.

According to Hardy-Weinberg equation, $p^2 + 2pq + q^2 = 1$

where, p = Frequency of M alleles,

p^2 = Frequency of homozygous dominant individuals.

q = Frequency of N alleles

q^2 = Frequency of homozygous recessive individuals.

$2Pq$ = Frequency of heterozygous individuals.

So, $(0.7)^2 + (0.3)^2 + 2\ pq = 1$

$0.49 + 0.09 + 2\ pq = 1$

$\therefore\ 2pq = 0.42$ = Frequency of heterozygous individuals.

i.e., 42%

19. **Following is the digrammatic representation of the operation of natural selection on different traits. Which of the following options correctly identifies all the three graphs *A*, *B* and *C*?** Competency Based Que.

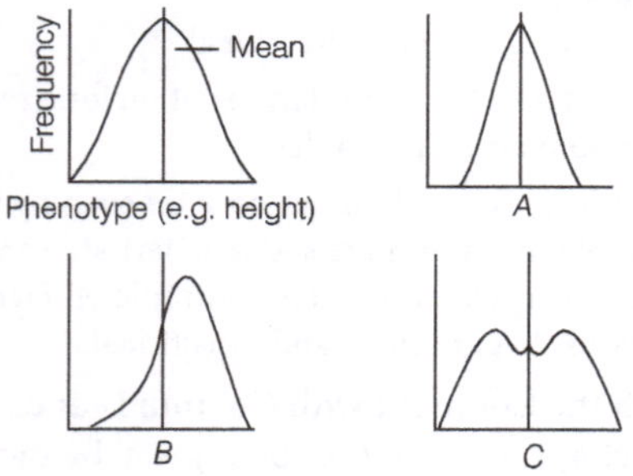

	A	*B*	*C*
(a)	Directional	Stabilising	Disruptive
(b)	Stabilising	Directional	Disruptive
(c)	Disruptive	Stabilising	Directional
(d)	Directional	Disruptive	Stabilising

Ans. (*b*)

20. **The common ancestor of mosses and tracheophytes are**

(a) *Psilophyton* (b) Chlorophyte ancestor
(c) Ferns (d) None of the above

Ans. (*b*)

21. **Herbaceous lycopods and arborescent lycopods evolved from**

(a) *Zosterophyllum* of Paleozoic era
(b) *Progymnosperms* of Mesozoic era
(c) *Psilophyton* of Paleozoic era
(d) Cycads of Mesozoic era

Ans. (*a*)

22. **Evolution of life shows that life forms had a trend of moving from** NCERT Exemplar

(a) land to water
(b) dry land to wet land
(c) freshwater to sea water
(d) water to land

Ans. (*d*) Evolution of life shows that life forms had a trend of moving from water to land. The early vertebrates were fishes which gradually changed into amphibians.

Certain amphibians then transformed into the reptiles, some of them latter finally evolved into birds and then mammals.

23. **Match the Column I with Column II and select the correct option from the codes given below.**

	Column I (Time periods in geological time scale)		Column II (Related to)
A.	Mesozoic	1.	First amphibians
B.	Paleozoic	2.	Extinction of thecodonts
C.	Cretaceous	3.	160 million years
D.	Permian	4.	Extinction of dinosaurs

Codes

	A	B	C	D
(a)	1	4	3	2
(b)	3	1	4	2
(c)	4	1	2	3
(d)	2	1	4	3

Ans. (*b*)

24. **The most primitive ancestor of humans is** CBSE 2024 C

(a) *Homo habilis* (b) *Australopithecus*
(c) *Ramapithecus* (d) *Homo neanderthalensis*

Ans. (*b*)

25. **At which stage during evolution did human use hides to protect their bodies and buried their dead?** CBSE 2023

(a) *Homo habilis* (b) Neanderthal man
(c) Java man (d) *Homo erectus*

Ans. (*b*)

26. **Match the Column I with Column II and select the correct option from the codes given below.**

	Column I (Primates)		Column II (Cranial capacities in cubic centimetres)
A.	Neanderthal man	1.	1400 cc
B.	*Australopithecus*	2.	500 cc
C.	*Homo habilis*	3.	700 cc
D.	*Homo erectus*	4.	900 cc

Codes

	A	B	C	D
(a)	4	3	2	1
(b)	2	3	4	1
(c)	1	2	3	4
(d)	3	2	1	4

Ans. (c)

27. The most accepted line of descent in human evolution is **NCERT Exemplar**

(a) *Australopithecus* → *Ramapithecus* → *Homo sapiens* → *Homo habilis*
(b) *Homo erectus* → *Homo habilis* → *Homo sapiens*
(c) *Ramapithecus* → *Homo habilis* → *Homo sapiens*
(d) *Australopithecus* → *Ramapithecus* → *Homo erectus* → *Homo habilis* → *Homo sapiens*

Ans. (c)

Assertion-Reason Questions

Direction (Q. Nos. 1-10) *In each of the following questions, a statement of Assertion (A) is given followed by corresponding statement of Reason(R). Of the statements, mark the correct answer*

(a) Both A and R are true and R is the correct explanation of A
(b) Both A and R are true, but R is not the correct explanation of A
(c) A is true, but R is false
(d) A is false, but R is true

1. Assertion (A) The first form of life arose gradually through evolutionary forces from non-living molecules.

Reason (R) The first form of life could have originated 4 billion years back.

Ans. (b)

2. Assertion (A) The theory of special creation states that God created life by his divine act of creation.

Reason (R) Louis Pasteur rejected the theory of spontaneous generation.

Ans. (b)

3. Assertion (A) The theory of spontaneous generation state that living organisms could arise from non-living matter.

Reason (R) Theory of spontaneous generation was supported by observations of organisms appearing in decaying substances, leading people to believe that life could spontaneously generate under certain conditions.

Ans. (a)

4. Assertion (A) Whales, bats, cheetah and humans, share similarities in the pattern of bone of forelimbs, although they perform different functions in them.

Reason (R) The same structures developed along different directions due to adaptations to different needs.

Ans. (a)

5. Assertion (A) Whales and mammals share similarities in the pattern of bones of forelimbs.

Reason (R) These organisms suggest occurrence of divergent evolution.

Ans. (b)

6. Assertion (A) Ernst Haeckel supported the embryological similarities as an evidence of evolution.

Reason (R) The embryos of all vertebrates including humans develop a row of vestigial gill slits which are absent in adult vertebrates.

Ans. (b)

7. Assertion (A) Nature selects for fitness.

Reason (R) The organism with better adaptive mechanisms and reproductive capacity get selected by nature.

Ans. (a)

8. Assertion (A) Variation due to mutation, recombination or gene flow results in changed frequency of genes and alleles in progeny.

Reason (R) Mutation caused speciation.

Ans. (b)

9. Assertion (A) Hugo de Vries said mutations cause speciation.

Reason (R) Mutations are slow directional changes.

Ans. (c) A is true, but R is false. A can be corrected as

Mutations are random and directionless, while Darwinian variations are small and directional.

10. Assertion (A) Common ancestor of ferns, conifers and seed ferns is *Psilophyton* .

Reason (R) The most recent ancestor of *Psilophyton* and seed fern is chlorophyte.

Ans. (c) A is true, but R is false. R can be corrected as

The most recent ancestor of *Psilophyton* and seed fern is *Rhynia* type plants.

Subjective Questions

Very Short Answer Type Questions

1. What was the important feature of the early atmosphere on earth?

Ans. An important feature of the early atmosphere was the absence of oxygen, which created a reducing atmosphere on the earth.

2. A frog can arise from the moist soil. The above example can be related to which theory of origin of life?

Ans. Theory of spontaneous generation.

3. The theory of spontaneous generation was rejected by whom and why?

Ans. Louis Pasteur rejected the theory of spontaneous generation and stated that life originates from pre-existing life.

4. The first cellular life form originated when and where?

Ans. The first life form originated 2000 million years ago in aquatic environment.

5. 'The earliest organisms that appeared on the earth were non-green and presumably anaerobes'. Is the above statement correct? Give reason.

Ans. True, the earliest organisms were anaerobic chemoautotrophs. They did not require O_2 and were able to adapt to earth's atmosphere at that time.

6. The first living organism which appeared on the earth would have adopted which mode of nutrition?

Ans. First living organism adopt heterotrophic nutrition as they obtained energy from complex organic substances.

7. State the significance of study of fossils in evolution.

Ans. Fossils helps to know about the geological period in which the organisms were present as well as to understand the process of the evolution.

8. What is the way to compute the age of a fossil? **NCERT Exemplar**

Ans. Radioactive dating is one of the way to compute the age of a fossil.

9. Name any two vertebrate's body parts that are homologous to human forelimbs (hands).

Ans. Flippers of whales and forelimbs of cheetah.

10. What can you infer about the structures shown in the image?

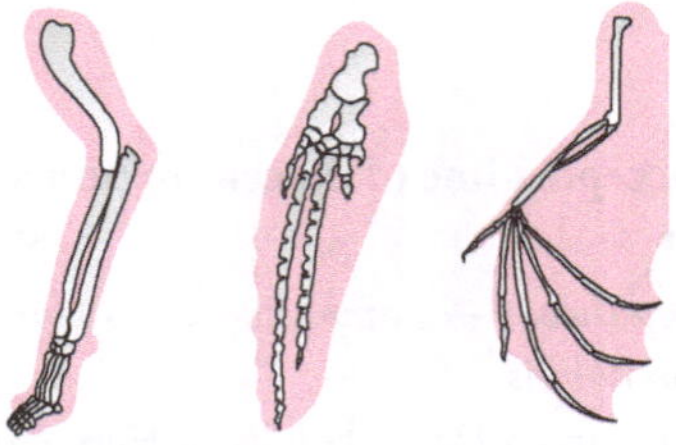

Ans. The given structures are homologous.

11. Select the homologous structures from the combinations given below and the kind of evolution they represent.

(a) Forelimbs of whales and bats

(b) Tuber of potato and sweet potato

(c) Eyes of *Octopus* and mammals

(d) Thorns of *Bougainvillea* and tendrils of *Cucurbita*

Ans. (a) and (d) represents homologous structures. They exhibits divergent evolution.

12. Why are analogous structures a result of convergent evolution?

Ans. When organisms of different geographical location converge to a restricted habitat, they develop adaptations to suit that location and develop analogous structures.

13. State the significance of biochemical similarities among diverse organisms in evolution.

Ans. Similarities in biochemicals such as DNA help in deriving the line of evolution. Organisms with more similar DNA sequences are considered close relatives or have evolved from the same ancestor.

14. Describe one example of adaptive radiation. **NCERT**

Ans. An example of adaptive radiation is Darwin's finches of the Galapagos Island, which once had a common ancestor, but with evolution, they modified into different types according to their food habits.

15. Name the placental mammals corresponding to the Australian spotted cuscus and Tasmanian tiger cat, which have evolved as a result of convergent evolution. **CBSE 2008 C**

Ans. Australian spotted cuscus–Lemur.
Tasmanian tiger cat–Bob cat.

16. What role does an individual organism play as per Darwin's theory of natural selection?

Ans. According to Darwin, each individual acts as a unit of selection, with variations influencing survival and reproductive success, ultimately driving the evolutionary process.

17. What is 'fitness of an individual' according to Darwin?

Ans. According to Darwin, fitness of an individual is its ability to reproduce successfully and leave a large number of progenies under a particular set of selection pressures.

18. The 'origin of species' was given by which scientist?

Ans. Charles Darwin

19. What do you understand by the concept of inheritance of acquired characters as proposed by Lamarck?

Ans. According to Lamarck, new traits are acquired by organisms during their life time and later passed on to the next generation.

20. Hugo de Vries gave the mutation theory. Name the plant he worked on.

Ans. Evening Primrose plant (*Oenothera lamarckiana*).

21. According to Hugo de Vries what is saltation?

Ans. According to Hugo de Vries, large step single mutation that causes speciation is saltation.

22. Attempt giving a clear definition of the term species. NCERT

Ans. A group of organisms capable of interbreeding and producing fertile offspring are called species.

23. Write down the consequence of absence of genetic variations among individual of a population.

Ans. In the absence of genetic variations, the rate of extinction of species would increase significantly as species would not be able to adapt in changing environment.

24. Rearrange the following in increasing order of evolution: Gnetales; Ferns; *Zosterophyllum; Ginkgo*.

Ans. The increasing order of evolution in plants is *Zosterophyllum*–Ferns–*Ginkgo*–Gnetales.

25. Coelacanth that was caught in 1938 in South Africa, was very significant in the evolutionary history of vertebrates. Why?

Ans. Coelacanth were lobefins, fish-like animals with stout and strong fins, that lived both in water as well as on land.

Their discovery was significant as they proved that amphibians have evolved from fish-like organisms.

26. Identify the examples of convergent evolution from the following.

(i) Flippers of penguins and dolphins.

(ii) Eyes of *Octopus* and mammals.

(iii) Vertebrate's brain.

Ans. (i) Flippers of penguins and dolphins.

(ii) Eyes of *Octopus* and mammals.

27. Name any two forms of extinct reptiles that evolved from synapsids.

Ans. *Pelycosaurs* and Therapsids. (½ + ½)

28. About 65 mya, the dinosaurs suddenly disappeared from the earth. What is the most likely reason for this disappearance?

Ans. The most likely reason to explain the disappearance of dinosaurs is the climatic change to which they could not adapt.

29. What did the first mammal look like?

Ans. First mammal looked like shrew.

30. Who among the *Dryopithecus* and *Ramapithecus* was more man-like? NCERT Exemplar

Ans. *Ramapithecus* was more man-like.

31. Write the names of the following.

(i) A 15 mya primate that was ape-like.

(ii) A 2 mya primate that lived in East African grasslands.

Ans. (i) *Dryopithecus*

(ii) *Australopithecines* (½ + ½)

32. Write the probable differences in eating habits of *Homo habilis* and *Homo erectus*. CBSE 2016

Ans. *Homo habilis* did not eat meat, while *Homo erectus* probably ate meat.

33. How many years back were the following developed in human evolution?

(i) Cave art

(ii) Agriculture

Ans. (i) Cave art : 18000 years ago

(ii) Agriculture : 10000 years ago (½ + ½)

Short Answer Type Questions

1. Give a brief account of origin of earth.

Ans. Refer to text on page no. 179.

2. When was earth formed? What were its conditions at that time? NCERT Exemplar

Ans. Refer to text on page no. 179.

3. Mention the three connotations of the theory of special creation.

Ans. Refer to text on page no. 179.

4. How did Louis Pasteur successfully demolish the popular theory of spontaneous generation?

Ans. Refer to text on page no. 179.

5. State two postulates of Oparin and Haldane's theory with reference to the origin of life. NCERT Exemplar

Ans. Refer to text on page no. 179.

6. Describe the experiment that helped Louis Pasteur to dismiss the theory of spontaneous generation of life.

Ans. Louis Pasteur rejected the theory of spontaneous generation and demonstrated that life came from pre-existing life. In his experiment, he kept killed yeast cells in pre-sterilised flask and an another flask which is kept open into air.

The life did not evolved in the former, but new living organisms evolved in the later flask.

7. State the theory of abiogenesis. How does Miller's experiment support this theory?

Ans. Refer to text on page no. 179-180.

8. Give the experimental setup for Miller's experiment.

Ans. Refer to text on page no. 179 and 180. Diksha

9. Explain how did the experiment conducted by SL Miller substantiate that life evolved from pre-existing non-living organic molecules. CBSE 2023

Ans. Refer to text on page no. 179 and 180

10. (i) Explain the significance of the experiment carried out by SL Miller. Name the scientists whose hypothesis prompted him to carry out this experiment.

(ii) How does meteorite analysis favour this hypothesis?

Ans. (i) SL Miller performed an experiment to demonstrate that UV radiations or electrical discharges or a combination of these can produce complex organic compounds from a mixture of CH_4 , NH_3 , H_2 and water vapour (H_2O) at 800°C. He observed the formation of amino acids, sugars, pigments, nitrogen bases and fats in the flask. This theory supported the theory of abiogenesis followed by chemical evolution.

Scientists whose hypothesis prompted him to carry out this experiment were Oparin and Haldane, who gave the theory that the first form of life came from pre-existing, non-living organic molecules (e.g. RNA, protein, etc.) (2½)

(ii) Analysis of meteorite content also revealed similar compounds indicating that similar processes are occurring elsewhere in space. (½)

11. Palaeontological evidence support the theory of organic evolution. Explain with an example.

Ans. The study of fossils, i.e. palaeontological evidences support theory of organic evolution, i.e. evolution in plants and animals. The transitional fossil organisms show evolutionary relationship between two groups and are called connecting links, e.g. *Archaeopteryx* is a connecting link between reptiles and birds.

12. State the modifications of forelimb in animals as an example of homology.

Ans. The forelimb of vertebrates are pentadactyl, consisting of same bones i.e., humerus, radius, ulna, carpals, metacarpals and phalanges, but differ in their function in different organisms. The forelimbs of the following animals got modified as follows.

(i) Whale for swimming.
(ii) Bat and bird for flying.
(iii) Horse for running.
(iv) Human for grasping.

This indicates common ancestry and homology based on divergent evolution.

13. Analogous organs are a result of convergent evolution whereas homologous organs are a result of divergent evolution. Justify with the help of suitable example for each. CBSE 2020

Ans. Refer to text on page no. 181-182.

14. How does analogous organ support the theory of organic evolution?

Ans. Analogous organs support theory of organic evolution because they show that organs in different organisms can evolve to perform similar functions even if they do not share a common ancestor.

15. Explain adaptive radiation with the help of a suitable example. CBSE 2015

Ans. Refer to text on page no. 183.

16. Explain the interpretation of Charles Darwin when he observed a variety of small black birds on Galapagos Island.

Ans. Refer to text on page no. 183.

17. Mention Darwin's observations made on finches during his visit to Galapagos Islands. Write the explanation given by Darwin on his observations. CBSE 2023

Ans. Refer to text on page no. 183.

18. Refer to the figure given below and answer the following questions.

Tasmanian wolf

(i) Identify the process by which Tasmanian wolf evolved.

(ii) Define the process identify in (i).

(iii) Apart from marsupials, this process was also observed in which other organism?

Ans. (i) Adaptive radiation. (1)

(ii) Refer to text on page no. 183. (1)

(iii) Finches. (1)

19. Name the ship in which Charles Darwin made his voyage. What was his conclusion about the life forms he observed?

Ans. Refer to text on page no. 184.

20. While creation and the presence of variation is directionless, natural selection is directional as it is in the context of adaptation. Comment. **NCERT Exemplar**

Ans. The creation and the presence of variations is directionless in regard that they occur randomly and spontaneously. The variations which are helpful in the adaptations of an organism towards its surroundings would be passed onto next generations.

Natural selection is the most critical evolutionary process, which can be considered directional as it leads to only one path that is selection and perpetuation of better adapted individuals. Natural selection leads to survival of the fittest and disappearance of all those organisms which do not fit in the prevailing environmental conditions. (3)

21. What do these pictures *A* and *B* illustrate with reference to evolution? Explain.

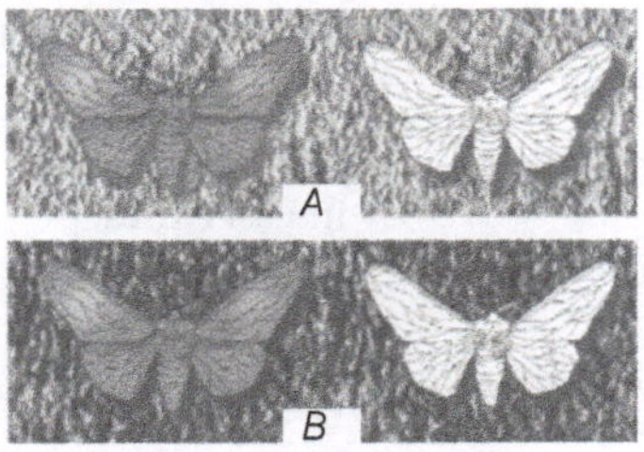

Ans. Refer to text on page no. 185.

22. State the reason for the increased population of dark coloured moths coinciding with the loss of lichens (on tree barks) during industrialisation period in England.

Ans. During post-industrialisation period, the tree trunks got dark because of industrial smoke and soot, so the dark coloured moths were able to hide without any risk of predation and survived, which led to increase in their population. While the white winged moths did not survive due to severe predation.

23. Industrial melanism in England after 1850 is an excellent example of natural selection. Explain how? **CBSE 2023**

Ans. Refer to text on page no. 185.

24. Explain the antibiotic resistance observed in bacteria in light of Darwinian selection theory. **NCERT**

Ans. Darwin's theory of natural selection states that the environment selects organisms with favourable variations and therefore, these organisms survive and reproduce successfully. It has been noticed that when bacterial populations are exposed to certain antibiotics, the sensitive bacteria could not tolerate and hence died due to the adverse environment. Whereas, some bacteria that developed mutation, became resistant to the particular antibiotics and survived. As a result, such resistant bacteria survived and multiplied quickly as compared to other sensitive bacteria. Thus, the whole population is regained by multiplication of resistant varieties and antibiotic resistant genes become widespread in the bacterial population.

25. With the help of any two suitable examples explain the effect of anthropogenic actions on organic evolution.

Ans. New species evolve in a short time scale, months or years due to anthropogenic actions or human activities. This hastens the evolutionary process. For example,

(i) Industrial melanism in peppered moth. Refer to text on page no. 185. (1½)

(ii) Chemical resistance in bacteria. Refer to text on page no. 185. (1½)

26. How do new species arise according to de Vries mutation theory of organic evolution?

Ans. Refer to text on page no. 186.

27. How is Darwin's concept of evolution different from that of de Vries?

Or

Differentiate between the explonation gien by darwin and devries respectively on the mechanism of evolution. Write any three differences. **CBSE 2024 C**

Ans. Differences between Darwin's concept and de Vries concept are as follows

Darwin's concept	de Vries concept
Variations causes minor heritable changes in characters among the individuals of a species.	Mutations are large differences in the characteristics of organisms, that occur suddenly and causes speciation.
Evolution was gradual. Speciation occurs through variations and natural selection over many generations.	Evolution occurs in a large single-step mutation. Single-step mutation cause speciation.

28. Have you heard of modern synthetic theory of evolution. What are the drawbacks of mutation theory that could lead to the formation of a new theory?

Ans. **Drawbacks of Mutation Theory** Mutations are not commonly occurring, most of them are negative. Mutations mostly are recessive however traits responsible for evolution are dominant.

29. With the help of an algebraic equation, how did Hardy-Weinberg explain that in a given population the frequency of occurrence of alleles of a gene is supposed to remain the same through generations?

Ans. Refer to text on page no. 186.

30. $p^2 + 2pq + q^2 = 1$. Explain this algebraic equation on the basis of Hardy-Weinberg's principle.

Ans. Refer to text on page no. 186.

31. Hardy-Weinberg's principle is stated in the following algebraic equation

$$p^2 + 2pq + q^2 = 1.$$

(i) State what do 'p' and 'q' denote in the equation.

(ii) State Hardy-Weinberg principle as indicated in the equation.

(iii) What would you interpret if the value of '1' in the equation gets deviated? **CBSE 2020**

Ans. Refer to text on page no. 186. (1×3)

32. Give difference between gene frequency and gene pool.

Ans. **Gene frequency** represent percentage of an allele in relation to total number of alleles in interbreeding population, while sum total of alleles in a population is called **gene pool**.

33. Disruptive selection is rarest form of selection. Give reason.

Ans. Disruptive selection is rare because it requires specific environmental conditions where intermediate traits are disadvantageous and the population must experience enough genetic isolation and stability to allow for the development of distinct phenotypic groups.

34. Refer the graph and answer the questions that follows.

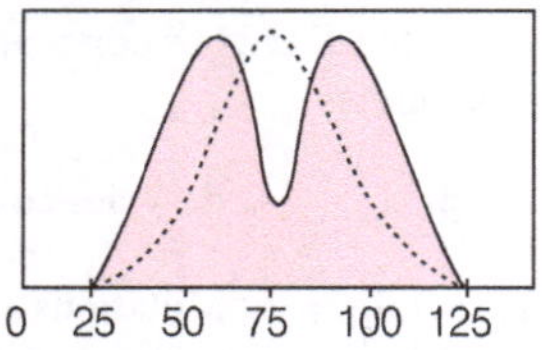

(i) The graph depicts which type of natural selection?

(ii) Explain the other two effects/types of natural selection.

Ans. (i) The graph depicts disruptive natural selection. This type of selection tends to eliminate intermediate types.

(ii) The other two types of natural selection are

(a) Directional Selection- Large number of individuals acquire value other than mean character value. (1)

(b) Stabilising Selection- Large number of individuals acquire mean character value. (2)

35. What are the periods in Paleozoic era and name the plant group that appeared in each of them?

Ans. The periods in Paleozoic era are

(i) **Silurian** *Zosterophyllum*.

(ii) **Devonian** Progymnosperms.

(iii) **Carboniferous** Seed ferns

(iv) **Permian** Arborescent lycopods. (½ × 4)

36. When did the following appear on the geological history?

(i) Invertebrates

(ii) Jawless fish

(iii) Sea weeds

Ans. (i) Invertebrates - 500 mya

(ii) Jawless fish - 350 mya

(iii) Sea weeds - 320 mya (1 × 3)

37. (i) Write two differences between *Homo erectus* and *Homo habilis*.

(ii) Rearrange the following from early to late geologic periods : Carboniferous, Silurian, Jurassic. **CBSE 2019**

Ans. (i) Differences between *Homo erectus* and *Homo habilis* are

Homo erectus	*Homo habilis*
Origin period is 1.5 mya.	Origin period is 1.6-2.3 mya.
Brain capacity-900 cc.	Brain capacity 650-800 cc.
They were carnivorous and ate meat.	They were herbivores.
Fossils were found in Java.	Fossils were found in East Africa.

(2)

(ii) The correct sequence of geological periods from early to late is

Silurian → Carboniferous → Jurassic. (1)

38. Mention the evolutionary significance of the following organisms

(i) Shrews

(ii) Lobefins

(iii) *Homo habilis*

(iv) *Homo erectus*

Ans. (i) Shrews were the first mammals.

(ii) Lobefins are ancestors of modern day frog.

(iii) *Homo habilis* are first hominid, i.e. human-like individuals.

(iv) *Homo erectus* started using tools and fire. (½ × 4)

39. Can we call human evolution as adaptive radiation? **NCERT**

Ans. No, we cannot call human evolution as adaptive radiation because *Homo sapiens* have evolved by progressive evolution from *Homo habilis* and *Homo erectus* lineage.

40. **Try to trace the various components of human evolution (hint : brain size and function, skeletal structure, dietary preference, etc.).** **NCERT**

Ans. With time, the brain size increased quite significantly. Skeletal structures has changed from ape-like, i.e. from a projecting jaw to broad forehead, to a well-developed chin and semi-erect posture provided the ability to walk on their two hindlimbs.

Long Answer Type Questions

1. (i) **How does the study of fossils help to understand evolution?**

(ii) **How did SL Miller provide an experimental evidence in favour of Oparin and Haldane's hypothesis? Explain.**

Ans. (i) Refer to text on page no. 180 and 181. (2½)

(ii) Refer to text on page no. 179-180. (2½)

2. (i) **List any four evidences of evolution.**

(ii) **Explain any one of the evidences that helps to understand the concept of evolution.**

Ans. Refer to text on page no. 180-182. (2+3)

3. **List 10 modern day animals and using the various resources available link it to a corresponding ancient fossil. Name both of them.** **NCERT**

Ans.

Animals	Ancient fossils
Horse	*Eohippus*
Camel	*Paracamelus*
Elephant	*Moeritherium*
Octopus	*Belemnite*
Whale	*Protocetus*
Giraffe	*Palaeotroagus*
Dog	*Leptocyon*
Man	*Ramapithecus*
Chimpanzee	*Dryopithecus*
Gorilla	*Dryopithecus*

(½ × 10)

4. (i) **Differentiate between analogy and homology giving one example each of plant and animal, respectively.**

(ii) **How are they considered as an evidence in support of evolution?** **CBSE 2016**

Ans. Refer to text on page no. 181 and 182. (4+1)

5. **Explain the process of divergent evolution in detail. Also, write down the driving force behind it.**

Ans. Refer to text on page no. 181 and 182

The driving force behind divergent evolution is adaptation to new habitat and changing environmental conditions.

6. (i) **How did Darwin explain adaptive radiation? Give another example exhibiting adaptive radiation.**

(ii) **Name the scientist who influenced Darwin and how?**

Ans. (i) Refer to text on page no. 183. (3½)

(ii) Darwin was influenced by Thomas Robert Malthus, a British economist. He put forward a theory of human population growth. He wrote the book *An Essay on the Principles of Population.* (1½)

7. (i) **Write and explain the conclusion Darwin arrived at, after observing the variations seen in the beaks of finches during his sea voyage.**

(ii) **Marsupials and Australian placental mammals exhibit convergent evolution. Explain how?**

Ans. (i) Refer to text on page no. 183. (2½)

(ii) Refer to text on page no. 183 and 184. (2½)

8. (i) **Explain the observations and the conclusion drawn by Darwin during his visit to Galapagos Islands.**

(ii) **Explain Lamarck's theory of acquired characters.**

Ans. (i) Refer to text on page no. 183. (3)

(ii) Refer to text on page no.186. (2)

9. (i) **How do the observations made during moth collection in pre and post-industrialised area in England support evolution by natural selection?**

(ii) **Explain the phenomenon that is well-represented by Darwin's finches other than natural selection.**

Ans. (i) Refer to text on page no. 185. (2½)

(ii) Refer to text on page no. 183. (2½)

10. **Write about the various theories of evolution.**

Ans. Refer to text on page no. 184-186.

11. **How does the process of natural selection affect Hardy-Weinberg equilibrium? Explain. List the other four factors that disturb the equilibrium.**

Ans. Refer to text on page no. 184-185

12. **Describe the factors that affects Hardy-Weinberg equilibrium.**

Ans. Refer to text on page no. 186 and 187.

13. (i) **Explain Darwinian theory of evolution with the help of one suitable example. State the two key concepts of the theory.**

(ii) **Mention any three characteristics of Neanderthal man that lived in near East and Central Asia.**

Ans. (i) Darwinian theory of evolution states that as a result of struggle for existence, only those organisms survive which have favourable variations.

Refer to text for example, theory of evolution on page no. 184 and 185.

The two key concepts of darkens theory are

(a) Branching of descent

(b) Natural selection (3½)

(ii) Three characteristics of Neanderthal man are

(a) Cranial capacity was 1400 cc and lived around 1,00,000-40,000 years back.

(b) Used hide to protect their body.

(c) Buried their dead. (1½)

14. Write the characteristics of *Ramapithecus, Australopithecines, Homo habilis, Dryopithecus* and Neanderthal man.

Ans. Refer to text on page no. 190. (1 × 5)

Source Based/ Case Based/ Passage Based Questions

1. A group of students perform the following experiment - Three plates of nutrient media were taken - *A, B* and *C* and studied for the extent of microbial growth in the plate post-incubation of 24 hours. **Competency Based Que.**

Plate	Column I (Primates)
A.	The sterile plate was sealed and incubated
B.	The sterile plate was not sealed and incubated
C.	A microbial culture was spread on the plate and it was sealed and incubated

(a) What would be the post-incubation results for the three plates?

(b) Which widely believed theory of the origin of life does this experiment disprove? Justify your answer.

Ans. (a) The post-incubation results for the three plates will be

"A" will show no microbial growth since it was sterile and sealed.

"B" will show microbial growth due to airborne contaminants reaching the nutrient media.

"C" will show microbial growth from the initially spread culture, as the sealed environment would prevent external contaminants from entering. (2)

(b) This experiment disproves the theory of spontaneous generation. The lack of microbial growth on the sterile, sealed plate (*A*) contradicts the idea of life spontaneously forming. (2)

2. Highly conserved proteins such as haemoglobin and cytochrome-*c* provide the best biochemical evidences to trace evolutionary relationships between different groups. Cytochrome-*c* is formed of 104 amino acids. Cytochrome-*c* is the respiratory pigment present in all eukaryotic cells. It has evolved at a constant rate during evolution. In chimpanzees and humans, cytochrome-*c* genes are identical. The given data shows the evolution of the cytochrome-*c* gene in different mammals from kangaroos, cows, rodents to humans **CBSE 2025**

Groups	Nucleotide substitution in the gene of cytochrome-*c*	Millions of years ago
Human/Kangaroo	100	125 mya
Human/Cow	75	120 mya
Human/Rodent	60	75 mya

(i) Select the correct option for the time of separation of two groups and the number of nucleotide substitutions in the gene of cytochrome-*c*.

Options	Time of separation of two groups during evolution	Number of nucleotide substitutions
(a)	Lesser	Greater
(b)	Greater	Lesser
(c)	Greater	Greater

(ii) What do you infer about the type of evolution (convergent or divergent) for the given pair of groups and why?

(a) Human and kangaroo

(b) Human and rodent

(iii) (a) Define convergent evolution.

Or

(b) Define divergent evolution.

Ans. (i) The correct option is (c) Greater-Greater.

The groups that separate earlier in evolution, accumulate more nucleotide substitutions in their cytochrome-*c* gene over time as compare to the group that separate later.

The table shows that human-kangaroo separated 125 mya with 100 substitutions, while human-rodent separated 75 mya with only 60 substitutions.

(ii) (a) Human and kangaroo: Divergent evolution is inferred. Since, humans and kangaroos share a common ancestor, but their lineages have diverged, accumulating differences in their cytochrome-*c* genes over time (125 million years ago).

(b) Human and rodent: Divergent evolution is also inferred. Humans and rodents also share a common ancestor, but their lineages have diverged, accumulating differences in their cytochrome-*c* genes over time (75 million years ago).

(iii) (a) Convergent evolution occurs when unrelated species develop similar traits due to similar environments, resulting in analogous structures. For example, the wings of birds and insects serve the same function, but evolved independently.

Or

(b) Divergent evolution occurs when species evolve from a common ancestor, but develop different traits due to environmental adaptation, leading to homologous structures. Examples include the forelimbs of whales, bats and humans, which share a common structure, but serve different functions. (2½+2½)

3. Refer to the given graph and answer the following questions. Competency Based Que.

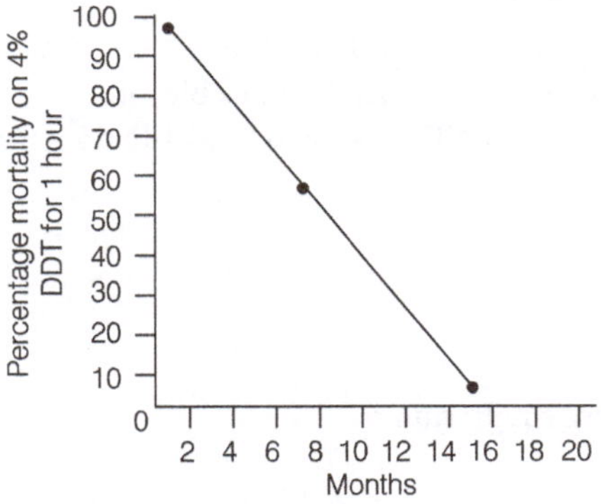

(i) What does the above graph shows?

(ii) Why DDT has now become almost ineffective against mosquitoes?

(iii) How do insects develop resistance to pesticides in terms of natural selection?

Or

(iii) Why is the evolution of pest resistance an example of natural selection caused by humans?

Ans. (i) The graph shows that DDT becomes ineffective quickly. (1)

(ii) DDT has now become almost ineffective against mosquitoes because introduction of DDT brought a change in gene frequency with a shift from DDT sensitive to DDT resistant mosquitoes. (2)

(iii) Selection for resistance can occur if a small proportion of the insect population is able to survive treatment with insecticide. These rare resistant individuals can reproduce and pass on their resistance to the offspring. (1)

Or (iii) We have simply caused pest populations to evolve, unintentionally applying artificial selection in the form of pesticides. Individuals with a higher tolerance for poisons survive and breed and soon resistant individuals out number the ones that can be controlled. (1)

4. A population of a certain plant species inhabits an area with variable water availability. The plant species carries a gene that influences drought resistance, with two alleles, D and d, where D confers extreme drought resistance and d confers poor drought resistance. Plants with the heterozygous genotype (Dd) were able to survive in different water conditions. In a population of 1000 plants, it was found that 250 plants had the DD genotype. Competency Based Que.

(i) Calculate the frequency of the DD, Dd and dd genotypes in the population. Show calculation.

(ii) Which kind of graph would it represent - stabilising, directional or disruptive? Justify your answer.

(iii) Due to climate changes, the frequency of drought periods has increased and the dd genotype is put under selective pressure. At this stage, which kind of graph would it represent - stabilising, directional or disruptive? Justify your answer.

Ans. (i) Frequency of DD = p^2 = 250/1000 = 0.25

p = 0.5

Therefore, q = 1 - p = 1 - 0.5 = 0.5

Frequency of dd = q^2 = 0.25

Frequency of Dd = 2pq = 2*0.5*0.5 = 0.5 (2)

(ii) It would represent stabilising evolution as the DD genotype (extreme drought resistance) and the dd genotype (poor drought resistance) are not favoured due to their disadvantages under varying water availability. The Dd genotype (intermediate drought resistance) has the highest fitness and is favoured, leading to a peak in the middle of the graph. (1)

(iii) In the scenario, where the frequency of drought periods is increasing and the dd genotype is under selective pressure, the situation would most likely represent directional selection. As due to the increased drought periods, the selective pressure will favour genotypes with better drought resistance (like DD and possibly Dd), reducing the frequency of the dd genotype, leading to a directional shift towards the D allele. (1)

SELF ASSESSMENT TEST

Multiple Choice Questions

1. Billions of years ago, when earth had a reducing atmosphere containing methane and ammonia along with high temperatures, the organisms that came to existence would have been
   (a) aerobic and chemo-autotrophic
   (b) anaerobic and chemo-heterotrophic
   (c) aerobic and chemo-heterotrophic
   (d) anaerobic and chemo-autotrophic
2. Homologous structures provide evidence for evolution because they
   (a) perform the same function in different species
   (b) indicate a common ancestry between species
   (c) are formed through convergent evolution
   (d) arise independently in unrelated species
3. The concept of "survival of the fittest" primarily refers to
   (a) the survival of the strongest individuals in a population.
   (b) the reproductive success of individuals best adapted to their environment.
   (c) the longevity of individuals within a species.
   (d) the preservation of species in a stable environment.
4. The Hardy-Weinberg principle is used to describe
   (a) the conditions under which evolution occurs
   (b) the genetic variation in a population at equilibrium
   (c) the process of natural selection in a population
   (d) the effects of mutations on allele frequencies
5. In pigeons, one gene controls the appearance of a crest on the head. The allele C (smooth head) is dominant to allele c (crested head). In a population of pigeons, the frequency of the allele responsible for a smooth head is 0.7 and for a crested head, it is 0.4. Which of the following conditions should be satisfied for the population to be in Hardy-Weinberg equilibrium?
   (a) The sum total of the frequency of C and c' is equal to 1
   (b) The sum total of the frequency of C and c' is less than 1
   (c) The sum total of the frequency of C and c' is more than 1
   (d) Cannot be said without knowing the frequency of Cc' individuals.
6. Which one of the following would lead to deviation from hardy-weinberg equilibrium?
   (a) Random mating
   (b) Lack of mutation
   (c) No gene flow
   (d) Natural selection
7. Which of the following phenomena significantly contributes to speciation?
   (P) Natural selection
   (Q) Genetic drift
   (R) Gene flow
   (S) Geographic isolation
   (T) Stabilising selection
   Choose the correct option
   (a) Q and S
   (b) R and T
   (c) P, Q and S
   (d) Q, R and T

Assertion-Reason Questions

Direction (Q. Nos. 8-11) *In each of the following questions, a statement of Assertion (A) is given followed by corresponding statement of Reason (R). Of the statements, mark the correct answer as*

(a) Both A and R are true and R is the correct explanation of the A.
(b) Both A and R are true, but R is not the correct explanation of the A.
(c) A is true, but R is false.
(d) A is false, but R is true.

8. **Assertion** (A) Homologous structures indicate common ancestry among species.
Reason (R) Homologous structures arise from different evolutionary paths but serve similar functions.

9. **Assertion** (A) The fossil record provides evidence for the theory of evolution.
Reason (R) Fossils show the gradual changes in species over time and the emergence of new species.

10. **Assertion** (A) Natural selection is a primary mechanism of evolution.
Reason (R) Natural selection acts on phenotypic variations that affect survival and reproduction.

11. **Assertion** (A) The number of white winged moths decreased drastically after industrialisation.
Reason (R) The white winged moths did not survived due to predators.

Very Short Answer Type Questions

12. State an example of plant exhibiting divergent evolution.
13. Which evolution is responsible for the existence of bob cat and Tasmanian tiger cat sharing the same habitat.
14. What role does an individual organism play as per Darwin's theory of natural selection?
15. Mention any one reproductive character that make reptile more successful than amphibians.

Short Answer Type Questions

16. What is biogenesis and how does it differ from abiogenesis in the context of the origin of life?
17. Difference between convergent and divergent evolution.
18. What does the following equation $p^2 + 2pq + q^2 = 1$ represents? Explain it.

Long Answer Type Questions

19. Discuss the theories regarding the origin of life on earth.
20. Discuss the mechanisms of evolution, focusing on natural selection, genetic drift and gene flow.
21. Describe the major geological eras of evolution, highlighting significant events and developments in each era.

Case Based Question

22. Study the graph and answer the questions that follows

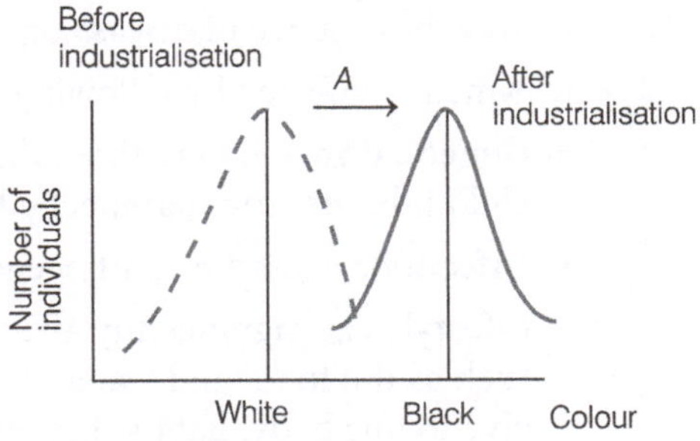

(i) Describe the phenomenon shown in the above graph.
(ii) What proves the above process as observed in pepper moths.
(iii) How would you link the above study with natural selection?

Answers

1. (b) 2. (b) 3. (b) 4. (b) 5. (a) 6. (d) 7. (c) 8. (c)
9. (a) 10. (a) 11. (a)

07

CHAPTER

Health as we know implies the concept of 'being well', in all the aspects of a person's life. With the advancement in science, it was stated that our immune system maintains our health and our mind influences it through the neuro-endocrine system.

YOUR STUDY GOALS

7.1 Health
7.2 Diseases
7.3 Immunity
7.4 Acquired Immuno Deficiency Sydrome (AIDS)
7.5 Cancer
7.6 Adolescence : Drug and Alcohol Abuse

YOUR PRACTICE GOAL

- Objective Type Questions (32 Qs ; MCQs, A-R)
- Case Based Questions (7)
- Subjective Type Questions (16 VSA, 72 SAs, 10 LAs)

Human Health and Diseases

In this chapter, we will be discussing about factors that affect health, common diseases in humans, different types of immunity and immune system, AIDS, cancer, adolescence and drug abuse.

7.1 Health

- According to World Health Organisation (WHO), health is a state of complete physical, mental and social well-being and not merely the absence of disease or physical fitness.
- It is mainly affected by following factors
  - **Genetic disorders** are those disorders deficiencies which the child inherits from parents by birth.
  - **Infections** caused by pathogens.
  - **Lifestyle** can significantly affect health by influencing factors such as the food and water we take, rest and exercise we give to our body, habits that we have or lack, etc.
- Good health can be achieved and maintained by
  - balanced diet, personal hygiene and regular exercise.
  - practicing regular yoga to achieve physical and mental health.
  - awareness about the diseases and their effects on body and its functions.

- vaccination (immunisation) against infectious diseases.
- proper disposal of wastes, control of vectors, maintenance of hygienic food and water resources.
- Schedule regular health check-ups to monitor overall health.

7.2 Disease

- Any change from normal state of the body that causes discomfort or disability in the body is called **disease.**
- In this condition, normal physiological functions of the body or an organ gets disturbed.
- Diseases are characterised by various signs and symptoms.

Types of Diseases

Diseases can be classified in following ways

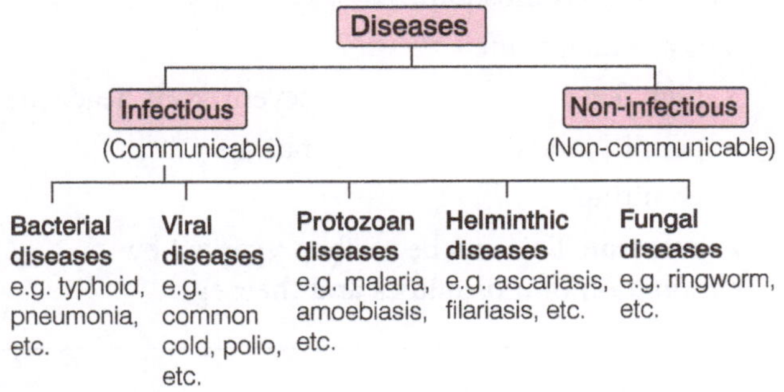

Infectious Diseases

- These diseases can be easily transmitted from one person to another.
- This transmission takes place by two ways, either through **direct transmission**, i.e. directly to human body without the involvement of any intermediate agent, e.g. smallpox or by **indirect transmission**, i.e. carried through intermediate agents called pathogens, e.g. typhoid, HIV.

Pathogens

- Disease causing microorganisms are called pathogens.
- These are of various types *viz.*, bacteria, virus, protozoans, helminthes, fungi, etc.
- Most of the pathogens are parasites. They can cause harm to the organism (host) by either living in (as **endoparasites**) or on them (as **ectoparasite**).
- They can enter the body by various means (air, water, food, etc.), multiply and interfere with the normal vital activities of the body, thus resulting in the morphological and functional damage.
- Certain pathogens can only survive as endoparasites. So, they need to adapt to the life within the environment of the host body.
- For example, pathogens that enter the gut must know a way of surviving in the stomach at low pH and show resistance to the various digestive enzymes.

Non-Infectious Diseases

- These diseases cannot be transmitted from one person to another and are not caused by pathogens.
- They occur either by nutritional deficiencies, malfunctioning of organs, etc., e.g. cancer, scurvy.

Common Infectious Diseases in Humans

On the basis of pathogen, the various infectious diseases as well as their causative agent, transmission, symptoms and preventions are as follows

Bacterial Diseases

Some bacterial diseases are given below

Typhoid

- **Causative agent** is bacterium *Salmonella typhi.*
- **Transmission** It enters the small intestine through contaminated water and food and then migrates to other organs of the body through blood.
- **Symptoms** include
  - high fever (39-40°C)
  - weakness
  - stomach pain
  - constipation
  - headache
  - loss of appetite.
  - In serious cases intestinal perforation and death may occur.
- **Detection** and **diagnosis** of typhoid fever could be confirmed by **Widal test**.

> **A Classic Case in Medicine**
>
> **Mary Mallon**, also named as Typhoid Mary, a cook by profession was a typhoid carrier. She continued to spread typhoid for several years unknowingly through the food she prepared.

Pneumonia

- **Causative agents** of pneumonia are *Streptococcus pneumoniae* and *Haemophilus influenzae.*
- Pneumonia infects alveoli of the lungs due to which alveoli get filled with a fluid thereby, leading to severe problems in breathing and respiration.
- **Transmission** The infection may spread by inhalation of the droplets/aerosols released by an infected person or even by sharing glasses and utensils with an infected person.
- **Symptoms** include
  - fever
  - chills
  - cough
  - headache.
  - In severe cases, lips and finger nails may turn greyish to bluish in colour.
- **Prevention** Avoid sharing personal belongings like glass, towel, clothes, etc., with the infected person. Wear mask to cover nose and mouth before coming in contact with the infected person.
- Dysentry, plague, diphtheria, etc., are some other bacterial diseases in human.

Viral Diseases

Some viral diseases are given below

Common Cold

- It is the most common viral infection found in case of humans.
- **Causative agent** of common cold is rhino virus.
- These viruses majorly affect the **nose** and the **respiratory passage** (but not the lungs).
- **Transmission** Infection is transmitted through droplets released by coughing or sneezing from an infected person, which are either inhaled directly or spread *via* contaminated objects such as pens, books, cups, doorknobs, computer keyboards, etc.
- **Symptoms** include
  - nasal congestion
  - nasal discharge
  - sore throat
  - hoarseness
  - cough
  - headache and tiredness, etc.
- These symptoms usually last for 3-7 days.
- **Prevention** In order to seek prevention from common cold, one should avoid sharing the personal belonging like glass, towel, etc. with an infected person.

While coming in contact with the infected person one should wear mask to cover their nose and mouth.

Chikungunya

- **Causative agent** is chikungunya virus.
- **Transmission** It is eventually transmitted by the bite of *Aedes aegypti* mosquito.
- **Symptoms** include
  - sudden onset of fever,
  - crippling joint pains,
  - nausea, fatigue, etc.
- **Prevention** It can be prevented by elimination of mosquitoes and their eggs.

Dengue Fever

- **Causative agent** of dengue fever is Flavi-ribo virus.
- **Transmission** It is also transmitted by the bite of *Aedes aegypti* mosquito.
- **Symptoms** include
  - high fever
  - severe front headache
  - pain in joints
  - nausea
  - vomiting
- **Prevention** This can be easily prevented by the elimination of mosquitoes and their eggs.

Quick Test 1

1. A person develops a chronic condition due to poor diet and lifestyle, without being exposed to an external pathogen. What type of disease is this?
2. An elderly patient is admitted to the hospital with a high fever, chills and difficulty in breathing. What infection is commonly seen in this cases?
3. **State True or False.**
   Antibiotics are not effective against cold.
4. **State True or False.**
   Both chikungunya and dengue are spread by the same species of mosquito.
5. The symptoms of disease 'X' include pain in joints, headache, vomiting, high fever and nausea. Identify 'X'.

Protozoan Diseases

Some protozoan diseases are given below

Malaria

- **Causative agent** of malaria is *Plasmodium*, a tiny protozoan.

- **Transmission** Its transmitting agent is female *Anopheles* mosquito that transfers the sporozoites of *Plasmodium.*
- Different species of *Plasmodium* are responsible for different types of malaria.
- These species are *P. vivax, P. falciparum* and *P. malariae.*

TEACHER'S TIP

The different species of *Plasmodium* genus have different symptoms of malaria such as *Plasmodium vivax* causes a mild form of malaria, *Plasmodium malariae* causes a milder form of malaria whereas *Plasmodium falciparum* causes the most deadly and prevalent malaria

Life Cycle of *Plasmodium*

The malarial parasite requires two hosts to complete its life cycle

- **Primary** or **definitive host** is the female *Anopheles* mosquito (vector or transmitting agent).
- The intermediate or secondary host is human being.

Life Cycle of *Plasmodium* in Human

- *Plasmodium* enters the human body as **sporozoites** (infectious form) through the bite of an infected female *Anopheles* mosquito.
- These **sporozoites** reach the liver through blood and multiply asexually within the liver cells and attack the Red Blood Cells (RBCs) resulting the rupture of RBC (which furthes infect new RBCs).
- The rupturing of RBCs is associated with the release of a toxin called **haemozoin,** which is responsible for chill (shivering) and the high fever recurring every 3-4 days.
- Gametocytes (sexual stages) develop in the RBCs of human host.

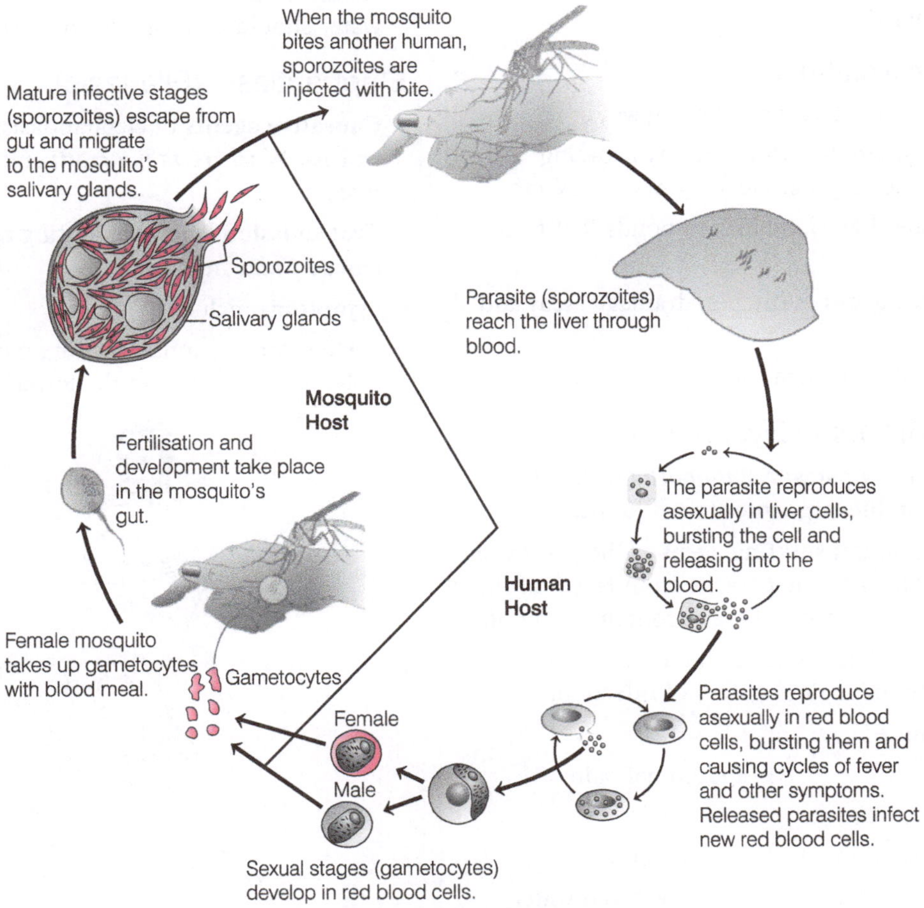

Fig. 7.1 Stages in the life cycle of *Plasmodium*

Life Cycle of *Plasmodium* in Female *Anopheles* Mosquito

- When female *Anopheles* mosquito bites the infected person, the gametocytes of parasite then enter into the mosquito's body alongwith the blood
- Further development occurs in the stomach wall of the mosquito, where the gametes fuse to form a zygote.
- The zygote undergoes further development in the body of the mosquito to form sporozoites.
- These sporozoites are then transported and stored in its salivary glands.
- When these mosquitoes bite a human, the sporozoites are introduced into the human's body through saliva.
- Thus, repeating the above mentioned cycle of events.

Symptoms

It include fever,

- shaking chills
- headache
- muscle ache
- nausea
- vomiting and diarrhoea

Prevention and Treatment

Malaria can be prevented by the following ways

- Controlling mosquito breeding sites by avoiding stagnation of water, regular cleaning of coolers, etc.
- Introducing fishes like *Gambusia* in ponds that feed on mosquito larvae.
- Spraying of insecticides in ditches, drainage areas and swamps, etc.
- By using mosquito repellents and mosquito nets.

Amoebiasis (Amoebic Dysentery)

- **Causative agent** is a parasite *Entamoeba histolytica*, which is found in the large intestine of humans.
- **Transmission** The transmitting agent of the pathogen is housefly. It transmits the parasite from faeces of the infected person to the food, thereby contaminating it.
- Drinking water and eating food contaminated with faecal matter are the major sources of infection.
- **Symptoms** include
  - constipation
  - abdominal pain
  - cramps
  - stools with excess mucus and blood clots.
- **Prevention** Intake of contaminated food and water should be avoided. Cooked food and drinking water should be properly covered.

Helminthic Diseases

Some helminthic diseases are given below

Ascariasis

- **Causative agent** of ascariasis is *Ascaris lumbricoides*, which is an intestinal parasite, commonly known as **roundworm**.
- **Transmission** Ascariasis is transmitted through contaminated water, vegetables, fruits, etc. Exposure to soil, water, plants, etc contaminated with the faeces of an infected person can spread this disease, as it contains the eggs of the parasite.
- **Symptoms** include
  - internal bleeding,
  - muscular pain
  - fever
  - anaemia and blockage of the intestinal passage.
- **Prevention** Intake of contaminated food and water should be avoided. Cooked food and drinking water should be properly covered.

Elephantiasis (Filariasis)

- **Causative agents** of elephantiasis are filarial worms, *Wuchereria bancrofti* and *Wuchereria malayi.*
- **Transmission** The transmitting agent/vector is female *Culex* mosquito.
- **Symptoms** include
  - slow chronic inflammation, mostly in the lymphatic vessels of the lower limbs.

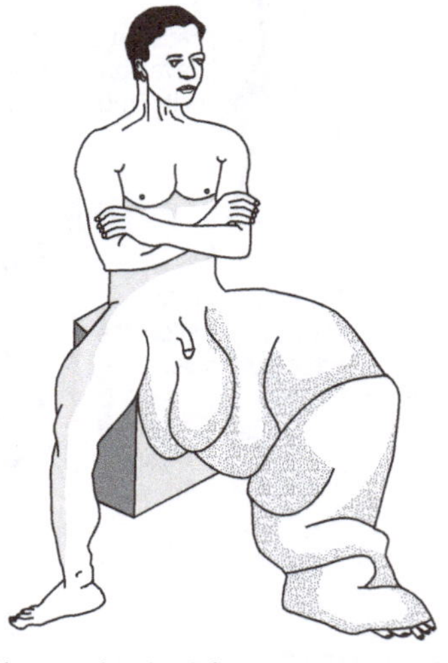

Fig. 7.2 Diagram showing inflammation in one of the lower limbs due to elephantiasis

- Genital organs are also often affected, resulting in gross deformites.
- **Prevention** Control or eliminate the vectors and their breeding places.

Fungal Disease

A common fungal disease is given below

Ringworms

- It is one of the most common infectious disease in man.
- **Causative agents** of ringworms are fungi belonging to genera *Microsporum, Trichophyton* and *Epidermophyton.*
- **Transmission** Ringworms are generally acquired from soil or by direct contact with contaminated articles (such as comb, towels) used by infected person.
- **Symptoms** include
  - dry, scaly lesions on various parts of the body such as skin, nails and scalp with intense itching.
- **Heat** and **moisture** help in growth of the fungi in the folds of skin, e.g. groin area, between the fingers of toe.
- **Prevention** Avoid sharing personal belonging with others.

Common Control Measures for Infectious Diseases

Maintenance of personal and public hygiene is extremely important for prevention and control of many infectious disease.

Some of the preventive measures that can be taken are as follows

- **For food and water borne diseases** like typhoid, amoebiasis, ascariasis.
  - **Maintenance of Personal Hygiene** Keeping the body clean, consumption of clean drinking water, food, vegetables, fruits, etc., prevents from catching several infectious diseases.
  - **Maintenance of Public Hygiene** Proper disposal of waste and excreta, periodic cleaning and disinfection of water reservoirs, pools, cesspools, tanks and observing standard practices of hygiene in public catering will help in preventing the spread of infection.
- **For air-borne diseases** like pneumonia, common cold. In addition to above measures, avoid contact with infected persons or their belongings to prevent catching infection.
- **For vector borne diseases** such as malaria, filariasis, dengue and chikungunya.
  - Eradication of vectors.
  - Destroying their breeding sites will aid in getting rid of such diseases.
- **Vaccination and Immunisation** These programmes for diseases should be strictly followed in order to stay disease free. They have enabled to completely eradicate a deadly disease like smallpox.

Quick Test 2

1. **State True or False.**
   Introducing *Gambusia* fish in ponds helps to reduce the chances of malaria.
2. Name the toxin responsible for appearance of symptoms of malaria in humans.
3. Life cycle of malarial parasite requires two host. Where does the sexual reproduction of malarial parasite takes place.
4. Name the human disease, spread by intake of water and food contaminated by human faecal matter.
5. Identify whether given statement is correct or incorrect. Using public showers without wearing flip-flops increases the risk of contacting ringworm.

7.3 Immunity

- The ability of the body (host) to fight against the disease causing agents is called **immunity**. It is of two types as shown below

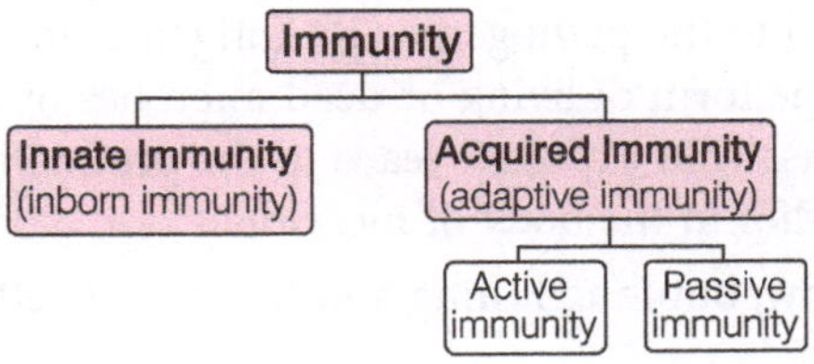

Innate Immunity

It is a non-specific type of defence system with which an individual is born. Innate immunity consists of different types of barrier systems that prevent the entry of pathogen or foreign element into the body.

Types of Barriers in Innate Immunity

Various types of barriers are as given below

- **Physical Barriers** Skin is the first line of defence which prevents the entry of the pathogens into the body. Mucus coating of epithelium lining the respiratory, gastrointestinal and urogenital tracts also helps in trapping microbes in the body.
- **Physiological Barriers** Body temperature, body pH and various body secretions prevent the growth of many harmful microorganisms. For example tears from the eyes, saliva in the mouth, acid in the stomach, etc.
- **Cellular Barriers** These include the special types of cells in our body which kill the disease causing agents. These cells include **WBCs like Polymorpho Nuclear Leukocytes** (PMNL–neutrophils), **monocytes** and **natural killer cells** (type of lymphocytes) in the blood and macrophages in tissues. They can phagocytose and destroy microbes.
- **Cytokine Barriers** Cells which are virus-infected release proteins called **interferons** that protect non-infected cells from further viral infection.

Acquired Immunity

It is pathogen specific immunity which is not present from birth and develops during an individual's lifetime. It is characterised by memory.

Types of Acquired Immunity

Acquired immunity can be classified as

Active Immunity

- It is the immunity developed by the body when it is exposed to the pathogen or its antigens, which may be in the form of living or dead microbes or other proteins. That exposure leads to the production of antibodies in the body of individual.
- It is slow, but long lasting and has no side effects.

Passive Immunity

- The type of immunity where readymade antibodies are directly given to the body in order to protect it against foreign agents. It is fast but lasts only for few days.
- Some examples of passive immunity are
  - Antibodies received by foetus from mother through placenta.
  - Antibodies in the colostrum (IgA rich). **Colostrum** is a yellowish fluid secreted by mother during the initial days of lactation.

Immune Responses

- The immune response is a reaction that occurs in the body as a result of encounter with foreign invaders.
- When the immune system encounters a pathogen for the first time, a **primary response** is produced which is of low intensity.
- On subsequent encounter with the same pathogen, a **secondary** or **anamnestic response** is produced.
- It is of very high intensity because of the memory of first encounter.
- Primary and secondary responses are carried out with the help of two types of lymphocytes, i.e. B-lymphocytes and T-lymphocytes.

Types of Immune Response

On the basis of type of cells produced, the immune responses are of two types

1. Humoral Immune Response

- These are mediated by antibody molecules that are secreted by plasma cells, thus also called **antibody-mediated immune response**.
- **B-lymphocytes** or **B-cells**, produce an army of proteins called **antibodies** in response to pathogens. These antibodies are found in blood.

2. Cell-Mediated Immune (CMI) Response

- It is mediated by T-lymphocytes, which also helps B-lymphocyte to produce antibodies. CMI plays an important role in **organ transplantation** and is responsible for body's ability to differentiate between 'self' and 'non-self'.
- In case of transplantation, the chances of graft rejection are very high. Hence, tissue matching and blood group matching are essential before transplantation of any organ or tissue.
- Even after successful transplant, the patient has to take immuno-suppressants throughout his/her life.

Antigens and Antibodies

- **Antigens** Substances that stimulate the production of antibodies upon entering the body.
- **Antibodies** Immunoglobulins (class of proteins) produced in response to antigenic stimulation.

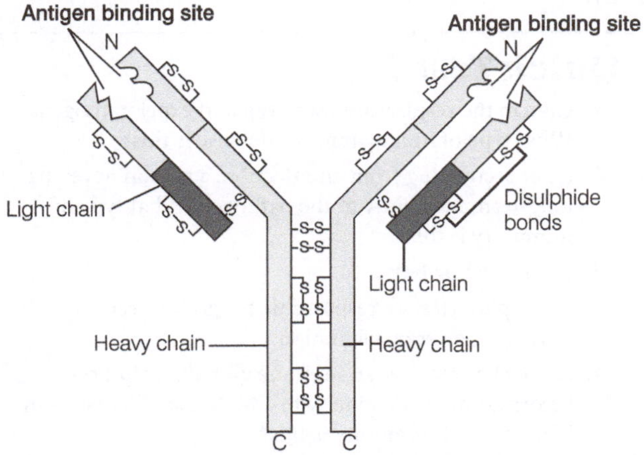

Fig. 7.3 Structure of an antibody molecule

- Each antibody molecule has four peptide chains, out of which two small chains are called **Light** (L) **chains** and two large chains are called **Heavy** (H) **chains**. Thus, an antibody is represented as H_2L_2.
- In human body, different types of antibodies are produced such as, IgG, IgA, IgM, IgE and IgD.

Vaccination and Immunisation

- The process of introducing antigenic proteins of a pathogen or an inactivated or weakened pathogen (vaccine), into the body to provide protection against a disease is called **vaccination.**
- **Immunisation** is the process by which the body produces antibodies against these antigens and develops the ability to neutralise pathogens during actual infection in the body (secondary response).
- The principle of immunisation or vaccination is based on the property of 'memory' of the immune system.
- Vaccine generates memory B and T-cells that recognise the pathogens quickly on subsequent exposure and produce an intense immune response by massive production of antibodies.
- Cases where quick immune response is required as in fatal infections like tetanus or snake bite, pre-formed antibodies or antitoxin (a preparation, containing antibodies to the toxin) are injected into the patient. This is called **passive immunisation.**
- Recombinant DNA technology has produced antigenic polypeptides of pathogen in bacteria or yeast. This allowed large scale production of vaccines, e.g. hepatitis-B vaccine produced from yeast.

Immune System in the Body

- Human immune system consists of lymphoid organs, tissues, immune cells and soluble molecules like antibodies.
- It has unique features of memory and identification of a large number of pathogens or antigens.
- Its main function is to recognise the foreign molecules (antigens), respond to them and to keep memory of these encounters.
- It also plays a crucial role in organ transplantation, allergic reactions and autoimmune diseases (explained later).

Lymphoid Organs

These are the organs where lymphocytes originate, proliferate and get matured. They can be categorised as

Primary Lymphoid Organs

In primary lymphoid organs, immature lymphocytes differentiate into mature, antigen sensitive lymphocytes. After maturation, lymphocytes migrate to secondary lymphoid organs.

The two primary lymphoid organs are as follows

1. Bone Marrow

It is the main lymphoid organ where all the blood cells including lymphocytes are produced. It is the major site of B-lymphocytes development and maturation.

2. Thymus

- It is a lobed organ, located near the heart and beneath the breastbone.
- It is large at the time of birth, but with age, the size keeps on reducing and becomes very small by the time puberty is attained.

- Both bone marrow and thymus provide micro-environments for the development and maturation of T-lymphocytes.

Secondary Lymphoid Organs

After maturation the B and T-lymphocytes move to secondary lymphocyte organs where they proliferated and differentiated. These organs also provide the sites for interaction of lymphocytes with the antigen.

The secondary lymphoid organs are as follows

1. Spleen

It is a large bean-shaped organ containing lymphocytes, phagocytes and large number of erythrocytes. It filtres the blood by trapping blood-borne microorganisms.

2. Lymph Nodes

- These are small solid structures located at different points along the lymphatic system. Their function is to trap the microorganisms or other antigens that enter the lymph and tissue fluid.
- Trapped antigens in the lymph nodes are responsible for the activation of lymphocytes present there and cause the immune response.
- Peyer's patches of small intestine, tonsils and appendix are secondary lymphoid organs.

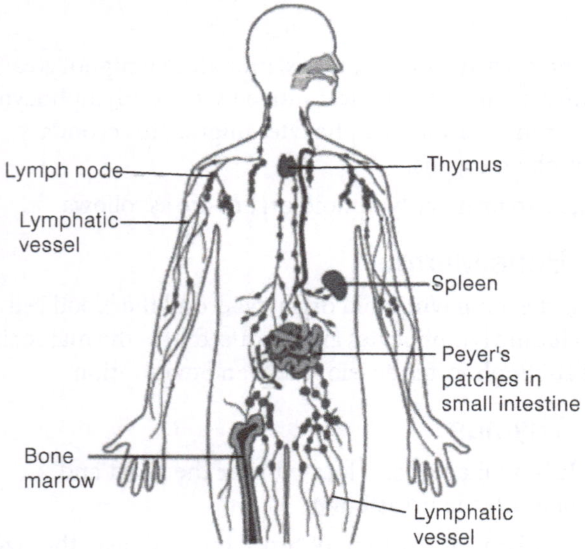

Fig. 7.4 Diagrammatic representation of human lymphatic system

3. Mucosal Associated Lymphoid Tissue (MALT)

It is located within the lining of major tracts in the body like respiratory, digestive, urogenital tracts. MALT constitutes about 50% of the lymphoid tissue in human body.

Quick Test 3

1. Cilia in the respiratory tract trap and expel pathogens. What type of innate immune defense is this?
2. After recovering from an infection, a person develops long-term immunity to the pathogen. What type of immunity is this?
3. **State True or False.**
   T-lymphocytes are responsible for graft rejection during organ transplantation.
4. A traveller receives an immune globulin injection before going to a region with a high risk of hepatitis-A. What type of immunity is this?
5. **State True of False.**
   Can removing the tonsils result in a higher susceptibility to infections.

Disorders of Immune System

Malfunctioning of the immune system is seen in following disorders

1. Allergies

- The exaggerated or hypersensitive response of the immune system to certain antigens present in the environment is called **allergy**.
- The agents that cause allergy are called **allergens** such as dust, mites, pollens, animal dander (old skin scales which are constantly shed), etc.
- The antibodies produced in response to allergens are of IgE type.
- **Symptoms** of allergic reaction include
  - sneezing
  - watery eyes
  - rashes
  - running nose
  - difficulty in breathing, etc.

- **Treatment** Allergy occurs due to the release of chemicals like histamine and serotonin from the mast cells. Thus, the drugs like anti-histamine, adrenaline and steroids quickly reduce the symptoms of allergy.
- Now-a-days, allergies are very common especially in children of metro cities which is a result of high sensitivity and lowering of immunity. It is due to the protected environment provided early in life.
- For determining the cause of allergy, the patient is exposed to or injected with very small doses of possible allergens and the reactions are studied.

2. Autoimmunity

- It is the memory-based acquired immunity in which an organism has the ability to differentiate between foreign organisms and self cells.
- Sometimes the body loses the ability to distinguish between self and non-self cells.
- The body's immune system goes off the track and start destroying self cells and molecules.
- This causes damage to the body resulting in **autoimmune diseases**, e.g. rheumatoid arthritis.

7.4 Acquired Immuno Deficiency Syndrome (AIDS)

- The word AIDS refers to the deficiency of immune system, that is acquired during an individual's life time. It is called a **syndrome** because it includes a group of symptoms associated with the disease.
- It is caused by **Human Immunodeficiency Virus** (HIV), which is a member of a group of viruses, called **retrovirus** which have an envelope enclosing the RNA genome.
- AIDS was first reported in 1981.

HIV Transmission

- It spreads only through body fluids. HIV gets transmitted generally by
  - sexual contact with infected person.
  - through infected needles especially in case of intravenous drug abusers.
  - transfusion of contaminated blood and blood products.
  - from infected mother to her child through placenta.
- HIV/AIDS is not transmitted by mere touch or any physical contact. It is hence, imperative for the physical and psychological well-being, that HIV/AIDS person should not be isolated from family and society.

High Risk Individuals

People at higher risk of getting infection includes

- Individuals who have multiple sexual partners.
- Drug addicts who take intravenous drugs.
- Individuals who require repeated blood transfusion.
- Children born to HIV infected mothers.

Life Cycle of HIV

- Virus enters into macrophages after entering body of the person.
- In macrophages the RNA genome gets replicated to form viral DNA by the enzyme **reverse transcriptase**.
- Viral DNA gets incorporated into the host cell's DNA and directs the infected cells to produce new viruses.
- Macrophages continue to produce virus particles, thus acting as HIV factory.
- At the same time, virus particles enter into helper T-lymphocytes (T_H cells) in the blood, where they continue to replicate and produce viral progenies.
- The progeny viruses released into the blood attack other T_H cells. Number of helper T-lymphocytes progressively decreases in the body of the infected person.
- The person experiences bouts of fever, diarrhoea and weight loss during this period.
- As the number of T-cells decreases, the immunity also decreases. As a result, affected individual cannot produce any immune response even against common bacteria like *Mycobacterium*, parasite like *Toxoplasma*, viruses and fungi.

- Therefore, there is always a time lag between infection and appearance of AIDS symptoms. This time lag can be from few months to many years (mostly 5-10 years).

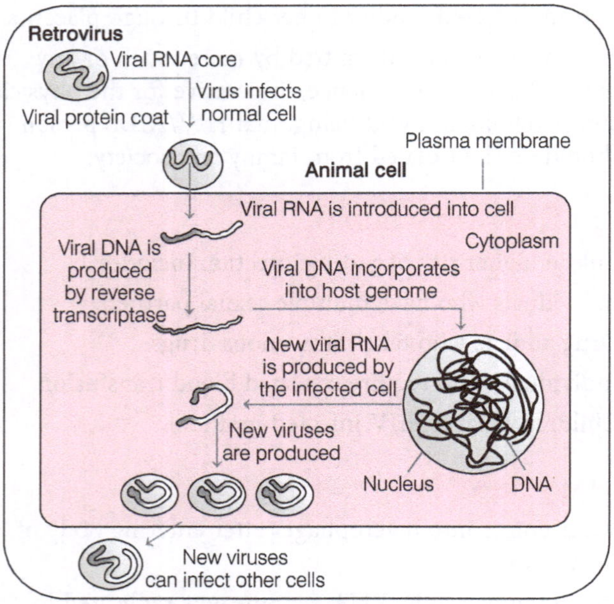

Fig. 7.5 Replication of retrovirus in a host cell

Note Infected cell can survive, while viruses are being replicated and released.

Diagnosis of AIDS

There are several methods for the diagnosis of HIV infection such as viral culture, **Enzyme Linked Immuno Sorbent Assay** (ELISA), PCR test, Western blotting, etc.

Treatment of AIDS

It has no cure. Use of anti-retroviral drugs can only prolong the life of the patient, but cannot prevent death, that is unavoidable.

Prevention of AIDS

- Awareness and precautions are the only option to prevent AIDS.
- In India, **National AIDS Control Organisation** (NACO) and many other NGOs are doing a lot to spread awareness.
- WHO has started a number of programmes to prevent the spread of HIV.

Some main strategies of prevention are as follows

- Ensuring that blood in blood bank is safe from HIV.
- Use of only disposable needles and syringes in public and private hospitals and clinics.
- Free distribution of condoms and advocating safe sex.
- Controlling drug abuse.
- Promoting regular check-ups for HIV in susceptible people.

7.5 Cancer

- It is one of the most dreaded diseases and is a major cause of death across the globe.
- The mechanism underlying the development of cancer or oncogenic transformation of cells, its treatment and control are some of the most intensely researched area in biology and medicine.

Biology of Cancer

- In normal cells, growth and differentiation is highly controlled and regulated. They show the property of contact inhibition by virtue of which contact with other cells stops their uncontrolled growth.
- Cancerous cells do not have this property. As a result, such cells continue to divide, producing a mass of cells called **tumours**. There is a breakdown of regulatory mechanisms in cancer cells.

Tumour

- It is an unorganised mass of cells, formed due to the uncontrolled division of cells.
- The tumour cells actively divide and grow they also starve the normal cells by competing for vital nutrients.
- Tumours are characteristic signs of cancerous growth. These are broadly divided into two major types

Benign tumour	Malignant tumour
It is non-cancerous.	It is cancerous.
It remain confined to its original location and do not spread to other parts of the body.	It is a mass of proliferating cells called neoplastic or tumour cells which grow very rapidly, invading and damaging the surrounding tissue.
It is less fatal to the body.	It is more fatal to the body.

- The cells of malignant tumour reach other regions of the body through blood flow and wherever they get lodged, they start a new tumour.

- This property is called **metastasis.** It is the most dangerous property of malignant tumours.

Causes of Cancer

Cancer causing agents are called **carcinogens.** They can be of the following types

- **Physical Agents** These include ionising radiations like X-rays, γ-rays and non-ionising radiations like UV-rays. These radiations can cause DNA damage leading to the neoplastic transformation.
- **Chemical Agents** These are present in tobacco smoke (major cause of lung cancer), benzene fumes, etc.
- **Biological Agents** These are cancer causing viruses called **oncogenic viruses.** They have genes called **viral oncogenes.**

  Certain other genes called **cellular oncogenes** (*c-onc*) or **proto-oncogenes** have been identified in normal cells, which when activated can lead to the tumour formation.

Cancer Detection and Diagnosis

Cancer should be detected early for its successful treatment. It can be detected by the following methods

- **Blood** and **bone marrow** tests to know increase in number of cell counts as in leukemia.
- **Biopsy** of a piece of suspected tissue is done by cutting it into thin sections, then staining and examining them under the microscope (histopathological studies).
- **Radiography** by X-rays, is done to detect cancer of the internal organs.
- **Computed Tomography** (CT) is done to generate a 3-D image of internal tissue by using X-rays.
- **Magnetic Resonance Imaging** (MRI) involves the use of non-ionising radiations and strong magnetic fields to detect pathological and physiological changes in a living tissue.
- **Antibodies** against cancer-specific antigens are also used for the cancer detection.
- **Molecular biology** can be applied to detect genes in individuals with inherited susceptibility to certain cancers.

Treatment of Cancer

Most cancers are treated by the combination of procedures, surgery, radiotherapy, chemotherapy and immunotherapy. These are explained below

- **Surgery** Tumours are removed by surgery to check further spread of cancer cells.
- **Radiotherapy** Tumour cells are irradiated by lethal doses of radiation while protecting the surrounding normal cells.
- **Chemotherapy** Several chemotherapeutic drugs are used to kill cancer cells. But their side effects like hair loss, anaemia are also reported. Some of these are specific for a particular tumour.
- **Immunotherapy** Biological response modifiers like **α-interferons** are used to activate the immune system and help in destroying the tumour.

Quick Test 4

1. A child experiences asthma symptoms after exposure to dust mites. What type of immune reaction is this?
2. A person's immune system becomes severely compromised due to the destruction of T-cells. What condition does this describe?
3. **State True or False.**

   In HIV infection, symptoms of AIDS appear immediately after the virus enters the body.
4. A patient experiences symptoms like weight loss, fatigue and pain due to a rapidly expanding tumour that invades nearby organs. What type of tumour does this describe?
5. Cancer detection using antibodies can only identify cancers that have already spread to other organs. Identify whether the given statement is correct or not.

7.6 Adolescence : Drug and Alcohol Abuse

- Adolescence refers to the period between 12-18 years of age, bridging the childhood and adulthood.
- It is a very vulnerable phase of mental and psychological development of an individual.
- In this age, use of drugs or alcohol occurs out of curiosity or experimentation which later turns to addiction.

- Drugs and alcohol when taken for the purpose other than medicine or taken in amounts or frequencies that disturbs the physical or psychological functions of body, then the condition is called **drug abuse** and **alcohol abuse**, respectively.

Drugs

The sources of drugs are mainly flowering plants and some fungi. They fall into following categories

Opioids

- It is white, crystalline, odourless and bitter compound.
- **Source** Heroin, commonly called smack (diacetylmorphine) is obtained by acetylation of morphine.
- Morphine is extracted from the latex of poppy plant *Papaver somniferum.*
- **Mode of Intake** Generally taken by snorting and injection.
- **Mode of Action** Opioids or opiates are the drugs that bind to specific opioid receptors present in our central nervous system and gastrointestinal tract.
- **Effects** Heroin slows down the body function as it is a depressant.

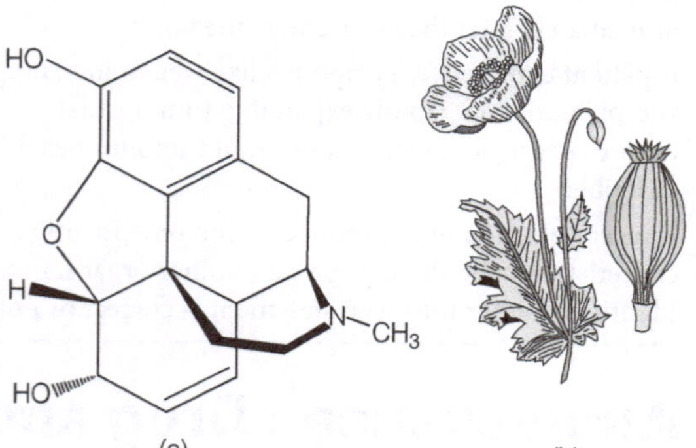

Fig. 7.6 (a) Chemical structure of morphine, (b) Opium poppy

Note Morphine is a very effective sedative and painkiller and is very useful in patients who have undergone surgery.

Cannabinoids

- **Source** Natural cannabinoids are obtained from the inflorescences of the plant *Cannabis sativa*. The flower tops, leaves and resins of *Cannabis* are used in various combinations for production of marijuana, hashish, charas and ganja.
- **Mode of Intake** These drugs are taken by inhalation and oral ingestion.
- **Mode of Action** Cannabinoid drugs bind to cannabinoid receptors present in the brain.
- **Effects** They affect cardiovascular system of the body. They are also being abused by some sport persons.

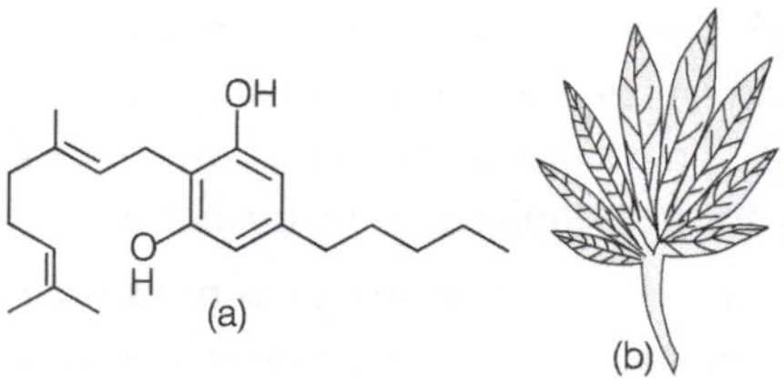

Fig. 7.7 (a) Skeletal structure of cannabinoid molecule (b) Leaves of *Cannabis sativa*

Coca Alkaloid or Cocaine

- It is commonly known as **coke** or **crack**
- **Source** It is obtained from the coca plant *Erythroxylum coca*, native to South America.
- **Mode of Intake** Usually taken up by snorting.
- **Mode of Action** Cocaine interferes with the transport of dopamine which is a neurotransmitter.
- **Effects** It stimulates the central nervous system and produces a sense of euphoria and excess of energy. Excessive dosage of cocaine cause hallucinogens.

Hallucinogens

- **Source** These are obtained from plants like *Atropa belladonna* and *Datura* species.
- **Mode of Action** These drugs act upon the cerebrum and sense organs.
- Drugs like barbiturates, amphetamines, benzodiazepines and other similar drugs, that are normally used as medicines to help patients cope with mental illnesses like depression and insomnia, are often abused.

Fig 7.8 Flowering branch of *Datura*

Tobacco

- **Source** It is obtained from tobacco plant.
- **Mode of Intake** It is smoked, chewed or used as a snuff.
- **Mode of Action** Tobacco contains large number of chemical substance which include nicotine, an alkaloid. Nicotine stimulates the adrenal gland to release adrenaline and nor-adrenaline into blood circulation resulting in increasing the blood pressure and heart rate.
- **Effects** Tobacco chewing has some adverse effects on health.
  - Tobacco can induce lung cancer.
  - Cancer of urinary bladder and throat.
  - Bronchitis
  - Emphysema
  - Coronary heart disease
  - Gastric ulcer
  - Oral cancer
  - Cause oxygen deficiency in the body by increasing carbon monoxide (CO) content in blood and reduces the concentration of haem-bound oxygen.

Reasons for Taking Drugs and Alcohol

Adolescents take drugs/alcohol due to following reasons

- Social and peer pressure.
- Curiosity and need for adventure and experiment.
- To avoid stress, depression and frustation.
- Stress, from pressures to excel in academics or examinations.
- Perception that it is cool or progressive. This perception is further promoted by TV, movies, newspapers and internet.

Addiction and Dependence

There are the two basic parameters which force a person to become addicted to one or the other forms of drugs.

Addiction

- It is a psychological attachment to certain effects such as euphoria and temporary feeling of well-being associated with drugs and alcohol.
- It makes the person to take up drugs on regular basis, even when they are not needed or even when their use becomes self-destructive.
- The repeated use of drugs and alcohol increases the tolerance level of the receptors present in the body.
- As a result, the receptors respond only to higher doses of drugs or alcohol leading to greater intake and addiction.
- Drugs consumed even once can cause addiction and pull the user in a vicious circle leading to regular abuse.

Dependence

- It is the tendency of the body to show unpleasant and characteristic **withdrawal syndrome**, if the dose of alcohol or drug is discontinued abruptly.
- Withdrawal symptoms include anxiety, shakiness, nausea and sweating.
- These may sometimes be life threatening too.
- Dependency pushes the person away from social norms and leads to social adjustment problems.

Effects of Drug and Alcohol Abuse

Effects of drug and alcohol abuse can be classified into two categories

Immediate Effects

- Reckless behaviour, vandalism and violence. Respiratory and heart failure, cerebral haemorrhage due to excessive doses of drugs may also lead to coma and death.
- Aggressive and rebellious behaviour, depression, fatigue, withdrawal and isolation.
- Deteriorating relationships with family and friends.
- Changes in sleeping pattern, fluctuation in weight, appetite and lack of personal hygiene.
- Drop in academic performance of students, absence from school /college and loss of interest in hobbies.

Far-Reaching Implications

- Habit of stealing on not getting money to buy drugs, alcohol, etc.
- Mental and financial distress not only to the addict, but to his/her entire family and friends as well.

- Alcohol use in adolescence may lead to heavy drinking in adulthood.
- Chronic use damages the nervous system and causes liver **cirrhosis.**
- Higher risk of infections like AIDS and hepatitis-B, which transmits through sharing of infected needle and syringes or sexual contact.
- The use of drugs and alcohol during pregnancy is also known to have adverse effects on foetus.
- Sports persons take up certain drugs, like narcotic analgesics, anabolic steroids, diuretics , etc., in order to enhance their performance. These drugs increase the muscle strength, thus increasing atheletic performance.
- These anabolic steroids have many side effects that may be permanent with prolonged use. In adolescents, severe facial and body acne, and premature closure of the growth centres of the long bone may result in stunted growth.

Side Effects of Drugs (Anabolic Steroids)

On male	On female
Acne, increased aggressiveness, mood swings, depression.	Masculinisation (features like males).
Reduction in the size of testicles.	Increased aggressiveness.
Decreased sperm production.	Mood swings and depression.
Potential for liver and kidney dysfunction.	Abnormal menstrual cycle.
Breast enlargement, premature baldness.	Excessive hair growth on the face and body.
Enlargement of prostate gland.	Enlargement of clitoris and deepening of voice.

Prevention and Control

- Prevention is always better than cure especially in case of drugs and alcohol abuse. People get addicted to drugs and alcohol at a young age. Therefore, parents and teachers have a very significant role in prevention and control of drug abuse.
- Some of the measures that will help in preventing the problem of drug and alcohol abuse among adolescents are

(i) **Avoid Undue Peer Pressure** Parents must understand the abilities and personality type of the child. A child should not be pushed unduly for studies or sports or other activities. Pressure from parents and teacher beyond threshold is not healthy for children.

(ii) **Education and Counselling** Parents and teachers should educate and counsel the child to face difficult situations as part of life.

Stress, disappointments and failure must be taken in a healthy way. Involvement in extra-curricular activities is a good distraction from daily stress. It channelise the child's energy in right direction.

(iii) **Seeking Help from Parents and Peers** In case of any academic or emotional problem, advice and guidance should be sought out from parents or trusted friends.

Besides solving problems, it also helps in venting out feelings of anxiety, fear and guilt.

(iv) **Looking for Danger Signs** Danger signs must be brought in light and must be told to parents and teachers if one find someone using drugs or alcohol. There should be no hesitation in informing the elders about this.

This helps in preventing the person from drug abuse and initiating remedial steps.

(v) **Seeking Professional and Medical Help** Affected people have a lot of help available in the form of doctors, psychologists, psychiatrists and rehabilitation programmes.

An addicted person can get completely rid of the problem and lead a perfectly normal and healthy life by getting help.

Quick Test 5

1. The drug '*X*' is prescribed to a patient for pain relief after surgery to reduce pain perception. What class of drug is '*X*'?
2. A sports person uses a substance derived from the coca plant to enhance performance by stimulating the central nervous system. What is this substance?
3. **State True or False.**
   Chewing tobacco can lead to emphysema and increase the risk of bladder cancer.
4. A heavy drinker suddenly quits alcohol and experiences symptoms like anxiety, tremors, and confusion. What condition is this person likely experiencing?
5. Anabolic steroids can increase masculinity in females. Is the given statement correct or incorrect.

Mind Map

Human Health and Diseases

Health

It is a state of complete physical, mental and social well-being and not merely the absence of disease.

Diseases

Condition of body or organ in which normal functions are disturbed or deranged.

Types of Diseases

- Communicable Disease (Infectious)
- Non-communicable Disease (Non-infectious)
- Congenital Disease (Genetic disorder)

Type	Diseases	Causal Organisms
Bacterial	Typhoid (Widal test)	*Salmonella typhi*
Bacterial	Pneumonia	*Streptococcus pneumoniae* *Haemophilus influenzae*
Viral	Common cold	Rhino viruses
Helminthic	Ascariasis	*Ascaris* (Intestinal parasite)
Helminthic	Filariasis (Elephantiasis)	Filarial worms or *Wuchereria* (*W. bancrofti* and *W. malayi*)
Fungal	Ringworm	*Microsporum*, *Trichophyton* and *Epidermophyton*
Protozoans	Amoebiasis (Amoebic dysentery)	*Entamoeba histolytica*
Protozoans	Malaria	*Plasmodium* sp. (*P. vivax*, *P. malariae* and *P. falciparum* ; fatal)

Cancer

- An uncontrolled proliferation of cells without any differentiation; shows no contact inhibition.

Types of Tumour (Masses of Cell)

- **Benign Tumour** Remains confined to their location and cause little damage.
- **Malignant Tumour** Neoplastic cell, grows very rapidly, invading and damaging surrounding normal tissue (metastasis).

Causes of Cancer

Agent Carcinogens
- Ionising radiation (X-rays and gamma rays)
- Non-ionising radiation (UV rays)
- Tobacco smoke

Detection
- Biopsy
- Histopathological studies

Treatment
- Immunotherapy
- Biological modifiers (α-interferon)
- Chemotherapy
- Radiation therapy

AIDS

- Syndrome caused by **HIV virus** (member of retrovirus).
- Generally transmitted by sexual contact, sharing infected needles, transfusion of blood and from infected mother to child through placenta.
- HIV virus enter the **macrophages,** where RNA replicates producing many particles. These enter T_H **cells** and decrease their number, thus decreasing immunity.

Adolescence and Drug/Alcohol Abuse

- **Adolescence Period :** 12-18 years
- **Addiction :** Physiological attachment to certain effects such as euphoria.
- **Withdrawal Syndrome :** If regular dose of drugs/alcohol is abruptly discontinued.
- **Effects :** More likely to acquire serious infections; damages nervous system and liver (cirrhosis).
- **Prevention :** Avoid undue peer pressure, education and counselling, seek help from parents and peers, looking for danger sign, seeking professional and medical help.

Immunity

- It is the ability of the body to fight against disease causing agents.
- It is of two types
  - **Innate Immunity** Present at the time of birth, inherited from parents. Four types are physical, physiological, cellular and cytokine barriers.
  - **Acquired Immunity** Developed during the lifetime. Specificity and memory are its characters.
- It is further of two types as : active and passive.

Immune Responses

- Two types, i.e. primary (encounter with pathogen for first time) and secondary (subsequent encounter).
- Lymphocytes involved are B-cells and T-cells.
- **Antibodies** Protein molecules, represented as H_2L_2. Five types of antibodies are IgG, IgM, IgA, IgE and IgD.

Vaccination and Immunisation

- **Vaccination** Introduction of vaccine into an individual to provide protection against a disease; extract of dead/attenuated pathogen.
- **Immunisation** Body produces antibodies against the preventable diseases through administration of specific vaccines.

Immune System in the Body

- **Human Immune System** Lymphoid organs, tissues, cells and antibodies.
- **Lymphoid Organs** Organs where origin and/or maturation and proliferation of lymphocyte occur.

Primary Lymphoid Organ

- **Bone Marrow** Main lymphoid organs : Blood cells and lymphocytes are produced.
- **Thymus** Lobed organ; near heart beneath breast bone, reduce in size with age.

Secondary Lymphoid Organ

- Spleen (Large reservior of erythrocytes)
- Lymph nodes (trap microorganisms)
- Peyer's patches of small intestine, appendix.
- **Lymphoid Tissue** Within the lining of the major tracts (respiratory, digestive and urogenital tract) called **MALT** (Mucosa Associated Lymphoid Tissue); (50% of lymphoid tissue)

Drugs

Addictive substances or Habituating substances.

Drugs	Sources	Examples
Opioids	Latex of poppy plant, *Papaver somniferum*	Morphine, heroin/smack (diacetylmorphine)
Cannabinoids	Inflorescence, flower tops, leaves and resin of *Cannabis* plant	Charas, hashish, ganja, marijuana
Stimulants	Coca plant, *Erythroxylum coca* (Native of South America)	Cocaine, coka, alkaloid, commonly called coke/crack
Hallucinogens	*Atropa belladona*	Cocaine
Other drugs	Synthetic	Barbiturates, benzodiazepines, amphetamines

EXAM PATTERN QUESTIONS

Objective Type Questions

Multiple Choice Questions

1. Which of the following systems affect and maintain our health?

(a) Neural system, immune system and circulatory system
(b) Neural system, endocrine system and circulatory system
(c) Immune system, endocrine system and neural system
(d) Immune system, endcorine system and digestive system

Ans. (*c*)

2. Fever, delirium, stomach pain and loss of appetite indicate the disease

(a) typhoid (b) measles
(c) tetanus (d) chicken pox

Ans. (*a*) Fever, delirium, slow pulse, abdominal tenderness and a rose-coloured rash indicate typhoid fever. Typhoid is a bacterial infection caused by *Salmonella typhi.*

3. Select the pathogen mismatched with the symptoms of disease caused by it from the given below. **CBSE 2023**

(a) *Entamoeba histolytica* : Constipation, abdominal pain
(b) *Epidermophyton*: Dry scaly lesions on nail
(c) *Wuchereria bancrofti* : Chronic inflammation of lymphatic vessels of lower limb
(d) *Haemophilus influenzae* : Blockage of the intestinal passage

Ans. (*d*)

4. Name the stage of malarial parasite that is responsible for infecting humans.

(a) Trophozoite (b) Gametocyte
(c) Gametophyte (d) Sporozoite

Ans. (*d*)

5. Which one of the following is not correctly matched?

(a) *Glossina palpalis* – Sleeping sickness
(b) *Culex pipiens* – Filariasis
(c) *Aedes aegypti* – Yellow fever
(d) *Anopheles* – Dengue

Ans. (*d*) Female *Anopheles* is a carrier of the protozoan *Plasmodium* that causes malaria.

6. The mosquito-borne disease in humans causing chromic inflammation of the lymphatic vessels is

(a) elephantiasis (b) ascariasis
(c) ringworm (d) amoebiasis

Ans. (*a*)

7. In which of the following option the two examples are correctly matched with their particular type of immunity.

	Examples	Types of immunity
(a)	Saliva in mouth and tears in eyes	Physical barriers
(b)	Mucus coating of epithelium lining the urogenital tract and HCl in stomach	Physiological barriers
(c)	PMNL and monocytes	Cellular barrier
(d)	Anti-tetanus and anti snake bite injection	Active barriers

Ans. (*c*)

8. The decrease in the T-lymphocytes count in human blood will result in **CBSE 2023**

(a) decrease in antigens (b) increase in antibodies
(c) decrease in antibodies (d) increase in antigens

Ans. (*c*) A decrease in the T-lymphocyte count in human blood will result in a decrease in antibodies. T-lymphocytes cells help to activate other immune cells such as B-lymphocytes, which produce antibodies. When the T-lymphocyte count decreases, B-lymphocytes are actively loss which leads to decrease in antibody production.

9. Immuno-suppressants are administered to patients post-organ transplantation and also to those suffering from auto-immune disorders. In which of the following ways are immuno-suppressants helpful? **Competency Based Que.**

(a) They trigger allergic response
(b) They eliminate unhealthy tissues
(c) They control the cell-mediated response
(d) They differentiate between self and non-self parts of the body

Ans. (*c*)

10. Tetanus antitoxin (Tetanus toxoid) when injected into the human body it immediately provides **CBSE 2023**

(a) innate immunity (b) passive immunity
(c) auto immunity (d) active immunity

Ans. (*b*)

11. As a part of increasing immunity against COVID-19, a small part of the virus is administered to people as a vaccine. Which of the following types of immunity is the above an example of? Competency Based Que.

(a) Naturally acquired active immunity
(b) Naturally acquired passive immunity
(c) Artificially acquired active immunity
(d) Artificially acquired passive immunity

Ans. (*c*)

12. Column I lists the components of body defence and Column II lists the corresponding descriptions. Match the two columns and choose the correct option from codes given below.

	Column I		Column II
A.	Active natural immunity	1.	Injection of gamma globulins
B.	First line of defence	2.	Complement proteins and interferons
C.	Passive natural immunity	3.	Direct contact with the pathogens that have entered inside the body
D.	Second line of defence	4.	Surface barriers
		5.	Antibodies transferred through the placenta

Codes

	A	B	C	D
(a)	4	3	5	2
(b)	3	4	2	5
(c)	3	4	5	2
(d)	5	3	2	1

Ans. (*c*)

13. Colostrum secreted by the mother's mammary glands in a human female during the initial days of lactation is rich in antibody. CBSE 2025

(a) IgE (b) IgD
(c) IgA (d) IgG

Ans. (*c*) Colostrum is rich in IgA, which provides passive immunity to the newborn.

14. The large bean-shaped organ acting as a filter of the blood in humans is CBSE 2025

(a) Liver (b) Thymus (c) Spleen (d) Heart

Ans. (*c*) The spleen, a large bean-shaped organ, filters blood by removing old RBCs, recycling iron, storing platelets and WBCs, and aiding immune responses.

15. Interferons are proteins. In humans they are secreted by CBSE 2023

(a) thymus gland (b) B-lymphocytes
(c) viral infected cells (d) tonsils

Ans. (*c*)

16. Given below is the diagrammatic representation of lymphatic system. Competency Based Que.

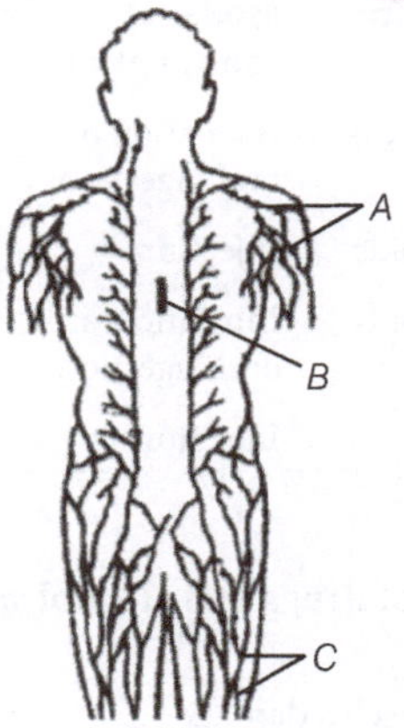

Label *A*, *B* and *C*.

(a) *A*–Lymph nodes, *B*–Thymus, *C*–Lymphatic vessels
(b) *A*–Lymphatic vessels, *B*–Thyroid, *C*–Lymph nodes
(c) *A*–Tonsils, *B*–Peyer's patches, *C*–Lymphatic vessels
(d) *A*–Tonsils, *B*–Thymus, *C*–Peyer's patches

Ans. (*a*)

17. MALT constitutes about .... per cent of lymphoid tissue in human body.

(a) 50% (b) 10%
(c) 70% (d) 20%

Ans. (*a*)

18. In which of the following condition/disease is there a substantial increase in the activity of mast cells observed in the human body ? CBSE 2024

(a) Typhoid (b) Allergy
(c) Ascariasis (d) AIDS

Ans. (*b*)

19. Time lag between the infection and appearance of AIDS symptoms Diksha

(a) 5-10 months (b) 6-11 months
(c) 5-20 years (d) 5-10 years

Ans. (*d*)

20. Drug called 'heroin' is synthesised by

(a) nitration of morphine
(b) glycosylation of morphine
(c) methylation of morphine
(d) acetylation of morphine

Ans. (*d*)

21. Refer to the structure of a drug given below.

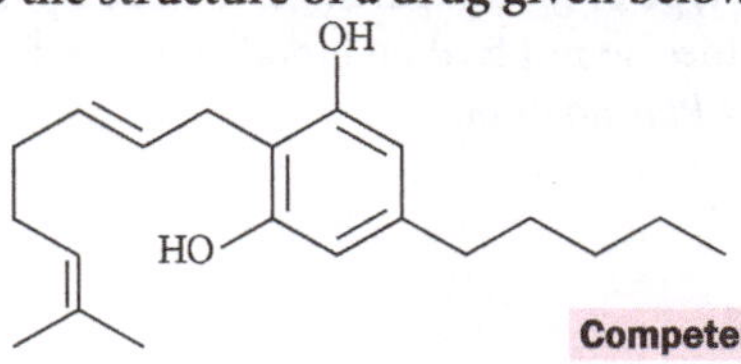

Competency Based Que.

Select the correct option accordingly.

	Group of drug	Modes of consumption	Affected organs
(a)	Hallucinogens	Inhalation or oral ingestion	Cardiovascular system
(b)	Cannabinoids	Injection	Nervous system
(c)	Cannabinoids	Inhalation or oral ingestion	Cardiovascular system
(d)	Opioids	Injection	Nervous system

Ans. (*c*)

22. Chronic use of drugs and alcohol specially causes

(a) cirrhosis
(b) cardiac muscles damage
(c) pulmonary system damage
(d) gametogenesis

Ans. (*a*)

Assertion-Reason Questions

Direction (Q. Nos. 1-10) *In each of the following questions, a statement of Assertion (A) is given followed by corresponding statement of Reason (R). Of the statements, mark the correct answer.*

(a) Both A and R are true and R is the correct explanation of A
(b) Both A and R are true, but R is not the correct explanation of A
(c) A is true, but R is false
(d) A is false, but R is true

1. Assertion (A) Streptococcus pneumoniae and Haemophilus influenzae are responsible for causing infectious diseases in human beings.

Reason (R) A healthy person acquires these infection by inhaling the droplets/aerosols released by an infected person.

Ans. (*a*)

2. Assertion (A) There is no chance of malaria to a man on the bite of male *Anopheles* mosquito.

Reason (R) Male *Anopheles* carries a non-virulant strain of *Plasmodium*.

Ans. (*c*) A is true, but R is false. R can be corrected as

The male *Anopheles* mosquito do not have piercing and sucking type of mouth parts. i.e. male *Anopheles* mosquitoes do not feed on blood and therefore cannot transmit *Plasmodium*.

3. Assertion (A) Filarial worms is transmitted to human by *Culex* mosquito.

Reason (R) *Culex* prefers to breed in freshwater.

Ans. (*c*) A is true, but R is false. R can be corrected as

Culex prefers to breed in dirty water near human habitation.

4. Assertion (A) Antibody mediated immune response is provided by B-cells.

Reason (R) B-cells work chiefly by secreting substances called antibodies into the body fluids.

Ans. (*a*)

5. Assertion (A) Interferons are a type of antibodies produced by body cells infected by bacteria.

Reason (R) Interferons interfere with viral replication at the site of injury.

Ans. (*d*)

6. Assertion (A) Artificially acquired passive immunity results when antibodies produced outside the host are introduced into a host.

Reason (R) Rabies immune globin given to a patient after a potential exposure to rabies virus is an example of artificially acquired passive immunity.

Ans. (*b*)

7. Assertion (A) In organ transplantation, donor and recipient should be genetically as close as possible.

Reason (R) Cell-mediated immune response is responsible for graft rejection in organ transplantation.

Ans. (*b*)

8. Assertion (A) Mast cells in the humans release excessive amount of chemicals like histamine, which cause allergy.

Reason (R) Allergens in the environment on reaching human body stimulate mast cells.

Ans. (*a*)

9. Assertion (A) Histamine is related to allergic and inflammatory reactions.

Reason (R) Histamine is a vasodilator.

Ans. (*b*)

10. Assertion (A) Malignant tumours are more dangerous to the affected organism than benign tumours.

Reason (R) Unlike malignant tumours that tend to stay localised in the same region, benign tumours spread to various body parts.

Ans. (*c*) A is true, but R is false. R can be corrected as

The benign tumours tend to stay localised, while malignant tumour spread to various body parts.

Subjective Questions

Very Short Answer Type Questions

1. Enumerate the factors that affect health.

Ans. Refer to text on page no. 206. (1)

2. Classify the following diseases under the headings 'transmissible' and 'non-transmissible'.
Lung cancer, whooping cough, rickets, arthritis, appendicitis, food poisoning, tuberculosis, measles, diabetes, anaemia, syphilis, influenza, AIDS, coronary heart disease and haemophilia. Competency Based Que.

Ans. Whooping cough, tuberculosis, measles, syphilis, influenza are transmissible diseases. All others are non-transmissible diseases.

3. Name the toxin released in man during malaria that causes fever and chills.

Ans. Heamozoin

4. Life cycle of malarial parasite requires two hosts. Where does the sexual reproduction of malarial parasite take place?

Ans. It takes place inside the gut of an *Anopheles* mosquito.

5. Name the fish that eat mosquito larve.

Ans. *Gambusia*

6. Name a human disease, which spread by intake of water and food contaminated by human faecal matter.

Ans. Amoebiasis.

7. How does saliva act in body defence?

Ans. Saliva in mouth prevents the growth of microbes.

8. Name the response triggered by the T-lymphocytes.

Ans. Cell-mediated immune response.

9. The figure given below shows an antibody molecule. Name the parts *A* and *B*.

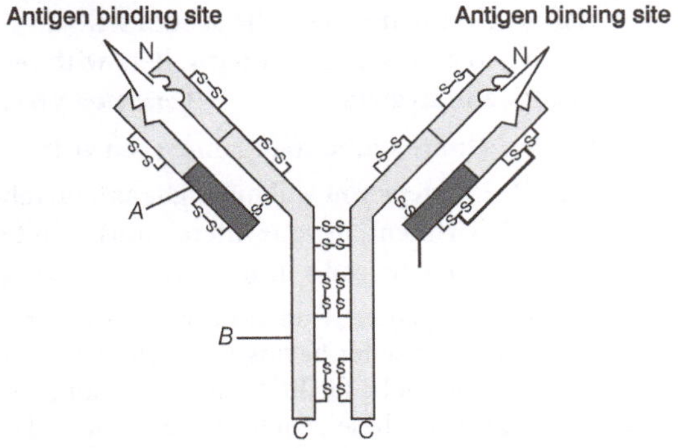

Ans. A–Light chain, B – Heavy chain

10. Why is an antibody molecule represented as H_2L_2? NCERT Exemplar

Ans. In an antibody molecule H_2 represents two large heavy chains and L_2 represents two small light chains.

11. Discuss with your teacher what does a 'suitable gene' means in the context of DNA vaccines. NCERT

Ans. A 'suitable gene' refers to a specific DNA segment which can be injected into the cells of the host body to produce specific protein.

This protein can kills or retard the disease causing organisms and provide immunity.

12. What happens when HIV virus enters into T-lymphocytes of a person? Diksha

Ans. It replicates and produces progeny viruses. These progeny viruses attack other resulting in progressive decrease in the number of T-lymphocytes.

13. Expand ELISA. Mention its applications.

Ans. ELISA stands for Enzyme Linked Immuno Sorbent Assay. It is used to diagnose diseases like AIDS.

14. Name the gene of a cancer causing virus responsible for tansformation.

Ans. Oncogenes

15. When is a tumour called malignant?

Ans. When the tumour cells proliferates and spreads to other parts of the body, it is called as malignant.

16. Why are sports persons tested strictly before an event? Competency Based Que.

Ans. To detect the presence of any performance enhancing drug.

Short Answer Type Questions

1. What are lifestyle diseases? How are they caused? Name any two such diseases. NCERT Exemplar

Ans. Lifestyle diseases are caused by unhealthy habits such as poor diet, lack of exercise, stress, etc.

Lifestyle diseases are caused by specific food habits, work related posture, exposure to harmful radiations or substances, lack of physical exercise, mental stress, etc., e.g. cancer, alcoholism, heart disease, etc. (1 + 1 + 1)

2. We all must work towards maintaining good health because 'health is wealth'. Enlist any six ways of achieving good health. CBSE 2023

Ans. Refer to text on page no. 206 and 207.

3. **Identify *A, B, C, D, E* and *F* in the table given below.**

Name of human diseases	Causative organisms	Symptoms
Pneumonia	*Streptococcus*	*A*
Typhoid	*B*	High fever, weakness, headache, stomach pain
Common cold	Rhino virus	*C*
Ringworm	*D*	Dry scaly lesions on body parts, redness, itching
Ascariasis	*Ascaris*	*E*
F	*Entamoeba histolytica.*	Constipation, cramps, stools with mucus and blood clots

Ans. *A* – Fever / chills / cough / headache / greyish blue lips and nails / severe problem in respiration

B– *Salmonella typhi*

C – Nasal congestion / discharge / sore throat / cough / hoarseness / tiredness

D– *Microsporum / Trichophyton / Epidermophyton,*

E – Internal bleeding / fever / muscular pain / anaemia / blockage of intestinal passage

F – Amoebiasis / amoebic dysentery (½ × 6)

4. **How does the transmission of each of the following takes place?**

Amoebiasis, malaria, ascariasis, pneumonia. **NCERT**

Ans.

Diseases	Modes of transmission
Amoebiasis	Transmitted by contaminated food and water. Vector involved is housefly.
Malaria	It is also a vector-borne disease that is usually spread by the biting of female *Anopheles* mosquito.
Ascariasis	Transmitted by contaminated food and water.
Pneumonia	It spreads by droplets/ aerosols released by an infected person.

(½ × 4)

5. **A person is suffering from a high-grade fever. Which symptoms will help to identify if he/she is suffering from typhoid, pneumonia or malaria?** **CBSE SQP 2022 Term-II**

Ans. If the person has sustained high fever (39° to 40°C), weakness, stomach pain, constipation, headache and loss of appetite, it is typhoid.

If the person has fever, chills, cough and headache and the lips and finger nails turn grey to bluish, it is pneumonia.

If the person has chills and high fever recurring every three to four days then, it is malaria. (1×3)

6. ***Plasmodium* protozoan needs both a mosquito and a human host for its continuity. Explain.** **CBSE 2023**

Ans. Refer to text on page no. 207-208.

7. **A patient complains of suffering from constipation, stomach ache, stool with blood clots and excess mucus. The physician diagnosed it as amoebiasis, after stool test.** **Competency Based Que.**

(i) Write the scientific name of the microbe identified in the stool sample.

(ii) How do you think, the patient must have contracted it?

(iii) Write your suggestions to the patient to avoid infection in future. **CBSE 2022 Term II**

Ans. (i) *Entamoeba histolytica* (1)

(ii) The patient would have contracted it through contaminated food and water. (1)

(iii) In order to avoid such an infection, the patient must avoid uncovered food as the infection spreads through houseflies. (1)

8. **Compare the symptoms of ascariasis, amoebiasis and elephantiasis.** **CBSE 2020**

Ans. Comparison between the symptoms of ascariasis, amoebiasis and elephantiasis are as follows

Ascariasis	Amoebiasis	Elephantiasis
Caused by *Ascaris lumbricoides.*	Caused by *Entamoeba histolytica.*	Caused by *Wuchereria bancrofti.*
Symptoms include internal bleeding, muscular pain, fever, anaemia, nausea, headache and blockage of intestinal passage.	Symptoms are abdominal pain, constipation, cramps, faeces with excess mucus and blood clots.	Symptoms include inflammation of organs in which the worms live for many years, normally affect lymph vessels of lower limbs resulting in swelling of feet and genitals.

(1 × 3)

9. **Community service department of your school plans a visit to a slum area near the school with an objective to educate the slum dwellers with respect to health and hygiene.** **Competency Based Que.**

(i) Why is there a need to organise such visits?

(ii) Write the steps you will highlight as a member of this department, in your interactions with them to enable them to lead a healthy life. **CBSE 2014**

Ans. (i) Slums are generally unauthorised and over crowded colonies having no public facilities. Due to lack of public facilities and education, the living standards of these people are very low and they are always at high risk. Thus, there is a need to organise visits to educate people of slum about sanitation and other health related issues in order to prevent massive spread of fatal diseases. (1)

(ii) Development of healthy life is a bidirectional process and needs the cooperation of both authorities and public of slum area. Steps that can be highlighted include
(a) interacting with people and understanding their needs,
(b) availability of funds,
(c) interaction with all concerned authorities,
(d) making a concrete plan of development. (½ × 4)

All these are required to handle the situation of slums and help them lead a healthy life.

10. What are the various public health measures, which you would suggest as safeguard against infectious diseases? NCERT

Ans. The various public health measures to safeguard against infectious diseases are as follows
(i) Implement widespread vaccination campaigns.
(ii) Promote personal hygiene.
(iii) Educate the public on disease prevention and the importance of seeking medical care.
(iv) Implement measures to isolate infected individuals.
(v) Ensure safe drinking water and proper sanitation facilities.

11. What measures would you take to prevent the water-borne diseases? NCERT

Ans. To prevent water-borne diseases, water bodies, ponds, water tanks, reservoirs in the city or village should be cleaned periodically. The proper disposal of domestic waste, excreta, sewage should be done. At personal level, boiling of water or using water purifier should be practiced.

12. Explain any three preventive measures to control microbial infections. NCERT Exemplar

Ans. Refer to text on page no. 211.

13. Why is it that during changing weather, one is advised to avoid closed, crowded and air conditioned places like cinema halls, etc? NCERT Exemplar, Competency Based Que.

Ans. During changing weather, one is advised to avoid crowded places because changing seasons are the time when infectious agents are more active as moist conditions favours the growth of pathogens. Also, people are more vulnerable as their body system is busy in adapting to the changing environmental conditions of temperature, humidity, etc. Thus, getting easily infected by various pathogens.

14. In which way has the biology helped us to control infectious diseases?

Ans. Study of biology helps to diagnose the pathogen in following ways.
(i) The mechanism of transmission is known.
(ii) Suitable medicine against infectious disease are suggested.
(iii) The life cycle of many pathogen is studied.
(iv) The preparation of vaccines against many pathogens also entitle the use of biology. (½×4)

15. 'Prevention is better than cure'. Comment. NCERT Exemplar

Ans. Prevention is always better than cure because some diseases cause extensive damage to the body tissues or organs and have a
(i) negative effect on their capacity to function.
(ii) permanent or long term debilitating effect.
(iii) negative mental and psychological effect.
(iv) financial burden.

Hence, it is said that prevention is easier and effective than cure of a disease.

16. Humans have innate immunity for protection against pathogens that may enter the gut along with food. What are the two barriers that protect the body from such pathogens? Competency Based Que, CBSE SQP 2022 Term-II

Ans. Innate immunity is inherited type of immunity and it protects an organism from birth throughout the life. It is not specific to a particular pathogen and consists of four types of barriers, i.e. physical, physiological, cellular and cytokine. The two innate immunity barriers that protect our body against the pathogen which enters the gut of humans along with food are as follows
(i) **Physical Barriers** Mucus coating of the epithelium and lining the gastrointestinal tract helps in trapping microbes entering our body.
(ii) **Physiological Barriers** Acid in the stomach, saliva in the mouth prevent microbial growth. (1×2)

17. Certain attributes of innate immunity are given in the table below. Identify *A*, *B*, *C*, *D*, *E* and *F* respectively in it.

	Types of barriers	Examples of the barrier	Functions
(i)	*A*	*B*	Prevent microbial growth
(ii)	*C*	Polymorpho nuclear leukocytes	*D*
(iii)	Cytokine	*E*	*F*

Ans. (i) *A* : Physiological barriers.
B : Acid in stomach. (½×2)
(ii) *C* : Cellular barriers.
D : Phagocytose and destroy microbes. (½×2)
(iii) *E* : Interferons
F : Prevention of viral infections (½×2)

18. What are interferons? How do interferons check infection of new cells? NCERT Exemplar

Ans. Refer to text on page no. 212.

Interferons check infections of new cells by triggering antiviral defenses in neighbouring cells.

19. Differentiate between the following with examples.
 (i) Innate and acquired immunity.
 (ii) Active and passive immunity. NCERT

Ans. (i) Differences between innate immunity and acquired immunity are as follows

Innate immunity	Acquired immunity
It includes the defence elements with which an individual is born.	It is immunity which is acquired after birth.
It consists of various types of barriers that prevent the entry of foreign agents.	It consists of specialised cells (T-cells and B-cells) and antibodies that circulate in the body fluid.
It remains throughout life.	It can be short lived or life long.
e.g. HCl acid in stomach and mechanism like phagocytosis.	e.g. Vaccine-induced immunity.

(1½)

(ii) Differences between active immunity and passive immunity are as follows

Active immunity	Passive immunity
It is developed by the body due to contact with pathogen or its antigen.	It is developed when ready-made antibodies are injected into the body.
It has no side effects.	It may cause a reaction.
It is slow but long lasting.	It is fast but lasts only for few days.
It takes time to develop its response.	It is used when the immune response has to be faster.
e.g. vaccination for polio, etc.	e.g. administration of tetanus antitoxins, etc.

(1½)

20. Recognition of an antigenic protein of a pathogen or exposure to a pathogen occurs during many types of immune responses, including active immunity and induced active immunity. Specify the types of responses elicited when human beings get encountered by a pathogen. Competency Based Que.

Ans. When body encounters an antigenic protein or a pathogen for the first time, it produces a response which is of low intensity. The body retains memory of the first encounter.

The subsequent encounter with the same pathogen elicits a highly intensified response carried out with the help of two special types of lymphocytes present in blood, i.e. B-lymphocytes and T-lymphocytes.

The B-lymphocytes produce an army of proteins in response to these pathogens into the blood to fight with them. These proteins are called antibodies. The T-cells themselves do not secrete antibodies, but help B-cells produce them.

21. What does the term 'memory of the immune system' mean? NCERT Exemplar

Ans. Refer to text on page no 212.

22. Name the two special types of lymphocytes in humans. How do they differ in their roles in immune response?

Ans. Two special types of lymphocytes in humans are B-lymphocytes and T-lymphocytes. B-lymphocytes execute antibody-mediated response, while T-lymphocytes show cell-mediated response. (1 + 1)

23. Name the types of acquired immune responses and the special types of lymphocytes involved in providing them.

Ans. Refer to text on page no 212.

24. Why is mother's milk considered the most appropriate food for a new born infant? NCERT Exemplar

Or **Why is colostrum a boon to the new born baby?**

Ans. Mother's milk is considered most appropriate or a boon for a newborn infant as it provides immunity in the initial period of baby's life. The yellowish fluid colostrum secreted by mother during the initial days of lactation has abundant antibodies (IgA) which protect the infant from various pathogens.

25. Draw a labelled diagram of an antibody molecule.

Ans. Refer to fig. 7.3 on page no. 213. NCERT

26. List all the types of antibodies produced in our body. Among all, which antibodies are produced during
 (i) allergic reactions
 (ii) transfusion reaction/rejection

Ans. Refer to text on page no. 213
 (i) Refer to text on page no. 214. (2)
 (ii) During transfusion reaction, the body produce antibodies like IgM and IgG. (1)

27. Mention one application for each of the following.
 (i) Passive immunisation **(ii) Antihistamine**
 (iii) Colostrum **(iv) Cytokinin barrier**

Ans. Applications of given components are as follows
 (i) **Passive immunisation** provides a faster immune response. (½)
 (ii) **Antihistamine** is used to reduce the symptoms of allergy such as sneezing, watery eyes, rashes, running nose, etc. (½)
 (iii) **Colostrum** consists of antibody (e.g. IgA) that provides immunity to an infant against infections. (½)
 (iv) **Cytokinin barrier** produces interferons and protects non-infected cells from further viral infection. (½)

28. A heavily bleeding and bruised road accident victim was brought to a nursing home. The doctor immediately gave him an injection to protect him against a deadly disease. Competency Based Que.

(i) **What did the doctor inject into the patient's body?**

(ii) **How do you think this injection would protect the patient against the disease?**

(iii) **Name the kind of immunity it provides.**

Ans. (i) The doctor must have injected the tetanus anti-toxin into the patient. (1)

(ii) The injection contain antibodies that fight against the tetanus toxin. (1)

(iii) The tetanus injection provides passive immunity. (1)

29. What are recombinant DNA vaccines? Give two examples of such vaccines. Discuss their advantages. NCERT Exemplar

Ans. Recombinant DNA vaccines are made up of a small circular DNA (plasmid) that has very tiny piece of pathogen DNA incorporated in it to produce one or two specific proteins of the pathogen.

This recombinant DNA is introduced into the bacteria or yeast cells, where it can use cell's machinery to produce polypeptides of pathogen. These are used as vaccines to trigger a range of immune responses. Vaccines produced by using this approach allow large scale production, e.g.

(i) Hepatitis-B vaccine produced from yeast.

(ii) Bird flu DNA vaccine. (1½)

Some advantages of recombinant DNA vaccines are as follows.

(i) Recombinant DNA vaccines are advantageous over killed or attenuated vaccines since they do not get virulent or mutated again as it is seen in case of attenuated vaccines.

(ii) Secondly, these are highly pure, specific and elicit strong immune response. (1½)

30. Explain giving two reasons, how immune response by 'vaccine' is different from that by 'antitoxin' in humans. CBSE 2022 Term II

Ans. Immune response by vaccine is different from that by antitoxin in humans in following two ways

(i) Vaccines give long term protection unlike antitoxins. (1)

(ii) Vaccines stimulate immune systen to recognise, destroy, kill or render a pathogen inactive, whereas antitoxins render a toxic substance harmless. (1)

31. What is the basic principle of vaccination? How do vaccines prevent microbial infections? Name the organism from which hepatitis-B vaccine is produced. NCERT Exemplar

Ans. Refer to text on page no. 213.

32. Following a road accident four injured persons were brought to a nearby clinic. The doctor immediately injected them with tetanus antitoxin.

(i) **What is tetanus antitoxin ?**

(ii) **Why were the injured immediately injected with this antitoxin ?**

(iii) **Name the kind of immunity this injection provided.**

Ans. (i) Tetanus antitoxin is a preparation containing antibodies to the toxin. It is produced by tetanus bacteria *Clostridium tetani*. (1)

(ii) Antitoxins neutralise the toxin produced by bacteria. Therefore, the injured persons are immediately injected with tetanus antitoxin for preventing any infection and septic. (1)

(iii) Tetanus antitoxin represents artificial passive immunisation where quick response is generated in the body. (1)

33. Give an account of the generalised structure of an antibody molecule produced by B-lymphocytes in response to the pathogen. CBSE 2025

Ans. An antibody is a Y-shaped glycoprotein produced by B-lymphocytes in response to pathogens. It consists of four polypeptide chains—two heavy chains and two light chains—which are held together by disulphide bonds. The variable region at the tips of the Y-shape forms the antigen-binding site, providing specificity for pathogens.

34. Name the primary and secondary lymphoid organs. NCERT

Or

Given below are some of the organs. Identify one primary and secondary lymphoid organ

Liver, thymus, stomach, thyroid, tonsils.

Ans. Refer to text on page no. 213-214.

35. 'Epithelial lining of our intestine is considered as secondary lymphoid organ'. Justify the statement. CBSE 2022 Term II

Ans. Lymphoid organs are the organs where origin, maturation and proliferation of lymphocytes occur.

They are of two types

(i) Primary lymphoid organs

(ii) Secondary lymphoid organs

Epithelial lining is considered as secondary lymphoid organ as it provides the site for lymphocyte-antigen interaction.

36. (i) **Explain the roles of (a) primary and (b) secondary lymphoid organs that are responsible for developing defence to combat the action of pathogens/foreign antigens which enter our body.**

(ii) **Doctors generally advise not to undergo surgery of tonsils. Why?**

Competency Based Que. CBES 2022 Term II

Ans. (i) Refer to text on page no. 213-214. (1½)

(ii) Doctors generally advise not to undergo surgery of tonsils because getting the tonsils removed leads to an increased rate of upper respiratory infections as tonsils are secondary lymphoid organ that possess more WBCs which help in killing germs. Removing tonsils would lead to higher infection rate. (1½)

37. Answer the following.

(i) Highlight the role of thymus as a lymphoid organ.

(ii) Give the name of the cells that are released from the above mentioned gland. Mention how they help in immunity?

Ans. (i) Thymus is a primary lymphoid organ. It is lobe-shaped and is known to be the site for growth and differentiation of antigen sensitive T-lymphocytes. (1½)

(ii) Thymus releases T-lymphocytes, which are involved in cell-mediated immunity and also help B-lymphocytes to produce antibodies. (1½)

38. (i) It is generally observed that the children who had suffered from chickenpox in their childhood may not contract the same disease in their adulthood. Explain giving reasons the basis of such an immunity in an individual. Name this kind of immunity. Competency Based Que.

(ii) What are interferons? Mention their role.

Ans. (i) When a child suffered from chickenpox for the first time, his/her body's immune system exhibited primary response. Along with that, the memory of chickenpox virus was stored by the immune system. Now, whenever the same virus will attack this child, the immune system will produce an intense response, preventing the body from getting chickenpox again. It is known as acquired immunity. (2)

(ii) Interferons are special kind of proteins secreted by virus infected cells. These protect the healthy cells from the virus attacks. (½ + ½)

39. A boy developed some allergic reactions when he straight entered into his air conditioned room after a game of football outside his house. Write any two symptoms that could be noticed in such condition. How does our body combat such conditions? Competency Based Que.

Ans. Two symptoms that the boy could develop in such situation are

(i) sneezing (ii) running nose (½ × 2)

Allergens produce exaggerated immune response in an individual. As a result, IgE antibodies are released in the body which bind to allergens and both then bind to mast cells. This binding causes the release of chemicals like histamine and serotonin from mast cells which cause reactions in the body. In order to reduce such reactions, antihistamines are usually taken. (2)

40. In the metropolitan cities of India, many children are suffering from allergy/asthma. What are the main causes of this problem? Give some symptoms of allergic reactions. NCERT Exemplar

Ans. In metropolitan cities, life style is responsible for lowering of immunity and high sensitivity to allergens.

It is due to the protected environment provided early in life. Some symptoms of allergic reactions are sneezing, watery eyes, running nose and difficulty in breathing.

41. What are the various routes by which transmission of Human Immunodeficiency Virus (HIV) takes place?

Ans. Refer to text on page no. 215. NCERT

42. (i) HIV and hepatitis-B are STDs. Mention the two other ways by which they can be transmitted to a healthy person.

(ii) Why is early detection of STD essential? What can it lead to otherwise?

Ans. (i) Refer to text on text on page no. 215. (1)

(ii) Early detection of STD is essential for timely cure. Otherwise this can lead to Pelvic Inflammatory Diseases (PIDs), abortions or even cancer of the reproductive tract. (1)

43. (i) What precaution(s) would you recommend to a patient requiring repeated blood transfusion?

(ii) If the advise is not followed by the patient there is an apprehension that the patient might contract a disease that would destroy the immune system of his/her body.

Explain with the help of schematic diagram only how the immune system would get affected and destroyed.

Ans. (i) Repeated blood transfusion may result in contracting diseases like AIDS. The recipient must ensure that the donor's blood is being screened for HIV and other pathogens. (1)

(ii) In the absence of such measures, the patient can get infected by HIV (Human Immunodeficiency Virus) which causes AIDS. It is a life threatening disorder that weakens the immune system by attacking helper T-cells in the body.

Refer to fig. 7.5 on page no. 216. (2)

44. What is the mechanism by which the AIDS virus causes deficiency of immune system of the infected person?

Ans. Refer to text on page no. 215-216. NCERT

45. How does human immunodeficiency virus cause immunodeficiency in the human body? Competency Based Que.

Ans. HIV virus enters into the macrophages after entering into the host body. RNA gets replicated to form viral DNA, with the help of an enzyme reverse transcriptase. Viral DNA gets incorporated into the host cell DNA and stimulates the production of virus particles. These particles enter the

T-lymphocytes and eventually destroy them with a decrease in number of T-lymphocytes, the immunity of an individual also decreases.

46. Name the type of cells attacked by AIDS virus in the human body. Also, explain the events in sequence undertaken by virus to increase its progeny.

Ans. Refer to text on page no. 215-216.

47. (i) Write the complete name of the diagnostic test for AIDS. Explain the principle it works on.

(ii) Name the type of genetic material present in AIDS causing pathogen. **CBSE 2022 Term II**

Ans. (i) There are several methods for the diagnosis of HIV infection like Enzyme Linked Immuno Sorbent Assay (ELISA), PCR test, Western blotting, etc. Out of these, ELISA and Western blotting are widely used.

ELISA is based on the principle of antigen-antibody interaction. Infection by pathogen can be detected by the presence of antigens like proteins and glycoproteins or by detecting the antibodies produced against the pathogen.

(ii) Genetic material present in AIDS causing pathogen is RNA. (2 + 1)

48. The following are some well known abbreviations, which have been used in this chapter. Expand each one to its full form.

(i) MALT (ii) CMI (iii) AIDS (iv) NACO (v) HIV **NCERT**

Ans. (i) **MALT** Mucosal Associated Lymphoid Tissue

(ii) **CMI** Cell-Mediated Immunity

(iii) **AIDS** Acquired Immuno Deficiency Syndrome

(iv) **NACO** National AIDS Control Organisation

(v) **HIV** Human Immunodeficiency Virus (2)

49. The immune system of a person is suppressed. In the ELISA test, he was found positive to a pathogen. **NCERT Exemplar**

(i) Name the disease the patient is suffering from.

(ii) What is the causative organism?

(iii) Which cells of body are affected by the pathogen?

Ans. . (i) The patient is suffering from AIDS.

(ii) AIDS is caused by Human Immunodeficiency Virus (HIV). It is a retrovirus containing RNA as genetic material.

(iii) Macrophages and helper T-cells are affected by the pathogen. (1 × 3)

50. Other than public awareness and counselling, enlist four measures taken up by NACO, WHO and other NGOs to prevent the spread of HIV infection in the society. **CBSE 2025**

Ans. Organisations like NACO, WHO and NGOs implement the following measures to prevent HIV transmission:

(i) Promotion of safe sex practices, including condom use.

(ii) Screening of blood before transfusion to ensure it is HIV-free.

(iii) Needle exchange programs to prevent sharing of infected syringes. (1+1)

51. Differentiate between benign tumour and malignant tumour. **NCERT Exemplar**

Ans. The differences between benign and malignant tumour are as follows

Benign tumour	Malignant tumour
It is a non-cancerous tumour.	It is a cancerous tumour.
Benign tumour does not show metastasis and is non-invasive.	It shows metastasis and thus invades other body parts.
It stops growing after reaching a certain size.	Malignant tumour shows indefinite growth.
It is less fatal to the body.	It is more fatal to the body.

(½×4)

52. Explain what is meant by metastasis. **NCERT**

Ans. When cells sloughed from a malignant tumour cells reaches other parts of body *via* blood and start a new tumour there, this condition is termed as metastasis. (2)

53. How do normal cells get transformed into cancerous neoplastic cells? Elaborate giving three examples of inducing agent. **Competency Based Que.**

Ans. Transformation of normal cells into cancerous neoplastic cells may be induced by the following physical, chemical or biological agents, causing DNA damage.

- Ionising radiations like X-rays and gamma rays, non-ionising radiations like UV rays.
- Chemical carcinogens present in tobacco smoke.
- Cellular oncogenes (*c-onc*) or proto-oncogenes, when activated under certain conditions cause cancer.
- Viruses with oncogenes can transform normal cells to cancerous cells. (any three) (1 × 3)

54. How do cancerous cells harm the normal cells? Explain the phenomenon. **NCERT**

Ans. Refer to text on page no. 216. (3)

55. What are interferons? State their role in the treatment of cancer. **CBSE 2022 Term II**

Ans. Interferons are a group of signalling proteins released by the host cells in response to the presence of several pathogens like viruses, bacteria, etc. (1)

Interferons mediate and regulate different aspects of cancer cells behaviour including proliferation and metastatic spreading. They play a key role in activating cellular immunity and increase host defence. (1)

56. (i) **Explain the property of contact inhibition and its effect on normal human cells and cancerous cells.**

(ii) **Why are biological modifiers like α-interferon required for cancer treatment? How do they act to treat the disease?** CBSE 2022 Term II

Ans. (i) In normal cells, the cell growth and differentiation is highly controlled and regulated as they show the property of contact inhibition. By virtue of this property, they contact with other cells, stop the uncontrolled cell growth.

Cancerous cells do not have this property, thus such cells continue to divide, producing a mass of cells called tumour.

Due to lack of contact inhibition, the cancerous cells damage the surrounding cells as they make them starve for nutrients. (1½)

(ii) Biological modifiers like α-interferons are a group of signalling proteins released by the host cells as a response to the presence of pathogens like viruses, bacteria, etc.

These regulate the different aspects of cancer cell's behaviour by keeping a check on their spread. This further leads to their controlled growth. Interferons also play a key role in activating cellular immunity of the host organism and increase host defence. (1½)

57. Name the plant source of the drug popularly called 'smack'. How does it affect the body of the abuser?

Ans. Smack is obtained from *Papaver somniferum*. It affects the Central Nervous System (CNS) and gastrointestinal system. It slows down the body functions and acts as a depressant. (1 + 1)

58. How are morphine and heroin related? Mention the effect each one of them has on the human body.

Ans. Both morphine and heroin are extracted from the latex of plant *Papaver somniferum*. (1)

Heroin is actually obtained from diacetylation of morphine. Thus, both are related. Morphine, is as an effective sedative and pain killer, while heroin acts as depressant and slows down body functions. (1)

59. Prior a sports event blood and urine samples of sports persons are collected for drug tests. Competency Based Que.

(i) **Why is there a need to conduct such tests?**

(ii) **Name the drugs the authorities usually look for.**

(iii) **Write the generic names of two plants from which these drugs are obtained.**

Ans. (i) It is necessary to conduct these tests as sports persons often take drugs to increase their performance. (1)

(ii) Cocaine and morphines are the drugs that authorities usually look for. (1)

(iii) Morphine is extracted from the latex of poppy plant *Papaver somniferum*. Cocaine is obtained from the coca plant *Erythroxylum coca*. (1)

60. Identify the compound whose chemical structure is shown below. State any three of its physical properties. Competency Based Que.

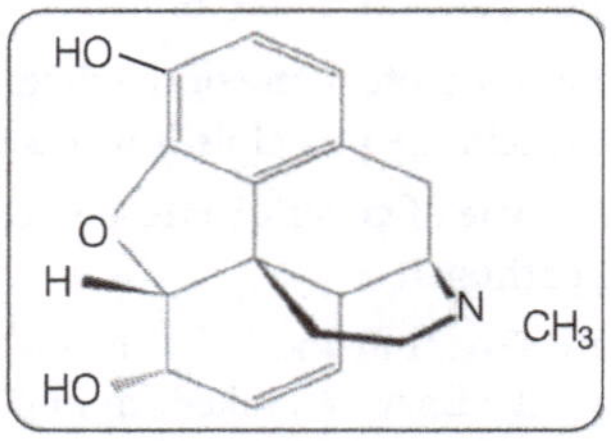

Ans. The chemical compound given is morphine. It is an effective sedative, analgesic and painkiller. (1)

Morphine is obtained from latex of poppy plant. It is crystalline, white in appearance and odourless. (1)

61. What is the mode of action of heroin in the body?

Ans. Refer to text on page no. 218.

62. Write the scientific name of the source plant of the drugs-marijuana and hashish and mention their effect on human body.

Ans. The scientific names of source plant of drugs marijuana and hashish is *Cannabis sativa*. They usually affect the cardiovascular system of human body. (1+1)

63. A team of students are preparing to participate in the inter school sports meet. During a practice session you find some vials with labels of certain cannabinoids. Competency Based Que.

(i) **Will you report to the authorities? Why?**

(ii) **Name a plant from which such chemicals are obtained.**

(iii) **Write the effect of these chemicals on human body.**

Ans. (i) Yes, I will report it to the authorities because cannabinoids are classified as drugs and taking them without medical supervision is illegal. (1)

(ii) Cannabinoids are obtained from various parts of the plant *Cannabis sativa*. (1)

(iii) The cannabinoids interact with cannabinoid receptors in the brain and affect the cardiovascular system of the body. (1)

64. Why cannabinoids are banned in sports and games? NCERT Exemplar

Or **Intake of cannabinoids should be banned. Justify giving reasons.** Competency Based Que.

Ans. Cannabinoids are banned in sports as athletes were misusing these drugs in order to enhance their performance. These prevent early exhaustion. These can also have a serious negative effect on their general health in long term, it can hamper the normal functioning of organ systems.

65. Drugs like LSD, barbiturates, amphetamines, etc., are used as medicines to help patients with mental illness. However, excessive doses and abusive usage are harmful. Enumerate the major adverse effects of such drugs in humans. NCERT Exemplar

Ans. Harmful effects of drugs like LSD, barbiturates, etc., are as follows

(i) Anxiety, shakiness, nausea, sweating and loss of control over the mind.
(ii) Reckless behaviour, vandalism and violence.
(iii) Lack of interest in personal hygiene, fluctuations in weight and appetite.
(iv) Social adjustment problems.
(v) Withdrawal, isolation, depression, fatigue, aggressive behaviour. These can be life threatening.
(vi) Excessive doses of drugs may lead to coma and death due to respiratory failure, heart failure or cerebral haemorrhage. ($\frac{1}{2} \times 6$)

66. In your view what motivates youngsters to take alcohol or drugs and how can this be avoided? NCERT

Or **Why do some adolescents start taking drugs. How can this be avoided?** NCERT Exemplar

Ans. Refer to text on page no. 219.

67. In your locality, if a person is addicted to alcohol, what kind of behavioural changes do you observe in that person? Suggest measures to overcome the problem. NCERT Exemplar

Ans. If a person is addicted to alcohol, it will give rise to some behavioural changes in that person. These are as follows

- Alcoholic drinks are costly and most drinkers because of their selfish habits, deprive their children and other members of the family of the basic needs.
- The drinking of alcohol is invariably associated with social crimes and dissolution of moral and cultural inhibitions.
- Violence and other corrupt practices in the community are often directly or indirectly caused by the consumption of alcohol. (1.5)

For measures to overcome the above mentioned problem, refer to text on page no. 219–220. (1.5)

68. What certain sportspersons do to enhance their performance? Write four side effects of the use of anabolic steroid on both male and female. Diksha

Ans. Some sportspersons take cannabinoids (drugs) to enhance their performance. Side effects of steroid on both male and female are as follows. (1)

Females Masculinisation, increased aggressiveness, mood swings, depression, abnormal menstrual cycle, excessive hair, deepeing of voice, etc. (1)

Males Increased aggressiveness, mood swings, depression, reduction of size of testicles, decreased sperm production, liver dysfunction, breast enlargement, premature baldness, etc. (1)

69. What happens to an individual when a regular dose of drugs/alcohol is abruptly discontinued? What characteristics manifest in the individual under such a situation? Competency Based Que.

Or **If a regular dose of drug or alcohol is not provided to an addicted person, he shows some withdrawal symptoms. List any four such withdrawal symptoms.** NCERT Exemplar

Ans. If the regular dose of drug or alcohol in an addicted person is discontinued abruptly, the body exhibits characteristic and unpleasant symptoms called 'withdrawal syndrome'.
This 'withdrawal syndrome' is characterised by symptoms like anxiety, nausea, fatigue and excessive sweating.

70. Why is that once a person starts taking alcohol or drugs, it is difficult to get rid of this habit? Discuss it with your teacher. NCERT

Ans. It is difficult to get rid of alcohol or drugs once a person starts taking them because their repeated use leads to addiction. It increases the tolerance level of these substances in the body and the receptors respond only to higher doses of alcohol and drugs which in turn increases the dosage and it becomes difficult to get rid of the habit.

71. List the harmful effects caused by the alcohol and drug abuse. NCERT

Ans. Refer to text on page no. 219-220.

72. Do you think that friends can influence one to take alcohol/drugs? If yes, how can one protect himself/herself from such an influence? NCERT

Ans. Yes, a friend can influence one to take alcohol/drugs.

Steps to avoid influence of drugs/alcohol are as follows

(i) Avoiding the company of friends who take drugs or alcohols.
(ii) Seeking help from parents, teachers and friends who do not indulge in alcohol/drug consumption.
(iii) Proper knowledge and awareness about alcohol and drug abuse.
(iv) Taking immediate medical help and counselling, if required. ($\frac{1}{2} \times 4$)

Long Answer Type Questions

1. A patient had tested positive to ELISA test. Identify the disease and the pathogen responsible, give reasons for the reduced/ weak immunity of the patient and trace the path, spread and effects of this pathogen in the human body.

Ans. Refer to text on page no. 215-216.

2. Identify and name the disease in which the patient's cells lose the property of contact inhibition. State its possible causes and explain any three methods to accurately detect the pathological and physiological changes that take place due to the disease in living tissues.

Ans. Refer to text on page no. 216 and 217.

3. (i) **Cancer is one of the most dreaded disease. Explain 'contact inhibition' and 'metastasis' with respect to the disease.**

(ii) **Name the group of genes that have been identified in normal cells that could lead to cancer. How do these genes cause cancer?**

(iii) **Name any two techniques that are useful in detecting cancers of internal organs.**

(iv) **Why are cancer patients often given α-interferon as part of the treatment?**

Ans. (i) **Contact Inhibition** Normal cells have the property of contact inhibition (stoppage of growth on coming in contact with other cells), but cancer cells do not have this property. As a result, cancer cells divide continuously to give rise to a mass of cells (tumours).

Metastasis This property is exhibited by malignant tumours. It is the pathological process of spreading of cancerous cells to different parts of the body. These cells divide uncontrollably, forming a mass of cells called tumour.

From the tumour, some cells get sloughed off and enter the bloodstream. From the bloodstream, these cells reach near by as well as distant parts of the body therefore, initiating the formation of new tumours by dividing actively. (2)

(ii) Refer to text on page no. 217. (1)

(iii) Refer to text on page no. 217. (1)

(iv) The biological response modifiers such as α-interferons are given to cancer patients as a part of their treatment because it activates patients's immune system and helps in destroying the tumour. (1)

4. (i) **How do normal cell become cancerous ?**

(ii) **Cancer can be treated successfully only if detected at an early stage. How do the following help in detecting cancer ?**

(a) CT scan (b) Antibodies

(iii) **Name any two methods that can possibly cure cancer.** **CBSE 2020**

Ans. (i) Normal cells have genes called **cellular oncogenes** (*c-onc*) or **proto-oncogenes**, which are present in inactive state. Also 'contact inhibition' is the property exhibited by normal cells.

It prevents their uncontrolled proliferation when they are in contact with other neighbouring cells.

Thus, when due to certain conditions like mutation, the oncogenes are turned on, this makes the cells to lose the property of contact inhibition and they continue to divide despite being in contact with other cell, which cause formation to masses of cells called tumours and lead to cancer. (2)

(ii) Cancer can be detected by the following methods

(a) **CT scan** It is used to generate a 3-D image of internal tissue using X-rays.

(b) **Antibodies** The presence of antibodies against cancer specific antigens in the body is also used for detection of cancer. (2)

(iii) **Treatment of Cancer** Refer to text on page no. 217. (1)

5. (i) **Name and explain the property present in normal cells, but is lost in cancer cells.**

(ii) **All normal human cells have genes that may become cancerous under certain conditions. Name them and explain how.**

(iii) **State the role of the following techniques in detection and diagnosis of cancer.**

(a) Biopsy and Histopathology

(b) Magnetic Resonance Imaging **CBSE 2024**

Ans. (i) Contact inhibition is present in normal cells, but not in cancer cells, when normal cells come in contact with other cells it inhibits their uncontrolled growth. (2)

(ii) Cellular oncogenes / Proto-oncogenes, when activated under certain conditions could lead to oncogenic transformation of the cells. (1)

(iii) (a) **Biopsy and Histopathology** A piece of suspected tissue cut into thin sections is stained and examined under microscope by pathologist for increased cell counts.

(b) **MRI** Detects cancer of internal organs ssing strong magnetic fields and non–ionising radiations to detect pathological and physiological changes in living tissue. (2)

6. State which of the following are incorrect along with proper explanation to your answer.

(i) **Alcohol precedes adolescence.**

(ii) **LSD is a hallucinogen.**

(iii) **Brown sugar is heroin.**

(iv) **Cocaine is obtained from *Thea sinensis*.**

(v) **Hallucinogens are called vision producing drugs.**

Ans. Statement (i) and (iv) are incorrect for the explanation.

Refer to text on page no. 217-218 for (i)-(v).

7. (i) **What is meant by addiction?**

(ii) **Mention any two ways in which opiate drugs affect human body.**

(iii) **Name any two opiate drug.**

Ans. (i) Refer to text on page no. 219. (2)

(ii) Refer to text on page no. 218. (2)

(iii) Heroin and morphine. (1)

8. Explain the mode of action and mode of intake of tobacco and also explain its effect on health (any six).

Ans. Refer to text on page no. 219.

9. (i) **Why is there a fear amongst the guardians that their adolescent wards may get trapped in drug/alcohol abuse?** **Competency Based Que.**

(ii) **Explain 'addiction' and 'dependence' in respect of drug/alcohol abuse in youth.**

Ans. (i) The period between 12-18 years of age is called adolescent period. There is always a fear amongst guardians that their adolescents may get trapped in drug/alcohol abuse due to following reasons

(a) Adolescence is accompanied by several biological and behavioural changes. It is a vulnerable phase of mental and psychological development of an individual in which an individual may get addicted to alcohol/drugs very easily.

(b) In this age, the first use of drugs or alcohol may be out of curiosity or experimentation, which later on turns into addiction.

(c) Adolescents usually take drugs due to social pressure, need of adventure, excitement, to avoid stress, depression and frustration. (3)

(ii) Refer to text on page no. 219. (2)

10. Explain the effects of alcohol on the

(i) kidney (ii) brain

(iii) heart (iv) liver (v) immunity

Or **Describe the ill-effects of alcohol on different parts of a body of an individual.**

Ans. (i) **Effect on Kidney** It reduces ADH secretion, which results in rapid dehydration.

(ii) **Effect on Brain** Reduced self control, judgement, loss of muscle coordination, in coherent speech, etc.

(iii) **Effect on Heart** Increased blood pressure which affects the activity of heart.

(iv) **Effect on Liver** Alcohol consumption cause liver cirrhosis.

(v) **Effect on Immunity** Alcoholism decreases the resistance to infection. (1 × 5)

Source Based/ Case Based/ Passage Based Questions

1. When a microorganism invades a host, a definite sequence of events usually occur leading to infection and disease, causing suffering to the host. This process is called pathogenesis. Once a microorganism overcomes the defence system of the host, development of the disease follows a certain sequence of events as shown in the graph. Study the graph given below for the sequence of events leading to appearance of a disease and answer the questions that follows

Competency Based Que.

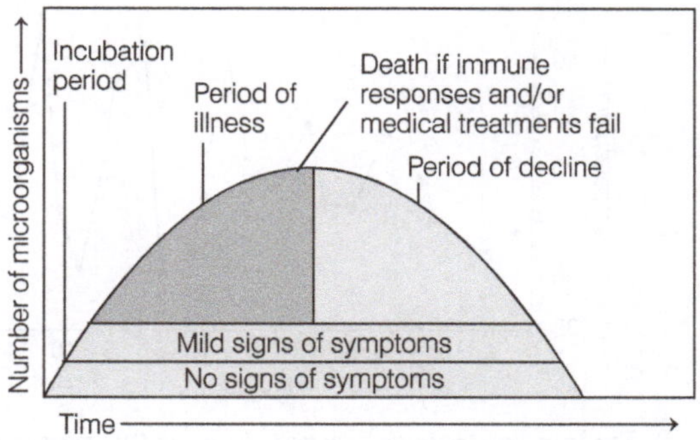

(i) In which period, according to the graph there are maximum chances of a person transmitting a disease/infection and why?

(ii) Study the graph and write what is an incubation period. Name a sexually transmitted disease that can be easily transmitted during this period. Name the specific type of lymphocytes that are attacked by the pathogen of this disease.

Or

(ii) Draw a schematic labelled diagram of an antibody.

(iii) In which period, the number of immune cells, forming antibodies, will be the highest in a person suffering from pneumonia? Name the immune cells that produce antibodies. **CBSE 2023**

Ans. (i) Period of illness. It is because the number of disease-causing microorganisms reaches maximum in the period of illness. (1)

(ii) The time between no signs and symptoms till mild signs and symptoms is called incubation period. AIDS is the sexually transmitted disease that can spread in this period. Macrophages are specific type of lymphocytes that are attacked by the pathogen of this disease. (2)

Or

(ii) Refer to fig. 7.3 on page no. 213. (2)

(iii) In period of illness the immune cells forming antibodies, will be the highest in a person suffering from pneumonia. The B-cells that produces antibodies are B-lymphocytes. (1)

2. Given below is the pattern of temperature in a person suffering from a non-viral disease transmitted by mosquitoes. Study the graph and answer the questions that follows. **Competency Based Que.**

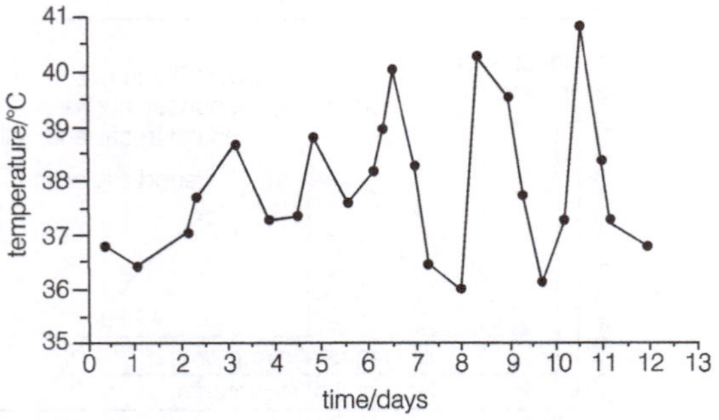

(i) **Explain the factor(s) responsible for this pattern of temperature.**

(ii) **How does this pathogen multiply in the human body?**

(iii) **How is this infection transmitted to humans?**

Or

(iv) **Which stages of the life cycle of this pathogen are completed in the mosquito's gut?**

Ans. (i) The rupture of RBCs associated with the release of toxic substance haemozoin is responsible for the chills and fever/recurring every 3-4 days. (1)

(ii) The parasite reproduces asexually in liver cells, bursting the cell and releasing into the blood. Parasite further reproduces asexually in red blood cells. Released parasite infects new red blood cells. Sexual stages (gametocytes) develop in red blood cells. (2)

(iii) The infection is caused by the bite of the female *Anopheles* mosquito which introduces the sporozoites in the human body. (1)

Or (iv) Fertilisation and development take place in the mosquito's gut. (1)

3. Refer to the graph given below and answer the questions that follows **Competency Based Que.**

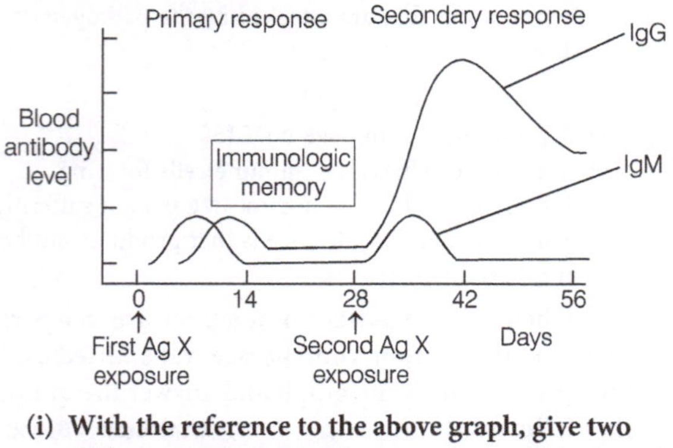

(i) **With the reference to the above graph, give two differences between primary and secondary immune response.**

(ii) **Trace the trajectory of the above graph.**

(iii) **IgG antibody level is higher in secondary response comment.**

Ans. (i)

Primary immune response	Secondary immune response
This occurs as a result of primary contact with antigen.	This occurs as a result of second and subsequent exposure of same antigen.
First antibody produced is IgM.	Mainly IgG is produced.

(1)

(ii) Trajectory of the above graph is explained as follows

In primary immune response the lag phase is often longer. Level of antibody reaches peak in 7 to 10 days. The first antibody produced is mainly IgM. Although small amount of IgG are also produced.

In secondary immune response lag phase is shorter (1-4 days) due to the presence of memory cell. Level of antibody reaches peak in 3-5 days. Mainly IgG is produced. Usually 1000 times more antibodies are produced here. (2)

(iii) IgG level is higher in secondary response as it can divide faster and produce high affinity antibodies in response to antigen. (1)

4. A senior student, sneezing very badly, with watery eyes and having difficulty in breathing was brought to the school medical room by his fellow friends. The medical room nurse enquired as to what had happened. One of the students said "after the football match we all were sweating profusely, one of our friends sprayed deodorant on us. Soon after the deodorant was sprayed on the senior boy, the symptoms appeared." **CBSE 2024 C**

(a) **What are the symptoms seen in the student indicative of ? Elaborate.**

(b) **State how the cause of such responses can be confirmed.**

(c) (i) **Name the cells in our body and the chemicals produced by them that are responsible for such reactions. Name any two drugs used to reduce these symptoms.**

Or

(c) (ii) **'In recent times there is a rise in such reactions amongst urban human population.' Do you agree ? Give three reasons in support of your answer.**

Ans. (a) The symptoms described — sneezing, watery eyes, and difficulty in breathing are indicative of an allergic reaction. (1)

(b) To confirm the cause of such allergic reactions, an allergy test can be conducted. This may involve blood tests to check for specific antibodies (IgE) produced in response to allergens like the chemicals in the deodorant. The test can help identify the specific substance that triggered the symptoms. (1)

(c) (i) The cells responsible for allergic reactions are mast cells and basophils. These cells release histamine and other chemicals in response to allergens. Histamine causes symptoms such as sneezing, itching, watery eyes, and difficulty breathing.

Two drugs commonly used to reduce these symptoms are:

- **Antihistamines** (e.g., cetirizine, loratadine) – These block the action of histamine and relieve allergy symptoms.
- **Corticosteroids** (e.g., prednisone) – These reduce inflammation and help manage severe allergic reactions. (2)

Or

(c) (ii) Yes, there is a rise in allergic reactions, especially in urban areas. Three reasons for this are:

- **Increased Exposure to Pollutants** Urban environments have higher levels of air pollution, which can trigger allergic reactions in sensitive individuals.
- **Changes in Lifestyle and Hygiene** Urban populations tend to have more exposure to chemical products, like deodorants, cleaning agents and perfumes, which can act as allergens.
- **Higher Stress Levels** Stress, more common in urban lifestyles, can weaken the immune system and increase the likelihood of allergic responses. (2)

5. An infection with HIV (Human Immunodeficiency Virus) can lead to AIDS (Acquired Immuno Deficiency Syndrome). It results in a gradual and persistent decline and failure of the immune system, resulting in heightened risk of life threatening infections and cancers.

The graph below given is showing the prevalence, new cases and death from HIV/AIDS, world 1990 to 2019. Observe it carefully and answer the questions that follows. **Competency Based Que.**

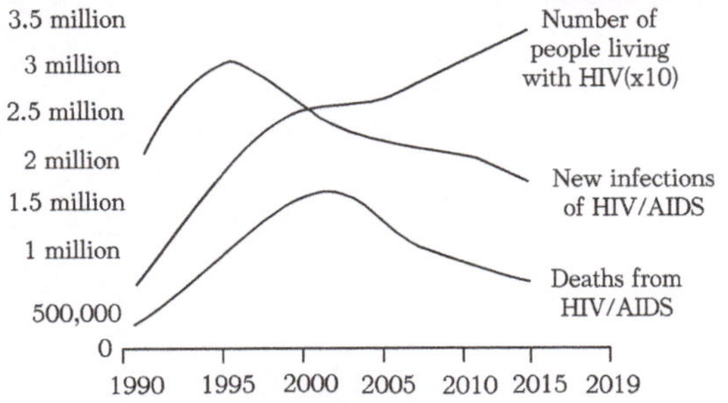

(i) What do you infer from the above graph?

(ii) List two ways by which the death from HIV/AIDS can be decreased.

(iii) Why in successive years (from the above graph) the survival rate has been increased?

Ans. (i) We infer that the number of people living with HIV is increasing in successive years which further leads to decreased deaths. (1)

(ii) Two ways by which the death from HIV/AIDS can be decreased

(a) Use condoms while having sex.

(b) Get tested and treated for STDs. (1)

(iii) Now-a-days, a person living with HIV has a similar life expectancy to an HIV negative person. This can happens when they are diagnosed in correct time, have good access to medical facilities and are able to adhere to their HIV treatment. However, death due to HIV is inevitable (2)

6. The graph given below is showing smoking, alcohol consumption and use of illicit drugs by people.

Study the graph given below and answer the following questions. **Competency Based Que.**

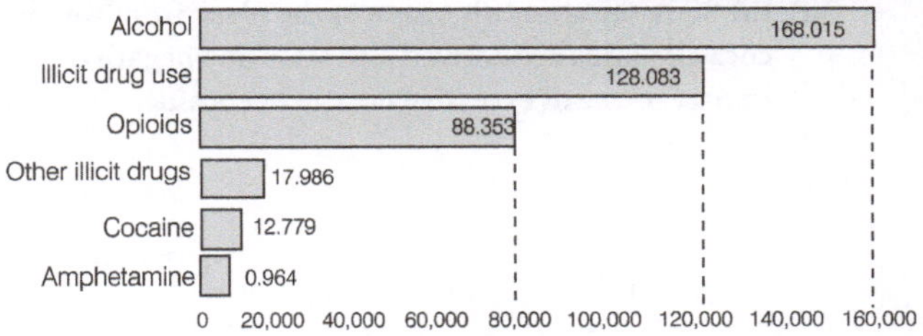

(i) Why did the alcohol consumption increase rapidly than the other drugs?

(ii) Will the adverse effects of opioids be more harmful than alcohol?

(iii) Why do atheletes use amphetamines?

(iv) What measure can be taken to decrease the drug and alcohol abuse?

Ans. (i) Alcohol consumption increases rapidly than other drugs is due to easy and increased availability of alcohol. (1)

(ii) Yes, at lower doses, opioids may make you feel sleepy but at higher doses, it can slow your breathing and heart rate, which may lead to death. (1)

(iii) Amphetamines are used by atheletes to reduce tiredness and fatigue and to increase alertness, competitiveness and aggressiveness. (1)

(iv) Refer to text on page no. 220. (1)

7. In 2021, 5.3 per cent of 15 to 16-year-olds worldwide (13.5 million individuals) had used *Cannabis* in the past year according to UNODC. The adolescent brain is still developing and drug use can have long-term negative effects. Early drug use initiation can lead to faster development of dependence than in adults and other problems in adulthood. Parts of the Amazon Basin are at the intersection of multiple forms of organised crimes that are accelerating devastation, with

severe implications for the security, health and well-being of the population across the region. The direct impact of coca cultivation on deforestation is minimal, but indirectly it acts as a catalyst for "Narco-deforestation". The laundering of drug trafficking profits into land speculation etc. is posing a growing danger to the world's largest rainforest.

CBSE 2025

(i) Which age group or period of growth people are more vulnerable to drug abuse?

(ii) Explain the negative impact of coca cultivation on the world's largest rainforest.

(iii) (a) From which part of the plant are cannabinoids mainly obtained? Mention any one negative effect of this drug on adolescents.

Or

(iii) (b) State the scientific name of the plant from which coca alkaloids are derived and state one negative impact of use of excessive dosage of cocaine.

Ans. (i) Adolescents aged 15 to 16 years are more vulnerable to drug abuse as their brains are still developing, making them more susceptible to dependence and long-term negative effects.

(ii) While coca cultivation has minimal direct impact on deforestation, it indirectly accelerates "Narco-deforestation" by facilitating land speculation and money laundering linked to drug trafficking. This leads to large-scale environmental destruction in the Amazon rainforest.

(iii) (a) Cannabinoids are mainly obtained from the resin of *Cannabis* plant. One negative effect of this drug on adolescents is impaired cognitive development, which can lead to memory loss and decreased learning ability.

Or

(iii) (b) Coca alkaloids are derived from the plant *Erythroxylum coca*. Excessive cocaine use can cause severe cardiovascular issues, including increased heart rate and high blood pressure, leading to potential heart failure.

SELF ASSESSMENT TEST

Multiple Choice Questions

1. What is the primary causative agent of malaria?
   (a) Virus (b) Bacteria (c) Protozoa (d) Fungus
2. Malignant malaria is caused by
   (a) *Plasmodium vivax* (b) *Plasmodium malariae*
   (c) *Plasmodium falciparum* (d) *Anopheles*
3. During plasma transfusions from healthy persons, individuals acquire all the components present in the plasma of the healthy person. Which of the following types of immunity is the above an example of?
   (a) Naturally-acquired active immunity (b) Artificially-acquired active immunity
   (c) Naturally-acquired passive immunity (d) Artificially-acquired passive immunity
4. Passive immunisation does not include
   (a) transfer of lymphocytes directly
   (b) use of colostrum by newborn baby
   (c) introduction of antibodies directly into the body
   (d) transfer of maternal antibodies across placenta to foetus
5. HIV primarily attacks which type of cells in the human body?
   (a) Red blood cells (b) White blood cells (c) Platelets (d) Neurons
6. Transformation of normal cells into cancerous neoplastic cells may be induced by some agents, which are called
   (a) carcinogens (b) oncogenes (c) oncogenic viruses (d) neoplasts
7. The flower tops, leaves and the resin of *Cannabis* plant are used in various combinations to produce
   (a) Marijuana (b) Hashish (c) Both (a) and (b) (d) Only (a)

Assertion-Reason Questions

Direction (Q. Nos. 8-11) *In each of the following questions, a statement of Assertion (A) is given followed by corresponding statement of Reason (R). Of the statements, mark the correct answer*

(a) Both A and R are true and R is the correct explanation of A.
(b) Both A and R are true, but R is not the correct explanation of A.
(c) A is true, but R is false.
(d) A is false, but R is true.

8. **Assertion** (A) Malaria is primarily transmitted through the bite of infected female *Anopheles* mosquitoes.

   Reason (R) Mosquitoes are vectors that carry and transmit pathogens to humans.
9. **Assertion** (A) The primary lymphoid organs are bone marrow and thymus.

   Reason (R) The bone marrow is the main lymphoid organ where all blood cells including lymphocytes are produced.
10. **Assertion** (A) Viruses secrete proteins called interferons.

    Reason (R) α-interferon activates the immune system and helps in destroying the tumour.
11. **Assertion** (A) Opioids are the drugs, which bind to specific opioid receptors present in the central nervous system and gastrointestinal tract.

    Reason (R) Opioids are chemically diacetylmethane which is a white, odourless, bitter crystalline compound.

Very Short Answer Type Questions

12. Immune responses to allergens are an example of active acquired immunity. Justify
13. What are non-infectious diseases? Give any two examples.
14. How does cancer spread in body?
15. Write any two symptoms of elephantiasis or filariasis.

Short Answer Type Questions

16. Draw a labelled diagram of life cycle of *Plasmodium*.
17. What is immunity? Write the difference between acquired and innate immunity.
18. From an immunological point of view, predict the consequences if a person is transplanted with a kidney without tissue matching.
19. What happens when:
    (a) A newborn is not breastfed. (b) A tumour cell enters the bloodstream.

Long Answer Type Questions

20. What are lymphoid organs? Explain primary and secondary lymphoid organ and their functions.
21. Discuss the similarities and differences between cancer and AIDS in terms of their causes, progression, and treatment.
22. Write a short note on
    (i) Opioids (ii) Cocaine (iii) Withdrawal syndrome or ascariasis.

Case Based Question

23. The graph given below shows the levels fo antibodies against a pathogen over a period of 30 years in a person's body.

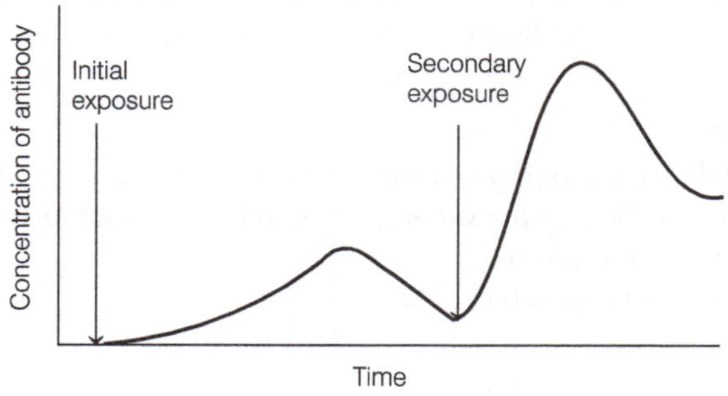

(i) What do the 2 peaks mean?
(ii) Explain the reason behind the difference in the size of the 2 peaks.
(iii) Explain the term antibody and name different types of antibodies found in human body.

Answers

1. (c)	2. (c)	3. (d)	4. (a)	5. (b)	6. (a)	7. (c)
8. (a)	9. (b)	10. (d)	11. (c)			

08

CHAPTER

Microbes are the major components of biological system on the earth. These are the microscopic organisms that are too small to be seen by the naked eyes.
The diverse forms of microbes include protozoans, bacteria, fungi, microscopic animal and plant along with viruses, viroids and prions (proteinaceous infectious agents).

▼ YOUR STUDY GOALS

8.1 Introduction
8.2 Microbes in Household Products
8.3 Microbes in Industrial Products
8.4 Microbes in Sewage Treatment
8.5 Microbes in Production of Biogas
8.6 Microbes as Biocontrol Agents
8.7 Microbes as Biofertilisers

▼ YOUR PRACTICE GOAL

- Objective Type Questions
  (38 Qs ; MCQs, A-R)
  Case Based Questions (5)
- Subjective Type Questions
- (17 VSA, 53 SAs, 9 LAs)

Microbes in Human Welfare

8.1 Introduction

- Microbes are present everywhere on earth, i.e. in soil, air, water, inside our body and that of other animals and plants.
- They are even present in extreme conditions like thermal vents (geysers) with high temperature as 100°C, under thick layers of snow and in highly acidic environments.
- The microbes like, fungi and bacteria can be cultured in laboratory on nutritive media to form colonies, that can be seen with the naked eyes. Such cultures are useful in scientific studies on microorganisms.
- Microbes are causal agents of large number of infectious diseases, but they also have been used by humans for many important processes in houses, industries, agriculture and also in sewage treatment.
- Some of the most important contributions of microbes to human welfare are discussed in this chapter.

8.2 Microbes in Household Products

- Microbes and their products are used by humans in everyday life for various purposes, e.g. they are used to ferment fish, bamboo shoots, soyabean etc. to make variety of foods.

- They are also used in production of curd, formation of dough and cheese etc.
- Let us now discuss these applications in detail.

Curd

- Microorganisms like *Lactobacillus*, commonly called **Lactic Acid Bacteria** (LAB) grow in milk and convert it into curd.
- As seen at home a starter is added to milk which turns it into curd. This starter is known as **inoculum** and it contains millions of LAB.
- At suitable temperature these bacteria grow and produce acids that coagulate and partially digest the milk proteins, thus converting milk to curd.
- They also improve nutritional quality by increasing vitamin-B_{12} content of the curd. A number of organic acids are also found in curd.
- LAB also play very beneficial role in checking disease causing microbes in our stomach.

Dough

- Foods like idli and dosa are prepared using dough fermented by bacterium.
- The puffed-up appearance of the dough is due to the production of CO_2 gas during fermentation by bacteria.
- In a similar way, dough used for bread making is fermented using baker's **yeast**, *Saccharomyces cerevisiae.*

TEACHER'S TIP

The CO_2 generated during the dough-making process is a result of alcoholic fermentation. Yeast in the dough breaks down sugar, producing both alcohol and CO_2. The CO_2 produced causes the dough to rise and give it a light, airy texture, While the alcohol evaporates during the baking process.

Toddy

- A number of traditional drinks are also made by fermentation.
- Toddy is a traditional drink of some parts of Southern India.
- It is made by fermenting sap from palm trees.

Cheese

- It is formed by the partial degradation of milk by different microorganisms.
- It is one of the oldest food item in which microbes were used.
- Different varieties of cheese are known by their texture, flavour and taste. This specificity is derived from the microbes used during manufacturing process. For example,
  - **Swiss cheese** with large holes is produced by *Propionibacterium sharmanii.* These holes are created due to the production of large amount of CO_2 by this bacterium.
  - **Roquefort cheese** are ripened by growing a specific fungi, *Penicillium roqueforti* on it, which gives it a particular flavour.

8.3 Microbes in Industrial Products

- A variety of microbes are used to synthesise a number of products valuable to human beings in industries, e.g. beverages and antibiotics.
- For industrial production, microbes are grown in very large vessels called **fermentors.**

Fig. 8.1 Fermentor

Fermented Beverages

- Microbes, especially yeasts have been used from time immemorial for the production of beverages like wine, beer, whisky, brandy and rum. For this purpose, the same yeast, *Saccharomyces cerevisiae* (also known as **Brewer's yeast**) is used for bread making.

- Fermentation of malted cereals and fruit juices results in the production of ethanol.
- Depending upon the type of raw material and processing (with or without distillation), different types of alcoholic drinks are prepared.
- Wine and beer are filtered and bottled without distillation. In contrast, whisky, brandy and rum are produced by distillation (to increase the alcoholic content) of fermented broth.

Antibiotics

- The term antibiotics is derived from the Greek word *Anti*–against and *bio*–life, together they mean **'against life'** (with reference to disease causing organisms).
- These are the chemical substances, produced by some microbes that can kill or retard the growth of other disease causing microbes.
- Antibiotics produced by microbes are regarded as one of the most significant discoveries of the 20th century.
- The first discovered antibiotic was **penicillin.**

Discovery of Penicillin

- **Alexander Fleming,** while working on *Staphylococci* bacteria, found a mould growing in one of his unwashed culture plates around which *Staphylococci* could not grow.
- This mould produced a chemical, which inhibits the bacterial growth. It was named as penicillin after the mould, *Penicillium notatum.*
- However, its full potential as an effective antibiotic was established much later by **Ernest Chain** and **Howard Florey**.
- Penicillin was extensively used in treating American soldiers wounded in World War-II.
- **Fleming, Chain** and **Florey** were awarded the Nobel Prize in 1945, for this discovery.
- Some other antibiotics were also purified after the successful discovery of *Penicillium*, e.g. fumagillin from *Aspergillus fumigatus.*
- Antibiotic have greatly improved the capacity to treat deadly diseases like plague, whooping cough (kali khansi), diphtheria (gal ghotu), leprosy (kusht rog) etc., which used to kill millions of people all over the world.

TEACHER'S TIP

Antibiotics are beneficial against bacteria, but inadequate against viruses because they target structures like cell walls and ribosomes in bacterial cells. On the other hand viruses lack these structures which make them resistance towards the antibiotics.

Judicious use of Antibiotics

- Judicious use of antibiotics is an important concern and thus it should be thoroughly taken care of.
- Excess antibiotic use is a well-documented risk factor for infection or development of resistant pathogens.
- The unnecessary use of antibiotics for viral illness is common and it has led to increasing rates of antibiotic resistance among *Streptococcus pneumoniae* and other community of acquired pathogens.
- Thus, appropriate doses of antibiotics should be taken for a specific duration of time as prescribed by the physician.
- Factors that contribute to antibiotic overuse include lack of education, patient's expectations and past experiences.

Chemicals, Enzymes and other Bioactive Molecules

- Microbes are being used for commercial and industrial production of certain chemicals like alcohols, organic acids, enzymes and other **bioactive molecules** (molecules which are functional in living systems or can interact with their components).
- Some of them are given below.

Organic acids produced by microbes and their uses

Organic acids	Microorganisms	Uses
Citric acid	*Aspergillus niger* (fungus)	Used for the preservation of food and candies
Acetic acid	*Acetobacter aceti* (bacterium)	Used in dyes and pharmaceuticals.
Butyric acid	*Clostridium butylicum* (bacterium)	Used as flavouring agent.
Lactic acid	*Lactobacillus* (bacterium)	Used in confectionery, curing of meat and as mordant in tanning.

Enzymes produced by microbes and their uses

Enzymes	Microorganisms	Uses
Lipases	*Candida lipolytica* (fungus)	Used in detergent formulations. They are helpful in removing oily stains from the laundry.
Pectinases and proteases	*Aspergillus* sp. (fungus)	Used in clearing of bottled juices.
Streptokinase	*Streptococcus* (bacterium)	Used as a 'clot buster' for removing clots from the blood vessels of heart patients, who have undergone myocardial infarction, leading to heart attack.

Bioactive molecules produced by microbes and their uses

Bioactive molecules (Products)	Microorganisms	Uses
Cyclosporin-A	*Trichoderma polysporum* (fungus)	Used as an immuno-suppressive agent in organ transplant patients.
Statins	*Monascus purpureus* (yeast)	Used as blood cholesterol lowering agents as it competitively inhibit the enzyme responsible for cholesterol synthesis.

Quick Test 1

1. In the process of curd formation, the decrease in pH is mainly due to the production of which component by LAB?
2. The production of CO_2 during dough-making is a direct outcome of which process in yeast cells?
3. Why are drinks like whisky and rum more intoxicating than wine?
4. **State True or False.**
   Using antibiotics in farming and agriculture can contribute to antibiotic resistance in humans.
5. Name the organic acid that is produced by a fungus and used for the preservation of candies.
6. A bioactive molecule, '*X*,' is commonly used in the treatment of organ transplant patients. Which microorganism is responsible for producing this molecule?

8.4 Microbes in Sewage Treatment

- **Sewage** refers to the municipal wastewater generated everyday in cities and towns. Human excreta is the major component of it.
- Besides it, sewage contains large amount of organic matter and microbes, out of which many are pathogenic. So, it cannot be discharged directly into natural water bodies like rivers, streams, etc.
- Before disposal, sewage has to be treated in **Sewage Treatment Plants** (STPs) in order to make it less polluting. The treatment of wastewater is done by the heterotrophic microbes, which are naturally present in the sewage.
- Sewage treatment is carried out in two stages as described below.

Primary Treatment

- It is also known as **physical treatment** because it basically involves the physical removal of small and large, floating and suspended solids from sewage through filtration and sedimentation.
- Initially, floating debris is removed by sequential filtration. Then, the **grit** (soil and small pebbles) are removed by sedimentation in settling tanks.
- All solids that settle form the **primary sludge,** which include lots of microbes and debris. The supernatant forms the **effluent**.
- This effluent is then taken from the primary settling tank for secondary treatment.

Secondary Treatment

- This treatment is also known as **biological treatment** because it involves the use of microbes for the treatment of sewage.
- The effluent from primary treatment is passed into large aeration tanks, where it is constantly, mechanically agitated and air is pumped into it.

Fig. 8.2 An aerial view of sewage treatment plant

- This air helps in the vigrous growth of useful aerobic microbes into **flocs** (masses of bacteria associated with fungal filament to form mesh-like structures). While growing, these microbes consume major part of the organic matter in the effluent. This significantly reduces the **Biochemical Oxygen Demand** (BOD) of the effluent.
- BOD refers to amount of oxygen that would be consumed if all the organic matter in one litre of water were oxidised by bacteria. So, the sewage water is treated till the BOD is reduced.

> The BOD test measures the rate of uptake of oxygen by microorganisms in a sample of water and thus, indirectly, BOD is a measure of the organic matter present in the water. The greater the BOD of waste water, more is its polluting potential.

- When the BOD of effluent is reduced significantly, it is then passed into a settling tank, where the bacterial 'flocs' are allowed to sediment. This sediment is called **activated sludge**.
- A small part of the activated sludge is then pumped back into the aeration tank to serve as the inoculum.
- The remaining part of the sludge is pumped into large tanks called **anaerobic sludge digesters**, in which other anaerobic bacteria (methanogens) are also present.
- They digest the organic mass as well as **aerobic microbes** (bacteria) and fungi of the sludge.

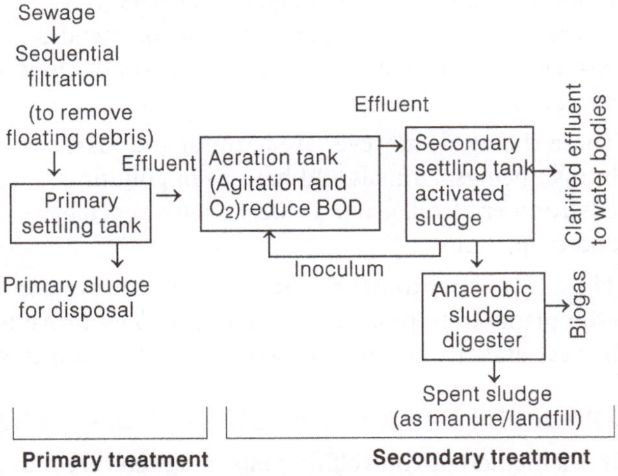

Fig. 8.3 Schematic representation of sewage treatment plant

- During the digestion, mixture of gases like methane (CH_4), hydrogen sulphide (H_2S), carbon dioxide (CO_2), etc., are produced by bacteria.
- These gases form **biogas** that is used as a source of energy because it is inflammable.
- The effluent from secondary treatment plant is released into natural water bodies like rivers and streams.

River Action Plan

- Currently, each country is producing several million gallons of wastewater everyday.
- However, the number of sewage treatment plants has not increased correspondingly. Due to this, untreated sewage is being discharged directly into river and water bodies which cause pollution and water-borne diseases.
- The **Ministry of Environment and Forests** initiated **Ganga Action Plan, Yamuna Action Plan, Sutlej Action Plan, Gomti Action Plan**, etc., to save these major rivers of our country from pollution.
- These plans are proposed to build a large number of sewage treatment plants, so that only treated sewage may be discharged into these rivers.

Quick Test 2

1. In a sewage treatment plant, which process is critical for reducing the load of large solids like grit, leaves and debris?
2. **State True or False.**
   Flocs are only effective in the removal of solid particles, not in the removal of dissolved organic matter.
3. Which parameter is commonly used to evaluate water quality in rivers or lakes impacted by organic waste?
4. River *A* has a BOD of 20 mg/L, while River *B* has a BOD of 60 mg/L. Based on BOD levels, which river is likely to have better water quality?
5. Identify whether the given statement is correct or incorrect.
   Flocs are digested by microorganisms during the final stage of sewage treatment.

8.5 Microbes in Production of Biogas

Fuels of biological origin, which are used for the production of heat and other form of energy are termed as **biofuels**.

The energy derived from the biofuels is called **bioenergy.** For example, Biogas is methane-rich fuel (source of bio energy) which is produced by microbial activity.

Biogas

- It is a mixture of gases in which the major content is methane. Biogas is produced by the anaerobic microbial activity during digestion of biomass. It is used as fuel.
- The type of gas produced by microbes during their growth and the organic substrates they utilise.
- Certain bacteria grow anaerobically on cellulosic material and produce large amount of methane along with CO_2 and H_2.
- These bacteria are called **methanogens** and one such common bacterium is *Methanobacterium*.
- They are generally present in anaerobic sludge during sewage treatment.
- Rumen (a part of stomach) of cattle also contains methanogens. Here, they help in the breakdown of cellulosic material in the food and thus play an important role in nutrition of cattle.

TEACHER'S TIP

Humans cannot digest cellulose because humans lack the enzyme **cellulase** that breakdown this complex substances. Undigestible cellulose is the fibre which aids in the smooth working of the intestinal tract.

- The excreta of cattle, commonly called **gobar**, is rich in methanogenic bacteria. Thus, cattle dung can be used for the generation of biogas, commonly called as **gobar gas**.
- Cattle dung is available in large quantities in rural areas, hence biogas plants are mostly functional in rural areas.

Biogas Plant

- A typical biogas plant (fig. 8.4) consists of a concrete tank (10-15 feet deep) in which bio-wastes are collected and slurry of dung is fed.
- A floating cover is placed over the slurry, which keeps on rising, as the gas is produced in the tank due to the microbial activity.
- The plant has an outlet which connects to a pipe that supply biogas to the nearby houses.
- The biogas thus, produced is used for cooking and lighting.
- There is another outlet from which spent slurry is removed. The slurry that can be used as fertiliser.
- Biogas production technology was developed in India mainly by **Khadi and Village Industries Commission** (KVIC) and **Indian Agricultural Research Institute** (IARI).

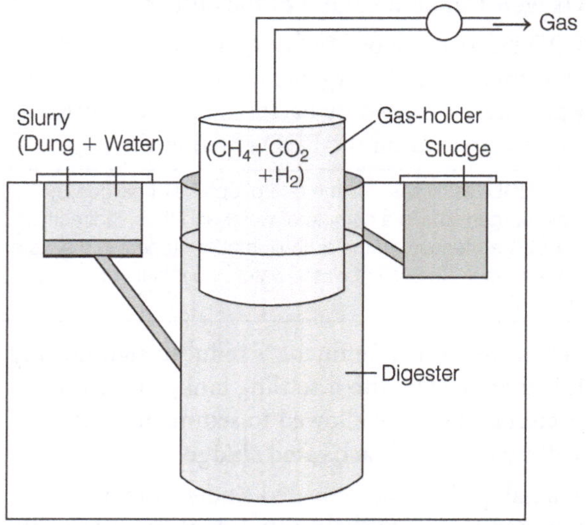

Fig. 8.4 A typical biogas plant

8.6 Microbes as Biocontrol Agents

- Biocontrol refers to the use of biological methods for controlling plant diseases and pests.
- In modern agricultural system, the farmers have increased the use of chemicals such as insecticides, pesticides, weedicides, etc., to control plant diseases and pests.
- These chemicals however are harmful and toxic for human beings, animals and have been polluting environment (soil, groundwater), fruits, vegetables and crop plants.
- Thus, it is better to use biological agents to save our crop plants from pests, etc. Certain microbes prove to be very effective biocontrol agents as explained below.

Biological Control of Pests and Diseases

- It is a method of controlling pests in agriculture that relies on natural predation and not on chemicals.

- Organic farmers believe that 'biodiversity furthers health'. The more diversity a landscape has, the more sustainable it is.
- Therefore, they work to create a system where the insects (pests) are not eradicated, but kept at manageable levels by a complex system of checks and balance within a living and vibrant ecosystem.
- Unlike 'conventional' farming practices where chemical methods are used to kill both useful and harmful life forms indiscriminately, this is a holistic approach.
- This method seeks to develop an understanding of the webs of interaction between the myriad of organisms, including both flora and fauna in the field.
- Biological farming approach requires familiarity with various life forms, their habitat, predators as well as pest, their life cycle, patterns of feeding, etc., to use them in biocontrol measures and reduce the dependence on chemicals and pesticides.

Examples of Biological Control Agents

Some examples of biological control agents are as follows.

- **Ladybird** and **dragonflies** are useful to get rid of aphids and mosquitoes, respectively.
- To control butterfly caterpillars, bacteria such as *Bacillus thuringiensis* are used in the form of sachets as dry spores.
  - These are mixed with water and sprayed onto vulnerable plants like brassicas and fruit trees, where these are eaten by the insects larvae. The alkaline pH of the insect gut solubilises the toxin crystals.
  - This kills the larvae due to the release of toxin in their gut, thereby eradicating the caterpillars, but leaving other insects unharmed.
  - *Bacillus thuringiensis* toxin genes are introduced into plants by using genetic engineering methods. Such plants are resistant to attack by insect pests. *Bt* cotton is one such example.
- *Trichoderma* species are free-living fungi that are very common in the root ecosystems. They are effective biocontrol agents of several plant pathogens.
- **Baculoviruses** belonging to genus- *Nucleopolyhedrovirus* are used as biological control agents.
  - They are pathogens that attack insects and other arthropods.
  - These viruses are excellent for species-specific, narrow spectrum insecticidal applications. Baculoviruses do not have any negative impact on plants, mammals, birds, fishes or even on non-target insects.
  - Thus, biological control agents are useful in overall Integrated Pest Management (IPM) programme, especially when beneficial insects have to be conserved or when an ecologically sensitive area is being treated.

8.7 Microbes as Biofertilisers

- The chemical fertilisers are being used in increasing amounts in order to increase the agricultural output.
- However, due to excessive use of these chemical fertilisers, there is increase in pollution.
- Thus, there is a pressure to switch to **organic farming** and to use biofertilisers.
- **Biofertilisers** are organisms that enrich the nutrient quality of soil by enhancing the availability of nutrients to the crops.
- The main sources of biofertilisers are as discussed below.

Bacteria

- Nitrogen-fixing bacteria fix atmospheric nitrogen into organic form, which is used by the plant as nutrient.
- For example, *Rhizobium* is a symbiotic bacterium that lives in the root nodules of legumes and fixes atmospheric nitrogen into organic compounds.
- *Azotobacter* and *Azospirillum* are free-living bacteria, that fix atmospheric nitrogen and convert it into nitrogen compounds.

Fungi

- They also form symbiotic association with plants, i.e. **mycorrhiza.**
- The fungal symbiont absorb phosphorus from soil and passes it to the plants.
- Many members of genus- *Glomus* form mycorrhiza. Plants with mycorrhizal association also show other benefits also such as
    - Resistance to root-borne pathogens.
    - Increased tolerance to salinity and drought.
    - Increase in overall plant growth and development.

Cyanobacteria

- These are autotrophic microbes found in aquatic and terrestrial environments. Most of them fix atmospheric nitrogen, e.g. *Anabaena, Nostoc, Oscillatoria*, etc.
- In paddy fields, cyanobacteria serve as important biofertiliser.
- Blue-Green Algae (BGA) also add organic matter to the soil. Thus, it increases soil fertility.

Quick Test 3

1. If *Methanobacterium* were removed from a biogas plant, how would the efficiency of biogas production and the overall methane yield be affected?
2. **State True or False.**
   The breakdown of cellulose is primarily responsible for the production of biogas in anaerobic digestion.
3. If *Bacillus thuringiensis* sachets are inhaled by a human, does it produce toxin?
4. An organism '*X*' forms a symbiotic association with legumes and fixes atmospheric nitrogen for the plant. Identify organism '*X*'.
5. Members of *Nucleopolyhedrovirus* do not harm birds, fishes and mammals. Identify, whether given statement is correct or not.

Mind Map

Microbes in Human Welfare

Microbes in Household Products

- **LAB (Lactic Acid Bacteria)** Grows in milk and converts it into curd; increases vitamin-B_{12} content.
- **Baker's Yeast** (*Saccharomyces cerevisiae*) Causes fermentation and produces carbon dioxide
- **Toddy** A traditional drink prepared by fermenting palm sap using microbes.
- **Swiss Cheese** Large holes due to CO_2 production by bacterium, *Propionibacterium sharmanii.*

Microbes in Industrial Products

Used to synthesise a number of valuable products such as

- **Fermented Beverage** Yeasts are used for production of wine, beer, whisky, etc.
- **Antibiotics** Chemical substances produced by microbes that kill or retard growth of other microbes, e.g. penicillin from *Penicillium notatum* (1st antibiotic discovered by **Alexander Fleming**).
- **Chemicals**, e.g. citric acid from *Aspergillus niger*, etc.
- **Enzymes**, e.g. lipases, pectinases.
- **Bioactive Molecules** Molecules that are functional in living systems or can interact with their components, e.g. cyclosporin-A from *Trichoderma polysporum* used as immuno suppressive agent.

Microbes in Sewage Treatment

Sewage is treated in STPs before disposal where treatment of wastewater is done by heterotrophic microbes, naturally present in sewage.

Sewage
↓
Sequential filtration (To remove floating debris)
↓
Primary setling tank → Effluent → Aeration tank (Agitation and O_2) reduce BOD → Effluent → Secondary Setling tank Activated sludge → Clarified effluent to water bodies

Primary setling tank → Primary sludge for diposal

Secondary Setling tank → Inoculum → Aeration tank

Secondary Setling tank → Anaerobic sludge digester → Spent sludge (as manure/landfill)

Primary Treatment | Secondary Treatment

Microbes in Production of Biogas

- **Biogas** is a methane rich mixture of gases produced by the anaerobic digestion of biomass with the help of methanogenic bacteria (methanogens).
- Methanogens grow anaerobically on cellulosic material producing CH_4 along with CO_2 and H_2. Also present in rumen of cattle.
- **Biogas plants** are functional in rural areas for generating biogas. Cattle dung rich in methanogens is used.

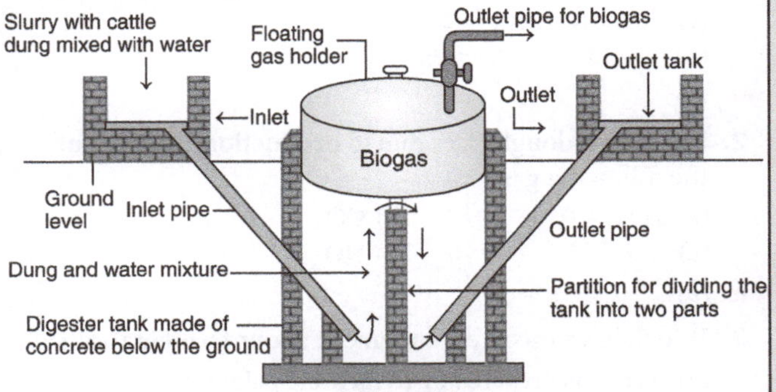

A Biogas Plant

Microbes as Biocontrol Agents

Biocontrol is the use of biological methods for controlling plant diseases and pests. For example,

- **Fungus**
  e.g. *Trichoderma* sp. → Kills root borne pathogens
- **Bacteria**
  e.g. *Bacillus thuringiensis* → Kills the pink bollworm attacking *Bt*-cotton by producing an insecticidal 'Cry' protein.
- **Viruses**
  e.g. *Nucleopolyhedrovirus* (Baculoviruses) → Attack specific insects and other arthropods.

Microbes as Biofertilisers

- Biofertilisers are organisms that bring about nutrient enrichment of soil.
- The main sources are
  - **Bacteria** such as *Rhizobium* (symbiotic) and *Azotobacter* (free-living) fix atmospheric nitrogen into organic form.
  - **Fungi** form symbiotic association with plants as mycorrhiza. Absorb phosphorus from soil, e.g. members of genus–*Glomus*.
  - **Cyanobacteria**, e.g. *Anabaena, Nostoc* can fix atmospheric nitrogen. Add organic matter to soil.

EXAM PATTERN QUESTIONS

Objective Type Questions

Multiple Choice Questions

1. *Lactobacillus* that sets milk into curd is categorised as **CBSE 2024**

(a) cyanobacteria
(b) Archaebacteria
(c) chemosynthetic bacteria
(d) heterotrophic bacteria

Ans. (*d*)

2. Idli – dosa dough rises due to production of which of the following gas?

(a) CO (b) CO_2
(c) NO (d) NO_2

Ans. (*b*)

3. Which is an incorrect statement about fermentation?

(a) Toddy is prepared by fermenting palm sap
(b) The *Propionibacterium* is used in fermentation of cheese
(c) Fermentation in muscles produces alcohol
(d) The production of CO_2 in dough causes puffed up appearance

Ans. (*c*)

4. A patient brought to a hospital with myocardial infarction is normally immediately given

(a) streptokinase (b) penicillin
(c) cyclosporin-A (d) statins

Ans. (*a*) In the case of a patient suffering with a myocardial infarction (heart attack), the immediate treatment typically involves the use of streptokinase. It is a thrombolytic agent, used to breakdown clots present in the blood vessels.

5. Which of the following bacteria has a role in removing clots in our blood vessels. **Diksha**

(a) *Bacillus thuringiensis* (b) *Clostridium butyricum*
(c) *Streptococcus* (d) *Lactobacillus*

Ans. (*c*)

6. Large scale industrial production of streptokinase for human welfare is done using the microbe **CBSE 2025**

(a) *Streptomyces* (b) *Streptococcus*
(c) *Streptobacilli* (d) *Streptopneumoniae*

Ans. (*b*) *Streptococcus* produces streptokinase, used in clot dissolution.

7. Large scale industrial production of butyric acid for human welfare is done using the microbes **CBSE 2025**

(a) *Aspergillus* sp. (b) *Streptococcus* sp.
(c) *Clostridium* sp. (d) *Trichoderma* sp.

Ans. (*c*) The large-scale industrial production of butyric acid is carried out using anaerobic bacteria, primarily *Clostridium* species. These bacteria ferment carbohydrates to produce butyric acid.

8. Given below are the list of the commercially important products and their source organisms. Select the option that gives the correct matches. **CBSE 2023**

	List A (Bioactive products)		List B Microbes (Source organism)
A.	Cyclosporin-A	1.	*Streptococcus*
B.	Statins	2.	*Trichoderma polysporum*
C.	Streptokinase	3.	*Penicillium notatum*
D.	Penicillin	4.	*Monascus purpureus*

Codes

	A	B	C	D		A	B	C	D
(a)	1	2	3	4	(b)	3	4	2	1
(c)	4	3	2	1	(d)	2	4	1	3

Ans. (*d*)

9. During the secondary treatment of sewage, which of the following change in the effluent occur due to flocs? **Competency Based Que.**

(a) Reduction in BOD (b) Increase in BOD
(c) Decrease in DO (d) No change in DO or BOD

Ans. (*a*) Flocs are aggregates of microorganisms that breakdown organic matter in sewage. As they metabolise this organic matter, the Biochemical Oxygen Demand (BOD) decreases, indicating improved water quality.

10. A scientist measured the BOD (Biochemical Oxygen Demand) of water from the following sources.
kitchen tap – Sample *P*
sewer pipe – Sample *Q* **Competency Based Que.**
Choose the correct statement.

(a) The BOD of sample *P* will be lesser than sample *Q*.
(b) The BOD of sample *P* will be greater than sample *Q*.
(c) The BOD of sample *P* will be equal to that of sample *Q*.
(d) The BOD of the two samples cannot be compared without additional data.

Ans. (*a*) Water from a kitchen tap (sample *P*) is generally cleaner and contains less organic matter compared to sewage from a sewer pipe (sample *Q*), which has a higher concentration of organic pollutants. Therefore, the BOD of the sample from the kitchen tap is expected to be lower than that from the sewer pipe.

11. Which one of the following statement regarding BOD is true?

(a) The greater the BOD of waste, less is its polluting potential
(b) The greater the BOD of wastewater, greater its polluting potential
(c) The lesser the BOD of wastewater more is its polluting potential
(d) All of the above

Ans. (*b*) A higher BOD indicates a higher concentration of organic pollutants, meaning that more oxygen will be required by microorganisms to breakdown this organic matter, which can lead to lower dissolved oxygen levels in the water.

12. Ganga action plan and Yamuna action plan have been initiated by the

(a) Ministry of Home Affairs
(b) Ministry of Agriculture
(c) Ministry of Environment and Forests
(d) Ministry of Chemical and Fertiliser

Ans. (*c*)

13. The technology of biogas production from cow dung was developed in India largely due to the efforts of **NCERT Exemplar**

(a) Gas Authority of India
(b) Oil and Natural Gas Commission
(c) Indian Agricultural Research Institute, Khadi and Village Industries Commission
(d) Indian Oil Corporation

Ans. (*c*)

14. The diagram given below represents a typical biogas plant. Select the correct option for *A*, *B* and *C* respectively.

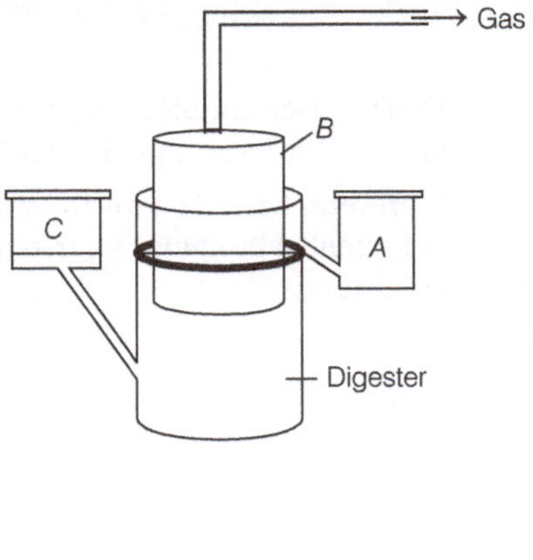

(a) *A*–Sludge, *B*–Dung + Water, *C*–$CH_4 + CO_2$
(b) *A*–Dung + Water, *B*–Sludge, *C*–$CH_4 + CO_2$
(c) *A*–Sludge, *B*–$CH_4 + CO_2$, *C*–Dung + Water
(d) *A*– $CH_4 + CO_2$, *B*–Dung + Water, *C*–Sludge

Ans. (*c*)

15. Methanogenic bacteria are not found in

(a) rumen of cattle
(b) gobar gas plant
(c) bottom of water logged paddy fields
(d) activated sludge

Ans. (*d*)

16. Read the given statements and choose the incorrect option with regard to the biocontrol agents.

(a) Biocontrol refers to the use of biological methods for the control of plant diseases and pests.
(b) Biocontrol refers to the use of natural predation to control plant diseases and pests.
(c) The chemical used are toxic and extremely harmful to human beings and animals.
(d) The use of biocontrol agents greatly reduce our dependence an toxic chemicals and pesticides.

Ans. (*c*)

17. Consider the following statements.

I. Ladybirds and dragonflies are used to get rid of aphids and mosquitoes.
II. The bacteria Bacillus thuringiensis **(*Bt*) are used to control caterpillars.**
III. *Trichoderma* sp., free-living fungi, are present in root ecosystem where they act against several plant pathogens.
IV. *Rhizobium* is a symbiotic bacterium that lives in the stem nodes of legumes.

Which of the statements given above are correct? **Competency Based Que.**

(a) I, II and III (b) I, III and IV
(c) II, III and IV (d) II and IV

Ans. (*a*)

18. *Bt* crops are resistant to pests. Identify the bacterium from whom the gene is isolated for pest resistance.

(a) *Bacillus thuringiensis* (b) *Bacillus thermus aquaticus*
(c) *Pseudomonas* (d) *Staphylococcus*

Ans. (*a*)

19. Select the biocontrol agents.

(a) *Trichoderma*, baculovirus, *Bacillus thuringiensis*
(b) *Oscillatoria, Rhizobium, Trichoderma*
(c) *Nostoc, Azospirillum, Nucleopolyhedrovirus*
(d) *Bacillus thuringiensis*, tobacco mosaic virus, aphids

Ans. (*a*)

20. Which of the following is not used as a biopesticide?
(a) *Bacillus thuringiensis*
(b) *Trichoderma harzianum*
(c) *Nucleopolyhedrovirus* (NPV)
(d) *Xanthomonas campestris*

Ans. (*d*)

21. The free-living fungus *Trichoderma* can be used for **NCERT Exemplar**
(a) killing insects
(b) biological control of plant diseases
(c) controlling butterflies
(d) producing antibiotics

Ans. (*b*)

22. Mycorrhiza does not help the host plant in **NCERT Exemplar**
(a) enhancing its phosphorus uptake capacity
(b) increasing its tolerance to drought
(c) enhancing its resistance to root pathogens
(d) increasing its resistance to insects

Ans. (*d*) Mycorrhiza primarily enhance plant health by improving nutrient and water uptake, increasing drought tolerance, and providing some protection against root pathogens. However, they do not specifically increase resistance to insect pests.

23. In plants, which one of the following helps in the absorption of phosporus from soil? **CBSE 2024 C**
(a) *Glomus* (b) *Rhizobium*
(c) *Frankia* (d) *Anabaena*

Ans. (*a*)

24. Which one of the following is not a nitrogen fixing organism? **NCERT Exemplar**
(a) *Anabaena* (b) *Nostoc*
(c) *Azotobacter* (d) *Pseudomonas*

Ans. (*d*)

Assertion-Reason Questions

Direction (Q. Nos. 1-14) *In each of the following questions, a statement of Assertion (A) is given by corresponding statement of Reason (R). Of the statements, mark the correct answer as*
(a) Both A and R are true and R is the correct explanation of A
(b) Both A and R are true, but R is not correct explanation of A
(c) A is true, but R is false
(d) A is false, but R is true

1. Assertion (A) Besides curdling of milk, LAB also improve curd's nutritional quality.

Reason (R) LAB, when present in human stomach, check disease causing microbes.

Ans. (*b*) Both A and R are true, but R is not the correct explanation of A. A can be explained as
Besides curdling of milk, LAB also improves curd's nutritional quality by increasing vitamin-B_{12}.

2. Assertion (A) Yeast, such as *Saccharomyces cerevisiae*, are used in baking industry.

Reason (R) Carbon dioxide produced by fermentation causes bread dough to rise by thermal expansion.

Ans. (*c*)

3. Assertion (A) Whisky and rum are produced by distillation of the fermented broth.

Reason (R) Ethanol is produced by fermenting malted cereals and fruit juices by yeast.

Ans. (*b*)

4. Assertion (A) Streptomycin is produced from *Streptomyces griseus*.

Reason (R) Streptomycin is given to patients suffering from pneumonia, meningitis and typhoid.

Ans. (*b*)

5. Given below is the visualisation of an antibiotic. Look at the image and comment upon the appropriateness of the Assertion and Reason. **Competency Based Que.**

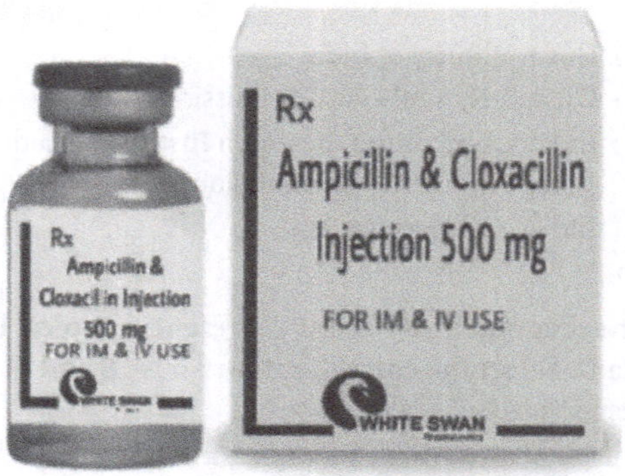

Assertion (A) The given antibiotic is primarily used during World War-II to treat wounded soldiers.

Reason (R) It prevents bacterial growth by preventing the synthesis of essential proteins required by bacteria to carry out vital functions.

Ans. (*b*)

6. Juices sold in the market are usually bottled or contained in tetrapacks. This calls for their hygienic importances. Carefully see the diagram below and comment upon the appropriateness of the Assertion and tl **Competency Based Que.**

Assertion (A) Bottled juices bought from market are clear as compared to those made at home.

Reason (R) Bottle juices are clarified by the use of pectinases and proteases.

Ans. (*a*)

7. Assertion (A) Indirectly, BOD is a measure of organic matter present in the water.

Reason (R) The BOD test measures the rate of uptake of oxygen by microorganisms in a sample of water.

Ans. (*a*)

8. Assertion (A) The Ganga action plans have been initiated by IARI and KVIC.

Reason (R) Ganga action plan and Yamuna action plan have been initiated to save these major river from pollution.

Ans. (*d*) A is false, but R is true. A can be corrected as

The Ministry of Environment and Forests has initiated Ganga action plan and Yamuna action plan to save these major rivers of our country from pollution.

9. Assertion (A) Biogas plants are more often built in rural areas.

Reason (R) The excreta or gobar of cattle is rich in *Methanobacterium*. **CBSE 2025**

Ans. (*b*)

10. Assertion (A) A floating cover placed over the slurry in a biogas plant keeps on rising.

Reason (R) This cover keeps on rising due to the gas produced in the tank by the microbial activity.

Ans. (*a*)

11. Assertion (A) Chemical pesticides are preferred over biopesticides.

Reason (R) Chemical pesticides are mostly expensive, hazardous and pollute the atmosphere.

Ans. (*d*) A is false, but R is true. A can be corrected as

Biopesticides are preferred over chemical pesticides.

12. Assertion (A) Disadvantages of synthetic pesticides can be overcome by the use of biopesticides.

Reason (R) Biopesticides control weeds and pest without causing any damage to other living organisms.

Ans. (*a*)

13. Assertion (A) Biocontrol refers to the use of biological methods for controlling pests and diseases.

Reason (R) Our dependence on toxins and chemicals will remain same even after introduction of biocontrol agents.

Ans. (*c*) A is true, but R is false and R can be corrected as

Our dependence on toxins and chemicals will decrease after introduction of biocontrol agents.

14. Assertion (A) Use of biofertilisers greatly enhances crop productivity.

Reason (R) Irrigation is very important in increasing crop productivity.

Ans. (*b*) Both A and R are true, but R is not the correct explanation of A. A can be explained as

The use of biofertilisers greatly enhances crop productivity because they enrich the soil with beneficial microorganisms that improve nutrient availability, promote plant growth and enhance soil health.

Subjective Questions

Very Short Answer Type Questions

1. **Bacteria cannot be seen with the naked eyes, but these can be seen with the help of a microscope. If you have to carry a sample from your home to your biology laboratory to demonstrate the presence of microbes under a microscope, which sample would you carry and why?** **NCERT**

Ans. Bacteria are present almost everywhere. To see them under microscope, we can take samples of tap water or curd because both of them can be easily mounted, stained and observed under a microscope.

2. **The sap of which tree is used to make toddy.**

Ans. Palm tree

3. **Why does Swiss cheese have big holes?** **NCERT Exemplar**

Ans. The large holes in Swiss cheese are due to production of a large amount of CO_2 by a bacterium *Propionibacterium shermanii.*

4. **Name a microbe used for the production of Swiss cheese.**

Ans. *Propionibacterium sharmanii*

5. **Which species of *Penicillium* produces Roquefort cheese?**

Ans. *Penicillium roqueforti*

6. **What are fermentors?**

Ans. For large scale production of biotechnological products in industries, microbes are grown in very large vessels called fermentors.

7. **Why is distillation required for producing certain alcoholic drinks?** **NCERT Exemplar**

Ans. Distillation increases the alcohol content in alcoholic drinks.

8. **Name any two industrially important enzymes.** **NCERT Exemplar**

Ans. Refer to text on page no. 244.

9. **Name any two species of fungus, which are used in manufacturing of antibiotics.** **NCERT**

Ans. *Aspergillus fumigatus* and *Penicillium notatum.* (1/2 × 2)

10. **Name a microbe used for statin production. How do statin lower blood cholesterol level?** **NCERT Exemplar**

Ans. Statin is produced by *Monascus purpureus*. It acts as a competitive inhibitor for the enzyme responsible for synthesis of cholesterol. (½ × 2)

11. **Name an immunosuppressive agent. Also state its function.** **NCERT Exemplar**

Ans. Refer to text on page no. 244.

12. **An antibiotic called wonder drug was used to treat the wounded soldiers of America during World War-II. Name the drug and the scientist, who discovered it.**

Ans. Penicillin was discovered by Alexander Fleming.

13. **The image below illustrates a specific stage of sewage treatment. Examine it closely and explain its importance.**

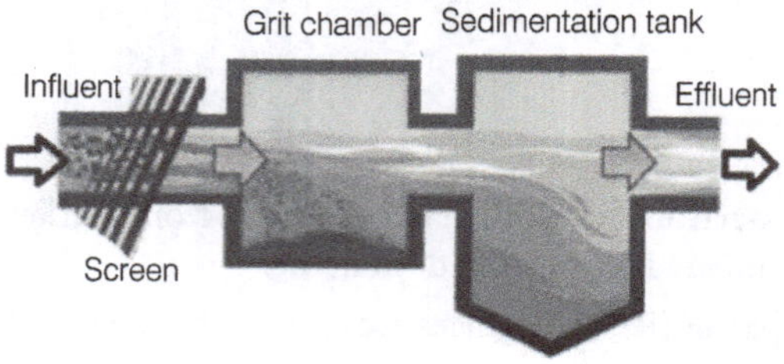

Ans. The image depicts primary treatment, which is crucial for removing suspended solids and large particles through physical processes like screening and sedimentation.

14. **Three water samples namely river water, untreated sewage water and secondary effluent discharged from a sewage treatment plant were subjected to BOD test. The samples were labelled *A*, *B* and *C*; but the laboratory attendant did not note which was which. The BOD values of the three samples *A*, *B* and *C* were recorded as 20mg/L, 8mg/L and 400mg/L, respectively. Which sample of the water is most polluted? Can you assign the correct label to each assuming the river water is relatively clean?** **Competency Based Que.**

Ans. Sample *C* is most polluted as it has highest BOD in all three samples. Therefore, it is untreated sewage. Sample *A* is the secondary effluent and Sample *B* is river water.

15. **How has the bacterium *Bacillus thuringiensis* helped us in controlling of caterpillars of insect pest?** **Competency Based Que.**

Ans. *Bacillus thuringiensis* produces endotoxins which when are ingested and released in the gut of the larvae of insect pest disrupts the insect gut lining thereby killing them.

16. ***Bacillus thuringiensis* is used in the form of sachets to control butterfly caterpillars. What triggers the activation of *Bt* toxin?**

Ans. A highly alkaline pH inside the insect gut triggers the activation of *Bt* toxin.

17. **Why do organic farmers not recommend eradication of insect-pests? Explain giving reason.**

Ans. Organic farmers do not recommend eradication of insect-pests as without them, the beneficial predator and parasitic insects which depend upon pests as food or hosts would not be able to survive.

Short Answer Type Questions

1. In which food would you find lactic acid bacteria? Mention some of their useful applications? NCERT

Or **Name the group of bacteria involved in setting milk into curd. Explain the process they carry in doing so. Write another beneficial role of such bacteria.**

Ans. Refer to text on page no. 242. (1+1)

2. Give examples to prove that microbes release gases during metabolism. NCERT

Ans. (i) Puffed up appearance of dough, which is used for making idli and dosa is due to release of CO_2 gas during fermentation by microbes.

(ii) Swiss cheese has large holes due to the production of CO_2.

(iii) Methanogens produce methane and CO_2. (1 ×3)

3. Name some traditional Indian food made of wheat, rice and Bengal gram, which involve use of microbes. NCERT

Ans. Wheat–Bread and cake.

Rice–Idli and dosa.

Bengal gram–Dhokla and khandvi. (1 × 3)

4. Why are some molecules called bioactive molecules? Give two examples of such molecules.

Ans. Molecules produced by a certain living organism perform functions in the body of other organisms and modify their metabolism. Hence, they are called bioactive molecules. Statins and cyclosporin-A are bioactive molecules. (1 + 1)

5. Find out the name of microbes from which cyclosporin- A (an immunosuppressive drug) and statins (blood cholesterol lowering agents) are obtained. NCERT Competency Based Que.

Ans. (i) Cyclosporin–A is obtained from the fungus *Trichoderma polysporum*. (1)

(ii) Statins are obtained from yeast, *Monascus purpureus*. (1)

6. A patient admitted in ICU was diagnosed to have suffered from myocardial infarction. The condition of coronary artery is depicted in the image below. Name two bioactive agents and their mode of action that can improve this condition. Competency Based Que.

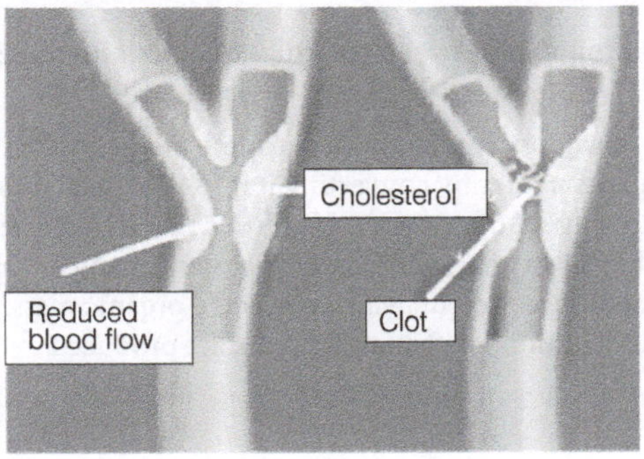

Ans. Two bioactive agents which can help the patient who suffered from myocardial infarction are

(i) **Streptokinase** It is produced by the bacterium *(Streptococcus)*. It can be used as a clot buster for removing clots from the blood vessels of the patient. (1)

(ii) **Statins** It is produced by the yeast *Monascus purpureus*. It act as blood cholesterol lowering agents and is given because the patient suffering from arteriosclerosis. (1)

7. In which way have microbes played a major role in controlling diseases caused by harmful bacteria? NCERT

Ans. Several microbes are used in preparing medicines. The most important medicines produced using microbes are antibiotics.

These are chemical compounds produced by some microbes and are used to kill or to subside the growth of other disease causing microbes. Streptomycin, tetracycline and penicillin are some of the commonly used antibiotics. These antibiotics have significantly contributed towards the welfare of the human society. (3)

8. Different species belonging to genus–*Trichoderma* are useful to humans as well as to plants. Justify their roles by giving one instance of each. CBSE 2022 Term II

Ans. Different species of the genus–*Trichoderma* are useful to both humans as well as plants. This can be understood as *Trichoderma polysporum* produces cyclosporin-A that acts as an immunosuppressive agent during organ transplant.

Apart from this, *Trichoderma* species promotes the growth of plants and limits the growth of plant pathogens. Thus, they effectively act as biofungicides and helps to degrade other fungi. (2)

9. Name the microbes that help in production of the following products commercially.

(i) Statin **(ii) Citric acid**
(iii) Penicillin **(iv) Butyric acid**

Ans. (i) Statin — *Monascus purpureus*

(ii) Citric acid — *Aspergillus niger*

(iii) Penicillin — *Penicillium notatum*

(iv) Butyric acid — *Clostridium butylicum* (1/2 ×4)

10. Mention a product of human welfare obtained with the help of each one of the following microbes.

(i) LAB
(ii) *Saccharomyces cerevisiae*
(iii) *Propionibacterium sharmanii*
(iv) *Aspergillus niger*

Ans.

Microbes	Products of human welfare
LAB	Curd
Saccharomyces cerevisiae	Bread, cakes, wines, beer
Propionibacterium sharmanii	Swiss cheese
Aspergillus niger	Citric acid

(½ × 4)

11. State the medicinal value and the bioactive molecules produced by *Streptococcus, Monascus* and *Trichoderma*.

Ans. Refer to tables on page no. 244. (1 ×3)

12. (i) Match the microbes listed under Column A with the products mentioned under Column B.

	Column A		Column B
A.	*Penicillium notatum*	(i)	Statin
B.	*Trichoderma polysporum*	(ii	Ethanol
C.	*Monascus purpureus*	(ii)	Antibiotic
D.	*Saccharomyces cerevisiae*	(i)	Cyclosporin-A

(ii) Why does 'Swiss cheese' develop large holes? CBSE 2019

Ans. (i) The correct matches are as follows

A.	*Penicillium notatum*	(iii)	Antibiotic
B.	*Trichoderma polysporum*	(iv)	Cyclosporin-A
C.	*Monascus purpureus*	(i)	Statin
D.	*Saccharomyces cerevisiae*	(ii)	Ethanol

(2)

(ii) Swiss cheese with large holes is produced by *Propionibacterium sharmanii*. Holes are created due to the production of large amount of CO_2 by this bacterium. (1)

13. Arrange the following in the decreasing order (most important first) of their importance, for the welfare of human society. Give reasons for your answers.

Biogas, citric acid, penicillin, curd. NCERT

Ans. Penicillin is the most important product. It is an antibiotic. It has been very helpful in curing many diseases. Next important is biogas, which is a clean and economical source of energy. Next in this order is citric acid, which is used as a food preservative. Least important in the list is curd, which is a food item obtained by the action of *Lactobacillus* on milk.

14. Find out the role of microbes in the following and discuss it with your teacher. NCERT

(i) Single Cell Protein (SCP) (ii) Soil

Ans. (i) Single Cell Protein (SCP) Microbes like bacteria and fungi convert waste materials into protein-rich biomass, providing a sustainable and nutritious food source.

(ii) Soil microbes decompose organic matter, recycle nutrients, improve soil structure, and suppress plant diseases, ensuring soil health and fertility. (1 × 2)

15. What is sewage? In which way can sewage be harmful to us? NCERT

Ans. Sewage is wastewater and organic matter from households, industries, and sewage systems. It can be harmful as it contaminate water sources, spreads diseases and harms aquatic life, leading to health risks and environmental degradation. (1 × 2)

16. What is the key difference between primary and secondary sewage treatment? NCERT

Ans. Differences between primary and secondary sewage treatment are as follows

Primary sewage treatment	Secondary sewage treatment
It is a physical process.	It is a biological process.
It involves physical removal of solid material.	It involves the action of microbes.
It is less complicated and not expensive.	It is a complicated and an expensive process.

(1 ×3)

17. Explain the different steps involved during primary treatment phase of sewage.

Ans. Refer to text on page no. 244.

18. Secondary treatment of the sewage is also called biological treatment. Justify this statement and explain the process. (1 × 2)

Ans. Refer to text on page no. 244-245. (2)

19. What are flocs? State their role in biological treatment of sewage. CBSE 2022 Term II

Or

Define flocs and state their importance in biological treatment of wastewater.

Ans. Flocs are masses of bacteria associated with the fungal filaments to form mesh-like structures during the secondary treatment of sewage. Flocs digest most of the organic material from the sludge. Thus, they help in reducing the Biochemical Oxygen Demand (BOD) of the effluent. This further helps in effective treatment of sewage. (1 × 2)

20. Distinguish between the roles of flocs and anaerobic sludge digesters in sewage treatments.

Ans. In sewage treatment, flocs consume major part of the organic matter by converting it into microbial biomass and releasing lot of minerals. It reduces the BOD of sewage. Whereas in anaerobic sludge digesters, many anaerobic bacteria are present, which digest the organic mass. During this digestion, methane, CO_2, etc., are produced.

21. (i) **Write the full form of BOD.**

(ii) **Define BOD. Explain how it is a measure of the organic matter present in the water body.** **CBSE 2025**

Ans. (i) BOD stands for Biochemical Oxygen Demand.

(ii) BOD is the amount of oxygen required by microorganisms to decompose organic matter in a water body. It indicates the level of organic pollution-higher BOD means more organic matter, leading to oxygen depletion and harm to aquatic life.

22. Water samples were collected at points *A*, *B* and *C* in a segment of a river near a sugar factory and tested for BOD level. The BOD levels of samples *A*, *B* and *C* were 400 mg/L, 480 mg/L and 8 mg/L, respectively. What is this indicative of? Explain why the BOD level gets reduced considerably at the collection point *C*?

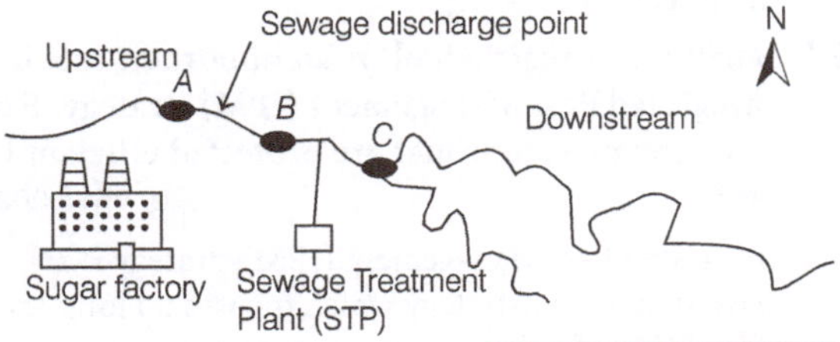

Competency Based Que.

Ans. The measurement of BOD helps to indicate the level of pollution in a water body. In the given results, at collection points *A* and *B*, the BOD level is high due to the high organic pollution caused by sugar factory and sewage discharge. (1½)

At the collection point *C*, the water was released after secondary treatment/biological treatment (where vigorous growth of useful aerobic microbes into flocs consume the major part of the organic matter present in the river water or effluent due to sugar factory and sewage discharge).

Therefore, BOD level gets reduced at the collection point *C*. (1½)

23. Give the name of the two different categories of microbes naturally occurring in sewage water. Explain their role in cleaning sewage water into usable water.

Ans. Two different categories of microbes naturally occurring in sewage water are aerobic and anaerobic microbes. (1)

(i) **Role of aerobic microbes in cleaning water** Aerobic microbes grow excessively in the aeration tank and consume a major part of the organic matter. It helps in reducing the BOD of the effluent. (1)

(ii) **Role of anaerobic microbes in cleaning water** In the settling tank, anaerobic microbes digest the aerobic bacteria and fungi and produce gases like CH_4, CO_2, H_2S, etc. It makes the water less polluted that could be released in the water bodies. (1)

24. Explain the function of 'anaerobic sludge digester' in a sewage treatment plant.

Ans. In anaerobic sludge digester, methanogens, i.e. anaerobic bacteria, digest the bacteria and fungi in the activated sludge. This produces mixture of methane, hydrogen sulphide and carbon dioxide, i.e. biogas. This gas is used as a source of energy as it is inflammable.

25. Mention the common bacterium found in the anaerobic sludge during sewage treatment and also in the rumen of cattle. How is this bacterium commercially useful? **CBSE 2022 Term II**

Ans. The common bacterium found in the anaerobic sludge during sewage treatment and also in the rumen of cattle is methanogen. (1)

These have become industrially important as their technical application lies in the production of biogas by digestion of organic substrates. Also, they find their role in the sewage treatment plants in order to filter the wastewater. (1)

26. (i) **What is activated sludge? How is it produced?**

(ii) **State some uses of biogas.**

Ans. (i) Refer to text on page no. 245. (2)

(ii) Refer to text on page no. 246 (1)

27. What role can an individual play in keeping our rivers clean? Is the government taking any action for the same? Explain. **NCERT Exemplar**

Ans. An individual can contribute better towards keeping the rivers and other water bodies clean. We can reduce the water pollution by not throwing plastic packets, wrappers and other waste materials in rivers. (1)

Yes, the government has also initiated many programmes for contributions in keeping water clean by starting programmes like Ganga Action Plan (GAP) and Narmada Action Plan. (NAP). (1)

28. Describe how biogas is generated from activated sludge? List the components of biogas.

Ans. Refer to text on page no. 246.

Biogas is a mixture of gases (methane-60%, CO_2-40%, traces of hydrogen and several other gases) produced by the microbial activity and may be used as fuel. (2)

29. Do you think microbes can be used as a source of energy? If yes how? **NCERT**

Ans. Yes, microbes can be used as a source of energy, e.g. methanogens like Methanobacterium are used to produce biogas, which is a source of energy. (1 × 2)

30. Give reasons, why?

(i) **Cow dung is preferred for biogas production.**

(ii) ***Saccharomyces cerevisiae*** **is commonly known as brewer's yeast.**

Ans. (i) Refer to text on page no. 246. (1)

(ii) Refer to text on page no. 242. (1)

31. Why are biogas plants considered more beneficial in rural areas? Competency Based Que.

Ans. The raw material for the biogas plant is mainly cow dung, which is available in plenty in rural areas where cattle are found in large quantity. The biogas is used for lighting and cooking in these areas. The slurry from the biogas plant is used as manure in agriculture; hence biogas plants are more suitable in rural areas. (2)

32. What are methanogens? How do they help to generate biogas?

Or **What are methanogens? Name the animals in which methanogens occur and the role they play there.**

Ans. Certain bacteria which grow anaerobically on cellulosic material, produce large amounts of methane along with CO_2 and H_2. These bacteria are called **methanogens** (one of the common bacterium is *Methanobacterium*). (1)

Methanogens are commonly found in the anaerobic sludge during sewage treatement and are also present in the rumen (a part of stomach) of cattle.

In rumen, methanogens help in the breakdown of cellulose and their excreta called gobar is rich in these bacteria. Therefore, dung can be used to produce biogas commonly called as **gobar gas**. (2)

33. Microbes can be used to decrease the use of chemical fertilisers and pesticides. Explain how this can be accomplished? NCERT

Ans. Microbes play an important role in organic farming, which reduce the use of chemical fertilisers, pesticides, etc. For instance (1)

(i) Biofertilisers are living organisms, which help in increasing the fertility of the soil. Beneficial microorganisms help in improving plant growth by supplying plant nutrients. Many species of bacteria and cyanobacteria help in fixing the nitrogen in the soil. (1)

(ii) Many biological agents like ladybird and *Bacillus thuringiensis*, etc., are useful in eradicating pests. Therefore, it is possible for microbes to reduce the use of chemical fertilisers and pesticides. (1)

34. How has the bacterium *Bacillus thuringiensis* helped us in controlling caterpillars of insect-pests?

Ans. Refer to text on page no. 247.

35. Certain specific bacterial spores are mixed in water and sprayed over *Brassica* crop to control butterfly caterpillars.

Name this bacterium and its mode of action on the butterfly caterpillar. CBSE 2023

Ans. To control butterfly caterpillars, bacteria such as *Bacillus thuringiensis* are used in the form of sachets as dry spores. These are mixed with water and are sprayed onto vulnerable plants like *Brassica* and fruit trees, where these are eaten by insects larvae. This kills the larvae due to the release of toxin in their gut, thereby eradicating the caterpillars, but leaving other insects unharmed.

36. On spraying *Bacillus thuringiensis* on an infected cotton crop field the pests are killed by the toxin, however the toxin although produced by the bacteria does not affect it. Explain giving reason. Competency Based Que., CBSE 2023

Ans. Some strains of *Bacillus thuringiensis* produce proteins that kill certain insects such as armyworm, beetles, flies, and mosquitoes. *B. thuringiensis* forms crystals of protein during their growth that comprise of a toxic insecticidal protein. The *Bt* toxin protein exist as inactive protoxins, but once an insect ingest the inactive toxin, it is converted into an active form of toxin due to the alkaline pH of the gut which solubilise the crystals. The activated toxin binds to the surface of midgut epithelial cells and create pores that cause cell swelling and lysis and eventually cause death of the insect.

37. *Bacillus thuringiensis* plays an important role in Integrated Pest Management (IPM) strategy. Explain how, any two crops that are protected efficient from pests. CBSE 2022 Term II

Ans. Integrated Pest Management (IPM) strategy is an ecosystem based strategy which focuses on long-term prevention of pests or their damage through a combination of techniques like biological control, use of resistant varieties, etc. In other words, it is an approach to control the pest in an integrated way.

Bacillus thuringiensis plays a major role in the integrated pest management strategy. It is used to control butterfly caterpillars. Dried spores of *Bt* are mixed with water and sprayed on plants in order to protect them from various pests (especially caterpillars). It also renders non-target insects beings unharmed. Thus, they are equally important in the IPM strategy. (2)

Two crops that are protected effectively from pests include *Brassica* and cotton. (1)

38. *Trichoderma* sp. which is mostly utilised in the medical and healthcare fields also acts as a biocontrol agent. State its significance as biocontrol Competency Based Que.

Ans. *Trichoderma* sp., is used in the medical and healthcare industry due to its ability to produce cyclosporin-A which is used as an immunosuppresive agent. It also acts as a biocontrol agent by inhibiting the growth of various microorganisms. This further enhances the plant growth. (1)

39. Organic farmer use *Trichoderma* and baculovirus as biological control agents. Explain. Competency Based Que.

Ans. Biocontrol refers to the use of biological methods for controlling plant diseases and pests. *Trichoderma* sp., are the most widely used fungal biocontrol agents. It is used against fungal disease of pulses, cotton, maize, etc. It has moderate effects on the soil balance and does not harm the beneficial organisms. Similarly, baculoviruses attack insects and other arthropods. They do not harm plants, fishes, birds and non-target organisms.

Thus, these are more often used in organic farming by the farmers.

40. Name the effective biocontrol agents of several plant pathogens belonging to group of viruses. Also write about the ways they support the environment. **CBSE 2022 Term II**

Ans. Baculoviruses are effective biocontrol agents of several plant pathogens. These belong to the genus– *Nucleopolyhedrovirus.* (1)

These are species specific, narrow spectrum insecticides which cause no harm to plants, mammals, birds, fishes and other non-target insects.

They are also beneficial in the integrated pest management programme. Thus, they support the environment. (2)

41. Name the genus to which baculoviruses belong. Describe their role in the integrated pest management programmes.

Ans. Baculoviruses belong to the genus– *Nucleopolyhedrovirus.*(1)

They control only species specific pests and do not affect non-target organisms or beneficial insects. So, they conserve the beneficial insects that aid in integrated pest management programmes. (1)

42. (i) Give an example of a genus of virus used as narrow spectrum insecticidal biocontrol agent.

(ii) How does its use serve as an aid in overall integrated pest management programme? **CBSE 2023**

Ans. (i) *Nucleopolyhedrovirus* (½)

(ii) Baculoviruses are the viruses belong the genus– *Nucleopolyhedrovirus*. These viruses attack the arthropods/insects. These viruses are excellent species specific, effective, narrow spectrum insecticidal biocontrol agent. This is especially important when treating an environmentally sensitive area or conserving beneficial insects to support an overall Integrated Pest Management (IPM) programme. (1½)

43. (i) Organic farmers prefer biological control of diseases and pests to the use of chemicals for the same purpose. Justify.

(ii) Give an example of a bacterium, a fungus and an insect that are used as biocontrol agents.

Ans. Refer to text on page no. 247.

44. (i) How do organic farmers control pests? Give two examples.

(ii) State the difference in their approach from that of conventional pest control methods.

Ans. (i) The organic farmers control pests by the use of insect pests resistant varieties. The two examples are (1)

(a) The Pusa Gaurav variety of *Brassica* is resistant to aphids.

(b) Pusa Sawani variety of okra is resistant to shoot and fruit borer. (1)

(ii) The use of resistant variety is safer to control the pests as it does not involve chemical pesticides which are used in conventional method of controlling pests. Thus, it is environmental friendly method and reduce soil pollution. (1)

45. How do biofertilisers enrich the fertility of the soil? **NCERT**

Ans. Biofertilisers are living organisms, that increase the fertility of the soil. These microbes help in supplying the nutrients to the plant by their natural biological activity. They mobilise the availability of the nutrients to the plants thus, improving the fertility of the soil.

Many species of bacteria and cyanobacteria help in fixing the nitrogen in the soil. Some bacteria stay in symbiotic relationship with legumes while, some are free-living nitrogen fixers.

Biofertilisers have additional advantage of being eco-friendly and effective. (3)

46. Name two organisms belonging to two different kingdoms, that are commonly used as biofertilisers, and how? **CBSE 2020**

Ans. Refer to text on page no. 247-248.

47. Choose any three microbes, from the following, which are suited for organic farming which is in great demand these days for various reasons. Mention one application of each one chosen.

Mycorrhiza, *Monascus, Anabaena, Rhizobium Methanobacterium, Trichoderma*

Ans. The three microbes that can be chosen for organic farming are as follows

(i) ***Rhizobium*** The nodules on the roots of leguminous plants are formed by the symbiotic association of *Rhizobium* bacteria. These bacteria fix atmospheric nitrogen into organic forms, which is used by the plants as nutrient.

(ii) **Mycorrhiza** Fungi form symbiotic association called mycorrhiza with plants. The fungal symbiont absorbs phosphorus from soil and passes it to the plant. Such plant shows resistance to root-borne pathogens, tolerance to salinity and drought as well as overall increase in plant growth and development.

(iii) ***Anabaena*** It is a cyanobacteria that is used as a biofertiliser. It fixes atmospheric nitrogen. (1 × 3)

48. Farmers are often suggested to use the following organisms in their cropland so as to improve the soil fertility.

(i) ***Rhizobium***

(ii) ***Anabaena*** **CBSE 2022 Term II**

Ans. Farmers are often suggested to use *Rhizobium* and *Anabaena* in their cropland so as to improve the soil fertility. Both *Rhizobium* and *Anabaena* act as biofertilisers. These enrich the nutrient quality of the soil.

(i) *Rhizobium* is a soil-dwelling bacteria that help in fixing atmospheric nitrogen in leguminous plants and thus help the plant grow well.

(ii) *Anabaena* is a cyanobacterium and adds organic matter to the soil, thus increase its fertility. (1 × 2)

49. How does the application of the fungal genus- *Glomus*, to the agricultural farm increase the farm output? **Competency Based Que.**

Ans. The application of *Glomus* to agricultural field increases the farm output by increasing the nutrient availability to the crops. *Glomus* develops symbiotic association with the roots of plants, called mycorrhiza. It absorbs phosphorus from the soil and passes it to the plants it associates with. In return, it derives sugars from the host plant cells for its survival.

50. How do mycorrhizal fungi help the plants harbouring them?

Ans. Refer to text on page no. 248.

51. (i) Give an example of a genus of fungi that forms mycorrhizial association with plants.

(ii) How does the plant derive benefits from this association? **CBSE 2023**

Ans. (i) The fungi which belongs to genus–*Glomus* forms mycorrhiza. (1)

(ii) The symbiotic association between fungi and plants are called as mycorrhiza in which fungi absorbs phosphorus from soil which is then used by plants as nutrients. (1)

52. List four advantages that a symbiotic mycorrhizal association provides to the host plant.

Or

How do plants benefit from having mycorrhizal symbiotic association?

Ans. Four advantages are as follows

(i) The fungus absorbs phosphorus from the soil and passes it to the plant.

(ii) Plants with mycorrhiza show resistance to root-borne pathogens.

(iii) They show increased tolerance to salinity and drought.

(iv) These show an overall increase in plant growth and development. (½ × 4)

53. Biofertilisers are organisms that enrich the nutrient quality in the soil. Explain the role of three main sources of biofertilisers.

Ans. Biofertilisers are natural organisms that enhance soil fertility. Here are three main sources and their role

(i) **Nitrogen-Fixing Bacteria**

Examples: *Rhizobium, Azotobacter.*

Role: Convert atmospheric nitrogen into usable forms for plants, enriching the soil and boosting crop yields.

(ii) **Mycorrhizal Fungi**

Examples: *Glomus* species.

Role: Form symbiotic relationships with plant roots, improving nutrient and water uptake, especially phosphorus.

(iii) **Phosphate-Solubilising Bacteria**

Examples: *Bacillus, Pseudomonas.*

Role: Solubilise insoluble phosphates, making them available to plants, crucial for energy transfer and growth. (1 × 3)

Long Answer Type Questions

1. Given below is a list of six microorganisms. State their usefulness to humans.

(i) ***Nucleopolyhedrovirus***

(ii) ***Saccharomyces cerevisiae***

(iii) ***Monascus purpureus***

(iv) ***Trichoderma polysporum***

(v) ***Penicillium notatum***

(vi) ***Propionibacterium shermanii***

Ans. (i) *Nucleopolyhedrovirus* is a widely used biopesticide in crop fields.

(ii) *Saccharomyces cerevisiae* commonly called **Brewer's yeast,** is used for fermenting malted cereals and fruit juices to ethanol.

(iii) Statins is produced by yeast *Monascus purpureus*. It have been commercialised as blood cholesterol lowering agents.

(iv) Cyclosporin-A is produced by the fungus *Trichoderma polysporum* and it is used as an immunosuppressive agent in case of organ transplants.

(v) *Penicillium notatum* is used for the production of penicillin an antibiotic. Antibiotics have helped in controlling, various harmful diseases.

(vi) Swiss cheese with large holes is produced by *Propionibacterium sharmanii.* Holes are created due to the production of large amount of CO_2 produced by this bacterium.

2. Explain the process of sewage water treatment before it can be discharged into natural water bodies. Why is this treatment essential?

Ans. The process of sewage water treatment before being discharged into natural water bodies.

Refer to text on page no. 244 and 245. (4)

The sewage treatment is essential before water is released into water bodies because sewage present in water causes water pollution and as a consequence, incidence of water borne diseases increases. (1)

3. **(i) Name the category of microbes naturally occurring in sewage and making it less polluted during the treatment.**

(ii) Explain the different steps involved in the secondary treatment of sewage.

Ans. (i) Refer to text on page no. 244-245. (2)

(ii) For different steps involved in secondary or biological treatment of sewage, refer to text on page no. 244-245. (3)

4. **Describe the process of wastewater (sewage) treatment under the following heads.**

(i) Primary treatment

(ii) Secondary treatment **Compartment 2024**

Ans. Refer to text on page no. 244-245.

5. **What is biogas? Explain its production with the help of a diagram.**

Ans. Refer to text on page no. 246.

6. **(i) Explain the sequence of events occurring in a biogas plant.** **CBSE 2024 C**

(i) Write the components of biogas.

(ii) Write any three advantages of using cow dung as the rew material

Ans. Refer to text on page no. 246.

7. **Describe the main idea behind the biological control of pests and diseases.**

Ans. Refer to text on page no. 246.-247.

8. **Large quantities of sewage are generated every day in cities as well as in towns and are treated in Sewage Treatment Plants (STPs) to make them less polluting. Given below is the flow diagram of stages of STP.** **CBSE 2024, Competency Based Que.**

Study the flow diagram and answer the questions that follow

Primary effluent passed into large aeration tanks

↓

Effluent passed into settling tanks to form 'sediment'

(i) (a) Why is primary effluent passed into large aeration tanks ?

(b) What is the sediment formed, referred to as ? Mention its significance.

(c) Explain the final step in the settling tank before the treated effluent is released into water bodies.

(ii) Name any two organisms commonly used as biofertilisers, belonging to different kingdoms. Write how each one acts as biofertiliser.

Ans. (i) (a) In aeration tanks there is a growth of aerobic microbes and fungi (flocs) that consume major part of organic matter in effluent thus reducing BOD.

(b) The sediment formed referred as activated sludge, it is used as inoculum in aeration tanks.

(c) Bacterial flocs are allowed to sediment. (Activated sludge) (1+1+1)

(ii) *Rhizobium* (Bacteria), live symbiotically in nodules of roots of leguminous plants and fix atmospheric nitrogen into organic form and provide nitrogen to the plant.

Glomus (fungi), live in symbiotic association with roots of higher plants and absorb phosphorus from the soil and passes it to plants. (1 × 2)

9. **What are biofertilisers? Name the categories of organisms used as biofertilisers with an example for each. How do they function in organic farming?**

Ans. Refer to text on page no. 247-248.

Source Based/ Case Based/ Passage Based Questions

1. ***Read the following passage and answer the questions given below.***

During the unfortunate corona virus lockdown, Kavita started cursing the existence of microbes on earth. On hearing this, Deepak told Kavita that not all the microbes are harmful for us. Many microbes are useful in producing medicines, bioactive molecules and household products.

(i) Antibiotics are produced by a living organism. What relationship do these share with target and non-target organisms?

(ii) Mention the source and functions of cyclosporin-A and statins.

(iii) Mention any two functions of fungal microbe *Saccharomyces cerevisiae*.

Ans. (i) Antibiotics are drugs/chemicals produced by a living organism. These adversely affect the target organism while generally being harmless to non-target organisms. (1)

(ii) Cyclosporin-A is produced by fungus *Trichoderma polysporum* and it is used as an immunosuppressive agent in organ transplant patients. Statins are produced by the yeast *Monascus purpureus* and they functions as blood cholesterol lowering agents. (1)

(iii) (a) It is used in bread making.

(b) It is used in the commercial production of ethanol. (1)

2. **Consider the given pie chart that shows different microorganisms which aid humans with their day-to-day living.**

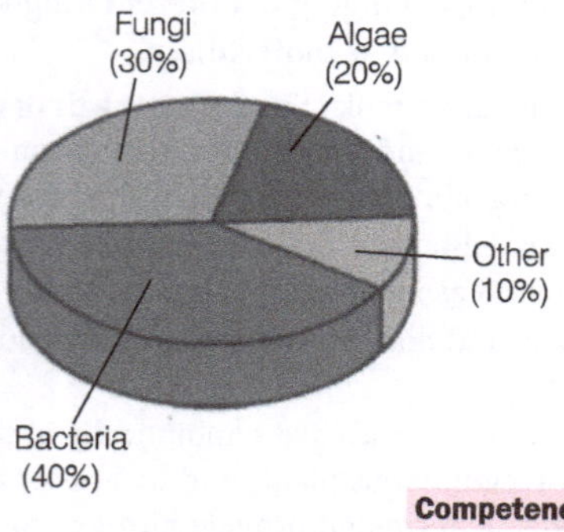

Competency Based Que.

Refer to the above pie chart and answer the following questions.

(i) In our lives, microbes contribute major role and are beneficial to us in many ways. On the other hand, a few microorganisms cause infections as well. Comment.

(ii) Are microorganisms industrially exploited ? Give one example.

Or

(ii) List out two ways in which certain microorganisms prove to be beneficial for us in the healthcare industry.

Ans. (i) Microorganisms play a very important role in our day-to-day life. They help us in our household work, e.g. *Lactobacillus* is used in the formation of curd from milk whereas dough which is used for making idlis and dosas is prepared using *Saccharomyces cerevisiae* (Bakers' yeast).

However, there are certain microbes like *Salmonella typhi* (bacterium), *Plasmodium* (protozoan), etc., which cause disease like typhoid, fever and malaria, respectively. (2)

(ii) Microorganisms are exploited industrially in a number of ways, e.g. the food and beverages industry exploits non-pathogenic microorganisms like *S. cerevisiae* in order to produce fermented food and beverages like wine and beer. (2)

Or

(ii) Two ways in which microorganisms have benefitted us in healthcare sector include

(a) Production of antibiotics, e.g. penicillin from *P. notatum*.

(b) Production of bioactive molecules like statins. (2)

3. **The graph shown below represents the production of streptomycin antibiotic, from the year 1944 and onwards till 2021.**

Study the graph given below and answer the following questions. **Competency Based Que.**

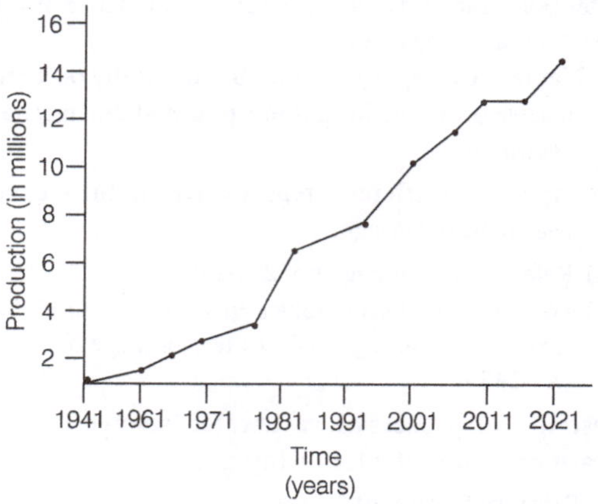

(i) What could infered from the above graph ?

(ii) Which microorganism has been exploited for extracting this valuable antibiotic ?

(iii) Overexploitation of an organism for the product it yields affects its population negatively. How far do you agree with this? Will the conclusion remain same in the above case?

Or **(iii) What would be the resulting effect, on the industrial preparations of antibiotic, of the population if its source declines rapidly ? Suggest any one alternative to it.**

Ans. (i) It could be infered that the production of streptomycin has been on a constant rise since its commercial use in 1944. (1)

(ii) The bacterium *Streptomyces griseus* has been exploited for extracting streptomycin. (1)

(iii) Yes, overexploitation of an organism for the product(s) it yields has a negative effect on the species population. This is because such organisms are used in large numbers in order to cope up with the industrial production of the products they yield. However, this is not true in the given case as the replication time of bacteria is fast and thus the population is not affected adversely. (2)

Or

(iii) In case the population of the source organism *Streptomyces griseus* declines rapidly, there would be a sharp decline in the industrial production of the antibiotic and its demand would increase. An alternate to this could be the discovery of another organism that yields this antibiotic. (2)

4. Study the picture of biogas plant given below and answer the questions that follows. **CBSE 2020**

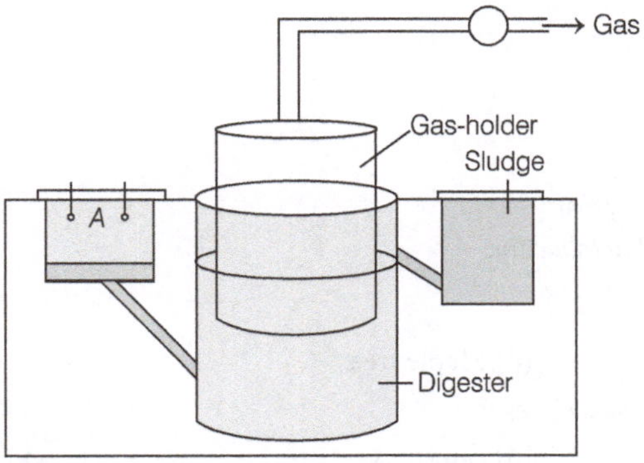

(i) **Name the components gaining entry from *A* into the chamber.**

(ii) **Mention the group of bacteria and the condition in which they act on the component that entered *A* in the digester.**

(iii) **Name the components that get collected in gas holder.**

Ans. (i) The dung and water are the components which gain entry from *A* point of the digestive chamber. (1)

(ii) Methanogens are the group of bacteria which act upon the dung matter to produce methane. The common methanogenic bacterium is *Methanobacterium*. These bacterium need anaerobic condition to digest cellulosic material present in cattle dung. (2)

(iii) The components that get collected in gas holder or chamber are mainly methane gas (CH_4) along with carbon dioxide (CO_2) and hydrogen (H_2) gases. (1)

5. Due to the increasing use of insecticides and pesticides in agricultural practices, government advised farmers to adopt organic farming and use of biocontrol agents. Farmers were also informed about various biocontrol agents and their target organisms.

(i) **Mention the use of these agents in agriculture.**

(ii) **Which agent is used to get rid of aphids and mosquitoes respectively?**

(iii) **Why baculoviruses are used as biocontrol agents?**

(iv) **In order to control butterfly caterpillars in *Brassica* and fruit trees, which biocontrol agent(s) can be used?**

Ans. (i) Biocontrol agents greatly reduce the dependency on toxic chemicals and pesticide. These are target specific and thus do not affect neighbouring flora and fauna. (1)

(ii) Ladybird is used to control aphids and dragonflies are used to control mosquitoes. (1)

(iii) Baculoviruses are pathogens, which attack insects and arthropods. They are used for narrow spectrum insecticidal applications. (1)

(iv) *Bacillus thuringiensis*. (1)

SELF ASSESSMENT TEST

Multiple Choice Questions

1. The microbes commonly used in kitchen are
   (a) *Lactobacillus* and yeast
   (b) *Penicillium* and yeast
   (c) *Microspora* and *E. coli*
   (d) *Rhizopus* and *Lactobacillus*

2. Toddy is traditionally produced from the sap of which type of plant?
   (a) Cactus (b) Bamboo (c) Palm tree (d) Maple tree

3. What is the primary fermentation agent used in the production of Swiss cheese?
   (a) Bacteria (b) Yeast (c) Mold (d) Enzymes

4. What is the primary purpose of using antibiotics in medicine?
   (a) To boost immunity
   (b) To kill or inhibit the growth of bacteria
   (c) To aid in digestion
   (d) To promote muscle growth

5. In sewage treatment, which process is primarily responsible for breaking down organic matter?
   (a) Filtration
   (b) Aerobic digestion
   (c) Chemical precipitation
   (d) Incineration

6. Read the following statements
   (A) BOD and polluting potential are inversely related.
   (B) BOD and polluting potential are directly related.
   (C) More the BOD, the easier it is to treat the water.
   (D) More the BOD, more will the harm if released in a water body.
   Which of these is true?
   (a) (A) and (C) are true and (C) is the reason for (A)
   (b) (B) and (C) are true and (C) is not related to (B)
   (c) (A) and (D) are true and (D) is not related to (A)
   (d) (B) and (D) are true and (D) is the reason for (B)

7. Biogas is primarily produced from the anaerobic digestion of
   (a) organic waste
   (b) minerals
   (c) heavy metals
   (d) plastics

Assertion-Reason Questions

Direction (Q. Nos. 8-12) *In each of the following questions, a statement of Assertion (A) is given followed by corresponding statement of Reason (R). Of the statements, mark the correct answer*

(a) Both A and R are true and R is the correct explanation of the A.
(b) Both A and R are true, but R is not the correct explanation of the A.
(c) A is true, but R is false.
(d) A is false, but R is true.

8. **Assertion** (A) The dough, which is used for making foods such as dosa and idli is fermented by a fungi.
   Reason (R) The puffed-up appearance of dough is due to the production of CO_2 gas.

9. **Assertion** (A) Toddy is a popular alcoholic beverage in many tropical regions.
   Reason (R) Toddy is produced from the fermentation of sap collected from palm trees, making it naturally sweet and refreshing.

10. **Assertion** (A) *Aspergillus niger* is a fungi.

Reason (R) *Aspergillus niger* produces acetic acid.

11. **Assertion** (A) In primary treatment small and large particles are removed from sewage.

Reason (R) Small pebbels are removed by filtration.

12. **Assertion** (A) Bacteria which grow anaerobically on cellulosic material, produce large amount of methane along with CO_2 and H_2, are collectively called methanogens.

Reason (R) Methanogens are commonly found in the anaerobic sludge during sewage treatment.

Very Short Answer Type Questions

13. Mention the importance of lactic acid bacteria in humans other than setting milk into curd.
14. Name one alcoholic drink produced by distillation and without distillation of fermented broth respectively.
15. The excreta of cattle does not contain any cellulose but human excreta may contain cellulose. Why.
16. Name the genus of baculovirus that acts as a biological agent in spite of being a pathogen.

Short Answer Type Questions

17. How does the pH of the system change during the conversion of milk into curd? Justify your answer.
18. Mention any three advantages that biological pesticides offer over chemical pesticides.
19. Write a short note on symbiotic N_2 fixation in cyanobacteria.

Long Answer Type Questions

20. How microbes are used in household and industrial product?
21. Explain the process of production of biogas, with the help of labelled diagram.
22. Describe the functions of microbes as biocontrol agents.

Case Based Question

23. In a wastewater treatment plant, sampling was done thrice at various stages in the treatment process indicated by *A*, *B* and *C* in the following diagram.

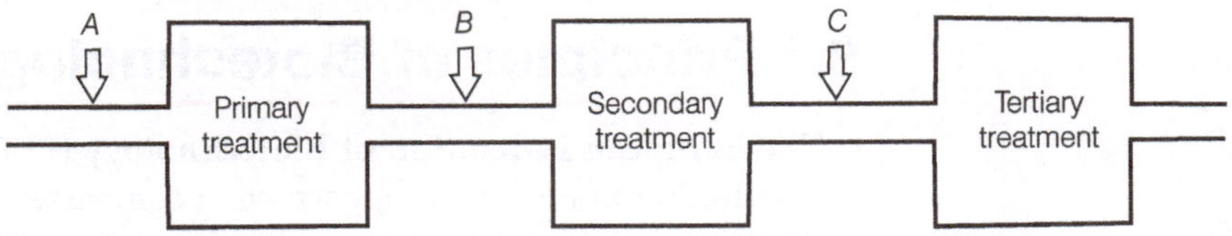

Each time the sample was taken, its BOD was measured, resulting in the following recorded values: 30 mg/L, 300 mg/L, 250 mg/L

(i) Define BOD and determine which of these BOD values correspond to stages *A*, *B* and *C* in the treatment process.

(ii) Based on (a), justify your answer for each value.

(iii) Why treatment of sewage water, before releasing it into natural water bodies, is necessary.

Answers

1. (a)	2. (c)	3. (a)	4. (b)	5. (b)	6. (d)	7. (a)	8. (d)
9. (a)	10. (c)	11. (b)	12. (b)				

09
CHAPTER

Biotechnology: Principles and Processes

Biotechnology is an integrated branch of biology which deals with the techniques of using living organisms (microbes, plant and animal cells) or enzymes from them in order to produce different products and processes useful to humans.

YOUR STUDY GOALS

9.1 Principles of Biotechnology
9.2 Tools of Recombinant DNA Technology
9.3 Processes of Recombinant DNA Technology

YOUR PRACTICE GOAL

- Objective Type Questions (42 Qs ; MCQs, A-R) Case Based Questions (9)
- Subjective Type Questions
- (21 VSAs, 47 SAs, 11 LAs)

- Human beings have been using biotechnology for thousands of years. For example, the production of curd, cheese, bread, vinegar, wine, etc. done by the process fermentation (microbe-mediated process) is one of the oldest biotechnology process.
- In this chapter, we will be discussing about various principles and processes of biotechnology.

9.1 Principles of Biotechnology

- The **European Federation of Biotechnology** (EFB) has given a definition of biotechnology which encompasses both traditional view and modern molecular biotechnology.
- It defines biotechnology as the integration of natural science and organisms, cells, parts thereof, and molecular analogues for products and services.
- Thus, we can conclude that biotechnology involves two factors, first the use of biological agents and second the product or service generated for the well-being of humans.
- For examples, *in vitro* fertilisation leading to a test tube baby, synthesising a gene and using it, developing a DNA vaccine or correcting a defective gene, are all part of biotechnology.

- Two core techniques that enabled birth of modern biotechnology are as follows

1. Genetic Engineering

It refers to the techniques used for modification of chemical nature of genetic material (DNA/RNA) and their introduction into another organism (host) to change the phenotypic characters of that organism.

2. Bioprocess Engineering

- These methods are used to maintain sterile (microbial contamination free) conditions in chemical engineering processes.
- It enables the growth and manipulation of only the desired microbes or eukaryotic cells.
- This method is used to get large quantities of biotechnological products like vaccines, enzymes, antibiotics, etc.

Conceptual Development of the Principle of Genetic Engineering

- Sexual reproduction permits variation by producing recombinants through crossing over during prophase-I of meiosis.
- This leads to formulation of unique combinations of genetic setup, some of which may be beneficial to the organism as well as the population.
- This method was used in traditional hybridisation procedures during plant and animal breeding, but very often it leads to inclusion and multiplication of undesirable genes along with the desired genes.
- The techniques of genetic engineering which include creation of **recombinant DNA**, use of **gene cloning** and **gene transfer** helps to overcome this limitation.
- It allows to isolate and introduce only one or a set of desirable genes without introducing undesirable genes into the target organisms.
  - During the process of genetic engineering the piece of DNA introduced into the alien (foreign) organism would not be able to multiply by its own. But when it gets incorporated into the genetic material (genome) of the recipient organism, it gets mutliplied and inherited along with the recipient chromosome.
  - A specific DNA sequence called **origin of replication** (*ori*) is present in a chromosomal DNA,which is responsible for initiating the process of replication.
- Thus, the foreign DNA linked with the origin of replication can replicate and make multiple, identical copies of itself in the host organism. This process is referred to as **cloning** or **making identical** copies of any template DNA.

Construction of an Artificial Recombinant DNA Molecule

The construction of an artificial recombinant DNA molecule include the following steps

- The recombinant DNA emerged from linking of a gene encoding antibiotic resistance with a native plasmid.
- A **plasmid** is an autonomously replicating extra-chromosomal circular DNA in some bacteria.
- **Stanley Cohen** and **Herbert Boyer** accomplished construction of *r*DNA molecule in 1972. They isolated the antibiotic resistance gene by cutting out a piece of DNA from a plasmid of *Salmonella typhimurium* with the help of restriction enzyme.
- The cut piece of DNA (antibiotic resistance gene) was then linked with plasmid DNA with the help of **DNA ligase**. The plasmid DNA acts as a vector to transfer the piece of DNA attached to it.
- This makes a new combination of circular self-replicating DNA created *in vitro* and is known as **recombinant DNA**.
- When this DNA is transferred into *Escherichia coli*, (a bacterium closely related to *Salmonella*) it could replicate using new host's DNA polymerase enzyme and will produce multiple copies.
- This ability to multiply and to produce multiple copies of antibiotic resistance gene in *E. coli* is called **cloning** of antibiotic resistance gene.
- Thus, genetic engineering include the three basic steps.
  - Identification of DNA with desirable genes.
  - Introduction of the identified DNA into a suitable host to form recombinant DNA (*r*DNA).
  - Maintenance of introduced DNA in the host and transfer of the DNA (gene transfer) to its progeny.

9.2 Tools of Recombinant DNA Technology

Genetic engineering or recombinant DNA technology can be accomplished only with the usage of key tools. The specific key tools are as follows

1. Enzymes

- There are various enzymes involved in genetic engineering which simplifies this complex process.
- The enzymes involved in genetic engineering are as follows

Restriction Enzymes (Molecular Scissors)

- The restriction enzymes are used for the cutting of DNA at specific locations during *r*DNA technology.
- In the year 1963, the two enzymes, responsible for restricting the growth of bacteriophage in *E. coli* were isolated. One of these added methyl groups to DNA , while the other cut DNA. The later was called **restriction endonuclease.**
- It was found that it always cuts DNA molecule at a particular point by recognising a specific sequence of DNA known as the **recognition sequence.**

  For example, the first restriction endonuclease, *Hind* II recognises a six base pair long recognition sequence.
- Besides *Hind* II, more than **900 restriction enzymes** are known today that have been isolated from over 230 bacterial strains. Each of which recognises different recognition sequences.
- Restriction endonucleases are not present in eukaryotic cells.
- These enzymes belong to a larger class called **nucleases,** which are of two types
  - **Exonucleases** remove nucleotides from the ends of the DNA (either 5′ or 3′).
  - **Endonucleases** make cuts at specific position within DNA.

Differences between Exonucleases and Endonucleases

Exonuclease	Endonuclease
They cleave base pairs of DNA at their terminal ends.	They cleave DNA at specific point except the terminal ends.
They act on single strand of double stranded DNA. 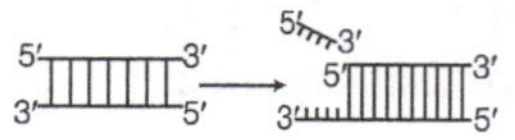	They cleave one strand or both strands of double stranded DNA. 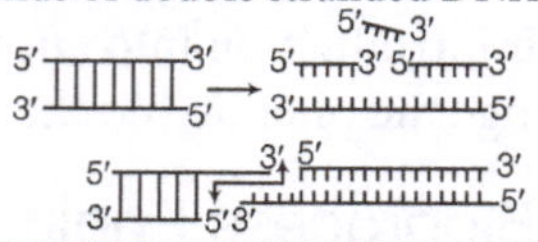
It is found in both eukaryotes and prokaryotes.	It is found only in prokaryotes.

Nomenclature of Restriction Enzymes

- The convention for naming these enzymes proceeds in a way that the first letter of the name comes from the **genus** and the second two letters come from the **species** of prokaryotic cell from which they were isolated, e.g.
  - In *Eco*RI, *Eco* comes from *E. coli,* the letter 'R' is derived from the name of **strain,** RY 13.
  - Roman number following the names that indicate the order in which the enzymes were isolated from that strain of bacteria.

Mechanism of Action of Restriction Endonuclease

- Each restriction endonuclease functions by 'inspecting' the length of a DNA sequence.
- Once it finds specific recognition sequence, it will bind to DNA and cut each of the two strands of double helix at specific points in their sugar phosphate backbones.
- Each restriction endonuclease recognises a specific **palindromic nucleotide sequences** in the DNA. **Palindromes** are the group of letters that form the same words when read both forward and backward, e.g. 'MALAYALAM'.
- As against a word-palindrome where the same word is read in both direction, the palindrome in DNA is a sequence of base pairs that reads same on the two strands when orientation of reading is kept same. e.g. the following sequences read the same on the two strands in 5′ ⟶ 3′ direction as well as 3′ ⟶ 5′ direction.

  5′ — GAATTC — 3′
  3′ — CTTAAG — 5′

- Restriction enzymes cut the strand of DNA a little away from the centre of the palindromic sites, but between the same two bases on the opposite strands.
- This leaves single-stranded portion at the ends. These are overhanging stretches called **sticky ends** present on each strand as shown in the fig. 9.1.
- These are named so because they form hydrogen bonds with their complementary cut counterparts. This stickiness of the ends facilitates the action of the enzyme DNA ligase.

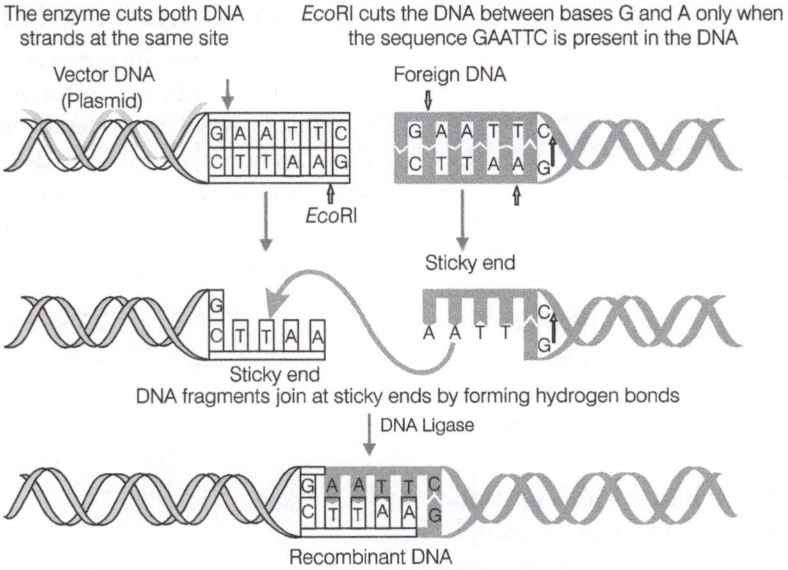

Fig. 9.1 Steps in formation of recombinant DNA by the action of restriction endonuclease enzyme *Eco*RI

- In genetic engineering, restriction endonucleases are used to form recombinant molecules of DNA, which are composed of DNA from different sources or genomes.
- In order to create a recombinant DNA molecule, it is necessary that the vector and the source DNA are cut with the same restriction enzyme.
- So, the resultant DNA fragments have the same sticky ends, which are complementary to each other and can be joined together (end-to-end) by using **DNA ligases.**

DNA Ligases (Molecular Glue)

- These enzymes repair broken DNA fragments by joining the sugar phosphate backbones of two adjacent nucleotides.
- It is used in genetic engineering to reverse the action of restriction enzymes, i.e. to join complementary DNA strands/ends together, e.g. T_4 DNA ligase.

DNA Polymerases

This enzyme helps in *in vitro* synthesis of complementary DNA (*c*DNA) strand from a DNA templates.

Quick Test 1

1. A 56 nucleotide base pair long piece of DNA, having desirable genes, was introduced into the host cell. Will it be able to multiply independently inside the host?
2. Mention the term used to describe the DNA construct formed when a gene of interest is ligated into a plasmid vector.
3. Mention the enzyme used to cut DNA at specific sites.
4. Suggest the name of the restriction enzyme isolated for the first time from the bacterium *Bacillus amyloliquefaciens* H.
5. **State True or False.**

   DNA ligase is used to break the phosphodiester bonds in the plasmid, ensuring the proper insertion of the gene of interest.

2. Cloning Vectors

- The DNA molecule that can carry a foreign DNA segment and replicate inside the host cell is called **vector**. These vectors have the ability to replicate with in bacterial cells independent of the control of chromosomal DNA.
- Following vectors are commonly used in recombinant DNA technology
  - **Plasmids** These are small, autonomously replicating usually circular, extrachromosomal double stranded DNA molecule that occurs in many bacteria and some yeasts.

    The plasmid molecules may be present as 1 or 2 copies or in multiple copies (500-700) inside the host organism.
  - **Bacteriophages** These are viruses that infect bacteria. They are used as the vector because of very high copy number (number of copies of vectors present in a cell) of their genome within the bacterial cells.
- If a foreign piece of DNA is linked with a plasmid, DNA or bacteriophage, its number can be multiplied and become equal to the copy number of the plasmid or bacteriophage.
- Vectors used at present, are engineered in such a way that they help easy linking of foreign DNA and selection of recombinants from non-recombinants.

Features of Cloning Vector

There are certain features that are required to facilitate cloning into a vector. These are as follows

Origin of Replication (*ori*)

- This is a sequence from where replication starts. Any piece of DNA, when linked to this sequence can be made to replicate within the host cells.
- This sequence is also responsible for controlling the copy number of the linked DNA.

Selectable Marker

- It helps in identifying or selecting transformants. These marker eliminate non-transformants by selectively permitting the growth of the transformants.
- **Transformation** is a procedure, through which a piece of DNA is introduced into the host bacterium.
- Normally, the genes encoding resistance to antibiotics such as ampicillin, chloramphenicol, tetracycline, kanamycin, etc. are considered as useful selectable markers for *E. coli*.
- The normal *E. coli* cells do not carry resistance against any of these antibiotics.

Cloning (recognition) Sites

- These are generally required to link the foreign or alien DNA with the vector. For this, the vector requires very few, preferably single recognition sites for commonly used restriction enzymes.
- If more than one recognition sites is present within the vector, it will generate several fragments. This will lead to more complication in gene cloning.

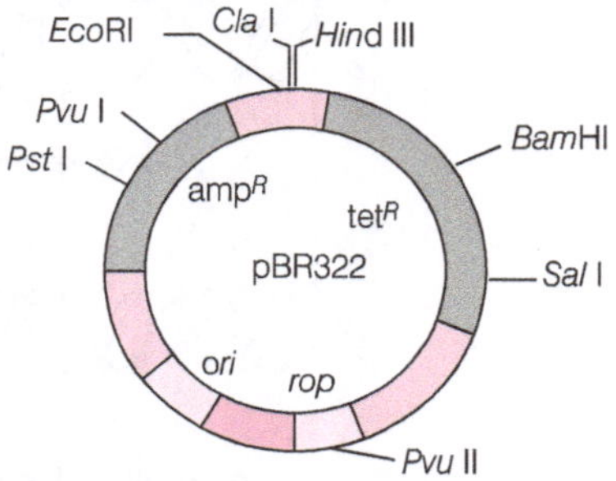

Fig. 9.2 *E. coli* cloning vector pBR322 showing restriction sites (*Hind* III, *Eco*RI, *Bam*HI, *Sal* I, *Pvu* II, *Pst* I, *Cla* I), *ori* and antibiotic resistance genes (amp^R and tet^R). *rop* codes for the proteins involved in the replication of the plasmid

- The **ligation** of the foreign DNA is carried out at a restriction site present in one of the two **antibiotic resistance genes**.

Selection between Recombinant and Non-recombinant

Selection of recombinants from non-recombinants can be done by one of the following methods, given below

(i) Inactivation of Antibiotic Resistance Gene

- If a foreign DNA is ligated at the *Bam*H I site of tetracycline-resistance gene in the vector pBR322, the recombinant plasmid will loose tetracycline resistance due to insertion of foreign DNA.
- But, it can still be selected out from non-recombinant ones by plating transformants on tetracycline containing medium.

- The transformants growing on medium, containing ampicillin, are then transferred on a medium, containing tetracycline.
- The **recombinants** will grow in ampicillin containing medium, but not on that containing tetracycline.
- On the other side, **non-recombinants** will grow on both media and thus, recombinants are selected.
- In this example, one antibiotic resistance gene helps in selecting the transformants whereas, the other antibiotic resistance gene gets inactivated due to insertion of alien DNA and helps in selection of recombinants.

(ii) Insertional Inactivation

- The selection of recombinants due to inactivation of antibiotic gene is a cumbersome procedure.
- As it requires simultaneous plating on two plates having different antibiotics.
- Therefore, the alternative selectable markers have been developed, which differentiate recombinants from non-recombinants.
- It is based on their ability to produce colour in the presence of **chromogenic substrate**.
- In this process, a recombinant DNA is inserted within the coding sequence of an enzyme β-**galactosidase**. This results into inactivation of the gene responsible for synthesis of this enzyme, which is referred to as **insertional inactivation**.
- Therefore, the bacterial colonies having an insert in their plasmid, shows no colouration (recombinant colonies) while, those without plasmid will show blue colour.
- Presence of insert results into insertional inactivation of the β- galactosidase gene and the colonies do not produce any colour, these are identified recombinant colonies.

Vectors for Cloning Genes in Plants and Animals

- In plants, *Agrobacterium tumifaciens* (a pathogen of several dicot plants) is able to deliver a piece of DNA known as 'T-DNA' (transfer-DNA) into plant cells.
- It transforms normal plant cells into tumour cells which produce chemicals required by pathogen.
- The tumour inducing (Ti) plasmid of *Agrobacterium tumifaciens* has been modified as a cloning vector. It is no longer pathogenic to the plants, but is still able to deliver genes of interest.
- Similarly, retroviruees, are also used as a cloning vectors in animals because of their ability to transform normal cells into **cancerous cells**.
- They are first disarmed and then used to transfer desirable gene to animal cells.

3. Competent Host (For Transformation with Recombinant DNA)

- DNA is a hydrophilic molecule, so it cannot pass through cell membranes. In order to force bacteria to take up the plasmid, the bacterial cells must first be made **competent**.

> **TEACHER'S TIP**
> The cell membrane is made up of lipids, which are hydrophobic in nature. This property does not allow hydrophilic molecules, like DNA, to pass through the membrane easily.

- The competency is the ability of a cell to take up foreign DNA. The cells can be made competent by following methods

Chemical Method ($CaCl_2$ Method)

- In this method, the cells are treated with a specific concentration of a divalent cation such as calcium. This increases the efficiency with which DNA enters into the bacterium through the pores in its cell wall.
- The cells are incubated with recombinant DNA on ice, followed by placing them briefly at 42°C (heat shock) and then putting them back on ice. This treatment enables the bacteria to take up the recombinant DNA.

Physical Method

The common physical methods for competency are as follows

- **Microinjection** This method is used to introduce foreign DNA into host cell. In this method, recombinant DNA is directly injected into the nucleus of an animal cell.
- **Biolistics** or **Gene Gun** It is another method which is suitable for introduction of DNA into plants. In this

method, cells are bombarded with high velocity microparticles of gold or tungsten coated with DNA.

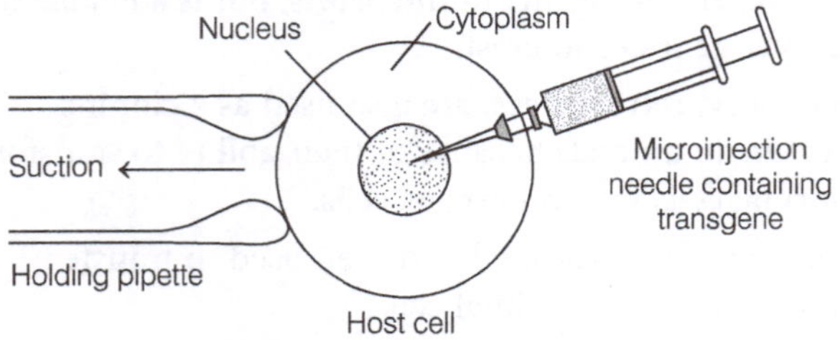

Fig. 9.3 Introduction of foreign DNA in a host cell with a microinjection needle

Disarmed Pathogen Vectors

In this method, the vectors that can cause infection are allowed to infect the cell to transfer the recombinant DNA into the host.

Quick Test 2

1. **State True or False.**
   Cloning vectors' ability to replicate independently within the host cell makes them efficient tools for gene cloning.
2. Name the site in the cloning vector that is essential for the replication of the gene of interest in the host cell.
3. A scientist constructs a cloning vector but forgets to add selectable markers. Is this vector suitable for gene cloning?
4. What are the sites in the plasmids where antibiotic resistance genes are inserted?
5. If a gene is inserted into the tetracycline resistance region of the pBR322 vector and transferred to *E. coli*, will the bacteria grow in tetracycline-containing medium?
6. Mention the type of host cells suitable to introduce the alien DNA through microinjection.

9.3 Processes of Recombinant DNA Technology

- **Recombinant DNA technology** involves the following steps in specific sequence.
  1. Isolation of the genetic material (DNA).
  2. Fragmentation of DNA by restriction endonucleases.
  3. Separation and isolation of a desired DNA fragment.
  4. Amplification of gene of interest using PCR.
  5. Ligation of the DNA fragment into a vector.
  6. Insertion of recombinant DNA into the host.
  7. Obtaining the foreign product by culturing the host cells on a suitable medium.

These steps are discussed in detail below

1. Isolation of the Genetic Material (DNA)

- Nucleic acid is the genetic material, in all living organisms. In majority of organisms, this is present in the form of **Deoxyribonucleic Acid** (DNA).
- In order to cut the DNA with restriction enzyme, it must be present in pure form, i.e. free from other macromolecules.
- This is done in the following sequence
  - Since, DNA is enclosed within the membranes, breaking of cell envelope is necessary in order to release DNA along with other macromolecules such as RNA, proteins, polysaccharides and lipids.
  - The bacterial cells, plant or animal tissues are treated with the enzyme such as lysozyme (bacteria), cellulase (plant cells), chitinase (fungus) to break the cell.
  - RNA can be removed by treating it with **ribonuclease**, whereas, proteins can be removed by its treatment with **protease**.
  - Other molecules can be removed by appropriate treatments. Now, purified DNA will precipitate out, after the addition of chilled **ethanol.**
  - This can be seen as collection of fine threads in the suspension which can be removed by **spooling.**

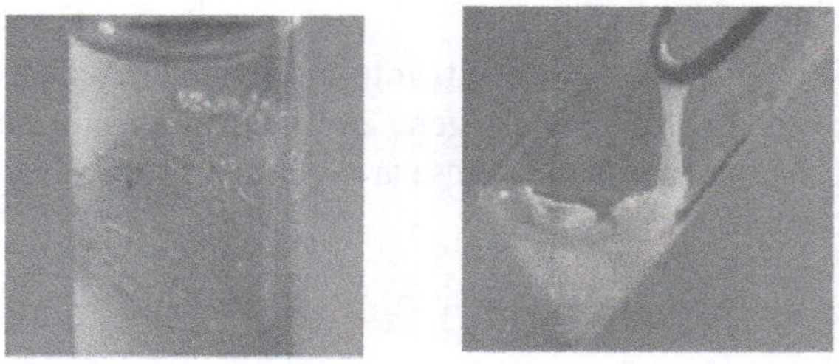

Fig. 9.4 DNA that separates out can be removed by spooling

2. Fragmentation of DNA by Restriction Endonuclease

- The digestion of DNA is performed by incubating purified DNA molecules with the restriction enzyme. This is done at the optimal conditions for that specific enzyme.

3. Separation and Isolation of DNA Fragments

- The cutting of DNA by restriction endonucleases results in the fragments of DNA which are separated by a technique known as **gel electrophoresis.**
- Since, the DNA fragments are negatively charged molecules, they can be separated by forcing them to move towards the anode (+) under an electric field through an appropriate medium or matrix.
- The most commonly used matrix is **agarose**, a natural polymer extracted from sea weeds.

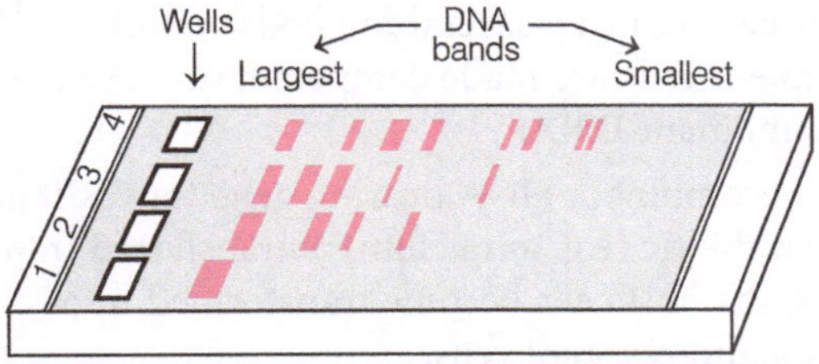

Fig. 9.5 A typical agarose gel electrophoresis showing migration of undigested (lane 1) and digested set of DNA fragments (lane 2-4)

- DNA fragments resolve (separate) according to their size through sieving effect provided by the agarose gel.
- Hence, smaller the fragment size, the farther it moves.
- The separated DNA fragments can be visualised only after staining the DNA with **Ethidium Bromide** (EtBr) followed by exposure to UV radiation.
- The bright orange coloured bands of DNA are seen when ethidium bromide stained gel is exposed to UV light.
- These separate stained bands of DNA are cut out from the agarose gel and extracted from the gel piece, by a process known as **elution.**
- Thus, the DNA fragments (containing gene of interest) are purified and used in the construction of recombinant DNA by joining them with cloning vectors in the presence of DNA ligase.

4. Amplification of Gene of Interest using PCR

- In **Polymerase Chain Reaction** (PCR), multiple copies of DNA (gene of interest) are synthesised *in vitro.*
- PCR uses two sets of primers and the enzyme DNA polymerase for the amplification of DNA.
- This technique was developed by **Kary Mullis**, who received Nobel Prize for this in 1993.

Requirements of PCR

The basic requirements of a PCR are discussed below

- **DNA Template** The double-stranded DNA that needs to be amplified.
- **Primers** These are chemically synthesised oligonucleotides (short segment of DNA) that are complementary to the regions of DNA template.
- **Enzymes** Commonly used enzymes in PCR is ***Taq* Polymerase** (DNA polymerase). It is isolated from a thermophilic bacterium, *Thermus aquaticus. Taq* polymerase has a property to remain active during the high temperature induced denaturation of double-stranded DNA. It also helps in the amplification of a segment of DNA.
- **Nucleotide Bases** These are added by DNA polymerase to the growing chain.

Steps Involved in PCR

Three main steps involved in the PCR technique are given below.

***Step* I Denaturation** The double-stranded DNA is denatured by subjecting it to high temperature, i.e. 95° C for 2-5 minutes. Now each separated single strand acts as a template for DNA synthesis.

***Step* II Annealing** Two sets of oligonucleotide primers are annealed (hybridised) to the separated single-strands. This step is carried out at a slightly lower temperature (40-60° C).

***Step* III Extension** The thermostable enzyme *Taq* DNA polymerase is used in this step.

- It extends the primers by adding *d*NTPs (deoxynucleotide triphosphates) complementary to those of the template DNA.
- Mg^{2+} is required as a cofactor for thermostable **DNA polymerase.** At this step, the temperature is raised to 72°C.
- These steps are repeated many times in order to obtain several copies of desired DNA (approximately 1 billion).
- Repeated amplification is achieved by using a thermostable DNA polymerase, which remain active during the high temperature induced the denaturation of *ds*DNA.

- The amplified fragment if desired can now be ligated to a vector for further cloning.

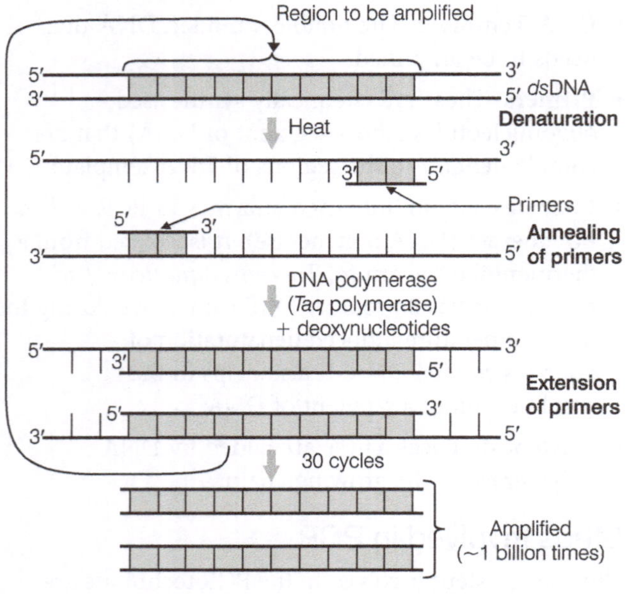

Fig. 9.6 Polymerase Chain Reaction (PCR)

Application of PCR

It has the following applications

- *r*DNA technology
- DNA sequencing
- DNA fingerprinting
- For diagnosis of infections and diseases.

Quick Test 3

1. Mention the enzyme used to isolate protoplasts from bacterial cells.
2. **State True or False.**
   The charge carried by DNA plays an important role in the separation of its fragments in the electrophoresis technique.
3. Name the dye that is used to visualise DNA fragments after electrophoresis.
4. Name the technique that employs the use of thermostable DNA polymerase.
5. At which step of gene amplification does Taq polymerase add bases to the template DNA?

5. Ligation of DNA Fragment into a Vector

- This process requires a vector DNA and a source DNA.
- In order to obtain sticky ends, both of these should be cut with the same endonuclease, after which, both are ligated by enzyme **DNA ligase** to form the **recombinant DNA/hybrid DNA.**

6. Insertion of Recombinant DNA into the Host Cell/Organisms

- This can occur by several methods, before which the recipient cells are made competent to receive the recombinant DNA.
- If a recombinant DNA bearing gene for resistance to an antibiotic (e.g. ampicillin) is transferred into *E. coli* cells, the host cells become transformed into ampicillin resistant cells.
- The ampicillin resistance gene in this case is called **selectable marker**. When transformed cells are grown on agar plates containing ampicillin, only **transformants** will grow and others will die.

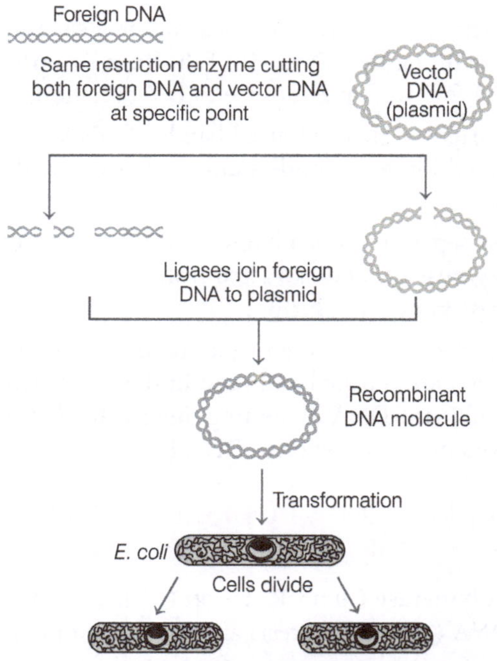

Fig. 9.7 Diagrammatic representation of recombinant DNA technology

7. Obtaining the Foreign Gene Product

- When a piece of foreign DNA is inserted into a cloning vector and transfered into cell (bacterial, plant, animal), the foreign DNA gets multiplied.
- In almost all *r*DNA technology, the ultimate aim is to produce a desirable protein. Hence, there is a need for the recombinant DNA to be expressed.
- The foreign DNA gets expressed under appropriate condition that involves many steps.
- After having cloned gene of interest and optimising the condition to induce the expression of target protein, it has to be produced on a large scale.
  - Any protein encoding gene expressed in a heterologous host, it is called **recombinant protein**.
  - The cells harbouring cloned genes of interest can grown on a small scale in the laboratory, (i.e. in appropriate nutrient medium at optimal conditions).
  - These cell cultures are used for extracting the desired protein which is purifying by using various separation techniques.
- Also, the cells can be multiplied in a **continuous culture** system. Here, the used medium is drained out from one side while, fresh is added from the other.
  - It is done to maintain the cells in their physiologically most active phase, i.e. exponential phase or active log phase.
  - This culturing method produces the larger biomass leading to higher yield of desired protein.

Bioreactors

- Small volume culture cannot yield satisfactory amount of product. To produce in large quantities, bioreactors are used.
- These are the large volume vessels approximately (100-1000 L) in which raw materials are biologically converted into specific products, individual enzymes, etc.
- It is done by using microbial, plant, animal or human cells.
- A **bioreactor** provides the optimal conditions for achieving the desired product by providing optimum growth conditions like temperature, pH, substrate, salts, vitamins and oxygen.

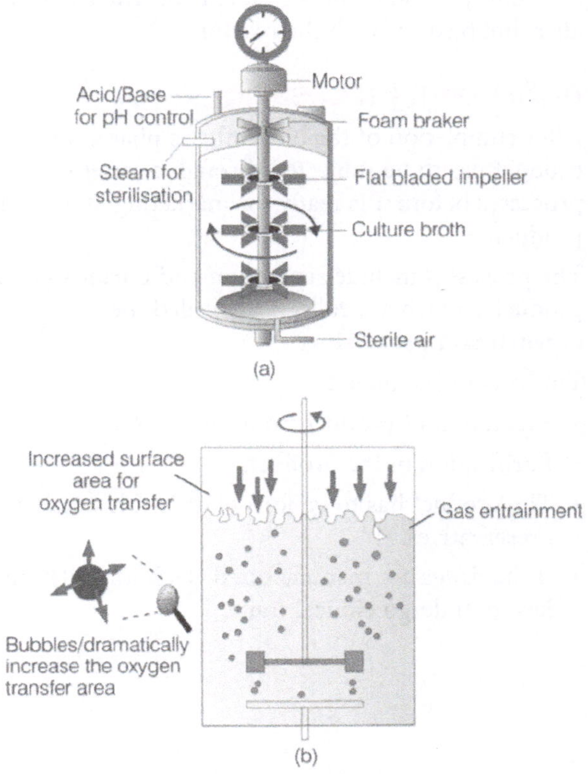

Fig. 9.8 (a) Simple stirred-tank bioreactor, (b) Sparged stirred-tank bioreactor through which sterile air bubbles are sparged

Components of Bioreactor

The components of a bioreactor are as follows

- An agitator system
- An oxygen delivery system
- A foam control system
- A temperature control system
- pH control system
- A sampling port to withdraw culture periodically.

Types of Bioreactor

The most commonly used bioreactors are of **stirring** type bioreactor. These are further of two types

- **A simple stirred-tank bioreactor** is usually cylindrical or with a curved base to facilitate even mixing of reactor contents.

- The **sparged- stirred-tank bioreactor** also facilitates the mixing of components and ensures oxygen availability throughout the bioreactor. Alternatively, air is bubbled through the reactor.

Downstream Processing

- After completion of the biosynthetic phase, the product has to be subjected through a series of processes before it is ready for marketing as a finished product.
- The processes include separation and purification of products, which are collectively called the **downstream processing**.
- This processing includes
  - Separation of product from the reactor.
  - Purification of the product.
  - The product has to be formulated with suitable preservatives.
  - If the drugs are manufactured, such formulations has to undergo clinical trails.
  - Strict quality control testing for each product is also required.
- The downstream processing and quality control testing vary from product to product.

Quick Test 4

1. In cell culturing, which phase exhibits the highest metabolic activity?
2. Name the instrument in which large volume of living cells are cultured in order to obtain a desired products.
3. Among a simple and a sparged stirred tank bioreactor, which is more suitable for the growth of aerobic bacteria?
4. What is the final step in recombinant DNA technology that involves the purification and preparation of the desired product?
5. **State True or False.**
   Downstream processing involves the steps of harvesting, purifying, and formulating the product.

Mind Map

Biotechnology : Principles and Processes

Biotechnology

Integration of natural science and organisms, cells, parts thereof and molecular analogues for the products and services (EFB).

Principles of Biotechnology

Genetic Engineering
- Modification of chemical nature of genetic material and its introduction into another organism.

Bioprocess Engineering
- To maintain the growth and manipulation of desired microbes in order to get large quantities of products.

Tools of Recombinant DNA Technology

- **Restriction Enzymes** Enzymes used for cutting of DNA at specific locations. Belong to a larger group of enzymes called **nucleases,** which are of two types; exonucleases and endonucleases.
- **Ligases** The resultant DNA fragments with same sticky ends formed by cutting of restriction endonucleases are joined together by DNA ligases.

Cloning Vectors

- DNA molecules that can carry foreign DNA segment into host cell, e.g. **plasmids** and **bacteriophages.**
- Features such as *ori*, **selectable marker** and cloning sites are required to facilitate for cloning into a vector.

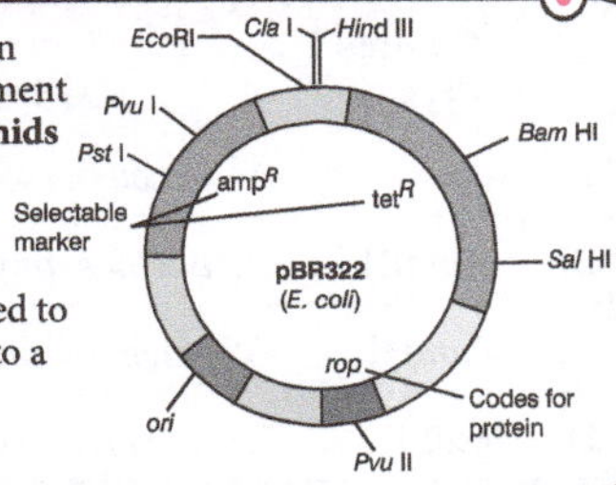

Competent Host

For Bacterial Cell
- Treat with Ca^{2+} → ice → heat shock → ice again.

For Plant Cell
- **Biolistics / Gene Gun** Plant cells are bombarded with high velocity micro particles of gold or tungsten coated with DNA.

For Animal Cell
- **Microinjection** DNA is directly injected in the nucleus of animal host cell.

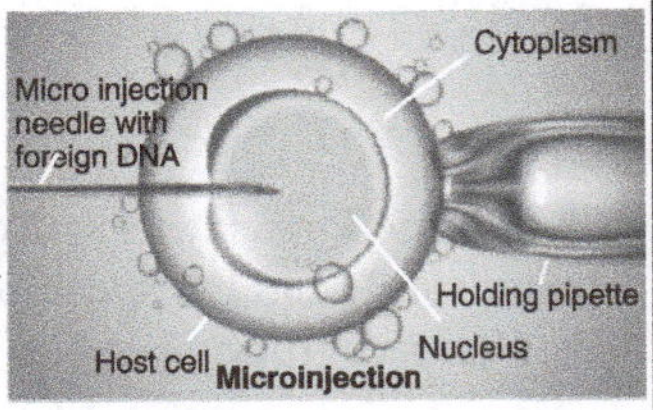

Bioreactors

Large volume vessels in which raw materials are biologically converted into specific products using microbial, plant, animal or human cell, e.g. stirring type bioreactor.

Processes of Recombinant DNA Technology

1. Isolation of genetic material (cell digestion)
   - Bacterial cells → Lysozyme
   - Plant cell → Cellulase
   - Fungal cell → Chitinase

   Spooling : Method to extract DNA from remains of the cell by treating it with chilled ethanol.
2. Cutting of DNA at specific location by restriction enzyme.
3. Separation and isolation of DNA by Gel Electrophoresis (GE).

   Agarose Gel Electrophoresis

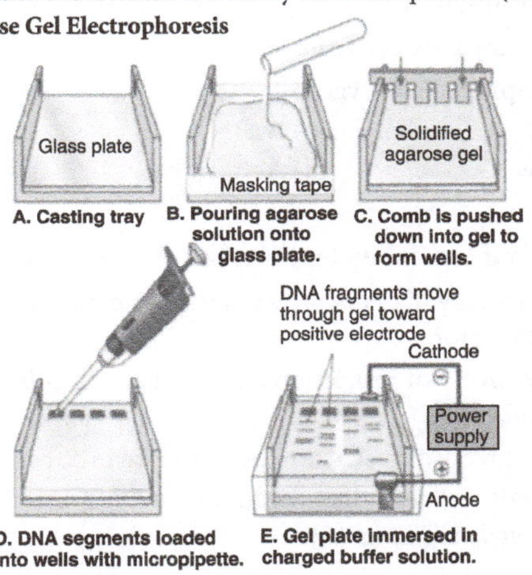

4. Amplification of gene of interest using **Polymerase Chain Reaction** (PCR) by **Kary Mullis.**

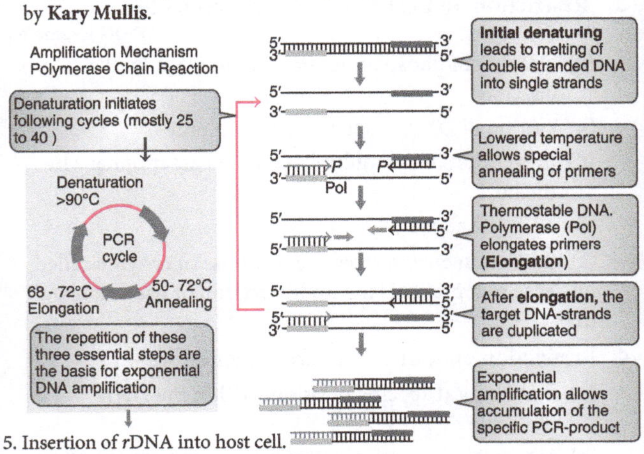

5. Insertion of *r*DNA into host cell.
6. Obtaining the foreign gene product.

Downstream Processing

- Series of processes for the recovery of finished product.
- Processes include separation and purification of product.

EXAM PATTERN QUESTIONS

Objective Type Questions

Multiple Choice Questions

1. The techniques or processes that are included under biotechnology are

A. *in vitro* fertilisation
B. synthesising a gene
C. chemical synthesis
D. correcting a defective gene
E. developing a DNA vaccine

(a) A, C, E (b) A, B, C
(c) B, D, E (d) A, B, D, E

Ans. (*d*)

2. In 1972, Stanley Cohen and Herbert Boyer achieved

(a) the discovery of nerve growth factor and epidermal growth factor
(b) the discovery of restriction endonuclease in *Salmonella typhimurium*
(c) the discovery of restriction exonuclease in *E. coli*
(d) the construction of first recombinant DNA involving *Salmonella typhimurium*

Ans. (*d*)

3. 'Restriction' in Restriction enzyme refers to **NCERT Exemplar**

(a) cleaving of phosphodiester bond in DNA by the enzyme
(b) cutting of DNA at specific position only
(c) prevention of the multiplication of bacteriophage by the host
(d) all of the above

Ans. (*c*) Restriction enzymes belong to a class of enzyme called nuclease that prevents the multiplication of bacteriophage in bacteria.

4. Restriction endonucleases are enzymes, which

(a) make cuts at specific positions within the DNA molecule
(b) recognise a specific nucleotide sequence for binding and then cleave both the strands of DNA
(c) restrict the action of the enzyme DNA polymerase
(d) remove nucleotides from the ends of the DNA molecule

Ans. (*a*)

5. An enzyme catalysing the removal of nucleotides from the ends of DNA is **NCERT Exemplar**

(a) endonuclease (b) exonuclease
(c) DNA ligase (d) *Hind* II

Ans. (*b*)

6. *Eco*RI cleaves the DNA strands to produce

(a) satellite ends (b) blunt end
(c) *ori* replication end (d) sticky ends

Ans. (*d*)

7. Restriction Endonuclease *Hind* II always cuts DNA molecules at a particular point by recognising a specific sequence of : **CBSE 2024**

(a) Six base pairs (b) Four base pairs
(c) Seven base pairs (d) Three base pairs

Ans. (*a*)

8. Match the following Column I with Column II and choose the correct option from the codes given below.

	Column I (Vectors)	Column II (Derivative microorganisms)
A.	EcoRI	1. *E. coli* R 245
B.	HindIII	2. *Bacillus amyloliquefaciens*
C.	BamHI	3. *Haemophilus influenzae*
D.	EcoRII	4. *Escherichia coli* RY13

Codes

	A	B	C	D		A	B	C	D
(a)	1	2	3	4	(b)	3	2	1	4
(c)	4	3	2	1	(d)	4	2	3	1

Ans. (*c*)

9. The restriction enzyme acts on recognition site which is palindromic and has specified base pairs. This means that the recognition site has **Competency Based Que.**

(a) base sequences identical to one another
(b) base sequences that consist of only four bases
(c) base sequences that reads same on the two strands when reading orientation is kept the same
(d) base sequence with attached probe

Ans. (*c*)

10. Given below is the restriction site of a restriction endonuclease *Pst* I and the cleavage sites on a DNA molecule. Competency Based Que, CBSE 2023

5′ C – T – G – C – A ↓ – G 3′
3′ G ↑ – A – C – G – T – C 5′

Choose the option that gives the correct resultant fragments by the action of the enzyme Pst I.

(a) 5′C – T – G   C – A – G 3′ C 5′
    3′ G – A – C – G – T
(b) 5′ C – T   G – C – A – G 3′ T – C 5′
    3′ G – A – G – C
(c) 5′ C – T – G – C   A – G3′
    3′ G – A – C – G   T – C 5′
(d) 5′ C – T – G – C – A   A – C – G – T – C 5′ G 3′
    3′ G

Ans. (*d*)

11. *Eco*RI cuts the DNA between bases G and A only when the sequence of GAATTC is present. The number of nucleotides present in the resultant sticky ends that will be formed in each of the two strands of DNA after this enzyme cuts the DNA will be: Competency Based Que.

	Vector DNA	Foreign DNA
(a)	1 and 5	5 and 1
(b)	2 and 4	4 and 2
(c)	2 and 5	5 and 2
(d)	3 and 4	4 and 3

Ans. (*a*)

12. In recombinant DNA technique, the term vector refers to a

(a) donor DNA, it is identified and picked up through electrophoresis
(b) plasmid, transfers DNA into living cell
(c) collection of entire genome in the form of plasmid
(d) enzyme that cuts the DNA at specific sites

Ans. (*b*)

13. Plasmids are vectors for the gene cloning because they

(a) replicate freely outside bacterial cell
(b) can autonomously replicate in bacterial cells
(c) can be multiplied in laboratories using enzymes
(d) can be multiplied in culture

Ans. (*b*)

14. An antibiotic resistance gene in a vector usually helps in the selection of NCERT exemplar

(a) competent bacterial cells
(b) transformed bacterial cells
(c) recombinant bacterial cells
(d) None of the above

Ans. (*b*) Selectable markers help in identifying and eliminating non-transformants and selectively permitting the growth of the transformants.

15. The sequence that controls the copy number of linked DNA in the vector is termed CBSE 2024 C

(a) selectable marker   (b) ori site
(c) palindromic sequence   (d) recognition site

Ans. (*b*)

16. The figure shows the structure of a plasmid Competency Based Que.

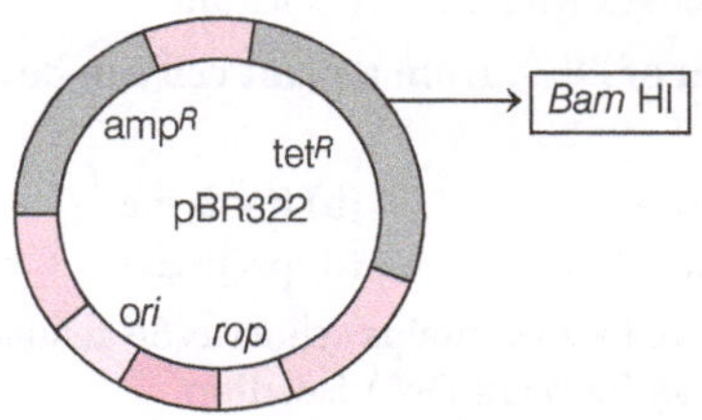

A foreign DNA was ligated at *Bam* HI. The transformants were then grown in a medium containing antibiotics tetracycline and ampicillin.
Choose the correct observation for the growth of transformed bacterial colonies from the given table. Competency Based Que.

	Medium with tetracycline	Medium with ampicillin
(a)	Growth	No growth
(b)	No growth	Growth
(c)	No growth	No growth
(d)	Growth	Growth

Ans. (*b*)

17. Identify *A*, *B*, *C* and *D* in the given diagram of *E. coli* cloning vector pBR322. Competency Based Que.

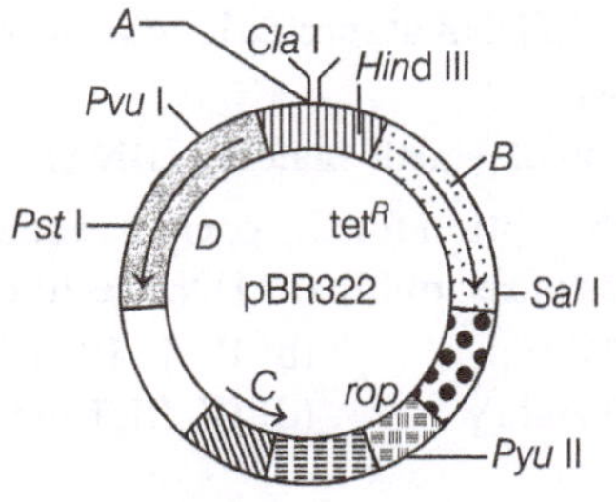

(a) *A*–*Eco*RI, *B*–*Bam*HI, *C*–*ori*, *D*–amp^R
(b) *A*–amp^R, *B*–*ori*, *C*–*Bam*HI, *D*–*Eco*RI
(c) *A*–*ori* , *B*–*Bam*HI, *C*–*Eco*RI, *D*–amp^R
(d) *A*–*Bam*HI, *B*–*Eco*RI, *C*–amp^R, *D*–*ori*

Ans. (*a*)

18. Recombinant colonies in insertional inactivation of β-galactosidase are differentiated on the basis of

(a) production of blue colour
(b) production of no colour
(c) production of red colour
(d) production of green colour

Ans. (*b*)

19. Isolation of DNA from a fungal cell can be achieved by using **CBSE 2025**

(a) cellulase (b) chitinase
(c) lysozyme (d) protease

Ans. (*b*) Fungal cell walls contain chitin, so chitinase is used to break them down for DNA isolation.

20. Isolation of DNA from a plant cell can be achieved by using **CBSE 2025**

(a) chitinase (b) lysozyme
(c) cellulase (d) pectinase

Ans. (*c*) Plant cell wall contains cellulase. So cellulase is used to breakdown for plant DNA isolation.

21. Microparticles coated with DNA to be bombarded with gene gun are made up of

(a) platinum or zinc
(b) silicon or platinum
(c) silver or platinum
(d) gold or tungsten

Ans. (*d*)

22. Which of the following is not used for introduction of alien DNA into host cells? **Diksha**

(a) Microinjection (b) Elution
(c) Gene gun (d) Competent bacteria

Ans. (*b*)

23. The process of recombinant DNA technology has following steps **Competency Based Que.**

I. Amplification of gene.
II. Insertion of recombinant DNA into the host cell.
III. Cutting of DNA at specific location using restriction enzyme.
IV. Isolation of genetic material (DNA).

Pick out the option for the correct sequence of step for the process of recombinant DNA technology.

(a) II, III, IV and I (b) IV, II, III and I
(c) I, II, III and IV (d) IV, III, I and II

Ans. (*d*)

24. Which of the following is not correctly matched for organism and its cell wall degrading enzyme?

(a) Algal-methylase (b) Bacteria-lysosyme
(c) Fungi-chitinase (d) Plant cells-cellulase

Ans. (*a*)

25. What is the criterion for DNA fragments movement on agarose gel during gel electrophoresis?

(a) The smaller the fragment size, the farther it moves
(b) Negatively charged fragments do not move
(c) Positively charged fragments move to the farther end
(d) The larger the fragment size, the farther it moves

Ans. (*a*)

26. Which of the following statement is correct in the context of observing DNA separated by agarose gel electrophoresis? **NCERT Exemplar**

(a) DNA can be seen in visible light
(b) DNA can be seen without staining in visible light
(c) Ethidium bromide stained DNA can be seen in visible light
(d) Ethidium bromide stained DNA can be seen under exposure to UV light

Ans. (*d*) The separated DNA fragments are visualised after staining the DNA with ethidium bromide followed by exposure to UV- radiation. These fragments are seen as orange coloured bands.

27. Which of the following steps are catalysed by *Taq* DNA polymerase in a PCR reaction? **NCERT Exemplar**

(a) Denaturation of template DNA
(b) Annealing of primers to template DNA
(c) Extension of primer end on the template DNA
(d) All of the above

Ans. (*c*) In polymerase chain reaction, polymerisation or extension step is catalysed by *Taq* polymerase enzyme.

28. Simple stirred-tank bioreactor is given below. Identify *A, B, C, D* and *E*.

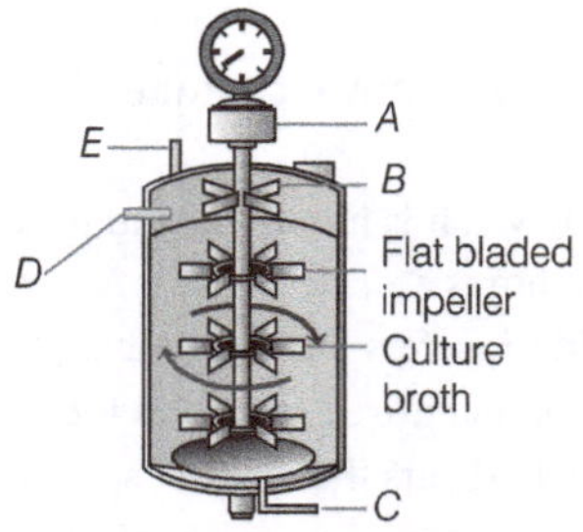

	A	*B*	*C*	*D*	*E*
(a)	Motor	Foam breaker	Sterile air	Steam for sterilisation	Acid/base for pH control
(b)	Foam breaker	Sterile air	Steam for sterilisation	Acid/Base for pH control	Motor
(c)	Acid/base for pH control	Motor	Foam breaker	Sterile air	Steam for sterilisation
(d)	Sterile air	Steam for sterilisation	Foam breaker	Motor	Acid/base for pH control

Ans. (*a*)

29. Which of the following is not a component of downstream processing?

(a) Separation and filtration.
(b) Purification and preservation.
(c) Clinical formulation and quality control testing.
(d) Expression of gene.

Ans. (*d*)

Assertion-Reason Questions

Direction (Q. Nos. 1-13) *In each of the following questions, a statement of Assertion (A) is given followed by corresponding statement of Reason (R). Of the statements, mark the correct answer.*

(a) Both A and R are true and R is the correct explanation of A
(b) Both A and R are true, but R is not the correct explanation of A
(c) A is true, but R is false
(d) A is false, but R is true

1. Assertion (A) Biotechnology deals with techniques that use living organism to produce products useful for humans.

Reason (R) Biotechnology uses only in unicellular organism.

Ans. (*c*) A is true, but R is false and R can be corrected as Biotechnology is used in unicellular as well as multicellular organism.

2. Assertion (A) The first restriction endonuclease was *Hind* II.

Reason (R) The *Hind* II always cut DNA molecule at particular point by recognising a specific sequence of 6-base pair.

Ans. (*b*)

3. Assertion (A) In *Eco*RI, the letter 'R' derived from the species of prokaryotic cell from which they were isolated.

Reason (R) Exonuclease and endonuclease are the types of nucleases enzyme.

Ans. (*d*) A is false, but R is true. A can be corrected as In *Eco*RI, the letter R is derived from the name of strain.

4. Assertion (A) Restriction enzymes cut the strand of DNA to produce sticky ends.

Reason (R) Stickiness of the end facilitates the action of enzyme DNA polymerase.

Ans. (*c*) A is true and R is false and R can be corrected as Stickiness of the end facilitates the action of enzyme DNA ligase.

5. Assertion (A) Foreign DNA and vector DNA are cleaved with the help of ligase.

Reason (R) Ligase acts by forming phosphodiester bonds.

Ans. (*d*)

6. Assertion (A) If one wants to recover many copies of target DNA it should be cloned in a vector whose origin support high copy number.

Reason (R) Cloning site is responsible for controling the copy number of the linked DNA/target DNA.

Ans. (*c*)

7. Assertion (A) *E. coli* having pBR322 with DNA insert at *Bam*HI site cannot grow in medium containing tetracycline.

Reason (R) Recognition site for *Bam*HI is present in tet^R region of pBR322.

Ans. (*a*)

8. Figure given below representing the insertional inactivation of lac z gene. Study the figure and comment upon the appropriateness of the Assertion and Reason.

Competency Based Que.

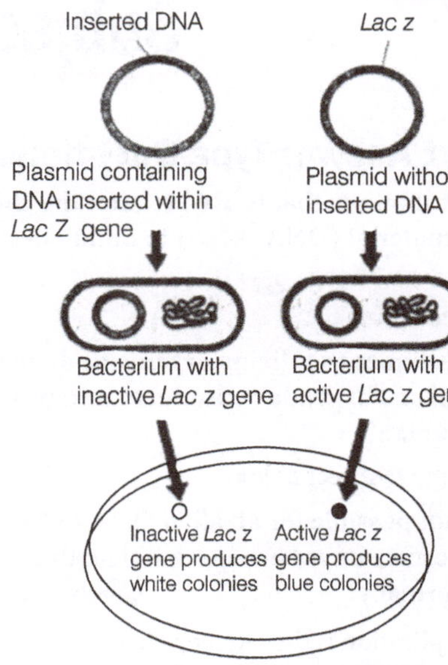

Assertion (A) Presence of insert in the above figure results in inactivation of enzyme β-galactosidase.

Reason (R) Insertion of recombinant DNA within the coding sequence of β-galactosidase results in colourless colonies.

Ans. (*b*)

9. Assertion (A) The tumour inducing plasmid (Ti- plasmid) of *Agrobacterium tumefaciens* acts as a cloning vector in recombinant DNA technology.

Reason (R) The Ti-plasmid which is used in the mechanisms of delivering genes to a cell remains pathogenic.

Ans. (*c*)

10. Assertion (A) *Agrobacterium tumefaciens* is a pathogen of several monocot plants.

Reason (R) *Agrobacterium tumefaciens* is able to deliver a piece of DNA known as T-DNA to transform normal plant cells into a tumor.

Ans. (*d*) A is false and R is true. A can be corrected as *Agrobacterium tumefaciens* is a pathogen of several dicot plants.

11. Given below is the figure of a method of gene transfer. Study the figure and comment upon the appropriatness of the Assertion and Reason. Competency Based Que.

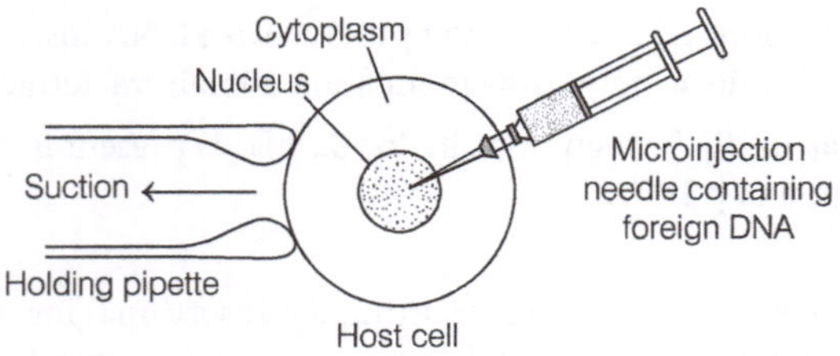

Assertion (A) The foreign DNA is injected directly into the nucleus.

Reason (R) This microinjection can puncture the plasma membrane.

Ans. (*b*)

12. Assertion (A) In gel electrophoresis, DNA fragments are separated.

Reason (R) DNA is negatively charged, so it moves towards anode under electric field.

Ans. (*a*)

13. Assertion (A) DNA fragments can be isolated by gel electrophoresis on the basis of their size.

Reason (R) The larger the fragment size, the faster it moves.

Ans. (*c*) A is true, but R is false and R can be corrected as The smaller the fragment size, the faster it moves.

Subjective Questions

Very Short Answer Type Questions

1. Name the technique that is used to alter the chemistry of genetic material (DNA, RNA) to obtain desired result.

Ans. Genetic engineering

2. Which techniques uses living organisms or enzymes from organisms to produce products and process useful to human?

Ans. Recombinant DNA technology

3. Why is it not possible for an alien DNA to become part of a chromosome anywhere along its length and replicate normally? Competency Based Que.

Ans. Origin of replication is the sequence from where replication start. An alien DNA must be linked to this sequence to be able to replicate within the host cell. (1)

4. Name the two components of first artificial recombinant DNA molecule constructed by Cohen and Boyer.

Ans. (i) A gene encoding antibiotic resistance

(ii) Native plasmid of *Salmonella typhimurium* (½ + ½)

5. What is meant by gene cloning? NCERT Exemplar

Ans. Gene cloning refers to the process of creating identical copies of a specific gene or DNA segment. It involve isolating the gene of intrest and inserting it into a carrier (vector) to enable its replication within the host organism.

6. Name the first restriction endonuclease discovered.

Ans. *Hind* II

7. State what happens when an alien gene is ligated at *Sal* I and *Pvu* I site of pBR322 plasmid? Competency Based Que.

Ans. In case of ligation at *Sal* I site, the transformant loses the tetracycline resistance while, in case of *Pvu* I, the transformant loses ampicillin resistance.

8. What modification is done on the Ti-plasmid of *Agrobacterium tumefaciens* to convert it into a cloning vector? NCERT Exemplar

Or **State how has *Agrobacterium tumefaciens* been made a useful cloning vector to transfer DNA to plant cells.** CBSE 2014

Ans. Tumour inducing (Ti) plasmid of *Agrobacterium tumefaciens* is modified into a cloning vector by removing/altering the gene responsible for its pathogenic property.

9. Name the commonly used vector for cloning genes into higher organisms.

Ans. The commonly used vectors for cloning genes into higher organisms are retrovirus, adenovirus, tobacco mosaic virus, papilloma virus, cauliflower mosaic virus, etc.

10. Name the host cells in which microinjection technique is used to introduce an alien DNA.

Ans. Animal cells.

11. **Name the enzymes that are used for the isolation of DNA from bacterial and fungal cells for recombinant DNA technology.**

Or

What is the role of enzymes like chitinase and lysozyme in genetic engineering? NCERT Exemplar

Ans. Lysozyme (for bacterial cell) and chitinase (for fungal cell) are used for isolating DNA for recombinant DNA technology.

12. **Write the significance of adding proteases at the time of isolation of genetic materials.**

Ans. Protease is added because it helps in digesting proteins and disrupting the plasma membrane by dissolving it.

13. **How can you remove DNA which is separated out from a cell suspension?**

Ans. By spooling method.

14. **Identify the process given below.** Competency Based Que.

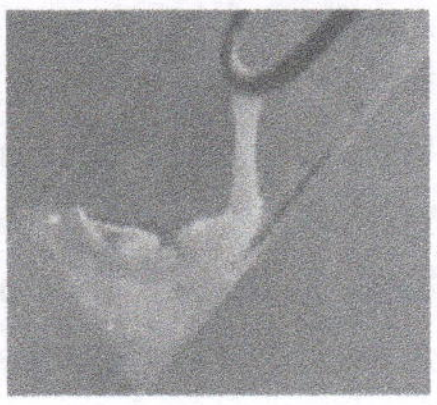

Ans. The given diagrams represent spooling in which the DNA that separates out as fine threads can be removed.

15. **Why do DNA fragments move towards the anode during gel electrophoresis?** Competency Based Que.

Ans. Since, DNA fragments are negatively charged molecules, they are forced to move towards the anode under an electric field through a matrix.

16. **Why is a thermostable DNA polymerase needed in amplification/genetic engineering?**

Ans. It remains active during high temperature induced denaturation of the double-stranded DNA.

17. **What is the purpose of using Mg^{2+} during annealing process of PCR?**

Ans. Mg^{2+} is required as a cofactor for the activity thermostable DNA polymerase.

18. **Write the function of a bioreactor.** CBSE 2017C

Ans. A bioreactor is a large vessel in which raw materials are biologically converted into specific products, such as individual enzymes, etc. using microbial plant, animal or human cell.

19. **What is the main function of sampling port in a bioreactor?**

Ans. The main function of sampling port is to withdraw culture periodically.

20. **Can you recall meiosis and indicate at what stage a recombinant DNA is made?** NCERT

Ans. Recombination of DNA occurs at the pachytene stage during the prophase-I by crossing over.

21. **What would be the molar concentration of human DNA in a human cell? Consult your teacher.** NCERT

Ans. 2.77×10^{23} moles

Short Answer Type Questions

1. **Name the scientists who constructed the first recombinant DNA. How?**

Ans. Cohen and Boyer constructed the first recombinant DNA in the 1970s through the following given steps: (1)

1. **DNA Isolation** They isolated DNA from a gene of interest.
2. **Restriction Enzymes** They used restriction enzymes to cut both DNA strands, creating sticky ends.
3. **Ligation** DNA ligase joined the plasmid and gene fragment, forming recombinant DNA.
4. **Transformation** The recombinant DNA was introduced into *E. coli* bacteria for its multiplication. (2)

2. **Do eukaryotic cells have restriction endonucleases? Justify your answer.** Competency Based Que., NCERT

Ans. No, eukaryotic cells do not have restriction endonucleases because DNA of eukaryotes is highly methylated.
Methylation in the cells protect the DNA from the activity of restriction enzymes.
All the restriction endonucleases have been isolated from various strains of bacteria. Prokaryotes/ bacteria have this enzyme as a defence mechanism to destroy the foreign DNA or to restrict the growth of bacteriophages.

3. **(i) Mention the difference in the mode of action of exonuclease and endonuclease.**

(ii) How does restriction endonuclease function?

Ans. (i) **Exonucleases** cleave base pairs of DNA at terminal ends (either 5′ or 3′) while, the **endonucleases** cleave DNA at any point within the DNA segment at specific position except terminal ends. (1)

(ii) Restriction endonuclease cuts the DNA strands a little away from the palindromic sequences, but between the same two bases on the two strands (1)

4. **(i) Explain the convention for naming *Eco*RI.**

(ii) With the help of an illustration only, show the action of *Eco*RI on a DNA Polynucleotide. CBSE 2024

Ans. (i) The name *Eco*RI comes from *Escherichia coli* RY13.
E represent genus-*Escherichia*, co represent species *coli*, R represent RY 13 strain, I represent order in which the enzyme was isolated from that strain of bacteria. (1½)

(ii) Refer to fig. 9.1 on page no. 269. (1½)

5. Collect five examples of palindromic DNA sequences by consulting your teacher. Better try to create a palindromic sequence by following base-pair rules. Competency Based Que., NCERT

Ans. Five examples of palindromic DNA sequences are as follows

(i) 5′—A A G C T T—3′ 3′—T T C G A A—5′
(ii) 5′—G G A T C C—3′ 3′—C C T A G G—5′
(iii) 5′—A G G C C T—3′ 3′—T C C G G A—5′
(iv) 5′—G A A T T C—3′ 3′—C T T A A G—5′
(v) 5′—A C T A G T—3′ 3′—T G A T C A—5′

6. What are sticky ends? State their significance in recombinant DNA technology.

Ans. Sticky ends are the overhanging stretches on each strand of DNA. These are formed when restriction enzymes cut the DNA strand a little away from the centre of palindrome sites, but between the same two bases on the opposite strands. (1)

Significance of Sticky Ends They form hydrogen bonds with their complementary counterparts and facilitate the action of DNA ligase enzyme. (1)

7. Make a chart (with diagrammatic representation) showing a restriction enzyme, the substrate DNA on which it acts, the site at which it cuts DNA and the product it produces. NCERT

Ans. Refer to fig. 9.1 on page no. 269.

8. Discuss with your teacher and find out how to distinguish between
(i) Plasmid DNA and chromosomal DNA.
(ii) RNA and DNA
(iii) Exonucleases and endonucleases. NCERT

Ans. (i) Differences between plasmid and chromosomal DNA are as follows

Plasmid DNA	Chromosomal DNA
A circular, extrachromosomal DNA.	Generally linear.
Contains very few genes, which may not be necessary for the cell.	Consists of complete genome vital for the cellular functions.
Present in only prokaryotic cell.	Presentr in both prokaryotes and eukaryotes. (1½)

(ii) The differences between RNA and DNA are as follows.

RNA	DNA
It is a single stranded molecule	It is a double stranded molecule
It has deoxyribose sugar.	It has ribose sugar
It is the genetic material in almost all organisms	It is the genetic material in only some viruses.

(iii) Refer to text on page no. 268. (1½)

9. Outline how restriction enzymes are used for removing sections of DNA from a chromosome.

Ans. Refer to text on page no. 268-269.

10. Only with the help of a labelled diagram, show the steps of formation of recombinant DNA by the action of restriction endonuclease enzyme *EcoRI*. CBSE 2022 Term II

Ans. Refer to fig. 9.1 page no. 269.

11. Why are bacteriophages used as vectors in RDT?

Ans. Bacteriophages are used as vectors because of very high copy number of their genome within the bacterial cells. Also they have the ability to gain an easy entry into the bacterial hosts in order to produce large number of recombinant DNA.

12. How is copy number of the plasmid vector related to yield of recombinant protein? NCERT Exemplar

Ans. The recombinant DNA can multiply as many times as the copy number of the plasmid vector, thereby determining the yield of recombinant protein. So, higher the copy number of the plasmid vector, higher will be the yield of recombinant protein.

13. What essential features must be present in a cloning vehicle/cloning vector?

Ans. Refer to text on page no. 270.

14. A vector is engineered with three features, which facilitates its cloning within host cell. List three features and explain each one of them.

Ans. Refer to text on page no. 270.

15. Write the role of '*ori*' and 'restriction site' in a cloning vector pBR322.

Ans. ***ori*** is the site where replication starts. This site is responsible for controlling the copy number of a vector.

Restriction site is the site of ligation of alien/foreign DNA in the vector which is recognised by restriction endonuclease.

16. All cloning vectors do have a selectable marker. Describe its role in recombinant DNA technology. CBSE 2020

Ans. Refer to text on page no. 270.

17. β-galactosidase enzyme is considered a better selectable marker. Justify the statement. Competency Based Que., CBSE 2019

Ans. Coding sequence of β-galactosidase is a better selectable marker, as the recombinants and non-recombinants are differentiated on the basis of their ability to produce colour in the presence of a chromogenic substrate, while the selection of recombinants due to the inactivation of antibiotic resistant gene is a tedious and time taking process as it include growing them simultaneously on two antibiotic plate.

18. **(i) Name the selectable markers in the cloning vector pBR322. Mention the role they play.**
(ii) Why is the coding sequence of an enzyme β-galactosidase a preferred selectable marker in comparison to the ones named above? CBSE 2016

Ans. (i) Refer to text on page no. 270. (1)
(ii) Refer to Q. no. 17. (2)

19. ***A* and *B* are two different cloning vectors in two different bacterial colonies cultured in chromogenic substrate. Bacterial colonies with cloning vector *A* were colourless, whereas those with *B* were blue coloured. Explain by giving reasons the cause of difference in colour that appeared.** Competency Based Que.

Ans. On the basis of colour production in the presence of chromogenic substrate, the recombinants and non-recombinants can be differentiated. In this, a desired DNA is inserted within coding sequence of an enzyme β-galactosidase, which results in inactivation of an enzyme. (2)

In plate *A*, the bacterial colonies having inserted plasmid, shows no colouration. While in plate *B*, insertion of gene does not occur, therefore it shows blue colour. (1)

20. **Can you think an answer, how a reporter enzyme can be used to monitor transformation of host cells by foreign DNA in addition to a selectable marker?** Competency Based Que., NCERT

Ans. A reporter gene is a gene in which scientist attaches a gene of interest. It can be used to monitor the transformed cells. The foreign gene is linked to the DNA construct along with reporter genes. These gene acts as a selectable marker for the transformed cells. An example of reporter gene includes *lac z* gene, which encodes for the enzyme β-galactosidase. This gene is not expressed in the transformed cell which results in the formation of white colonies. In non- transformed cells, the gene is expressed, resulting in the formation of blue colonies.

21. **Expand 'BAC' and 'YAC'. What are they and what is the purpose for which they are used?** CBSE 2019

Ans. 'BAC' stands for Bacterial Artificial Chromosome and 'YAC' stands for Yeast Artificial chromosome. These are vectors used in cloning DNA.

Purpose of these vectors (1)

YAC and BAC are used for cloning large DNA fragments in yeast and bacteria respectively.

They are widely used in creating genomic libraries and for large-scale genome sequencing projects. (2)

22. ***Agrobacterium tumefaciens* is considered as a good cloning vector. Explain why?**

Ans. Refer to text on page no. 271.

23. **Why is making host cells 'competent' essential for *r*DNA technology?**
Mention any two ways by which this can be achieved. CBSE 2024 C

Ans. Refer to text on page no. 271.

24. **Describe the role of $CaCl_2$ in the preparation of competent cells.** NCERT Exemplar

Ans. $CaCl_2$ is known to increase the efficiency of DNA uptake to produce transformed bacterial cells. The divalent Ca^{2+} ions create transient pores on the bacterial cell wall by which the entry of foreign DNA is facilitated into the bacterial cells.

25. **Write any four ways used to introduce a desired DNA segment into a bacterial cell in recombinant DNA technology experiments.** CBSE 2013

Ans. . (i) Microinjection
(ii) Biolistics/gene gun
(iii) Heat-shock method
(iv) Using disarmed pathogen vectors. (½ ×4)

26. **State the steps involved in the recombinant DNA technology.** Diksha

Ans. Recombinant DNA technology involves following steps

- Isolation of genetic material (DNA)
- Cutting of DNA at specific locations by restriction endonuclease.
- Isolation and amplification of gene of interest using polymerase chain reaction.
- Ligation of DNA fragment into a vector and insertion of *r*DNA into the host.
- Obtaining the foreign gene product (recombinant protein) using bioreactors.
- Downstream processing. (½ × 6)

27. **(i) State the principle involved in separation of DNA fragments using gel electrophoresis.**
(ii) How are DNA fragments visualised once they are separated by gel electrophoresis? CBSE 2023

Ans. (i) DNA is negatively charged, therefore when an electric current is applied to the gel, DNA will migrate towards the positively charged electrode. Shorter strands of DNA move more quickly through the gel than longer strands resulting in the fragments being arranged in order of size. (1)

(ii) The separated DNA fragments can be visualised only after staining the DNA with a compound known as ethidium bromide followed by exposure to UV radiation, as pure DNA fragments can not be seen in the visible light and without staining. (1)

28. (i) **Given below is the stepwise schematic representation of the process of electrophoresis. Identify the 'alphabets' representing (a) Anode end, (b) smallest/lightest DNA strand in the matrix, (c) Agarose gel.** Competency Based Que.

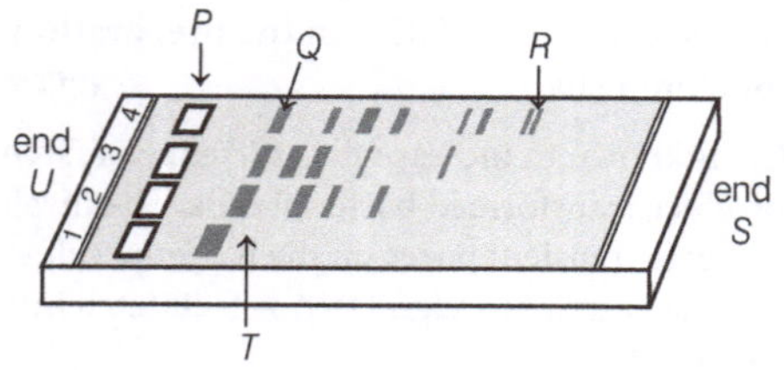

(ii) **What is elution? State the importance of elution in this process.** CBSE 2022 Term II

Ans. (i) (a) Alphabet 'S' represents anode end.

(b) Alphabet 'R' represents smallest/lightest DNA strand.

(c) Alphabet 'T' represents agarose gel. (1½)

(ii) The process of separating or cutting of DNA out from the agarose gel and extracting from the gel pieces is called **elution**.

Importance Elution is crucial for separating and purifying specific components from a mixture allowing for their identification or recovery. It enhances the efficiency of processes like chromatography, DNA extraction and protein purification. (1½)

29. (i) **Mention the importance of gel electrophoresis in biotechnology.**

(ii) **Explain the process of this technique.** CBSE 2019

Ans. (i) DNA fragments formed by the use of restriction endonucleases are separated by gel-electrophoresis. (1)

(ii) The process of gel electrophoresis is as follows.

(a) DNA fragments are negatively charged molecules. Thus, they move towards the anode under electric field through the medium.

(b) DNA fragments separate according to their size due to seiving effect of agarose gel.

(c) The separated DNA fragments can be viewed by staining the DNA with ethidium bromide followed by exposure to UV radiation.

(d) The separated bands of DNA are cut and extracted from gel piece. This is known as elution. (2)

30. Explain how PCR technique can be used for amplification of a small amount of DNA template.

Ans. PCR stands for Polymerase Chain Reaction. In this reaction, multiple copies of the gene (or DNA) of interest are synthesised *in vitro* using two sets of primers (small chemically synthesised oligonucleotides that are complementary to the regions of DNA) and the enzyme DNA polymerase. The enzyme extends the primers using the nucleotides provided in the reaction and the genomic DNA as template.

If the process of replication of DNA is repeated many times, the segment of DNA can be amplified to approximately billion times, i.e. 1 billion copies are made. Such repeated amplification is achieved by the use of a thermostable DNA polymerase (isolated from a bacterium, *Thermus aquaticus*), which remains active during the high temperature induced denaturation of double stranded DNA.

31. A plasmid DNA and a linear DNA (both of the same size) have one site for a restriction endonuclease. When cut and separated on agarose gel electrophoresis, plasmid shows one DNA band while, linear DNA shows two fragments. Explain. Competency Based Que., NCERT Exemplar

Ans. The plasmid is a circular DNA molecule. When cut with enzyme, it becomes linear, but does not get fragmented. Whereas, a linear DNA molecule gets cut into two fragments. Hence, a single DNA band is observed for plasmid while, two DNA bands are observed for linear DNA in agarose gel.

32. Any recombinant DNA with desired gene is required in billion copies for commercial use. How is the amplification done? Explain. CBSE 2010C

Or **Suggest and describe a technique to obtain multiple copies of a gene of interest *in vitro*.** CBSE 2016

Ans. Amplification of a gene is done by using Polymerase Chain Reaction (PCR). (1)

Refer to text on page no. 273. (2)

33. How and why is the bacterium *Thermus aquaticus* employed in DNA technology? Explain. Competency Based Que.

Or **Name the source of the DNA polymerase used in PCR technique. Mention why it is used ?** CBSE 2013

Or **Give the name of the organism from where the thermostable DNA polymerase is isolated. State its role in genetic engineering.**

Or (i) **Write the scientific name of the source organism of the thermostable DNA polymerase used in PCR.**

(ii) **State the advantage of using thermostable DNA polymerase.** CBSE 2023

Ans. Bacterium *Thermus aquaticus* is a source of enzyme *Taq* polymerase. As it is a thermostable enzyme and work at high temperature, it is used to amplify DNA *in vitro* by PCR. The amplified fragment of desired DNA can be used to ligate with the vector for further cloning.

34. The basic scheme of the essential steps involved in the process of recombinant DNA technology is summarised below in the form of a flow diagram. Study the given flow diagram and answer the questions that follow.

Step 1 **Plasmid DNA** (cut using restriction enzyme *Eco*RI) + **Foreign DNA** (cut using restriction enzyme *Eco*RI)

↓ DNA ligase

Step 2 Recombinant DNA molecule

↓

Step 3 Transfer of recombinant DNA molecule to the host cell

↓

Step 4 Replication of recombinant DNA molecule in the host cell

(i) Name the specific enzyme that might have been used to make the multiple copies of foreign DNA before undergoing step-1 of the process.

(ii) How does the use of restriction enzyme EcoRI in step-1facilitate the action of DNA ligase to form the recombinant DNA molecule?

(iii) Name the most commonly used host in the above process. **CBSE 2025**

Ans. (i) The enzyme used to make multiple copies of foreign DNA before step-1 is DNA polymerase (*Taq* Polymerase). It is used in Polymerase Chain Reaction (PCR) to amplify the DNA sequence.

(ii) *Eco*RI is a restriction enzyme that cuts DNA at specific sequences, producing sticky ends. These sticky ends help in the easy ligation of foreign DNA with plasmid DNA using DNA ligase, forming a stable recombinant DNA molecule.

(iii) The most commonly used host in this process is *Escherichia coli* (*E. coli*), as it is easy to culture, grows rapidly, and accepts recombinant DNA efficiently. (2)

35. Describe the process of amplification of 'gene of interest' using PCR technique. **CBSE 2019**

Ans. Amplification of gene is done using Polymerase Chain Reaction (PCR). It is carried out in the following steps:

(i) **Denaturation** The double-stranded DNA is denatured by applying high temperature of 95°C for 2-3 minutes. Each separated strand acts as a template. (1)

(ii) **Annealing** Two sets of primers are added, which anneal to the 3′ end of each separated strand. (1)

(iii) **Extension** DNA polymerase extends the primers by adding nucleotides complementary to the template provided in the reaction. *Taq* polymerase is used in the reaction, which can tolerate heat. All these steps are repeated many times to get several copies of the desired DNA. (1)

36. Rearrange the following in the correct sequence to accomplish an important biotechnological reaction:

(i) *In vitro* synthesis of copies of DNA of interest

(ii) Chemically synthesised oligonucleotides

(iii) Enzyme DNA–polymerase

(iv) Complementary region of DNA

(v) Genomic DNA template

(vi) Nucleotides provided

(vii) Primers

(viii) Thermostable DNA–polymers (From *Thermus aquaticus*)

(ix) Denaturation of *ds*DNA **CBSE 2015**

Ans. Genomic DNA template

↓

Denaturation of *ds*DNA

↓

Primers

↓

Chemically synthesised oligonucleotides

↓

Complementry region of DNA

↓

Enzyme DNA polymerase

↓

Thermostable DNA polymerase (from *Thermus aquaticus*)

↓

Nucleotides provided

↓

In vitro synthesis of copies of DNA of interest

37. Causative agents of HIV-AIDS and Covid-19 belong to the same group of viruses. To diagnose and amplify the genetic material for further study of Covid-19 virus, 'RT-PCR' test is carried out. **CBSE 2022 Term II**

(i) What does 'RT-PCR' stand for?

(ii) Explain the various steps of PCR technique.

Ans. (i) RT-PCR stands for Reverse Transcription Polymerase Chain Reaction. (1)

(ii) Refer to text on page no. 273-274. (1)

38. Explain the contribution of *Thermus aquaticus* in the amplification of a gene of interest.

Ans. Refer to text on page no. 273.

39. Describe the roles of (i) high temperature, (ii) primers and (iii) bacterium- *Thermus aquaticus* in carrying the process of polymerase chain reaction. **CBSE 2019**

Ans. (i) **Role of High Temperature** In PCR (*in vitro*), the DNA strands are separated by heating at 95°C for two minutes. Heating breaks the H-bonds between bases of two strands causing unwinding of DNA helix. (1)

(ii) **Role of Primers** Primers are short lengths of DNA about 20bp long that are required to start DNA polymerisation in PCR. The primers hybridise to their complementary sequence on the DNA strands at 40-50°C temperature and help in DNA polymerisation. (1)

(iii) **Role of *Thermus aquaticus*** An enzyme called *Taq* polymerase is isolated from *Thermus aquaticus*. Since, this bacteria thrives in temperature as high as 95°C, this enzyme can also tolerate high temperature without undergoing denaturation. Therefore, this enzyme is used in PCR instead of normal DNA polymerase. (1)

40. Mention three uses of PCR. CBSE 2009

Ans. Three uses of PCR are as follows

(i) It is used to during *r*DNA for production of newer and desired DNA. (1)

(ii) It is used for DNA sequencing. (1)

(iii) It is used in DNA fingerprinting. (1)

41. How is a continuous culture system maintained in bioreactors and why ? CBSE 2019

Ans. The cells can be multiplied in a continuous culture system. In this, the used medium is drained out from one side, while fresh medium is added from the other side to maintain the cells in their physiologically most active (log/exponential) phase. This type of culturing method produces a larger biomass leading to higher yields of desired products. (1 + 1)

42. Give the name of the type of bioreactor shown. Write the purpose for which it is used. Competency Based Que.

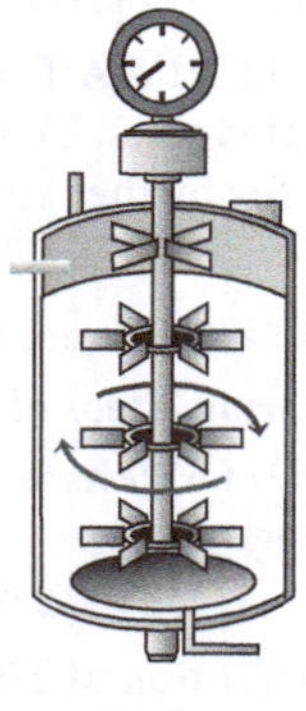

CBSE 2011

Ans. The bioreactor shown in the figure is the simple stirred-tank type bioreactor. (1)

Its purpose is large scale production of recombinant protein or enzymes, using microbial plants, animals and human cells. (1)

43. Besides better aeration and mixing properties, what other advantages do stirred-tank bioreactors have over shake flasks? NCERT

Ans. The stirred-tank bioreactor facilitate even mixing and oxygen availability throughout the bioreactor. It also has an oxygen delivery system, a foam control system and a temperature controller. Small volumes of cultures can be periodically withdrawn from the reactor for sampling.

The shake flask method is used for a small-scale production on the other hand bioreactors are used for a large scale production.

44. Draw a labelled sketch of sparged-stirred tank bioreactor. Write its application. CBSE 2015

Ans. Refer to fig. 9.8 (b) on page no. 275. (2)

Application These bioreactors are used to produce large quantities of products, enzymes, etc., using microbial, plant, animal or human cells. (1)

45. State the differences between simple stirred-tank bioreactor and sparged stirred-tank bioreactor.

Ans. Refer to text on page no. 275-276.

46. Can you list 10 recombinant proteins which are used in medical practice? Find out where they are used as therapeutics (use the internet). NCERT

Ans.

Recombinant proteins	Therapeutic use
Insulin (Humulin)	Helps in the treatment of type-I diabetes mellitus
DNAse I	Cystic fibrosis treatment
Interferon-α	Treatment of cancer
Bovine	It is used as a growth hormone.
Interferon-β	It is used for multiple sclerosis.
Hirudin	Used as anticoagulent
Coagulation factor IX	Haemophilia B treatment
Human recombinant growth hormone	Used to promote growth
Anti-thrombin III	Used to prevent blood clotting.
Tissue plasminogen activator	Acute myocardial infarction treatment

47. From what have you learnt, can you tell whether enzymes are bigger or DNA is bigger in molecular size? How did you know? NCERT

Ans. DNA molecules are bigger in molecular size as compared to the enzymes. Small segment of the DNA called genes, controls the synthesis of proteins and enzymes. DNA is made up of sugar, phosphate and nitrogen while enzyme is made up of only protein molecule.

Long Answer Type Questions

1. (i) **'*Eco*RI' has played very significant role in *r*DNA technology.**

(a) Explain the convention for naming *Eco*RI.

(b) Write the recognition site and the cleavage sites of this restriction endonuclease.

(ii) **What are the protruding and hanging stretches of DNA produced by these restriction enzymes called ? Describe their role on formation of *r*DNA.** **CBSE 2023**

Ans. (i) (a) *Eco*RI comes from *Escherichia coli* RY13 strain. In *Eco*RI, '*E*' comes from the genus '*Escherichia*' and '*co*' comes from the species name '*coli*'. The genus and species names should be in italics. The letter 'R' is derived from the name of the strain RY13. Roman numbers following the names indicate the order in which the enzymes were isolated from that strain of bacteria. (1)

(b) *Eco*RI is a restriction enzyme that cuts only at the restriction site with the 5'-GAATTC-3' sequence. It chops the DNA at a specified location, resulting in sticky ends. (1)

*Eco*RI has a palindrome recognition site that cuts DNA following G, creating sticky ends with AATT. It is a six-nucleotide sequence with GAATTC in the 5' to 3' direction and CTTAAG in the 3' to 5' direction on the complementary strand. (1)

(ii) The protruding and hanging stretches of DNA produced by these restriction enzymes are called sticky ends. They are important in the formation of *r*DNA because they form hydrogen bonds with their complimentary counter parts. This stickiness of the ends facilitates the action of the enzyme DNA ligase. (2)

2. Explain the roles of the following with the help of an example each in recombinant DNA technology
(i) Restriction enzymes (ii) Plasmids **CBSE 2018**

Ans. (i) Refer to text on page no. 268. (2½)

(ii) **Plasmids** These are extrachromosomal, self-replicating, double-stranded, closed and circular DNA molecules. It is found only in bacteria.

Role of Plasmid in DNA Recombinant Technology
These are used as vectors to carry the desired gene (foreign genes) into the desired organisms.e.g. pBR322 is widely used plasmid vector. This plasmid has genes for resistance against ampicillin and tetracycline. They have restriction sites for enzymes like *Pvu* I, *Pst* I, *Sal* I, *Bam*HI. Refer to fig. no. 9.2 on page no. 270. (2½)

3. What is genetic engineering? List the steps involved in *r*DNA technology.

Ans. Genetic engineering is *in vitro* manipulation of genetic material It involves the techniques to alter the chemistry of genetic material (DNA and RNA), to introduce into the host organisms and thereby change the phenotype of the host organism. (2)

Steps of *r*DNA technology Refer to text on page no. 272. (3)

4. If a desired gene is identified in an organism for some experiments, explain the process of the following.

(i) Cutting this desired gene at specific location.

(ii) Synthesis of multiple copies of this desired gene.

Competency Based Que., CBSE 2011

Ans. (i) The desired gene is cut by using the enzymes restriction endonucleases. Firstly, the restriction endonucleases that recognise the palindromic nucleotide sequence of the desired gene is identified. The endonuclease inspects the entire DNA sequences to find and recognise the site. It cuts each of the double helix at a specific point, which is a little away from the centre of the palindromic site. The cutting site is between the same two bases on the opposite strands. This results in over-hanging of single stranded stretches, which act as sticky ends. (2½)

(ii) Multiple copies of the desired gene are synthesised by Polymerase Chain Reaction (PCR) method. In this method, the desired gene is synthesised *in vitro*. The double-stranded DNA is denatured using high temperature of 95° C and the strands are separated. Each separated strand acts as a template.

Two sets of oligonucleotide primers are annealed to the denatured DNA strands. The thermostable *Taq* polymerase extends the primers using nucleotides provided in the reaction mixture. Finally, the amplified fragments are ligated into recipient cells.

Refer to fig. 9.6 on page no. 274. (2½)

5. In a pathological lab, a series of steps were undertaken for finding the gene of interest. Describe the steps, or make a flow chart showing the process of amplification of this gene of interest.

Ans. Polymerase Chain Reaction (PCR) is a technique, used to obtain multiple copies of a gene of interest *in vitro*. This technique helps to amplify DNA through a simple enzymatic reaction. (1)

The steps of PCR Refer to text on page no. 272-274. Refer to fig. 9.6 page 274. (4)

6. Explain briefly **NCERT**

(i) PCR **(ii) Restriction enzymes and DNA**

(iii) Chitinase

Ans. (i) Refer to text on page no. 273-274. (2)

(ii) Restriction enzymes are used in genetic engineering to cut the large DNA molecule into smaller fragments.

When DNA from two different sources are cut by the same restriction enzyme, the resultant DNA fragments have the same kind of 'sticky-ends' and these can be joined together (end-to-end) using DNA ligases. (2)

(iii) Chitinase is an enzyme that breaks down chitin, a component of the fungal cell wall. It is useful for isolating the fungal cell DNA. (1)

7. Explain how more than a billion copies of a fragment of DNA are formed using the technique of PCR. **CBSE 2025**

Ans. Polymerase Chain Reaction (PCR) is a technique used to generate billions of copies of a specific DNA fragment *in vitro*. It involves three key steps

(i) **Denaturation** The double-stranded DNA is heated to a high temperature (~94–98°C) to break hydrogen bonds, separating it into single strands.

(ii) **Annealing** The temperature is lowered (~50–65°C), allowing two primers (short, complementary DNA sequences) to bind to the target DNA.

(iii) **Extension** DNA polymerase (*Taq* polymerase), a heat-stable enzyme from *Thermus aquaticus*, extends the primers by adding free nucleotides, synthesising new DNA strands.

By repeating this cycle multiple times, the DNA segment is exponentially amplified, producing nearly a billion copies of the desired gene. The amplified DNA can be ligated into a vector for further cloning and genetic studies.

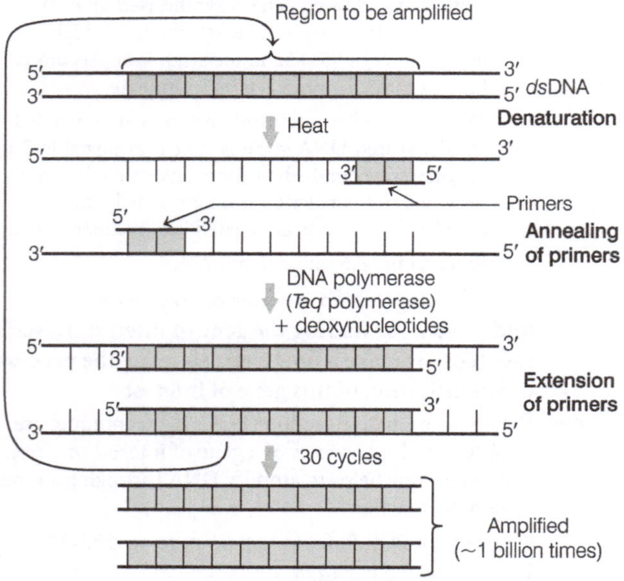

8. (i) How has the development of bioreactor helped in biotechnology?

(ii) Name the most commonly used bioreactor and describe its working. **CBSE 2018**

Ans. (i) Bioreactors are the large volume vessels approximately (100-1000 L) in which raw materials are biologically converted into specific products, individual enzymes, etc., using microbial, plant, animal or human cells. A bioreactor provides the optimal conditions for achieving the desired product by providing optimum growth conditions like temperature, pH, substrate, salts, vitamins and oxygen. The cells can also be multiplied in a continuous culture system. In this, the used medium is drained out from one side while fresh medium is added from the other side to maintain the cells in their physiologically most active log/exponential phase.

This type of culturing method produces a larger biomass leading to higher yields of desired protein. Thus, it plays a very important role in biotechnology. (2½)

(ii) The most commonly used bioreactor is simple stirred tank bioreactor. It is usually cylindrical or with a curved base to facilitate the mixing of the reactor contents. The stirrer activity facilitates even mixing and availability of O_2 throughout the bioreactor.

Alternatively air can also be bubbles into the medium. It has an agitator system, a temperature control system, a pH control system and sample ports so that small samples can be withdrawn periodically.

Refer to fig. no. 9.8 (a) on page no. 275. (2½)

9. Bioreactors are the containment vehicles of any biotechnology-based production process. For large scale production and for economic reasons the final success of biotechnological process depends on the efficiency of the bioreactor.
Answer the following questions w.r.t. the given paragraph.

(i) List the operational guidelines that must be adhered to so as to achieve optimisation of the bioreactor system. Enlist any four.

(ii) Mention the phase of the growth we refer to in the statement "Optimisation of growth and metabolic activity of the cells".

(iii) Is the biological product formed in the bioreactor suitable for the intended use immediate? Give reason in support of your answer.

Competency Based Que., CBSE 2023

Ans. (i) The operational guidelines that must be adhered to so as to achieve optimisation of the bioreactor system are as follows

(a) Monitoring and control of key parameters.
(b) Optimisation of mixing and aeration.
(c) Minimising contamination.
(d) Maintenance and cleaning of the bioreactor. (2)

(ii) The phase of the growth referred to in the statement "Optimisation of growth and metabolic activity of the cells" is the exponential phase of growth. (1)

(iii) In many cases, further processing and purification of the biological product are required before it can be used for its intended purpose. This is because the product may contain impurities or other components that could be harmful or interfere with its activity. (2)

10. Describe the structure and working of a sparged stirred-tank bioreactor. **CBSE 2025**

Ans. Structure of a Sparged Stirred-Tank Bioreactor

Cylindrical Vessel The bioreactor has a cylindrical shape, designed for efficient mixing and large-scale production.

Stirrer (Impeller) A rotating stirrer inside the tank ensures uniform mixing of the culture medium and enhances oxygen distribution.

Sparger (Gas Inlet) A sparger at the bottom introduces air or oxygen into the medium in the form of tiny bubbles, increasing the surface area for oxygen transfer.

Gas Entrainment The movement of the stirrer helps in proper gas mixing and ensures effective oxygen supply to the microorganisms.

Increased Surface Area for Oxygen Transfer The formation of bubbles significantly enhances oxygen transfer, which is crucial for microbial or cell growth.

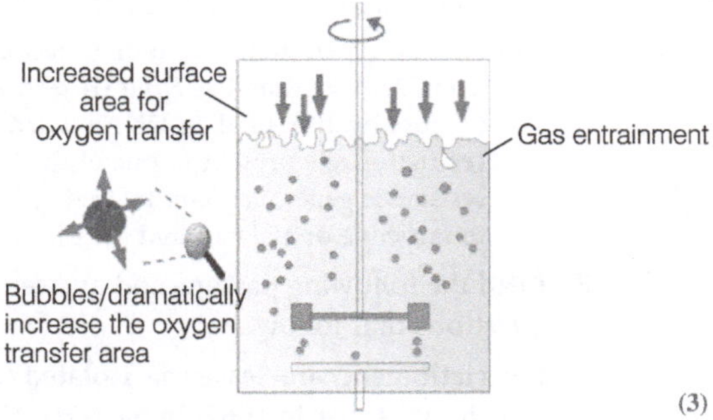

(3)

Working of Sparged Stirred Tank

The sparger releases small air bubbles into the culture medium, which are evenly distributed by the stirrer (impeller). This ensures that oxygen is efficiently dissolved in the medium, promoting microbial or cell growth. The continuous mixing also helps in maintaining a uniform distribution of nutrients and prevents sedimentation. Waste gases like CO_2 are released through an exhaust system, ensuring proper aeration. This controlled environment allows for maximum yield of the desired product. (2)

11. Describe briefly the following. **NCERT**

(i) **Origin of replication** (ii) **Bioreactors**

(iii) **Downstream processing**

Ans. (i) **Origin of Replication** It is a specific sequence of nucleotides in a DNA molecule where the replication process begins. In plasmids and chromosomes, this site serves as the starting point for DNA synthesis. It contains necessary elements for the binding of initiator proteins, which then recruit other enzymes to unwind the DNA and synthesise new strands. The origin of replication is crucial for ensuring that genetic material is accurately copied and passed on during cell division. (2)

(ii) **Bioreactors** are vessels or containers in which biological reactions occur, typically used in biotechnology and bioprocessing to cultivate desired products or enzymes. They provide controlled conditions (such as temperature, pH and oxygen levels) to optimize growth and product formation. Common types include stirred tank bioreactors and sparged stirred tank bioreactor, which are essential for producing pharmaceuticals, biofuels, and other bioproducts on an industrial scale. (2)

(iii) **Downstream processing** refers to the process of purification and separation of products of recombinant DNA technology. Suitable preservatives are added to the product. Proper quality check is maintained. In the case of drugs and medicines proper clinical trials are conducted. Pure homogeneous products are obtained which are free of other molecules. (1)

Source Based/ Case Based/ Passage Based Questions

1. Read the following passage and answer the questions given below.

Some restriction enzymes break a phosphodiester bond on both the DNA strands, such that only one end of each molecule is cut and these ends have regions of single-stranded DNA. *Bam*HI is one such restriction enzyme which binds at the recognition sequence, 5'-GGATCC- 3' and cleaves these sequences just after the 5'- guanine on each strand.

(i) What is the objective of this action?

(ii) Explain how the gene of interest is introduced into a vector.

(iii) A sequence of DNA is shown below.

5' ATTTTGAGGATCCGTAATGTCCT 3'

3' TAAAACTCCTAGGCATTACAGGA 5'

If this DNA was cut with *Bam*HI, how many DNA fragments would you expect? Write the sequence of these double-stranded DNA fragments with their respective polarity. **Competency Based Que.**

***Or* (iii) A gene M was introduced into *E. coli* cloning vector pBR322 at *Bam*HI site. What will be its impact on the recombinant plasmids?**

Give a possible way by which you could differentiate non-recombinant to recombinant plasmids.
Competency Based Que.

Ans. (i) Restriction enzymes helps to break phosphodiester bond on both the DNA strands. These are used in recombinant DNA technology. By this method desired compatible ends of DNA can be recombined. (1)

(ii) Restriction enzyme cuts the DNA of the vector and then ligates the gene of interest into the DNA of the vector. (1)

(iii) *Bam*HI recognition sequence is 5'-GGATCC-3' and it cleaves these sequence just after the 5'-guanine. In the given sequence the restriction will work as follows

↓

5' ATTTTGAGGATCCGTAATGTCCT 3'

3' TAAAACTCCTAGGCATTACAGGA 5'

↓ 2 fragments

5'-ATTTTGAG-3' 5'GATCCGTAATGTCCT-3'

3'-TAAAACTCCTAG-5' 3'- GCATTACAGGA 5' (2)

Or

(iii) *Bam*HI site will affect tetracycline antibiotic resistance gene, hence the recombinant plasmids will lose tetracycline resistance due to the inactivation of resistance gene. Recombinants can be selected from non-recombinants by plating them into a medium containing tetracycline as the recombinants will not grow in the medium because the tetracycline resistance gene is inactivated. (2)

2. Gene of interest/alien gene is introduced by a cloning vector into a host cell to bring about a desired phenotypic expression in a host cell. The cloning vectors used are plasmid and bacteriophages. Biotechnologists in their labs, for desired results engineered specialised cloning vectors. One such vector is pBR322. Study the diagram carefully and answer the questions that follow. **CBSE 2022 Term II**

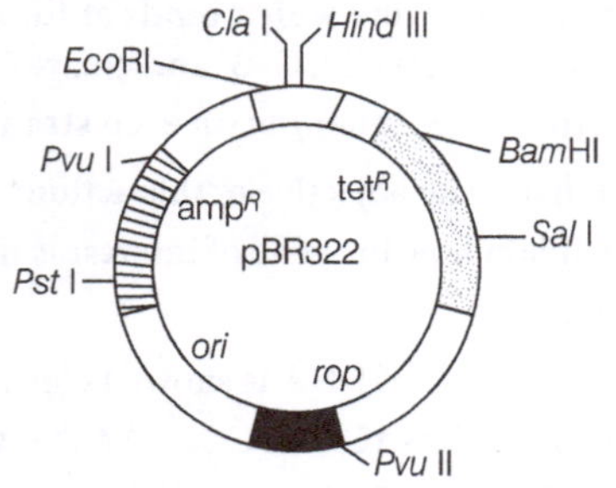

(i) What do '*Eco*RI', '*Bam*HI' and '*Hin*d III' represent? State their functions.

(ii) Identify the gene you would select for the role of a selectable marker in pBR322. Explain why?

(iii) Write the property/characteristic of plasmid and bacteriophage that makes them efficient cloning vectors.

(iv) Biotechnologists always insert '*ori*' gene in their engineered cloning vector. Justify the statement.

(v) Will the experiment be successful if the alien DNA is ligated at *Hin*d III restriction site? Give reason in support of your answer.

Ans. (i) '*Eco*RI', *Bam*HI' and '*Hin*d III' are restriction sites where restriction enzymes make cut at specific positions within the DNA. It produces sticky ends of DNA which ligates to gene of interest. Therefore, these restriction sites are used to assist insertion of gene into plasmid vector. (1)

(ii) The genes encoding resistance to antibiotics such as ampicillin, and tetracycline, can be considered a useful selectable markers for *E.coli* cloning vector pBR322 because the *E. coli* cells do not carry resistance against any of these antibiotics. (1)

(iii) The property/characteristics of plasmid and bacteriophage that makes them efficient cloning vector are as follows

(a) Plasmids are small autonomously replicating usually circular, extra chromosomal double stranded DNA molecule that occurs in many bacteria and some yeasts.

(b) Bacteriophages are viruses that infects bacteria and are used as vector because of very high copy number of their genome within the bacterial cell. (1)

(iv) Biotechnologist always insert '*ori*' gene in their engineered cloning vector because this is the sequence from where the replication starts and any piece of DNA when, linked to this sequence can be made to replicate within the host cells. This sequence is also responsible for controlling the copy number of the linked DNA. (1)

(v) No, the experiment will not be successful if the alien DNA is ligated at *Hind* III restriction site because ligation of alien DNA is carried out at restriction site present in one of the two antibiotic resistance genes, i.e. *Bam* HI and *Sal* I for tetracycline or at *Pvu* I and *Pst* I for ampicillin. (1)

3. Read the following passage and answer the questions that follow.

Restriction endonuclease was isolated for the first time by W Arber in 1962, in bacteria. DNA, the genentic material can be manipulated by addition or substitution of the desired gene by using a specific restriction endonuclease resulting in *r*DNA. This is one of the major steps in biotechnology.

(a) Name the first isolated restriction endonuclease. Why are restriction endonucleases so called?

(b) Write the palindrome recognised by *Eco*RI.

(c) (i) How does restriction endonuclease function? Explain.

Or **(c) (ii) Write the convention for naming a restriction endonuclease with the help of an example.** **CBSE 2024 C**

Ans. (a) • *Hin*d II

• The restriction enzyme are so called because they restricts the growth of bacteriophage in bacteries *E. coli*.

(b) 5′–GAATTC–3′
3′–CTTAAG–5′

(c) (i) Restriction endonuclease first inspects the length of a DNA sequence and binds to specific recognition palindromic sequence. It then cut each of the two strands at specific points in the sugar-phosphate backbones.

Or (c) (ii) In *Eco*RI (comes from *Escherichia coli* RY13)

- *E* represent Genus Escherichia,
- *co* represent species *coli*,
- R represent RY 13 strain,
- I represent order in which the enzyme were isolated from that strain of bacteria.

4. Study the diagram given below that shows the steps involved in the procedure of selecting transformed bacteria and answer the questions that follow :
CBSE 2024, Competency Based Que.

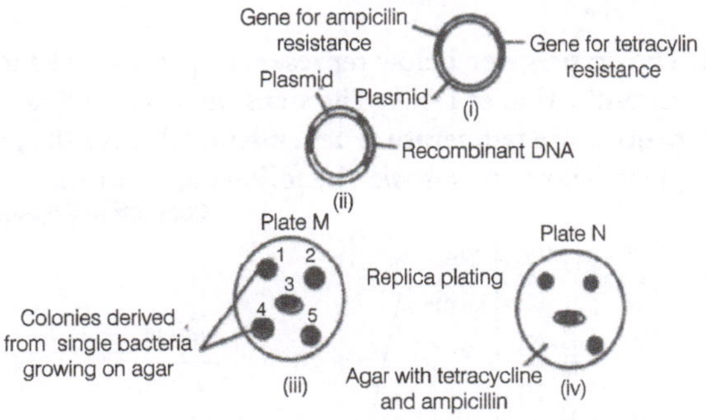

(i) Identify the colony that has got transformed. Justify your answer.

(ii) What are the sites in a plasmid called where ampicillin and tetracycline resistance genes are inserted ? State their role in genetic engineering.

(iii) Name two enzymes playing an important role in genetic engineering.

***Or* (iv) State the role of β-galactosidase in insertional inactivation.**

Ans. (i) Colony 4 is transformed with plasmid containing recombinant DNA, as they will not show resistance towards tetracycline. (1)

(ii) In genetic engineering, plasmids are commonly used as vectors to introduce foreign gene into organisms. The plasmids of ten contain multiple cloning sites, which are short regions containing several restriction enzymes recognition sites. These sites allows the insertion of specific gene, like the ampicillin resistance gene and tetracycline resistance gene. (2)

(iii) Restriction endonuclease / ligase/Taq DNA Polymerase (1)

Or (iv) Insertional inactivation of gene encoding for β-galactosidase will lead to colourless bacterial colonies (recombinant). (1)

5. Refer to the following flow diagram and answer the questions that follows. **Competency Based Que.**

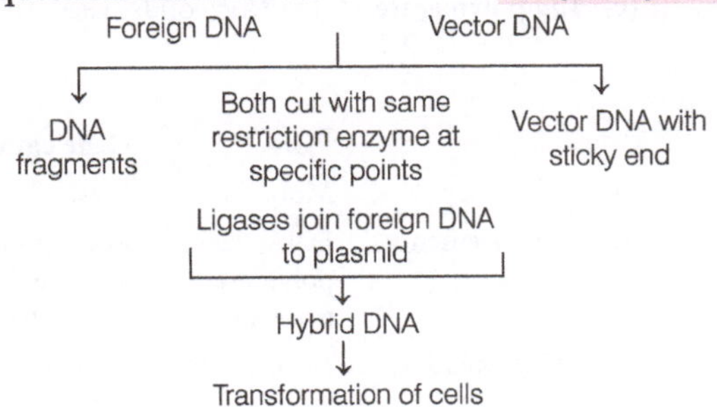

(i) A plasmid DNA and a linear DNA (both of same size) have one site for a restriction endonuclease. When cut and separated on agarose gel electrophoresis, plasmid shows one DNA band, while linear DNA shows two fragments. Justify.

(ii) How are transformed cells selected?

Ans. (i) Plasmid is a circular DNA molecule. When cut with enzyme, it becomes linear, but does not get fragmented. Whereas, a linear DNA molecule gets cut into two fragments. Hence, a single DNA band is observed for plasmid, while two DNA bands are observed for linear DNA in agarose gel. (2)

(ii) The genes called selectable marker help in selecting those host cells, which contain the foreign gene (transformants) and eliminate non-transformants. (2)

6. The image below depicts the result of gel electrophoresis.

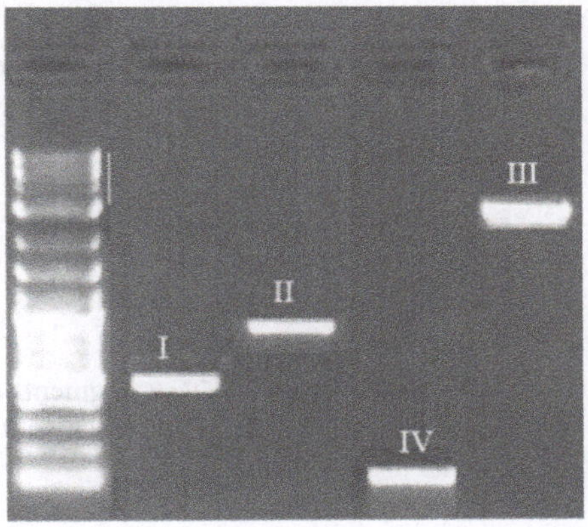

If the ladder represents sequence length upto 3000 base pairs (bp),

(i) Which of the bands (I - IV) correspond to 2500 bp and 100 bp, respectively?

(ii) Explain the basis of this kind of separation and also mention the significance of this process.
CBSE SQP 2022 Term-II

Ans. (i) Band III is 2500 base pairs and band IV is 100 bp. (1)

(ii) The DNA fragments separate (resolve) according to their size through the sieving effect provided by the agarose gel, during electrophoresis. The smaller the fragment size, the farther it moves. So, band III corresponds to 2500 bp as it is more close towards the cathode and band IV is 100 bp as it had moved farther, i.e. towards anode. (2)

The significance of electrophoresis is to purify the DNA fragments for constructing recombinant DNA by joining them with cloning vectors. (1)

7. Given below is the graph representing the relationship between DNA fragment size and distance migrated in gel electrophoresis. Observe the graph given below and answer the questions that follows.

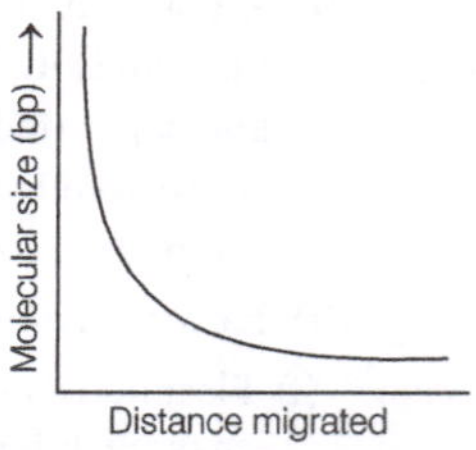

(i) **With the reference to the above graph, explain the relationship between DNA fragment size and distance migrated.**

(ii) **When you should use agarose gel electrophoresis ?**

(iii) **How will you determine the exact size of separated DNA fragments in the gel electrophoresis ?**

Competency Based Que.

Or

(iii) **Why is DNA size standard used in gel electrophoresis?**

Ans. (i) The smaller molecule, migrate through the gel more quickly and therefore travel further than larger fragments. The larger molecules migrate more slowly and therefore will travel a shorter distance. (1)

(ii) Gel electrophoresis can be used for the following purposes

(a) To analyse the integrity quality of DNA samples

(b) To analyse the PCR products. (2)

(iii) The exact sizes of separated DNA fragments can be determined by using DNA ladder which contains DNA fragments of known sizes. (1)

Or

(iii) The DNA size standards are used as positive controls for electrophoresis and for determining the size of unknown DNA fragments. (1)

8. Enzyme *Taq* polymerase, is extracted from an eubacterial microorganism *Thermus aquaticus* from Yellowstone National Park in Montana, USA and isolated by Chien *et at.*, (1976). *Taq* polymerase successfully replaced the DNA polymerase from *E. coli* that was being used in PCR earlier and this shift revolutionised the PCR technique.

(i) ***Taq* polymerase after its discovery replaced *E. coli.* DNA polymerase in PCR technique. Explain giving reasons why was the need felt for the change?**

(ii) **What is a primer and its importance in PCR?**

(iii) **Write the importance of PCR as a diagnostic tool.**

CBSE 2022 Term II

Ans. (i) *Taq* polymerase is isolated from a thermophilic bacterium, i.e. *Thermus aquaticus* and has a property to remain active during the high temperature induced denaturation of double-stranded DNA. Therefore, it replaced *E. coli* DNA polymerase in PCR technique (2)

(ii) Refer to text on page 273. (1)

(iii) Polymerase chain reaction is an important diagnostic tool because it allows for the rapid accurate detection of specific genetic material enabling the identification of pathogen, genetic mutation and diseases at an early age. (2)

9. The graph given below represents a process used for the amplification of DNA. The steps involved in this process are temperature dependent. Observe the graph given below and answer the following questions.

Competency Based Que.

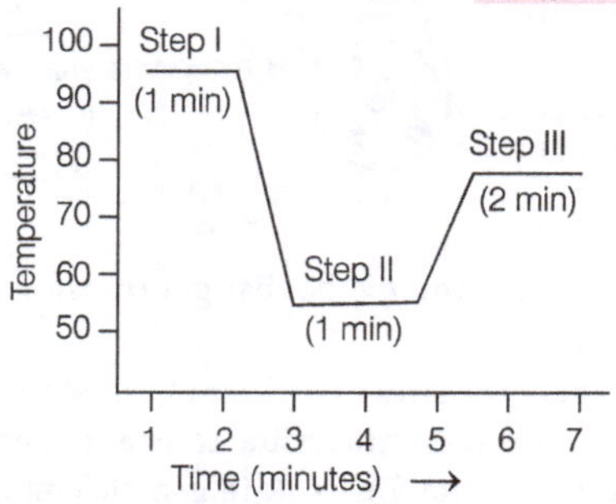

(i) **On the basis of the above graph, what conclusion can you draw about the temperature dependence of different steps involved in the given process ?**

(ii) **If we are not able to maintain high temperature at step I, how this process will be affected ?**

(iii) **Mention the basic requirements involved in this process?**

Or (iii) **How this process is differ from conventional gene cloning ?**

Ans. (i) The given process, PCR is a temperature dependent process. Its efficiency depends on precise temperature control. The step 1 (denaturation) requires highest temperature, followed by step III (extension) and then step II (annealing) require lowest temperature. (1)

(ii) The first step in PCR is denaturation. If the temperature at step I is too low, the DNA will not completely denature and amplification efficiency will be low. (1)

(iii) The basic requirements of PCR reactions are

(a) DNA template (b) Primers

(c) *Taq* polymerase (d) Nucleotide bases (2)

Or

(iii)

		PCR	Gene cloning
(a)	Efficiency	More	Less
(b)	Requirements	DNA, *Taq* polymerase primers	Restriction enzyme, ligase, vector, bacteria
(c)	Manipulation	*In vitro* only	*In vivo* and *in vitro*
(d)	Time required	4 hours	2-4 days

(2)

SELF ASSESSMENT TEST

Multiple Choice Questions

1. Which of the following is correct regarding plasmid DNA?
   (a) Plasmid DNA is typically circular and found in the nucleus of eukaryotic cells
   (b) Plasmids can replicate independently of chromosomal DNA in bacteria
   (c) Plasmids are always linear and much larger than the chromosomal DNA
   (d) Plasmids are composed solely of RNA

2. Match the following columns.

	Column I		Column II
A.	Restriciton enzyme	1.	Joins DNA fragments
B.	DNA polymerase	2.	Synthesises new DNA strands
C.	Ligase	3.	Cuts DNA at specific sites
D.	Origin of replication	4.	Controls the copy number of linked DNA

   (a) A-1,B-3,C-4,D-2 (b) A-1,B-2, C-3, D-4 (c) A- 3,B-2,C–1,D-4 (d) A- 4,B-2,C–1,D-3

3. What is the function of a selectable marker in recombinant DNA technology?
   (a) To differentiate between transformed and non-transformed cells
   (b) To help in DNA replication
   (c) To amplify the DNA
   (d) To join DNA fragments together

4. pBR322 plasmid is resistant to which of the following antibiotics?
   (a) Ampicillin (b) Tetracycline (c) Penicillin (d) Both (a) and (b)

5. Which restriction site is not present in pBR322 plasmid?
   (a) *Eco*RI (b) *Hind* III (c) *Hind* II (d) *Sal* I

6. What is the purpose of gel electrophoresis in biotechnology?
   (a) To clone DNA (b) To separate DNA fragments based on size
   (c) To amplify DNA (d) To insert DNA into cells

7. Which of the following methods is used to introduce foreign DNA into a animal cell?
   (a) Microinjection (b) Bacteriophages transfection
   (c) *Agrobacterium tumefaciens* (d) All of the above

Assertion-Reason Questions

Direction (Q. Nos. 8-11) *In each of the following questions, a statement of Assertion (A) is given followed by corresponding statement of Reason (R). Of the statements, mark the correct answer If*
   (a) Both A and R are true and R is the correct explanation of the A.
   (b) Both A and R are true, but R is not the correct explanation of the A.
   (c) A is true, but R is false.
   (d) A is false, but R is true.

8. **Assertion** (A) Restriction enzymes recognise palindromic sequence.
   Reason (R) Palindromic sequences read same in both directions of the two strands.

9. **Assertion** (A) Foreign DNA and vector DNA are cleaved with the help of ligase.
   Reason (R) Ligase act on sugar phosphate backbone of DNA.

10. **Assertion** (A) In gel electrophoresis, DNA fragments are separated, based on size.

Reason (R) DNA is negatively charged, so it moves towards anode under electric field.

11. **Assertion** (A) A temperature control system is essential in a bioreactor.

Reason (R) It is crucial for the efficiency, productivity, and safety of bioprocesses in bioreactors.

Very Short Answer Type Questions

12. Give the palindromic sequence recognised by *Eco*RI.
13. What does *rop* codes for in plasmid pBR322?
14. Name the technique that helps in separating DNA fragments formed by the use of restriction endonuclease.
15. Name the bacterium that carries the Ti plasmid, enabling it to cause tumor formation in plants.

Short Answer Type Questions

16. Explain the significance of palindromic nucleotide sequences in the formation of recombinant DNA.
17. All cloning vectors have a selectable marker. Describe its role in recombinant DNA technology.
18. What is elution? State its importance.

Long Answer Type Questions

19. Explain the mechanism of action of restriction endonuclease.
20. What is cloning vectors? Explain its feature.
21. Explain in brief.

I. Stirred tank bioreactor II. Insertion of *r*DNA into host cell

Case Based Question

22. The large-scale production of an organism is generally done in a bio-processor unit. The given fig represents growth curve of a bacteria that is being used for the production of a recombinant molecule. Maintaining sterile conditions is of utmost importance in a bio-processor unit

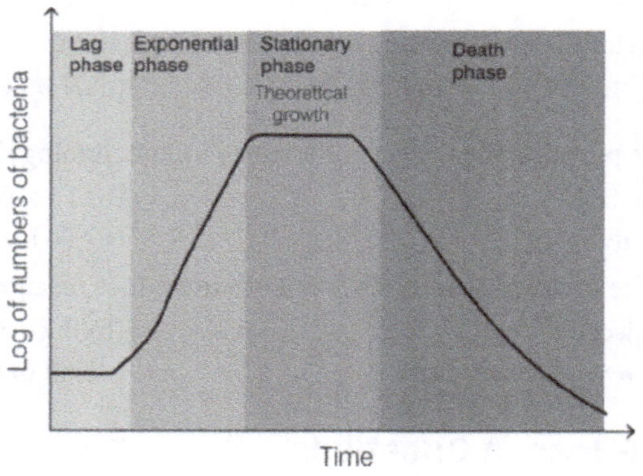

(i) In which phase are the cells likely to be producing a larger concentration of the recombinant molecule? Why?

(ii) In cases where the culture in the bio-processor unit reaches the death phase, identify one strategy that can help revive the bio-processing to restart production of the recombinant molecule.

(iii) What does a sterile condition mean?

(iv) State one reason why the bacteria that are producing the recombinant molecule are not harmed during the process of sterilisation.

Answers

1. (b)	2. (c)	3. (a)	4. (d)	5. (c)	6. (b)	7. (a)	8. (b)
9. (d)	10. (a)	11. (a)					

10

CHAPTER

Biotechnology and Its Applications

Biotechnology is useful to humans in producing various products by utilising microbes, plants, animals and their metabolic machinery.
This became possible due to Recombinant DNA Technology (RDT) in which valuable and useful manipulation of genes, in various living species, is done to obtain desirable products at large scale.

YOUR STUDY GOALS

10.1 Biotechnological Applications in Agriculture

10.2 Biotechnological Applications in Medicine

10.3 Transgenic Animals

10.4 Ethical Issues

YOUR PRACTICE GOAL

- Objective Type Questions (44 Qs ; MCQs, A-R) Case Based Questions (6)
- Subjective Type Questions
- (32 VSAs 51 SAs, 13 LAs)

- The applications of biotechnology include therapeutics, diagnostics, Genetically Modified (GM) crops for agriculture, processed food, bioremediation, waste treatment and energy production.
- Three critical research areas of biotechnology are as follows
  - To provide the best catalyst in the form of improved organism, usually a microbe or a pure enzyme.
  - To create optimal conditions through engineering for a catalyst to act.
  - Downstream processing technologies to purify the organic compounds or proteins.

10.1 Biotechnological Applications in Agriculture

- To feed the increasing population of the world, we need to enhance our food production. This can be done by applying any of the following options.
  - Agrochemical based agriculture
  - Organic agriculture
  - Genetically engineered crop based agriculture

- As traditional breeding techniques failed to keep pace with demand and to provide sufficiently fast and efficient systems for crop improvement, another technology called **tissue culture** was developed during 1950's.

Plant Tissue Culture

- It is the technique of maintaining and growing plant cells, tissues or organs in nutrient media under controlled environmental conditions.
- The plant part taken out to be grown in a test tube, in special nutrient media under sterile conditions, is called **explant.**
- The capacity of producing a whole plant from this explant is called **totipotency**.
- The nutrient media for the growth of explant must provide a carbon source (such as sucrose), inorganic salts, vitamins, amino acids and growth regulators such as auxins, cytokinins, etc.
- The application of tissue culture for the production of a large number of plants in a short duration in floriculture (flower farming) and horticulture (farming of both edible and ornamental plants) industries, is known as **micropropagation**.
- The resultant plants, are genetically similar to the original plant from which they are grown, so they are called **somaclones.**
- To recover healthy plants from diseased plants, a technique called **meristem culture** is commonly practiced.
- **Meristem** (axillary and apical) remains free from pathogens due to the absence of vascular supply.
- Plants which are commonly developed from meristems are banana, sugarcane, potato, etc.

Advantages of Tissue Culture

- A large number of plants can be grown in a short period of time.
- Healthy plants can be developed from diseased plants.
- Plants without seeds can be multiplied.
- It is useful where sexual reproduction is not possible.

Somatic Hybridisation

- Somatic hybrids are formed through the fusion of protoplasts of two plants belonging to different varieties, species and even genera.
- The process through which somatic hybrids are formed is know as **somatic hybridisation.**
- In this, isolated protoplasts from two different varieties of plants having desirable characters, are selected.
- It is carried out in the following main steps
  - Single cells are isolated from selected plants.
  - Cell walls of these single cells are digested by the enzymes like pectinase and cellulase, to expose the naked protoplasts.
  - Naked protoplasts are then isolated, which are surrounded by plasma membrane.
  - After that, the isolated protoplasts are fused together in order to obtain the hybrid protoplasts in a special nutrient medium, under sterile conditions.
    The fusion of parent protoplasts is induced by **Polyethylene Glycol** (PEG) solution.
  - Hybrid protoplasts thus, obtained are cultured in a suitable medium to form new plants.

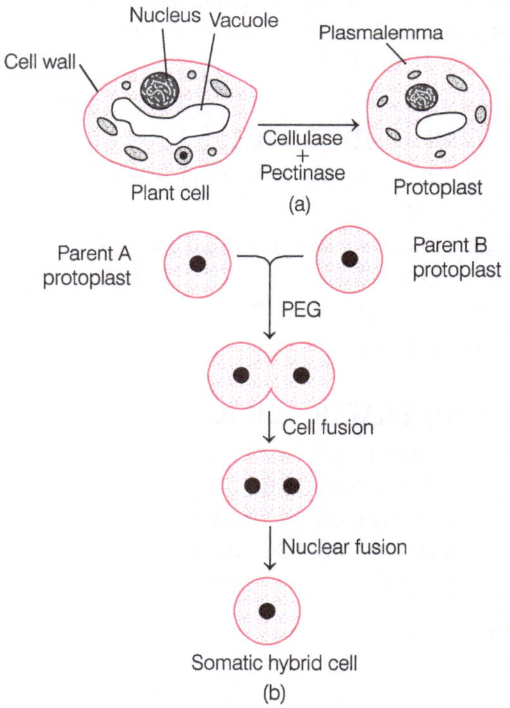

Fig. 10.1 (a) Isolation of protoplast, (b) Somatic hybridisation

- **Pomato** is a somatic hybrid which is produced by the fusion of protoplasts of tomato and potato.
- Unfortunately, this plant do not have all the desired characteristics for its commercial utilisation.

Green Revolution

- It refers to increase in the production of food grains through agricultural practices introduced in the mid 20th century which significantly boosted food production.
- The revolution succeeded in enhancing the food supply to three folds, but yet it was not enough to feed the rapidly growing human population.
- It has increased the yield of crops mainly due to the use of improved varieties of crops, agrochemicals (fertilisers and pesticides) and better management practices.
- Most agrochemicals used to increase the yield have harmful effects on the environment and are expensive for farmers in developing countries.
- Therefore it becomes difficult to further increase the yield with existing varieties using conventional breeding.
- Therefore, the best solution to overcome all these issues is to develop and use Genetically Modified (GM) crops.

Genetically Modified Organisms (GMOs)

- The plants, bacteria, fungi and animals whose genes have been altered by manipulation are called **Genetically Modified Organisms** (GMOs).
- These are also called **transgenic organisms**, as they contain and express one or more foreign genes called **transgenes**.

Importance of GM Plants

Genetic modification has brought the various changes and made plants useful in many ways, which are as follows

- **Tolerance to Abiotic Stresses** Crops became more tolerant to abiotic stresses like cold, drought, salt and heat.
- **Reduced Dependence on Chemical Fertilisers** Dependence on chemical pesticides has reduced, by the production of pest-resistant crops.
- **Decline Post-harvest Losses** It helped to reduce post-harvest losses.
- **Increased Mineral Uptake Efficiency** Efficiency of mineral usage is increased in plants. This prevents early exhaustion of fertility of soil.
- **Enhanced Nutritional Value** Because of genetic modification, crops have enhanced nutritional content, e.g. vitamin-A enriched rice (Golden rice).
- Other than the above mentioned uses, genetic modifications have been used to create tailor-made plants. These plants supply alternative resources to the industries in the form of starches, fuels and pharmaceuticals.

Biopesticides

- An application of biotechnology in agriculture is the production of pest-resistant plants which could decrease the amount of pesticides being used.
- *Bt* toxin is produced by a bacterium called *Bacillus thuringiensis.*
- *Bt* toxin gene has been cloned from the bacteria and been expressed in plants to provide resistance against the insects without the need for insecticides.
- Therefore, it is named as biopesticide, e.g. *Bt* cotton, *Bt* corn, rice, tomato, potato and soybean, etc.

Bt Cotton

It is a genetically modified pest resistant variety of cotton plant and possess the following characteristics

- *Bt* cotton is created by using some strains of bacterium, *Bacillus thuringiensis* (*Bt* is a short form). This bacterium produces a protein that kills certain insects such as lepidopterans (tobacco budworm, armyworm), coleopterans (beetles) and dipterans (flies, mosquitoes).
- *Bacillus thuringiensis* forms protein crystals (Cry) during a particular phase of their growth.
- These crystals contain a toxic **insecticidal protein**. This toxin does not kill the *Bacillus* (bacterium), because *Bt* toxin protein exists as inactive protoxins.
- However, when an insect ingests the inactive toxin, it is converted into its active form due to the **alkaline pH** of insect's gut which solubilises the crystals.
- The activated toxin binds to the surface of midgut epithelial cells and creates pores that cause cell swelling and lysis, thus leading to the death of an insect.
- Most *Bt* toxins are effective against specific insect groups and the selection of gene depends upon the crop and the targeted pest. The toxin is encoded by

the *cry* genes, which are insect group specific. For example,

- *cry* IAc and *cry* IIAb control cotton bollworms.
- *cry* IAb controls corn borer.

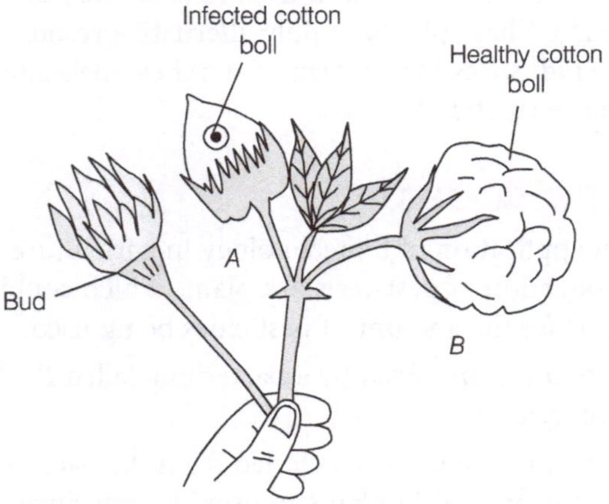

Fig. 10.2 Cotton boll, A. Destroyed by bollworms; B. Fully mature cotton boll (uninfected)

Pest Resistant Plants

The techniques for modifying plants genetically has contributed much to the production of pest resistant plants as described below

- A wide variety of plants and animals including human beings are infected by nematodes.
- A nematode, *Meloidegyne incognitia* infects the roots of tobacco plants which thus reduces the production of tobacco.
- The strategy adopted to prevent this infection is based on the process of **RNA interference** (RNAi). This process takes place in all eukaryotic organisms as a method of cellular defence.
- RNAi method involves silencing of a specific *m*RNA by the complementary *ds*RNA molecules that binds to and prevents the translation of *m*RNA (gene silencing).
- The source of this complementary RNA could be from an infection by viruses having RNA genomes or transposons (mobile genetic elements). These transposons replicate *via* RNA intermediate.
- *Agrobacterium* vectors are used to introduce this nematode-specific genes into the host plant. The DNA was introduced in such a way that it produces both sense and anti-sense RNA into the host plant.
- These two RNAs are complementary to each other and form a double-stranded RNA (*ds*RNA) that initiates RNAi.
- This further silences the specific *m*RNA of the nematode.
- As a results, the parasite fails to survive in the hosts and the transgenic plant gets itself protected from the parasite.

Quick Test 1

1. 100 years-old plant is suffering from a viral infection. To preserve its genetic material, scientists decide to create its clones. Which part of the plant should be used to generate them?
2. Name the technique used to fuse two protoplasts under controlled conditions, resulting in the formation of a hybrid.
3. If a plant contains the *cry*1Ac gene, will it provide resistance to all types of insect larvae?
4. **State True or False.**
   RNA interference (RNAi) is a natural defence mechanism found in a variety of organisms, including plants, animals and bacteria.
5. Mention the scientific name of the bacteria that can be used as a natural genetic engineer for the production of transgenic plants.

10.2 Biotechnological Applications in Medicine

- The recombinant DNA technological processes have made immense impact in the area of healthcare by enabling mass production of safe and more effective **therapeutic drugs**.
- Further the recombinant therapeutics do not induce unwanted immunological responses as in common case of similar products isolated from non-human sources.
- At present, about **30 recombinant therapeutics** have been approved for human use all over the world. Out of these, **12 are marketed in India**.

Genetically Engineered Insulin

- β-cells of the pancreas secrete a hormone called **insulin**. This hormone is responsible for controlling the blood sugar level in a person.

- Insufficient secretion of insulin often leads to diabetes. This is where genetically engineered insulin comes into play.
- It has lead to the sufficient availability of insulin for the management of adult onset diabetes.
- Insulin used for diabetes was earlier extracted from the pancreas of slaughtered cattle and pigs.
- This insulin caused patients to developed an allergy or other types of reactions due to the foreign protein.

TEACHER'S TIP

Insulin cannot be administered orally to diabetic people because it is a protein that would be broken down in the digestive system by the enzymes present in stomach and intestine. Therefore; insulin is typically delivered via injection to ensures that it directly enters the bloodstreams.

Structure of Insulin

- It consists of two short polypeptide chains, i.e. chain 'A' and chain 'B' that are linked together by disulphide bridges.
- In mammals, including humans, insulin is synthesised as a **pro-hormone** (needs to be processed before it becomes a fully mature and functional hormone) which contains an extra stretch called the **C-peptide**.
- This C-peptide is not present in the mature insulin and is removed during the maturation.
- Therefore, the main challenge for the production of insulin using *r*DNA techniques was getting insulin assembled into a mature form.

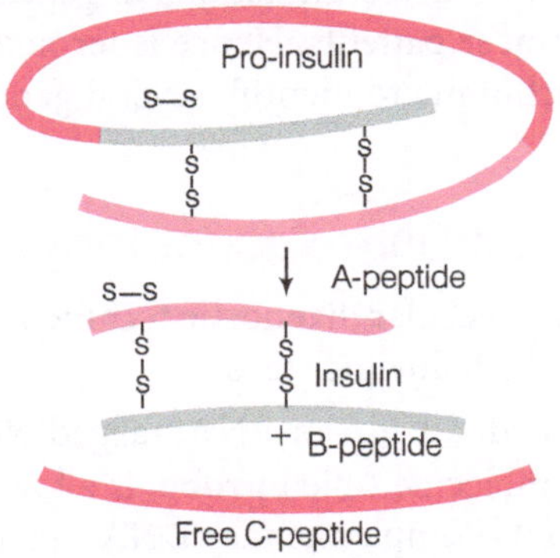

Fig. 10.3 Maturation of pro-insulin into insulin after the removal of C-peptide (simplified)

Production of Human Insulin (Humulin)

- In 1983, **Eli Lilly**, an American company prepared two DNA sequences corresponding to A and B-chains of human insulin and introduced them in the plasmids of *E. coli* to produce insulin chains.
- These chains (A and B) were produced separately, extracted and combined by creating disulphide bonds to form human insulin called **humulin**.

Vaccine Production (Recombinant Vaccine)

- The vaccines produced through genetic engineering methods are called recombinant vaccines or '**second generation vaccines**'.
- They have gene inserts for the surface proteins of a pathogen that elicit immunity, but do not result in infection.
- These plasmids are inserted in bacteria or yeast cells that express the viral proteins. These proteins are purified and used to formulate vaccines which are then injected into the human host.
- In human body, they are recognised as foreign material and an immune response is elicited.
- Recombinant hepatitis-B vaccine and polio vaccine are the examples of recombinant DNA vaccine.

Stem Cell Technology

- Stem cells are the biological cells that are capable of renewing themselves *via* mitosis and differentiating into specialised cells.
- These cells are found in multicellular organisms and are of two types
  - **Embryonic Stem Cells** These are isolated from the inner cell mass of blastocysts and the undifferentiated cells of embryo of 5-6 days.
  - **Adult Stem Cells** They exist throughout the body after embryonic development and are found inside different tissues, like brain.
- These stem cells, at present are grown rapidly and transformed into specialised cells like muscles, glands, tissues, etc.

- The technology used to treat a variety of diseases (both malignant and non-malignant) using stem cells is termed stem cell technology.

Applications of Stem Cell Technology

These include the following

- Treatment of diabetes
- Treatment of leukemia (from umbilical stem cells)
- Treatment of cardiac tissue damage
- Treatment of Alzheimer's, Parkinson's and genetic diseases like cystic fibrosis, etc.
- Organ repair and replacement.

Gene Therapy

- It is a collection of methods which allows correction of a gene defect that has been diagnosed in a child or embryo.
- Gene therapy involves delivery of normal gene into the individual/embryo. This normal gene compensates the function of defective or non-functional gene.
- The first clinical gene therapy was attempted in 1990 to a 4 years old girl with **Adenosine Deaminase** (ADA) **deficiency**. This particular enzyme is crucial for the immune system to function.

Causes and Cure for ADA Deficiency

- This disorder is caused due to the deletion of the gene for **adenosine deaminase**.
- In some children, ADA deficiency can be cured by bone marrow transplantation and in others by enzyme replacement therapy in which functional ADA is given to the patient by injection.
- But, the problem with both of these approaches is that these are not completely curative.
- This is why, gene therapy was introduced to cure this ailment.
- Steps followed in gene therapy are given below
  - In first step of gene therapy, lymphocytes from the blood of the patient are extracted and grown in a culture outside the body.
  - A functional ADA *c*DNA (using a retroviral vector) is then introduced into these lymphocytes which are subsequently returned in the patient's body.
  - As these cells are not immortal, the patient requires periodic infusion of such genetically engineered lymphocytes.
    But if the gene isolated from bone marrow cells producing ADA is introduced into cells at early embryonic stages, it could be a permanent cure.

Molecular Diagnosis

- For the effective treatment of diseases, early diagnosis and understanding its pathophysiology is very important.
- By using conventional methods of diagnosis (serum and urine analysis), early detection of diseases is not possible.
- Some techniques used for early diagnosis are as follows

Polymerase Chain Reaction (PCR)

It is one of the important technique that serves the purpose of amplification of nucleic acid.

- PCR helps in early detection of disease or pathogen.
- The presence of a pathogen (bacteria, viruses, etc.) is suspected only when the pathogen has produced a disease symptoms. But by that time, the number of pathogens is already very high in the body.
- However, PCR can detect even very low concentrations of these pathogens by amplification of their nucleic acid.
- This technique can be used routinely to detect HIV in suspected AIDS patients.
- It is also used to detect mutations in genes in suspected cancer patients. Hence is termed a powerful technique to identify several genetic disorders.

Recombinant DNA Technology

It is a modern molecular diagnostic technique that is carried out in the following steps

- A single-stranded DNA or RNA, tagged with a radioactive molecule called **probe,** is allowed to hybridise to its complementary DNA in a clone of cells.
- The cells are then detected by autoradiography.
- The mutated gene is not observed on the photographic film because the probe does not show complementarity with the mutated gene.

- The site where the DNA probe had hybridised with the target sequence appear as dark bands.

Enzyme Linked Immuno-Sorbent Assay (ELISA)

- This diagnostic method relies upon the principle of antigen-antibody interaction.
- Infection by pathogen can be detected by the presence of antigens like proteins and glycoproteins or by detecting the antibodies synthesised against the pathogen.

Quick Test 2

1. Mention the name of the company which started selling human insulin in 1983.
2. Name the technique that can be employed to detect low concentrations of pathogens in humans.
3. **State True or False.**
   Stem cell technology has the potential to regenerate damaged tissues and organs, but it cannot be used to treat genetic disorders.
4. Name the technique used to cure a patient of a genetic disease in the embryonic stage, leading to a complete recovery.
5. Which biological molecule is commonly targeted in ELISA to detect infections or immune responses?

10.3 Transgenic Animals

- Animals that have their DNA manipulated to possess and express an extra (foreign) gene are known as **transgenic animals**, e.g. transgenic rats, rabbits, pigs, sheep, cows and fishes.
- Over 95% of all the existing transgenic animals are mice.
- There are several benefits of transgenic animals. Some of them are as follows

1. Normal Physiology and Development

- Transgenic animals can be specifically designed to allow the study of how genes are regulated and how they affect the normal functioning of the body and its development.
- For example, the study of complex factors involved in growth such as insulin like growth factors.
- By introducing genes from other species that alter the formation of this factor and studying the biological effects that result, information is obtained about the biological role of the factor in the body.

2. Study of Disease

- Many transgenic animals are designed to increase the understanding of how genes contribute to the development of diseases such as cancer, cystic fibrosis, rheumatoid arthritis and Alzheimer's.
- These are specially made to serve as models for human diseases, so that investigation of new treatments for diseases is made possible.

3. Biological Products

- Human diseases can be treated by medicines that contain biological products, but such products are often costly to make.
- Transgenic animals that produce useful biological products can be created by the introduction of the portion of DNA or genes that code for a particular product such as **human protein (α-1-antitrypsin)** which is used to treat **emphysema.**
- Similar attempts are being made for the treatment of **Phenylketonuria** (PKU) and **cystic fibrosis.**
- For example, in 1997 the first transgenic cow **Rosie** produced human protein enriched milk (2.4 g/L).
- The milk contained the human **alpha lactalbumin** and was nutritionally more balanced product for human babies than natural cow's milk.

4. Vaccine Safety

- Transgenic mice are being used for testing the safety of vaccines before they are used on humans, i.e. polio vaccine.
- If found reliable and successful, they could replace the use of monkeys in order to test the safety of batches of the vaccine.

5. Chemical Safety Testing

- It is also known as **toxicity** or **safety testing.** It is similar to the procedure used for testing toxicity of drugs.
- Transgenic animals are made that carry the genes, which make them more sensitive to toxic substances than the non-transgenic animals.

- They are then exposed to toxic substances and effects are studied. This allows us to obtain results in less time.

10.4 Ethical Issues

- Manipulation of living organisms by the human race can be unethical and should not go unregulated.
- The genetic modification of organisms can have unpredictable results, when such organisms are introduced into the ecosystem.
- The modification or usage of living organisms for public services has also created problems with patents granted for the same.
- Therefore, there is a need for some ethical standards to evaluate our actions.
- These sets of standards that are used to regulate our activities in relation to biological world are called **bioethics**.
- The public is very much concerned that certain companies are being granted patents for the products and technologies that make use of the genetic materials, plants and other biological resources that have long been identified, developed and used by the farmers and indigenous people of a specific region or country.
- In order to control these issues, the Indian Government has setup the **Genetic Engineering Approval Committee** (GEAC), which makes all decisions regarding the validity of GM research and the safety of introducing GMOs for public services.

Patent

- It is a set of exclusive rights granted by a government to the inventors or their assignee to prevent others from commercialising their invention.
- When patent is granted for biological entities and for products derived from them, they are called **biopatents.**
- Primarily USA, Japan and members of European Union are awarding biopatents.

Biopiracy

- Biopiracy refers to as theft of genetic resources that are indigenous to a country.
- The majority of industrialised nations are financially rich, but poor in biodiversity and traditional knowledge, in comparison to developing and underdeveloped countries.
- There has been growing realisation of the injustice, inadequate compensation and benefit sharing between developed and developing countries.
- Therefore, some nations are developing laws to prevent such unauthorised exploitation of their bioresources and traditional knowledge.
- Traditional knowledge related to bio-resources can be exploited to develop modern applications and can save time, efforts and expenditure during their commercialisation.
- Many multinational companies and other organisations exploit biological resources of other nations without proper authorisation from the countries and people concerned without compensatory payment.
- The Indian Parliament has recently cleared the second amendment of the Indian Patents Bill.
- It takes consideration of such issues including patent terms, emergency provisions, research and development initiative.

Controversies in India Regarding Patent and Biopiracy

- When a patent is taken out on plants and seeds derived from Indian biological resources, biopiracy occurs.
- Challenging and stopping such biopiracy is the duty of government. Following are the plants on which controversies have occurred in India.

Basmati Rice

- Rice has been used for thousands of years in Asia's agricultural history. There are an estimated 2,00,000 varieties of rice in India alone.

- Basmati is unique for its aroma and flavour and 27 documented varieties of Basmati are cultivated in India.
- An American company, **Rice Tec** won a patent on Basmati rice lines and grains in 1997 through the **US Patent** and **Trademark Office** and was allowed to sell a 'new variety' in US and Abroad.
- This new variety of Basmati was actually derived from the Indian farmer's varieties.
- Indian Basmati was crossed with semi-dwarf varieties and claimed as an invention or a novelty by the American company.
- The patent extends to functional equivalents implying that other people selling Basmati rice could be restricted by the patent.

Turmeric and Neem

- In 1995, the US Patent Office granted a patent for 'Use of Turmeric in Wound Healing' to the University of Mississippi Medical Center.
- In 1994, another patent was granted to the firm of **WR Grace** and **Co.**, by the European Patent Office, Munich for 'fungicidal uses of neem oil'.
- Thus, if we do not pay attention or counter these patent applications, our rich legacy will be encashed by other countries and individuals.

Quick Test 3

1. Mention a transgenic animal-derived protein that is used to treat lung damage in emphysema.
2. **State True or False.**
   Transgenic animals in chemical safety testing help evaluate toxicity by predicting human reactions through genetic modifications.
3. Name the committee set up by the Indian government to monitor GM research.
4. Can biopiracy be prevented by recognising indigenous knowledge and rights?
5. Name two plants with medicinal properties that were granted patents without proper consent from indigenous communities.

Mind Map

Biotechnology and Its Applications

Applications in Agriculture

- Agro-chemical based
- Organic agriculture
- Genetically engineered crop based agriculture
- **Green Revolution** Introduction of High Yielding Varieties (HYVs) seeds for increasing the food supply three times.
- **Tissue Culture**

Explant (meristematic tissue) → Totipotency → Micro-propagation 1000 plants → Somaclones

Somatic Hybridisation

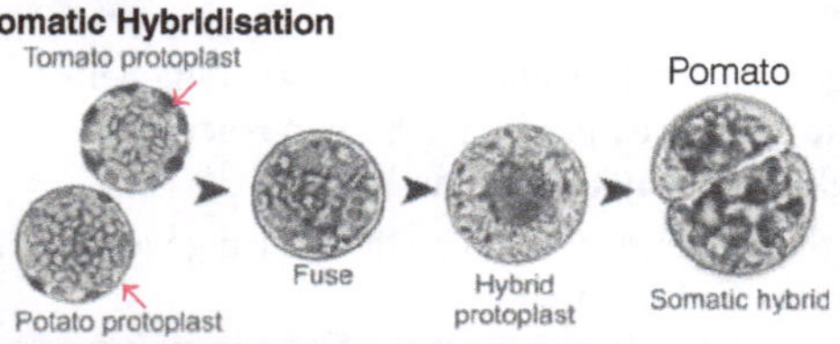

Genetically Modified Organisms (GMOs)

- Tolerant to abiotic stresses
- Pest-resistant crops
- Reduce post-harvest losses (*Flavr Savr* tomato)
- Efficiency of mineral usage by plants
- Enhanced nutritional value of food (Golden rice)

Insect Resistant Plants

- Plants have characters that enable plant to avoid insect attack. e.g. *Bt* gene from *Bacillus thuringiensis* provides resistance to insects.
- This bacterium is used to produce plants such as *Bt* cotton, *Bt* corn, etc.

Pest-Resistant Plants

Tobacco plant produced by using RNA interference method to silence the *m*RNA of nematode *Meloidegyne incognita.*

Ethical Issues

- **Bioethics** The set of guidelines for the genetic modification of organisms and the patents granted for the same.
- The GEAC in India makes all decisions regarding the GM research validity.

Biopatent

It is a set of exclusive rights granted by a state or national government, to an inventor or their assignee for a limited period of time for a public disclosure of an invention.

Biopiracy

Use of bioresources by multinational companies and other organisations without any payment and proper authorisation from the countries and people concerned.

Controversies in India

Basmati rice, turmeric and neem are some of the plants for which controversies occurred in India, regarding their patent.

Production of Transgenic Animals

Animal whose genome has been altered.
e.g. transgenic cattle, transgenic mice (95%), etc.

Benefits of Transgenic Animals

- To study normal physiology and development
- **To Study Biological Products**
  Examples
  - Human protein (α-antitrypsin) used to treat emphysema.
  - **Rosie** (first transgenic cow) produced human protein-enriched milk (2.4 gm per litre)
- Vaccine safety testing.
- Chemical safety testing.

Applications in Medicine

- 30 recombinant therapeutics in world, 12 in India.
- **Humulin** Genetically engineered by **Eli Lilly** (1983).

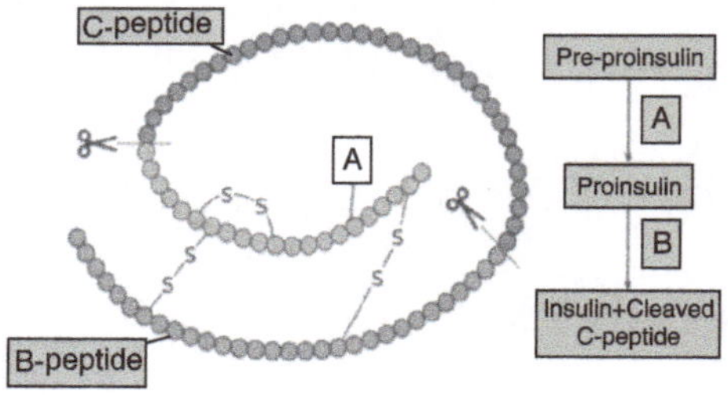

Plasmid of *E. coli* —Produce→ Chain-A and B separate —Extracted and combine by disulfide bond→ Humulin

Gene Therapy

- The first clinical gene therapy was given in 1990, to a 4-years old girl with **Adenosine Deaminase** (ADA) deficiency.
- This enzyme is very important for the immune system to function. SCID is caused due to defect in the gene for the enzyme adenosine deaminase.

Bone marrow transplantation }
Enzyme replacement therapy } Both are not completely curative

- **ADA** introduced into cells at early embryonic stage (permanently curable).
- **Molecular Diagnosis** Detect the presence of pathogen, e.g. *r*DNA technology, PCR, ELISA (Ag-Ab interaction).
- **Stem Cell Technology** Uses stems cells for organ and tissue regeneration, brain disease treatment, etc.

EXAM PATTERN QUESTIONS

Objective Type Questions

Multiple Choice Questions

1. In some areas, farmers who grow Genetically Modified (GM) corn have to make sure there is a gap between non-GM crops and GM crops. What is the reason for leaving a gap between the crops? **Competency Based Que.**

(a) To prevent pest attacking crops
(b) To prevent cross-pollination between GM and non-GM crops
(c) To prevent spread of disease between crops
(d) So they can get large machinery into the fields

Ans. (*b*) To avoid unwanted outcome and undesired effect it is advisable to not mix GMO with non-GMO. If they cross-pollinate and result in successful fertilisation, they can produce variation which might be harmful for the farmers' business and/or to the ecosystem.

2. Which one of the following is a correct statement?

(a) Somatic hybridisation involves the fusion of two complete plant cells carrying desired gene
(b) *Bt* toxin gene has been cloned from plants and expressed in bacterium
(c) '*Bt*' in '*Bt* cotton' shows that it is genetically modified organism, produced through biotechnology
(d) Genetic modification have reduced dependence on chemical fertilisers

Ans. (*d*)

3. Any part of plant, i.e. meristem of shoot or node of stem can be used to grow a new plant under sterile conditions in artificial nutrient media. This method and the part of plant which is used are known as

(a) tissue culture and explant
(b) cell culture and callus
(c) tissue culture and callus
(d) cell culture and explant

Ans. (*a*)

4. The apical meristemic cells of a flowering plant can be artificially cultivated in a nutrient media to grow multiple plants in a very short time. The potential of these cells to make a whole new plant is called

(a) explant (b) totipotency
(c) micropropagation (d) somatic hybridisation

Ans. (*b*)

5. An improved variety of transgenic rice

(a) gives high yield and rich in vitamin-A
(b) gives high yield, but has no characteristic aroma
(c) does not require chemical fertiliser and growth hormone
(d) is completely resistant to all insect pest and disease of paddy

Ans. (*a*) Golden rice are vitamin-A enriched rice.

6. The improved trait that is found in the genetically modified transgenic crop Golden rice is **CBSE 2024**

(a) high lysine content (b) insect resistant
(c) high protein content (d) high vitamin-A content

Ans. (*d*)

7. Match the Column I with Column II and choose the correct answer from the codes given below.

	Column I		Column II
A.	Lepidopterans	1.	Tobacco budworm and armyworm
B.	Coleopterans	2.	Beetles
C.	Dipterans	3.	Flies and mosquitoes

Codes

	A	B	C
(a)	1	2	3
(b)	2	3	1
(c)	3	2	1
(d)	1	3	2

Ans. (*a*)

8. Crystals of *Bt* toxin produced by some bacteria do not kill the bacteria themselves because **CBSE 2024 C**

(a) bacteria are resistant to toxin
(b) toxin is immature
(c) toxin is inactive
(d) bacteria encloses toxin in a special sac

Ans. (*c*) The *Bt* toxin produced by *Bacillus thuringiensis* is produced in an inactive form, known as a protoxin. It only becomes active when ingested by certain insects, where it is activated by the alkaline conditions of the gut. This mechanism protects the bacteria from the toxic effects of the toxin they produce.

9. **Consider the following statements.**

I. ***Bt* toxin gene has been cloned from the bacteria.**

II. **Genetic engineering works only on animals and has not yet been successfully used on plants.**

III. **Strains of *Bacillus thuringiensis* are used in producing bioinsecticidal plants.** Competency Based Que.

Which of the above statements are correct?

(a) I and II (b) I and III
(c) II and III (d) I, II and III

Ans. (*b*)

10. **Which of the following genes were used in case '*b*' to protect '*b*' from cotton bollworms?**

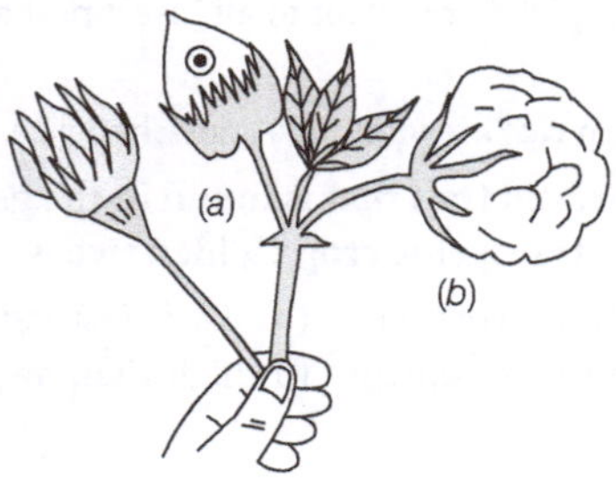

(a) *cry* I Ac and *cry* II Ab (b) *cry* I Ac and *cry* I Ab
(c) *Bt* Ac and *Bt* Ab (d) *Bt* Ac and *Bt* II Ab

Ans. (*a*)

11. **RNA interference involves**

(a) synthesis of *m*RNA from DNA
(b) interference of RNA synthesis of DNA
(c) synthesis of *c*DNA and RNA using reverse transcriptase
(d) silencing of specific *m*RNA due to complementary *ds*RNA

Ans. (*d*)

12. **To produce insulin *via* a non-human cell, which of the following would be required to be inserted in the vector is plasmid?** Competency Based Que.

(a) An enzyme
(b) A molecule of insulin
(c) A segment of DNA from another bacterium
(d) A segment of DNA from a human

Ans. (*d*)

13. **C- peptide of human insulin is** NCERT Exemplar

(a) a part of mature insulin molecule
(b) responsible for formation of disulphide bridges
(c) removed during maturation of pro-insulin to insulin
(d) responsible for its biological activity

Ans. (*c*)

14. **A collection of methods that allows correction of a gene defect in a child/embryo is called as** Diksha

(a) gene therapy (b) silencing
(c) ELISA test (d) electrophoresis

Ans. (*a*)

15. **An example of gene therapy is**

(a) production of test tube babies by artifically insemination and implantation of fertilised eggs
(b) introduction of gene of adenosine deaminase in person suffering from Severe Combined Immuno Deficiency (SCID)
(c) production of injectable hepatitis-B vaccine
(d) production of vaccine in food crops like potatoes which can be eaten

Ans. (*b*)

16. **The first clinical gene therapy was given in 1990 to a 4 years old girl with enzyme deficiency of**

(a) moanmire oxidase
(b) glutamate dehydrogenase
(c) adenosine deaminase
(d) tyrosine oxidase

Ans. (*c*) The first clinical gene therapy was given in 1990 to a 4 years old girl with ADA deficiency. This enzyme is very important for the immune system to function. ADA deficiency can lead to severe combined immuno deficiency.

17. **The first clinical gene therapy was done for the treatment of** NCERT Exemplar

(a) AIDS
(b) Cancer
(c) Cystic fibrosis
(d) SCID (Severe Combined Immuno Deficiency resulting form deficiency of ADA)

Ans. (*d*)

18. **What is the permanent cure for ADA deficiency?** Diksha

(a) Enzyme replacement therapy
(b) Bone marrow transplantation
(c) Introduction of the gene isolated from marrow cells producing ADA at early embryonic stage
(d) Introduction of lymphocytes containing functional ADA cDNA into the patient

Ans. (*c*)

19. **The site of production of ADA in the body is** NCERT Exemplar

(a) erythrocytes (b) lymphocytes
(c) blood plasma (d) osteocytes

Ans. (*b*)

20. ADA is an enzyme which is deficient in a genetic disorder SCID. What is the full form of ADA?

(a) Adenosine deoxyaminase **NCERT Exemplar**

(b) Adenosine deaminase

(c) Aspartate deaminase

(d) Arginine deaminase

Ans. *(b)*

21. Which one of the following molecular diagnostic techniques is used to detect the presence of a pathogen in its early stage of infection?

(a) Angiography

(b) Radiography

(c) Enzyme replacement technique

(d) Polymerase Chain Reaction (PCR)

Ans. *(d)*

22. Which of the following is commonly used as a vector for introducing a DNA fragment in human lymphocytes?

(a) Retrovirus (b) pBR322

(c) α-phage (d) Ti-plasmid

Ans. *(a)*

23. Transgenic animals can be used to **Competency Based Que.**

I. **study normal physiology**

II. **study vaccine safety**

III. **produce biological products**

IV. **study chemical safety**

V. **produce organs for organ transplantation in sheep**

Correct answer is

(a) I, II, IV and V (b) I, II, III and IV

(c) I, II and III (d) I, II, III, IV and V

Ans. *(b)*

24. α-1 antitrypsin is **NCERT Exemplar**

(a) an antacid

(b) an enzyme

(c) used to treat arthritis

(d) used to treat emphysema

Ans. *(d)*

25. Which one of the following transgenic animals is being used to test the safety of the polio vaccine?

(a) Sheep (b) Goat **CBSE 2024**

(c) Pig (d) Mice

Ans. *(d)*

26. Gene introduced in the first transgenic cow is

(a) human α-lactalbumin (b) β-1-antitrypsin

(c) α-1-antitrypsin (d) *cry* I Ac

Ans. *(a)*

27. In 1997, the first transgenic cow, Rosie produced

(a) human protein enriched milk (2.4 g/L)

(b) human protein enriched milk (2.8 g/L)

(c) human calcium enriched milk (2.4 g/L)

(d) human calcium enriched milk (2.8 g/L)

Ans. *(a)*

28. The decisions regarding the validity of GMOs (Genetically Modified Organisms) research and the safety of introducing GM organisms and their product for the public services in India is taken by **Competency Based Que.**

(a) Genetic Engineering Approval Committee

(b) Department of Recombinant DNA Technology

(c) Department of Science and Biotechnology

(d) National Biotechnology Board

Ans. *(a)* Genetic Engineering Approval Committee (GEAC) makes decisions regarding the validity of GM research and the safety of introducing GM organisms for public services.

29. Biopiracy is related to which of the following?

(a) Traditional knowledge

(b) Biomolecules and regarding bioresources

(c) Bioresources

(d) All of the above

Ans. *(d)*

30. Which Indian plants has not either been patented nor attempts have been made to patent them by Western nations for their use?

(a) Basmati rice (b) Turmeric

(c) Neem (d) Corn

Ans. *(d)*

Assertion-Reason Questions

Direction (Q. Nos. 1-14) *In each of the following questions, a statement of Assertion (A) is given followed by corresponding statement of Reason (R). Of the statements, mark the correct answer*

(a) Both A and R are true and R is the correct explanation of A

(b) Both A and R are true, but R is not the correct explanation of A

(c) A is true, but R is false

(d) A is false, but R is true

1. Assertion (A) To generate only a part of the plant from a cell is totipotency.

Reason (R) Suitable special nutrient media and sterile conditions are required in '*in vitro*' conditions for the division of cells in explants. **CBSE 2025**

Ans. (*d*) A is false, but R is true, A can be corrected as Totipotency is the ability of a single cell to regenerate an entire plant.

2. Assertion (A) GM foods are facing widespread resistance by the people.

Reason (R) Some people believe that human should not interfere with the natural genetic makeup of an organism.

Ans. (*a*)

3. Assertion (A) Biotechnology produces transgenic micro-organisms that act as microfactories for proteins.

Reason (R) To produce proteins for human use like insulin, transgenic microorganisms can be developed. **CBSE 2024 C**

Ans. (*b*)

4. Assertion (A) Transgenic plant production can be achieved *via* recombinant DNA technology.

Reason (R) An organism that contains and expresses a transgene is called transgenic organism.

Ans. (*b*)

5. Assertion (A) In recombinant DNA technology, human genes are generally transferred into bacteria (prokaryotes) or yeasts (eukaryotes).

Reason (R) Both bacteria and yeast multiply very fast to form huge population which express the desired gene.

Ans. (*a*)

6. Assertion (A) A crop expressing a *cry* gene is usually resistant to a group of insects.

Reason (R) Cry proteins produced from *Bacillus thuringiensis* are toxic to larvae of certain insects.

Ans. (*b*)

7. Study the diagram given below and answer the question that follows. **Competency Based Que.**

Assertion (A) Insect resistant transgenic cotton has been produced by inserting *Bt* gene.

Reason (R) *Bt* gene is derived from a bacterium.

Ans. (*b*)

8. Assertion (A) *Agrobacterium tumefaciens* is popular in genetic engineering because this bacterium is used to transfer foreign gene to the host plant.

Reason (R) Using *Agrobacterium* as vector nematodes specific genes were introduced into the host plant.

Ans. (*b*)

9. Assertion (A) RNA interference (RNAi) is used to protect plants against nematode infestation.

Reason (R) RNAi method involves silencing of a specific *m*RNA by a complementary *ds*RNA molecule that binds to and prevents translation of the *m*RNA. **Competency Based Que.**

Ans. (*a*)

10. Assertion (A) Management of adult onset diabetes is possible by taking insulin at regular time intervals.

Reason (R) Insulin used for diabetes was earlier extracted from the pancreas of slaughtered cattle and dogs.

Ans. (*c*) A is true, but R is false. R can be corrected as

Insulin used for diabetes was earlier extracted from pancreas of slaughtered cattle and pigs.

11. Assertion (A) The ADA gene provides instruction for producing the enzyme adenosine deaminase.

Reason (R) Adenosine deaminase is found throughout the body, but is most active in lymphocytes.

Ans. (*b*)

12. Assertion (A) ELISA has been used to detect mutations in gene of suspected cancer patients.

Reason (R) Very low concentration of bacteria or virus (at a time when the symptoms of the disease are not yet visible) can be detected by amplification of their nucleic acid by PCR.

Ans. (*d*) A is false, but R is true. A can be corrected as

PCR is used to detect mutations in gene of suspected cancer patients.

13. Assertion (A) First transgenic cow, Rosie produced milk which was enriched in human alpha lactalbumin.

Reason (R) Animals that have their DNA manipulated to possess and express foreign gene are called transgenic animals.

Ans. (*b*)

14. Assertion (A) Indian Government has set up an organisation known as GEAC to decide the validity of GM research.

Reason (R) Genetic modification of organisms has no effect when such organisms are introduced in the ecosystem.

Ans. (*c*) A is true, but R is false. R can be corrected as

Genetic modification can have significant effects on ecosystems when GM organisms are introduced. These effects can include changes in biodiversity, impacts on non-target species, etc.

Subjective Questions

Very Short Answer Type Questions

1. What is the major advantage of producing plants by micropropagation? NCERT

Ans. Micropropagation is used to produce thousands of plants in very short durations of time.

2. In which form does *Bt* toxin exists in bacterium?

Ans. Inactive form, i.e. protoxins.

3. *Bt* cotton is resistant to pests, such as lepidopterans, dipterans and coleopterans. Is *Bt* cotton resistant to other pests as well? Competency Based Que.

Ans. *Bt* cotton is made resistant to only certain specific taxa of pests. It is quite likely that in future some other pests may infest this *Bt* cotton.

4. Give the name of the source organism of the gene *cry* IAc and its target pest.

Ans. Source–*Bacillus thuringiensis*. Target pest–cotton bollworms. (½ + ½)

5. Name the *cry* genes that control cotton bollworm and corn borer, respectively.

Ans. *cry* I Ac and *cry* II Ab control cotton bollworm and *cry* I Ab controls corn borer. (½ + ½)

6. What are *cry* genes? In which organisms they are present?

Ans. *cry* genes are genes that are found in the bacterium '*Bacillus thuringiensis*'. These genes encode for protein crystals that contain a toxic insecticidal protein called *Bt* toxin. (½ + ½)

7. Mention a method of cellular defence which works in all eukaryotic organisms.

Ans. RNA interference

8. State the role of transposons in silencing of *m*RNA in eukaryotic cells.

Ans. Transposons are the source of complementary RNA that binds to and prevents the translation of specific *m*RNA.

9. How does *ds*RNA gain entry into eukaryotic cell to cause RNA interference? Competency Based Que.

Ans. *ds*RNA gain entry into eukaryotic cell through the following ways

(i) Infection by virus having RNA genome.

(ii) Mobile genetic elements (transposons) that replicate *via* an RNA intermediate. (½ + ½)

10. Name the bond which joins chains '*A*' and '*B*' in insulin.

Ans. Disulphide bond

11. The diagram given below is a biomolecule required for sugar metabolism in humans. Identify the biomolecule and state whether it is inactive form or active form. Competency Based Que.

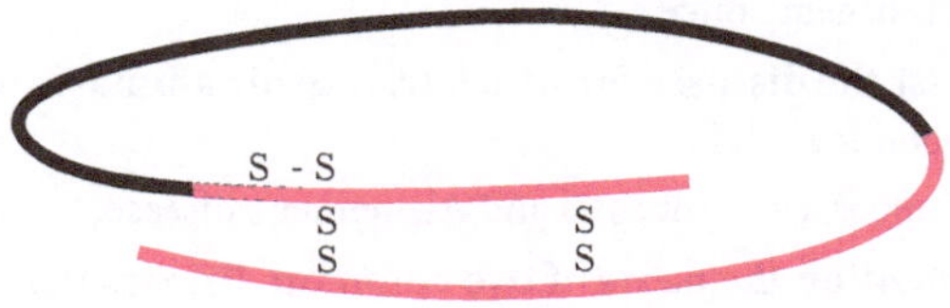

Ans. The given biomolecule is insulin. It is present in its inactive form. (½ +½)

12. State the role of C-peptide in human insulin.

Ans. C-peptide is an extra stretch of polypeptide which makes the insulin molecule inactive.

13. Name the source used to produce hepatitis-B vaccine using *r*DNA technology. CBSE 2015C

Ans. The source used to produce the hepatitis-B vaccine using *r*DNA technology is the yeast.

14. State the cause of adenosine deaminase enzyme deficiency.

Ans. The adenosine deaminase enzyme deficiency is caused by the deletion of a gene for ADA, an enzyme crucial for the immune system to function.

15. Suggest any two possible treatments that can be given to a patient exhibiting adenosine deaminase deficiency.

Ans. Bone marrow transplantation and enzyme replacement therapy. (½ + ½)

16. Why do children cured by enzyme-replacement therapy for adenosine deaminase deficiency need periodic treatment? Competency Based Que.

Ans. Children cured by enzyme-replacement therapy for adenosine deaminase deficiency need periodic treatment. It is because such type of treatment uses genetically engineered lymphocytes that are mortal.

17. Name any two techniques that serve the purpose of early diagnosis of some bacterial/viral human diseases.

Ans. The two techniques that serve the purpose of early diagnosis are

(i) Polymerase Chain Reaction (PCR)

(ii) ELISA (½ + ½)

18. Name any one diagnostic kits based upon antigen-antibody interaction.

Ans. ELISA

19. Explain the term 'pathophysiology'. NCERT Exemplar

Ans. Pathophysiology is the study of functional changes in the body of the host that occur in response to any disease or injury, e.g. if someone ingests a toxin, it may result into a variety of physical changes, such as inflammation in the stomach lining.

20. Name a transgenic animal being used in testing the safety of polio vaccine.

Ans. Transgenic mice.

21. List the diseases for which transgenic animals are being used for trials.

Ans. Cancer, cystic fibrosis and Alzheimer's disease.

22. Mention the name of two common diseases that can be treated by medicines that contain biological products of transgenic animals.

Ans. Phenylketonuria and cystic fibrosis. (½ + ½)

23. Emphysema causes breakdown of alveoli cells thus, reducing surface area for gaseous exchange. Which human protein is used to treat the disease?

Ans. Human protein α-1-antitrypsin is used to treat emphysema

24. Name the first transgenic cow that produced human protein enriched milk.

Ans. Rosie produced human protein enriched milk (2.4 g/L) in 1997.

25. Give specific content of milk produced by transgenic cow Rosie.

Ans. It contains human alpha lactalbumin (2.4 g/L) and was nutritionally more balanced product for human babies.

26. State the role of GEAC in the field of biotechnology.

Ans. GEAC or Genetic Engineering Approval Committee makes all decisions regarding the validity of GM research and the safety of introducing GMOs for public services.

27. What is biopiracy? CBSE 2017

Ans. Biopiracy refers to the use of bioresources by multinational companies and other organisations without proper authorisation from the countries and people concerned without any payment.

28. A multinational company outside India tried to sell new varieties of turmeric without proper rights. What is such an act referred to?

Ans. Biopiracy

29. Why biopiracy should be prevented?

Ans. Biopiracy should be prevented to stop the unauthorised exploitation of bioresources.

30. Why has the Indian Parliament cleared the second amendment of the country's patents bill? NCERT Exemplar

Ans. Amendments to the patent bill has empowered India to prevent unauthorised exploitation of our bio-resources and traditional knowledge by other countries.

This bill also considers patent terms and initiates research development in this field.

31. Name the Indian variety of rice patented by an American company.

Ans. Basmati rice.

32. Name any two Indian traditional herbal medicines.

Ans. Turmeric and neem. (½ + ½)

Short Answer Type Questions

1. Find out, what are the various components of the medium used for the propagation of an explant *in vitro*. NCERT

Ans. The various components are water, agar, a source of carbon (e.g. sucrose), inorganic salts, vitamins, amino acid and growth hormones (e.g. auxins, cytokinin, etc).

2. Which part of the plant is best suited for making virus-free plants and why? NCERT

Or

How can healthy potato plants be obtained from a desired potato variety which is viral infected? Explain. CBSE 2014

Ans. Refer to text on page no. 298.

3. Why are plants obtained by protoplast culture called somatic hybrids? NCERT Exemplar,

Ans. Plants obtained by protoplast culture are called somatic hybrids because they are formed by the fusion of isolated protoplasts from two different varieties of plants.

4. Expand GMO. How is it different from a hybrid? NCERT Exemplar

Ans. GMO stands for Genetically Modified Organism.

It differs from a hybrid because in a hybrid, cross is done between total genomes of two species or strains. In contrast, in a GMO, foreign genes from an entirely different species are introduced in the organism and are usually maintained as extrachromosomal entity or are integrated into the genome of the organism. (1+2)

5. What is GMO? List any five possible advantages of a GMO to a farmer.

Or

List any four ways by which GMOs have been useful for enhanced crop output. CBSE 2019

Or **Why GMOs are so called ? List the different ways in which GMO plants have benefitted and have become useful to humans.** CBSE 2020

Ans. The plants, bacteria, fungi and animals whose genes have been altered are called Genetically Modified Organisms (GMOs).

Advantages of GMOs to a farmer are as follows

(i) Crops become more tolerant to abiotic stresses like cold, drought, salt and heat.

(ii) Dependence on chemical pesticides has reduced, i.e. pest-resistant crops.

(iii) Helped to reduce post-harvest losses.

(iv) Efficiency of mineral usage increased in plants, preventing early exhaustion of fertility of soil.

(v) Enhanced nutritional value of food, e.g. vitamin-A enriched rice. (1+2)

6. 'Genetically modified plants are considered to be superior to non-genetically modified plants'. Explain giving three reasons why? **CBSE 2022 Term II**

Ans. Refer to Q. no. 5 on page no. 313.

7. People are quite apprehensive to use GM crops. Give three arguments in support of GM crops so as to convince the people in favour of such crops.

Or

Enlist three advantages of genetically modified plants. **CBSE 2025**

Ans. Genetically modified crops are genetically engineered crops with altered genetic make up. They are also called transgenic plants.

GM crops are beneficial in many ways because

(i) the agro-chemicals used in agriculture are too costly.

(ii) excess use of chemicals in field adversely affects our environment by causing pollution.

Advantages of GM crops are as follows

(i) Tolerance against abiotic stresses, such as cold, drought, salt, heat.

(ii) Reduce dependence on chemical pesticides.

(iii) Reduce post-harvest losses.

(iv) Increase efficiency of mineral usage by plants.

8. Compare and contrast the advantages and disadvantages of the production of genetically modified crops. **NCERT**

Ans. For advantages of GM crops are refer to Q. no. 7 on page no. 313.

Disadvantages of GM crops are as follows

(i) Transgenic genes in genetically modified crops endanger native species.

(ii) They cause damage to the natural environment by reducing biodiversity.

(iii) They may also cause human health problems due to altered genes and transferred antibiotic resistance. (1½ + 1½)

9. While creating genetically modified organisms, genetic barriers are not respected. How can this be dangerous in the long run? **NCERT Exemplar**

Ans. Genetic engineering involves the deliberate introduction of genes from one organism to another, often crossing natural species boundaries.

This genetic modification of organisms can have unpredictable results when such organisms are introduced into the ecosystem. Because the real effects of gene manipulation are visible only when such organisms interact with other components and organisms of the ecosystem.

10. (i) Name (a) a GM cereal crop having enhanced nutritional value, (b) the nutrient is rich in.

(ii) State any two benefits of genetically modified crops. **CBSE 2023**

Ans. (i) (a) A GM cereal crop with enhanced nutritional value is Golden rice.

(b) It is rich in vitamin-A. (½ + ½)

(ii) The two benefits of genetically modified crops are as follows

(a) They can improve the yield which can meet the increasing demand of the population.

(b) These crops are less dependent on pesticide and insecticides as they are genetically pest-resistant. (2)

11. Find out from the internet what is Golden rice? **NCERT**

Ans. Golden rice is a genetically modified rice with high levels of β-carotene and other carotenoids. This rice is modified in order to enhance the quantity of vitamin-A in it. It is called golden due to the gold-like colour it gets from β-carotene. (2)

12. Certain cotton plants are called *Bt* cotton. Explain.

Ans. Refer to text on page no. 299-300.

13. Differentiate the terms 'Cry' and '*cry*'.

Ans. *cry* is the gene that codes for *Bt* toxin. It is usually written in Italics. On the other hand, Cry is the protein encoded by the *cry* genes. It is written in Roman letters with first letter capital. (1+1)

14. (i) Which insects are killed by *Bacillus thuringiensis*?

(ii) The *Bt* binds to which cells?

(iii) In which plants *Bt* toxin is used?

Ans. Refer to text on page no. 299.

15. What are Cry proteins? With the help of a suitable example, explain how it acts as a biological pesticide. **CBSE 2022 Term II**

Ans. Cry proteins are toxin proteins, called insecticidal proteins which are secreted in crystal form by *Bacillus thuringiensis* during a specific growth process. (1)

This toxic protein is coded by different form of a gene called *cry* gene, i.e. *cry* IAc and *cry* II Ab. When these genes are incorporated in the plant through genetic engineering, they provide resistance against insects and act as biological pesticides, e.g. *Bt* cotton.

It is a genetically modified crop in which the *Bt* genes are incorporated due to which when insects such as lepidopterans, coleopterans and dipterans ingest it, the inactive toxin gets converted into active toxin due to the alkaline pH of the gut, which solubilise the crystal. After activation, these crystals bind with the receptors present on the gut epithelial cells. As a result, the membrane swells and pores are created. These pores lead to bursting of cell and soon the insect dies. (2)

16. Why does *Bt* toxin not kill the bacterium that produces it, but kills the insect that ingests it?

Ans. *Bt* toxin is produced by a soil bacterium called *Bacillus thuringiensis*. This toxin does not kill the bacterium which produces it, because it is present in an inactive and crystalline form. It becomes active and toxic only when it is consumed by insects such as lepidopterans, etc., due to the alkaline pH of their gut.

17. What are Cry proteins? Name an organism that produces it. How has man exploited this protein to his benefit? **NCERT**

Ans. The proteins encoded by the gene named *cry* are called Cry proteins. Organism that produces Cry proteins is *Bacillus thuringiensis*. (1½)

The *cry* genes are incorporated in several crop plants, which then develop resistance to a specific targeted pest, e.g. *cry* I Ac and *cry* II Ab control the cotton bollworms and *cry* I Ab controls corn borer. (1½)

18. Why do lepidopterans die when they feed on *Bt* cotton plant? Explain how does it happen.

Ans. *Bt* cotton plants are the transgenic plants that express a *Bacillus thuringiensis* gene called *cry* gene.

This gene encodes for protein crystals having insecticidal properties against insects like Lepidopterans, Dipterans and Coleopterans. Inside the bacterium, these proteins remain inactive and do not harm the bacteria. However, these inactive crystals can get activated in the alkaline pH of the gut of insects upon ingestion.

After activation, these crystals binds to the receptors present on the membranes of gut epithelial cells. Due to this binding, the membrane swells and pores are created on them. These pores lead to bursting of cell. Hence, soon the lepidopteran dies due to starvation. (1½ + 1½)

19. You have identified a useful gene in a bacteria. Make a flowchart of the steps that you would follow to transfer this gene to a plant. **NCERT Exemplar**

Ans. After identifying a useful gene in bacteria, following steps should be undertaken.

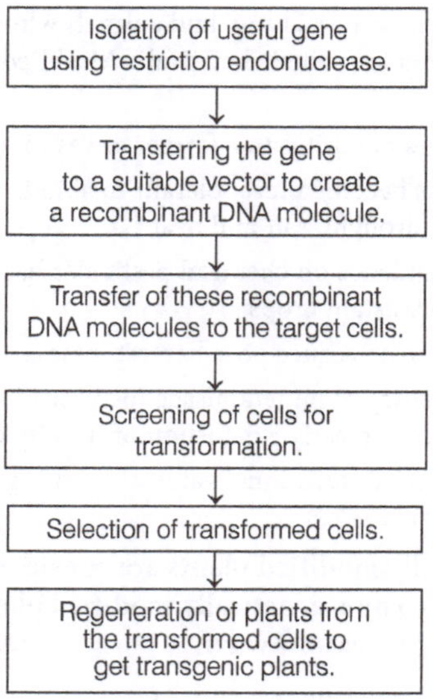

20. How are tobacco plants benefitted when nematode specific genes are introduced into them using certain vectors?

Ans. Refer to text on page no. 300.

21. "RNA interference has been used to produce transgenic tobacco plants to protect them from the infestation by specific nematodes." Explain the novel strategy exploited by the biotechnologists. **CBSE 2023**

Ans. Refer to text on page no. 300.

22. Correct the following statement by giving reason.

The mature insulin molecule consists of three short polypetide chains.

Ans. Refer to text on page no. 301.

23. List the advantages of recombinant insulin.

Ans. The advantages of recombinant insulin are as follows

- It does not require the sacrifice of animals such as pigs and cows.
- It is safe and has the least side effects, unlike the insulin obtained from non-human sources such as pigs and cows.
- It can be synthesised in large quantities in a short period of time.
- It has increased shelf life and does not degrade rapidly.

(½ ×4)

24. Eli Lilly's contribution for diabetic patients through *r*DNA technology has been overwhelmingly accepted. Explain how. **CBSE 2023**

Ans. Refer to text on page no. 301.

25. Write the difference between the proinsulin and mature insulin. **CBSE 2020**

Ans. Insulin is a hormone secreted by pancreas. It consists of two short polypeptide chains, i.e. chain-A and B, linked together by disulphide bridges. In mammals, insulin is synthesised as a prohormone, i.e. it needs to be processed before it becomes fully mature and functional hormone. This prohormone contains an extra stretch called the C-peptide. This is known as proinsulin. (1+1)

26. Explain the various steps involved in the production of artificial insulin.

Or **With the help of a story board or a flowchart only, explain all the stages of how human insulin is produced through *r*DNA technology?** **CBSE 2022 Term II**

Or **Recombinant DNA technology is of great importance in the field of medicine. With the help of a flowchart, show how this technology has been used in preparing genetically engineered human insulin?**

Ans. Insulin production by using recombinant DNA technology is shown in flowchart below

DNA sequences corresponding to the two polypeptides, i.e. A and B-chains of insulin are synthesised *in vitro*

↓

They are introduced into plasmid DNA of *E. coli*

↓

This bacterium is cloned under suitable conditions

↓

The transgene is expressed in the form of polypeptides, i.e. A and B-chains secreted into the medium

↓

They are extracted and combined by creating disulphide bridge to form human insulin.

27. Hormones are broadly categorised as steroid hormones and protein hormones. Patients with type 2 diabetes, generally, have to take insulin externally. Researchers across the world believe that if insulin can be given orally it would be ideal as it would closely mimic the movement of natural insulin. Yet, injectable insulin is commonly prescribed by doctors.

What type of a hormone is insulin and why cannot it be administered orally?

Ans. Insulin is a protein hormone. If taken orally, they will get digested by pepsin and trypsin in the stomach and small intestine into their simpler forms, thereby losing their function. Hence, it cannot be administered orally.

28. What is gene therapy? Name the first clinical case in which it was used. **CBSE 2014**

Or **What is gene therapy? Illustrate using the example of Adenosine Deaminase (ADA) deficiency?** **NCERT**

Or **(a) What is gene therapy?**

(b) Describe the procedure of such a therapy that could be a permanent cure for a genetic disease. Name the genetic disease. **CBSE 2024 C**

Ans. Refer to text on page no. 302.

29. Write the function of adenosine deaminase enzyme. State the cause of ADA deficiency in humans. Mention a possible permanent cure for an ADA deficiency patient.

Ans. Refer to text on page no. 302. (3)

30. Two girls, *A* and *B* aged 4 and 5 years respectively visited a hospital with a similar genetic disorder. The girl *A* was provided enzyme-replacement therapy and was advised to revisit periodically for further treatment. The girl *B* was, however given a therapy that did not require revisit for further treatment.

(i) Name the ailments the two girls were suffering from?

(ii) Why did the treatment provided to girl *A* required repeated visits?

(iii) How was the girl *B* cured permanently? **CBSE 2019**

Ans. (i) Both girls suffer from adenosine deaminase deficiency due to probable deletion of gene that codes for ADA production. (1)

(ii) Girl *A* was treated with injections of functional ADA or bone marrow transplant. These techniques are not completely curative as these lymphocytes are not immortal and require repeated treatment. (1)

(iii) Girl *B* was treated using gene therapy where the gene isolate from marrow cells producing ADA was introduced into cells at an early embryonic stage for a possible permanent cure. (1)

31. Explain enzyme replacement therapy to treat adenosine deaminase deficiency. Mention two disadvantages of this procedure.

Ans. In enzyme replacement therapy, the patient is given functional ADA (Adenosine Deaminase) by injection. (1)

Disadvantage

(i) The patient does not completely recover from the disease.

(ii) It needs periodic injections of the enzyme to the patients. (1)

32. Why is molecular diagnosis preferred over conventional methods? Name any two techniques giving one use of each.

Ans. Using conventional methods of diagnosis (serum and urine analysis), early detection of diseases is not possible. To overcome this problem, some molecular diagnosis techniques were developed that provide early detection of diseases.

These are as follows (1)

(i) **Polymerase Chain Reaction** (PCR) helps in early detection of diseases or pathogens by the amplification of their nucleic acid.

PCR can amplify nucleic acids of pathogens even when their concentration is very low.

This technique can be used for detecting HIV in suspected AIDS patients, genetic mutations in suspected cancer patients and in identifying genetic disorders. (1)

(ii) **Enzyme Linked Immuno Sorbent Assay** (ELISA) is based on the principle of antigen-antibody interaction. Infection by pathogen can be detected by the presence of antigens (proteins, glycoproteins, etc.) or by detecting the antibodies synthesised against the pathogen. (1)

33. How is PCR used to detect gene mutation in case of suspected cancer patient?

Ans. Refer to text on page no. 302.

34. How is recombinant DNA technology helpful in detecting the presence of mutated genes in the cancer patients?

Ans. Molecular diagnosis by recombinant DNA technology uses a single-stranded DNA or RNA tagged with a radioactive molecule. It is allowed to hybridise its complementary DNA in a clone of cells followed by detection using autoradiography. The clone having the mutated gene will not appear on the photographic film, because the probe used will not be complementary to the mutated gene. In this way, presence of mutated genes can be detected. (2)

35. Give the full form of ELISA. Which disease can be detected using it? Discuss the principle underlying the test.

Ans. ELISA can be used for diagnosing several disease such as HIV, hepatitis, etc. For full form and principle of ELISA Refer to text on page no. 303. (½ + ½ +1)

36. ELISA is a test used for early detection of an infection.

(i) What components of a disease can be detected using ELISA?

(ii) Describe the components that can be checked if one wants to identify whether an individual is allergic to pollen or not.

(iii) Given below is an image of an ELISA test result with two of its cells marked P and Q. A coloured cell indicates a positive result whereas an uncoloured cell is a negative result.

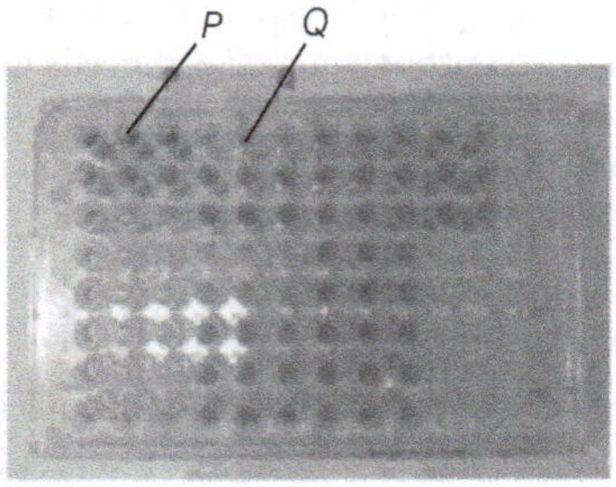

The colour of *P* is darker than the colour of *Q*. What could this possibly indicate? Competency Based Que.

Ans. (i) Presence of antigen/antibodies to an antigen can be detected using ELISA. (1)

(ii) Presence of IgE antibodies can be used. (1)

(iii) *P* may have more antibodies as compared to *Q*. (1)

37. What are transgenic animals? Give an example. CBSE 2016

Ans. Animals which have manipulated DNA and express an extra (foreign) gene are known as transgenic animals, e.g. transgenic rats, rabbits, pigs, etc. (1+1)

38. With respect to understanding diseases, discuss the importance of transgenic animal models. NCERT Exemplar

Ans. Transgenic animals are important in the following fields

(i) They are being used in basic science research to elucidate the role of genes in the development of diseases like cancer, cystic fibrosis, rheumatoid arthritis and Alzheimer's.

(ii) They are valuable tools in testing safety of vaccines

(iii) Transgenics can produce medicines or human proteins (insulin, growth hormone, etc.) in large quantities. (1 × 3)

39. Explain alpha lactalbumin. Where is it produced in human body? CBSE 2010

Ans. Alpha lactalbumin is a human milk protein which helps to increase the production of lactose in the body. It is produced in mammary glands. (1+1)

40. Describe how biotechnology has helped in producing more nutritionally balanced milk.

Ans. Biotechnology leads the production of transgenic cow, Rosie that produced around 2.4 g/L human protein enriched milk. This milk contained the human alpha lactalbumin and was nutritionally more balanced than a natural cow's milk.

41. Why are certain animals called 'transgenic'? Give an example of such animals that is being used for testing the vaccine safety for a specific human disease. Name the disease. CBSE 2020

Ans. Certain animals are called transgenic because their DNA is manipulated to possess and express an useful and extra (foreign) gene. (1)

Transgenic mice are being used for testing the vaccine safety for the polio disease, before being used in humans. It can replace the use of monkeys to test the safety of batches of the vaccine. (1)

42. What are transgenic animals ? How was the first transgenic cow found to be more useful than the normal cow, for humans? CBSE 2020

Ans. Transgenic animals are those animals that have had their genome, i.e. DNA manipulated to possess and express a useful and foreign gene, e.g. transgenic cow, transgenic rat, etc. (1)

The transgenic cow 'Rosie' produced human protein enriched milk (2.4 gm/L). It contained the human α-lactalbumin and was nutritionally more balanced for human babies than normal cow's milk. (1)

43. How are transgenic animals used in chemical safety testing?

Ans. Transgenic animals are employed for testing the safety of various chemicals (drugs, etc.) before being released for public use. It is also called as toxicity or safety testing. Transgenic animals are developed carrying the genes which makes them more susceptible to the chemical substances than others. These animals are then exposed to the chemicals under test and effects generated are studied.

These studies helps in identifying the desirable and harmful effects of the chemical substances and their further improvement.

44. Mention two objectives of setting up GEAC by our government.

Or

Describe the responsibility of GEAC setup by the Indian government.

Ans. The two objectives of setting up Genetic Engineering Approval Committee (GEAC) by the Indian Government are as follows

(i) To make decisions regarding the validity of GM research.

(ii) To make decisions regarding the safety of introducing GM organisms for public services. (1+1)

45. A patent is a legal document that safeguards the rights of the inventors. What is the purpose of introducing patenting in biology? Write any one abuse of biopatents.

Ans. A patent refers to the exclusive rights over any idea or invention. In case of biology, this patent is called biopatent. The main purpose of introducing patenting in biology is to ensure that there is financial security to the investors. The major abuse of biopatenting is that large profits can be made by charging royalties or hiking up prices for their inventories. These may not be fulfilled by other.

46. Write a self-explanatory note on biopatent.

Ans. Refer to text on page no. 304.

47. Write a short note on biopiracy highlighting the exploitation of developing countries by the developed countries. NCERT Exemplar

Ans. Refer to text on page no. 304.

48. Differentiate between bioethics and biopatent.

Ans. Refer to text on page no. 304.

49. Write about the amendment passed by the Indian Parliament regarding patent issues.

Ans. Refer to text on page no. 304. (2)

50. In 1997, an American company obtained patent rights on Basmati rice, allowing them to market a 'new' strain of Basmati rice in the United States and overseas. This 'new' Basmati strain was really derived from Indian farmer's varieties.

(i) What is this unauthorised act called? Define it.

(ii) State one measures that different countries are taking to prevent such unauthorised exploitation of their bio-resources.

Ans. (i) This act is called biopiracy. It refers to the use of bio-resources by multinational companies and other organisations without proper authorisation from the countries and people concerned, without compensatory payment. (1)

(ii) By implementing laws for issues such as patent terms emergency provisions research and development initiative countries can safeguard their resources from unauthorised exploitation. (1)

51. Does our blood have proteases and nucleases? NCERT

Ans. Yes, human blood contains both proteases and nucleases. . Proteases are enzymes that breakdown proteins into smaller peptides or amino acids, playing vital roles in digestion, immune response and tissue repair. On the other hand, nucleases degrade nucleic acids (DNA and RNA) into nucleotides, which is important for removing damaged DNA and regulating RNA turnover.

Long Answer Type Questions

1. Diagrammatically represent the experimental steps in cloning and expressing a human gene (say the gene for growth hormone) into a bacterium like *E. coli*. NCERT

Ans. The multiple identical copies of specific template DNA can be produced by DNA cloning. It can be carried out by the use of a vector to carry specific foreign DNA fragment into the host cell. The mechanism of cloning and transfer of a gene for human growth hormone into *E. coli* is diagrammatically represented below.

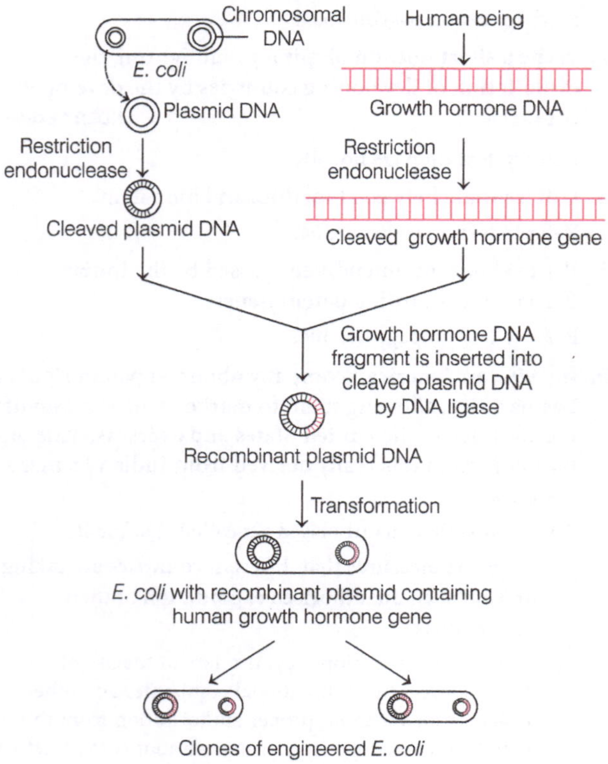

2. How has the study of biotechnology helped in developing pest resistant cotton crop? Explain.

Or **One of the major contribution of biotechnology is to develop pest resistant varieties of cotton plants. Explain how it has been made possible.**

Ans. The pests that destroy the cotton bolls are cotton bollworms and corn borer. The study of biotechnology has helped in developing pest resistant varieties of cotton. *Bt* cotton, a product of biotechnology is created by using some strains of a bacterium, *Bacillus thuringiensis* (*Bt* is short form).

(i) This bacterium produces protein that kills certain insects such as lepidopterans (tobacco budworm and armyworm), coleopterans (beetles) and dipterans (flies and mosquitoes).

(ii) *Bacillus thuringiensis* forms protein crystals during a particular phase of their growth. These crystals contain a toxic insecticidal protein.

(iii) *Bt* toxin protein exists as inactive protoxins in bacteria, but once an insect ingests this inactive toxin, it is converted into an active form due to the alkaline pH of the gut, which solubilises the crystals.

(iv) The activated toxin binds to the surface of midgut epithelial cells and creates pores that cause cell swelling and lysis, leading to the death of insect.

(v) Specific *Bt* toxin genes were isolated from *Bacillus thuringiensis* and incorporated into several crop plants.

(vi) Most *Bt* toxins are insect-group specific. The toxin is coded by a gene named *cry*. For example, the proteins encoded by the genes *cry* I Ac and *cry* II Ab control the cotton bollworms and *cry* I Ab controls corn borer. (2 + 3)

3. (i) Name the insect that attacks cotton crops and causes lot of damage to the crop. How has *Bt* cotton plant overcome this problem and saved the crop ? Explain.

(ii) Write the role of gene *cry* IAb. CBSE 2020

Ans. (i) The insect that attacks cotton crops is cotton bollworms and corn borers. (1)

Bt cotton is made by using a bacterium called as *Bacillus thuringiensis*. This bacterium produce a protein that kills certain insects. *B. thuringiensis* forms protein crystals (Cry) during a phase of its growth. These crystals contain a toxic insecticidal protein. Specific *Bt* toxin genes were isolated from *Bacillus thuringiensis* and incorporated into cotton.

This *Bt* toxin does not kill the *Bacillus* because it exists as inactive protoxins in its body. However, when an insect ingest the inactive toxin, it gets exposed to the alkaline pH of the gut, which solubilise the crystals and convert it into active form.

The activated toxin binds to the surface of midgut epithelial cells and create pores that cause cell swelling and lysis and eventually causes death of the insect. In this manner, the crop is saved from insects and a large yield is obtained. (3)

(ii) Gene *cry* I Ab secretes a protein that inhibits the growth of corn borer insects. (1)

4. Explain how the process of RNA interference technology is used effectively to prevent infestation of the roots of tobacco plant by the nematode *Meloidogyne incognita*. CBSE 2025

Ans. RNA interference (RNAi) technology is used to prevent root infestation of tobacco plants by the nematode *Meloidogyne incognita* through gene silencing. In this method, nematode-specific genes are introduced into the tobacco plant using *Agrobacterium* vectors. These genes are designed to produce both sense and antisense RNA, which form a double-stranded RNA (*ds*RNA) inside the plant cells. The *ds*RNA triggers RNAi, leading to the silencing of the nematode's specific *m*RNA, thereby preventing the synthesis of essential proteins required for its survival. As a result, the nematode fails to infect the transgenic tobacco plant, providing protection against infestation.

5. What is meant by the term biopesticide? Name and explain the mode of action of a popular biopesticide.

Ans. Refer to text on page no. 299.

6. Mention some therapeutical applications that are related to biotechnology.

Ans. Refer to text on page no. 300-302.

7. Explain how advent of biotechnology has helped in preventing infestation by nematodes and thereby increasing crop yield. **CBSE SQP 2024**

Ans. Several nematodes infects a wide variety of plants and animals including human beings.

- A nematode *Meloidegyne incognita* infects the roots of tobacco plants and causes a great reduction in yield.
- A novel strategy was adopted to prevent this infestation which was based on the process of RNA interference (RNAi).
- RNAi takes place in all eukaryotic organisms as a method of cellular defence.
- This method involves silencing of a specific *m*RNA due to a complementary *ds*RNA molecule that binds to and prevents translation of the *m*RNA (silencing).
- The source of this complementary RNA could be from an infection by viruses having RNA genomes or mobile genetic elements (transposons) that replicate *via* an RNA intermediate.
- Using *Agrobacterium* vectors, nematode-specific genes were introduced into the host plant.
- The introduction of DNA was such that it produced both sense and anti-sense RNA in the host cells.
- These two RNA's being complementary to each other formed a double-stranded RNA (*ds*RNA) that initiated RNAi and thus silenced the specific *m*RNA of the nematode.
- The consequence was that the parasite could not survive in a transgenic host expressing specific interfering RNA. The transgenic plant therefore got itself protected from the parasite.

8. In the future, genetic therapies may be used to prevent, treat, or cure certain inherited disorders in humans. Justify the statement with a suitable example. **CBSE SQP 2024**

Ans.
- Gene therapy is a collection of methods that allows correction of a gene defect that has been diagnosed in a child/embryo. Here, genes are inserted into a person's cells and tissues to treat a disease.
- Correction of a genetic defect involves delivery of a normal gene into the individual or embryo to take over the function of and compensate for the non-functional gene.
- The first clinical gene therapy was given in 1990 to a 4-years old girl with Adenosine Deaminase (ADA) deficiency. This enzyme is crucial for the immune system to function.
- The disorder is caused due to the deletion of the gene for adenosine deaminase.
- In some children ADA deficiency can be cured by bone marrow transplantation; in others it can be treated by enzyme replacement therapy, in which functional ADA is given to the patient by injection.
- But the problem with both of these approaches is that they are not completely curative.
- As a first step towards gene therapy, lymphocytes from the blood of the patient are grown in a culture outside the body.
- A functional ADA cDNA (using a retroviral vector) is then introduced into these lymphocytes, which are subsequently returned to the patient.
- However, as these cells are not immortal, the patient requires periodic infusion of such genetically engineered lymphocytes.
- However, if the gene isolate from marrow cells producing ADA is introduced into cells at early embryonic stages, it could be a permanent cure.

9. What is ADA deficiency and how can it be cured?

Ans. Refer to text on page no. 302 (Gene therapy).

10. How is PCR technique and *r*DNA technology beneficial in biotechnology?

Ans. Refer to text on page no. 302-303.

11. Define transgenic animals. Explain in detail any four areas where they can be used for human benefit. **CBSE 2025**

Ans. Refer to text on page no. 303.

12. Highlight five areas, where biotechnology has influenced our lives. **NCERT Exemplar**

Ans. Biotechnology has influenced our lives in following ways

(i) It has provided us with genetically modified crops of better quality and high nutrient value.

(ii) It has made available better and safer recombinant vaccines.

(iii) It has helped to develop transgenic animals that can produce human proteins.

(iv) It has enabled gene therapy for curing genetic diseases.

(v) Environment pollution has also been taken care of with the help of genetically engineered microbes. (1 × 5)

13. **How are the developed countries related to biopiracy cases? Explain with an example.**

Ans. Refer to text on page no. 305.

Source Based/Case Based/ Passage Based Questions

1. **The graph given below represents the production of genetically modified plants (in millions) starting from 1996 to 2016, i.e. a timespan of 20 years. Study the given graph and answer the following questions.**

Competency Based Que. CBSE SQP 2022 Term-II

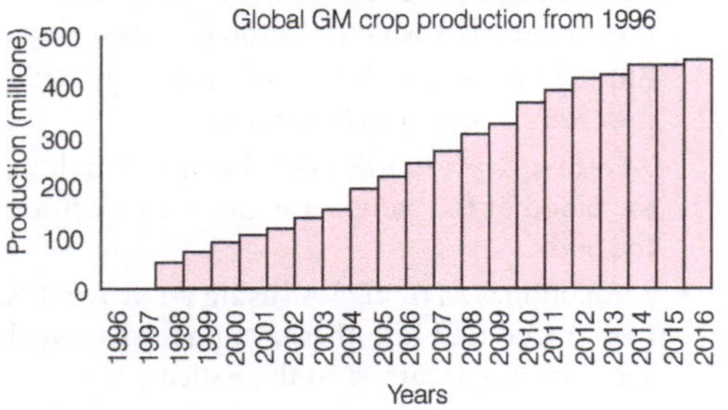

(i) **State the relationship between increased production of genetically modified crops with time. How for do you agree with the current circumstances?**

(ii) **Do genetically modified crops favour post-harvest losses?**

(iii) **State any two advantages of genetically modified crops.**

Or

(iii) **Are there any adverse effects of transgenic crops on humans?**

Ans. (i) The production of genetically modified crops has increased with increasing timespan due to the benefits that the GM crops give. Therefore, this scenario is completely justified. GM plants have benefitted by humans increasing yield and qualities like stress tolerance, etc., therefore growing GM crops has become favourable for the farmers as they bring much benefits. (1)

(ii) No, genetically engineered crops do not favour/offer post-harvest losses. They help farmers in minimising crop losses which occur due to insects and/or diseases. (1)

(iii) Two advantages of genetically modified crops are as follows

(a) Production of disease and drought resistant plants.

(b) Increased production of food with longer self life. (2)

Or (iii) Transgenic plants/crops have certain adverse effects on humans. These include

(a) They may cause allergic reactions in humans.

(b) They may transfer antibiotic resistance to humans. (2)

2. **The graph given below represents yields of both *Bt* and non-*Bt* cotton in China during a timespan of eight years.**

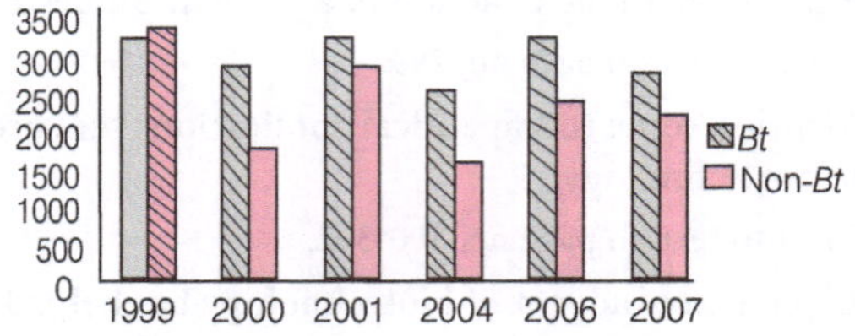

Study the graph and answer the following questions.

Competency Based Que. CBSE SQP 2022 Term-II

(i) **Which of the above given years show the maximum difference between growth of *Bt* and non-*Bt* cotton?**

(ii) **The bar representing *Bt* cotton is always longer than that representing non-*Bt* cotton. Give reason.**

(iii) **Is the transgenic variety of cotton still in use? What benefits have the farmers growing this variety gained?**

Or

(iii) **How is the conventional variety of cotton different from *Bt* cotton variety?**

Ans. (i) The year 2000 shows the maximum difference (1100 kg/hect.) between growth of *Bt* and non-*Bt* cotton crop. (1)

(ii) This is because *Bt* cotton crop has provided much benefits not only in terms of quantity, but also in terms of quality. Thus, it has become the first choice for farmers growing cotton in their fields. (1)

(iii) Yes, the transgenic variety of cotton crop is still in use. In fact, the genetically modified variety of cotton is preferred over conventional cotton because of benefits like

(a) **Increased Pest Resistance** This results in enhancement of crop quality.

(b) **Higher Yield** Due to increased crop resistance, the crop yield is also enhanced. (2)

Or

(iii) *Bt* cotton plants have one or more foreign genes derived from *Bacillus thuringensis*, thus they are called transgenic plants. Also, due to inbuilt resistance, *Bt* cotton requires fewer pesticides. Thus, it provides a better yield. On the other hand, conventional variety of cotton does not passes these qualities/characters and hence is different from transgenic variety. (2)

3. GM crops especially *Bt* crops are known to have higher resistance to pest attacks. To substantiate this an experimental study was conducted in 4 different farmlands growing *Bt* and non-*Bt* cotton crops.

The farmlands had the same dimensions, fertility and were under similar climatic conditions. The histogram below shows the usage of pesticides on *Bt* crops and non-*Bt* crops in these farmlands.

Competency Based Que. CBSE SQP 2022 Term-II

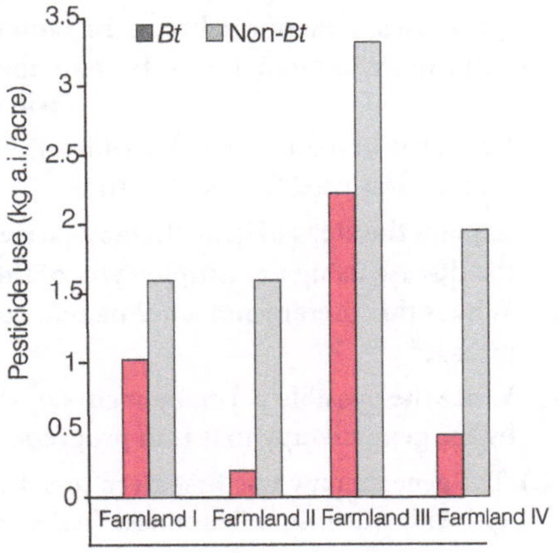

(i) Which of the above 4 farmlands has successfully applied the concepts of biotechnology to show better management practices and use of agrochemicals? If you had to cultivate, which crop would you prefer (*Bt* or non- *Bt*) and why?

(ii) Cotton bollworms were introduced in another experimental study on the above farmlands where in no pesticide was used. Explain what effect would a *Bt* and non- *Bt* crop have on the pest.

Ans. (i) From the given 4 farmlands, the farmland II has successfully applied the concepts of biotechnology to show better management practices and use of agrochemicals. Because their pesticide use is the least out of four.

If we were given preference between *Bt* and non-*Bt* crops, we will cultivate *Bt* crop.

This is because use of pesticide is highly reduced for growing *Bt* crop. (1)

(ii) If cotton bollworms were introduced in the experimental farmland, they will show following effects

(a) **Effect on *Bt* Crop** In *Bt* crop, a *cry* gene has been introduced from bacterium, *Bacillus thuringiensis* (*Bt*) which causes synthesis of a toxic protein. This protein becomes active in the alkaline gut of bollworm feeding on cotton. It leads to the formation of holes in their gut lining, causing death of the insect.

(b) **Effect on Non-*Bt* Crop** A non-*Bt* crop will have no effect on the cotton bollworm. The yield of cotton will decrease and non-*Bt* crop will succumb to pest attack. (3)

4. There are two different farmlands, one where *Bt* cotton crop was cultivated and the other where non-*Bt* cotton crop (indigenous) was cultivated. Farmers responsible for this experimental cultivation were free to use the farming practices of their choice. During the cultivation period, the data was collected with respect to the amount of pesticide use, water required for irrigation and at harvesting time, the crop productivity. Based on the data collected, a bar graph was plotted which is shown below. **CBSE 2022 Term II**

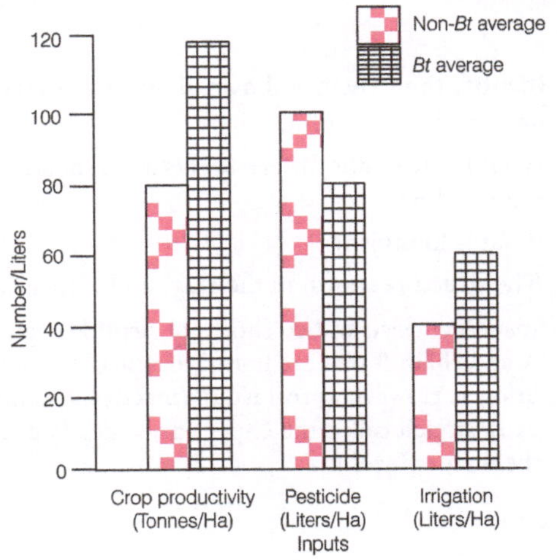

Answer the following questions

(i) Write your interpretation with reason, on the basis of the three parameters plotted in the graph.

(ii) Which one of the crops would you like to cultivate in your farm and why?

(iii) Which one out of these two crops would a farmer from Rajasthan like to cultivate and why?

Ans. (i) On comparing non-*Bt* average and *Bt* average crops, the following three inferences can be drawn

(a) With regard to crop productivity, the number of *Bt* average crops was found to be greater than that of non-*Bt* crops since the former were genetically modified and the latter were destroyed by cotton bollworms.

(b) Growing *Bt* crops requires less conventional or chemical pesticides because of the genetic modifications in them, whereas in non-*Bt* crops the use of pesticides is higher.

(c) Genetically modified crops (*Bt* here) require more water for irrigation when compared to normal or non-*Bt* crops, since they show resistance to biotic and abiotic stress. (2)

(ii) It is better to cultivate *Bt* crops in our farms as they provide many advantages such as
- Better yield/high productivity
- Resistance to pests and insects
- Control of soil pollution (1)

(iii) A farmer from Rajasthan would like to cultivate non-*Bt* crops as it requires less water for irrigation (since Rajasthan is a state with less water availability). (1)

5. Refer to the diagram given below and answer the questions that follows

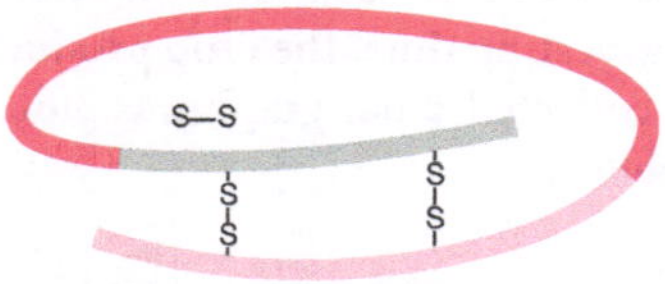

(i) Identify the structure shown above in the diagram, as pro-insulin or insulin.

(ii) What is the major difference between insulin and pro-insulin?

(iii) What is humulin?

Ans. (i) The structure shown in the diagram is pro-insulin. (1)

(ii) Insulin consists of two short polypeptide chains, i.e. chain A and chain B that are linked together by disulphide bridges. However, pro-insulin (inactive insulin) contains an extra stretch called the C-peptide, which is not present in the mature insulin. (2)

(iii) In 1983, Eli Lilly, prepared two insulin chains, i.e. chain A and chain B. These chains were extracted and combined by creating disulphide bonds to form human insulin (humulin). (1)

6. Read the following paragraph and answer the questions given below.

Biotechnology revolves around the "gene of interest" with an objective to open various avenues for human welfare in health, medicine, pharma, agriculture, etc., using different techniques, tools and processes. One of the break through of biotechnology in medicine is the gene therapy.

CBSE 2022 Term II

(i) Name the human disease for which the gene therapy was used for the first time.

(ii) Explain the steps of gene therapy carried to cure the disease using the lymphocytes of the patient. Why is this therapy not a permanent cure of the disease?

(iii) Write the possible permanent cure of the disease by the gene therapy that is in progress.

Ans. (i) The gene therapy was first given to a 4 years old girl with Adenosine Deaminase (ADA) deficiency. (1)

(ii) For steps involve in gene therapy, Refer to text on page no. 302. (2)

(iii) Refer to text on page no. 302. (1)

SELF ASSESSMENT TEST

Multiple Choice Questions

1. What is the primary purpose of using the explant in plant tissue culture?
   (a) To increase plant height
   (b) To obtain a source of genetic material
   (c) To initiate the growth of a new plant
   (d) To enhance flower colour
2. Which of the following is a commonly used growth regulator in plant tissue culture?
   (a) Ethylene
   (b) Auxin
   (c) Cytokinin
   (d) Both (b) and (c)
3. Tobacco plants resistant to a nematode have been developed by the introduction of DNA that produced (in the host cells)
   (a) Both sense and anti-sense RNA
   (b) a particular hormone
   (c) an antifeedant
   (d) a toxic protein
4. Which of the following is a major advantage of using recombinant insulin over traditional insulin sources?
   (a) It is cheaper to produce
   (b) It is less effective in lowering blood sugar
   (c) It eliminates the risk of allergic reactions
   (d) It has a shorter shelf life
5. Which organism is commonly used in the production of recombinant human insulin?
   (a) Yeast (b) *E. coli* (c) Mice (d) Plants
6. Transgenic mice are often used in research because they can be used to
   (a) study human diseases
   (b) produce pharmaceuticals
   (c) enhance agricultural traits
   (d) All of these
7. Which of the following is a potential benefit of transgenic animals in agriculture?
   (a) Increased resistance to diseases
   (b) Higher nutritional value of products
   (c) Enhanced microbe growth
   (d) Both (a) and (b)

Assertion-Reason Questions

Direction (Q. Nos. 8-11) *In each of the following questions, a statement of Assertion (A) is given followed by corresponding statement of Reason (R). Of the statements, mark the correct answer*

(a) Both A and R are true and R is the correct explanation of A.
(b) Both A and R are true, but R is not the correct explanation of A.
(c) A is true, but R is false.
(d) A is false, but R is true.

8. **Assertion** (A) Plant tissue culture allows for the rapid propagation of disease-free plants.

   Reason (R) In tissue culture, small explants are grown in a controlled, sterile environment that minimises the risk of pathogen contamination.
9. **Assertion** (A) Transgenic plant production can be achieved through recombinant DNA technology.

   Reason (R) A transgenic organism is one that contains and express a transgene.
10. **Assertion** (A) ADA deficiency leads to Severe Combined Immuno Deficiency (SCID) in affected individuals.

    Reason (R) ADA gene gives instruction for producing the enzyme adenosine deaminase.
11. **Assertion** (A) Transgenic animals help scientists to study human diseases and creat treatments.

    Reason (R) These animals have genes from other species added to them, which helps researchers to understand diseases better and test new medicines.

Very Short Answer Type Questions

12. Mention the groups of insects that are affected by Cry protein.
13. What is the cause of ADA deficiency in humans?
14. State the importance of first transgenic cow.
15. How are transgenic animals proved to be beneficial in chemical safety testing?

Short Answer Type Questions

16. Explain somatic hybridisation.
17. How genetically modified plants are useful?
18. Mention four benefits derived from transgenic animals.
19. Describe the function of PCR and ELISA.

Long Answer Type Questions

20. Describe the method of micropropagation.
21. What are pest resistant plant? Give examples.
22. What is gene therapy explain in brief?

Case Based Question

23. Given below is an image of a hormone which is required for the treatment of a disease.

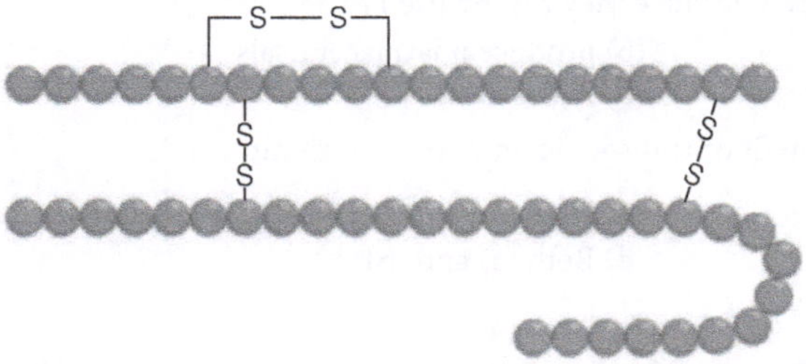

(i) Identify the hormone and the disease that is caused due to its insufficient secretion.

(ii) State whether the following statement about this hormone is true or false. Justify if true, correct if false.
'The structure in the image is a protein and is the precursor form of the hormone.'

(iii) Which characteristic helped you arrive at your answer in (ii).

(iv) Describe the challenges in larges scale production of this hormone using *r*DNA techniques and how it was overcome.

Answers

1. (c)	2. (d)	3. (a)	4. (c)	5. (b)	6. (a)	7. (d)	8. (a)
9. (a)	10. (b)	11. (a)					

11 CHAPTER

A single organism cannot exist alone, due to which it forms a dynamic inter-relationship with its surrounding.
Ecology is the study of interactions among organisms and between the organism and its physical (abiotic) environment.

YOUR STUDY GOALS

11.1 Populations
11.2 Population Interactions

YOUR PRACTICE GOAL

- Objective Type Questions (36 Qs ; MCQs, A-R)
  Case Based Questions (5)
- Subjective Type Questions
- (20 VSAs, 32 SAs, 13 LAs)

Organisms and Populations

Ecology basically concerned with four levels of biological organisation, i.e. organisms, populations, communities and biomes.

In this chapter, we will explore ecology at population levels.

11.1 Populations

- Population is a set of individuals of a particular species, found in a particular geographical area, sharing and competing for similar resources and can interbreed.
- Population ecology is an important area of ecology because it links ecology to population genetics and evolution.

Population Attributes

A population has certain attributes that an individual organism does not have. Some of them are given below

1. Population Size or Density

- It is defined as the number of individuals of a species per unit area or volume.

- Population Density (D)

$$= \frac{\text{Number of individuals in a region } (N)}{\text{Area of the region } (S)};$$

$$D = \frac{N}{S}$$

- However, population density need not necessarily be measured in numbers only.
- Although, the total number is the most appropriate measure of population density, but it is difficult to determine in some cases, e.g. there are 200 *Parthenium* (carrot grass) plants, but only a single huge banyan tree with large canopy.
- This states that the population density of banyan tree is relatively low as compared to that of *Parthenium*.
- In such cases, the per cent cover or biomass is a more meaningful measure of the population size/density.
- In some ecological studies, relative population densities are as effective as absolute densities.
- For instance, the number of fish caught per trap is good enough measure of its total population density in the lake.
- The population size can also be estimated indirectly, without actually counting them or seeing them.
- The tiger census in national parks and tiger reserves is often based on pug marks and faecal pellets.

2. Birth Rate or Natality

It is the number of births per 1000 individuals of a population per unit time, e.g. if in a pond, there are 20 lotus plants last year and through reproduction, 8 new plants are added, taking the current population to 28. Then, birth rate = 8/20 = 0.4 offspring per lotus per year.

3. Death Rate or Mortality

It is the number of deaths per 1000 individuals of a population per unit time due to environmental changes, such as competition, predation, etc., e.g. if in a laboratory, population of 40 fruitflies, 4 died during a week, then the death rate = 4/40 = 0.1 individuals per fruitfly per week.

4. Sex Ratio

It is the number of females per 1000 males of a population in a given time.

Age Pyramid

- Population at any given time is composed of individuals of different age groups.
- When the age distribution (per cent individuals of a given age or age group) is plotted for the population, it is called **age pyramid**.
- The age pyramids of human population generally shows the age distribution of males and females in a combined diagram.
- The growth status of the population is reflected by the shape of the pyramids.
- The three types of age pyramids are as follows

1. Expanding Age Pyramid

- In this type of pyramid, the number of pre-reproductive individuals is very large.
- The number of reproductive individuals is moderate, whereas post-reproductive individuals are minimum or few.
- This shows a growing population. It is **triangular shaped** pyramid.

2. Stable Age Pyramid

- In this type of pyramid, the number of pre-reproductive and reproductive individuals are almost equal while the post-reproductive individuals are comparatively fewer.
- Thus, population size remains stable. This represents a **bell-shaped pyramid.**

3. Declining Age Pyramid

- A declining age pyramid is characterised by a population structure where the number of individuals in the pre-reproductive phase is smaller than those in the reproductive phase with a significantly fewer than those in the post-reproductive phase.
- This pyramid is **urn-shaped.**

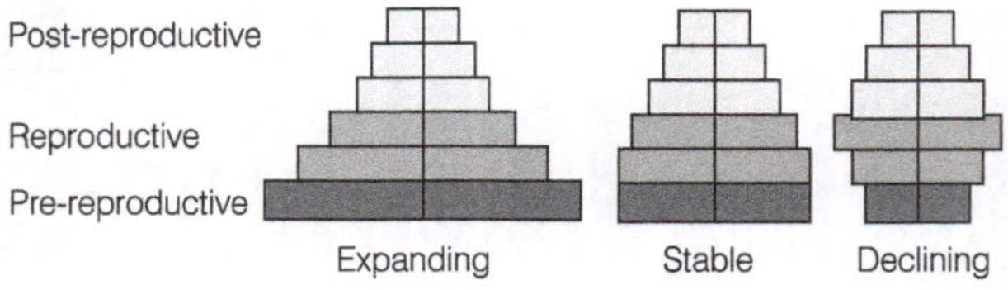

Fig. 11.1 Representation of age pyramids for human populations

Population Growth

- The population size of any species is not a static parameter and keeps on changing with time.
- It depends on the factors such as food availability, predation pressure and adverse weather.
- The density of a population in a given habitat during a given period fluctuates due to the four basic processes. These are as follows
  - **Natality** It refers to the number of births during a given period.
  - **Mortality** It is the number of deaths in the population during a given period.
  - **Immigration** It is the number of individuals of the same species that have come into the habitat from elsewhere during the time period under consideration.
  - **Emigration** It is the number of individuals of the population who left the habitat and moved elsewhere during a given time period.

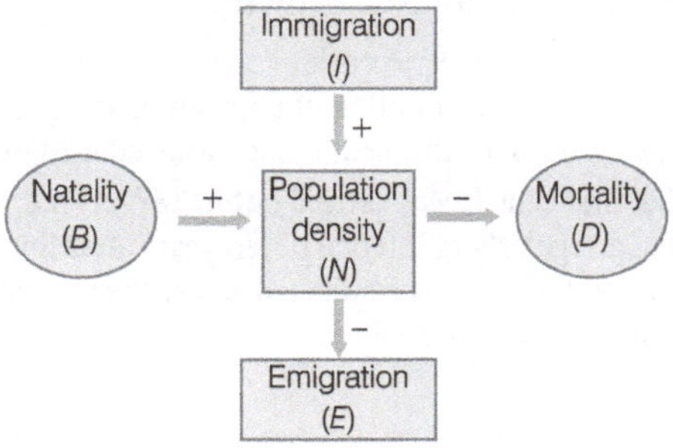

Fig. 11.2 Factors influencing population density

- Out of these four, natality and immigration contribute to an increase in population density.
- While, mortality and emigration contribute to the decrease in population density.
- So, if **N** is the population density at time *t*, then its density at time $t+1$ is

$$N_{t+1} = N_t + [(B+I) - (D+E)]$$

Where, B = Birth rate, I = Immigration, D = Death rate and E = Emigration.

- From the above equation, it can be seen that population density will increase, if $(B+I)$ is more than $(D+E)$.
- Under normal conditions births and deaths are the most important factors influencing population density, the other two factors assuming importance only under special conditions.
- For instance, if a new habitat is just being colonised immigration may contribute more significantly to population growth than birth rates.

Growth Models

- A growth model of a population describes how the size of a population changes over time based on factors like birth rates, death rate, immigration and emigration.
- A population growth model tries to predict how populations will evolve under different environmental conditions.
- The two models of population growth are given below

Exponential Growth

- The availability of resources (food and space) is essential for the growth of population.
- Their unlimited availability results in population's exponential or geometric growth. Each species has the ability to realise fully its innate potential to grow in number as Darwin observed while proposing theory of natural selection.
- The increase or decrease in population size during a unit time period (t) is calculated as

$$dN/dt = (b-d)N$$

Let $(b-d) = r$, then, $dN/dt = rN$

where, N is population size, b is birth per capita, d is death per capita, t is time period and r is intrinsic rate of natural increase.

TEACHER'S TIP

The intrinsic rate of natural increase (r) is a measure of how fast a population is growing. It is calculated as the difference between the birth and death rate.

- The r is an important parameter that assesses the effects of biotic and abiotic factors on population growth.
- It is different for different organisms, e.g. its value is 0.015 for Norway rat and 0.12 for flour beetle.

- In 1981, the value of r for human population in India was 0.0205.
- The equation of exponential growth results in a **J-shaped** curve as shown in the graph

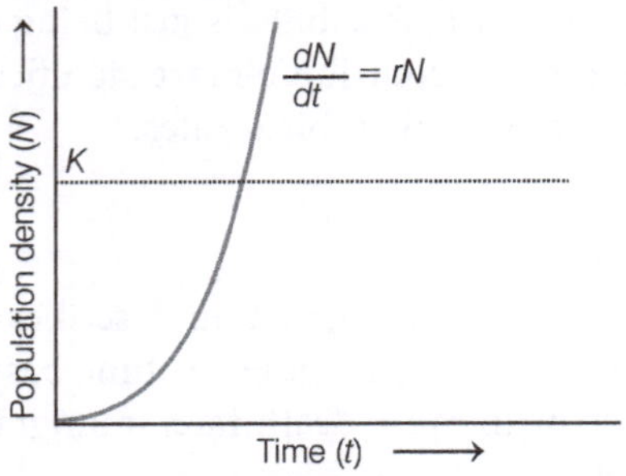

Fig. 11.3 Population growth curve showing exponential growth

- Integral form of exponential growth equation is

$$N_t = N_0 e^{rt}$$

where, N_t = Population density after time t
N_0 = Population density at time zero
r = Intrinsic rate of natural increase
e = Base of natural logarithms (2.71828).

- Any species growing exponentially under unlimited resource conditions without any check, can reach enormous population densities in a short time.

Logistic Growth

- There is no population, of any species, in nature that possess unlimited resources to permit exponential growth.
- This leads to the competition among the individuals and eventually the 'fittest' individual will survive and reproduce.
- In nature, a given habitat has enough resources to support a maximum possible number, beyond which no further growth is possible.
- This is called the **carrying capacity** (K) for the species in that habitat.
- A population growing in a habitat with limited resources shows initially a **lag phase** followed by phases of **acceleration**, **deceleration** and finally an **asymptote**, when the population density reaches the carrying capacity (K).
- When N is plotted in relation to time t, the logistic growth shows **sigmoid curve** and this type of growth is called **Verhulst-Pearl logistic growth**.

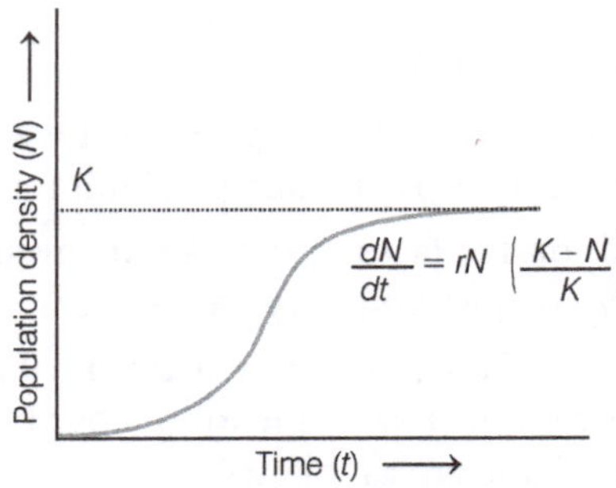

Fig. 11.4 Population growth curve showing logistic growth

It is calculated as

$$dN/dt = rN\left(\frac{K-N}{K}\right)$$

where, N is population density at time t, K is carrying capacity and r is intrinsic rate of natural increase.

- This model is more **realistic** in nature because no population growth can sustain exponential growth indefinitely as there will be competition for the basic needs due to finite resources.
- The human population growth curve follows an **S-shaped**, under logistic growth.

> **Census** is an official counting of population and preparing data about age groups, births, deaths, sex ratio, education, etc.
> In India, first census was carried out in 1872. It has been conducted regularly at interval of ten years after this, the last being in 2011. Census is conducted as per the provisions made under the Census Act, 1948.

Life History Variations

- Populations evolve to maximise their **reproductive fitness** or **Darwinian fitness** (high r value) in the habitat where they live.
- Under a particular set of selection pressures, organisms evolve towards the most efficient reproductive strategy.
- The rate of breeding varies from species to species, such as
  - Some species breed only once in their lifetime, e.g. Pacific salmon fish and bamboo, while some breed many times in their lifetime, e.g. most birds and mammals.
  - Some organisms produce a large number of small-sized offsprings, e.g. oysters and pelagic fishes, whereas others produce a small number of large-sized offsprings, e.g. birds and mammals.

- According to ecologists, life history traits of organisms have evolved in relation to the constraints imposed by the biotic and abiotic components of habitats in which they live.

Quick Test 1

1. In a pond, there were 60 fishes. Through reproduction, 20 more fishes were added in a pond. Calculate the birth rate of the population.
2. In a country where the number of pre-reproductive individuals surpasses that of reproductive individuals, what type of age pyramid would be observed?
3. If individuals begin to leave the habitat, which of the four factors affecting population growth would have the most significant impact?
4. If N is the population density at a time t, mention the formula to show its density at time $t+1$.
5. Give two examples of organism that breed only once in their lifetime.

11.2 Population Interactions

- No natural habitat on earth is inhabited by a single species.
- The minimal requirement for a species is another species on which it can feed upon.
- Even a plant species cannot survive alone. It needs soil microbes to breakdown the organic matter in soil and return the inorganic nutrients for absorption.
- This concludes that in nature, living organisms such as animals, plants and microbes, cannot live in isolation but interact in various ways to form a biological community.
- **Interspecific interactions** arise from the interaction of populations of two different species living together within a community.
- These interactions could be beneficial (+), detrimental (–) or neutral (0) as shown in table

Population Interactions and their Effects

Name of Interactions	Effect on Species A	Effect on Species B
Mutualism	+	+
Competition	–	–
Predation	+	–
Parasitism	+	–
Commensalism	+	0
Amensalism	–	0

Predation

- It is an interspecific interaction, where an animal called **predator** kills and consumes the other weaker animal called **prey**.
- It is the nature's way of transferring energy to higher trophic levels, which is fixed by plants at the first trophic level, e.g. tiger (predator) and deer (prey).
- This is also a biological control method of prey population.
- Important roles of predators are as follows
  - In the absence of predators, prey species could achieve very high population densities and cause ecosystem instability.
    So, besides acting as 'conduits' for energy transfer across trophic levels, predators play very important role in providing population stability.
  - They help in **maintaining species diversity** in a community, by reducing the intensity of competition among competing prey species, e.g. predator starfish *Pisaster* in the rocky intertidal communities of American Pacific Coast.
    In a field experiment, when all the starfish were removed from an enclosed area, more than 10 species of invertebrates became extinct within a year, because of interspecific competition.
  - When certain exotic species are introduced into a geographical area, they become invasive and start spreading fast because the invaded land does not have natural predators, e.g. prickly pear cactus introduced in Australia in early 1920s caused havoc by spreading rapidly into millions of hectares of rangeland. It was brought under control by introducing its predator (i.e. a moth) in the country.
  - This method is used in biological control of weeds and pests, which is based on the prey-regulating ability of the predator.

Defencive Measures of Prey Against Predator

- If a predator is too efficient and over exploits its prey, then the prey might become extinct.
- Following it, the predator will also become extinct because of the lack of food.
- This is why predators are prudent in nature.
- Prey species have evolved various defence mechanisms to lessen the impact of predation. These defense mechanisms are as follows

In Animals

- Some species of insects and frogs are cryptically coloured (**camouflaged**) to avoid being detected easily by the predator.
- Some organisms are poisonous and therefore avoided by the predators. For example
  - Monarch butterfly is highly distasteful to its predators (birds) because of a special chemical present in its body.
  - The butterfly acquires this chemical during its caterpillar stage by feeding on a poisonous weed.

In Plants

- For plants, herbivores are the predators.
- Nearly 25% of all insects are known to be **phytophagous** (feeding on plant sap and other parts of plants). Since, plants cannot run away from their predators unlike animals. So, they have evolved various defences against them, e.g. thorns of *Acacia* and cactus are the most common morphological means of defence.
- Some plants produce highly poisonous chemicals, like **cardiac glycosides** produced by weed *Calotropis*, that makes the herbivore sick. That is why cattlles and goats are never seen browsing on this plant.
- Chemicals like nicotine, caffeine, quinine, strychnine, opium, etc., are actually defence mechanisms against grazers and browsers.

Competition

- It is generally believed to occur when closely related species compete for the same resources that are limiting. However, this is not always true.
- Some totally unrelated species could also compete for the same resources, e.g. in some shallow South American lakes, visiting flamingoes and resident fishes compete for their common food, i.e. **zooplanktons**.
- Resources need not be limiting for competition to occur.
- In **interference competition**, the feeding efficiency of one species might be reduced due to the interferring and inhibitory presence of the other species even if the resources are abundant.
- For example when goats were introduced in **Galapagos Islands**, the **Abingdon tortoise** became extinct within a decade due to greater browsing efficiency of the goats.
- Therefore, competition can be best defined as a process in which the fitness of one species (measured in terms of its *r*, the intrinsic rate of increase) is significantly lower in the presence of another species.

Note Darwin's concept of the struggle for existence and survival of the fittest in nature reflected that interspecific competition is a potent force in organic evolution.

Evidences of Competition

Following are the evidences related to competition

1. Competitive Release

It is a phenomenon, in which a species whose distribution is restricted to a small geographical area because of the presence of a competitively superior species, is found to expand its distributional range dramatically, when the competing species is experimentally removed.

2. Connell's Elegant Field Experiments

It showed that on the rocky sea coasts of Scotland, the larger and competitively superior barnacle *Balanus* dominates the intertidal area and excludes the smaller barnacle *Chathamalus* from that zone.

Gause's competitive exclusion principle states that two closely related species competing for the same resources cannot co-exist indefinitely and the competitively inferior one will be eliminated eventually. This may hold true in case of limited resources, but not in other cases.

Mechanism to Avoid Competition

- **Resource partitioning** is a mechanism evolved by competiting species for co-existence.
- This means that if two species compete for the same resource, they could avoid competition by choosing, for instance, different times of feeding or different foraging patterns.
- In this relation, **MacArthur** showed that five closely related species of warblers living on the same tree were able to avoid competition and co-exist due to behavioural differences in their foraging activities.

Parasitism

- It is the mode of interaction between two species in which one species (parasite) depends on the other species (host) for food and shelter.

- In this process, one organism is benefitted (parasite), while the other is being harmed (host).

Adaptation in Parasite

- Generally parasites are host-specific in which both host and parasite tends to co-evolve.
- This means that if the host evolves special mechanisms for resisting or rejecting a parasite, the latter has to evolve mechanisms to counteract and neutralise them.
- According to its lifestyle, a parasite evolved special adaptations such as
  - Loss of unnecessary sense organs.
  - Presence of adhesive organs or suckers for clinging on to the host.
  - Loss of digestive system.
  - High reproductive capacity.

Life Cycle of Parasite

- The life cycles of parasites are often complex, involving one or two intermediate hosts or vectors to facilitate parasitisation of its primary host. For example,
  - **Human liver fluke** (a trematode parasite) depends on two intermediate hosts (a snail and a fish) to complete its life cycle.
  - **Malarial parasite** (*Plasmodium*) needs a vector (mosquito) to spread to other hosts.

Methods to Harm the Host

Majority of parasites harm the host. The harm is done in the following ways

- They reduce the survival, growth and reproductive ability of the host.
- They reduce its population density.
- They might render the host more vulnerable to predation by making it physically weak.

Types of Parasites

Parasites are broadly divided into following two types

1. Ectoparasites

- They feed on the external surface of the host organism for food and shelter, e.g. lice on humans, ticks on dogs, copepods on marine fishes.
- *Cuscuta*, a parasitic plant that grows on hedge plants loses its chlorophyll and leaves during evolution. It derives its nutrition from the host plant.

2. Endoparasites

- They live inside the host's body at different sites like liver, kidney, lungs, etc., for food and shelter, e.g. tapeworm, liver fluke, *Plasmodium*, etc.
- The life cycles of endoparasites are more complex because of their extreme specialisation.
- Their morphological and anatomical features are generally simplified with emphasising their reproductive potential.

Brood Parasitism

It is an example of parasitism in which one organism (parasite) lays its eggs in the nest of another organism (host) and let the latter to incubate them.

The eggs of parasitic birds have evolved to resemble the host's egg to reduce the chances of host bird detecting and ejecting the parasitic eggs from nest, e.g. cuckoo (koel, parasite) and crow (host) during breeding season (spring to summer).

Commensalism

It is the interaction between two species, where one species is benefitted and the other is neither harmed nor benefitted. Some examples of commensalism are as follows

- An **orchid** growing as an epiphyte on a **mango tree** gets shelter and nutrition from mango tree, while the mango tree is neither benefitted nor harmed.
- **Barnacles** growing on the back of **whale** are benefitted by getting moved to different locations for food as well as shelter, while the whale is neither benefitted nor harmed.
- **Egrets** always forage close to area where the **cattle** are grazing.
  - The cattle egrets are benefitted by the cattle through easy detection of the insects.
  - When the cattle stir up the bushes, insects are flushed out from the vegetation.
  - This makes it easy for the cattle egrets to catch them.
- **Sea anemone** has stinging tentacles and the **clown fish** lives among them.
  - The fish gets protection from predators, which stay away from the stinging tentacles.
  - The anemone does not appear to derive any benefit by hosting the clown fish.

Mutualism

It refers to an symbiotic interaction between two organisms belonging to different species in which both the partners are benefitted.

Some examples of mutualism are as follows

- **Lichens** represent an intimate mutualistic relationship between a fungus and photosynthesising algae or cyanobacteria.

  Here, the fungus helps in the absorption of nutrients and provides protection, while algae prepare the food.
- **Mycorrhizae** is a close mutual association between fungi and the roots of higher plants.

  Fungi help the plant in absorption of nutrients, while the plant provides energy yielding carbohydrates for the fungus, e.g. many members of genus–*Glomus*.
- Plants need help from animals for pollination and dispersal of seeds. In return, plants provide nectar and pollens for pollinators, and fruits to seed dispersers.

To safeguard this mutually beneficial system against cheaters, animals that try to stel nectar without aiding in pollination. The plant-animal interactions involve co-evolution of the mutualists, i.e. the evolution of the flower and its pollinator species are tightly linked with one another. For example,

- In many species of **fig** there is a tight one-to-one relationship with pollinator species of **wasp**.
- It means that a given fig species can be pollinated only by its partner wasp species and no other species. The female wasp uses the fruit as an oviposition (egg-laying) site, and also uses the developing seeds within the fruit for nourishing its larvae.

  In return, the wasp pollinates the fig inflorescence, while searching for suitable egg-laying sites.
- **Mediterranean orchid** *Ophrys* employs 'sexual deceit' to get pollinated by a species of bee.
  - One petal of its flower bears an uncanny resemblance to the female of the bee in size, colour and markings.
  - The male bee is attracted to what it perceives as a female and 'pseudocopulates' with the flower.
  - During this process, pollens are dusted from the flower onto the male bee.
  - When the same bee pseudocopulates with another flower, it transfers pollens to it and thus pollinates the flower.
- Here, both the species show co-evolution, i.e. if the female bee's colour patterns change even slightly for any reason during evolution, pollination success will be reduced unless the orchid flower co-evolves to maintain the resemblance of its petal to the female bee.

Quick Test 2

1. In an area, if two species choose different foraging patterns to avoid competition, what ecological mechanism is this?
2. **State True or False.**

   In the presence of limited resources, the competitively superior species will always eliminate the other species.
3. Name two intermediate host on which the human liver fluke depends to complete its life cycle as to facilitate parasitisation of its primary host.
4. Name the interaction that exist between barnacles and whale.
5. If an organism relies on its host for a period of time, can this relationship be classified as mutualism?

Mind Map

Organisms and Populations

Organisms and Its Environment

Ecology

- Branch of biology that studies the interactions among organisms and its abiotic environment.
- It is basically concerned with
  - **Organisms** Basic unit of ecological hierarchy.
  - **Population** Organisms of same kind capable of interbreeding among themselves.
  - **Communities** Assemblage of different species of population in an area.
  - **Biomes** Large unit, consist of major vegetation type and associated fauna.

Age Pyramids

- It is the age distribution of per cent individuals of a given age (or age group) plotted for the population.
- The growth status of the population is reflected by the shape of age pyramid as expanding, stable or declining.

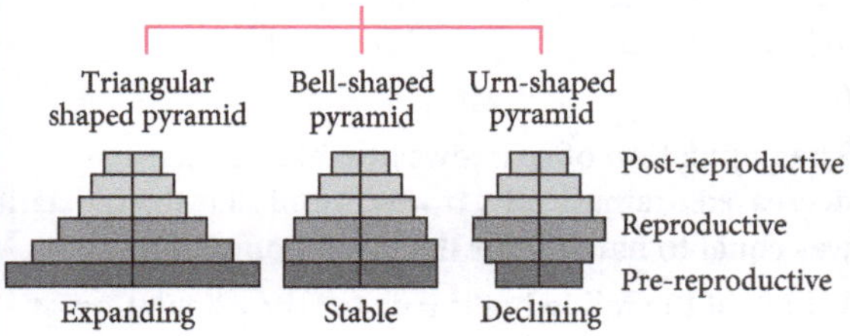

Population Interactions

Interspecific interactions occur between populations of two different species living together within a community. These interactions could be

Positive
- Mutualism
- Commensalism

Negative
- Competition
- Predation
- Parasitism

Species A	Species B	Name of Interaction
+	+	Mutualism
–	–	Competition
+	–	Predation
+	–	Parasitism
+	0	Commensalism

Population Size

Generally represented an number of individuals in a population.

Population Attributes

- Population Density (D) = $\frac{\text{Number of individuals in a region } [N]}{\text{Size of unit area in a region } [S]}$
- Natality (Birth rate)
- Mortality (Death rate)
- Sex ratio

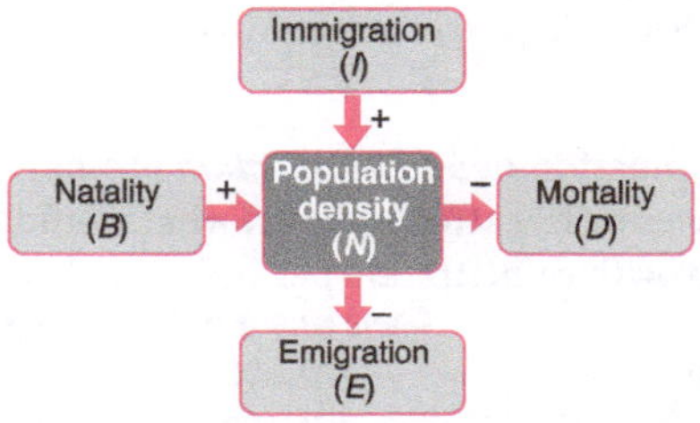

Population Growth

- Size of a population keeps on changing due to food availability, predation pressure and weather.
- Density of a population [N] in a given habitat during a given period fluctuates due to natality [B], mortality [D], immigration [I] and emigration [E].
- $N_{t+1} = N_t + [(B + I) - (D + E)]$

Growth Models

Exponential (unrestricted) Growth	Logistic (restricted) Growth
• Unlimited resources	• Limited resources
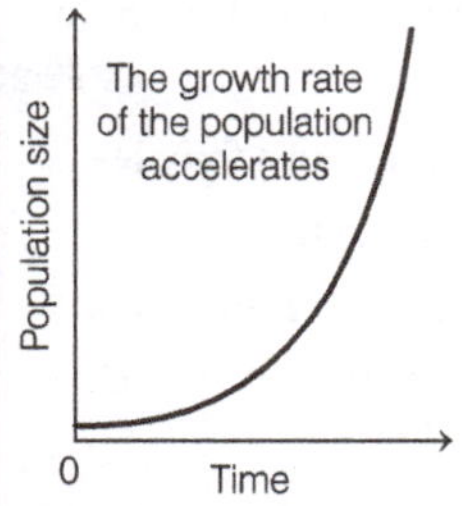	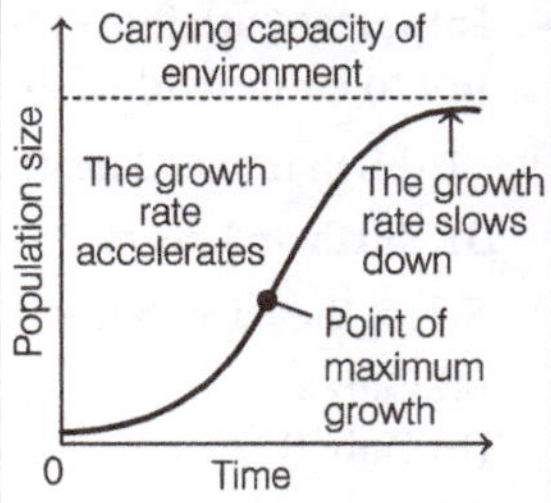
• Mathematically, expressed as $N_t = N_o e^{rt}$	• Mathematically, expressed as $dN/dt = rN\left(\frac{K-N}{K}\right)$
• J- shaped curve	• Sigmoid curve

EXAM PATTERN QUESTIONS

Objective Type Questions

Multiple Choice Questions

1. Population ecology is an important area of ecology because it links

(a) ecology to population genetics and evolution
(b) ecology to biochemistry
(c) ecology to global ecology and deep ecology
(d) global ecology to community ecology

Ans. (*a*)

2. If a population of 50 *Paramecium* present in a pool increases to 150 after an hour, what would be the per cent growth or birth rate per individual per hour? Competency Based Que., NCERT Exemplar

(a) 100 (b) 200
(c) 50 (d) 150

Ans. (*b*) Birth rate

$$= \frac{\text{Number of births in a given time period}}{\text{Initial population}} \times 100$$

$$= \frac{150-50}{50} \times 100 = 200\%$$

Therefore, the birth rate per individual per hour is 200%.

3. Which of the following does not relate to population attributes?

(a) Mortality (b) Number of educated people
(c) Sex ratio (d) Population size

Ans. (*b*)

4. Important attributes belonging to a population, but not to an individual are CBSE 2023

I. birth rate and death rate II. male and female
III. birth and death IV. sex ratio

Select the correct answer from the given options.

(a) Only I (c) II and III
(b) Only II (d) I and IV

Ans. (*d*)

5. A biologist studied the population of rats in a barn. He found that the average natality was 250, average mortality 240, immigration 20 and emigration 30. The net increase in population is Competency Based Que.

(a) 15 (b) 0
(c) 10 (d) 5

Ans. (*b*)

6. Match the following columns.

Column I (Attributes of Population Growth)		Column II (Features)	
A.	Mortality	1.	Individuals of same species going out from population.
B.	Immigration	2.	Individuals of same species coming in population.
C.	Emigration	3.	Numbers of deaths in population during given period.

Codes

	A	B	C		A	B	C
(a)	1	3	2	(b)	2	3	1
(c)	3	2	1	(d)	2	1	3

Ans. (*c*)

7. The population of sparrows inhabiting a garden decreased dramatically. It was found that the mortality was equal to natality for the given population.

Which of the following is true for the population of sparrows? Competency Based Que.

(a) The number of emigrants was equal to immigrants.
(b) The number of emigrants was less than immigrants.
(c) The number of emigrants was more than immigrants.
(d) The population of sparrows was unaffected by emigrants and immigrants.

Ans. (*c*) Since, mortality equals natality, the population should remain stable. However, the population decreased dramatically, which suggests that more sparrows were leaving (emigrating) than entering (immigrating), causing the population to decline.

8. A population has more young individuals compared to the older individuals. What would be the status of the population after some years? NCERT Exemplar

(a) It will decline
(b) It will stabilise
(c) It will increase
(d) It will first decline and then stabilise

Ans. (*c*) A population of more young individual than older individuals, will show positive growth in future, i.e. it will increase after some time.

9. The bell-shaped polygonal pyramid indicates

(a) low percentage of pre-reproductive individuals
(b) low percentage of young individuals
(c) high percentage of old individuals
(d) moderate percentage of young individuals

Ans. (*d*)

10. In 2005, for each of the 14 million people present in a country, 0.028 were born and 0.008 died during the year. Using exponential equation, the number of people present in 2015 is predicted as NCERT Exemplar

(a) 25 millions (b) 17 millions
(c) 20 millions (d) 18 millions

Ans. (*b*) Exponential equation

$dN/dt = (b-d)N$

$dN/10 = (0.028 - 0.008) \times 14$

$dN/10 = 0.28$

$dN = 0.28 \times 10$

$dN = 2.8$

= 14 million + 2.8 million

= 16.8 million or 17 million

11. Logistic growth is represented by which of the following equation?

(a) $\frac{dN}{dt} = rN\left[\frac{K-N}{K}\right]$ (b) $\frac{dN}{dt} = rN\left[\frac{K}{K+N}\right]$

(c) $\frac{dN}{dt} = rN\left[\frac{K-N}{N}\right]$ (d) $\frac{dN}{dt} = rN\left[\frac{K+N}{K}\right]$

Ans. (*a*)

12. A population growth curve is given below. It indicates

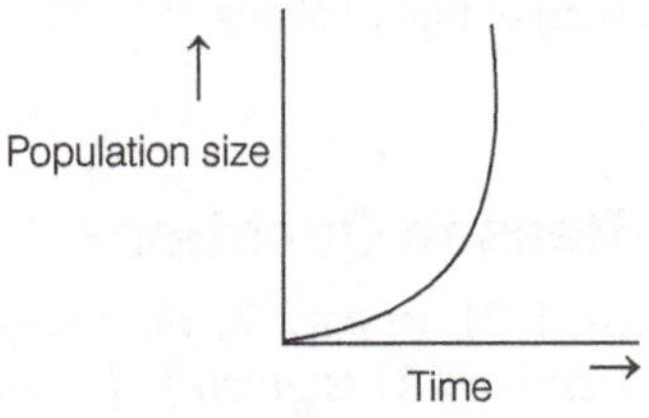

(a) Exponential growth curve
(b) Logistic growth pattern
(c) J-shaped curve
(d) Both (a) and (c)

Ans. (*d*)

13. Logistic growth occurs when there is

(a) no resistance from increasing population
(b) unlimited food
(c) fixed carrying capacity
(d) All of the above

Ans. (*c*)

14. The equation of the exponential growth curve of the population has 'r' which is

(a) extrinsic rate of natural increase
(b) an important parameter for assessing impacts of only biotic factors on population growth
(c) for Norway rat, it values 0.15
(d) for flour beetle, it values 0.12

Ans. (*d*)

15. Which is correctly labelled as per the given diagram?

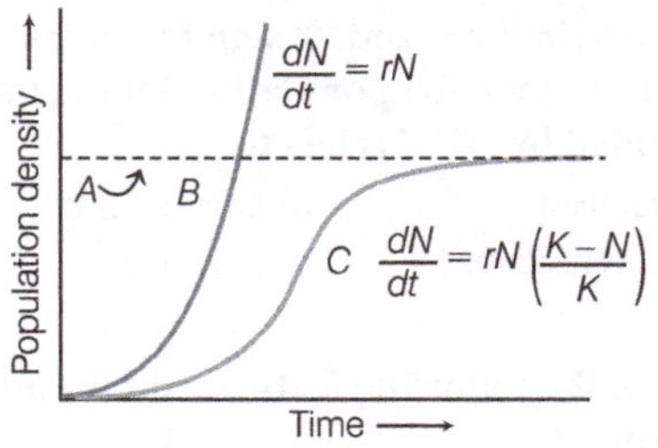

(a) *B*–Logistic curve
(b) *C*–Carrying capacity
(c) *C*–Exponential curve
(d) *A*–Carrying capacity

Ans. (*d*)

16. Choose the incorrect match for the life history variations in various organisms.

(a) Breeds only once in their life – Pacific salmon fish
(b) Produce small number of large sized offspring – Mammals
(c) Breeds many time during lifetime –Mammals
(d) Produce large number of small sized offspring – Birds

Ans. (*d*)

17. The Abingdon tortoise in Galapagos Island became extinct within a decade after goats were introduced on the Island due to Competency Based Que.

(a) superiority of goats
(b) greater browsing efficiency of goats
(c) higher value
(d) competitve release

Ans. (*b*)

18. Through resource partitioning

(a) two species can compete for the same prey
(b) slight variation in the niche allow closely related species to co-exist in the same habitat
(c) competitive exclusion results in the success of superior species
(d) two species undergo character displacement

Ans. (*b*)

19. Which of the following showed that five closely related species of warblers living on the same tree were able to avoid competition and co-exist due to behavioural difference in their foraging activities?

(a) Gause's competitive exclusion
(b) Mac Arthur's resource partitioning
(c) Gause's resource partitioning
(d) Mac Arthur's competitive exclusion

Ans. (*b*)

20. If '+' sign is assigned to beneficial interaction, '–' sign to detrimental and '0' sign to neutral interaction, then the population interaction represented by '+' '–' refers to

(a) mutualism (b) amensalism
(c) commensalism (d) parasitism

Ans. (*d*)

21. Which of the following features are the adaptations in parasites? **Competency Based Que.**

I. Loss of unnecessary organs.
II. Presence of adhesive organs.
III. Origin of suckers to cling to host.
IV. Loss of digestive system.
V. High reproductive capacity.

Choose the correct option.

(a) I, III and IV (b) II, IV and V
(c) I, IV and V (d) I, II, III, IV and V

Ans. (*d*)

22. Many copepods live on the body surface of marine fish. This relationship is an example of **CBSE 2023**

(a) commensalism (b) parasitism
(c) amensalism (d) mutualism

Ans. (*b*)

23. Select the statement which explains best parasitism. **NCERT**

(a) One organism is benefitted.
(b) Both the organisms are benefitted.
(c) One organism is benefitted, other is not affected.
(d) One organism is benefitted, other is affected.

Ans. (*d*)

24. Interaction between clown fish living among the stinging tentacles of sea anemone is an example of **CBSE 2023**

(a) amensalism (b) parasitism
(c) mutualism (d) commensalism

Ans. (*d*)

25. The population interaction where one species is harmed and the other is unaffected is

(a) Amensalism (b) Commensalism
(c) Parasitism (d) Predation

Ans. (*a*)

26. The black walnut plant secretes juglone, a chemical substance that destroys other plants like pepper growing within its root zone. Which type of population interaction does the above statement represent? **Competency Based Que.**

(a) Predation
(b) Competition
(c) Mutualism
(d) Amensalism

Ans. (*d*)

27. Amensalism is an association between two species where **NCERT Exemplar**

(a) one species is harmed and other is benefitted
(b) one species is harmed and other is unaffected
(c) one species is benefitted and other is unaffected
(d) Both the species are harmed.

Ans. (*b*) When one species is harmed and other is unaffected, in an association between two species, it is called amensalism.

28. A tight one-to-one relationship between many species of fig tree and certain wasps is an example of **CBSE 2023**

(a) commensalism
(b) parasitism
(c) amensalism
(d) mutualism

Ans. (*d*)

29. Mycorrhiza represents an intimate mutualistic relationship between

(a) fungi and stem of higher plants
(b) fungi and roots of higher plants
(c) algae and roots of higher plants
(d) algae and stem of higher plants

Ans. (*b*)

Assertion-Reason Questions

Direction (Q. Nos. 1-7) *In each of the following questions, a statement of Assertion (A) is given followed by corresponding statement of Reason (R). Of the statements, mark the correct answer as.*

(a) Both A and R are true and R is the correct explanation of A
(b) Both A and R are true, but R is not the correct explanation of A
(c) A is true, but R is false
(d) A is false, but R is true

1. Assertion (A) Natality rate increases the population size and population density.

Reason (R) Natality increases the number of individuals in an area by births.

Ans. (*a*)

2. Assertion (A) In nature, animals, plants and microbes cannot live in isolation.

Reason (R) For any species, the minimal requirement is one more species on which it can feed.

Ans. (*a*)

3. Refer to the figure given below and comment upon the appropriateness of Assertion and Reason.

Assertion (A) Predation is an interspecific interaction with a feeding strategy.

Reason (R) Predators and their prey maintain fairly stable population through time and rarely one population become abundant or scarce.

Ans. (*b*)

4. Assertion (A) Brood parasitism is a reproductive strategy observed in certain species.

Reason (R) In brood parasitism, the parasitic bird lays its eggs in the nest of another species, relying on the host species to incubate and raise its chick.

Ans. (*a*)

5. Assertion (A) The life cycle of parasites are often complex.

Reason (R) They involve two or more intermediate hosts to facilitate parasitisation.

Ans. (*a*)

6. Assertion (A) Fig species and wasp shows tightly linked relationship.

Reason (R) Angiosperms and insects are co-evolved to perform a plant pollinator interaction.

Ans. (*b*)

7. Assertion (A) In commensalism, one organism is benefitted and other is unaffected.

Reason (R) Cattle egret bird and cattle is an example of commensalism.

Ans. (*b*)

Subjective Questions

Very Short Answer Type Questions

1. List the attributes that populations possess, but not individuals. NCERT

Ans. Birth rate, death rate, population density and sex ratio are the attributes that population possess, but not individuals.

2. Provide an instance where the population size of species can be estimated indirectly, without actually counting them or seeing them.

Ans. Tiger population in national parks is based on pug marks.

3. Sex ratio is defined as the number of females per 1000 males in the population. It is important to know about sex ratio. Give reason.

Ans. It is important to know about sex ratio because it is an important social indicator to measure the extent of equality between males and females at a given time in the society.

4. Factors like immigration and emigration collectively determine the growth of a population. Comment. Competency Based Que.

Ans. Populations gain individuals through birth and immigration and lose individuals through deaths and emigration. Thus, the two factors immigration and emigration collectively determine the rate of population growth. (½ × ½)

5. What would be the growth rate pattern, when the resources are unlimited? NCERT Exemplar

Ans. In case of unlimited resources, the pattern of growth rate is exponential.

6. Write the mathematical equation for the following graph.

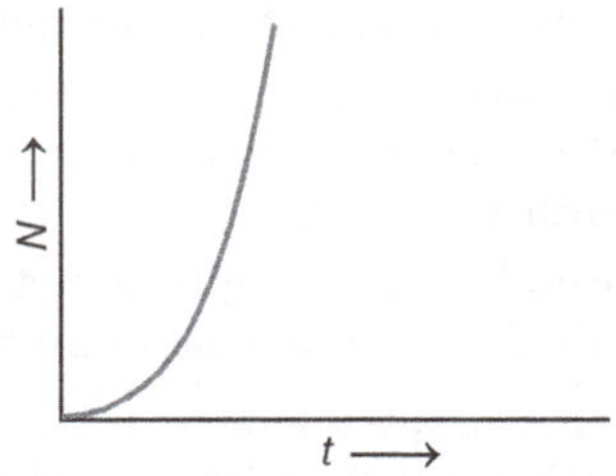

Ans. Exponential equation for J-shaped growth form is

$$\frac{dN}{dt} = rN$$

where, dN/dt is the rate of change in population size, 'r' is intrinsic rate of natural increase and 'N' is the population size.

7. What would be the growth rate pattern when the resources are limited?

Ans. Logistic growth.

8. Define the terms 'acceleration' and 'deceleration' with respect to logistic growth curve of population.

Ans. **Acceleration** Increasing rate of populations.

Deceleration Decreasing rate of populations. (½ × 2)

9. What are the organisms that feed on plant sap and other plant parts called? NCERT Exemplar

Ans. The organisms that feed on plant sap and other parts of plants are termed as phytophagous.

10. Why the *Calotropis* plants are not grazed by goats and cattle? Competency Based Que.

Or **Cattle and goats do not browse the *Calotropis* plant. Justify the statement giving reason.** CBSE 2023

Ans. *Calotropis* produces highly poisonous cardiac glycosides that can make the herbivore sick and hence they are not grazed by goats and cattle.

11. Why did the Abingdon tortoise in Galapagos Island become extinct?

Ans. Abingdon tortoise became extinct due to greater browsing efficiency of goats that were introduced in Galapagos Island.

12. State Gause's competitive exclusion principle.

Ans. Gause's competitive exclusion principle states that two closely related species competing for the same resources cannot co-exist indefinitely and the competitively inferior one will be eliminated eventually by the superior one.

13. Do only closely related species compete for same resources? If no, comment. Competency Based Que.

Ans. No, some totally unrelated species can also compete for the same resources, e.g. in some shallow South American lake visiting flamingoes and resident fishes compete for a common food, i.e. zooplanktons.

14. Mention how closely related species of warblers are able to co-exist in a competitive environment.

Ans. The warblers species are able to co-exist in a competitive environment due to behavioural differences in their foraging activities.

15. What is the ecological principle behind the biological control method of managing pest insects? NCERT

Ans. The ecological principle behind the biological control of pest insects is based on the ability of predator to reduce prey population in a habitat.

16. State the type of interaction that exists between ticks and dogs.

Ans. Parasitism (Ectoparasite).

17. Give the name of two parasitic plants and two parasitic animals.

Ans. Parasitic plants are *Cuscuta* and *Viscum* and parasitic animals are mites and lice. (½ + ½)

18. Give a suitable example for commensalism. NCERT Exemplar

Ans. An interaction between blue whale and the barnacle growing on its back is an example of commensalism between them.

19. What advantage does the sea anemone get in the sea anemone-hermit crab interaction as facultative mutualism?

Ans. The sea anemone is transported on the back of hermit crab for reaching new food sources.

20. Name the association between fungus and roots of higher plants.

Ans. Mutualism.

Short Answer Type Questions

1. Define population and community. NCERT

Ans. A population is a group individuals of the same species living in the same area.

A community is a group individuals of different species living in the same area. (1+1)

2. List any three important characteristics of a population and explain. NCERT

Ans. Refer to text on page no. 325-326.

3. Population density need not necessarily be measured in numbers only. Explain.

Ans. Refer to text on page no. 326.

4. What are the different attributes of population? What is meant by sex ratio? Is it a characteristic of an individual or a population?

Ans. Refer to text on page no. 325-326.

5. The following diagrams are the age pyramids of different populations. Comment on the status of these populations. NCERT Exemplar

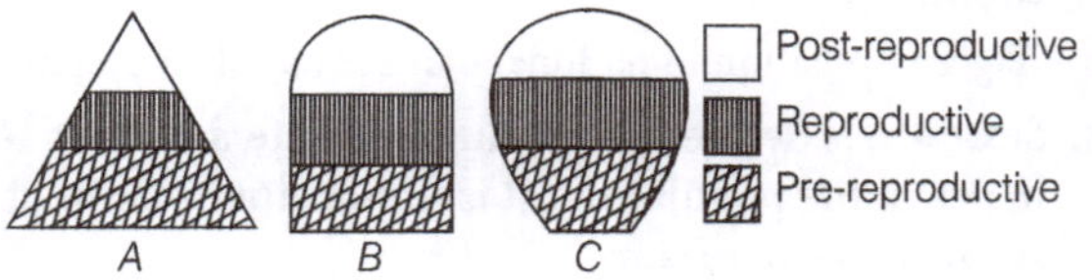

Ans. **Figure** *A* It is a triangular shaped age pyramid. In this figure, the base, i.e. pre-reproductive stage is very large as compared to the reproductive and post-reproductive stages of the population. This type of age structure indicates that the population would increase rapidly.

Figure *B* It is an bell-shaped pyramid. In this figure, the number of individuals pre-reproductive and reproductive stages are same. This type of age structure indicates that the population is stable.

Figure *C* It is an urn-shaped pyramid. In the figure, the number of individuals in pre-reproductive stage are less than the reproductive stages. In this population, more older people are present. This type of age structure indicates that the population definitely is declining. (1 × 3)

6. Analysis of age pyramids for human population can provide important inputs for long terms planning strategies. Explain. **Competency Based Que.**

Ans. When a population at any given time is plotted against the age distribution, the resulting structure is called age pyramid.

The shape of the pyramids shows the growth of the population whether it is growing, stable or declining. Age pyramids show age distribution of males and females in a combined diagram. Pyramid also indicate the ratio of pre-reproductive, reproductive, post-reproductive individuals in a population.

Refer to fig. 11.1 on page no. 326. (½ + 1½)

7. Study the three different pyramids for human population given below and answer the following questions. **Competency Based Que.**

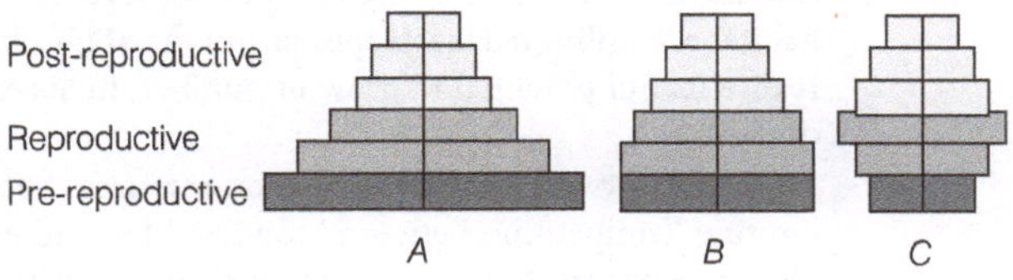

(i) **Write the names given to each of these age pyramids.**

(ii) **Mention the one which is ideal for human population and why?**

(iii) **What would be the growth rate pattern when the resources are limited?**

Ans. (i) *A*-Expanding pyramid,
B- Stable pyramid
C-Declining pyramid

(ii) Stable pyramid is ideal for human population because it maintain the stability in all phases.

(iii) When resources are limited the growth rate of population follows a pattern called logistic growth. (1 × 3)

8.

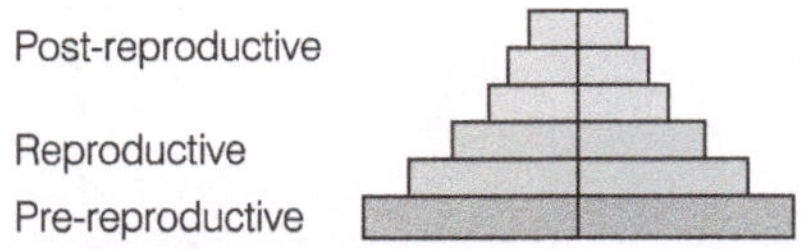

Identify the type of pyramid given above. Write the identifying features on the basis of which you identified it. **CBSE 2022 Term II**

Ans. The type of pyramid given is expanding. This type of pyramid is triangle in shape and depicts populations with higher percentage of pre-reproductive or younger people in the age groups. (1)

The identifying features of the pyramid are as follows

(i) Birth rate
(ii) Reproductive rate
(iii) Number of old age people (1)

9. List any four characteristics that are employed in human population census. **NCERT Exemplar**

Ans. A population has the following characteristics that are employed in human population census

(i) Natality and mortality
(ii) Sex ratio
(iii) Population density
(iv) Age distribution (½ × 4)

10. As per a recent newspaper report, a particular country showed declining population growth rate. According to you, what could be the two most possible reasons for this decline and why?
Competency Based Que., CBSE 2022 Term II

Ans. Growth rate refers to the percentage change of a specific variable within a specific time period. In case of declining population growth rate, the two possible reasons could be

(i) **Death Rate** (mortality) Number of deaths during a given period. This affects the overall population of a country. Increasing death rate could be due to several factors like bad medical services, etc.

(ii) **Emigration** It is the number of individuals of a population who left the habitat and gone elsewhere in search of food, jobs or many other factors. (1+1)

11.

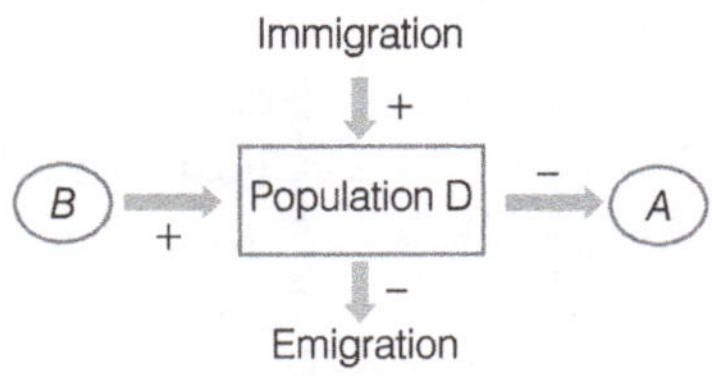

Observe the schematic representation given and answer the following questions.

(i) **Identify** ***A*** **and** ***B*****.**

(ii) **Calculate the growth rate of bacteria in a curd sample, where 1 million bacteria increased to 2 million, within a period of one hour.**
Competency Based Que., CBSE 2022 Term II

Ans. (i) *A* – Mortality, *B* – Natality (½ + ½)

(ii) Given that number of bacteria (initially) = 10,00,000
Final number of bacteria = 20,00,000
Time taken for doubling = 60 minutes (1 hour)
Growth rate can be calculated by the formula

$$N_t = N_o \times (1+r)^t$$

where, N_t = amount at time 't'
N_o = amount at time 0
r = growth rate
t = time passed

$$\Rightarrow 20{,}00{,}000 = 10{,}00{,}000 \times (1+r)^t$$
$$\Rightarrow 2 = (1+r)^{60} = (1+r) = (2)^{1/60}$$
$$r = (2)^{1/60} - 1$$
$$\Rightarrow r = 0.0116$$ (1)

12. If a population growing exponentially doubles in size in three years. What is the intrinsic rate increase (*r*) of the population? **Competency Based Que., NCERT**

Ans. In case of exponential growth of population,

$$N_t = N_0 e^{rt} \quad ..(i)$$

where, N_t = Population density at time t

N_0 = Population density before time t.

r = Intrinsic rate of increase.

We can also write equation (i) as $\frac{N_t}{N_0} = e^{rt}$

Given, $\frac{N_t}{N_0} = 2, t = 3$ yrs $\Rightarrow 2 = e^{rt}$

Taking $\log_e$ on both sides,

$ln\, 2 = rt \quad [\log_e = ln; ln\, e^x = x]$

$$\Rightarrow r = \frac{ln\, 2}{t}$$
$$= \frac{ln\, 2}{3} = \frac{0.69314}{3} = 00.23104$$

Intrinsic increase rate (r %) = 0.23104 × 100 = 23.10%.

13. The graphs given below, *A* and *B* represent population of elephants in two different National Parks (a hypothetical situation) at different times.

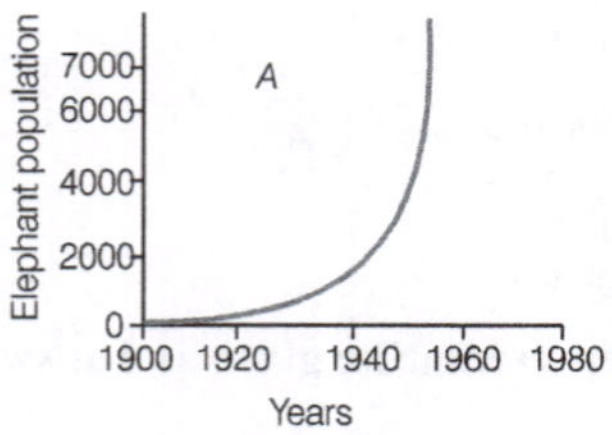

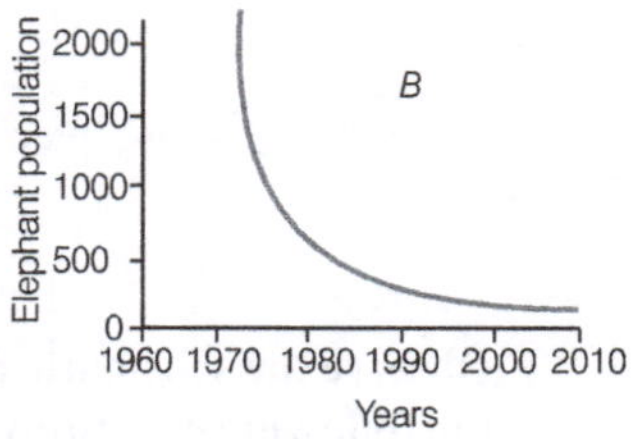

Study the graphs and comment upon the pattern of growth observed. Mention the possible reason for such patterns seen in nature.
Competency Based Que., CBSE 2022 Term II

Ans. In graph *A* the population of elephants shows an increase in number with increasing years or timespan.

Reasons for increase in elephant population (graph *A*) could be

- Afforestation
- Ban on illegal poaching activities. (1½)

In graph *B* the situation is just opposite to that shown in graph *A*. With the increasing timespan, the population of elephants has first shows a decline and then a constant growth rate (from year 2000 to 2010).

Possible reasons for decreasing population (graph *B*) could be

- Habitat loss and fragmentation
- Hunting and poaching (1½)

14. Study the population growth curve given below and answer the questions that follows.

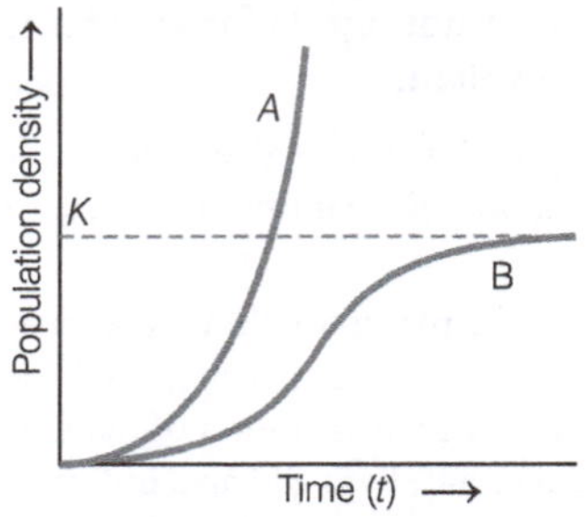

(i) Identify *A* and *B* in the graph.

(ii) When and why do such curves occur in a population?

Ans. (i) *A*-Exponential growth curve, *B*-Logistic growth curve (½ + ½)

(ii) *A*-Exponential growth curve exists when resources (food/space) are not limiting or when resources in the habitat are unlimited, each species has the ability to realise its full potential to grow in number, in absence of checks.

B-Logistic growth curves exists when resources become limiting, competition between individual for limited resources occurs, the fittest individuals will survive and reproduce. (2)

15. Logistic model is more realistic is nature. Justify.

Ans. Refer to text on page no. 328.

16. Study the table showing the population interaction between species *Z* and *Y*, respectively. Assign the appropriate +/– signs for *A*, *B*, *D*, *E* and respective interactions for *C* and *F*. **CBSE 2020**

Species Z	Species Y	Name of Interaction
A	*B*	Mutualism
–	–	*C*
D	*E*	Parasitism
+	0	*F*

(½ × 6)

Ans.

Species Z	Species Y	Name of Interaction
+(*A*)	+ (*B*)	Mutualism
–	–	Competition (*C*)
+ (*D*)	– (*E*)	Parasitism
+	0	Commensalism (*F*)

17. Fill in the blanks. **NCERT Exemplar**

Species A	Species B	Types of Interaction	Examples
+	−	____	____
+	+	____	____
+	____	Commensalism	____

Ans.

Species A	Species B	Types of Interaction	Examples
+	−	Predation	Phytophagous animal and plants.
+	+	Mutualism	Mycorrhiza
+	0	Commensalism	An orchid growing as an epiphyte on a mango tree.

(½ × 6)

18. Why are predators considered to be 'prudent' in nature? Explain. **CBSE 2022 Term II**

Ans. Refer to text on page no. 329-330.

19. What is 'predation'? Explain with the help of suitable examples.

Ans. **Predation** is an interaction where one organism (predator) kills and eats the other weaker organism called prey. Predation is a natural way of transferring the energy fixed by plants, to higher trophic levels. Examples of predation include snake eating a frog, tiger killing and eating a deer. Predators keep prey population under control which otherwise could achieve very high population densities and cause instability in ecosystem.

They also help in maintaining a species diversity in a community by reducing the intensity of competition among competing prey species. (1+2)

20. 'Some species of insects and frogs have evolved with various specific features that help them from being detected.' **CBSE 2023**

(i) Justify the statement giving reasons.

(ii) Mention any two such features.

Ans. (i) This is done when predator is too efficient and over exploits its prey. The prey species, thus evolves various defence mechanism to lessen the impact of predation. For example, some species of insects and frogs avoid being detected easily by the predators by camouflage technique. (1)

(ii) Two other such features are given below

(a) Some species become poisonous and therefore avoided by the predators. For example, the monarch butterfly that is highly distasteful to its predators.

(b) Nearly, 25% of all insects are known to be phytophagous (feeding on plant sap and other parts of plants). So, plants evolved various defences against them, e.g. thorns of *Acacia* and cactus are the most common morphological means of defence. (1+1)

21. Name important defence mechanisms in plants against herbivory. **NCERT**

Ans. Refer to text on page no. 329-330.

22. 'Abingdon tortoise in Galapagos Islands became extinct within a decade on introduction of goats in the Island.' Explain giving reason. **CBSE 2023**

Ans. The competitive exclusion principle state that two species competing for same limiting resources cannot coexist. Eventually one will outcompete the other and drive it to extinction.

For example, tortoises greatly depended upon the grass of the Galapagos Islands for their food. On the introduction of goats, the goats competed in their eating habits with the tortoises and consumed the grasses more rapidly than the tortoises. As a result, there was less food available for the tortoises to eat and they slowly died out of hunger and became extinct.

23. (i) Diagram given below depicts different species of warbler birds feeding on different regions on a spruce tree. Explain the mechanism which helps them to co-exist. **Competency Based Que.**

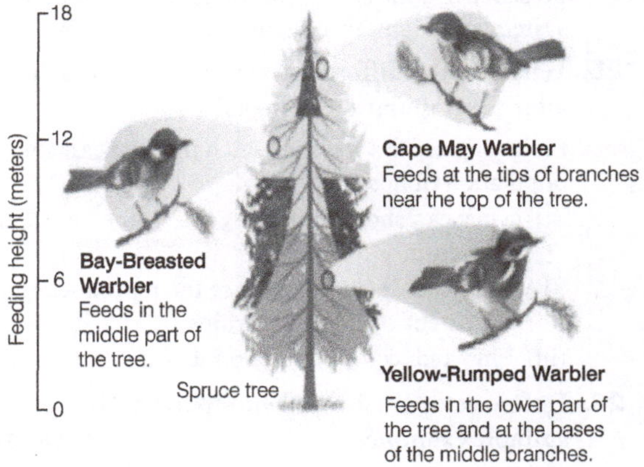

(ii) What does Gause's exclusion principle state? Does it apply in the case shown above? Explain. **CBSE SQP 2024**

Ans. (i) They are able to co-exist by the mechanism of 'resource partitioning'. The two species competing for the same resource can avoid competition by choosing different foraging patterns.

MacArthur showed that five closely related species of warblers living on the same tree were able to avoid competition and co-exist due to behavioural differences in their foraging activities. (1½)

(ii) Gause's Competitive Exclusion Principle' states that two closely related species competing for the same resources cannot co-exist indefinitely and the competitively inferior one will be eliminated eventually.
No, it does not apply in the case shown above because the warbler species are not competing for the same exact resources in the same niche. Instead, they are utilising different parts of the spruce tree and are thus able to co-exist without one species outcompeting the others. (1½)

24. Explain co-evolution with reference to parasites and their hosts. Mention any four special adaptive features evolved in parasites for their parasitic mode of life.

Or

Explain parasitism and co-evolution with the help of one example of each.

Ans. Co-evolution is a phenomenon where many parasites have evolved to be host-specific in such a way that both the host and the parasite tend to co-evolve, i.e. if the host develops/ evolves special mechanism for rejecting or resisting the parasite, latter has to evolve mechanism to counteract and neutralise them to succeed with the same host species, e.g. malarial parasite.
Parasites have special adaptations according to their lifestyles such as; loss of unnecessary sense organs, presence of adhesive organs or suckers, loss of digestive system and high reproductive system.

25. What are the different ways in which parasite can alter the population of hosts?

Ans. Following are the ways in which parasite can alter the population of host
(i) They can shorten the life cycle of the host and can weaken it.
(ii) They can drastically reduce the reproduction rate to the extent of causing sterility.
(iii) They reduce its population density. (1 × 3)

26. Define ectoparasite and endoparasite and give suitable examples. NCERT Exemplar

Ans. Ectoparasite feeds on the external surface of the host organism, e.g. lice on humans and ticks on dogs. Many marine fishes are infested with ectoparasitic copepods.
Endoparasite live inside the host body at different sites (liver, kidney, lungs, red blood cells, etc.), such as malarial parasite *P. vivax*, gut parasites, i.e. tapeworm. (1½ × 2)

27. Explain 'brood parasitism' with the help of an example.

Ans. Brood parasitism is a natural phenomenon in which the parasitic bird lays its egg in the nest of its host and let the host incubate them.
Example cuckoo (koel) lays their egg in the nest of crow which resemble the host's egg in size and colour/Any other correct example.

28. An orchid plant is growing on the branch of mango tree. How do you describe this interaction between the orchid and mango tree? NCERT

Ans. Orchid is an epiphytic plant that grows on a mango tree branch and they together show commensalism. In this interaction, orchid is benefitted and the mango tree is neither harmed nor benefitted at all.

29. (i) Give an example of a genus of fungi that forms mycorrhizal association with plants.
(ii) How does the plant drive benefits from this association? CBSE 2023

Ans. (i) The fungi which belongs to genus–*Glomus* forms mycorrhiza.
(ii) The symbiotic association between fungi and plants are called as mycorrhiza in which fungi absorbs phosphorus from soil which is then used by plants as nutrients. (1 × 2)

30. Name and explain the type of interaction that exists in mycorrhizae and between cattle egret and grazing cattle.

Ans. Mycorrhizae is an association between fungi and roots of higher plants. It is an example of mutualism. The fungi help plant in the absorption of essential nutrients from the soil, while in turn plant provides the fungi with energy yielding carbohydrates. Both partners are benefitted.
The cattle egret and grazing cattle share commensalism type of relationship. The grazing cattle flush out insects from grass while grazing. So, it becomes easier for egret to catch and feed on them. In this, one partner gets benefitted, while other remains unaffected. (1½ × 2)

31. Describe the mutual relationship between the fig tree and wasp and comment on the phenomenon that operates in their relationship.

Or **Explain how the interaction between a fig tree and its tight one to one relationship with the pollinator species of wasp is one of the best examples of mutualism.** CBSE 2025

Ans. The relationship between fig tree and wasp shows mutualism. The wasp while searching for sites to lay its eggs, pollinates the fig's inflorescence.
On the other hand, the fig not only provides shelter (fruit) for oviposition, but also allows wasp's larva to feed on its seeds.

32. Comment on the interaction between a fig tree and wasp. Mention the phenomenon that operates in their relationship.

Ans.
- They show mutualism, where female wasp uses the fruit not only as an oviposition (egg laying) site but uses the developing seeds within the fruit for nourishing its larvae, in return the wasp pollinates the fig inflorescence.
- Co-evolution is the phenomenon that operates in their relationship.

Long Answer Type Questions

1. (i) List the different attributes that a population has and not an individual organism.

(ii) What is population density? Explain any three different ways the population density can be measured, with the help of an example each.

Ans. (i) Refer to text on page no. 325-326.

(ii) Refer to text on page no. 325-326.

2. (i) What is 'population' according to you as a biology student?

(ii) 'The size of a population for any species is not a static parameter'. Justify the statement with specific reference to fluctuations in the population density of a region in a given period of time. **CBSE 2019**

Ans. (i) Refer to text on page no. 325.

(ii) Refer to text on page no. 327.

3. 'Analysis of age pyramids for human population can provide important inputs for long-term planning strategies'. Explain. **Competency Based Que.**

Ans. Analysing age pyramids provides key insights for long-term population and economic planning in the following ways

- A youthful population signals the need for investments in education, childcare, and future job creation, while an ageing population requires more focus on healthcare, retirement systems, and elderly care.
- A shrinking or ageing population can lead to labour shortages and economic challenges, highlighting the need for policies that support higher birth rates, immigration, or workforce productivity.
- Understanding these trends also helps in forecasting future demand for housing, transportation and social services.
- By anticipating demographic shifts, governments can plan for sustainable development, ensuring resources are allocated effectively.
- This analysis is key to maintaining economic stability and meeting future needs of society. (1 × 5)

4. (i) Study the flowchart given below and complete the equation that follows by identifying 1, 2, 3 and 4.

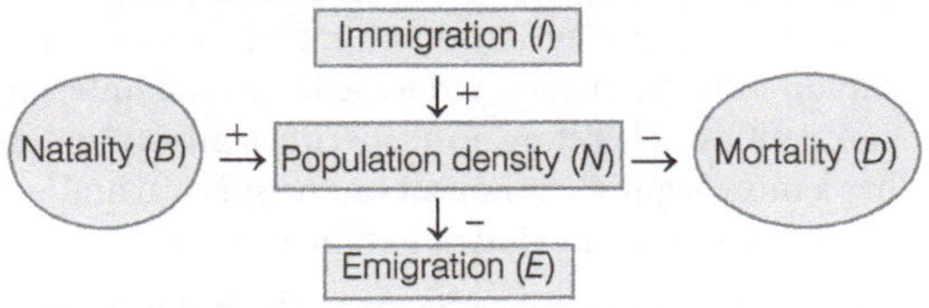

$$N_{t+1} = N_t + [(1+2) - (3+4)]$$

(ii) Mention the different ways by which the population density of different species can be measured.

Competency Based Que., CBSE 2019

Ans. (i) If N is the population density at time t, then its density at time $t+1$ is

$N_{t+1} = N_t + [(B+I) - (D+E)]$

The population density will increase if the number of births and the number of immigrants, i.e. $(B+I)$ is more than the number of death and the number of emigrants, i.e. $(D+E)$. (2)

(ii) Population density is the number of individuals per unit area at a given time/period. Different ways of measuring population density are as follows

(a) Biomass or percentage cover, e.g. hundred *Parthenium* plants and one huge banyan tree.

(b) By measuring relative density, e.g. the number of fish caught per trap from a lake.

(c) Numbers, e.g. human population.

(d) Indirect estimation, e.g. without seeing or actually counting population sizes, e.g. the tiger census is often based on pug marks and faecal pellets. (3)

5. (i) Compare giving reasons, the J-shaped and S-shaped models of population growth of a species.

(ii) Explain 'fitness of a species', as mentioned by Darwin.

Ans. (i) Comparison between J-shaped and S-shaped models of population growth is as follows

J-shaped Population Growth	S-shaped Population Growth
Population growth occurs in J-shaped manner when resources are unlimited in a habitat.	Population growth occurs in S-shaped manner when resources are limited in a habitat.
A stationary or steady phase is seldom achieved.	A stationary or steady phase is reached.
Population crashes ultimately due to mass mortality.	Population seldom crashes.
The growth curve is characterised by initial lag phase followed by acceleration phase.	The growth curve initially depicts a lag phase followed by acceleration phase, deceleration phase and an upper asymptote that represents the carrying capacity. (2½)

(ii) **Fitness of a Species as Mentioned by Darwin**

Darwinian fitness (high '*r*' value) states that the population evolves to maximise its reproductive fitness in the habitat where it lives. Under a particular set of selection pressure, organisms evolve towards the most efficient reproductive strategy.

The rate of breeding varies from species to species. Some species breed only once in their lifetime (Pacific salmon fish and bamboo), while some breed many times in their lifetime (birds and mammals). Some organisms produce a large number of small-sized offsprings (oysters), whereas other produce a small number of large-sized offspring (birds and mammals). (2½)

6. With the help of suitable diagram describe the logistic population growth curve. NCERT

Ans. Refer to text on page no. 328 (fig. 11.4).

7. (i) Describe the population growth curve applicable in a population of any species in nature that has unlimited resources at its disposal.

(ii) Explain the equation of this growth curve.

(iii) Name the growth curve and depict a graphical plot for this type of population growth. CBSE 2025

Ans. (i) When a species has unlimited resources, its population grows exponentially, following the J-shaped growth curve. Initially, the population grows slowly (lag phase), but as reproduction increases, growth accelerates rapidly (exponential phase) without any environmental restrictions.

(ii) The exponential growth equation is:

$$dN/dt = rN$$

where dN/dt is the rate of population growth, is the intrinsic growth rate, and N is the population size. This equation shows that as population size increases, the growth rate also increases.

(iii) This type of population growth is called the exponential growth curve. It is represented as a J-shaped curve when plotted graphically, showing rapid and continuous growth.

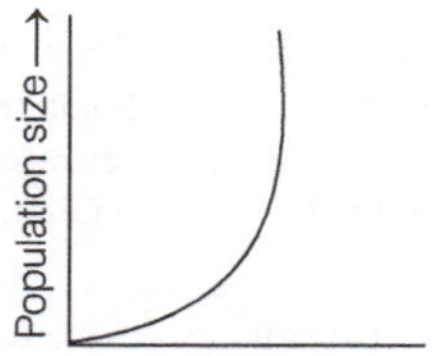

8. 'Predation is beneficial in long run'. Comment.

Ans. Refer to text on page no. 329-330.

9. Justify the statement 'Besides acting as conduits for energy transfer across trophic levels predator play other important roles in an ecosystem. Diksha

Ans. Besides acting as conduits for energy transfer across trophic levels, predators play several other important roles in an ecosystem as given below

(i) **Population Control** Predators help to regulate the populations of prey species. By keeping prey numbers in check, they prevent overgrazing or overpopulation, which can lead to habitat degradation and resource depletion.

(ii) **Biodiversity Maintenance** By controlling the populations of certain species, predators help to maintain a balance in the ecosystem. This promotes biodiversity, as it allows various species to thrive without being dominated by a single prey species.

(iii) **Behavioural Adaptations** The presence of predators can influence the behaviour of prey species. Prey may develop adaptations such as camouflage, increased vigilance, or altered feeding patterns, which can lead to evolutionary changes over the time.

(iv) **Nutrient Cycling** Predators contribute to nutrient cycling through their waste and the decomposition of their remains after death. This process enriches the soil and supports plant growth, benefitting the entire ecosystem. (5)

10. Differentiate between

(i) Predator and parasite.

(ii) S-shaped and J-shaped growth curve.

Ans. (i) The differences between parasites and predators are as follows

Parasites	Predators
The parasite does not kill the host right away, the host may die as a result of prolonged exploitation.	It kills the other organism.
They are weaker than host.	They are stronger than prey.
They are two types, i.e. endo parasites and ectoparasite.	They are also two types, i.e. herbivore and carnivore.
e.g. protozoan parasites.	e.g. hawk, rabbit. (2½)

(ii) Refer to Q. No. 6 on page no. 344. (2½)

11. Name two basic types of competition among organisms. Which one of them is more intense and why?

Ans. The two basic types of competition among organisms are as follows

(i) **Intraspecific Competition** Competition among individuals of the same species for identical resources (e.g. food, space, mates).

(ii) **Interspecific Competition** Competition between individuals of different species for similar resources. (2)

Intraspecific competition is generally more intense than interspecific competition. This is because individuals of the same species have identical or very similar resource requirements, leading to direct competition for the same limited resources. As a result, when population densities are high, the competition for resources becomes particularly fierce. In contrast, in interspecific competition, species may differ in their resource needs or exploit different niches, reducing the overall intensity of competition. Therefore, intraspecific competition usually has a more significant impact on the survival and reproduction of individuals within a species. (3)

12. How do parasites cause harm to the host? Name two categories. Differentiate between them with examples.

Ans. Refer to text on page no. 330-331.

13. **Define the following terms and give one example of each.**

(i) **Commensalism** (ii) **Parasitism**

(iii) **Camouflage** (iv) **Mutualism**

(v) **Interspecific competition** **NCERT**

Ans. .(i) **Commensalism** Refer to text on page no. 331.

(ii) **Parasitism** Refer to text on page no. 330-331.

(iii) **Camouflage** It is a phenomenon of blending of an organism with the surrounding due to similar colour, marking and shape, so as to avoid the predators, e.g. leaf-like insects such as grasshopper.

(iv) **Mutualism** Refer to text on page no. 332.

(v) **Interspecific Competition** It is the competition among the members of different species for limited natural resources. The Abingdon tortoise in Galapagos Islands became extinct within a decade after goats were introduced on the Island, apparently due to the greater browsing efficiency of the goats. (1 × 5)

Source Based/Case Based/ Passage Based Questions

1. **The given graph shows the population of a state according to the age group. Consider the graph given below and answer the following questions.**

Competency Based Que.

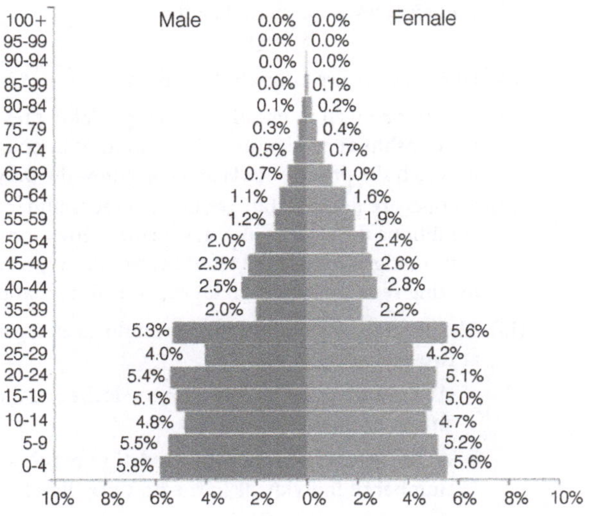

(i) **What information can be inferred from the above graph?**

(ii) **What according to you can be the reason for this expanding population? State any two.**

(iii) **This kind of graph is often referred to as expanding in terms of age pyramid. How far do you agree? Give reason.**

Or (iii) **Suppose that a line graph is made taking any one of the two individuals (male/female), will the graph then follow an exponential growth? Why?**

Ans. (i) The information that can be inferred from the above graph is that there is a difference in number of males and females in every age group. (1)

(ii) There can be many reasons for this expanding population. Two of these are

(a) Increased rate of natality (b) Immigration (1)

(iii) Yes, this kind of graph completely represents the expanding age pyramid.

It can be concluded because in this the people of pre-reproductive age group are the highest in number followed by people of reproductive age group. The people in post-reproductive age group are the least. This scenario is in complete sync with the expanding age pyramid. (2)

Or (iii) No, the graph will not follow an exponential growth pattern. This is because exponential growth is favoured by availability of unlimited resources. This is only followed under ideal conditions and is not practical. (2)

2.

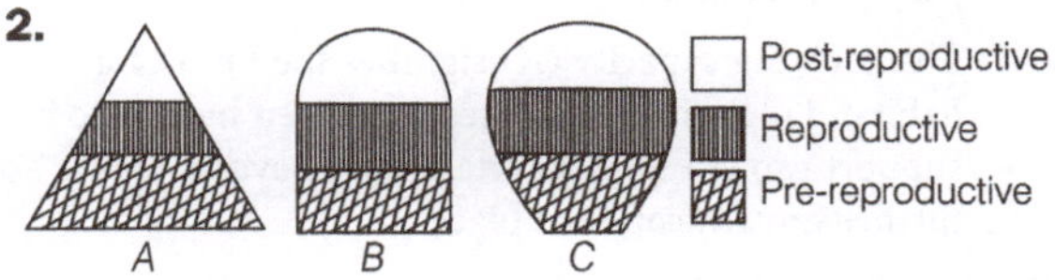

With reference to the above schematic representation of *A*, *B* and *C*, answer the following questions.

(i) **What is depicted in all these three figures? Explain.**

(ii) **Which of the above mentioned structures, shows expanding population and why?**

(iii) **Which shape is obtained for zero population growth rate?**

Ans. (i) The structures *A*, *B* and *C* depicts age pyramids. The age pyramids of human population generally shows the age distributionship of males and females in a combined diagram. (2)

(ii) Age pyramid *A* shows expanding population because more members of pre-reproductive age groups are seen. (1)

(iii) An inverted bell-shaped age pyramid is obtained for zero population growth rate. (1)

3. Study the graph given below and answer the questions that follows

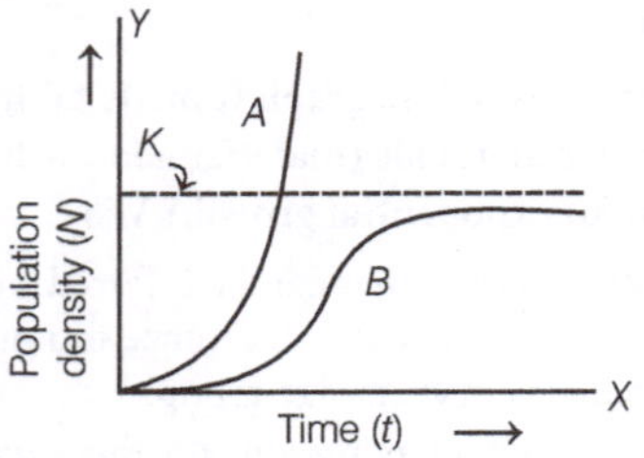

(i) Write the status of food and space in the curves A and B.

(ii) In the absence of predators, which one of the two curves would appropriately depict the prey population?

(iii) Time has been shown on X-axis and there is a parallel dotted line above it. Give the significance of this dotted line. **Competency Based Que.**

Ans. (i) The status of food and space in curve *A* is unlimited, while in curve *B*, the sources of food and space are limited. (1)

(ii) In the absence of predators, the curve *B* would depict the competition for limited food and shelter within the prey population. (1)

(iii) The carrying capacity (*K*) signifies the limit of a habitat, i.e. limited resources in a given habitat to support growth upto a certain level beyond which no further growth can take place. (2)

4. Study the graph given below and answer the questions that follows.

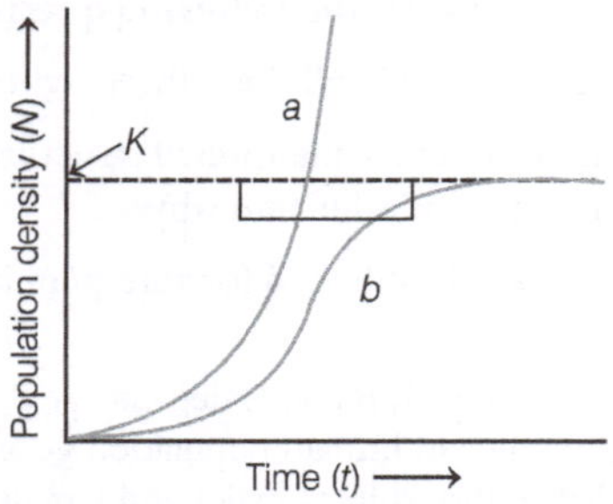

(i) The curve *b* is described by the following equation

$$\frac{dN}{dt} = rN\left\{\frac{K-N}{K}\right\}$$

What does '*K*' stand for in this equation? Mention its significance.

(ii) Which one of the two curves is considered a more realistic one for most of the animal populations?

(iii) Which curve would depict the population of a species of deer if there are no predators in the habitat? **CBSE 2019**

Ans. (i) Refer to text on page no. 328. (2)

(ii) Logistic growth curve (b) is more realistic in nature. (1)

(iii) Since, there are no predators in the habitat, the population of a species of deer will show logistic growth curve (b). (1)

5. The following represents a general graph of interaction that happens between zebras and lions over time in Savanna. The zebra population is represented in dotted line and the simple line shows the lion population. **Competency Based Que.**

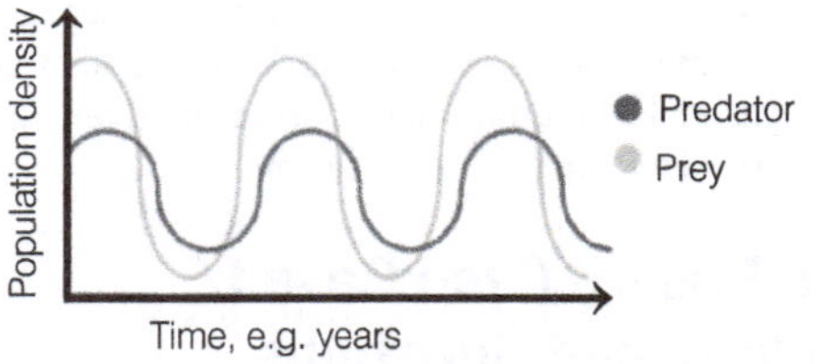

(i) What relationship does the above graph show?

(ii) Humans consuming sprouts is also an example of predation. Do you agree?

(iii) The above interaction influences organisms at two ecological levels. Explain briefly.

Or

(iii) All predators are animals. Comment.

Ans. (i) The graph given in question shows predator-prey relationship or predation. It is the kind of interaction in which the predator kills and consumes the prey. (1)

(ii) Sprouts are nothing, but germinated seeds under ideal conditions these grow into new plants. However, consuming seed kills the plant before it can grow, thus making seed consumption an example of predation. (1)

(iii) The given interaction (predation) influences organisms at two ecological levels.

- At the individual level it causes a decline in the fitness of the individual.
- At the level of community, predation reduces the number of individuals in the prey population. (2)

Or

(iii) The prey-predator interaction or predation is found in both animal and plant kingdom. Carnivorous plants like venus flytrap consume insects by capturing it. Thus, it fulfills the condition of predation. (2)

SELF ASSESSMENT TEST

Multiple Choice Questions

1. Which of the following factors is likely to contribute to an increase in the growth rate of a population?
   (a) High emigration and low immigration
   (b) High natality and low mortality
   (c) Low natality and high mortality
   (d) High emigration and high mortality
2. Darwinian fitness is represented by
   (a) high K value (b) low r value (c) high r value (d) low K value
3. When Darwin spoke of the struggle for the existence and survival of the fittest in the nature, he was convinced that
   (a) intraspecific competition is a potent force in organic evolution.
   (b) interspecific competition is a potent force in organic evolution.
   (c) intensive reproduction is the potent force in organic evolution.
   (d) intensive predation is the potent force in organic evolution.
4. In a field experiment where all the *Pisaster* starfish were removed from an enclosed intertidal area, the result was
   (a) extinction of many vertebrate species
   (b) decreased invertebrate diversity
   (c) decreased mussel populations
   (d) increased biodiversity in the intertidal community
5. What is characterised as a rivalry between members of two different species for the use of the same resources in the same territory?
   (a) Apparent competition
   (b) Interspecific competition
   (c) Interference competition
   (d) Intraspecific competition
6. What is the name of the interaction between species when one' s fitness dominates the other's existence and fitness?
   (a) Competition (b) Mutualism (c) Parasitism (d) Commensalism
7. Mutualism is what form of interaction?
   (a) Positive intraspecific (b) Negative interspecific (c) Positive interspecific (d) Negative intraspecific

Assertion-Reason Questions

Direction (Q. Nos. 8-11) *In each of the following questions, a statement of Assertion (A) is given followed by corresponding statement of Reason (R). Of the statements, mark the correct answer.*

(a) Both A and R are true and R is the correct explanation of A.
(b) Both A and R are true, but R is not the correct explanation of A.
(c) A is true, but R is false.
(d) A is false, but R is true.

8. **Assertion** (A) The shape of an age pyramid can indicate whether a population is growing, stable or declining.
   Reason (R) Age pyramids visually represent the distribution of age groups within a population, revealing trends in birth rates and mortality rates.
9. **Assertion** (A) The population size of a species directly determines its overall health and viability.
   Reason (R) A larger population size always indicates better health.
10. **Assertion** (A) Logistic growth model is considered a more realistic as compared to exponential growth model.
    Reason (R) Resources for growth for most animal population are finite and becomes limiting sooner or later.

11. **Assertion** (A) Interspecific interactions can significantly influence community dynamics and species distribution.
Reason (R) Interspecific interactions impact resource availability, reproductive success and survival rates, thereby shaping ecological community, structure and composition.

Very Short Answer Type Questions

12. A new infectious disease breaks out in a city with a population of 5,00,000 people. Over the course of one month, 3,500 individuals die from the disease. Calculate the death rate for this disease in the city.
13. Construct an age pyramid which reflect a stable growth status of human population.
14. Clown fish living among the tentacles of sea anemone.' Name the interaction between tentacles and sea anemone.
15. Certain wasp species frequently visit flowering fig trees. What type of interaction is seen between them and why?

Short Answer Type Questions

16. A forest can accommodate a maximum of 500 deer (i.e. its carrying capacity). If the initial population size is 100 deer and the maximum per capita growth rate is 0.05 per year, calculate the rate of change of the population size of deer for given time period.
17. What is mutualism? Mention any two examples where the organisms involved are commercially exploited in nature.

Long Answer Type Questions

18. How do factors like birth rates, death rates, immigration and emigration influence population growth trends in ecosystems?
19. How do exponential and logistic growth models show different patterns of population growth and what factors affect these models in real life?

Case Based Question

20. Given graph represents the predator-prey relationship. Answer the questions that follows.

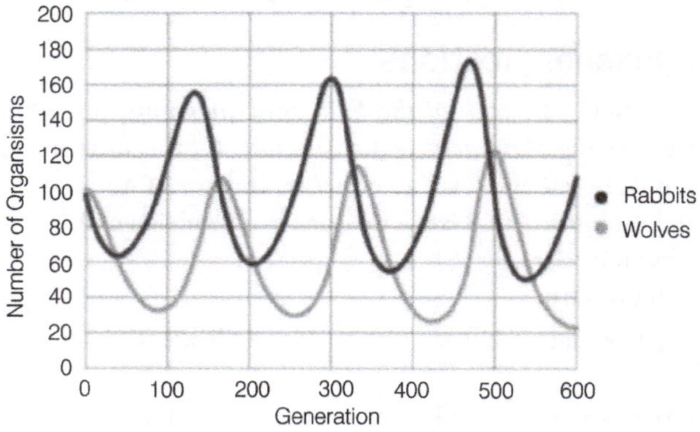

   (i) Give one evidence that the ecosystem is stable.
   (ii) What will be effect of migration of rabbits on the population of wolves and why?
   (iii) Name and describe one adaptation that helps preys escape predation.
   (iv) In a hypothetical scenario, all wolves vanish from the ecosystem. What will be the consequence on the vegetation present in the ecosystem and why?

Answers

1. (b)	2. (c)	3. (b)	4. (b)	5. (b)	6. (a)	7. (c)
8. (a)	9. (a)	10. (a)	11. (a)			

12

CHAPTER

An ecosystem is a functional unit of nature, where living organisms interact among themselves and also with their surrounding physical environment. The term 'ecosystem' was coined by AG Tansley (1935).

▼ **YOUR STUDY GOALS**

12.1 Introduction
12.2 Ecosystem : Structure and Function
12.3 Productivity
12.4 Decomposition
12.5 Energy Flow
12.6 Ecological Pyramids

▼ **YOUR PRACTICE GOAL**

- Objective Type Questions (37 Qs ; MCQs, A-R)
  Case Based Questions (2)
- Subjective Type Questions
- (23 VSAs, 26 SAs, 6 LAs)

Ecosystem

12.1 Introduction

- Ecosystem is an open system. It receives input in the form of solar energy and inorganic nutrient which results in productivity or synthesis of food.
- The food with its contained energy passes through various components of the ecosystem through food chain/web.
- As the matter circulates in the ecosystem, it gives out energy and matter as its output.
- Ecologist consider the entire biosphere as a global ecosystem, which comprises of many local ecosystems on the earth.
- These ecosystems vary in size from a small pond to a large forest or a sea. Since, this system is very large and complex, it cannot be studied at one time.

Types of Ecosystem

It is convenient to divide an ecosystem into two basic categories.

- **Natural Ecosystem** These are capable of maintaining and operating themselves, without the interference of human. They are further classified as
  - **Terrestrial ecosystem**, e.g. forest, grassland, desert, etc.
  - **Aquatic ecosystem**, e.g. pond, lake, river, wetland, estuary, etc.

- **Artificial or Man-made Ecosystem** These are maintained and manipulated by human for different purposes, e.g. cropland, aquarium, etc.

Components of Ecosystem

An ecosystem has two major components as discussed below

1. Abiotic Components

The abiotic or non-living components consist of temperature, water, light, etc.

2. Biotic Components

The various biotic or living components of an ecosystem are further classified as

- **Producers** All green plants are called producers. In terrestrial ecosystem, herbaceous and woody plants are producers. In aquatic ecosystem, phytoplanktons, some algae and higher plants are producers. They are also called as **autotrophs**.
- **Consumers** All animals which depend directly or indirectly on plants (autotrophs) for their food requirements are called consumers. They are also called as **heterotrophs**.
- **Decomposers** These are also called **saprobes** or **saprophytes** or **mineralisers**. Moulds and mushrooms are among largest decomposers in a forest.

12.2 Ecosystem : Structure and Function

- Interaction of biotic and abiotic components results in physical structure that is the characteristic of each type of ecosystem.
- The two important structural features of an ecosystem are
  - **Species Composition** It includes identification and enumeration of plant and animal species of an ecosystem.
  - **Stratification** It is the vertical distribution of different species occupying different levels in an ecosystem.
    For example, trees occupy top vertical strata or layer of a forest, shrubs occupies the second and herbs and grasses occupy the bottom (third) layers.
- The important functional aspects of an ecosystem are
  (i) productivity (ii) decomposition
  (iii) energy flow (iv) nutrient cycling
- To understand the concept of an aquatic ecosystem, let us take a small pond ecosystem as an example.

Pond Ecosystem

- A pond is fairly a self-sustainable unit, that explains even the complex interactions that exist in an aquatic ecosystem.
- It is a shallow water body in which all the above mentioned basic structural and functional components are present.
- Pond has both abiotic and biotic components, which are discussed below

1. Abiotic Component

- It include water with all the dissolved inorganic and organic materials and soil deposited at its bottom.
- The solar input, the cycle of temperature, day-length and other climatic conditions regulate the rate of function of the entire pond.

2. Biotic Component

- The various biotic components of pond ecosystem are as follows
  - **Autotrophic components** like phytoplanktons, some algae and the floating, submerged and marginal plants. These are found at the edges of the pond.
  - **Consumers** like zooplanktons, the free-swimming and bottom dwelling forms.
  - **Decomposers** like fungi, bacteria and flagellates are found abundantly in the bottom of the pond.
- This pond ecosystem performs all the functions of an ecosystem and of the biosphere as a whole.
- The autotrophs convert inorganic materials into organic material with the help of solar energy.
- The heterotrophs consume autotrophs while decomposers breakdown and mineralise dead organic materials to release nutrients back for their reuse by the autotrophs.
- These events are repeated over and over again.
- The energy flow is unidirectional towards the higher trophic levels.

- At each trophic level, a part of energy is dissipated and is lost as heat to the environment.

12.3 Productivity

- A constant input of solar energy is the basic requirement for any ecosystem to function and sustain.
- Productivity of an ecosystem can be categorised into primary and secondary productivity.

1. Primary Productivity

- The amount of biomass or organic matter produced per unit area over a time period by plants during photosynthesis is called **primary production**.
- It is expressed in terms of **weight** (gm^{-2}) or **energy** ($kcal\ m^{-2}$).
- The rate of biomass production is called **productivity**.
- It is expressed in terms of $gm^{-2}\ yr^{-1}$ or $(kcal\ m^{-2})\ yr^{-1}$.
- The primary productivity has two aspects as discussed below

(i) Gross Primary Productivity (GPP)

It is the rate of production of organic matter during photosynthesis. A considerable amount of GPP is utilised by plants during respiration.

(ii) Net Primary Productivity (NPP)

- It is the available biomass for consumption by heterotrophs (herbivores and decomposers).
- It is actually the amount of energy left in the producers after the utilisation of some energy during respiration.
- Thus, Gross Primary Productivity (GPP) minus the respiration losses gives the Net Primary Productivity (NPP).

$$\text{GPP} - R = \text{NPP}$$

where, R = Respiration losses.

- The annual net primary productivity of the whole biosphere is approximately 170 billion tonnes of the dry organic weights.
- Despite covering about 70% of the earth's surface, the productivity of the oceans are only 55 billion tons.

Factors Affecting Primary Productivity

- Primary productivity depends on the plant species inhabiting a particular area.
- Various environmental factors also affect the primary productivity. Some of them are as follows
  - **Light** Sunlight is the ultimate source of energy.
    - Due to the less availability of light in an aquatic ecosystem, its productivity is less than terrestrial ecosystem.
    - Maximum light is available in tropics while poles receive the minimum light, therefore productivity is comparatively low at the poles.
  - **Temperature** It controls the enzyme mediated dark reaction of photosynthesis.
    - Temperate forests have lesser productivity than tropical rainforest.
    - Also alpine and arctic zone have less productivity due to low temperature throughout the year.
  - **Moisture** Rain (humidity) increases the productivity of the ecosystem, but tends to decrease with the scarcity of water.
    Therefore, deserts have the lowest primary productivity as soil is deficient in moisture.
  - **Nutrients Availability** Nutrients are essential for the growth of producers.
    - In ocean, deficiency of nitrogen limits the productivity in an aquatic ecosystem.
    - Estuaries and coral reefs are highly productive as the nutrient supply is rich, whereas desert soil are less productive.
    - Thus, higher availability of nutrients ensure greater primary productivity.
  - **Photosynthetic Efficiency of Plants** (Producers) C_4 plants are more productive as compared to C_3 plants because they are more efficient at trapping sunlight, which allows them to accumulate higher productivity.

TEACHER'S TIP
The main reason for low productivity in oceans is the limited availability of nutrients. While sunlight supports photosynthesis, important nutrients like nitrogen and phosphorus are often scarce, especially in the open ocean. This lack of nutrients limit the growth of plants and algae, which are essential for productivity.

2. Secondary Productivity

It is the rate of assimilation and formation of new organic matter by consumers. It is small as compared to primary productivity and tends to decrease with an increase in the trophic level.

Quick Test 1

1. The organism '*X*' is primarily responsible for absorbing sunlight and converting it into chemical energy in a pond ecosystem. Identify '*X*'.
2. Name the term used for the storage of organic matter by producer for the consumptions of heterotrophs.
3. How would an increase in plant respiration impact the Net Primary Productivity (NPP) of an ecosystem?
4. **State True or False.**
   Temperate forest have lesser productivity than tropical rainforest.
5. In a pond, if herbivores consume 2000 kcal/m^2/year and convert 500 kcal/m^2/year into their biomass, what is the secondary productivity?

12.4 Decomposition

- The breakdown of complex organic matter into inorganic substances like carbon dioxide, water and nutrients is called **decomposition**.
- This process is carried out by decomposers.
- **Detritus** is the raw material for decomposition. It includes dead remains of plants (leaves, bark and flowers) and animals, including faecal matter.
- Different steps involved in the process of decomposition are as follows
  - **Fragmentation** It is the process of breakdown of detritus into smaller particles by detritivores (e.g. earthworm).

    Earthworm is also referred to as the farmer's friend as it helps in the breakdown of complex organic matter as well as loosening of the soil.

  - **Leaching** It is the process by which water-soluble inorganic nutrients go down into the soil horizon and get precipitated as unavailable salts.

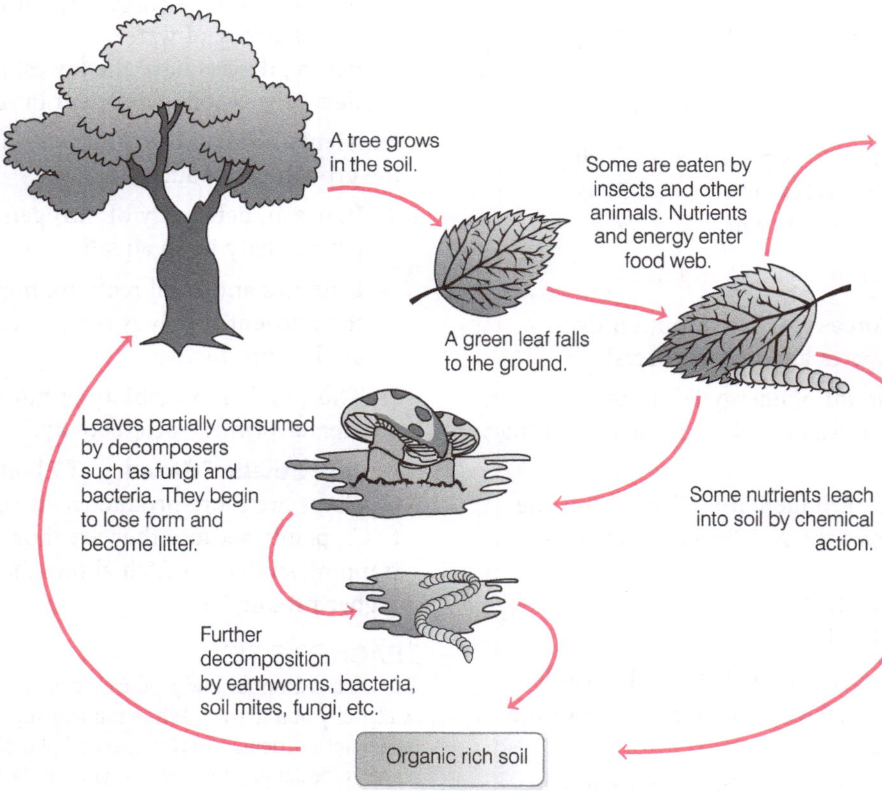

Fig. 12.1 Diagrammatic representation of decomposition cycle in a terrestrial ecosystem

- **Catabolism** It is the process of degradation of detritus into simple inorganic material by the action of bacterial and fungal enzymes.
- **Humification** It is a process that leads to the accumulation of a dark coloured amorphous and colloidal substance called **humus**.
  - It is highly resistant to microbial action and undergoes decomposition at a very slow rate.
  - Being colloidal in nature, it serves as a reservoir of nutrients.
- **Mineralisation** It is a process of degradation of humus by microbial action and release of inorganic nutrients.

Factors Affecting the Rate of Decomposition

- Decomposition is largely an aerobic process, i.e. requires oxygen for its processing.
- The rate of decomposition is controlled mainly by the following two factors

Chemical Composition of Detritus

- The rate of decomposition is slower, if detritus is rich in lignin and chitin.
- While, it is quicker if it is composed of nitrogen and water-soluble substances like sugars.

Climatic Factors

- Temperature and soil moisture are the most important climatic factors that controls decomposition.
- Warm and moist environment favours decomposition, while low temperature and anaerobiosis, i.e. anaerobic conditions (unavailability of oxygen) inhibit decomposition thus resulting in the build up of organic materials.

12.5 Energy Flow

- Sun is the only source of energy for all the ecosystems on earth, except for deep sea hydrothermal ecosystem.
- Of all the total solar radiation incident on earth, less than 50% is **Photosynthetically Active Radiation** (PAR).
- Plants are able to trap only 2-10% of PAR and this small amount of energy sustain the entire living world.
- No energy that is trapped into an organism remains in it forever.
- Plants as well as other producers like photosynthetic bacteria (autotrophs) fix sun's radiant energy to make food from simple inorganic molecules and all the other organisms are dependent on producers either directly or indirectly for their food.
- This shows that flow of energy in an ecosystem is unidirectional, i.e. it flows from the sun to producers and then to consumers and thus maintains the **first law of thermodynamics**.
- Moreover, all ecosystems need a constant supply of energy to synthesise the required molecules in order to counteract the universal tendency towards increasing disorderliness.
- This is in correlation with **second law of thermodynamics**.
- The energy trapped by the **producers**, is either passed on to higher trophic level or the organism dies and release energy.

Trophic Level

- All organisms occupy a particular place in their natural surrounding or in a community according to their feeding relationship among the other organisms.
- Based on the relationship among the organisms and the source of their nutrition or food, organisms occupy a specific place in the food chain that is known as their trophic level.
- It is divided into
  - **First Trophic Level** Producers occupy the first trophic level. Thus, use inorganic molecules to prepare food.
  - **Second Trophic Level** Primary consumer occupy the second trophic level.
    - The consumers that feed on producers or their products directly, are called **primary consumers** or **herbivores**.
    - Some common herbivores in terrestrial ecosystem are insects, birds and mammals.
    - Molluscs are the common herbivores in aquatic ecosystem.

- **Third Trophic Level** Secondary consumer occupy the third trophic level.
- These organisms eat primary consumer to obtain energy.
- They are also referred to as **primary carnivore** or **secondary consumer**.
- **Fourth Trophic Level** It is occupied by the tertiary consumer.
  - These are the organisms who feed upon secondary consumers to obtain their energy.
  - Tertiary consumers are also referred to as **secondary carnivores**.

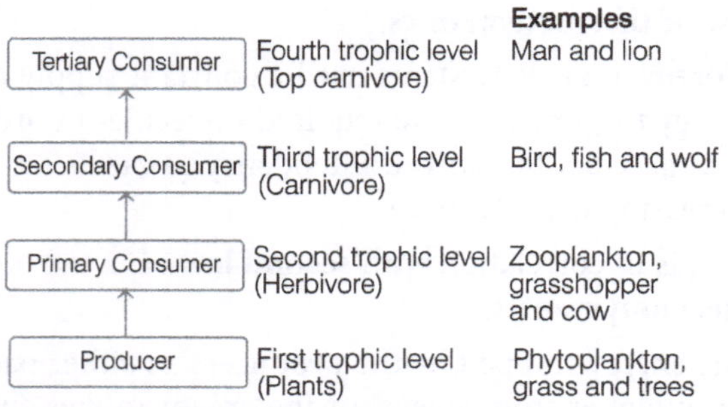

Fig. 12.2 Diagrammatic representation of trophic levels in an ecosystem

- **Standing Crop** It is the mass of living material at a particular trophic level at a specific time.
  - Standing crop is measured as the mass of living organisms **(biomass)** or the number in an unit area.
  - The biomass of a species is expressed in terms of fresh or dry weight.
- It is to be noted that the amount of energy decreases at successive trophic levels.
- When any organisms dies it is converted into detritus or dead biomass that serves as an energy source for decomposers.
- Organisms at each trophic level depend on those at the lower trophic level for their energy demands.
- Hence, due to this interdependence of food/energy between organisms, the chains or webs are formed in the ecosystem.

Food Chain

The sequence of organisms through which the energy is transferred from one organism to another at different trophic levels form a food chain.

Types of Food Chain

There are mainly two types of food chains which are as follows

Grazing Food Chain (GFC)

- A grazing food chain is a linear sequence of organisms where energy is acquired from producers or from the lowest trophic levels.
- In an grassland ecosystem, the GFC is the major channel for energy flow.

Grass (Producer) → Goat (Primary consumer) → Man (Secondary consumer)

Detritus Food Chain (DFC)

- It begins with dead organic matter and is made up of decomposers which are heterotrophic organisms, mainly **fungi** and **bacteria**.
- They are also known as **saprotrophs** (*Sapro* – to decompose).
- They fulfill their energy and nutrient requirements by degrading the dead organic matter.
- Decomposers secrete digestive enzymes that breakdown dead and waste matter into simple inorganic materials, which are later absorbed by them.

Dead leaves (Producer) → Woodlouse (Primary consumer) → Black bird (Secondary consumer)

- A much larger fraction of energy flows through Detritus Food Chain (DFC) than the Grazing Food Chain (GFC) in a terrestrial ecosystem.

Food Web

- It consists of many food chains. The food web reflects that GFC is connected to DFC at some level.
- Hence, some organisms of DFC are the prey of GFC organisms. Also, some organisms like cockroaches, crows, etc. feeds on both plants and animals. These are known as **omnivorous animals** or **omnivores**.

- Therefore, the naturally interconnected food chains constitute a food web.

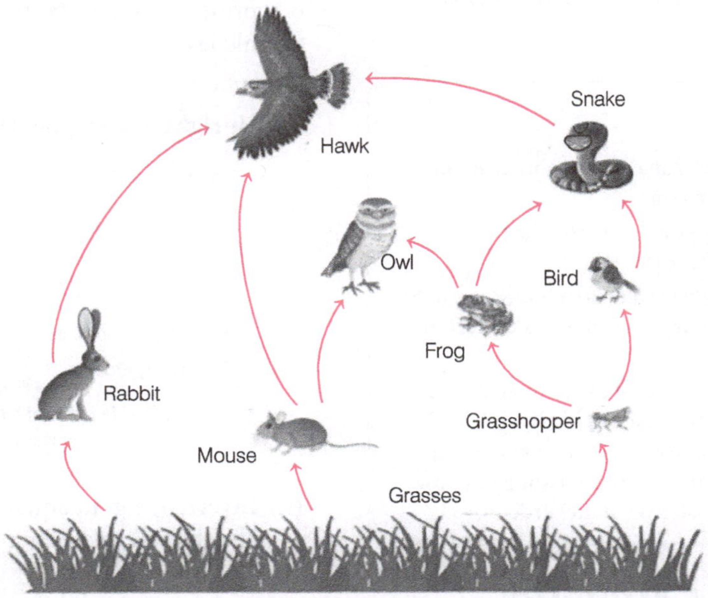

Fig. 12.3 Food web

Ten Per Cent Law (10% Law)

- According to this law, in each step of food chain when energy is being transferred from one trophic level to the next trophic level, some energy is lost as heat and only 10% of the energy is transferred to the next level, as shown in fig. 12.4.

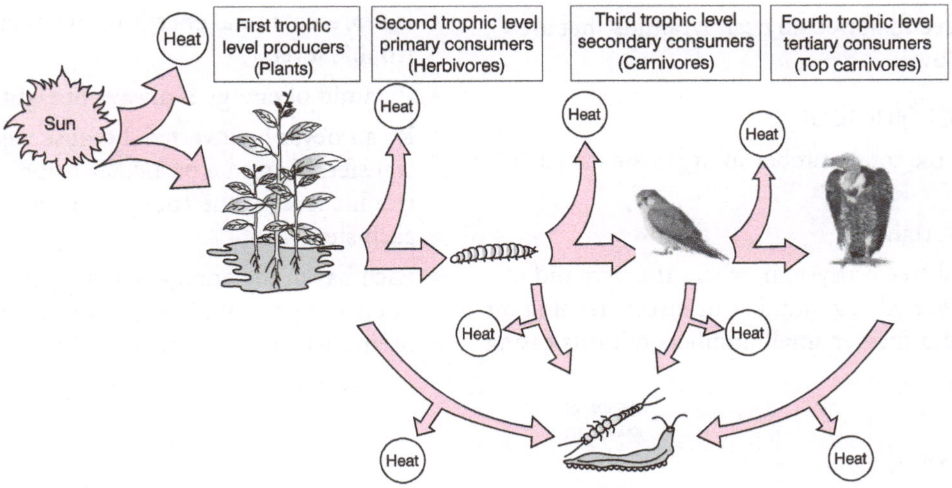

Fig. 12.4 Energy flow through different trophic levels

- Due to this, the number of trophic levels in the grazing food chain is restricted as the transfer of energy follows 10% law.

Quick Test 2

1. Name an organism which can occupy more than one trophic level in the ecosystem?
2. Mr. Galgotia eats curd/yogurt. Mention the trophic level he will occupy in this case.
3. Comment whether the given statement 'humans can be both primary and secondary consumers' is correct or not.
4. Which is more stable: a food chain with three trophic levels or a food chain with eight trophic levels?
5. In a grassland, a grasshopper consumes 2000 kcal of energy from grass. If a bird eats the grasshopper, how much energy will be transferred to the bird?

18.6 Ecological Pyramids

- These are the diagrammatic illustrations of connection between different trophic levels in terms of energy, biomass and number of organisms.
- The base of each pyramid represents the producers or the first trophic level.
- Apex represents tertiary or top level consumers.
- There are three major ecological pyramids that are discussed below

1. Pyramid of Number

- It represents the total number of organisms at each trophic level.
- It is always upright.
- Exception is a tree ecosystem, where the pyramid of number is inverted, e.g. number of insects feeding on a large tree and further small numbers of birds eating these insects.

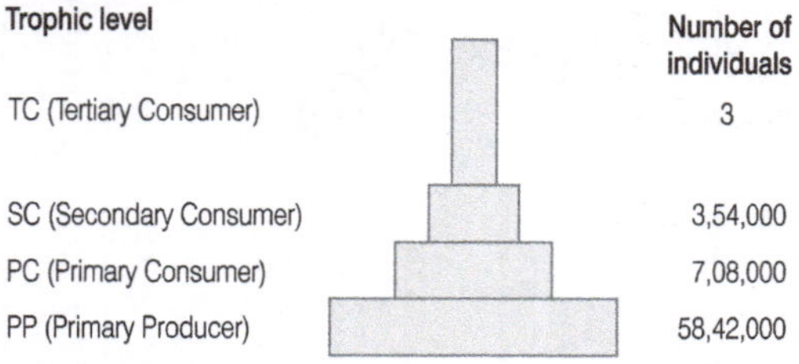

Fig. 12.5 Pyramid of numbers in a grassland ecosystem. Only three top carnivores are supported in an ecosystem based on the production of nearly 60 lakh plants (6 millions).

2. Pyramid of Biomass

- It represents total weight of the organisms in each trophic level.
- It can be
  (i) **Upright**, e.g. in grasslands ecosystem.

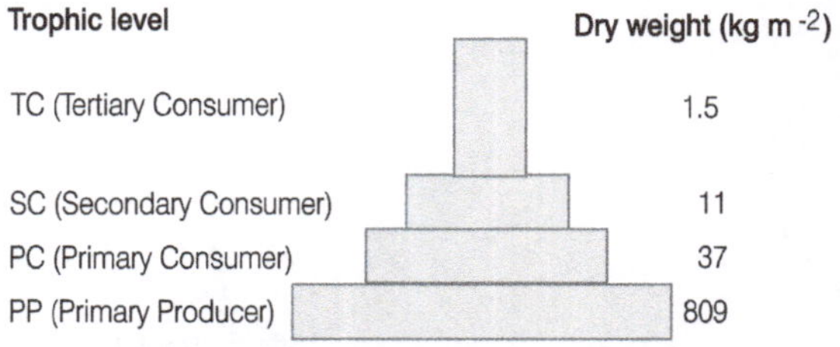

Fig. 12.6 Pyramid of biomass shows a sharp decrease in biomass at higher trophic levels

  (ii) **Inverted,** e.g. in aquatic sea ecosystem (biomass of fishes far exceeding that of phytoplanktons).

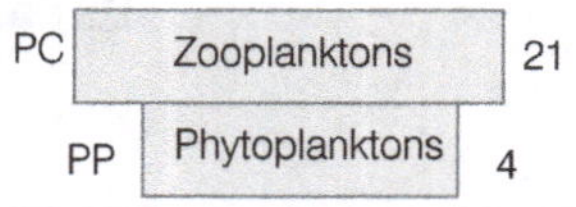

Fig. 12.7 Inverted pyramid of biomass shows a small standing crop of phytoplanktons supports the large standing crop of zooplanktons

3. Pyramid of Energy

- It represents total energy of the organisms in each trophic level.
- Pyramid of energy is always **upright**.
- It can never be inverted, because when energy is transferred from a particular trophic level to the next trophic level, some energy is always lost as heat at each step.
- Each bar in the energy pyramid indicates the amount of energy present at each trophic level in a given time or annually per unit area.

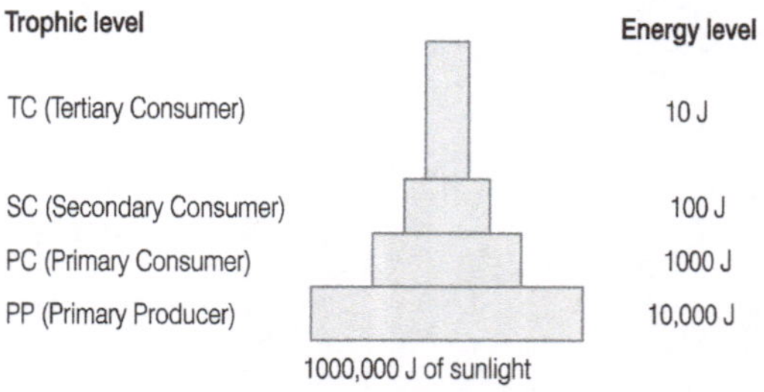

Fig. 12.8 An ideal pyramid of energy with primary producers storing only 1% of solar energy as NPP

Some Important Points about Ecological Pyramids

Some important points about ecological pyramids are given below

- A trophic level represents a functional level, not a species as such.
- A given species may occupy more than one trophic level in the same ecosystem at the same time, e.g. a sparrow is primary consumer, when it eats seeds, fruits, peas, etc., and a secondary consumer when it eats insects and worms.
- In most ecosystems, all the pyramids of number, biomass, energy are upright, i.e. producers are more in number and biomass than the herbivores and herbivores are more in number and biomass than carnivores. However, there are few exceptions to this generalisation.
- Energy at lower trophic level is always more than at a higher trophic level.
- Any calculation of energy content, biomass or number has to include all organisms at that trophic level. If only few individuals are taken into account, no generalisation will be true.

Limitations of Ecological Pyramids

- It never takes into account the same species belonging to two or more trophic levels.
- It assumes a simple food chain, something that almost never exists in nature.
- It does not accommodate a food web.
- Saprophytes are not given any place in ecological pyramids even though, they play an important role in the ecosystem.

Quick Test 3

1. In a pyramid of numbers, how many producers are typically required to support two top carnivores?
2. In a pyramid of biomass, which level typically has the smallest biomass in an aquatic ecosystem?
3. **State True or False.**
   Primary producers store only 1% of solar energy as NPP.
4. Among lion, deer, earthworm, fungi, which animals is not typically represented in ecological pyramids?
5. Analyse the following ecological pyramid and provide an example of an ecosystem where this type of pyramid structure is typically observed.

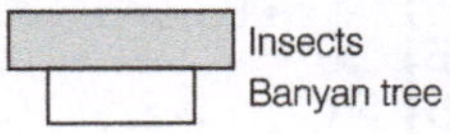

Mind Map

Ecosystem

Ecosystem

An interactive system where biotic and abiotic components interact with each other *via* energy exchange and flow of nutrients.

Classification of Ecosystem

- Terrestrial
  - Natural e.g. forest
  - Man-made e.g. crop fields
- Aquatic
  - Natural e.g. pond
  - Man-made e.g. aquarium

Components of Ecosystem

Biotic
- Producers (autotrophs)
- Consumers (heterotrophs)
- Decomposers (reducers)

Abiotic
- Light
- Wind
- Soil
- Temperature
- Water

Structural Aspects of Ecosystem

Species composition (identification and enumeration of plant and animal species) and **stratification** (vertical distribution of different species occupying different levels).

Decomposition

- Process of decomposition is as follows

Fragmentation → Leaching → Catabolism → Humification → Mineralisation

- **Conditions Favouring Decomposition** Nitrogen rich detritus, water-soluble substances like sugars, warm moist environment.
- **Conditions Inhibiting Decomposition** Lignin and chitin rich detritus, low temperature and anaerobiosis.

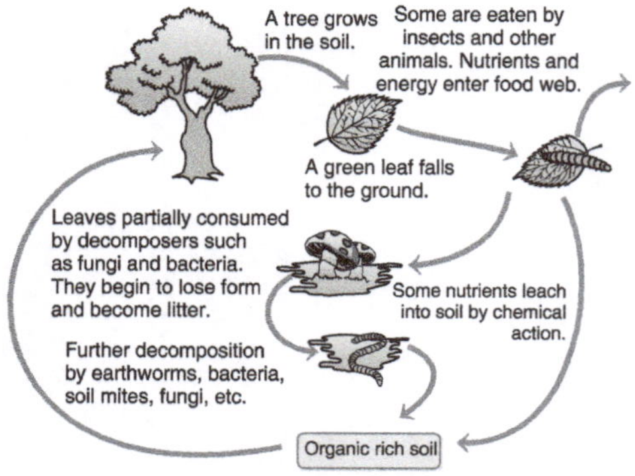

Decomposition cycle

Productivity

Expressed in terms of $gm^{-2}\ yr^{-1}$ or $(kcal\ m^{-2})\ yr^{-1}$

Types of Productivity

- **Primary Productivity**
  - **Gross Primary Productivity** (GPP)
  - **Net Primary Productivity** (NPP)
- **Secondary Productivity**

$$NPP = GPP - R$$

(Net Primary Productivity) (Gross Primary Productivity) (Respiratory loss)

Ecological Pyramid

Pyramid of Number

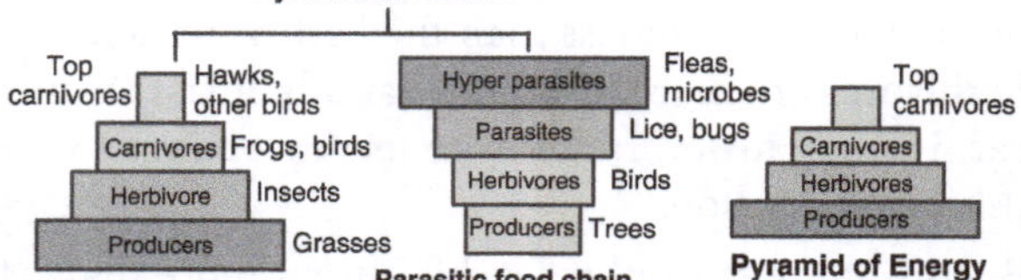

Grasslands (Upright) | **Parasitic food chain** (Inverted) | **Pyramid of Energy** (Always upright)

Pyramid of Biomass

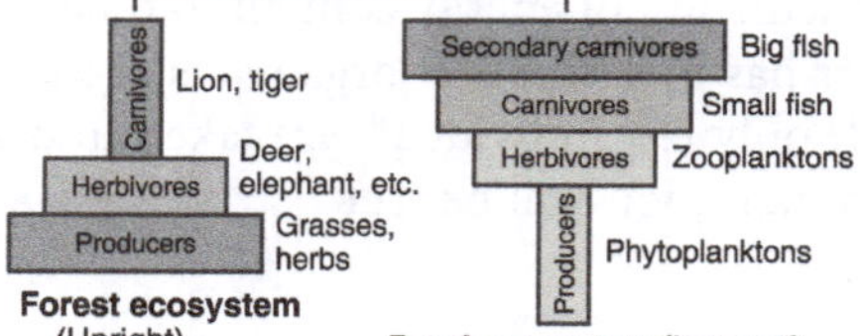

Forest ecosystem (Upright) | **Pond ecosystem** (Inverted)

Energy Flow

- Unidirectional in an ecosystem.
- **Trophic Level** Specific place of an organism in a food chain characterised by their source of nutrition.

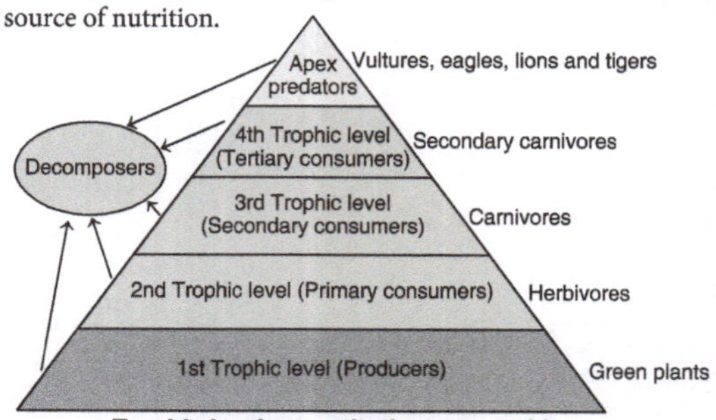

Trophic levels constituting a pyramid

- **Food Chain** Sequence of transfer of nutrients and energy in the form of food from organism to organism.
- **Types of Food Chain**
  - **Grazing Food Chain (GFC)**
    Grass → Caterpillar → Frog → Snake → Owl
  - **Detritus Food Chain (DFC)**
    Detritus → Earthworm → Sparrow → Falcon

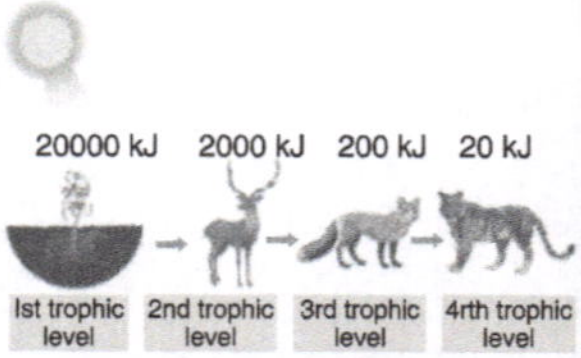

10% energy transfer at successive trophic levels

EXAM PATTERN QUESTIONS

Objective Type Questions

Multiple Choice Questions

1. A functional unit of nature, where living organisms interact among themselves and also with the surrounding physical environment is

(a) biosphere (b) ecosystem
(c) environment (d) None of these

Ans. (*b*)

2. The two important components of an ecosystem includes which out of these?

(a) Plants and animals
(b) Weeds, trees, animals and man
(c) Energy flow and mineral cycling
(d) Biotic and abiotic

Ans. (*d*)

3. Vertical distribution of different species occupying different levels in a biotic community is known as

(a) divergence (b) stratification
(c) zonation (d) pyramid

Ans. (*b*)

4. Which out of the following statements are true regarding a pond ecosystem?

(a) It is a shallow water body with all basic four components of an ecosystem
(b) Water is the biotic component
(c) Day length, cycle of temperature do not regulate rate of function of a bond
(d) The consumers are represented by phytoplanktons

Ans. (*a*)

5. Which one of the following has the largest population in a food chain? **NCERT**

(a) Producers
(b) Primary consumers
(c) Secondary consumers
(d) Decomposers

Ans. (*a*) In a food chain, producers (like plants) typically have the largest population, as they form the base of the food chain and provide energy for primary consumers.

6. Secondary producers are **NCERT**

(a) herbivores (b) producers
(c) carnivores (d) None of these

Ans. (*d*)

7. Which of the following is not a functional unit of ecosystem?

(a) Decomposition (b) Productivity
(c) Stratification (d) Energy flow

Ans. (*c*)

8. Which of the following utilises inorganic materials?

(a) Autotrophs (b) Saprotrophs
(c) Heterotrophs (d) Decomposers

Ans. (*a*)

9. Match the Column I with Column II and choose the correct answer from the codes given below.

	Column I (Components of Ecosystem)		Column II (Feeding Habits)
A.	Scavengers	1.	Autotrophs
B.	Parasites	2.	Heterotrophs
C.	Producers	3.	Consumers that feed on a living being
D.	Phagotrophs	4.	Consumers of dead bodies

Codes

	A	B	C	D		A	B	C	D
(a)	4	3	1	2	(b)	3	1	2	4
(c)	1	2	4	3	(d)	4	3	2	1

Ans. (*a*)

10. The primary productivity in an ecosystem is expressed as

(a) $gm^{-2}\ yr^{1}$ (b) $gm^{-2}\ yr$
(c) $kcal\ m^{-2}\ yr^{-1}$ (d) $kcal\ m^{-2}$

Ans. (*c*)

11. How much of the net primary productivity of a terrestrial ecosystem is eaten and digested by herbivores? **Competency Based Que.**

(a) 1% (b) 40%
(c) 90% (d) 10%

Ans. (*d*)

12. Energy stored at the consumer level is

(a) gross primary productivity
(b) net primary productivity
(c) net productivity
(d) secondary productivity

Ans. (*d*)

13. **The breakdown of detritus into small particles by detrivores is called**
(a) leaching (b) humification
(c) fragmentation (d) catabolism

Ans. (*c*)

14. **Of the following which ecosystem will show lowest primary productivity?** **Diksha**
(a) Marsh (b) Desert
(c) Swamp (d) Tropical rainforest

Ans. (*b*) Deserts generally show the lowest primary productivity. This is primarily due to their extreme aridity, limited water availability and harsh climatic conditions, which restrict plant growth and biomass production.

15. **The rate of formation of new organic matter by consumers and the biomass available for consumption of herbivores as well as decomposers are referred to as** **CBSE 2024**
(a) gross primary productivity and net primary productivity
(b) net primary productivity and secondary productivity
(c) secondary productivity and net primary productivity
(d) secondary productivity and gross primary productivity

Ans. (*c*)

16. **Each trophic level has a certain mass of living material at a particular time called**
(a) standing crop (b) biomass
(c) branching lines (d) progressive straight line

Ans. (*a*)

17. **The second trophic level in a lake is** **NCERT**
(a) phytoplankton (b) zooplankton (c) benthos (d) fishes

Ans. (*b*)

18. **What is the percentage of Photosynthetically Active Radiation (PAR) in the incident solar radiation?** **NCERT**
(a) 100% (b) 50% (c) 1-5% (d) 2-10%

Ans. (*b*)

19. **In a food chain, the largest population is that of**
(a) decomposers (b) producers
(c) primary consumers (d) tertiary consumers

Ans. (*b*)

20. **Identify the correct type of food chain shown below.** **Competency Based Que.**

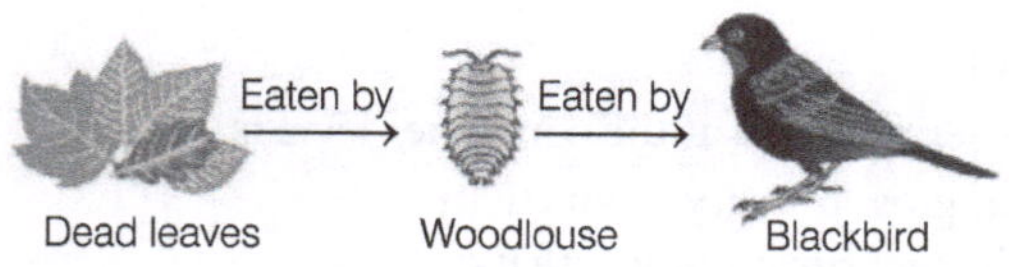

(a) Grazing food chain (b) Detritus food chain
(c) Aquatic food chain (d) None of these

Ans. (*b*)

21. **Which of the following food chain is the major conduit for energy flow in terrestrial and aquatic ecosystems, respectively?**

	Terrestrial ecosystem	Aquatic ecosystem
(a)	Grazing	Grazing
(b)	Detritus	Detritus
(c)	Detritus	Grazing
(d)	Grazing	Detritus

Ans. (*c*)

22. **Study the following statements regarding food chain and select the correct ones.** **Competency Based Que.**

I. Removal of 80% tigers from an area resulted in greatly increased growth of vegetation.
II. Removal of most of the carnivores resulted in an increased population of deers.
III. The length of food chains is generally limited to 3-4 trophic levels due to energy loss.
IV. The length of food chains may vary from 2-8 trophic levels.

(a) I and II (b) II and III (c) I and III (d) III and IV

Ans. (*b*) Statements II and III are correct, while statements I and IV are incorrect. The incorrect statements can be corrected as

- The removal of 80% of tigers from an area can lead to decreased vegetation due to rise in herbivore population.
- The length of a food chain may vary from 3 to 5 trophic levels.

23. **In the given food web, an increase in the population of hawks will not result in** **Competency Based Que.**

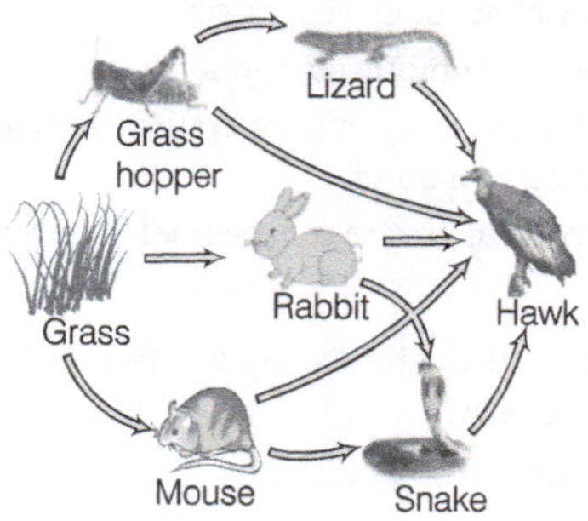

(a) decrease in the population of lizards
(b) increase in the population of grasshoppers
(c) decrease in the population of rabbits and snakes
(d) decrease in the population of mouse

Ans. (*b*)

24. **The 10% law for energy transfer in food chains was given by**
(a) Stanley (b) Tansley (c) Lindemann (d) Weismann

Ans. (*c*)

25. If 20 J of energy is trapped at producer levels, then how much energy will be available to peacock as food in the following chain? **Competency Based Que.**

Plant → Mice → Snake → Peacock

(a) 0.0002 J (b) 0.02 J (c) 0.002 J (d) 0.2 J

Ans. (*b*) Energy available to mice (primary consumers) = 20 J×0.1=2 J

Energy available to snakes (secondary consumers) = 2 J×0.1=0.2 J

Energy available to peacock (tertiary consumers) = 0.2 J×0.1=0.02 J

So, the energy available to the peacock will be 0.02 J.

26. The upright pyramid of number is absent in

(a) forest (b) lake (c) grassland (d) pond

Ans. (*a*)

Assertion-Reason Questions

Direction (Q. Nos. 1-11) *In each of the following questions, a statement of Assertion (A) is given and followed by corresponding statement of Reason (R). Of the statements, mark the correct answer.*

(a) Both A and R are true and R is the correct explanation of A

(b) Both A and R are true, but R is not the correct explanation of A

(c) A is true, but R is false

(d) A is false, but R is true

1. Assertion (A) An ecosystem is an interaction between biotic and abiotic components.

Reason (R) AG Tansley coined the term ecosystem.

Ans. (*b*)

2. Assertion (A) Complex interactions occurs in a pond ecosystem.

Reason (R) Pond ecosystem is a self-sustainable unit.

Ans. (*b*)

3. Assertion (A) Gross primary productivity is always less than net primary productivity.

Reason (R) Rate of synthesis of organic matter by consumers is known as secondary productivity. **Compartment 2024**

Ans. (*d*)

4. Assertion (A) Decomposition process is slower if detritus is rich in lignin and chitin.

Reason (R) Decomposition is largely an oxygen requiring process. **Delhi 2023**

Ans. (*b*)

5. Assertion (A) Lignin slow down the process of decomposition.

Reason (R) Lignin is a water-soluble substance in detritus.

Ans. (*c*) A is true, but R is false and R can be corrected as Lignin is hydrophobic substance. It contributes to the structural integrity of plant cell walls, making it more difficult for decomposers to break it down.

6. Assertion (A) Energy trapped in autotrophs does not get circulated.

Reason (R) Autotrophs trap energy from the sun.

Ans. (*d*)

7. Assertion (A) Herbivores are also called as first order consumers.

Reason (R) Herbivores obtain their food directly from plants.

Ans. (*a*)

8. Assertion (A) The standing crop is measured as the mass of living organisms.

Reason (R) It represents the entire living matter in a specific population at a particular time.

Ans. (*a*)

9. Assertion (A) In a terrestrial ecosystem, detritus food chain is a major conduict for energy flow.

Reason (R) Solar energy is a direct source of energy supply in the detritus food chains.

Ans. (*c*) A is true, but R is false and R can be corrected as Detritus food chains rely on energy stored in dead organic matter, not directly on solar energy.

10. Assertion (A) A network of food chains existing together in an ecosystem is known as a food web.

Reason (R) A bird like kite cannot be a part of a food web.

Ans. (*c*) A is true, but R is false and R can be corrected as

A bird like a kite can certainly be part of a food web as it may be a predator of various organisms, depending on the ecosystem.

11. Given below is the pond ecosystem, showing the complex interaction between biotic and abiotic factors. Study the ecosystem shown and comment upon the appropriateness of the Assertion and Reason.

Competency Based Que.

Assertion (A) The pyramid of number of the above ecosystem is upright.

Reason (R) Phytoplanktons are most abundant organisms, while secondary consumers are lesser in number in given ecosystem.

Ans. (*a*)

Subjective Questions

Very Short Answer Type Questions

1. Is an aquarium a complete ecosystem?

Or **Can an aquarium be considered a complete ecosystem?** **Competency Based Que.**

Ans. Yes, aquarium is a man-made ecosystem (artificial). If an ecosystem possesses all physical and biological components, then it is said to be complete.
Since, aquarium has both biotic components (plants and fishes) and abiotic components (air and water), so it is a complete ecosystem.

2. Name the basic component of the ecosystem.

Ans. Biotic and abiotic factors. (½ × 2)

3. What two abiotic factors might affect

(i) an animal living at bottom of the sea?

(ii) a plant growing on a mountain side?

Ans. (i) Light (ii) Temperature (½ × 2)

4. 'Ecosystem is called an interactive system'. Name a functional aspect of ecosystem which justifies the above statement. **Competency Based Que.**

Ans. An ecosystem is called an interactive system because it involves dynamic interactions between living organisms and their physical environment, where energy flow and nutrient cycling maintain balance and support life.

5. How is stratification represented in an ecosystem?

Ans. Stratification is the way in which different species in an ecosystem are placed or arranged vertically, occupying different levels. It is a way of minimising competition for limited resources vital for survival.

6. Write the equation that helps in deriving the net primary productivity of an ecosystem.

Or **How is the net primary productivity of an ecosystem derived?**

Ans. Net Primary Productivity (NPP) is the weight of the organic matter stored by the producers which is available to heterotrophs for consumption. It is equal to the rate of organic matter produced during photosynthesis (GPP) minus respiratory losses (R), i.e. $\text{NPP} = \text{GPP} - R$.

7. What does 'R' represent in the given equation for productivity in an ecosystem?

$$\text{GPP} - R = \text{NPP}$$

Ans. In the given equation for productivity in an ecosystem, 'R' represents the energy utilised by plants or producers in respiration. It is also referred to as respiratory losses.

8. All primary productivity is not available for herbivores. Give one reason.

Ans. Some of the gross primary productivity gets lost in the form of respiration, that is why all primary productivity is not available for herbivores.

9. Why is the rate of assimilation of energy at the herbivore level called secondary productivity?

Ans. The rate of assimilation of energy at herbivore (primary consumer) level is called secondary productivity because the biomass available to the organisms of this trophic level is a resultant of the primary productivity, which is formed by autotrophs (plants).

10. Why are oceans least productive? Explain.

Ans. Oceans are least productive because

(i) there is insufficient radiation as sunlight decreases with the increasing depth of the ocean.

(ii) oceans are nitrogen deficient which is an important nutrient for plants. (½ × 2)

11. Why are green algae not likely to be found in the deepest strata of the ocean? **Competency Based Que.**

Ans. Green algae are autotrophic organisms, i.e. they synthesise their own food during photosynthesis. At deepest layers of ocean, light is absent. So, photosynthesis does not take place there and hence green algae are not found in deep strata of the ocean.

12. How does the dead organic matter get decomposed in nature? Explain.

Ans. In nature, the decomposers like bacteria and fungi act on the dead organic matter and decompose it. Decomposition is a process of breaking down of complex organic matter into inorganic substances like CO_2, water and nutrients.

13. Which two major groups of organisms make up the bulk of decomposers?

Ans. Fungi and bacteria. (½ × 2)

14. Name the common detritivores in an ecosystem.

Ans. Earthworms.

15. Which are more numerous, secondary consumers or tertiary consumers?

Ans. Secondary consumers.

16. State what does standing crop of a trophic level represent.

Ans. Standing crop represents total amount of living matter or organic matter present in an ecosystem in an unit area and at a specific time.

17. List any two ways of measuring the standing crop of a trophic level.

Ans. Two ways of measuring the standing crop of a trophic level are

(i) biomass of living organisms.

(ii) number in an unit area. (½ × 2)

18. What is the starting point of a grazing food chain?

Ans. Producers.

19. Why is a food web formed in nature?

Ans. Many organisms occupy positions in different food chains and several food chain become inter-connected to form food web.

20. The energy flow in an ecosystem is unidirectional'. Justify the statement.

Or **Give an account of energy flow in an ecosystem.** **NCERT**

Ans. Energy in an ecosystem flows from producers to primary consumers, then from primary consumers to secondary consumers and so on. There is never a back flow of energy, i.e. energy cannot come back to a trophic level it has already passed. Therefore, the energy flow is unidirectional in an ecosystem. (1)

21. The diagram shows the flow of energy through an ecosystem.

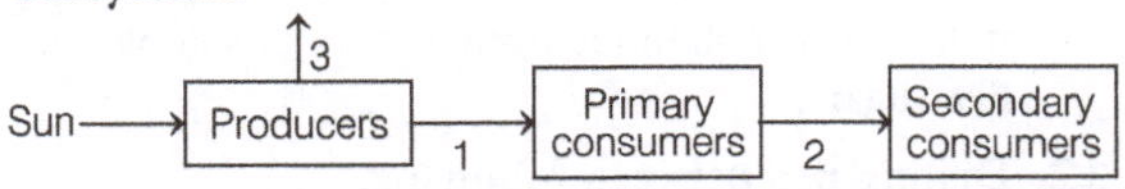

Which arrows represent the smallest amount of energy transferred between organisms and the largest amount of energy lost to the ecosystem? **Competency Based Que.**

Ans. The smallest amount of energy transferred is represented by arrow 2 and largest energy loss by arrow 3. (½ × 2)

22. In which case, the pyramid of number is inverted?

Ans. In a tree ecosystem.

23. What does the base tier of ecological pyramid represent?

Ans. Producer or first trophic level.

Short Answer Type Questions

1. What is natural ecosystem? Explain with the help of suitable example.

Ans. Refer to text on page no. 349.

2. Describe components of an ecosystem. **NCERT**

Ans. Refer to text on page no. 350.

3. Which of the following ecosystems will be more productive in terms of primary productivity? Justify your answer. A young forest, a natural old forest, a shallow polluted lake, alpine meadow. **NCERT Exemplar**

Ans. So, primary productivity varies from ecosystem to ecosystem. The ecosystem which possesses more producers will be more productive in terms of primary productivity. So, a natural old forest will be more productive in terms of primary productivity. The young forest is still developing, so it may contain fewer trees compared to the old forests.

The young forests therefore will not quench the solar radiation as much as old forests. Hence, old forest is more productive as compared to young one.

The shallow polluted lake will be less productive because of less number of producers and high amount of dead organic matter. Alpine meadows have a short growing period. They do not have trees, but contain simple plants such as grasses, hence they have low productivity. (1½ × 2)

4. Mention any two reasons, why the primary productivity varies in different types of ecosystems.

Ans. The primary productivity varies in different types of ecosystems as

(i) It depends upon plant species (producers) of a given ecosystem and their photosynthetic capacity.

(ii) It is dependent on various environmental factors like availability of nutrients, etc. (1 × 2)

5. (i) It was estimated that if an evergreen forest has a GPP of 400 J/m^2/day and 150 J/m^2 /day worth of carbon dioxide flows out of that forest, what is the NPP in that forest?

(ii) Explain why pyramids of energy must always be upright. **Competency Based Que.**

Ans. (i) NPP = GPP – *R*;

Given GPP = 400 J/m^2/day, R = 150 J/m^2/day, NPP = 400 J/m^2/day – 150 J/m^2 /day = 250 J/m^2 /day (1)

(ii) As energy flows from one trophic level to the next trophic level. Some amount of energy is lost in each trophic level in the form of heat. Therefore, the pyramid of energy is always upright and can never be inverted.

6. (i) Assume that, GPP forest A = GPP forest B = GPP forest C, If forest A has NPP = 1254 J/m^2/day; forest B, NPP =2157 J/m^2 /day; and forest C, NPP = 779 J/m^2 /day, which one of these forests has maximum energy loss by respiration? Give reason.

(ii) Draw an ecological pyramid of number of the following food chains

(a) Grass — Animal —Fleas on the host animal

(b) Tree — Insects — Woodpecker **CBSE SQP 2024**

Ans. (i) If GPP is equal, then we can manipulate the NPP equation and solve.

NPP = GPP – Respiration of plants;

Respiration of plants = GPP – NPP.

This means that the smallest NPP corresponds to the largest respiration. That is forest C. (1)

(ii)

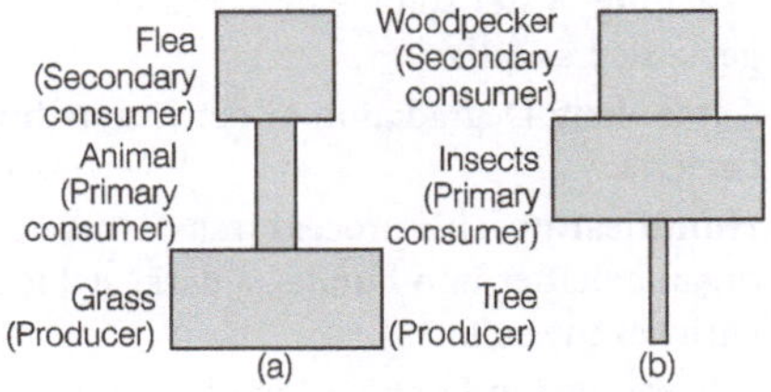

(½ × 2)

7. How would you differentiate between gross primary productivity from net primary productivity and secondary productivity of an ecosystem? CBSE 2020

Ans. The difference between gross primary productivity, net primary productivity and secondary productivity is as follows

Gross Primary Productivity	Net Primary Productivity	Secondary Productivity
It is the rate of production of biomass/organic matter by producers during photosynthesis.	It is equal to gross primary productivity minus respiration losses by the plants. The energy which is finally available to the consumers.	It is defined as the rate of production of organic matter by consumers over a period of time.

(1 × 3)

8. Differentiate between carnivores and consumers.

Ans. Refer to text on page no. 354 and 350.

9. How does a detritivore differ from a decomposer? Explain with an example.

Ans. The differences between detritivores and decomposers are as follows

Detritivores	Decomposers
These are soil dwelling small worm-like animals.	These are microorganisms.
These animals can ingest the food materials in their bodies.	They secrete their digestive enzymes over the matter to decompose it.
Ecologically, they cause fragmentation of detritus.	These organisms cause humification and mineralisation of organic matter.
e.g. earthworm.	e.g. bacteria, fungi.

(½ × 4)

10. Define decomposition and describe the processes and products of decomposition. NCERT

Ans. Decomposition is the process of disintegration of the complex organic matter to obtain water, carbon dioxide and nutrients with the help of decomposers. (1)

Process of Decomposition

(i) **Fragmentation** Detritivores breakdown large organic materials into smaller pieces, increasing surface area for microbial action.

(ii) **Leaching** Water soluble nutrients enters into the soil and get sealed as salts.

(iii) **Catabolism** Degradation of detritus by fungi and bacteria.

(iv) **Humification** This process transforms decomposed organic matter into humus, a dark, stable substance that enriches the soil.

(v) **Mineralisation** Degradation of humus to release inorganic nutrients such as water, carbon dioxide and nutrients into the soil. (1)

The products of decomposition include nutrients that enrich the soil, supporting plant growth and gases like carbon dioxide that are released into the atmosphere. Overall, decomposition is essential for nutrient cycling and maintaining ecosystem health. (1)

11. Describe how do oxygen and chemical composition of detritus control decomposition.

Ans. **Effect of Oxygen** The decomposition of detritus is an energy requiring process. Most of the decomposers (bacteria and fungi) are aerobic organisms. They require oxygen for their cellular activities, while acting on dead organic matter. (1)

Effect of Chemical Composition Decomposition rate is slower, if detritus is rich in lignin and chitin. It is quicker if detritus is rich in nitrogen and water soluble substances like sugars. (1)

12. Distinguish between following.

(i) Production and decomposition

(ii) Litter and detritus

(iii) Primary and secondary productivity NCERT

Ans. (i) Differences between production and decomposition are as follows

Production	Decomposition
It is the process of formation of organic matter.	It is the process of breaking down of complex organic matter into simpler inorganic compounds like water, carbon dioxide, other nutrients, etc.
It is dependent on photosynthesis, done by producers.	It is dependent on the decomposers.
For primary productivity, sunlight is required.	For decomposition, sunlight is not required.

(ii) Differences between litter and detritus are as follows

Litter	Detritus
It is composed of ground waste that has been disposed improperly.	It constitutes the remains of dead plants and animals.
It contains biodegradable and non-biodegradable material.	It contains mostly biodegradable material.

(iii) Difference between primary and secondary productivity is as follows

Primary Productivity	Secondary Productivity
It is the amount of organic matter produced by producers per unit area over a period of time.	It is defined as the rate of production of organic matter by consumers over a period of time.

(1 × 3)

13. Why is earthworm considered as farmer's friend? Explain humification and mineralisation occurring in a decomposition cycle. Competency Based Que.

Ans. Earthworms are farmer's friend because these help in fragmentation of detritus and loosening of the soil. Both of these processes are helpful for the decomposition of dead organic matter at a faster rate. (1)

Humification and mineralisation which occur during decomposition cycle are as follows

Humification It is the process of accumulation of dark coloured amorphous substance called humus. It is highly resistant to microbial action and undergoes decomposition at very slow rate.

Mineralisation It is the process by which organic matter is degraded by some microbes to release inorganic substances. (2)

14. Discuss the factors which affect the rate of decomposition.

Ans. Refer to text on page no. 353.

15. 'The energy flow in the ecosystem follows the second law of thermodynamics.' Explain. NCERT Exemplar

Ans. According to the second law of thermodynamics, every activity involving energy transformation is accompanied by the dissipation of some energy as heat and increase in disorderliness.

This can be explained as follows

Out of the total PAR only 2-10% is captured by photosynthetic organisms during the synthesis of organic matter. And further this energy is used during various metabolic processes for the formation of food and very little is stored as biomass.

This trapped energy as biomass is transferred to the next trophic level according to Lindemann's law. Only 10% of the stored energy is passed from one trophic level to successive trophic level, while rest is used for metabolic processes or lost as heat.

16. It is possible that a species may occupy more than one trophic level in the same ecosystem at the same time. Explain with the help of one example. Competency Based Que.

Ans. Yes, the trophic level of species represents its functional level in the energy flow. The preference of food habit depends on the available food. A single species may occupy more than one trophic level at the same time in an ecosystem. For example, sparrow is primary consumer when it eats seeds and secondary consumer when feeds on insects and worms.

17. 'In a food chain, a trophic level represents a functional level, not a species.' Explain. Competency Based Que.

Ans. All organisms occupy a particular place in their natural surrounding or in a community according to their feeding relationship with other organisms and the source of their nutrition or food.

In a food chain one trophic level is occupied by more than one species. For example, in a grassland ecosystem, rabbits and insects occupy the same trophic level, while both are different species. Therefore, one trophic level contains more than one species and is a functional level of different species rather than only one. (2)

18. Name the type of food chains responsible for the flow of larger fraction of energy in an aquatic and a terrestrial ecosystem, respectively.

Ans. Food chain operating in an aquatic ecosystem is the grazing food chain and in a terrestrial ecosystem is detritus food chain. (2)

19. Discuss the relationship between detritus food chain and grazing food chain in a terrestrial ecosystem.

Ans. The producers occupy the first trophic level in terrestrial ecosystem and thus, make the base of food chain. These producers (plants) are grazed upon by the grazers (herbivores) so herbivores are primary consumers. Primary carnivores prey upon herbivores and are eaten up by the secondary carnivores.

The top carnivores are ferocious and are not eaten up by any other animal. The decomposers act on all dead animals/plants and return nutrients stored in them to the soil. These nutrients are then again used up by the plants and cycle goes on. This way the grazing food chain and detritus food chains are linked up.

20. Organisms at a higher trophic level have less energy available. Comment. NCERT Exemplar

Ans. The energy flow in the ecosystem follows Lindemann's 10% energy law. According to this law, only 10% of the energy available at each trophic level, gets transferred to the next trophic level, the rest is lost in the environment as heat.

As we move to higher trophic levels, the energy available to organisms keeps on decreasing. Thus, the top carnivore gains the least energy in a food chain.

21. The number of trophic levels in an ecosystem are limited. Comment. NCERT Exemplar

Ans. The number of trophic levels in an ecosystem are limited and are not more than 3-4. It is because that the amount of energy flow decreases with successive trophic level. Only 10% of energy is transferred from one trophic level to the next trophic level and rest of the energy is lost in the form of respiration and other vital activities to maintain life. If more trophic levels are present, the residual energy will be limited and will decrease to such an extent that it cannot further support any trophic level. So, the food chain is generally limited to 3-4 trophic levels only.

22. (i) How many primary producers do you think would be needed to support six tertiary consumers in a grassland ecosystem?

(ii) Draw a grassland pyramid to substantiate answer. CBSE 2020

Ans. (i and ii) In grassland ecosystem, the number of producers (plants) is highest to support fewer herbivores (primary consumers) and carnivores (secondary and tertiary consumers). This can be understood by the following pyramid of number in a grassland ecosystem.

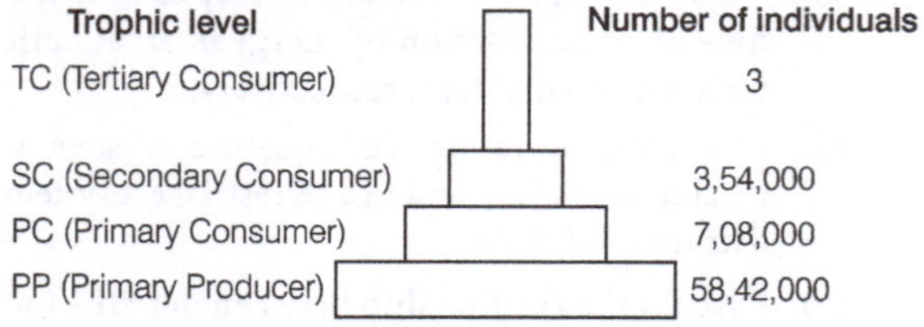

Pyramid of numbers in a grassland ecosystem

Only three top carnivores are supported in an ecosystem based on the production of nearly 60 lakh plants. As mentioned above, three tertiary consumers are supported by 60 lakh plants. Six tertiary consumers will be supported by 120 lakh plants. (1½ × 2)

23. Distinguish between

(i) Grazing food chain and detritus food chain. **CBSE 2024C NCERT**

(ii) Upright and inverted pyramid.

(iii) Food chain and food web.

Ans. (i) Refer to text on page no. 354. (1)

(ii) Differences between upright and inverted pyramid are as follows

Upright Pyramid	Inverted Pyramid
In this type of pyramid, the number and biomass of organisms at producer level is highest and keeps on decreasing at each trophic level.	In this type of pyramid, the number and biomass of organisms at producer level is lowest and keeps on increasing at each trophic level.
Energy pyramid is always upright.	Pyramid of number and pyramid of biomass can be inverted.

(1)

(iii) Differences between food chain and food web are as follows

Food Chain	Food Web
It is a linear sequence of organisms.	It is an interconnection of many food chains.
Members present at higher trophic level feeds on single type of organisms.	One organism has alternate food sources.
The energy flow can be easily calculated.	Energy flow is difficult to calculate.

(1)

24. Construct an ideal pyramid of energy when 10,00,000 J of sunlight is available. Label all its levels. **Competency Based Que.**

Ans.

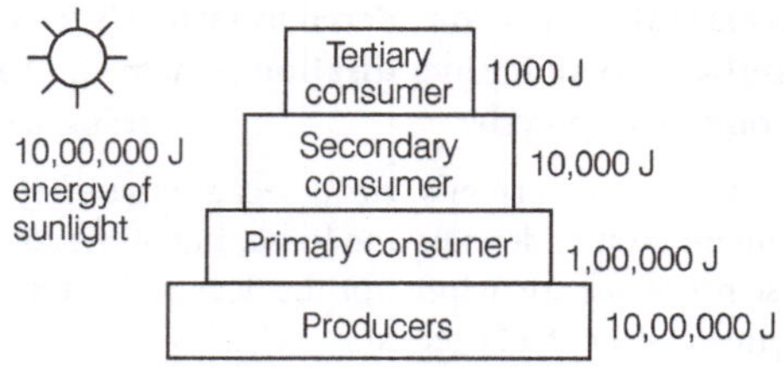

Ideal pyramid of energy

25. Study the diagram of a pyramid of biomass given below. Name the two standing crop that could be occupying level A and level B in it. Name this type of pyramid and the ecosystem in which it is found. **CBSE 2024**

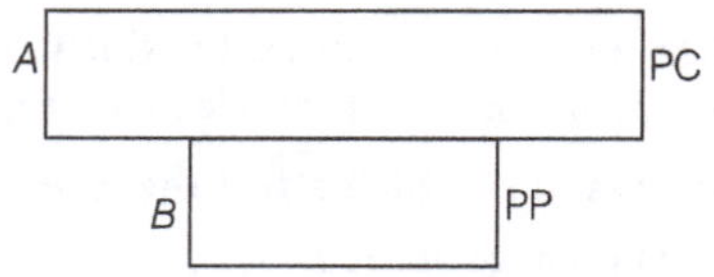

Ans. *A* – Zooplankton , *B* – Phytoplankton (½ × 2)

This is the inverted pyramid of biomass. It is found in sea ecosystem/ aquatic ecosystem. (1)

26. Correctly depict (also indicate the trophic level) and describe the ecological pyramid of number with 32 birds dependent on 20 insects feeding on one banyan tree. **CBSE 2025**

Ans.

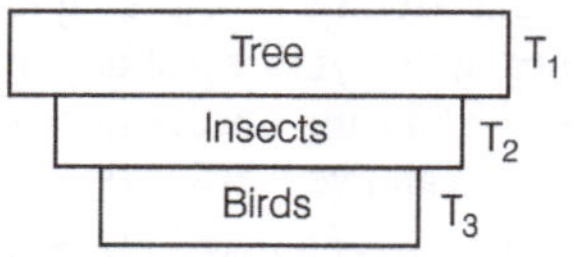

The pyramid of number represents the number of individuals at each trophic level. In this pyramid, the banyan tree (producer) is at the base, supporting many consumers. 20 insects (primary consumers) feed on the banyan tree. 32 birds (secondary consumers) feed on the insects. This pyramid is inverted since a single tree supports a larger number of consumers.

Long Answer Type Questions

1. What is primary productivity? Give brief description of factors that affect primary productivity. **NCERT**

Or **Describe the various environmental factors affecting primary productivity.**

Ans. Refer to text on page no. 351.

2. (i) Taking example of a small pond, explain how the four components of an ecosystem function as a unit.

(ii) Name the type of food chain that is major conduit of energy flow in a pond.

Ans. (i) Refer to text on page no. 350. (4)

(ii) Grazing food chain exists in a pond. (1)

3. Given below is a list of autotrophs and heterotrophs. With your knowledge about food chain, establish various linkages between the organisms on the principle of 'eating and being eaten'. What is this inter-linkage established known as?

Algae, *Hydrilla*, grasshopper, rat, squirrel, crow, maize plant, deer, rabbit, lizard, wolf, snake, peacock, phytoplankton, crustaceans, whale, tiger, lion, sparrow, duck, crane, cockroach, spider, toad, fish, leopard, elephant, goat, *Nymphaea*, *Spirogyra*.

Competency Based Que.

Ans. A straight line sequence of 'who eats whom' or eating and being eaten in an ecosystem is called a food chain.

A network of cross connecting food chains involving producers, consumers and decomposers is termed as a food web. (1)

Lion and tiger – Top carnivores (Top trophic level). (1)

Spider, cockroach, lizard, wolf, snake, toad, fish and crane – Secondary consumers (IIIrd trophic level). (1)

Crustaceans, grasshopper, deer, mouse, squirrel, rabbit, elephant and goat – Primary consumers (IInd trophic level). (1)

Phytoplankton, algae, *Hydrilla*, maize plant, *Nymphaea* and *Spirogyra* – Producers (Ist trophic level). (1)

4. (i) What is a trophic level in an ecosystem? What is 'standing crop' with reference to it?

(ii) Explain the role of the 'first trophic level' in an ecosystem.

(iii) How is the detritus food chain connected with the grazing food chain in a natural ecosystem?

Ans. (i) **Trophic Level** Organisms occupy a place in the natural surroundings or in a community according to their feeding relationship with the other organisms. The specific place occupied by organisms, in the food chain, on the basis of their nutrition or food is known as their trophic level.

Standing crop is the mass of a living material at a particular time in a trophic level. (1½)

(ii) **First Trophic Level** It consists of producers. These are autotrophs. They trap the light energy and convert it into chemical energy.

The organisms of other trophic levels, i.e. consumers, depend on them for their energy and food requirement. Thus, first trophic level plays a very important role in the ecosystem. (1½)

(iii) Grazing food chain starts from green plants and ends at carnivores by passing through the herbivores. It is the major conduit of energy flow in aquatic. It binds up inorganic nutrients.

Given below is the grazing food chain.

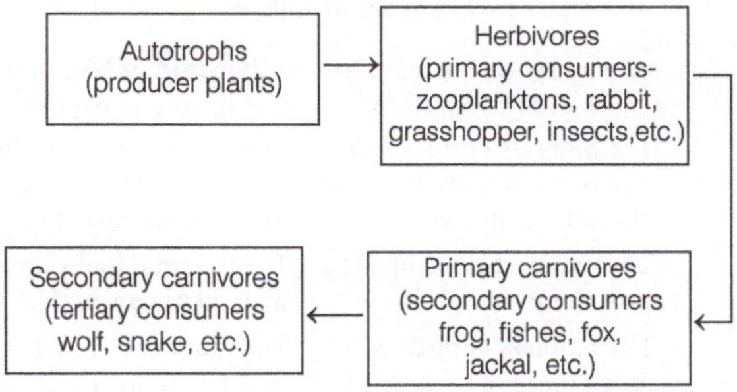

Detritus food chain begins from dead organic matter or detritus. The microbes degrade dead organic matter and are also known as **saprotrophs** or **decomposers**. This food chain helps in releasing inorganic nutrients to the cycling pool.

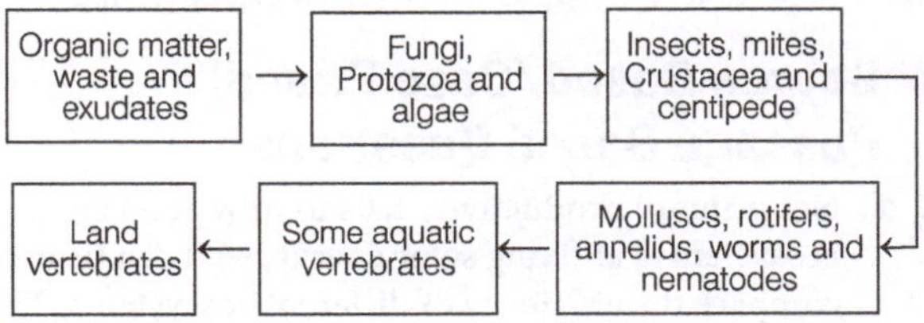

Connection Nutrients released by decomposers of detritus food chain are utilised by plants or autotrophs of grazing food chain. These plants inturn transfer these nutrients to other organisms. The dead remains of these organisms are source of food for the decomposers. (2)

5. (i) Draw a pyramid of numbers of a situation, where a large population of insects feeds upon a very big tree. The insects inturn are eaten by small birds, which inturn are fed upon by big birds.

(ii) Differentiate giving reason, between the pyramid of biomass of the above situation and the pyramid of numbers that you have drawn.

Or **In a botanical garden of a city there is a huge banyan tree growing on which hundreds of birds and thousands of insects live. Draw the pyramids of numbers and also biomass represented by this community. Comment giving reasons on the two different pyramids drawn.**

Ans. (i) Structure of a pyramid of number is given below

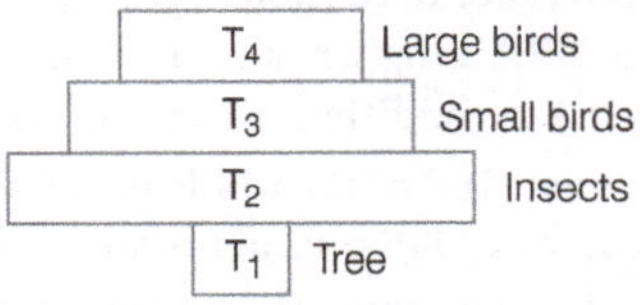

Pyramid of number

(2)

(ii) Differences between pyramid of biomass and number in a tree ecosystem are as follows

Pyramid of Biomass in a Tree Ecosystem	Pyramid of Number in a Tree Ecosystem
The biomass of the single tree is much more than the biomass of insects.	The base is much smaller with a single tree compared to the thousands of insects.
The pyramid looks upright with these two levels.	The pyramid looks inverted with these two levels.
The biomass of birds is much more than those of insects.	The number of birds feeding on the insects is less than that of insects.

(1 × 3)

6. Define ecological pyramids and describe with examples, pyramids of number and biomass. NCERT

Ans. Refer to text on page no. 356 (Ecological pyramid.)

Source Based/Case Based/ Passage Based Questions

1. Net primary productivity tells us how good an ecosystem is at fixing solar energy, so it can be used to compare the efficiency of different ecosystems. This graph shows the NPP of a variety of ecosystems. Competency Based Ques.

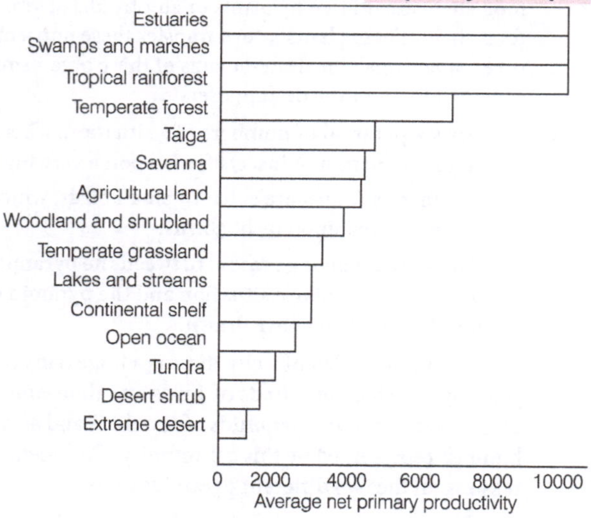

(i) With reference to the above graph, give reason why average NPP is higher in topical rainforest when compared to conditions of extreme desert.

(ii) The annual NPP of the whole biosphere is approximately 175 billion tonnes of organic matter. Out of this the productivity of ocean is only 55 billion tons. Give reason.

(iii) Compare the NPP of temperate forest to that of temperate grassland and answer which of these two has a higher NPP?

Or

(iii) Which factor would affect net primary productivity the most?

Ans. (i) Net primary productivity is affected by temperature, water availability and nutrients all of which are abiotic factors. In tropical rainforests, water, sunlight and high temperature are consistent as compared to desert. Therefore, concentration of plant is present, causing both GPP and NPP to be highs. (2)

(ii) In ocean, the limiting factor for productivity is light as producers depend on light which is scanty in deeper layers. Also the amount of minerals in oceanic water is low. (1)

(iii) Temperate forests have higher NPP compared to temperate grassland due to greater biomass and more energy capture through photosynthesis. (1)

Or

(iii) Sunlight is the main factor that would affect net primary productivity the most. (1)

2. Observe the given diagram and answer the questions that follows Competency Based Que.

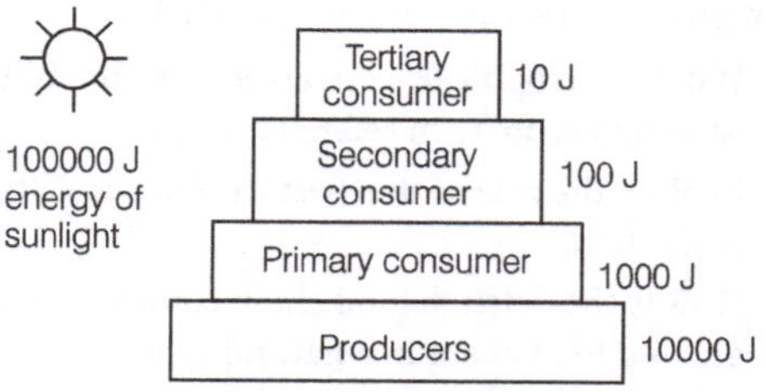

(i) Energy is lost as heat at each step of trophic level. What does it depicts?

(ii) Can a given species occupy more than one trophic level in the same ecosystem at the same time?

(iii) Enlist any two limitations of ecological pyramids.

Ans. (i) At each step of food chain when food energy is transferred from one trophic level to the next higher trophic level, some energy is lost as heat and only 10% of the energy is transferred to the next level. (1)

(ii) Yes, a sparrow is a primary consumer when it eats seeds, fruits, peas and a secondary consumer when it eats insects and worms. (1)

(iii) (a) It does not take into account the same species belonging to two or more trophic levels. (1)

(b) It assumes a simple food chain, which never exists in nature. (1)

SELF ASSESSMENT TEST

Multiple Choice Questions

1. Which of the following factors does not directly influence an ecosystem's productivity?
   (a) Latitude
   (b) Water availability
   (c) Soil pH
   (d) Temperature
2. Which of the following is not a characteristic of a stable ecosystem?
   (a) High biodiversity
   (b) Resilience to disturbances
   (c) Constant energy flow
   (d) Low productivity
3. In a food chain, which of the following represents a tertiary consumer?
   (a) Grasshopper
   (b) Frog
   (c) Snake
   (d) Hawk
4. If a specific ecosystem has a high diversity of primary producers, what effect is likely observed at the secondary consumer level?
   (a) Decreased biomass of secondary consumers
   (b) Increased competition among secondary consumers
   (c) Increased biomass of secondary consumers
   (d) No effect on secondary consumers
5. What is the primary factor limiting the number of trophic levels in an ecosystem?
   (a) Nutrient availability
   (b) Energy loss at each trophic level
   (c) Competition among species
   (d) Habitat size
6. In a typical food chain, what is the primary reason that energy transfer from one trophic level to the next is inefficient?
   (a) Energy is lost as heat through metabolic processes.
   (b) Not all organisms at the lower trophic levels are consumed.
   (c) Some energy is used for reproduction.
   (d) Both (a) and (b)

Assertion-Reason Questions

Direction (Q. Nos. 7-11) *In each of the following questions, a statement of Assertion (A) is given followed by corresponding statement of Reason (R). Of the statements, mark the correct answer.*

(a) Both A and R are true and R is the correct explanation of A.
(b) Both A and R are true, but R is not the correct explanation of A.
(c) A is true, but R is false.
(d) A is false, but R is true.

7. **Assertion** (A) Energy transfer between trophic levels is typically around 10%.

   Reason (R) Only a fraction of energy from one trophic level is converted into biomass at the next level.
8. **Assertion** (A) Trophic levels do not vary significantly in aquatic ecosystems compared to terrestrial ecosystems.

   Reason (R) Aquatic ecosystems often have a higher efficiency of energy transfer due to lower resistance in water.

9. **Assertion** (A) Biotic factors include all living components of an ecosystem, such as plants and animals.
Reason (R) Biotic factors are solely responsible for shaping the physical environment of an ecosystem.

10. **Assertion** (A) Overfishing can lead to the collapse of marine trophic levels.
Reason (R) Removing top predators disrupts the balance and affects the population of primary producers.

11. **Assertion** (A) In a forest ecosystem, the presence of large herbivores can influence the growth patterns of vegetation.
Reason (R) Herbivores act as biotic factors that primarily compete with each other for resources, affecting the distribution of plant species.

Very Short Answer Type Questions

12. Which is the important link between the abiotic and biotic components of ecosystem?
13. The Tundra desert's Gross Primary Productivity (GPP) is 800 kilocalories/m^2 and respiration losses are about 200 kilocalories. What is the net primary productivity of the desert?
14. Give reason 'Mass lost in faeces is considered available biomass for decomposers.

Short Answer Type Questions

15. Compare the stability of a food chain with 4 trophic levels to one with 7 trophic levels.
16. The first law of thermodynamics states that energy can neither be created nor destroyed, only altered in form. Does the energy flow in an ecosystem follow this rule? Justify.
17. What is the term for the mass of living material at each trophic level at a given time and how is it measured?
18. What does the pyramid of biomass represent in an ecosystem?

Long Answer Type Questions

19. What are the key components of a pond ecosystem and how do biotic and abiotic factors interact to maintain its balance?
20. What role does decomposition play in ecosystems and how do decomposers contribute to the process of decomposition, soil health and overall ecosystem productivity?
21. What is energy flow in ecosystems and how does it transfer through different trophic levels? How does the 10% rule illustrate the energy loss at each trophic level?

Case Based Question

22. Given below is the approximate percentage content of cellulose, hemicellulose and lignin composition of the same mass of dried grass and coconut husks.

	Cellulose	Hemicellulose	Lignin
Dried grass	40%	40%	20%
Coconut husks	25%	20%	50%

(i) Considering ambient climatic conditions, which of these will take longer to decompose and why?
(ii) If these materials are found in marshy soils, would overall decomposition be faster? Justify.
(iii) How would the presence of microorganisms affect the decomposition rate of these materials? Explain.

Answers

1. (a) 2. (d) 3. (d) 4. (c) 5. (b) 6. (d) 7. (a) 8. (d)
9. (c) 10. (a) 11. (b)

13 CHAPTER

Biodiversity and Its Conservation

There are millions of plant and animals present on earth with every distinct geographical location having its own set of flora and fauna.
This immense diversity exists at all levels of biological organisation from micromolecules within the cell to biomes.
This **variety** and **variability** of living organisms on the earth is referred to as **biodiversity.**
It can also be defined as the variety of life forms, gene pools and habitats found in an ecosystem.

YOUR STUDY GOALS

13.1 Levels of Biodiversity
13.2 Magnitude of Biodiversity
13.3 Patterns of Biodiversity
13.4 Loss of Biodiversity
13.5 Biodiversity Conservation

YOUR PRACTICE GOAL

- Objective Type Questions (35 Qs ; MCQs, A-R) Case Based Questions (4)
- Subjective Type Questions
- (25 VSAs, 47 SAs, 10 LAs)

- The term 'biodiversity' was popularised by sociobiologist **Edward Wilson** to describe the combined diversity at all the levels of biological organisation.
- In this chapter, we will be studying about the different levels of biodiversity, its magnitude, its distribution patterns and the causes of its loss.

13.1 Levels of Biodiversity

The biodiversity has three inter-related components or hierarchical levels of biological organisation which are described below

Genetic Diversity

- It is the diversity in the number and types of genes among individuals of a species.
- Genetic diversity is useful as it enables the adaptation to changing environmental condition.

- A single species might show high diversity at the genetic level over its distributional range.
- For example,
  - India has more than 50,000 genetically different strains of rice and 1000 varieties of mango.
  - *Rauwolfia vomitoria*, a medicinal plant growing in different Himalayan ranges shows genetic variation in terms of concentration and potency of the active chemical (reserpine) that the plant produces.

Species Diversity

- It is the diversity at the species level or the measure of the variety of species and their relative abundance within a region, e.g. Western Ghats have more amphibian species diversity than Eastern Ghats.
- There are more than 20,000 species of ants, 3,00,000 species of beetles, 28,000 species of fishes and nearly 20,000 species of orchids.
- Two important measures of species diversity are
  - **Species Richness** It refers to the number of species per unit area. Species diversity increases, if the species richness is higher.
  - **Species Evenness** It refers to the relative abundance of species in an area.
  - The number of individuals and variety determine the level of diversity of an ecosystem.

Ecological Diversity

- It refers to the diversity at ecosystem level.
- Due to the presence of a greater variety of ecosystems and habitats, i.e. rainforest, desert, wetlands, mangroves, coral reefs and alpine meadows, India has a greater ecological diversity than Scandinavian countries (e.g. Norway).

13.2 Magnitude of Biodiversity

- According to **International Union for Conservation of Nature and Natural Resources** (IUCN) 2004, the total number of plant and animal species described so far is more than 1.5 million.
- For many taxonomic groups, species inventories are more complete in temperate than in tropical countries.
- Assuming that a large number of species are still undiscovered in the tropics, biologists make a statistical comparison of the temperate-tropical species richness of an exhaustively studied group of insects and extrapolate this ratio to other groups of animals and plants.
- This leads to a gross estimate of the total number of species on earth, that ranges from 20-50 million.
- A more conservative and scientifically sound estimate by **Robert May** places the global species diversity at about 7 million.

Some Important Aspects About Global Species Diversity

- More than 70% of all the species recorded are animals, while plants comprise not more than 22% of the total.
- Insects are the most species rich taxonomic group in animal kingdom, making more than 70% of the total animals. It means, out of every 10 animals, 7 are insects on the earth.
- Number of fungi species in the world is more than the total number of species of fishes, amphibians, reptiles and mammals.

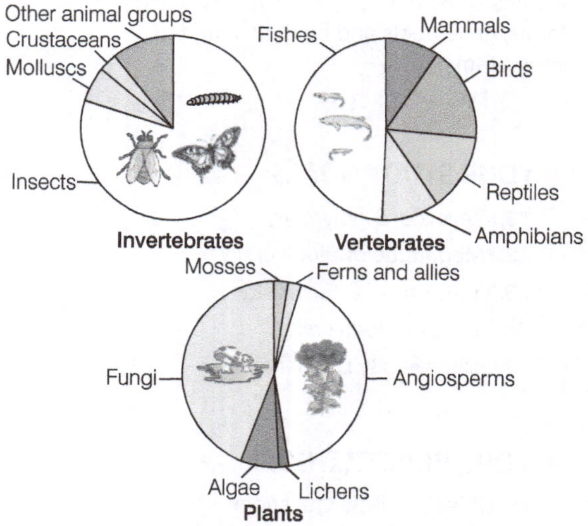

Fig. 13.1 Representation of global biodiversity of major taxa of invertebrates, vertebrates and plants

- But biologists are still not sure about the diversity of prokaryotic species like protists, and bacteria, etc. This is because of the following reasons
  - The conventional taxonomic methods are not sufficient for identifying these microbial species.

- Most of the species cannot be cultured under laboratory conditions.
- If molecular and biochemical criteria are adopted for delineating microbial species their diversity could reach into millions.

Some Important Aspect About Indian Species Diversity

- India is one of the 12 megadiverse countries of the world.
- All though India has only 2.4% of the world's land, but it shares an impressive 8.1% of the world's species diversity.
- Nearly 45,000 species of plants and twice as many of animals have been recorded from India.
- If we accept Robert May's global estimation then only 22% of species have been recorded.
- India probably has more than 1,00,000 species of plants and 3,00,000 species of animals yet to be discovered and described.

Quick Test 1

1. Identify the term which refers to the number of different species in a specific area?
2. Name the term that is used for the genetic differences observed in *Rauwolfia vomitoria* and rice strains.
3. Write the level of biodiversity represented by a mangrove.
4. **State True or False.**
   (i) Western Ghats have more species diversity than Eastern Ghats.
   (ii) India has 4.2 per cent of the world's land, but it shares an impressive 8.1 per cent of the world's.
5. Which taxonomic group accounts for over 70% of the animal species?

13.3 Patterns of Biodiversity

- Biodiversity is not uniform throughout the world, but shows a rather uneven distribution.
- It varies with the changes in latitude and altitude.
- For many groups of animals and plants, there are specific patterns of diversity.
- Two of them are discussed below

1. Latitudinal Gradients

- Species diversity decreases as we move away from the equator towards the poles.
- It means biodiversity is more at lower latitude (equator) than the higher latitude (poles).
- Tropics (latitudinal range of 23.5°N to 23.5°S) harbour more species than temperate or polar areas. Pattern of distribution of some birds are given below
  - Colombia located near the equator, has 1,400 species of birds, New York located at 41°N has 105 species of birds, while Greenland at 71°N has only 56 species of birds.
  - India, with most of its land area in tropical latitude has more than 1,200 species of birds.
- A forest of equal area in tropical region (like equator) has ten times more species of vascular plants than in temperate region like Mid-West of USA.
- The largely tropical **Amazonian rainforest** in South America has the greatest biodiversity on the earth with more than 40,000 species of plants, 3,000 of fishes, 1,300 of birds, 427 of mammals and amphibians, 378 of reptiles and more than 1,25,000 of invertebrates.
- About 2 million species of insects are still waiting to be discovered and named in these rainforests as estimated by scientists.

Reasons for Greater Biodiversity in Tropics

Ecologists and evolutionary biologists have proposed various hypothesis, some important ones are given below

- Temperate regions were subjected to frequent glaciation in the past while the tropics have remained undisturbed for million of years, providing more evolutionary time for species diversification.
- Tropical environments are less seasonal, relatively more constant and predictable as compared to temperate regions.
  Such constant environments have promoted niche specialisation and thus lead to greater species diversity.
- More solar energy is available in tropics, which contributes to the higher productivity and indirectly to greater species diversity.

- Resource availability is higher and rate of extinction is low in tropics.

2. Species-Area Relationships

- **Alexander von Humboldt** (German naturalist and geographer), while explorings the wilderness of South American jungles observed that within a region, species richness increased with increasing explored area, but only upto a limit.
- The relationship between species richness and area for wide variety of taxa (e.g. birds, bats, fishes in freshwater) turns out to be a rectangular hyperbola.
- On a logarithmic scale, the relationship is a straight line and is described by the following equation

$$\text{Log } S = \log C + Z \log A$$

where, S = Species richness, A = Area
Z = Slope of the line (regression coefficient)
C = Y-intercept

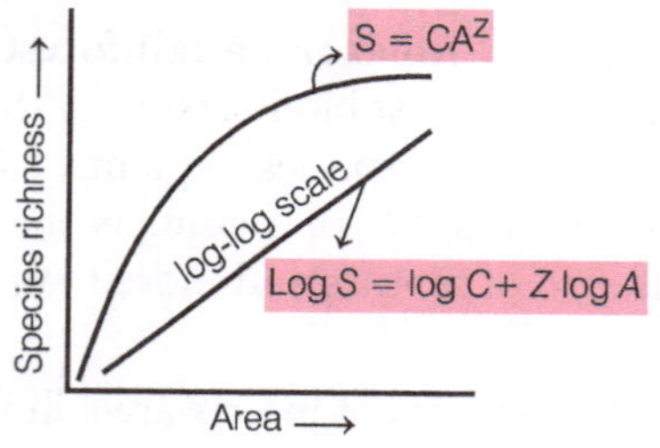

Fig. 13.2 A graph showing species-area relationship which becomes linear on log scale

- The value of Z lies between 0.1-0.2 regardless of the taxonomic group or the region, whether it is plants in Britain, bird in California or molluscs in New York state.
- But for species-area relationship among very large areas like continents, the slope of the line will be much steeper.
- Here, the value of Z lies in the range of 0.6-1.2, e.g. for fruit eating (frugivorous) birds and mammals in tropical forests of different continents, the slope is found to be 1.15.

Importance of Species Diversity to the Ecosystem

- Ecologists believed that communities with more species tend to be more stable than those with less species.
- A stable community shows following characteristics
  - It does not show too much of variations in the year-to-year productivity.
  - It must be either resistant or resilient to occasional disturbance (man-made or natural).
  - It must be resistant to invasion by alien species.
- This was confirmed by **David Tilman.** Through his long-term ecosystem experiments using outdoor plots he provided some concrete evidences of link between species richness and stable community.
- According to him, diverse communities show almost constant productivity in total biomass and also contributes to higher productivity.

Rivet Popper Hypothesis

- Rich biodiversity is not only essential for ecosystem health, but also imperative for the very survival of the human race on this planet.
- However, the loss of species at present disrupts the stability of an ecosystem.
- **Paul Ehrlich** proposed rivet popper hypothesis for the effect of decrease in biodiversity of an ecosystem.
- According to this hypothesis, ecosystem is like an aeroplane and all its parts are joined together using thousands of rivets (species).
- If every passenger, travelling in it, starts popping a rivet to take home (causing a species to become extinct), it may not affect flight safety (proper functioning of the ecosystem), but as more and more rivets are removed the plane becomes dangerously weak over a period of time.
- Moreover, which rivet is removed is also crucial, e.g. loss of rivet on the wings (key species that drive major ecosystem functions) is a more serious threat than loss of rivets on seats or windows inside the plane.

13.4 Loss of Biodiversity

- Biological wealth of earth is declining rapidly.
- Human activities are the major reasons for it, e.g. the colonisation of tropical Pacific Islands by humans has led to the extinction of more than 2,000 native bird species.
- **IUCN Red List** of threatened species is an inventory of global conservation status of biological species, which is compiled in **Red Data Book**.

- IUCN Red list (2004) enlists the extinction of 784 species (including 338 vertebrates, 359 invertebrates and 87 plants) in the last 500 years.
- Some examples of recent extinction are
    - Dodo (Mauritius), quagga (Africa), thylacine (Australia), Steller's sea cow (Russia) and three sub-species of tiger (Bali, Javan and Caspian).
    - About 27 species have disappeared from the world in the last 20 years in the world, with more than 15,500 species being endangered.
    Presently 12% of all bird species, 23% of all mammal species, 32% of all amphibian species and 31% of all gymnosperms species are facing threat of extinction.

Note **Endangered species** are those species which are facing a high risk of extinction in the near future.

Extinction in Biodiversity

- Study of fossil record reveals that large scale loss of species had also occurred earlier, even before humans appeared on the scene.
- There have been five episodes of **mass extinctions** during the long period of >3 billion years due to natural calamities, e.g. extinction of dinosaurs.
- Currently, the earth is heading towards the **sixth extinction**, which is different from the previous episodes in the rates.
- The current species extinction rates are estimated to be 100-1,000 times faster than in the pre-human times and human activities are responsible for the faster rates.
- If the present rate of species extinction goes on, 50% of the species might be wiped out within next 100 years.
- In general, loss of biodiversity may lead to
    - decline in plant production.
    - lower resistance and resilience to environment perturbations such as drought.
    - increased variability in ecosystem processes such as plant productivity, water use, pest and disease cycles, etc.

Causes of Loss of Biodiversity

- Human activities have accelerated the rate of extinction of species from the earth.
- The four major causes also called the **evil quartet** responsible for the loss of biodiversity are as follows

1. Habitat Loss and Fragmentation

- Destruction of habitat is the most important cause of extinction of both plant and animal species.
- The most dramatic example of habitat loss is tropical rainforests (once covering more than 14% of the earth's land surface is now limited to only 6% in the last few years).
- The **Amazon rainforest** (lungs of the planet) are also being cut and destroyed for cultivation of soybean or is converted to grasslands for raising beef cattle.
- Besides total loss, the degradation of many habitats by pollution also threatens the survival of many species.
- When large habitats are broken up into small fragments, mammals and birds requiring large territories and certain animals with migratory habits are badly affected, leading to their population decline.

2. Overexploitation

- Humans are always dependent on nature for food and shelter.
- But when human needs turn into greed, it leads to the overexploitation of natural resources.
- Many species that have gone extinct in last 500 years were due to overexploitation, e.g. Steller's sea cow, passenger pigeon, etc.
- Presently many marine fishes are overharvested, which is threatening the existence of some commercially important species.

3. Alien (Exotic) Species Invasions

- Introduction of alien species also causes the risk of extinction.
- When alien species are introduced, some of them turn invasive and cause decline or extinction of indigenous species.

- Some examples of alien species invasion are as follows
  - The **Nile perch**, a large predator fish when introduced into the lake Victoria in East Africa, eventually led to the extinction of an ecologically unique assemblage of more than 200 species of cichlid fish in the lake.
  - Water hyacinth (*Eichhornia*) was introduced in Indian water resulting in death of several aquatic plant and animals.
  - *Lantana* and *Parthenium* had caused immense environmental damage and posed threat to native species.
  - The recent illegal introduction of African catfish (*Clarias gariepinus*) for aquaculture purpose is posing a threat to the indigenous catfishes of Indian rivers.

4. Co-extinctions

- When a species becomes extinct, the plant and animal species associated with it, in an obligatory way also become **extinct**, e.g. if a species of fish becomes extinct, all the parasites unique/specific to that fish also face extinction.
- Similarly, in case of a co-evolved plant pollinator (mutualism), extinction of one species invariably leads to the extinction of the other.

Quick Test 2

1. Name the region which generally harbors more species than temperate or polar areas.
2. Identify the term that refers to the pattern of species diversity decreasing from the equator toward the poles.
3. **State True or False.**
   (i) Colombia, located near the equator, has fewer bird species than New York.
   (ii) The Amazon rainforest is home to the greatest biodiversity on earth.
4. Name the invasive weed species which is known for its environmental damage and threat to native species.
5. The term *X* refers to species that cause the decline or extinction of native species after being introduced, identify *X*.

13.5 Biodiversity Conservation

- Conservation of biodiversity is protection, upliftment and scientific management of biodiversity.
- It maintains the biodiversity at the optimum level and derive sustainable benefits for the present as well as future generations.

Reasons for Conserving Biodiversity

- There are many reasons for conservation of biodiversity and all reasons are equally important.
- They can be grouped into three categories which are as follows

1. Narrowly Utilitarian Argument

- These are based on obvious reasons.
- Humans derive countless direct economic benefits from the nature like food (cereals, pulses and fruits), firewood, fibre, construction material, industrial products (tannins, lubricants, dyes, resins and perfumes) and products of medicinal importance.
- More than 25% of the drugs currently sold in the market worldwide are derived from plants and 25,000 plant species are used as traditional medicines used by native people around the world.
- Moreover, biodiversity rich countries expect to reap more benefits from the increasing resources put into **bioprospecting**, i.e. exploration of molecular, genetic and species-level diversity for obtaining products of economic importance.

2. Broadly Utilitarian Argument

According to this argument, biodiversity plays a major role in ecosystem services that nature provides. Some of these are

- Production of oxygen, e.g. Amazon forests produce 20% of the total oxygen in the earth's atmosphere *via* photosynthesis.
- Pollination of flowers, without which fruits and seeds are not produced is provided by pollinator layer, i.e. bees, bumble bees, birds and bats.
- Control of floods and soil erosion.
- Intangible benefits of nature like aesthetic pleasures of watching spring flower in full bloom, walking through thick forest, listening to bulbul's song, etc.

3. Ethical Argument

- Every species has an intrinsic value, even if it is not of any economic value to us.
- It is our moral duty to care for their well-being and pass on our biological legacy in good order to future generations.
- Moreover, many plants like tulsi and peepal have religious importance as well.

How do We Conserve Biodiversity?

- Biodiversity can be conserved by protecting its whole ecosystem.
- There are two basic approaches for conservation of biodiversity.

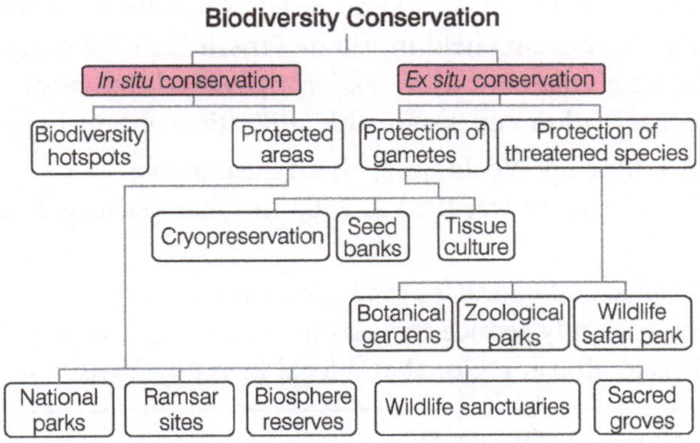

I. *In Situ* (On-site) Conservation

- This conservation strategy involves conservation of living organisms within their natural habitats.
- The *in situ* conservation allows the population to maintain itself with in its community environment.
- However, it is not economically feasible to conserve all the biological wealth at all the existing ecosystems. Methods used in *in situ* conservation are

1. Biodiversity Hotspots

- These are regions with very high levels of species richness, high degree of **endemism** (species confined to a region and not found anywhere else) and accelerated habitat loss. Thus, these areas are identified for maximum protection.
- Initially, 25 biodiversity hotspots were identified.
- Now, there are 34 hotspots all over the world.
- Out of these, hotspots in India lie in Western Ghats and Sri Lanka, Indo-Burma and Eastern Himalaya.
- If all the biodiversity hotspots are put together, they cover less than 2% of the earth's land area, but harbour extremely high diversity.
- Ongoing mass extinctions could be reduced by 30% through strict protection of these hotspots.

2. Protected Areas

- These are especially dedicated areas for protection and maintenance of ecologically unique and biodiversity rich regions.
- Protected areas are classified as

(i) National Parks

- Activities such as cultivation, grazing, forestry and habitat manipulation are not allowed here.
- India has 90 national parks.

(ii) Wildlife Sanctuaries

- Activities like collection of forest products, harvesting of timber, private ownership of land, tilling of land, etc., are allowed here.
- There number is 448 in India.

(iii) Biosphere Reserves

- People are an integral component of the system and play a major role. In these areas, multiple use of a single land is permitted.
- There are 14 biosphere reserves in India.

> **TEACHER'S TIP**
> A biosphere reserve consists of three zones as shown below
> - **Core Zone** No human activity is allowed in this zone.
> - **Buffer Zone** Limited activity is permitted.
> - **Transition Zone** Several human activites are allowed.

(iv) Sacred Groves

- These are tracts of forests with special religious importance in a particular culture and are also of mythological importance.
- These are undisturbed forests without any human interventions and include a number of rare, endangered and endemic species.
- Sacred groves are found in Khasi and Jaintia Hills in Meghalaya, Aravalli Hills of Rajasthan, Western Ghat regions of Karnataka and Maharashtra and the Sarguja, Chanda and Bastar areas of Madhya Pradesh.

- These are protected by native people as a part of cultural traditions.
- In Meghalaya, the sacred groves are the last refuges for a large number of rare and threatened plants.

(v) Ramsar Sites

- Ramasar sites are wetlands of international importance, designated under the Ramsar convention.
- These sites are recognised for their ecological value, supporting biodiversity water purification and flood control.
- Some of the Ramsar sites in India are Ashtamudi wetland (Kerala), Sambhar lake (Rajasthan), Chilika lake (Odisha), Renuka wetland (Himachal Pradesh), etc.

II. *Ex Situ* (Off-site) Conservation

This approach involves placing the threatened animals and plants in special care units for their protection.

Protection of Threatened Species

- It is done by relocating of wild and domesticated species from their natural habitates to specialised settings like in botanical gardens, zoological parks, wildlife safari parks, etc.
- There are many animals that have become extinct in the wild, but continued to maintained in zoological parks.

Protection of Gametes

The protection and maintenance of gametes is done by adopting following methods

- **Seed Banks** The storage of different genetic strains of threatened or commercially important plants in the form of seeds is one of the most widespread and valuable *ex situ* approaches of the conservation strategy.
- **Tissue Culture** Plant tissue culture is widely used to produce clones of a plant by a method known as **micropropagation**.

  This method is useful in maintaining a large number of genotypes in small area, rapid multiplication of even endangered species and for hybrid rescue, e.g. banana and potato.
- **Cryopreservation** It is a method of *in vitro* conservation of gametes of threatened species in viable and fertile condition for long periods.

International Initiatives

- Biodiversity conservation is a collective responsibility of all the nations.
- The historic convention on Biological Diversity (**The Earth Summit**) held in Rio de Janerio in 1992 called upon all the nations to take initiative in biodiversity conservation and sustainable utilisation of benefits.
- A follow up World Summit on Sustainable Development was held in 2002 in Johannesburg, South Africa.
- In this, 190 countries made commitments to significantly reduce the current rate of biodiversity loss at global, regional and local levels by 2010.

Quick Test 3

1. Name the procedure which involves the conservation of living organism in their natural habitat.
2. *X* represents the zone of biodiversity in which no human activity is allowed. Identify the zone.
3. Name the term which refers to protected forest areas considered holy by local communities.
4. Name the technique which is used to preserve gametes of threatened species in viable and fertile condition for long periods.
5. **State True or False.**

   Tissue culture is widely used for the production of clones of an animal.

Mind Map

Biodiversity and Conservation

Biodiversity
It is the variety and variability of living organisms on earth.

Levels of Biodiversity
It includes three levels as
- **Genetic Diversity** Diversity at the gene level, e.g. 1000 varieties of mango in India.
- **Species Diversity** Diversity in the number and richness of species within a region, e.g. greater number of amphibian species in Western Ghats than Eastern Ghats. Its important measures are species richness and species evenness.
- **Ecological Diversity** It is related to the different type of ecosystems/habitats, e.g. India has greater ecosystem diversity than any scandinavian country.

Global Biodiversity
- **Robert May** places global species diversity at about 7 million (only 22% of total sp.)
- Of the named species, more than 70% are animals, while plants are no more than 22%.
- 70% are insects (most species rich group).

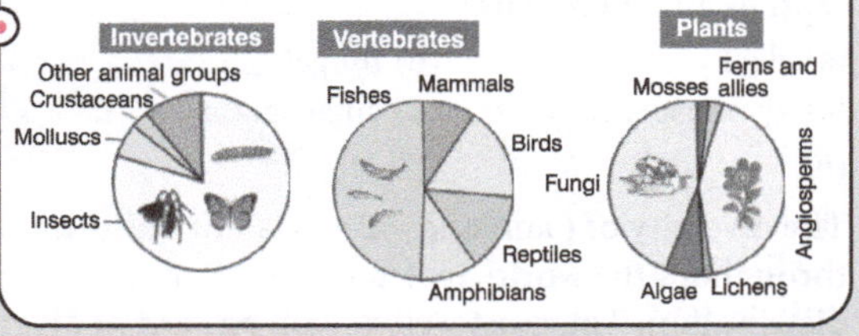

Indian Biodiversity
India with 2.4% of world's land shares, 8.1% of world species diversity. It is one of the 12 megadiversity countries of the world.

Patterns of Biodiversity
It has been described below
- **Latitude Gradient** Species diversity decreases as we move from the equator toward the poles, e.g. greatest biodiversity on earth in Amazon rainforest,
  Greater biodiversity at tropics is due to more solar energy, less seasonal variation, etc.
- **Species-area Relationship** Species richness increase in an area upto a certain limit **(Alexander von Humboldt)**.
  Relationship Straight line on a logarithmic scale;
  $\log S = \log C + Z \log A$.

Where,
S = Species richness
A = Area
Z = Slope of the line
C = Y-intercept
- The value of Z ranges between 0.1 to 0.2.

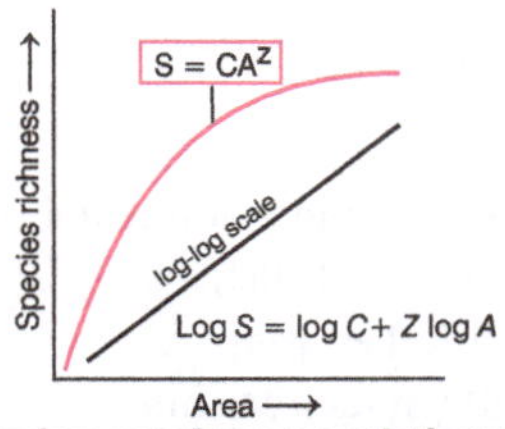

Showing species-area relationship

Note that on log scale the relationship becomes linear.

Loss of Biodiversity
- Human activities are the major reason.
- Extinction of species is most serious aspect. IUCN Red List enlists extinction of 784 species in last 500 years, e.g. dodo, quagga.
- The present rates of extinction, largely attributed to human activities, are 100-1000 times faster.
- Biodiversity loss leads to decline in plant production, perturbations such as drought, etc.
- The four major causes also called **the evil quartet** responsible for the loss of biodiversity are as follows
  - Habitat loss and fragmentation
  - Over-exploitation
  - Alien species invasion
  - Co-extinctions

Biodiversity Conservation
Protection, management or restoration of wildlife and their natural habitat.

Reasons for Conserving Biodiversity
It can be grouped into the following categories
- **Narrowly Utilitarian** Based on direct countless economic benefits that humans derive from nature.
- **Broadly Utilitarian** Based on intangible benefits obtained from biodiversity, e.g. O_2 production, aesthetic pleasures, etc.
- **Ethical Argument** Based on intrinsic value of every species and our moral duty to care for them.

Conservation Strategies
- ***In situ*** (Conservation in natural habitat)
  - Hotspots
  - Protected areas
    - Wildlife sanctuaries
    - Biosphere reserves
    - Natural parks
- ***Ex situ*** (Conservation outside natural habitat)
  - Seed bank, gene bank, cryopreservation, tissue culture, orchards
  - Botanical garden, arboreta, zoological parks

International Efforts
- **The Earth Summit** (1992) in Rio de Janeiro was held to take appropriate measures for biodiversity conservation and utilisation of its benefits.
- **World Summit** was also held on sustainable development (2002), in Johannesburg, South Africa.

Importance of Species Diversity to Ecosystem
- Communities with more species tend be more stable (David Tilman).
- **Rivet Popper Hypothesis By Paul Enrlich** According to this hypothesis, ecosystem is like an airplane, all the parts are joined together using thousands of rivets (species).

EXAM PATTERN QUESTIONS

Objective Type Questions

Multiple Choice Questions

1. Genetic diversity is the measure of

(a) varieties of the species and their relative abundance present within a region
(b) variety in the genetic information contained in the organisms
(c) diversity of the genes at community and ecosystem levels
(d) All of the above

Ans. (*b*)

2. Genetic diversity refers to the diversity in genetic makeup of organisms that are capable of interbreeding. What component of an ecosystem does genetic diversity directly impact? **Competency Based Ques.**

(a) Ecosystem diversity
(b) Species diversity
(c) Species richness
(d) Ecological niche

Ans. (*b*)

3. The active chemical drug reserpine is obtained from **NCERT Exemplar**

(a) *Datura* (b) *Rauwolfia*
(c) *Atropa* (d) *Papaver*

Ans. (*b*) *Rauwolfia vomitoria* is the source of active chemical drug reserpine, which is prescribed in hypertension and act as tranquiliser.

4. The greatest threat to genetic diversity in agriculture crop is

(a) extensive use of insecticides and pesticides
(b) extensive mixed cropping
(c) introduction of high yield varieties
(d) extensive use of fertilisers

Ans. (*c*)

5. The Western Ghats have a greater amphibians diversity than the Eastern Ghats. It is an example of

(a) species diversity
(b) genetic diversity
(c) ecological diversity
(d) None of the above

Ans. (*a*)

6. Choose the option which is correct with regard to ecological diversity.

(a) India has a greater ecosystem diverisity than a Scandinavian country like Norway
(b) India has a lesser ecosystem diversity than a Scandinavian country like Norway
(c) Australia has a greater ecosystem diversity than India
(d) Deserts, rainforests, coral reefs are the part of Norway diveristy

Ans. (*a*)

7. Read the given sentence.

The number of ...... species in the world is more than the combined total of the species of fishes, amphibians, reptiles and mammals.

(a) algal (b) fungal
(c) gymnosperms (d) angiosperms

Ans. (*b*)

8. The diversity of plant and animal is not uniform throughout the world, instead shows uneven distribution. The most well knwon pattern of diversity is

(a) latitudinal gradients
(b) species area relationship
(c) speciation
(d) species diversity

Ans. (*a*)

9. Which of the following naturalist studied this kind of relationship as shown in the graph given below? **Competency Based Que.**

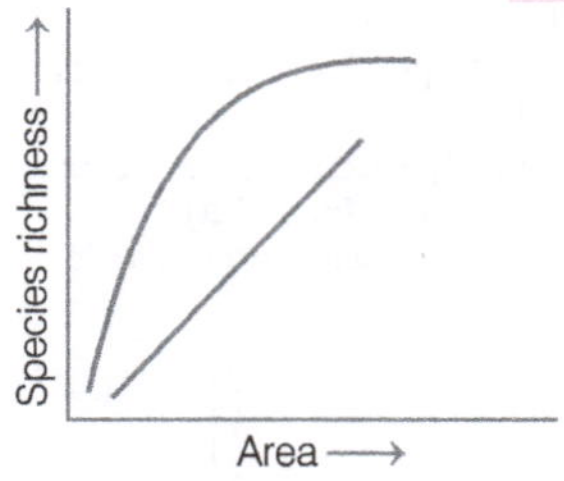

(a) Alexander von Humboldt
(b) Paul Ehrlich
(c) Robert May
(d) Ramdeo Mishra

Ans. (*a*)

10. **Match the Column I with Column II and choose the correct option from the codes given below.**

	Column I		Column II
A.	Rivet popper hypothesis	1.	Paul Ehrlich
B.	Communities with more species	2.	Edward Wilson
C.	Communities with less species	3.	Less stable
D.	Term biodiversity	4.	More stable

Codes

	A	B	C	D		A	B	C	D
(a)	2	4	3	1	(b)	1	4	3	2
(c)	1	3	4	2	(d)	1	4	2	3

Ans. (*b*)

11. **The organisation which publishes the Red List of species is**

(a) ICFRE (b) IUCN
(c) UNEP (d) WWF

Ans. (*b*)

12. **The IUCN Red Data List (2004) in the last 500 years documents the extinction of nearly 784 species including** **CBSE 2023**

(a) 330 invertebrates (b) 338 invertebrates
(c) 359 invertebrates (d) 362 invertebrates

Ans. (*c*)

13. **Which one of the following is an endangered plant species of India?** **NCERT Exemplar**

(a) *Rauwolfia serpentina*
(b) *Santalum album* (sandal wood)
(c) *Cycas beddomei*
(d) All of the above

Ans. (*d*) All of the above mentioned plants are endangered plant species of India. *Rauwolfia serpentina* (sarpgandha), *Santalum album* (sandal wood) and *Cycas beddomei* are facing the threat of extinction due to their medicinal and commercial importance.

14. **Dodo, passenger pigeon and Steller's sea cow became extinct in the last 500 years due to**

(a) habitat destruction
(b) overexploitation
(c) bird flu virus infection
(d) pollution

Ans. (*b*)

15. **Which of the following statements describe natural extinction?** **Competency Based Que.**

I. Extinctions abetted by human activities.
II. Slow replacement of existing species.
III. Also known as background extinction.
IV. It occurs over long period of time.

(a) I and II (b) I, II and III
(c) II, III and IV (d) All of these

Ans. (*c*)

16. **Which of the following is not an invasive alien species in the Indian context?**

(a) *Lantana* (b) *Cynodon*
(c) *Parthenium* (d) *Eichhornia*

Ans. (*b*)

17. **The reasons behind conserving biodiversity can be grouped into categories, which include**

I. broadly utilitarian arguments
II. narrowly utilitarian arguments
III. universal utilitarian arguments
IV. ethical arguments

Choose the correct option.

(a) I, II, III and IV (b) II, III and IV
(c) I, II and IV (d) I, III and IV

Ans. (*c*)

18. **Match the Column I with Column II and choose the correct option from the codes given below.**

	Column I		Column II
A.	Dodo	1.	*Rauwolfia*
B.	Reserpine	2.	Mauritius
C.	Nile perch in lake Victoria	3.	Habitat destruction
D.	Main cause for biodiversity loss	4.	Alien species

Codes

	A	B	C	D		A	B	C	D
(a)	4	2	1	3	(b)	2	1	4	3
(c)	2	4	3	1	(d)	3	2	1	4

Ans. (*b*)

19. **Match the Column I with Column II and choose the correct option from the codes given below.**

	Column I		Column II
A.	Hotspots	1.	Areas maintained by government for the betterment of wildlife.
B.	Protected areas	2.	Areas of high endemism and high level of species richness.
C.	National parks	3.	Biogeographical areas where biological diversity along with natural and cultural resources is protected, maintained and managed.
D.	Biosphere reserves	4.	Multipurpose protected areas, which are meant for preserving genetic diversity in the ecosystem of various natural biomass and unique biological communities.

Codes

	A	B	C	D
(a)	1	2	3	4
(b)	3	1	2	4
(c)	2	3	1	4
(d)	4	2	3	1

Ans. (*c*)

20. Sacred groves in India are related with

(a) cultural tradition
(b) it is the place where threatened species are protected
(c) it is the place where only artificial animal breeding is allowed
(d) forest patches around the places of worship

Ans. (*d*)

21. Which of the following is an example of *ex situ* conservation?

(a) Sacred groves (b) National park
(c) Biosphere reserve (d) Seed bank

Ans. (*d*)

22. What is common to the techniques **NCERT Exemplar**

(i) *in vitro* fertilisation,
(ii) cryopreservation,
(iii) tissue culture?

(a) All are *in situ* conservation methods
(b) All are *ex situ* conservation methods
(c) All require ultra modern equipment and large space
(d) All are methods of conservation of extinct organisms

Ans. (*b*) All the three above mentioned techniques are *ex situ* conservation methods.

At present gametes of threatened species can be preserved in viable conditions for longer duration by cryopreservation method.

Fertilisation can be achieved *in vitro* and species can be improved or propagated by tissue culture method, a plant breeding principle.

23. The historic convention on biological diversity held in Rio de Janeiro in 1992 is known as

(a) CITES convention
(b) The Earth summit
(c) G-16 summit
(d) MAB programme

Ans. (*b*)

24. World summit on sustainable development was held in

(a) USA (b) South Africa
(c) South Korea (d) UK

Ans. (*b*)

Assertion-Reason Questions

Direction (Q. Nos. 1-11) *In each of the following question, a statement of Assertion (A) is given and followed by corresponding statement of Reason (R). Of the statements, mark the correct answer*

(a) Both A and R are true and R is the correct explanation of A
(b) Both A and R are true, but R is not the correct explanation of A
(c) A is true, but R is false
(d) A is false, but R is true

1. Assertion (A) Tropical rainforests are disappearing fast from developing countries such as India.

Reason (R) No value is attached to these forest because they are poor in diversity.

Ans. (*c*) A is true, but R is false and R can be corrected as Tropical rainforests are rich in biodiversity and host many unique species.

2. Assertion (A) Tropical latitudes have greater biological diversity than temperate latitudes.

Reason (R) Tropical regions remain relatively undisturbed for millions of years.

Ans. (*a*)

3. Given below is the graph showing species-area relationship. Alexander van Humboldt observe the relationship between species richness and area for a wide variety of taxa, turns out to be hyperbola. Observe the graph and answer the question. **Competency Based Que.**

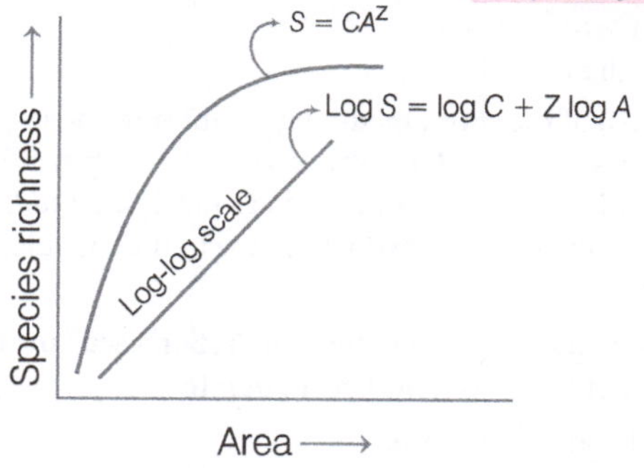

Assertion (A) If the species-area relationships are analysed among very large areas like the entire continents, the value of *Z*, i.e. slope of line lies in the range of 0.1 to 0.2.

Reason (R) Larger is the explored area more is the steepness of slope of line.

Ans. (*d*)

4. Assertion (A) Communities that comprise of more species tend to be more stable.

Reason (R) A higher number of species results in less annual variation in total biomass.

Ans. (*a*)

5. Assertion (A) The process of extinction is random.

Reason (R) Any species that is not adapted to its environmental conditions cannot survive.

Ans. (*d*) A is false, but R is true and A can be corrected as The process of extinction is not random.

6. Assertion (A) Species with low genetic variability are usually at a great risk of extinction.

Reason (R) Low genetic variability increases vulnerability to diseases, environmental changes and predators.

Ans. (*a*)

7. Assertion (A) The presently occurring species extinction is different from the earlier mass extinction.

Reason (R) Present species extinction is due to natural causes, whereas the earlier extinction was due to the man-made causes.

Ans. (*c*) A is true, but R is false and R can be corrected as Present species extinction is largely driven by human activities, such as habitat destruction, pollution.

8. Assertion (A) Currently the sixth extinction is in progress.

Reason (R) The current species extinction rates are estimated to be 100 to 1000 times faster than in the pre human times and our activities are responsible for the faster rates.

Ans. (*a*)

9. Assertion (A) In case, a species becomes extinct, the plant and animal species associated within an obligatory way also become extinct.

Reason (R) When a host fish species becomes extinct, its unique assemblage of parasites also become extinct.

Ans. (*b*)

10. The figure given below is showing the zonation in a terrestrial biosphere reserve. It consists of core, buffer and transition zones. Study the figure and comment upon the appropriateness of Assertion and Reason.

Competency Based Que.

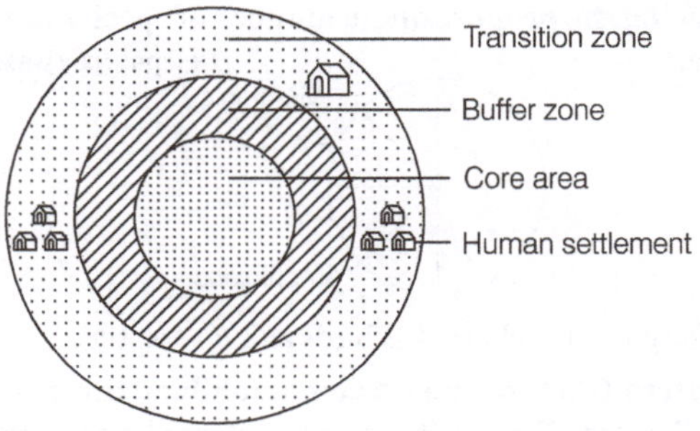

Assertion (A) Biosphere reserve is a specified area in which multiple use of land is permitted by dividing it into zones.

Reason (R) These are the spaces where sustainable economic practices are developed.

Ans. (*b*)

11. Assertion (A) *Ex situ* conservation removes threatened species from the wild and places them in the controlled environment for protection.

Reason (R) Technique like cryopreservation and *in vitro* fertilisation help to conserve species outside their habitat.

Ans. (*b*)

Subjective Questions

Very Short Answer Type Questions

1. Name the sociobiologist who popularised the term biodiversity.

Ans. Edward Wilson

2. India has more than 50,000 strains of rice. Mention the level of biodiversity it represents.

Ans. More than 50,000 strains of rice represent genetic biodiversity.

3. Why is genetic variation important in the plant *Rauwolfia vomitoria*? **NCERT Exemplar**

Ans. Genetic variation is important as it affects the production of the drug reserpine in the medicinal plant *Rauwolfia*.

4. What is the expanded form of IUCN? **NCERT Exemplar**

Ans. IUCN stands for 'International Union for Conservation of Nature and Natural Resources'.

5. Identify *A* and *B* in the figure given below representing proportionate number of major vertebrate taxa.

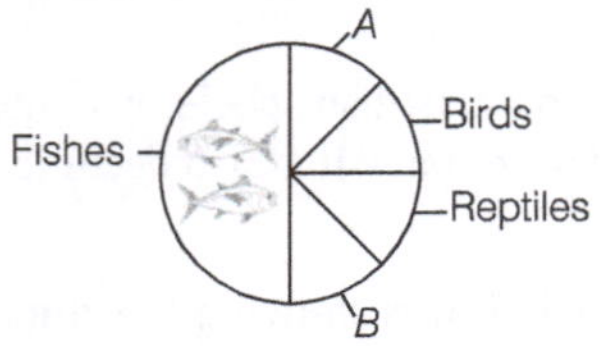

Ans. In the given pie chart, *A* is mammals and *B* is amphibians. (½ × 2)

6. Name the unlabelled areas *A* and *B* of the pie chart representing biodiversity of vertebrates showing the proportionate number of species of major taxa. **Competency Based Que.**

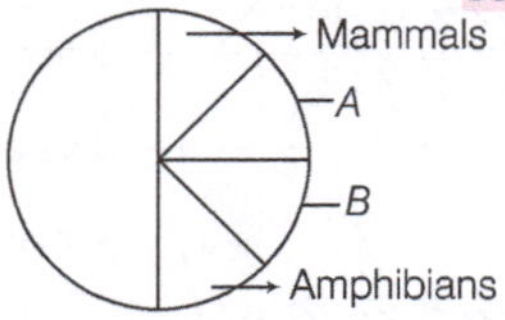

Ans. In the given pie chart, *A* is birds and *B* is reptiles. (½ × 2)

7. Western Ghats have a greater amphibian diversity than the Eastern Ghats. What can be inferred from this statement?

Ans. Western Ghats have high levels of species diversity than the Eastern ghats. (1)

8. Which rainforest is called as 'Lungs of the planet'?

Ans. Amazon rainforest in South America.

9. The Amazon rainforest is referred to as the 'lungs of planet'. Mention any one human activity which causes loss of biodiversity in this region. **Competency Based Que.**

Ans. Human activities causing loss of biodiversity in Amazon rainforest are

(i) Many plants are cut for cultivation of soybean.

(ii) Forests are converted to grasslands for raising beef cattle. (½ + ½)

10. Give the name of a bird, which recently became extinct.

Ans. Dodo

11. What do you mean by the term 'alien species'?

Ans. Alien species are plants, animals or microorganisms that are transported and established in a new area beyond their natural range.

12. About 200 species of cichlid fish became extinct when a particular fish was introduced in lake Victoria of Africa. Name the invasive fish.

Ans. Nile perch

13. Give the names of some invasive species in India.

Ans. Invasive species in India are weed species like carrot grass (*Parthenium*), *Lantana*, water hyacinth (*Eichhornia*) and African catfish (*Clarias gariepinus*).

14. Can you think of a situation where we deliberately want to make a species extinct? How would you justify it? **NCERT**

Ans. Pathogens and their vectors, like the *Plasmodium* species causing malaria, are harmful to humans. These pathogens do not play a role in food chains and their extinction would likely have no negative impact on ecosystems. Therefore, eradicating them could be justified. (½ × 2)

15. Enumerate any one reason for the conservation of biodiversity.

Ans. Refer to text on page no. 376 and 377.

16. Among the ecosystem services are control of floods and soil erosion. How is this achieved by the biotic components of the ecosystem? **NCERT**

Ans. Biotic components, especially plants, play a crucial role in controlling floods and soil erosion. Their roots hold soil particles together, it preventing erosion by wind and water. Additionally, roots enhance soil porosity, allowing groundwater infiltration and mitigating floods.

17. How much area of earth's land surface is covered by hotspots?

Ans. Less than 2% area.

18. Give the names of biodiversity rich zones in India.

Ans. Western Ghats and Eastern Himalayas. (½ × 2)

19. Why Western Ghats in India have been declared as biological hotspots? **Competency Based Que.**

Ans. Western Ghats are biological hotspots because they have high levels of species richness and endemism.

20. What are protected areas?

Ans. Areas that protect and maintain ecological uniqueness and biodiversity rich regions.

21. How many biosphere reserves have been established in India?

Ans. There are 14 biosphere reserves established in India.

22. What is common to the species shown in figures *A* and *B*? **NCERT Exemplar**

A

B

Ans. Both the species are conserved in their natural habitats.

23. Apart from conserving individual plants and animals, what else needs to be conserved?

Ans. Viable seeds and gametes.

24. Write the importance of cryopreservation in the conservation of biodiversity. CBSE 2023, 11

Ans. In cryopreservation method, seeds of plants, eggs and sperms of animals of threatened species or the species at the urge of extinction can be preserved for a long time. Hence, serving the purpose of *ex situ* conservation.

25. Name the historic convention on biological diversity held at Rio in 1992. NCERT Exemplar

Ans. The Earth Summit (1992).

Short Answer Type Questions

1. Name the three important components of biodiversity. NCERT

Ans. The three important components of biodiversity are

(i) Genetic diversity

(ii) Species diversity

(iii) Ecosystem diversity (1 × 3)

2. Explain the levels of biodiversity at genetic, specific and ecological levels with the help of one example each.

Ans. **Genetic Diversity** A single species shows diversity at the genetic level over its distributional range. For example, the genetic variation showed by the plant *Rauwolfia vomitoria* growing in the different Himalayan ranges might be in terms of the potency and concentration of reserpine.

Species Diversity It is the diversity at the species level or the measure of the variety of species and their relative abundance with the region. For example, the Western Ghats have a greater amphibian species diversity than the Eastern Ghats.

Ecological Diversity At the ecosystem level, India shows diversity with its deserts, rainforests, mangroves, coral reefs and alpine meadows. (1 × 3)

3. Mention the kind of biodiversity represented by more than 1000 varieties of mangoes in India. How is it possible?

Ans. Refer to text on page no. 371-372. (1 + 1)

4. (i) 'India has greater ecosystem diversity than Norway.' Do you agree with the statement? Give reasons in support of your answer.

(ii) Write the differences between genetic biodiversity and species biodiversity that exists at all the levels of biological organisation. Competency Based Que.

Ans. (i) India is one of the twelve megadiversity regions of the world with 8.1% of genetic resources of the world. Since, India is placed in the tropical part of the world it exhibits more species diversity than the regions of temperate zones.

India, with much of its land area in the tropical latitudes, has more species diversity than Norway which is away from tropics and hence exhibits less biodiversity. (1½)

(ii) Differences between genetic and species diversity are as follows

Genetic Diversity	Species Diversity
It is related to the number of genes and their alleles found in organisms.	It is related to the number and distribution of species found in an area.
It is trait of a species.	It is a trait of community.
It influences adaptability and distribution of species in diverse habitats.	It influences biotic interactions and stability of the community.

(1½)

5. The species diversity of plants (22 per cent) is much less than that of animals (72 per cent). What could be the explanations to how animals achieved greater diversification? NCERT

Ans. Plants are stationary, limiting their ability to spread to new habitats compared to animals. On the other hand animals can migrate, encountering different environments and interacting with various organisms. This movement leads to changes in their genetic makeup, increased genetic diversity and the emergence of new species. Therefore, mobility is the main reason for greater genetic diversity in animals than in plants.

6. How do ecologists estimate the total number of species present in the world? Competency Based Que., NCERT

Ans. Ecologists make a statistical comparison of the species richness of systematically studied groups of insects of the temperate and tropical regions and extrapolate this ratio to the other groups of animals and plants.

This is how they calculate the gross estimate of the total number of species existing on this planet.

7. What accounts for the greater ecological diversity in India? NCERT Exemplar

Ans. Refer to text on page no. 372.

8. Species diversity decreases as we move away from the equator towards the poles. What could be the possible reasons? NCERT Exemplar

Ans. Species diversity decreases as we move towards the poles, because

(i) Temperature decreases and conditions become harsh.

(ii) Both the amount and intensity of solar radiation decrease.

(iii) Vegetation decreases.

(iv) Less resources available to support species.

Speciation is generally a function of time and environmental stability, so if conditions are too harsh, it is difficult for the species to survive and adapt. This results, decrease in biodiversity towards the poles.

9. Give three reasons as to why prokaryotes are not given any figures for their diversity.

Ans. Refer to text on page no. 372 and 373.

10. Explain giving three reasons why tropics show, greatest level of species diversity.

Or **Give three hypothesis for explaining why tropics show greatest level of species richness.** NCERT

Ans. Refer to text on page no. 373.

11. Is it true that there is more solar energy available in the tropics? Explain briefly. NCERT Exemplar

Ans. Yes, there is more solar energy available in the tropics because

(i) As one moves from equator to the polar regions, the length of the day decreases and the length of the night increases.

(ii) In the tropical regions, the length of the day is almost equal to the length of the night, hence it has more solar energy available. (1 × 2)

12. (i) Write the inference drawn by Alexander von Humboldt after his extensive explorations of South American jungle.

(ii) Study the graph given below

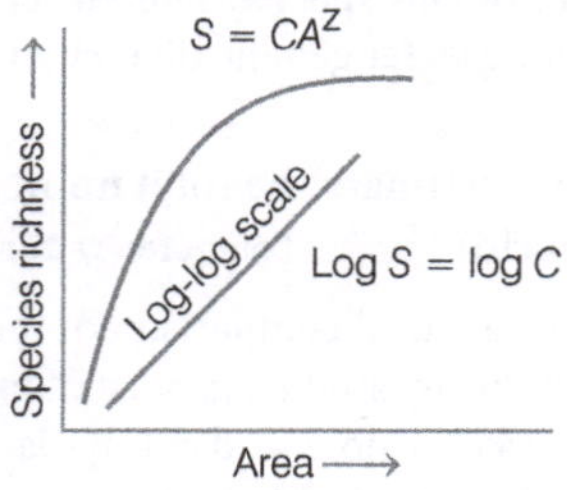

As per Alexander von Humboldt, what do the symbols *S*, *A*, *Z* and *C* in the graph stand for, in respect of a species and area relationship?

Competency Based Que., Delhi 2022 Term II

Ans. (i) German naturalist and geographer, Av Humboldt during his exploration in South American jungles made two inferences

(a) Within a region, species richness increased with increasing explored area, but only upto a limit.

(b) The relationship between species richness and area for a wide variety of taxa (angiospermic plants, birds, bats, freshwater fishes) turns out to be a rectangular hyperbola. (1½)

(ii) According to Humboldt, in respect of a species and area relationship, the meanings of the symbols are as follows

S – Species richness; *A* – Area

Z – Slop of line (Regression coefficient)

C – Y-intercept (1½)

13. What is the significance of the slope of regression in a species-area relationship? NCERT

Ans. Slope of regression represents the changes in the species richness with the area. Species richness decreases with the decrease in area. The value of 'Z' (regression coefficient) lies in between 0.1-0.2, regardless of the taxonomic groups in the region. For very larger areas like continents, the slope of the line becomes much steep with the *Z* values in the range of 0.6-1.

14. The graph given below shows species-area relationship of a certain region.

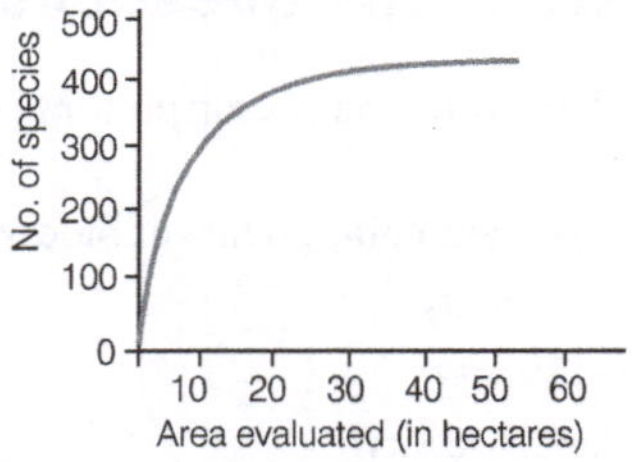

(i) Study the graph and explain what it represents.

(ii) After a while, a small area was taken for constructing a road which divided the region into two. Write the impact of this construction would have on species richness of the region. CBSE 2022 Term II

Ans. (i) The given graph represents species-area relationship. It shows that within an area (region), the species richness increases with the increase in explored area, but only to a certain limit. Thus, it becomes constant after a certain time period. (2)

(ii) If a small area is taken for constructing a road, thus dividing the region into two, the species richness will become less. (1)

15. How did Dr. David Tilman relate experimentally, the stability of a community and its species richness? Explain. All India 2022 Term II

Ans. Dr. David Tilman's long term ecosystem experiments using outdoor plots provided some tentative answers on the relation of stability of a community and its species richness. He showed that stability of a community depends on its species richness by using outdoor plots. Each plot had a different number of species. Tilman found that plots with more species showed less year to year variation in total biomass. He also showed experimentally that increased diversity contributed to higher productivity.

16. Write the importance of species diversity to the ecosystem. Support your answer with the finding of Tilman.

Ans. Importance of species diversity for the ecosystem are

(i) Ecologists for many years, believe that communities with species are more stable than those with less species.

(ii) A stable biological community does not show too much variation in production from year-to-year. It must be resistant or resilient to occasional disturbance and must also be resistant to invasions by alien species. (1½)

David Tilman's long term ecosystem experiments using outdoor plots provided answers to stability of a biological community and species richness in that community. Tilman found that plots with more species showed less year-to-year variation in total biomass. He also showed in his experiments that increased diversity contributed to higher productivity. (1½)

17. What is mass extinction? Give an example.

Ans. Refer to text on page no. 375. (2)

18. Since the origin of life on earth, there were five episodes of mass extinction of species.

(i) How is the 'sixth extinction', presently in progress, different from the previous episodes?

(ii) Who is mainly responsible for the 'sixth extinction'?

(iii) List any four points that can help to overcome this disaster. **Competency Based Que.**

Ans. (i) The current species extinction rates are estimated to be 100-1000 times faster than in pre-human times. (½)

(ii) Human activities (½)

(iii) To prevent sixth extinction to take place we would

(a) Preventing habitat loss and fragmentation

(b) Checking overexploitation

(c) Preventing alien species invasion

(d) Preventing co-extinction

(e) Conservation and preservation of species. (2)

19. Extinction of a species is classified into three types, i.e. natural extinction, mass extinction and anthropogenic extinction. Classify the following examples on this basis

(i) Animals lost due to inbreeding depression.

(ii) Disappearance of dinosaurs.

(iii) Extinction of passenger pigeon.

(iv) Extinction of marine invertebrates.

(v) Extinction of tiger. **Competency Based Que.**

Ans. (i) Natural extinction

(ii) Mass extinction

(iii) Anthropogenic extinction

(iv) Natural extinction

(v) Anthropogenic extinction

20. What characteristics make a community stable? **NCERT Exemplar**

Or **List the features that make a stable biological community.**

Ans. The characteristic feature that make a community stable are

(i) Less variation in productivity from year-to-year.

(ii) Resistance or resilience to occasional disturbances (natural or man-made).

(iii) Resistance to invasions by alien species.

21. What are the major causes of species losses in a geographical region? **NCERT, CBSE 2008C**

Or **List four causes of biodiversity loss.**

Ans. The major causes of species losses in a geographical region are

(i) Habitat loss and fragmentation.

(ii) Overexploitation of natural resources.

(iii) Alien species invasions that can cause decline or extinction of indigenous species.

(iv) Co-extinctions, i.e. when a species become extinct, the plant and animal species associated with it in an obligatory way, also become extinct. (½ × 4)

22. Explain the status of Indian biodiversity. Give a brief account of loss of diversity.

Ans. Refer to text on page no. 373. (1)

For causes of loss of biodiversity, refer to text on page no. 374-375.

23. Name and describe any three causes of biodiversity losses.

Ans. Refer to text on page no. 375-376.

24. Explain how the loss of habitat and fragmentation drives plants and animals to extinction with the help of an example of habitat loss in the Tropical Rain Forest. Also write the effect of fragmentation of a habitat on the population decline. **CBSE 2025**

Ans. Loss of habitat and fragmentation are major causes of species extinction. When natural habitats are destroyed due to deforestation, urbanisation or agriculture, plants and animals lose their shelter, food sources and breeding grounds, leading to a decline in population and eventual extinction.

For example, in the Tropical Rainforests of Amazon, large-scale deforestation for agriculture and logging has led to the loss of biodiversity. Many species, including the golden lion tamarin and jaguar, are endangered due to habitat destruction.

Habitat fragmentation breaks large ecosystems into smaller, isolated patches, reducing genetic diversity and making species more vulnerable to predators, climate change and human interference. Smaller populations face a higher risk of extinction due to limited resources, inbreeding and difficulty in finding mates.

25. Justify with the help of an example where a deliberate attempt by humans leads to the extinction of a particular species. **Competency Based Que.**

Ans. When Nile perch, a large predator fish was introduced in lake Victoria, it started feeding on native fish, cichlid fish. As a result, cichlid fish become extinct.

26. Explain giving one example, how co-extinction is one of the cause of biodiversity loss? List the other three causes also.

Ans. Refer to text on page no. 375-376.

27. Discuss one example based on your day-to-day observations, showing how loss of one species may lead to the extinction of another. NCERT Exemplar

Ans. Co-extinction is the extinction of two mutually related or inter-related species, for instance a host fish extinction leads to the extinction of all those parasites exclusively found on it.

Another example is plant pollinator (mutualism) where extinction of one leads to the extinction of other.

28. Explain the concept of 'coextinction' by taking two examples. CBSE 2022 Term II

Ans. Refer to text on page no. 376.

29. Explain how biodiversity is important for human.

Or **Humans benefit from diversity of life. Give two examples.** NCERT Exemplar

Ans. (i) Humans derive numerous economic benefits directly from diversity of organisms such as

(a) Food products (cereals, pulses and fruits), firewood and fibre (cotton, jute from plants and silk, wool from animals).

(b) Construction material (timber for making furniture, houses and sports goods), industrial products (tannis, lubricant, dyes, resins and perfumes) and products of medicinal importance (about 25,000 plants are used in traditional medicine). (1½)

(ii) There are huge indirect benefits that humans derive from the diversity of life. These are pure oxygen, natural pollinators, flood and soil erosion control, nutrient replenishment, waste recycling by microbes and aesthetic pleasure and mental peace. (1½)

30. Why should biodiversity be conserved? Explain giving three reasons.

Ans. Biodiversity should be conserved for the following reasons

(i) The broadly utilitarian argument says that biodiversity plays a major role in many ecosystem services that nature provides.

(ii) The narrow utilitarian argument says that humans derive countless direct economic benefits from nature and products of medicinal importance.

(iii) The ethical argument for conserving biodiversity relates to what we owe to millions of plant, animal and microbe species with whom we share this planet. (1 × 3)

31. Biodiversity plays a major role in many ecosystem services that nature provides.

(i) Describe any two broadly utilitarian arguments to justify the given.

(ii) State one ethical reason of conserving biodiversity. CBSE 2023

Ans. (i) Refer to text on page no. 376.

(ii) Refer to text on page no. 377.

32. (i) What are two types of desirable approaches to conserve biodiversity? Explain with examples, bringing out the difference between two types.

(ii) What is the association between the bumble bee and its favourite orchid *Ophrys*? How could extinction or change of one would affect the other?

Ans. . (i) Refer to text on page no. 377. (1½)

(ii) The association between the bumble bee and the orchid *Ophrys* is an example of commensalism, where the two species have a mutual relationship.

Extinction of one species could disrupt the entire mutualistic relationship, potentially leading to extinction of the other. This is referred to as co-extinction. (1½)

33. Suggest two practices giving one example of each, that help to protect rare or threatened species.

Ans. Refer to text on page no. 377-378.

34. *In situ* conservation can help endangered/threatened species. Justify the statement.

Ans. *In situ* conservation involves the protection of species in their natural habitats. It helps in the conservation of threatened/endangered species *via* following means

(i) **Biodiversity hotspots** are regions with high levels of species richness and high degree of endemism (i.e. species confined to that region are not found anywhere else). These hotspots can reduce the ongoing mass extinctions by almost 30%.

(ii) **Protected areas** are ecologically unique and biodiversity rich regions. These are legally protected as biosphere reserves, national parks and sanctuaries. Hence, can help in conservation of endangered species.

(iii) **Sacred groves** are forest areas set aside, all the trees and wildlife within it are venerated and given total protection. These are religious and cultural places, which are protected for conservation of endangered species. (1 × 3)

35. (i) Explain the concept of endemism.

(ii) Name four regions around our country that are considered hotspots. CBSE 2020

Ans. Refer to text on page no. 377.

36. Regions with high endemism are choosen as hotspots. Why?

Ans. Hotspots are the regions with high endemism. The endemic species are mostly rare and its crucial to conserve them. Hence, the areas with high endemism are choosen as hotspots and given high protection.

37. (i) (a) What are 'biodiversity hotspot' regions? Mention any two criteria used for determining any reigion as a 'hotspot'.

(b) Name any two hotspots of India.

Or (b) Explain giving three reasons, why tropics show greatest level of species diversity.

Ans. (i) (a) Biodiversity hotspots are the regions with very high level of species richness and high degree of endemism.

Criteria used for determining any region as a hot spot-species richness, endemism.

(b) Western Ghats and Sri Lanka, Indo-Burma and Himalayas.

Tropics show greatest level of species diversity because of the following reason.

Or (b)
- Tropical latitude have remained undisturbed and have had a long evolutionary time for species diversification.
- Tropical environments have less seasonal variations with more constant and predictable environmental conditions to promote niche specialisation for greater diversity.
- There is more availability of solar energy which contributes to higher productivity.

38. Why are sacred groves highly protected?

Ans. Sacred groves are small patches of forest with special religious importance in a particular culture. These are highly protected as these forests include a number of rare, endangered and endemic species.

39. What are sacred groves? Where are they found in India? Explain their importance in conservation.

Ans. Refer to text on page no. 377-378. **NCERT**

40. Explain any three ways other than zoological parks, botanical gardens and wildlife safaries, by which threatened species of plants and animals are being conserved '*ex situ*'. **CBSE 2020**

Ans. Refer to text on page no. 378.

41. There are many animals that have become extinct in the wild, but continue to be maintained in zoological parks.

(i) Which type of biodiversity conservation is observed in this case?

(ii) Explain any two other ways, which help in this type of conservation.

Ans. (i) It is an example of *ex situ* (off-site) conservation. In this approach, threatened plants and animals are taken out of their natural habitat and placed in suitable settings and given special care. (1)

(ii) Cryopreservation and tissue culture are two ways that help in *ex situ* conservation. Refer to text on page no. 375. (2)

42. Express your opinion on removal of tribal people out of forest due to developmental activities in the forest.

Ans. Recently, it has been a trend of removing the tribal people out of the forest in the name of conservation measures. To ensure conservation of habitat and prevention of any sort of danger to biodiversity, government tends to seclude even tribal people from their home. It is an ethical issue. Tribal people are equally a part of the forest. They have lived there for years and have evolved along with the forest.

They share a mutual relationship with the biodiversity present there.

In their unique ways, they also conserve and protect the diversity. Therefore, we must make policies, which include tribals in the conservation measures and utilise their indigenous knowledge as a conservation tool.

43. Differentiate between *in situ* and *ex situ* approaches of biodiversity conservation.

Ans. Refer to text on page no. 377-378.

44. Many plant and animal species are on the verge of their extinction because of loss of forest land by indiscriminate use by the humans. As a biology student what method would you suggest along with its advantages that can protect such threatened species from getting extinct? **Competency Based Que.**

Ans. As a biology student, I would suggest *ex situ* conservation approach for such animals.

It involves placing the threatened animals and plants in special care units for their protection. It includes off-site collections (botanical gardens, zoological parks, etc.) and gene banks (seedbank, tissue culture, etc). (1)

Advantages of *ex situ* conservation are

(i) Off-site collection can be used to restock depleted population, reintroduce species in the wild and restore degraded habitats.

(ii) It is useful in maintaining a large number of genotypes in small area, rapid multiplication of even endangered species through tissue culture, etc. (2)

45. List six advantages of '*ex situ*' approach to conservation of biodiversity. **CBSE 2019**

Ans. *Ex situ* conservation has various advantages. It helps

(i) To conserve those animals that have become extinct in wild, but can be maintained in zoological parks.

(ii) To protect and conserve the endangered animals in the artificial habitats.

(iii) To preserve gametes of threatened species in viable condition through cryopreservation.

(iv) To propagate threatened plants *via* tissue culture.

(v) To conserve seeds of commercially important plants in seed banks.

(vi) To save endangered or threatened plant that needs urgent measure to save it from extinction in botanical gardens. ($\frac{1}{2} \times 6$)

46. List any four techniques where the principle of *ex situ* conservation of biodiversity has been employed.

Ans. Four techniques where principle of *ex situ* conservation of biodiversity has been employed are

(i) Tissue culture (ii) Cryopreservation

(iii) Botanical gardens

(iv) Zoological parks (½ × 4)

47. (i) Seeds of different genetic strains are kept for long periods in seed banks. Explain the conservation strategy involved in this.

(ii) Can an extinction of one insect pollinator affect the whole ecosystem? If yes. Explain.

Ans. (i) Refer to text on page no. 378.

(ii) Refer to text on page no. 376.

Long Answer Type Questions

1. How is biodiversity important for ecosystem functioning? NCERT

Ans. Biodiversity is very important for ecosystem functioning. More diverse ecosystems are considered more stable. Stable communities are resilient and resistant to change.

Hence, diversity stabilises the community and also helps in increasing the productivity. Higher the biodiversity of an ecosystem, higher the number of species and therefore, lower is the rate of extinction. While, in case of low biodiversity, there are higher chances of extinction.

Extinction of even one or two key species has negative impacts on the entire ecosystem.

Thus, the diversity ensures the stability and proper functioning of the entire ecosystem as explained *via* the 'Rivet popper hypothesis'.

Refer to text on page no. 374.

2. (i) Explain the conclusion drawn by Alexander von Humboldt during his extensive explorations in the wilderness of South American jungles.

(ii) Give the equation of the Species-Area relationship.

(iii) Draw a graphical representation of the relation between species richness and area for a wide variety of taxa such as birds, bats, etc. CBSE 2025, NCERT Exemplar

Ans. (i) Alexander von Humboldt observed that species richness increases with an increase in the explored area but up to a certain limit. He concluded that within a habitat, larger areas support more species due to greater habitat diversity and resource availability.

(ii) The Species-Area relationship is mathematically expressed as:

$$\text{Log } S = \text{Log } C \;\; Z \text{ Log } A$$

where S is species richness, A is area, C is a constant, and Z represents the slope of the curve.

(iii) The graphical representation of species richness vs. area is a curve that rises steeply at first and then levels off, forming a rectangular hyperbola.

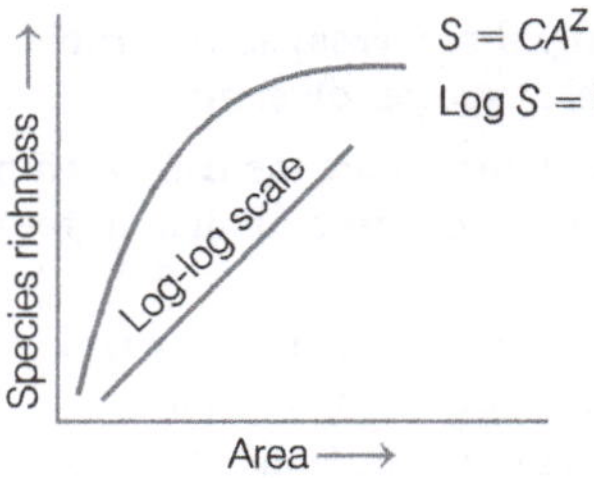

(2½)

3. Of the four major causes for the loss of biodiversity (alien-species invasion, habitat loss and fragmentation, overexploitation and co-extinctions) which according to you is the major cause for the loss of biodiversity? Give reasons in support.

Competency Based Que., NCERT Exemplar

Ans. Out of the four major causes for the loss of biodiversity, loss of habitat and fragmentation is the major cause as

(i) Habitat loss and fragmentation caused by clearing and overexploitation of forest areas for agriculture, urbanisation and industrialisation, results in destruction of natural habitats.

(ii) Increasing human population has overburdened the forest resources and have destroyed forest land, which means loss of habitat for several species.

(iii) In addition, large habitats are broken up into small fragments, because of which mammals and birds requiring large territories and migratory habits are badly affected, leading to decline in population.

(iv) Increase in industrialisation and habit degradation by pollution also possess threat to survival of many species.

4. How can you as an individual prevent the loss of biodiversity? NCERT Exemplar

Ans. Biodiversity is the occurrence of different type of species, habitat, ecosystem, gene, gene pool in a particular place and various parts of earth.

As an individual, biodiversity can be conserved with conservation strategies and management of both biotic and abiotic resources. (2)

Some of the conservation strategies are as follows

(i) Protection of useful animals and plants in their natural habitat or *in situ* conservation.

(ii) Preservation of critical habitats like feeding and breeding areas and resting area of endangered species to promote their growth and multiplication.

(iii) Hunting should be banned or regulated.

(iv) Habitat of migratory animals should be protected by bilateral or multilateral agreements.

(v) People should be made aware of the importance of biodiversity and its conservation.

(vi) Overexploitation of natural resources must be avoided. (½ × 6)

5. (i) **Indiscriminate human activities such as alien-species invasion, fragmentation and habitat loss have accelerated the loss of biodiversity. Justify by taking one example for each.**

(ii) **State the importance of (a) IUCN Red Data List and (b) Hotspots in conservation of biodiversity.**

Ans. (i) Refer to text on page no. 375-376. (3)

(ii) (a) IUCN Red list of threatened species is a critical tool for informing and catalysing action to protect the world's biodiversity.

(b) Refer to text on page no. 377. (2)

6. (i) **What are endangered species and how they are different from rare species?**

(ii) **What are the different causes of accelerated rates of species extinction the world is facing?** Diksha

Ans. (i) Endangered species are those at risk of extinction due to a variety of factors, such as habitat loss, pollution, overexploitation and climate change. Organisations like the International Union for Conservation of Nature and Natural Resources (IUCN) classify them based on their population size and the threats they face.

Endangered species are often listed on conservation lists to help prioritise efforts for their protection.

Rare species, on the other hand, are not necessarily endangered, but are uncommon or limited in distribution. They may have small populations or restricted habitats, but might not be at immediate risk of extinction. The key difference is that all endangered species are rare, but not all rare species are classified as endangered. (2½)

(ii) The accelerated rate of species extinction is driven by several interconnected factors

(a) **Habitat Loss** Urbanisation, deforestation, agriculture and infrastructure development reduce the natural habitats that species depend on for survival.

(b) **Pollution** Contaminants in air, water and soil can harm or kill species, disrupt reproductive systems and alter ecosystems.

(c) **Climate Change** Global warming affects habitats and alters weather patterns, impacting species' migration, breeding and food availability.

(d) **Overexploitation** Unsustainable hunting, fishing and harvesting of plants and animals can deplete populations faster than they can recover.

(e) **Invasive Species** Non-native species can outcompete, prey on, or bring diseases to native species, disrupting local ecosystems.

(f) **Human Population Growth** Increasing human populations lead to greater resource demands, further stressing ecosystems and wildlife. (2½)

7. (i) **Why is there a need to conserve biodiversity? (Any two reasons)**

(ii) **Name and explain any two causes that are responsible for the loss of biodiversity.** Competency Based Ques.

Ans. (i) There are three main reasons for conserving the biodiversity which have been classified into the following categories

Narrowly Utilitarian Arguments Human beings derive direct economic benefits from nature, like food, firewood, fibre, construction material, industrial products (resins, gums, dyes, tannins, etc.) and medicinally important products.

Broadly Utilitarian Arguments Biodiversity plays a major role in maintaining and sustaining supply of goods and services from various species as well as ecological systems. The different ecological services provided are

- Amazon forest is estimated to contribute 20 per cent of the total oxygen in the atmosphere on earth.
- Pollinators like bee, bumble bees, birds and bats pollinate plants to form fruits and seeds.
- Aesthetic pleasures like bird watching, spring flowers in full bloom, walking through the thick forest, waking up to a bulbul's song, etc., are some other benefits of the ecosystem.

Ethical Reasons There are thousands of plants, animals and microbes on this earth which are not useless. Everyone has some intrinsic value even if it is not of any economic value to us. It is, therefore our moral duty to ensure well-being of all the living creatures for the utilisation of future generations. (3)

(ii) There are four major causes of biodiversity loss. These are also known as '**The Evil Quartet**'.

Habitat Loss and Fragmentation Destruction of habitat is the primary cause of extinction of species. When large-sized habitats are broken or fragmented due to human settlements, building of roads, digging of canals, etc., the population of animals requiring large territories and some animals with migratory habitats declines.

Overexploitation When biological system is overexploited by man for the natural resources, it results in degradation and extinction of the resources. For example, Steller's sea cow, passenger pigeon and many marine fishes. (2)

8. (i) **Name the two types of desirable approaches to conserve biodiversity. Explain with examples bringing out the difference between the two types.**

(ii) **State the features of a stable biological community.**

Ans. (i) The two desirable approaches to conserve biodiversity are as follows

In Situ Conservation	*Ex Situ* Conservation
It is conservation and protection of biodiversity in its natural habitat.	It is conservation of selected threatened plant and animal species in places outside their natural habitat.
Population is conserved in the surroundings where they have developed their distinctive features.	Population is conserved under simulated conditions that closely resemble their natural habitats.
e.g. national parks, biosphere reserves, wildlife sanctuaries, etc.	e.g. botanical gardens, zoological parks, wildlife safari, gene banks, etc.

(3)

(ii) A stable community should not show too much variation in productivity from year-to-year; it must be either resistant or resilient to occasional disturbances (natural or man-made) and it must also be resistant to invasions by alien species. (2)

9. Describe the consumptive use value of biodiversity as food, drugs and medicines, fuel and fibre with suitable examples. NCERT Exemplar

Ans. Biological resources are the basis of life forms on this planet. The countries with maximum biodiversity possess better potential to compete with the rest of the world. Biodiversity has great economic importance to mankind due to its many uses, some of, which with consumptive values are following.

Food is obtained from biodiversity sources like livestock, forestry and fish. Biodiversity in modern agriculture is beneficial due to the source of new crops, e.g. just three cereals crop like wheat, rice and maize account for about 55% of protein and 60% of calories in humans.

Drugs such as morphine (*Papaver somniferum*), quinine (*Cinchona ledgeriana*), reserpine (*Rauwolfia vomitoria*), belladonna (*Atropa belladonna*), etc., are derived from plants.

About 70-80% of entire population is dependent on plants or its extract for medicine. Penicillin (*Penicillium notatum*), tetracycline (bacteria), digitalin (*Digitalis*) are some examples of active ingredients of medicinal plants.

Plant like *Corchorus, Gossypium* are sources of fibre, while *Jatropha* is a source of biofuels. Fossils fuels (e.g. petroleum) are obtained from fossils of organisms.

10. (i) Why should we conserve biodiversity? How can we do it?

(ii) Explain the importance of biodiversity hotspots and sacred groves.

Or **Why should we conserve biodiversity? Why is it a moral as well as social duty to contribute towards its protection?**

Ans. (i) Refer to text on page no. 376-377. (3)

(ii) **Importance of Biodiversity Hotspots and Sacred Groves** Biodiversity hotspots are the regions with high level of species richness and high degree of endemism. These can reduce the ongoing mass extinctions by almost 30%. Sacred groves are important in biodiversity conservation, as these are naturally protected by the native population without much effort. In Meghalaya, the sacred groves are the last refuges for large number of rare and threatened plants. (2)

Source Based/Case Based/ Passage Based Questions

1. Observe the global biodiversity distribution of the major plant taxa in the given diagram and answer the questions accordingly. Competency Based Que.

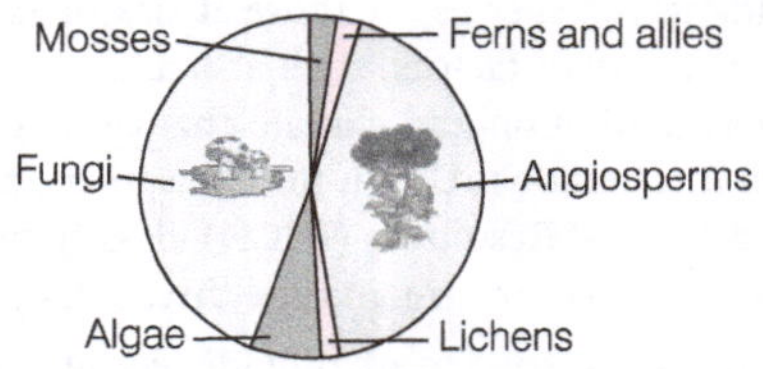

(i) Which group of plants are the most endangered?

(ii) Why are mosses/ferns so few? Give reason.

(iii) How do fungi that are heterotrophs sustain themselves as a large population?

(iv) Which group of plants is most advanced and which one is most primitive?

Ans. (i) Lichens.

(ii) Mosses and ferns are very few as they need humid conditions in forests and forests are disappearing.

(iii) Fungi are able to sustain themselves as a large population because of their wider adaptability to the changing environmental conditions.

(iv) Most advanced group is of angiosperms and most primitive group is of algae. (1 × 4)

2. The following graph shows the species-area relationship. Answer the following questions as directed.

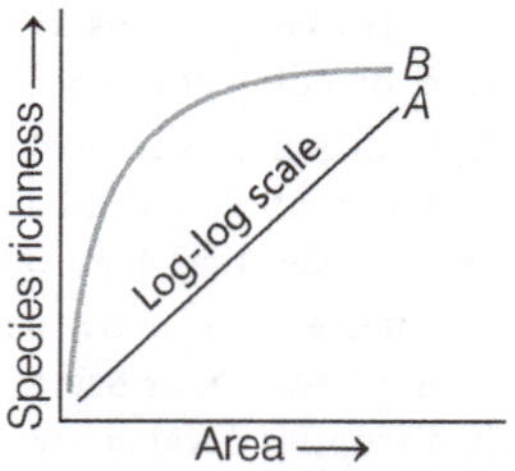

(i) Name the naturalist who studied the kind of relationship shown in the graph. Write the observations made by him.

(ii) Write the situations as discovered by the ecologists when the value of Z (slope of the line) lies between (a) 0.1 and 0.2 (b) 0.6 and 1.2. What does Z stand for?

(iii) When would the slope of the line B become steeper?

Ans. (i) Alexander von Humboldt studied the relationship shown in the graph. He observed that species richness increased within an explored area, but only upto a limit. (1)

(ii) (a) Value of Z lies between 0.1-0.2, when area is small to normal.

(b) Value of Z lies between 0.6-1.2, when area is very large.

Z is slope of the line which is regression coefficient. (2)

(iii) Slope of the line B becomes steeper when area is very large like continents. (1)

3. Read the following passage and answer the questions that follows.

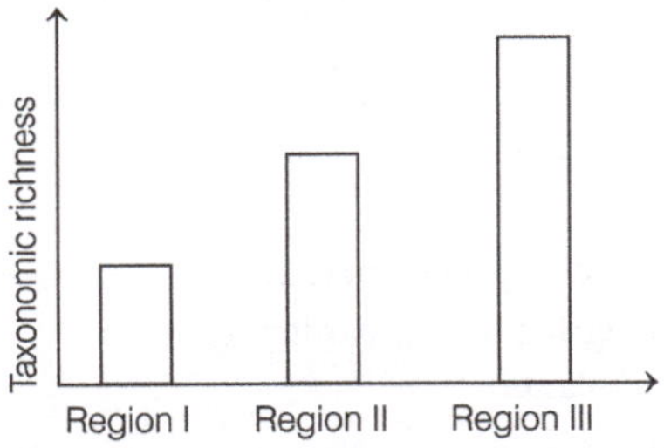

It is incredible that India's land area is only 2.4 % in the world's total land area, whereas its share of the global species diversity is an impressive 8·1 per cent. However, in these estimates of species, prokaryotes do not figure anywhere. Biologists are always keep on collecting data with respect to species diversity observed in different regions of the world. The data collected based on the survey conducted for species richness of groups of mammals in three different regions of the world is shown in the bar graph given below

(i) Why is the species richness maximum in Region III in the bar graph?

Or

(i) Why is the species richness minimum in Region I in the bar graph?

(ii) Plants and animals do not have uniform diversity in the world, but show rather uneven distribution. Mention what this kind of diversity is referred to as.

(iii) Why is it that prokaryotes do not have an estimated number of their species diversity as seen in plants and animals ? Explain. **CBSE 2024**

Ans. (i) This region is less seasonal with constant and more predictable environment. It represent tropical latitudes which remain relatively undisturbed for millions of years and had a long evolutionary time for species diversification. **Competency Based Que.**

Or

(i) Region I represent temperate region subjected to frequent glaciation and get lesser evolutionary time for species diversification or has more seasonal with less constant and less predictable environment which lead to lower species diversification. (1½)

(ii) Latitudinal gradient in diversity. (1)

(iii) Conventional taxonomic methods are not suitable for identifying microbial species and many species are not cultured under laboratory conditions. Due to this, prokaryotes do not have estimated number of their species diversity. (1½)

4. The graph given below represents the database of animal species that fall into different risk categories in India. Observe the graph and answer the following questions. **Competency Based Que.**

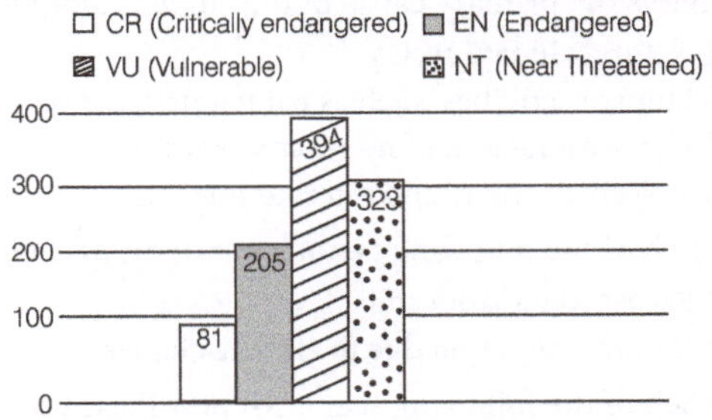

(i) What do you infer from vulnerable species? Why is the bar of such species high?

(ii) What activities of the humans have led to a rise in the number of endangered animals in India?

Or

(ii) What steps can be taken at individual levels in order to save species from getting endangered?

Ans. (i) Vulnerable species are those species which are not currently endangered, but face high risk of endangerment in the near future if the factors do not favour them.

The bar of such species is the highest because a lot of species are currently getting endangered due to harmful human activities and other factors. (2)

(ii) A number of human activities which include exploitation of plant/animal species, e.g. hunting and poaching, deforestation, pollution, etc., have led to a rise in the number of endangered species. (2)

Or (ii) Steps that can be taken to save species include

(a) Preventing deforestation and encouraging reforestation.

(b) Stopping activities like hunting and poaching that harm the animal population.

(c) Spreading awareness about the importance of saving such species and encouraging others to do so. (2)

SELF ASSESSMENT TEST

Multiple Choice Questions

1. Which of the following levels of biodiversity refers specifically to the variety of genes within a particular species?
   (a) Ecosystem diversity
   (b) Species diversity
   (c) Genetic diversity
   (d) Community diversity
2. The loss of genetic diversity within a species can lead to
   (a) increased adaptability to changing environments
   (b) enhanced survival rates in changing conditions
   (c) increased susceptibility to diseases and environmental changes
   (d) greater reproductive success in offspring
3. Which of the following levels of biodiversity is most directly affected by habitat destruction?
   (a) Genetic diversity (b) Species diversity (c) Ecosystem diversity (d) All of these
4. What is the primary cause of the current biodiversity crisis, often referred to as the sixth mass extinction?
   (a) Natural climate cycles
   (b) Human activities, such as habitat destruction and pollution
   (c) The introduction of non-native species
   (d) Volcanic activity and asteroid impacts
5. Which of the following is not a common mechanism through which an invasive species spread?
   (a) Ballast water from ships
   (b) Intentional release for agriculture or gardening
   (c) Natural migration due to climate change
   (d) Contaminated soil and plants
6. Which of the following scenarios best illustrates the concept of co-extinction?
   (a) The extinction of a predator leading to a population explosion in its prey
   (b) The decline of a plant species resulting in the extinction of a specific pollinator that relies on it
   (c) The introduction of an invasive species that causes multiple native species to decline
   (d) The loss of habitat due to climate change affecting an entire ecosystem
7. Which of the following is not an example of *ex situ* conservation?
   (a) Botanical gardens maintaining plant species
   (b) Wildlife reserves protecting animals in their natural habitats
   (c) Seed banks storing genetic material of various plants
   (d) Breeding of endangered species in zoo

Assertion-Reason Questions

Direction (Q. Nos. 8-11) *In each of the following questions, a statement of Assertion (A) is given followed by corresponding statement of Reason (R). Of the statements, mark the correct answer as*

(a) Both A and R are true and R is the correct explanation of A.
(b) Both A and R are true, but R is not the correct explanation of A.
(c) A is true, but R is false.
(d) A is false, but R is true.

8. **Assertion** (A) Climate change possess a direct threat to biodiversity.

   Reason (R) Species cannot adapt quickly enough to the rapid changes in their environments caused by climate change.
9. **Assertion** (A) Invasive species can lead to significant declines in native biodiversity.

   Reason (R) Invasive species often have no natural predators in their new environments.

10. **Assertion** (A) Overexploitation of a species reduces the size of the population eventually leading to its extinction.

Reason (R) Steller's sea cow is on the verge of extinction due to overexploitation.

11. **Assertion** (A) *Ex situ* conservation methods, such as seed banks are sufficient on their own to protect biodiversity.

Reason (R) *In situ* conservation is often limited by habitat destruction.

Very Short Answer Type Questions

12. What is red data book?
13. Give any two examples of alien-species invasion.
14. What is overexploitation?
15. What are the characteristics of stable community?

Short Answer Type Questions

16. Explain rivet popper hypothesis.
17. Write a short note on
   (i) Habitat loss
   (ii) Overexploitation
18. Explain ethical argument.

Long Answer Type Questions

19. Discuss the patterns of biodiversity observed across different ecosystems and geographic regions.
20. Analyse the effectiveness of *ex situ* versus *in situ* conservation methods. Define both terms and provide examples of each approach. Discuss the advantages and disadvantages of each method.
21. Examine the concept of biodiversity hotspots and their significance in conservation efforts.

Case Based Question

22. The pie chart given below represents the biodiversity of vertebrates showing the proportionate number of species of major taxa.

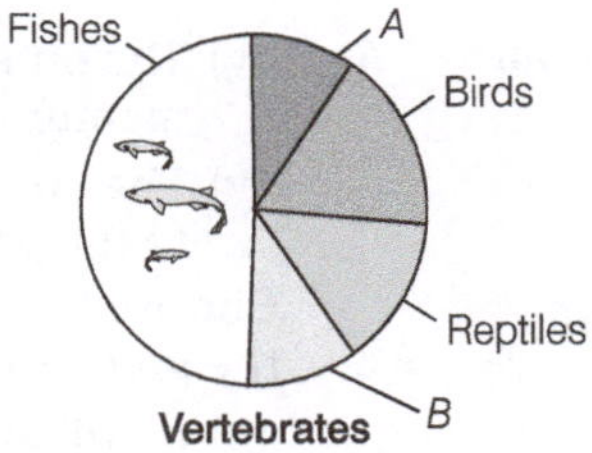

Vertebrates

   (i) Name the unlabelled areas, *A* and *B*.
   (ii) Extinction of species across taxa is not random. Which group among vertebrate is more vulnerable to extinction? Give reason.
   (iii) Among *A* and *B*, which group of vertebrates is least endangered?
   (iv) Give one example each of the recent extinction of species in Russia and Australia.

Answers

1. (c)	2. (c)	3. (d)	4. (b)	5. (c)	6. (b)	7. (b)	8. (a)
9. (b)	10. (b)	11. (d)					

CBSE

EXAMINATION PAPER 2025

BIOLOGY

Time : 3 Hours **Max. Marks : 70**

General Instructions

1. This question paper contains 33 questions. All questions are compulsory.
2. Question paper is divided into **five** sections-Sections A, B, C, D and E.
3. **Section-A-** question number 1 to 16 are multiple choice type questions. Each question carries 1 mark.
4. **Section-B-** question number 17 to 21 are very short answer type questions. Each question carries 2 marks.
5. **Section-C-** question number 22 to 28 are short answer type questions. Each question carries 3 marks.
6. **Section-D-** question number 29 and 30 are case-based questions. Each question carries 4 marks. Each question has sub-parts with internal choice in one sub-part.
7. **Section-E-** question number 31 to 33 are long answer type questions. Each question carries 5 marks.
8. There is no overall choice. However, an internal choice has been provided in Sections B, D and E of the question paper. A candidate has to write answer for only one of the alternatives in such questions.
9. Wherever necessary, neat and properly labelled diagrams should be drawn.

SET - I (Code 57/5/1)

Section-A ($16 \times 1 = 16$)

Question nos. 1 to 16 are multiple choice type questions, carrying 1 mark each. Choose the best option.

1. The histone core in a nucleosome of chromatin thread is a/an
   (a) pentamer (b) hexamer
   (c) heptomer (d) octamer

2. Given below are few statements with reference to the uterus in the female reproductive system.
   (i) The myometrium exhibits strong contractions during the delivery of the baby.
   (ii) The uterus opens into the cervix through a narrow opening called vagina.
   (iii) The cavity of the cervix and the vagina forms the birth canal.
   (iv) The outermost layer of uterus is a thin membranous perimetrium.
   (v) The uterus is supported by tendons attached to the pelvic wall.

   Choose the option with all true statements from the given options.
   (a) (i), (ii) and (iv) (b) (ii), (iii) and (v)
   (c) (ii), (iv) and (v) (d) (i), (iii) and (iv)

3. During the process of transcription, after binding to a promoter, RNA polymerase catalyses and makes the bases in the template strand of DNA available for base pairing with the bases of
   (a) deoxyribonucleotide triphosphate
   (b) deoxyribonucleoside triphosphate
   (c) ribonucleotide triphosphate
   (d) ribonucleoside triphosphate

4. Which of the following is not an example of aneuploidy?
   (a) Turner's syndrome
   (b) Down's syndrome
   (c) Phenylketonuria
   (d) Klinefelter's syndrome

5. Colostrum secreted by the mother's mammary glands in a human female during the initial days of lactation is rich in antibody.
   (a) IgE (b) IgD
   (c) IgA (d) IgG

6. Select the statements that are true for pollination mechanism in flowering plants from the given options.
   (i) In *Vallisneria*, the female flowers are pollinated by pollen grains inside the water.
   (ii) In *Zostera*, pollen grains are released on the surface of water.
   (iii) In most of the water-pollinated species, pollen grains are covered by a mucilaginous coating.
   (iv) Pollination by water is quite rare and limited to about 30 genera.
   Choose the correct answer.
   (a) (i) and (ii)
   (b) (ii) and (iii)
   (c) (iii) and (iv)
   (d) (i) and (iv)

7. Which of the following combinations is a correct example of convergent evolution in Australian marsupials and Placental mammals?

	Australian Marsupials	Placental Mammals
(a)	Lemur	Spotted cuscus
(b)	Tasmanian tiger cat	Anteater
(c)	Bobcat	Lemur
(d)	Numbat	Anteater

8. Isolation of DNA from a fungal cell can be achieved by using
   (a) cellulase (b) chitinase
   (c) lysozyme (d) protease

9. During a monohybrid cross involving a tall pea plant with a dwarf pea plant, the offspring populations were tall and dwarf in equal ratio. Find out the genotype of parent pea plants.
   (a) Tt × tt (b) TT × Tt
   (c) tt × tt (d) Tt × Tt

10. What would happen if a gene encoding a polypeptide of 50 amino acids, 25th Codon (UAU) is mutated to 'UAA'?
   (a) A polypeptide of 49 amino acids will be formed.
   (b) A polypeptide of 25 amino acids will be formed.
   (c) A polypeptide of 24 amino acids will be formed.
   (d) A polypeptide of 50 amino acids will be formed.

11. Large scale industrial production of butyric acid for human welfare is done using the microbe.
   (a) *Aspergillus* sp.
   (b) *Streptococcus* sp.
   (c) *Clostridium* sp.
   (d) *Trichoderma* sp.

12. The correct depiction of the centrifugation step of the experiment conducted by Alfred Hershey and Martha Chase on using radioactive labelled phages to prove that DNA is the genetic material is:

(a)
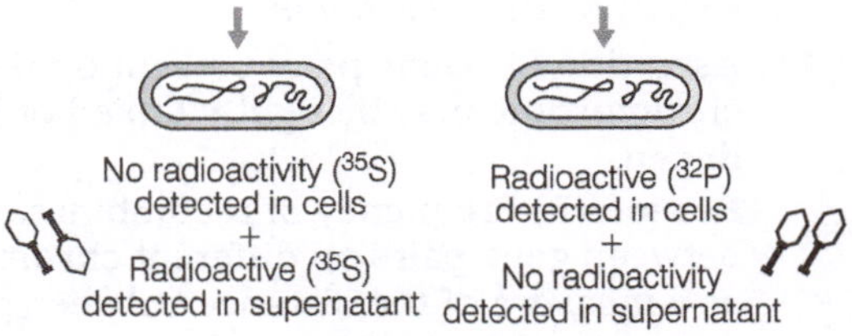

(b)
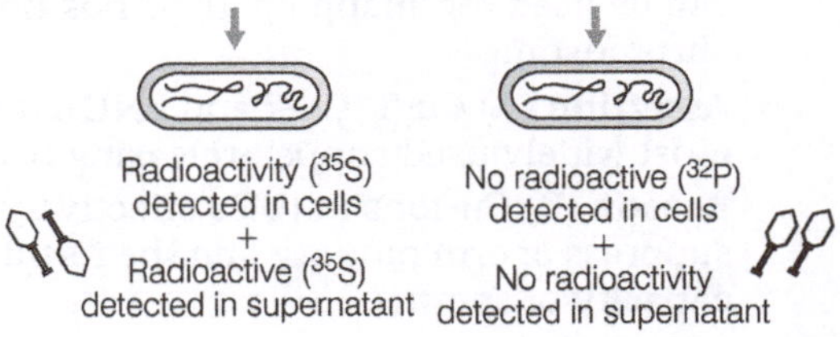

(c)
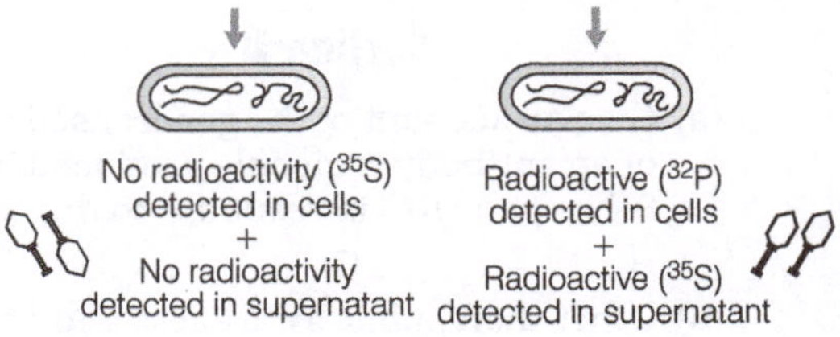

(d)
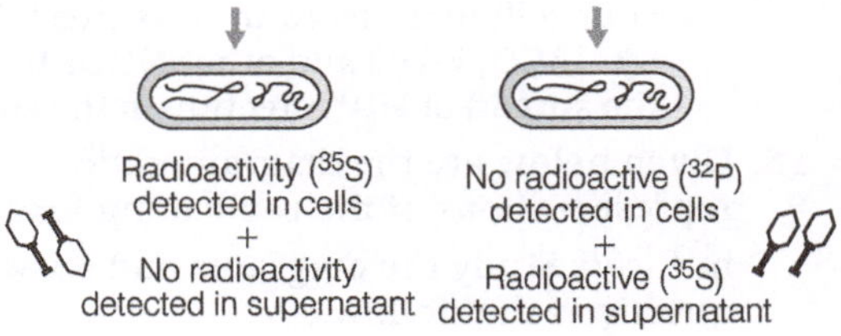

Assertion-Reason Based Questions

For questions number 13 to 16, two statements are given one labelled as Assertion (A) and the other labelled as Reason (R). Select the correct answer to these questions from the codes (a), (b), (c) and (d) are given below.

(a) Both Assertion (A) and Reason (R) are true and Reason (R) is the correct explanation of the Assertion (A).

(b) Both Assertion (A) and Reason (R) are true, but Reason (R) is not the correct explanation of the Assertion (A).

(c) Assertion (A) is true, but Reason (R) is false.

(d) Assertion (A) is false, but Reason (R) is true.

13. **Assertion** (A) To generate only a part of the plant from a cell is totipotency.
Reason (R) Suitable special nutrient media and sterile conditions are required in '*in vitro*' conditions for the division of cells in explants.

14. **Assertion** (A) Biogas plants are more often built in rural areas.
Reason (R) The excreta or gobar of cattle is rich in *Methanobacterium*,

15. **Assertion** (A) Gene pairs present on the same chromosome may be tightly linked or loosely linked.
Reason (R) Frequency of recombination between gene pairs on different chromosomes as a measure of the distance between genes can be used for 'mapping' their position on the chromosomes.

16. **Assertion** (A) Cu-T, Cu-7 and LNG-20 are the most widely used copper-releasing IUDs.
Reason (R) Cu-ions in IUDs effectively suppress sperm motility and the fertilising capacity of sperms.

Section-B

17. (a) Give an account of the generalised structure of an antibody molecule produced by B-lymphocytes in response to the pathogen.

Or

(b) Other than public awareness and counselling, enlist four measures taken up by NACO, WHO and other NGOs to prevent the spread of HIV infection in the society.

18. Given below are the diagrammatic representations of the replicating fork of DNA in *E. coli*. Study the diagrams and answer the questions that follow.

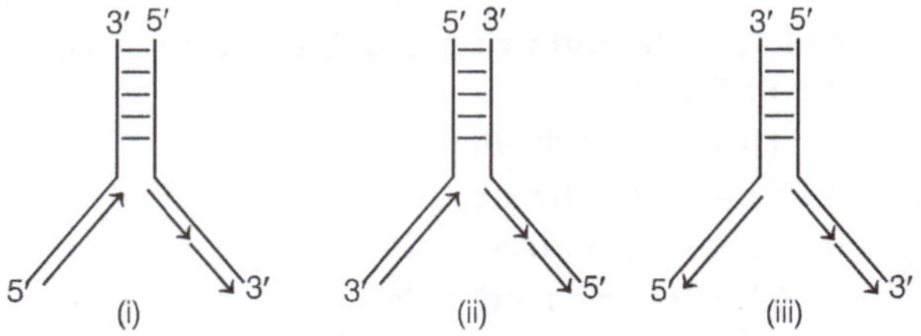

(a) Which one of the three diagrams (i), (ii) or (iii) is the correct representation of the replicating fork of DNA replication? Explain your answer.

(b) Name the enzyme used in *E. coli* to join the newly synthesised fragments of DNA.

19. (a) Explain what is meant by the term amniocentesis. How is this technique misused in India?

Or

(b) Name any two VDs which might occur in a human female. State any two complications in a female if it is left untreated.

20. The basic scheme of the essential steps involved in the process of recombinant DNA technology is summarised below in the form of a flow diagram. Study the given flow diagram and answer the questions that follow.

Step-1 Plasmid DNA (cut using Restriction Enzyme *Eco* RI) + Foreign DNA (cut using Restriction Enzyme *Eco* RI)

↓ DNA ligase

Step-2 Recombinant DNA molecule

↓

Step-3 Transfer of recombinant DNA molecule to the host cell

↓

Step-4 Replication of recombinant DNA molecule in the host cell

(a) Name the specific enzyme that might have been used to make the multiple copies of foreign DNA before undergoing Step-1 of the process.

(b) How does the use of restriction enzyme *Eco* RI in Step-1 facilitate the action of DNA ligase to form the recombinant DNA molecule ? Explain.

(c) Name the most commonly used host in the above process.

21. (a) Explain how the interaction between a fig tree and its tight one-to-one relationship with the pollinator species of wasp is one of the best examples of mutualism.

Or

(b) Correctly depict (also indicate the trophic level) and describe the ecological pyramid of number with 32 birds dependent on 20 insects feeding on one banyan tree.

Section-C

22. Explain the neuroendocrine mechanism involved in the process of parturition in a human female leading to the expulsion of the baby out of the uterus through the birth canal.

23. During a medical investigation, an infant was found to possess an extra copy of chromosome no. 21. Identify the disorder the child is suffering from. Describe the symptoms the child is likely to develop later in life.

24. (a) Write the full form of BOD.

(b) Define BOD. Explain how it is a measure of the organic matter present in the water body.

25. Enlist three advantages of genetically modified plants.

26.

Genotype	RBC	Phenotype
I^AI^A	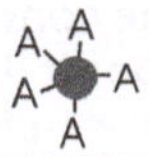	A
I^Ai		A
I^BI^B	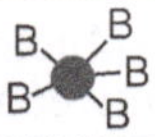	B
I^Bi	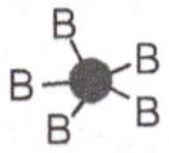	B
I^AI^B	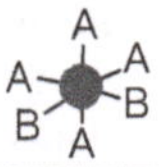	AB
ii		O

Study the diagram above and answer the following questions.

(a) How many alleles are involved in blood grouping?

(b) A person having 'AB' blood group has both dominant alleles. What is this inheritance type called?

(c) A man with 'A' blood group marries a woman with 'B' blood group. Can they have a child with 'O' blood group? Explain with the help of a cross.

27. Explain how the loss of habitat and fragmentation drives plants and animals to extinction with the help of an example of habitat loss in the tropical rain forest. Also write the effect of fragmentation of a habitat on the population decline.

28. Many of the flowering plants producing hermaphrodite flowers have developed many devices to discourage self-pollination and to encourage cross-pollination. Given below is a picture of one such outbreeding device in a flowering plant. Study the picture and answer the questions that follow.

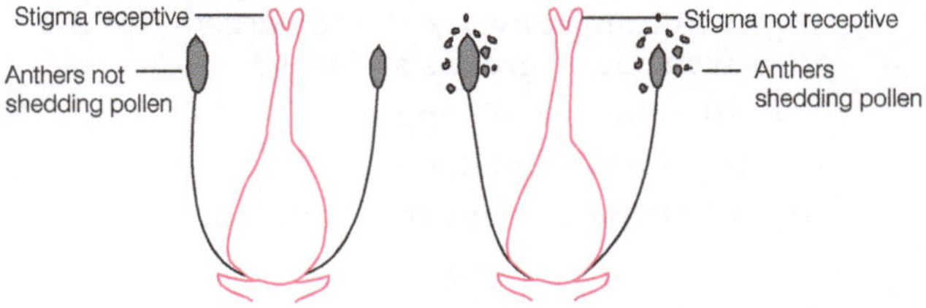

Flowers present on different plants of same species

(a) Explain how the given type of pollination is advantageous to the plant.

(b) Can this flowering plant show geitonogamy? Justify your answer.

Section-D

Question no. 29 and 30 are case-based questions. Each question has 3 sub- questions with internal choice in one sub- question.

29. Highly conserved proteins such as haemoglobin and cytochrome-*c* provide the best biochemical evidences to trace evolutionary relationships between different groups. Cytochrome-*c* is formed of 104 amino acids. Cytochrome-*c* is the respiratory pigment present in all eukaryotic cells. It has evolved at a constant rate during evolution. In chimpanzees and humans, cytochrome-*c* genes are identical. The given data shows the evolution of the cytochrome-*c* gene in different mammals from kangaroos, cows, rodents and humans.

Groups	Nucleotide substitution in the gene of cytochrome-c	Millions of years ago
Human/Kangaroo	100	125 mya
Human/Cow	75	120 mya
Human/Rodent	60	75 mya

(a) Select the correct option for the time of separation of two groups and the number of nucleotide substitutions in the gene of cytochrome-*c*.

Options	Time of separation of two groups during evolution	Number of nucleotide substitutions
(i)	Lesser	Greater
(ii)	Greater	Lesser
(iii)	Greater	Greater

(b) What do you infer about the type of evolution (convergent or divergent) for the given pair of groups and why?
  (i) Human and Kangaroo
  (ii) Human and Rodent

(c) (i) Define convergent evolution.

Or

(ii) Define divergent evolution.

30. In 2021, 5-3 percent of 15 to 16-year-olds worldwide (13.5 million individuals) had used *Cannabis* in the past year according to UNODC. The adolescent brain is still developing and drug use can have long-term negative effects. Early drug use initiation can lead to faster development of dependence than in adults and other problems in adulthood. Parts of the Amazon Basin are at the intersection of multiple forms of organised crimes that are accelerating devastation with severe implications for the security, health and well-being of the population across the region. The direct impact of coca cultivation on deforestation is minimal, but indirectly it acts as a catalyst for "Narco-deforestation". The laundering of drug trafficking profits into land speculation, etc., is posing a growing danger to the world's largest rainforest.

(a) Which age group or period of growth people are more vulnerable to drug abuse?

(b) Explain the negative impact of coca cultivation on the world's largest rainforest.

(c) (i) From which part of the plant are cannabinoids mainly obtained? Mention any one negative effect of this drug on adolescents.

Or

(c) (ii) State the scientific name of the plant from which coca alkaloids are derived and state one negative impact of use of excessive dosage of cocaine.

Section-E

31. (a) Define transgenic animals. Explain in details any four areas where they can be used for human benefit.

Or

(b) Describe the structure and working of a sparged stirred-tank bioreactor.

32. (a) (i) Describe the population growth curve applicable in a population of any species in nature that has unlimited resources at its disposal.
  (ii) Explain the equation of this growth curve.
  (iii) Name the growth curve and depict a graphical plot for this type of population growth.

Or

(b) (i) Explain the conclusion drawn by Alexander von Humboldt during his extensive explorations in the wilderness of South American jungles.
  (ii) Give the equation of the species-area relationship.
  (iii) Draw a graphical representation of the relation between species richness and area for a wide variety of taxa such as birds, bats, etc.

33. (a) (i) Explain the structure of a typical monocotyledonous embryo of a flowering plant.
  (ii) How are multiple embryos formed in a citrus fruit? What is the mechanism known as?

Or

(b) (i) Name and explain the structural organisation of the male sex accessory ducts in the human male reproductive system.
  (ii) Describe the role of gonadotropin FSH in the regulation of spermatogenesis.

Set - II (Only Uncommon Questions from Set-I) (Code 57/5/2)

Section-A

Question nos. 1 to 16 are multiple choice type questions, carrying I mark each. Choose the best option. **(16 × 1 = 16)**

1. In *E. coli*, a DNA sequence that specifies where RNA polymerase will bind and initiate transcription of a gene is

(a) start codon (b) stop codon
(c) terminator (d) promoter

2. Given below are few statements with reference to the major events in the menstrual cycle of a human female

(i) During the follicular phase, the primary follicles grow to become a Graafian follicle.
(ii) Gonadotropins FSH and progesterone stimulate follicular development during the follicular phase.
(iii) LH surge induces rupture of Graafian follicle thereby releasing the corpus luteum.
(iv) Progesterone released by corpus luteum is essential for maintenance of endometrium.
(v) Both LH and progesterone attain a peak level in the middle of the cycle.

Choose the option with all true statements from the given options:

(a) (i), (ii) and (iv) (b) (ii), (iii) and (v)
(c) (ii), (iv) and (v) (d) (i), (iii) and (iv)

3. The approach used in HGP of identifying all the genes that are expressed as RNA is referred to as

(a) SNPs (b) YACs
(c) ESTs (d) BACs

4. Study the pedigree chart of a family showing the inheritance of myotonic dystrophy

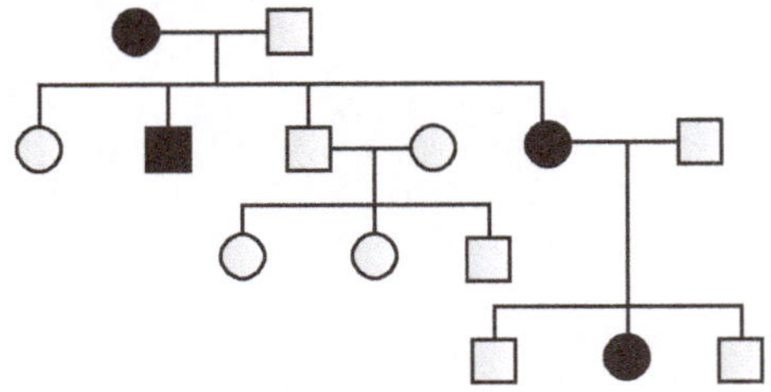

The trait under study is

(a) dominant *X*-linked trait
(b) recessive *X*-linked trait
(c) autosomal dominant trait
(d) autosomal recessive trait

5. The large bean-shaped organ acting as a filter of the blood in humans is

(a) liver (b) thymus
(c) spleen (d) heart

6. Select the following statements that are **true** for insect pollinated flowers from the given options.

(i) Majority of these flowers are large, colourful and rich in nectar.
(ii) Nectars and seeds are usual floral rewards to attract insects for pollination.
(iii) Pollen grains of these flowers are generally mucilaginous so as to stick to the body of the insects.
(iv) A foul odour is emitted by some flowers to attract flies and beetles.

Choose the correct answer:

(a) (i) and (ii) (b) (ii) and (iii)
(c) (iii) and (iv) (d) (i) and (iv)

7. Which of the following combinations is a correct example of convergent evolution in Australian marsupials and Placental mammals?

	Australian Marsupials	Placental Mammals
(a)	Tasmanian tiger cat	Lemur
(b)	Tasmanian tiger cat	Numbat
(c)	Spotted cuscus	Lemur
(d)	Spotted cuscus	Numbat

8. 'AGGTATCGCAT' is a sequence from the coding strand of a gene. What will be the corresponding sequence of the transcribed *m*RNA?

(a) AGGUAUCGCAU
(b) ACCUAUGCGAU
(c) UGGTUTCGCAT
(d) UCCAUAGCGUA

9. Removal of RNA polymerase-III from nucleoplasm of a eukaryotic cell will affect the transcription of which of the following?

(a) *t*RNA (b) *hn*RNA
(c) *m*RNA (d) *r*RNA

10. Large scale industrial production of streptokinase for human welfare is done using the microbe

(a) *Streptomyces*
(b) *Streptococcus*
(c) *Streptobacilli*
(d) *Streptopneumoniae*

11. Isolation of DNA from a plant cell can be achieved by using
(a) chitinase (B) lysozyme
(c) cellulase (D) pectinase

12. In a pea plant (*Pisum sativum*), green pod colour is dominant over yellow pod colour. The expected ratio of the phenotypes of the offsprings in a cross between parents with heterozygous green pod colour and homozygous yellow pod will be
(a) 1 : 1 (B) 2 : 1
(c) 3 : 1 (D) 4 : 1

Assertion-Reason Based Question

14. **Assertion** (A) Mode of action of pills and implants/injectables is similar.
Reason (R) The effective period of pills is much longer as compared to implants/injectables.
(a) Both Assertion (A) and Reason (R) are true and Reason (R) is the correct explanation of the Assertion (A).
(b) Both Assertion (A) and Reason (R) are true, but Reason (R) is not the correct explanation of the Assertion (A).
(c) Assertion (A) is true, but Reason (R) is false.
(d) Assertion (A) is false, but Reason (R) is true.

Section-B

21. (a) Give an account of the generalised structure of an antibody molecule produced by B-lymphocytes in response to the pathogen. (2)

Or

(b) Other than public awareness and counselling, enlist four measures taken up by NACO, WHO and other NGOs to prevent the spread of HIV infection in the society. (2)

Section-C

25. Name one commonly occurring genetic disorder in humans which is caused due to monosomy (one chromosome less than the normal number of chromosomes) of sex chromosome. Give its two symptoms. (3)

Section-E

32. (a) Explain how the process of RNA interference technology is used effectively to prevent infestation of the roots of tobacco plant by the nematode Meloidegyne incognitia (5)

Or

(b) Explain how more than a billion copies of a fragment of DNA are formed using the technique of PCR. (5)

Answers

Set-I

1. (d) Refer to Q. no. 7 on page no. 153.
2. (d) Refer to Q. no. 6 on page no. 49.
3. (c) Refer to Q. no. 14 on page no. 154.
4. (c) Refer to Q. no. 31 on page no. 111.
5. (c) Refer to Q. no. 13 on page no. 223.
6. (c) Refer to Q. no. 20 on page no. 20.
7. (d) Refer to Q. no. 9 on page no. 193.
8. (b) Refer to Q. no. 19 on page no. 280.
9. (a) Refer to Q. no. 2 on page no. 107.
10. (c) Refer to Q. no. 24 on page no. 155.
11. (c) Refer to Q. no. 7 on page no. 250.
12. (a) Refer to Q. no. 9 on page no. 153.
13. (d) Refer to Q. no. 1 on page no. 309.
14. (b) Refer to Q. no. 9 on page no. 253.
15. (c) Refer to Q. no. 6 on page no. 111.
16. (c) Refer to Q. no. 8 on page no. 79.
17. (a) Refer to Q. no. 33 on page no. 229
Or (b) Refer to Q. no. 50 on page no. 231.
18. Refer to Q. no. 20 on page no. 162.
19. (a) Refer to Q. no. 10 on page no. 81.
Or (b) Refer to Q. no. 36 on page no. 84.
20. Refer to Q. no. 34 on page no. 287.
21. (a) Refer to Q. no. 31 on page no. 342.
Or (b) Refer to Q. no. 26 on page no. 366.
22. Refer to Q. no. 42 on page no. 59.
23. Refer to Q. no. 65 on page no. 122.
24. Refer to Q. no. 21 on page no. 257.
25. Refer to Q. no. 7 on page no. 313.
26. Refer to Q. no. 25 on page no. 117.
27. Refer to Q. no. 24 on page no. 387.
28. Refer to Q. no. 17 on page no. 26.
29. Refer to Q. no. 2 on page no. 202.
30. Refer to Q. no. 7 on page no. 237.
31. (a) Refer to Q. no. 11 on page no. 319.
Or (b) refer to Q. no. 10 on page no. 290.
32. (a) Refer to Q. no. 7 on page no. 344
Or (b) Refer to Q. no. 2 on page no. 390.
33. (a) Refer to Q. no. 19 on page no. 32.
Or (b) Refer to Q. no. 3 on page no. 60

Set-II

1. (d) Refer to Q. no. 13 on page no. 154.
2. (d) Refer to Q. no. 15 on page no. 50.
3. (c) Refer to Q. no. 27 on page no. 156.
4. (c) Refer to Q. no. 23 on page no. 109.
5. (c) Refer to Q. no. 14 on page no. 223.
6. (b) Refer to Q. no. 21 on page no. 20.
7. (c) Refer to Q. no. 10 on page no. 193.
8. (a) Refer to Q. no. 15 on page no. 154
9. (a) Refer to Q. no. 17 on page no. 154.
10. (b) Refer to Q. no. 6 on page no. 250.
11. (c) Refer to Q. no. 20 on page no. 280.
12. (a) Refer to Q. no. 4 on page no. 107.
14. Refer to Q. no. 10 on page no. 79.
21. (a) Refer to Q. no. 33 on page no. 229.
Or (b) Refer to Q. no. 50 on page no. 231.
25. Refer to Q. no. 66 on page no. 122.
32. (a) Refer to Q. no. 4 on page no. 318.
Or (b) Refer to Q. no. 7 on page no. 290.

SAMPLE QUESTION PAPER 1

A Highly Simulated Sample Question Paper for CBSE Class XII Examination

BIOLOGY

Time : 3 Hours **Max. Marks : 70**

General Instructions

1. All questions are compulsory.
2. The question paper has five sections and 33 questions.
3. Section-A has 16 questions of 1 mark each; Section-B has 5 questions of 2 marks each; Section-C has 7 questions of 3 marks each; Section-D has 2 case-based questions of 4 marks each; and Section-E has 3 questions of 5 marks each.
4. There is no overall choice. However, internal choices have been provided in some questions. A student has to attempt only one of the alternatives in such questions.
5. Wherever necessary, neat and properly labelled diagrams should be drawn.

Section-A

1. A female was incapable of producing ovum, but can provide suitable environment for fertilisation. Out of the options given below, select the correct method suggested by the doctors for successful results?

(a) IUD (b) GIFT
(c) IUI (d) ICSI

2. Given below are four reproductive stages and their sites of occurrence.

	Stages		Sites of Occurrence
A.	Fertilisation	1.	Ampulla of oviduct
B.	Cleavage	2.	Isthmus of oviduct
C.	Blastocyst	3.	Cervix
D.	Parturition	4.	Uterine wall

How many pairs are correctly matched?

(a) 1 (b) 2 (c) 3 (d) 4

3. Which one of the following correctly describes the homologous structure?

(a) Organs with anatomical similarities, but performing different functions
(b) Organs with anatomical dissimilarities, but performing same function
(c) Organs that have not function now, but had an important function in ancestor
(d) Organs appearing only in embryonic stage and disappearing later in the adult

4. The gene disorder phenylketonuria is an example for

(a) multiple factor (b) multiple allelism
(c) pleiotropy (d) polygenic inheritance

5. Smoking is not socially acceptable as it has greater risk to human health. Identify the type of cancer caused by smoking and the main component for this case.

	Cancer	Component
(a)	Lung	Carbon dioxide
(b)	Throat	Carbon monoxide
(c)	Lung	Tar
(d)	Throat	Nicotine

6. In order to activate the immune system and destroy tumour, which of the following substances are given to cancer patients?

(a) Histamine
(b) Interleukin
(c) α-interferon
(d) Morphine

7. **Which of the following microorganisms shows the correct relationship between the production of bread and alcohol?**

	Microorganisms	Bread	Alcohol
(a)	*Lactobacillus*	Yes	No
(b)	*Saccharomyces cerevisiae*	Yes	Yes
(c)	*Propionibacterium shermanii*	No	Yes
(d)	*Trichoderma polysporum*	Yes	No

8. **The process of recombinant DNA technology has following steps**

I. Amplification of gene.
II. Insertion of recombinant DNA into the host cell.
III. Cutting of DNA at specific location using restriction enzyme.
IV. Isolation of genetic material (DNA).

Pick out the option for the correct sequence of step for the process of recombinant DNA technology.

(a) II, III, IV and I (b) IV, II, III and I
(c) I, II, III and IV (d) IV, III, I and II

9. **The population of a species *P* in a certain community was constant until a population species Q from a distant land was subsequentally introduced into that community. The interaction between the two population is reflected in the graph below.**

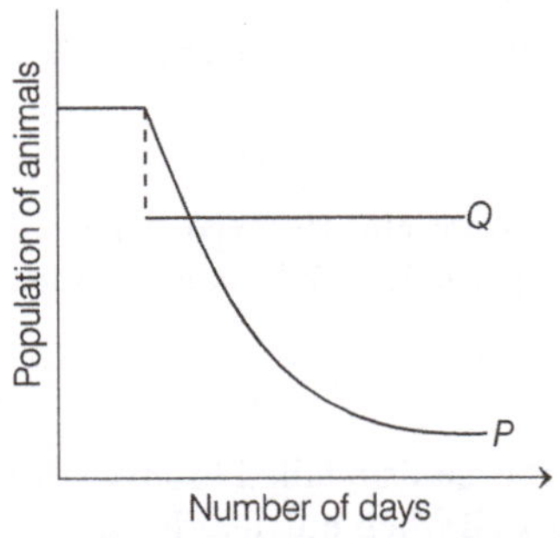

What could be the possible reason for the decrease in population of species *P* over a number of days?

(a) Species *Q* is a predator of species *P*.
(b) Species *Q* is a prey species which wraped out the population of species *P*.
(c) Species *P* and *Q* compete for space, but feeds on different food.
(d) None of the above

10. **In grasslands, cows belong to a particular trophic level. Identify the organism present that are equivalent to this trophic level in an aquatic ecosystem.**

(a) Phytoplanktons (b) Large fishes
(c) Sea gulls (d) Zooplanktons

11. **Which of the following is correct about the species diversity as one moves from high to low altitudes and away from equator or towards poles?**

	High altitude to low altitude	Equator towards poles
(a)	Increase	Decrease
(b)	Increase	Increase
(c)	Decrease	Decrease
(d)	Decrease	Increase

12. **Select the strategies for *ex situ* conservation out of the list given below.**

I. Zoological parks
II. Sacred groves
III. Gene bank
IV. Botanical garden

(a) II, III and IV
(b) I, II and III
(c) I, III and IV
(d) I, II, III and IV

Question Nos. 13 to 16 *consist of two statements, Assertion (A) and Reason (R). Answer these questions selecting the appropriate option given below.*

(a) Both Assertion and Reason are true and Reason is the correct explanation of Assertion
(b) Both Assertion and Reason are true, but Reason is not the correct explanation of Assertion
(c) Assertion is true, but Reason is false
(d) Assertion is false, but Reason is true

13. **Assertion (A) In females, parturition is the act of giving birth to a baby.**

Reason (R) Signals for parturition originates from the placenta and fully developed foetus.

14. **Assertion (A) In pigeons, females are heterogametic and males are homogametic.**

Reason (R) In pigeons, females have ZW sex chromosomes and males have ZZ sex chromosomes.

15. **Assertion (A) A bacterial cell with no restriction enzymes could easily get infected and lysed by bacteriophages.**

Reason (R) Restriction enzymes catalyses the synthesis of protection coat around bacterial cells that prevent bacteriophage attack.

16. **Assertion (A) The pyramid of energy is always upright.**

Reason (R) The flow of energy is unidirectional.

Section-B

17. A schematic representation of Polymerase Chain Reaction (PCR) upto the extension stage is given below. Answer the questions that follow.

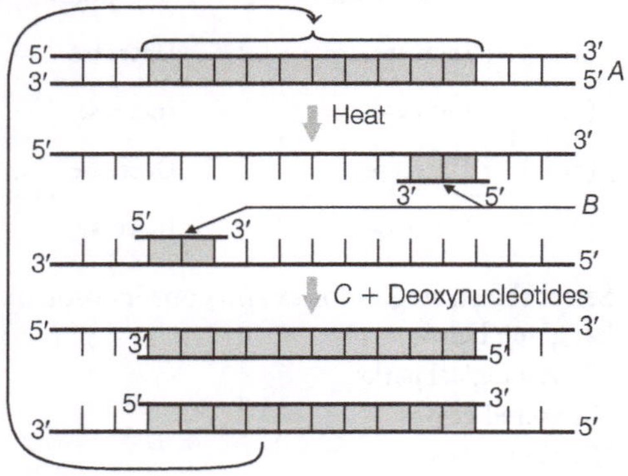

(i) Identify *A* and *B*.

(ii) Identify *C* and mention its importance in PCR.

18. In a habitat with unlimited resources, which type of population growth can be observed and describe the number of growth phases present.

19. A. Biomass of a standing crop of phytoplankton is 5 kg/m^2. It supports a large standing crop of zooplankton having a biomass 12 kg/m^2. This is consumed by small fishes having biomass 26 kg/m^2, which are then consumed by large fishes with the biomass 38 kg/m^2.

(i) Draw an ecological pyramid indicating the biomass at each stage and also name the trophic levels.

(ii) Mention whether it is an upright or inverted pyramid.

Or

B. Use the information provided in the table given below to answer the following questions

Trophic Level	Net Productivity ($KJm^{-2}Y^{-1}$)	Respiration ($KJm^{-2}Y^{-1}$)
Top carnivore	60	45
Carnivores	520	478
Herbivores	5590	50211
Producers	46,000	40,367

(i) Calculate the gross primary productivity.

(ii) Analyse the trend in the net production from producers to top carnivore. Give a reason for your observation.

20. A woman took a pregnancy test, which showed a positive result. Pregnancy tests typically give positive result after implantation.

(i) Name the site where implantation of blastocyst occur in the female reproductive system.

(ii) Name the structure that supports the developing embryo after implantation.

Or

(i) Where do the signals for parturition originate in humans?

(ii) Why is it important to feed the newborn babies on colostrum?

21. (i) Given below is a representation of dinucleotide. Name the type of sugar to which a guanine base is found attached to. Also name the linkage connecting the two nucleotides.

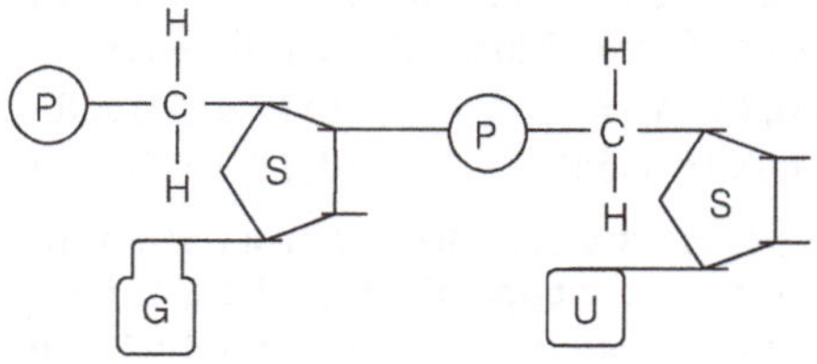

(ii) Identify the 3' end of the dinucleotide. Give a reason for your answer.

Identify the type of genetic material shown in the figure.

Or

An organism is able to survive on a culture medium, containing nutrient *A*, by the enzyme catalysed reaction.

$$A \xrightarrow{p} B \xrightarrow{q} C \xrightarrow{r} D$$

A mutant organism failed to survive on this medium, but grew well when nutrient *B* was added to it.

(i) Which gene of this mutant organism is defective?

(ii) What does such a condition indicate of ?

Section-C

22. Explain one application of each one of the following terms.

(i) Amniocentesis

(ii) Lactational amenorrhea

(iii) ZIFT

23. State the structure and function of the *t*RNA in a prokaryote.

24. (i) Observe the diagram of the factors influencing population density and define immigration and emigration.

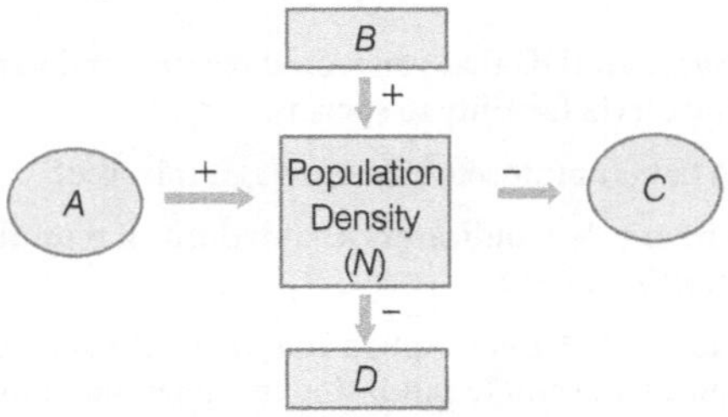

(ii) Name the factors on which the size of a population for any species depends? Also, give the mathematical expression for the change in population size.

25. In embryonic stage, the embryo gets implanted in the uterine wall. Explain the process of implantation.

26. Study the figure given below and answer the questions that follows.

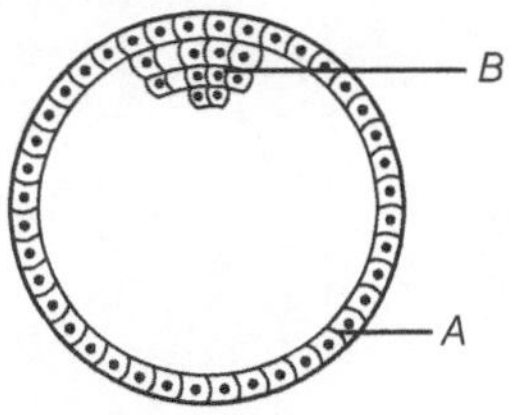

(i) Name the stage of human embryo the figure represents.

(ii) Identify '*A*' in the figure and mention its function.

(iii) Where are the stem cells located in this embryo?

27. Study the schematic representation of gene, involved in the *lac* operon, given below and answer the questions that follows

(i) Identify the region where the repressor protein will attach normally.

(ii) Under certain condition repressor is unable to attach at their site. Explain.

(iii) If repressor fails to attach to the said site what products will be formed by *z*, *y* and *a*?

28. Explain the effect of the deletion of the ADA gene in an individual. Does gene therapy help in this case?

Section-D

29. Study the given pedigree chart, which shows the occurrence of colour blindness in one family.

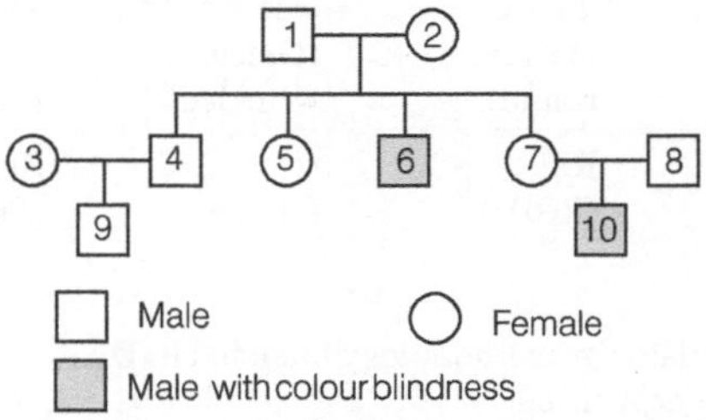

(i) On the basis of the inheritance pattern exhibited in this pedigree chart, what conclusion can be drawn about the allele of colour blindness? [1]

(ii) With reference to the above given pedigree, using the symbols R for dominant allele and r for the recessive allele, state the genotypes of the individuals shown in 2 and 4. [2]

(iii) It is often said that females are less likely to be affected by the disease than male. Explain why is it so in regard of the above drawn pedigree? [1]

Or (iii) If the first generation have a carrier female, then state the genotype of 6 and 7. [1]

30. Once Gita asked Sarita about her adrenaline and steroid medication. Sarita told Gita that she is allergic to pollens and mites. Sarita also mentioned that she became allergic due to the protected environment provided to her in early life. Upon further conversation, Gita discussed that she is suffering from an autoimmune disease.

(i) Name the antibody which is produced in response to allergens. [1]

(ii) Mention few symptoms of allergic reactions. [1]

(iii) How adrenaline and steroids would help Gita to relieve allergy? [2]

Or

(iii) What is an autoimmune disease? Give two examples of autoimmune diseases. [2]

Section-E

31. Three different type of crosses were made between plants P_1 and P_2 for different characters.

(i) The F_1-generation obtained is tabulated below.
Mention the various laws of inheritance associated with cross 1 and cross 2.

(ii) Also find the phenotypic ratio of F_2- generation of each cross.

Crosses	Parent (P_1)	Parent (P_2)	F_1	F_2
1.	YYRR (Yellow, round)	yyrr (Green, wrinkled)	YyRr (Yellow, round)	–
2.	RR (Red)	rr (White)	Rr (Pink)	–

Or

(i) Explain the methodology included in DNA fingerprinting.

(ii) Explain DNA polymorphism.

32. A pregnant woman went to the hospital for an ultrasound. Where the doctor told her about the different changes occurring in the foetus developing inside her.

(i) Name the embryonic stage that gets implanted in the uterine wall.

(ii) Name the hormones that are produced by placenta.

(iii) Explain the process of implantation.

Or

(i) Name an IUD that you would recommend to promote the cervix hostility to sperms.

(ii) What is amniocentesis? How is it misused?

(iii) List any two 'indicators' that indicate a reproductively healthy society.

33. (i) How did Darwin explain adaptive radiation? Give another example exhibiting this phenomenon.

(ii) Name the scientist who influenced Darwin and how?

Or

(i) How do the observations made during moth collection in pre and post-industrialised era in England support evolution by natural selection?

(ii) Explain the phenomenon that is well-represented by Darwin's finches other than natural selection.

Answers

1. (b) 2. (b) 3. (a) 4. (c) 5. (c) 6. (c) 7. (b) 8. (d) 9. (a) 10. (d)
11. (a) 12. (c) 13. (b) 14. (a) 15. (c) 16. (a)

SAMPLE QUESTION PAPER 2

A Highly Simulated Sample Question Paper for CBSE Class XII Examination

BIOLOGY

Time : 3 Hours **Max. Marks : 70**

General Instructions

1. All questions are compulsory.
2. The question paper has five sections and 33 questions.
3. Section-A has 16 questions of 1 mark each; Section-B has 5 questions of 2 marks each; Section-C has 7 questions of 3 marks each; Section-D has 2 case-based questions of 4 marks each; and Section-E has 3 questions of 5 marks each.
4. There is no overall choice. However, internal choices have been provided in some questions. A student has to attempt only one of the alternatives in such questions.
5. Wherever necessary, neat and properly labelled diagrams should be drawn.

Section-A

1. If any extinction of a mutualistic pollinator takes place, what would be its effect on the plants where it pollinate?

(a) Decreased pollination
(b) No effect because substitute pollinator is available
(c) The plant would not be pollinated
(d) None of the above

2. Given below are the four products and the bacteria by which they are produced.

Product	Curd	Swiss cheese	Penicillin
Bacteria	*Lactobacillus*	*Propionibacterium sharmanii*	*Saccharomyces cerevisiae*

Which of the following are incorrectly matched?

(a) 1 (b) 2
(c) 3 (d) None of these

3. The testes in humans are present outside the abdominal cavity in a pouch like structure called scrotum. This anatomical adaptation

(a) is a secondary sexual feature exhibiting maleness
(b) helps in escaping any possible compression caused by visceral organs
(c) maintains scrotal temperature 2°C lower than the internal body temperature
(d) neutralise the effect of any acid or urine in the urethra

4. $p^2 + 2pq + q^2 = 1$**, this equation cannot operate in a population if**

(a) frequent mutations occur among the gene pool
(b) there is no migration to a new habitat for a long time
(c) free interbreeding occurs among all individuals
(d) is isolated from other populations

5. Which of the following type of drug obtained form the plant which is shown below?

(a) Hallucinogen (b) Pain killer
(c) Stimulant (d) Depressant

6. ***Bt*** **toxin gene isolated from a bacterium, is cloned and inserted in plants like cotton, soybean, tobacco to develop resistance to insects. The bacteria is**

(a) *Bacillus subtilis*
(b) *Bacillus thermus aquaticus*
(c) *Bacillus thuringiensis*
(d) *Meloidogyne incognita*

7. In the given diagram which of the following correctly represent the part labelled as 5 and 4?

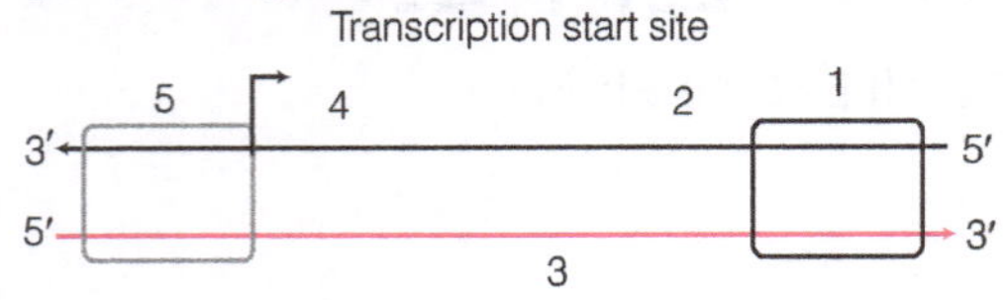

(a) Promoter site and structural gene
(b) Promoter site and terminator site
(c) Structural gene and coding strand
(d) Coding strand and template strand

8. Study the shape of age pyramid given below.

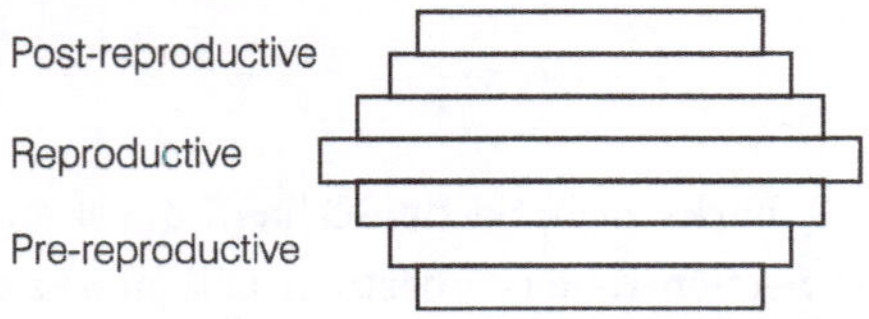

What does this shape of pyramid reflects with respect to population of the area under study?

	Shape of pyramid	Observation
(a)	Triangular	The population is expanding
(b)	Bell-shaped	The number of pre- reproductive and reproductive individual is almost equal. The population is stable.
(c)	Urn-shaped	The population is declining with negative growth
(d)	Triangular	The population growth is slow and stable.

9. A male having abnormal arrangement of chromosome is sterile. He also shows feminine development due to abnormal presence of a Barr body. Mention the chromosomal disorder from which he suffers.

(a) Turner's syndrome (b) Down's syndrome
(c) Klinefelter's syndrome (d) Haemophilia

10. Rate of production of organic matter by producers per unit time and area is

(a) GPP (b) NPP
(c) NPP–R (d) GPP + R

11. Which of the following statement regarding diseases and their causes is correct?

(i) Infectious diseases are caused only by viruses and bacteria.

(ii) Non infectious diseases can be caused by genetic factors lifestyle choices or environmental factors.

(iii) Malaria is caused by bacteral infection transmitted by the bite of an infected mosquito.

(iv) Tuberculosis is primarily caused by human Immunodeficiency virus (HIV).

Select the correct option.

(a) I and II (b) II only
(c) III only (d) III and IV

12. The method(s) that is/are used to differentiate between recombinants and non-recombinants is/are

(a) antibiotic affected gene (b) insertional inactivation
(c) gene cloning (d) Both (a) and (b)

Question Nos. *13 to 16 consist of two statements, Assertion (A) and Reason (R) answer these questions selecting the appropriate option given below.*

(a) Both A and R are true and R is the correct explanation of A
(b) Both A and R are true, but R is not the correct explanation of A
(c) A is true, but R is false
(d) A is false, but R is true

13. Assertion (A) Diaphragms, cervical caps and vaults are the barriers made up of rubber.

Reason (R) Diaphragms, cervical caps and vaults are used to cover the male copulatory organ during coitus.

14. Assertion (A) Turner's syndrome is caused due to the absence of the X-chromosome.

Reason (R) Such individuals have rudimentary ovaries and lack secondary sexual characteristics.

15. Assertion (A) *t*RNA recognises its corresponding codon in *m*RNA.

Reason (R) For each codon, there is an individual RNA.

16. Assertion (A) The pyramid of energy is always upright.

Reason (R) The flow of energy is unidirectional.

Section-B

17. Assess how the sequencing of human genome has opened new windows for the treatment of various genetic disorders.

18. The figure given below depicts a diagrammatic sectional view of the female reproductive system of humans.

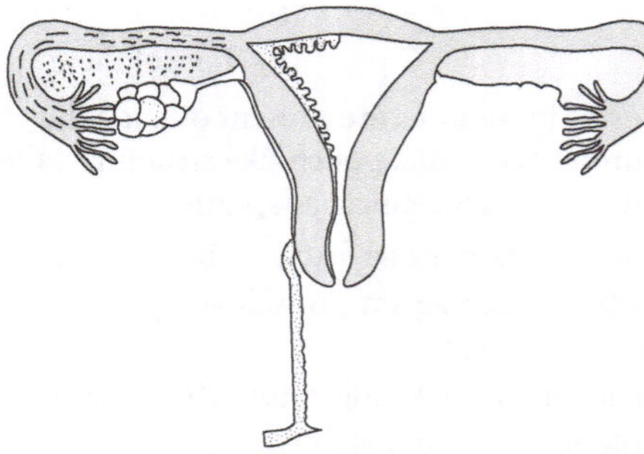

(i) Identify and name the site where implantation of the blastocyst occurs.

(ii) What is the function of *D* in reproduction?

Or

Observe the figure that given below and answer the questions that follows

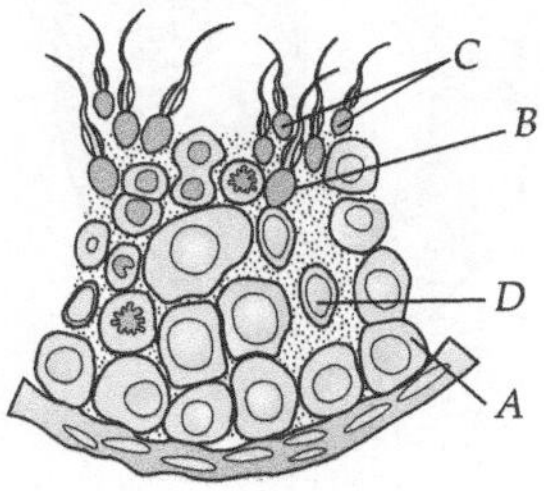

(i) Identify the parts *A*, *B*, *C* and *D* from the figure.

(ii) Write the functions of *A* and *D*.

19. The diagram given below depicts the ovule structure which is formed immediately after the completion fertilisation.
(Note PEN refers to Primary Endosperm Nucleus).

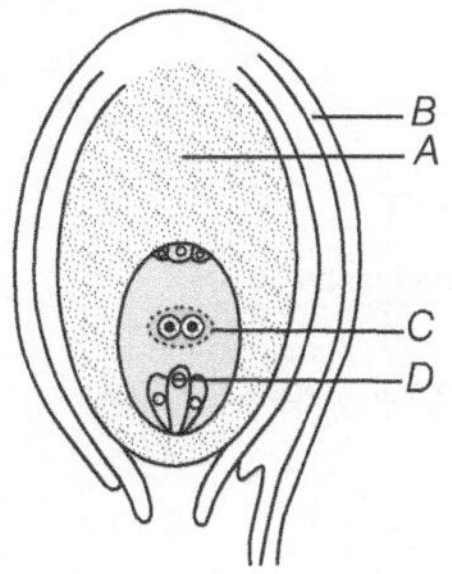

(i) What does the structures labelled *A-D* depict?

(ii) Mention the role played by the parts labelled as *A* and *B*.

20. (i) State what does standing crop of a trophic level represent?

(ii) What is a detritus food chain made up of?

How does the organisms in detritus food chain meet their energy and nutritional requirements?

Or

Organisms occupy a place in the natural surroundings or in a community according to their feeding relationships with other organisms.

Based on the source of the nutrition or food, organisms occupy a specific place in a food chain.

(i) Can we say that 'man can be primary as well as secondary consumer'? Justify this statement.

(ii) Which trophic level is oceupied by zooplanktons and phytoplankton?

21. The distance between genes *A* and *B* is 20 Map units, genes *B* and *C* is 10 Map units while, between genes *A* and *C* is 30 Map units.

(i) Based on the above information, construct a linkage map.

(ii) Find out the possible order of the genes *A*, *B* and *C* in the map.

Or

(i) In the experiment performed by Miller and Urey, name the gases used in order to simulate the primitive atmosphere.

(ii) State the significance of the experiment done by Miller and Urey.

Section-C

22. Study the pedigree chart and answer the questions that follows.

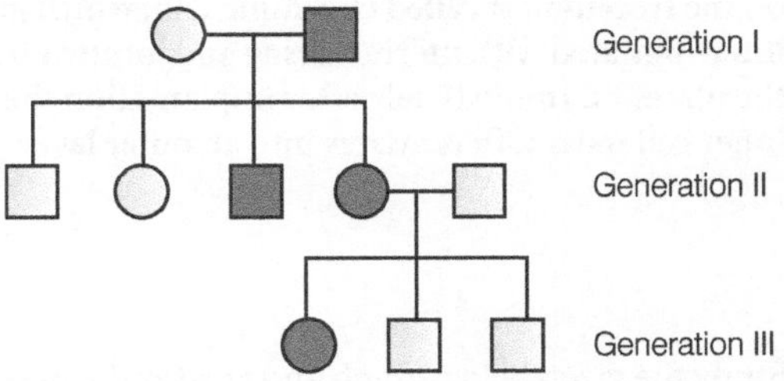

(i) Is the trait shown above dominant or recessive?

(ii) Is the trait shown above autosomal or sex-linked?

(iii) Predict the genotypes of the parents shown in generation I and their third child shown in generation II and first grand child in generation III.

23. Explain the role of tapetum during microsporogenesis.

24. Evolution is any cumulative change in the characteristics of organisms over many generations. Based on this, answer the questions related to evolution.

(i) List any four evidences of evolution.

(ii) How does homology lead divergent evolution? Give an example of homology in plants.

25. Observe the diagram given below and answer the questions that follows.

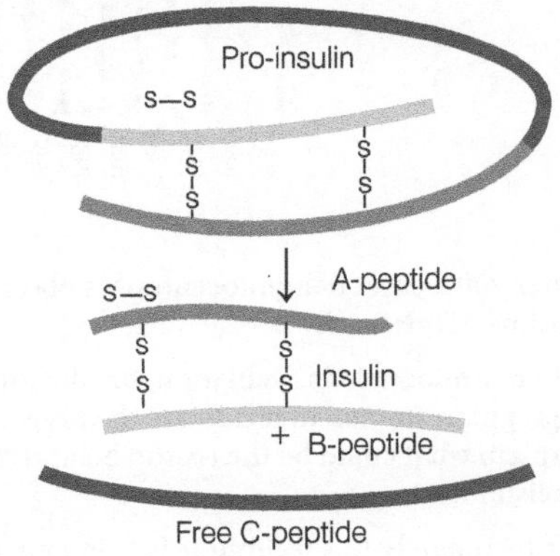

(i) Name the protein that was synthesised by this technique.

(ii) What was the major challenge, faced by the scientists while producing the above mentioned protein by using this technique?

(iii) Mention the name of an organism, which improved the procedure for the production of this protein.

26. In some children, ADA (Adenosine Deaminase) deficiency can be cured by bone marrow transplantation and in other enzyme replacement therapy can be opted alternatively. However, both these approaches are not completely curative. Suggest an alternate method to improve the approach towards a more permanent cure.

27. After implantation, finger-like projections appear on the trophoblast called chorionic villi, which get inter-digitated with uterine tissue and jointly form the placenta. Immediately after implantation the inner cell mass differentiates into an outer layer called ectoderm and an inner layer endoderm. A mesoderm soon develops between ectoderm and mesoderm.

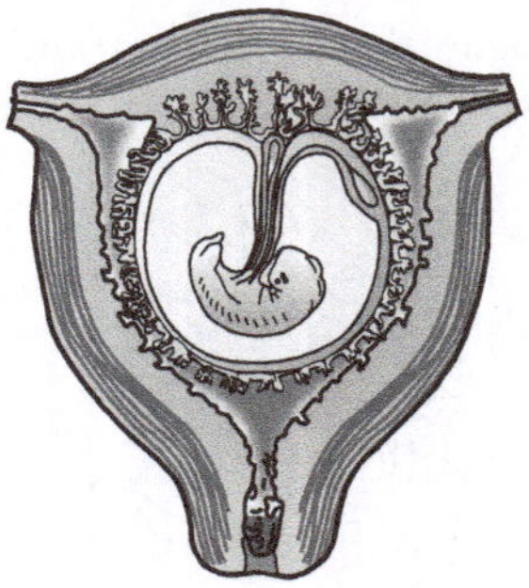

(i) Name the structures formed by

(a) Ectoderm (b) Mesoderm

(ii) Mention any two functions of human placenta.

28. What is PCR? Describe its underlying principles and steps involved in it. Mention any two of its applications.

Section-D

29. Study the given below graph and answer the questions that follows.

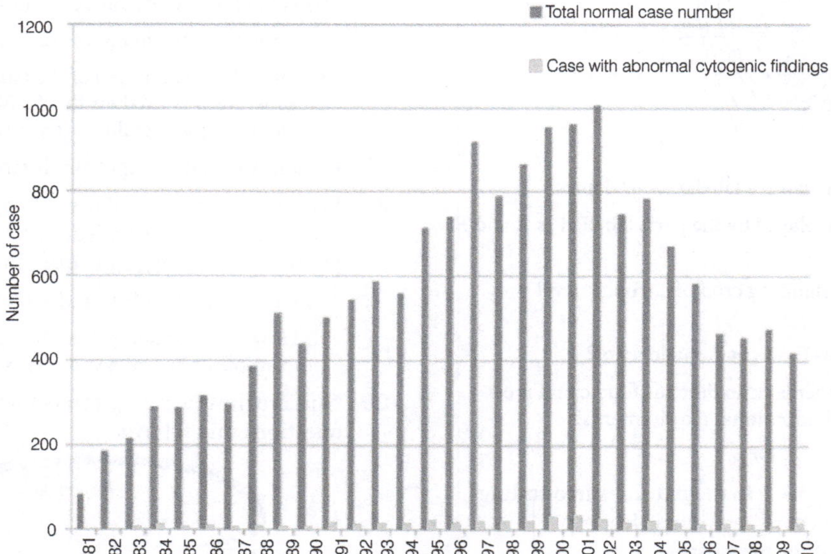

(i) After 2002, cases of amniocentesis is observed to be decline. Explain why? [1]

(ii) After amniocentesis evaluation, the doctor advised a pregnant women to terminate the pregnancy. Explain what could be the reason behind this decision. [1]

(iii) 'Unfortunately this technique is being misused'. Elaborate the context of this statement. [2]

Or (iii) Amniocentesis is a pre-natal diagnostic procedure to asses chromosomal abnormalities and foetal infections. How is this made possible? [2]

30. Due to the increasing use of insecticides and pesticides in agricultural practices, government advised farmers to adopt organic farming and use of biocontrol agents. Farmers were also informed about various biocontrol agents and their target organisms.

(i) Mention the use of biocontrol agents in agriculture. [2]

(ii) Which biocontrol agents are used to get rid of aphids and mosquitoes? [1]

(iii) Why baculoviruses are used as biocontrol agents? [1]

Or (iii) In order to control butterfly caterpillars in brassicas and fruit trees, which biocontrol agent(s) can be used? [1]

Section-E

31. Black eyes are dominant over blue eyes and black hair is dominant over red hair.

A man with pure blue eyes and pure black hair marries a woman with black eyes and red hair.

(i) How can we say that a given trait is dominant or recessive?

(ii) What could be the genotypes of male and female partner in the case discussed above?

(iii) What will be the probabilities of phenotypes of the children of this couple?

Or Read the sequence of the nucleotides in the given segment of *m*RNA and the respective amino acid sequence in the polypeptide chain.

								X
*m*RNA	AUG	UAC	CCU	AAU	GGC	GUU	UCU	CUC UGA
	1	2	3	4	5	6	7	8

Polypeptide P → Tyr → Pro → Asp → Gly → Val → Ser → Leu

(i) Draw the nucleotide sequence of the DNA strand from which this *m*RNA was transcribed.

(ii) A mutation occurred at 6th codon in the *m*RNA where 'G' was replaced by 'A'. What is this type of mutation called and how will it affect the polypeptide chain?

(iii) What does P coded by AUG represents? If AUG is replaced by UAA, how will translation of *m*RNA chain suffer?

(iv) If CUC gets replaced with CUG and no change is occurs in the polypeptide chain. What does this indicate about the nature of codon?

32. (i) How does smoking tobacco in human lead to oxygen deficiency in their body?

(ii) How does moderate and high dosage of cocaine affect the human body?

(iii) (a) Name the causative agent of typhoid in humans.

(b) Name the test administered to confirm the disease.

(c) How does the pathogen gain entry into the human body? Write the diagnostic symptoms and mention the body organ that gets affected in severe cases?

Or

(i) The three microbes are listed below. Name the product produced by each one of them and mention their use.

(a) *Aspergillus niger*

(b) *Trichoderma polysporum*

(c) *Monascus purpureus*

(ii) Name the category of microbes naturally occurring in sewage and making it less polluted during the treatment.

(iii) Write the scientific name of the microbe used for fermenting malted cereals and fruit juices.

33. How can you as an individual prevent the loss of biodiversity?

Or

'Analysis of age pyramids for human population can provide important inputs for long-term planning strategies'. Explain.

Answers

1. (c) 2. (c) 3. (c) 4. (a) 5. (a) 6. (c) 7. (a) 8. (c) 9. (c) 10. (a)
11. (b) 12. (b) 13. (c) 14. (a) 15. (c) 16. (a)

SAMPLE QUESTION PAPER 3

A Highly Simulated Sample Question Paper for CBSE Class XII Examination

BIOLOGY

Time : 3 Hours **Max. Marks : 70**

General Instructions

1. All questions are compulsory.
2. The question paper has five sections and 33 questions.
3. Section-A has 16 questions of 1 mark each; Section-B has 5 questions of 2 marks each; Section-C has 7 questions of 3 marks each; Section-D has 2 case-based questions of 4 marks each; and Section-E has 3 questions of 5 marks each.
4. There is no overall choice. However, internal choices have been provided in some questions. A student has to attempt only one of the alternatives in such questions.
5. Wherever necessary, neat and properly labelled diagrams should be drawn.

Section-A

1. Lactational amenorrhea as a means of contraception refers to

(a) absence of menstruation since ovulation does not occur during breastfeeding
(b) reduced efficiency of pregnancy hormones
(c) unsuitable uterus
(d) suppressed sperm motility

2. Given below are some chromosomal abnormalities and chromosomal complement.

	1	2	3
Chromosomal abnormalities	Down's syndrome	Klinefelter's syndrome	Turner's syndrome
Chromosomal complement	Trisomy 21	44 + XXY	44 + OX

Which of the chromosomal abnormality incorrectly represent their chromosomal complement?

(a) 1 (b) 2
(c) 3 (d) 4

3. Choose correct option for *A, B, C* and *D* in the given figure.

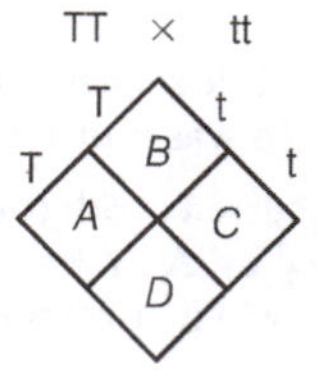

(a) *A*–tt, *B*–TT, *C*–TT, *D*–TT
(b) *A*–Tt, *B*–Tt, *C*–Tt, *D*–Tt
(c) *A*–TT, *B*–TT, *C*–Tt, *D*–TT
(d) *A*–Tt, *B*–Tt, *C*–Tt, *D*–TT

4. The presence of both a leading and a lagging strand is observed during DNA replication. This is because

(a) RNA primers are not sufficient enough to facilitate replication of both strands
(b) only one DNA template is available for reading at a time
(c) DNA polymerase can catalyse synthesis of one strand at a time.
(d) DNA polymerase reads only in 5′ –3′ direction

5. **Consider the following statements.**

I. **Ladybirds and dragonflies are used to get rid of aphids and mosquitoes.**

II. **The bacteria *Bacillus thuringiensis* (*Bt*) are used to control caterpillars.**

III. ***Trichoderma* sp., free-living fungi, are present in root ecosystem where they act against several plant pathogens.**

IV. ***Rhizobium* is a symbiotic bacterium that lives in the stem nodes of legumes.**

Which of the statements given above are correct?

(a) I, II and III (b) I, III and IV
(c) II, III and IV (d) II and IV

6. **The sequence of human evolution is correctly depicted in**

(a) *Dryopithecus* → *Homo erectus* → *Homo habilis* → Cro-Magnon man
(b) *Australopithecus* → Neanderthal man → *Homo erectus* → Modern man
(c) *Homo sapiens* → *Dryopithecus* → *Homo erectus* → *Autralopithecus*
(d) *Australopithecus* → *Homo erectus* → Neanderthal man → *Homo sapiens*

7. **The table below highlights differences between PCR and gene cloning. Which of the following options highlights a correct difference?**

	Characteristics	Gene cloning	PCR
(a)	Efficiency	More	Less
(b)	Manipulation	Both *in vivo* and *in vitro*	*in vivo* only
(c)	Error probability	More	Less
(d)	Materials required	Different enzymes, vectors, bacterial host, etc.	Only the gene of interest and subject

8. **Study the given figure carefully.**

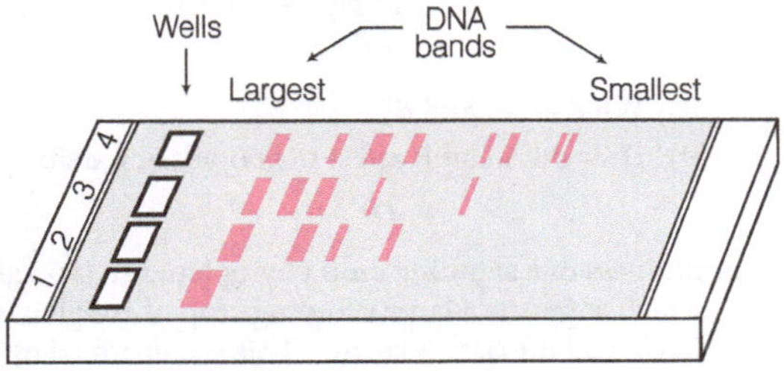

A fragment of DNA molecule on cutting with restriction enzyme yielded 4 fragments of sizes 3 kb, 2.5 kb, 8 kb, 6.7 kb.

Having become an expert on gel electrophoresis, you are asked to examine a gel. Identify where would you find these segments of DNA.

	DNA fragments	Location
(a)	3 kb	Near the positive electrode, farthest from wells
(b)	6.7 kb	Near the negative electrode, close to wells
(c)	8 kb	Near the positive electrode, farthest from wells
(d)	2.5 kb	In middle, stones down after few minutes

9. **Transgenic animals are generally created for a variety of medical reasons except**

(a) for testing vaccine safety
(b) for manufacturing of physiologically important proteins
(c) stimulation of pathogenicity
(d) for toxicity tests

10. **Purified DNA ultimately precipitates out and this can be seen as collection of fine threads in the suspension as seen in the figure. It refers to**

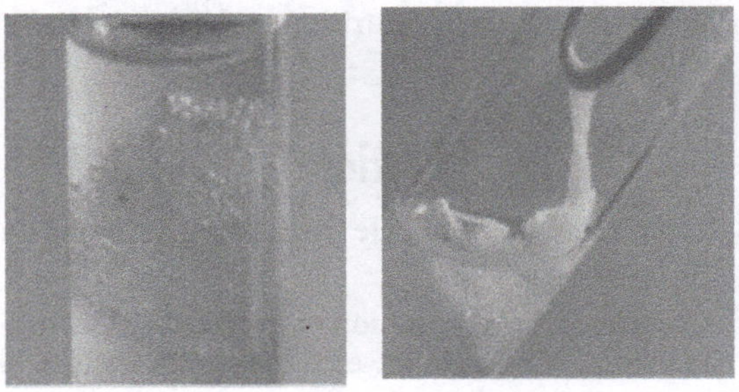

(a) DNA spooling (b) DNA digestion
(c) DNA recognition (d) DNA bands

11. **Exotic species sometimes become invasive and starts spreading fast because of**

(a) natural predators
(b) abundant natural competitor
(c) invaded land not having its natural predators
(d) mutation in their genome

12. **Which of the following is an example of *ex situ* conservation strategy?**

(a) Biosphere reserves (b) Sacred groves
(c) Hotspots (d) Zoological park

Question Nos. *13 to 16 consist of two statements, Assertion (A) and Reason (R). Answer these questions selecting the appropriate option given below.*

(a) Both A and R are true and R is the correct explanation of A.
(b) Both A and R are true, but R is not the correct explanation of A
(c) A is true, but R is false
(d) A is false, but R is true

13. **Assertion (A) Our immune system always recognise the 'self cells' and destroys the foreign proteins.**

Reason (R) When it fails to recognise the 'self' from 'non-self', it starts destroying the body's own proteins.

14. **Assertion (A) The distance between two polynucleotide chains in DNA remains almost constant.**

Reason (R) A purine is paired with pyrimidine with hydrogen bonds.

15. **Assertion (A) Constant gene frequencies over several generations indicate an absence of evolutionary progress.**

Reason (R) Evolution occurs when genetic equilibrium is absent.

16. **Assertion (A) Endosperm development precedes embryo development.**

Reason (R) It assures nutrition to the developing embryo.

Section-B

17. **Explain the role of follicle stimulating hormone during the menstrual cycle.**

18. **A schematic representation of Polymerase Chain Reaction (PCR) upto the extension stage is given below. Answer the questions that follows.**

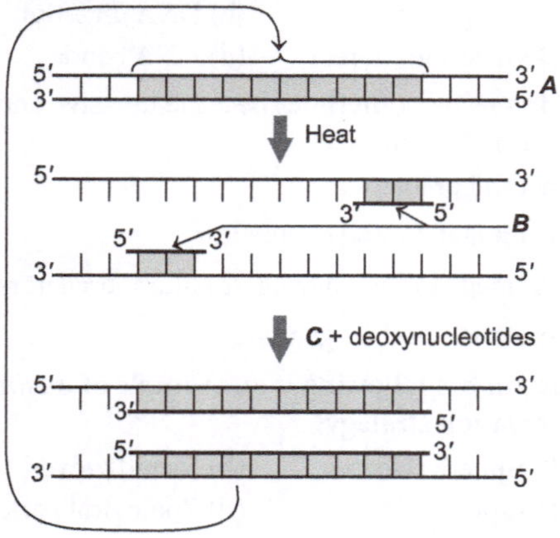

(i) Name the process *A*.

(ii) Identify *C* and mention its importance in PCR.

19. **A cross is made between the following plants with different phenotypic characteristics.**

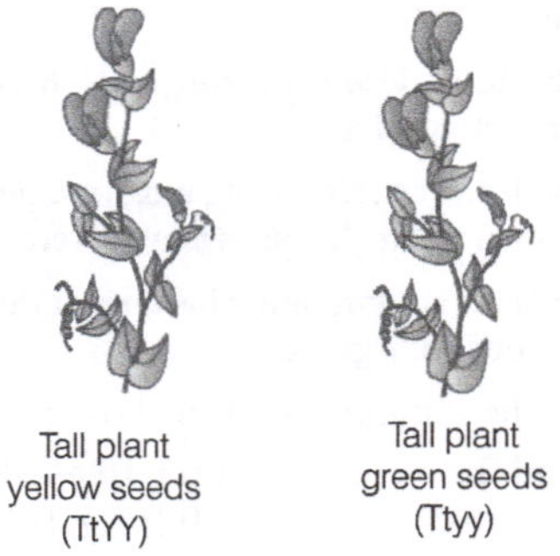

What will be the proportions of phenotypes of their offspring in F_1?

Or **Study the given pedigree chart and answer the questions that follow.**

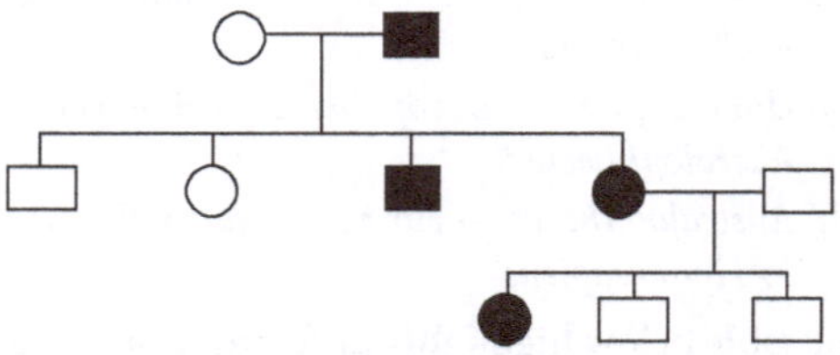

(i) Is the trait recessive or dominant?

(ii) Give the genotypes of the parents shown in generation-I and their third child shown in generation-II and the first grandchild shown in generation-III.

20. **Mention any one importance of lactic acid bacteria to humans other than converting milk into curd.**

Or

Give the scientific name of the microbes from which cyclosporin-A and statin are obtained.

21. **A. The density of a population in any given habitat during a specific period fluctuates. These changes are associated with phenomena *A* and *B* as shown below.**

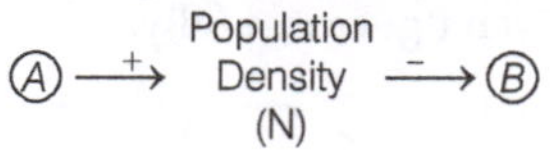

(i) What are *A* and *B*?

(ii) How do *A* and *B* affect the population density?

Or

B. Biomass of a standing crop phytoplankton is 6 kg/m^2 which supports a large standing crop of zooplankton having a biomass 13 kg/m^2. This is consumed by small fishes having biomass 27 kg/m^2 which are then consumed by large fishes with the biomass 39 kg/m^2.

(i) Draw an ecological pyramid indicating the biomass at each stage and also name the trophic levels.

(ii) Mention whether it is an upright or inverted pyramid.

Section-C

22. **Observe the image carefully and answer the questions that follows.**

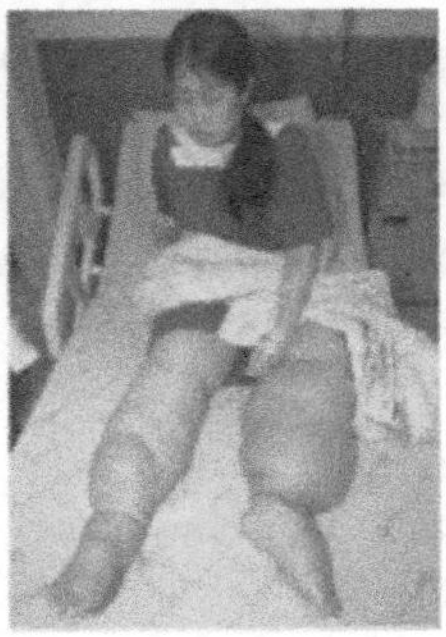

(i) Identify the disease in the above diagram and mention its causative organism.

(ii) Can this disease be transmitted directly by coming in contact with infected person. Support your answer with a brief explanation.

(iii) Mention any two symptoms associated with this disease.

23. **Explain the process of spermatogenesis in human.**

24. **Given below is a diagrammatic representation of the experimental setup used by SL Miller for his experiment.**

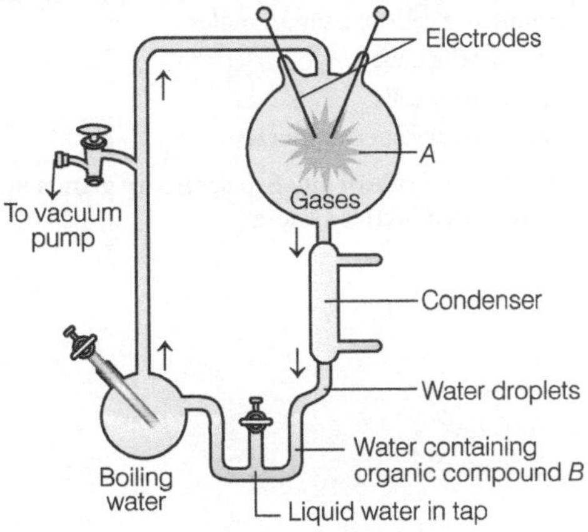

(i) Write the names of different gases contained and the conditions set for the reaction in the flask *A*.

(ii) State the type of organic molecule he collected in the water at *B*.

(iii) Write the conclusion he arrived at.

25. **Observe the diagram given below and answer the questions that follows.**

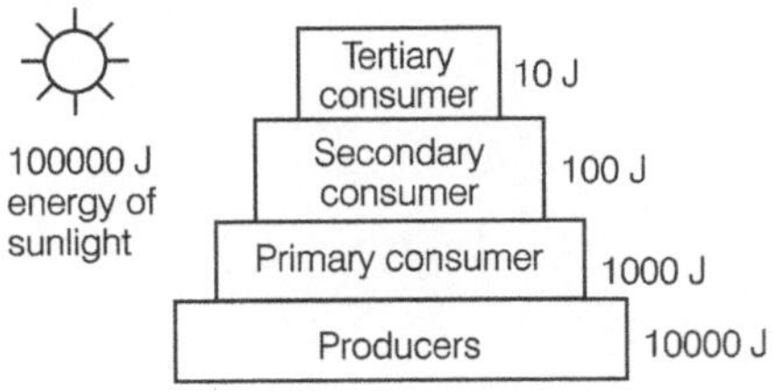

(i) Identify the ecological pyramid shown above. Is it always upright?

(ii) Energy is lost as heat at each step of trophic level. What does it depicts ?

(iii) Can a given species occupy more than one trophic level in the same ecosystem at the same time ?

26. **Explain the role of *ori, rop* and selectable marker in *E. coli* cloning vector pBR322.**

27. ***cry* I Ac and *cry* II Ab are introduced in a plant to prevent infestation by cotton bollworms.**

(i) What would be the result of this process?

(ii) Summarise the action of this gene in the host in which it is introduced.

(iii) In which organism these genes are present?

28. **Discuss how the loss of habitats has affected the animal population and describe any two instances where the introduction of a non-natives plant or crop has resulted in extinction of native species.**

Section-D

29. **A chromosomal disorder associated either with an extra chromosome 21 or an effective trisomy for chromosome 21. Clinical manifestation include short stature, protruding tongue, small ears, short broad hands, fifth finger clinodactyly and moderate to revere mental retardation.**

(i) On the basis of the given information, name the disorder. [1]

(ii) What type of mutation is seen in this syndrome? [1]

(iii) If this syndrome is recognised during birth. What are the physical traits that can be seen? [2]

30. **Bar graph shows reason for not using of modern contraception methods among current married women.**

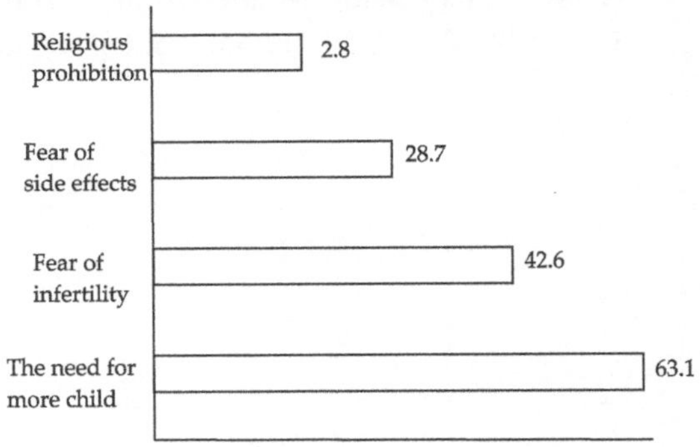

(i) On the basis of the above histogram, what will be the impact of this scenario on the population of a country? [1]

(ii) What can be the ideal contraceptive method for them? Support your answer by giving a suitable reason. [1]

(iii) Why is birth control so important? [2]

Or

(iii) Give the example of following [2]

(a) Non-medicated IUDs

(b) Barrier method

Section-E

31. Study the inheritance chart for colour blindness in a couple, where no history of this disease is present in the female partner.

Parents XX (Normal woman) X^cY (Colourblind man)

♀ \ ♂	X^c	Y
X	XX^c	XY
X	XX^c	XY

All carrier daughters, All normal sons

(i) What is the probability of their grandchildren being colourblind.

(a) Carrier daughter marries a normal man.

(b) Carrier daughter marries a colourblind man. [2]

(ii) What would be the condition of all their sons? [1]

(iii) The gene for colour blindness is present on X-chromosome. How does this affect its inheritance? [1]

(iv) Name another genetic disorder showing similar trait. [1]

Or (i) Name the kind of disease/ disorder and one symptom that are likely to occur in humans if

(a) mutation in the gene that codes for an enzyme phenylalanine hydroxylase occurs.

(b) trisomy of chromosome 21

(c) presence of additional copy of X-chromosome

(ii) Mention the type of allele that expresses itself only in homozygous state in an organism.

(iii) Pea flowers produce assured seed sets. Give a reason.

32. Explain the adaptive immunity with emphasis on its properties, activation and its role in vaccination.

Or

Briefly explain the life cycle of HIV, mention its mode of transmission and the precautionary measures that should be taken to avoid such infections.

33. (i) Explain the following phases in the menstrual cycle of a human female.

(a) Menstrual phase

(b) Follicular phase

(c) Luteal phase

(ii) A proper understanding of menstrual cycle can help immensely in family planning. Do you agree with the statement? Provide reasons for your answer.

Or

(i) Write the specific location and the functions of the following cells in human males

(a) Leydig cells

(b) Sertoli cells

(c) Primary spermatocytes

(ii) Explain the role of any two accessory glands in human male reproductive system

Answers

1. (a) 2. (c) 3. (b) 4. (d) 5. (a) 6. (d) 7. (c) 8. (b) 9. (c) 10. (a)
11. (c) 12. (d) 13. (b) 14. (a) 15. (a) 16. (a)